Multidisciplinary Perspectives on Cross-Border Trade and Business

Asmat-Nizam Abdul-Talib
University Utara Malaysia, Malaysia

Norhayati Zakaria
University of Wollongong in Dubai, UAE

Samshul-Amry Abdul-Latif
Universiti Utara Malaysia, Malaysia

IGI Global
PUBLISHER of TIMELY KNOWLEDGE

A volume in the Advances in Business Strategy and Competitive Advantage (ABSCA) Book Series

Published in the United States of America by
IGI Global
Business Science Reference (an imprint of IGI Global)
701 E. Chocolate Avenue
Hershey PA, USA 17033
Tel: 717-533-8845
Fax: 717-533-8661
E-mail: cust@igi-global.com
Web site: http://www.igi-global.com

Library of Congress Cataloging-in-Publication Data

Names: Asmat-Nizam Abdul-Talib, editor. | Norhayati Zakaria, 1969- editor. | Abdul-Latif, Samshul-Amry, 1978- editor.
Title: Multidisciplinary perspectives on cross border trade and business / Asmat-Nizam Abdul-Talib, Norhayati Zakaria, and Samshul Amry Abdul Latif, editor.
Description: Hershey, PA : Business Science Reference (an imprint of IGI Global), [2022] | Includes bibliographical references and index. | Summary: "Cross border business transactions have become increasingly important due to new norms of doing business so this book captures the multi-faceted outlook on international business phenomena particularly when cross border businesses were severely affected by the worldwide pandemic"-- Provided by publisher.
Identifiers: LCCN 2021031938 (print) | LCCN 2021031939 (ebook) | ISBN 9781799890713 (hardcover) | ISBN 9781799890720 (paperback) | ISBN 9781799890737 (ebook)
Subjects: LCSH: International trade. | International business enterprises.
Classification: LCC HD62.4 .M78 2022 (print) | LCC HD62.4 (ebook) | DDC 658/.049--dc23
LC record available at https://lccn.loc.gov/2021031938
LC ebook record available at https://lccn.loc.gov/2021031939

This book is published in the IGI Global book series Advances in Business Strategy and Competitive Advantage (ABSCA) (ISSN: 2327-3429; eISSN: 2327-3437)

British Cataloguing in Publication Data
A Cataloguing in Publication record for this book is available from the British Library.

For electronic access to this publication, please contact: eresources@igi-global.com.

Advances in Business Strategy and Competitive Advantage (ABSCA) Book Series

Patricia Ordóñez de Pablos
Universidad de Oviedo, Spain

ISSN:2327-3429
EISSN:2327-3437

Mission

Business entities are constantly seeking new ways through which to gain advantage over their competitors and strengthen their position within the business environment. With competition at an all-time high due to technological advancements allowing for competition on a global scale, firms continue to seek new ways through which to improve and strengthen their business processes, procedures, and profitability.

The **Advances in Business Strategy and Competitive Advantage (ABSCA) Book Series** is a timely series responding to the high demand for state-of-the-art research on how business strategies are created, implemented and re-designed to meet the demands of globalized competitive markets. With a focus on local and global challenges, business opportunities and the needs of society, the **ABSCA** encourages scientific discourse on doing business and managing information technologies for the creation of sustainable competitive advantage.

Coverage

- Joint Ventures
- Strategy Performance Management
- Competitive Strategy
- Ethics and Business Strategy
- Differentiation Strategy
- Foreign Investment Decision Process
- Strategic Alliances
- Core Competencies
- Tacit Knowledge
- Co-operative Strategies

IGI Global is currently accepting manuscripts for publication within this series. To submit a proposal for a volume in this series, please contact our Acquisition Editors at Acquisitions@igi-global.com or visit: http://www.igi-global.com/publish/.

The Advances in Business Strategy and Competitive Advantage (ABSCA) Book Series (ISSN 2327-3429) is published by IGI Global, 701 E. Chocolate Avenue, Hershey, PA 17033-1240, USA, www.igi-global.com. This series is composed of titles available for purchase individually; each title is edited to be contextually exclusive from any other title within the series. For pricing and ordering information please visit http://www.igi-global.com/book-series/advances-business-strategy-competitive-advantage/73672. Postmaster: Send all address changes to above address.

Titles in this Series

For a list of additional titles in this series, please visit: http://www.igi-global.com/book-series/advances-business-strategy-competitive-advantage/73672

Cases on Digital Strategies and Management Issues in Modern Organizations
José Duarte Santos (Instituto Superior Politecnico, Spain)
Business Science Reference • © 2022 • 365pp • H/C (ISBN: 9781799816300) • US $195.00

Employee Share Ownership and Impacts on Organizational Value and Behavior
Sara Elouadi (Hassan II University, Casablanca, Morocco)
Business Science Reference • © 2022 • 255pp • H/C (ISBN: 9781799885573) • US $215.00

ICT as Innovator Between Tourism and Culture
Célia M.Q. Ramos (University of Algarve, Portugal) Silvia Quinteiro (University of Algarve, Portugal) and Alexandra R. Gonçalves (University of Algarve, Portugal)
Business Science Reference • © 2022 • 319pp • H/C (ISBN: 9781799881650) • US $215.00

Handbook of Research on Big Data, Green Growth, and Technology Disruption in Asian Companies and Societies
Patricia Ordóñez de Pablos (The University of Oviedo, Spain) Xi Zhang (Tianjin University, China) Mohammad Nabil Almunawar (Universiti Brunei Darussalam, Brunei) and José Emilio Labra Gayo (University of Oviedo, Spain)
Business Science Reference • © 2022 • 415pp • H/C (ISBN: 9781799885245) • US $295.00

Driving Factors for Venture Creation and Success in Agricultural Entrepreneurship
Mohd Yasir Arafat (Aligarh Muslim University, Aligarh, India) Imran Saleem (Aligarh Muslim University, Aligarh, India) Jabir Ali (Indian Institute of Management, Jammu, India) Adil Khan (O.P. Jindal University, Raigarh, India) and Hamad Hussain Balhareth (Saudi Electronic University, Saudi Arabia)
Business Science Reference • © 2022 • 356pp • H/C (ISBN: 9781668423493) • US $215.00

Handbook of Research on Emerging Business Models and the New World Economic Order
Jose Manuel Saiz-Alvarez (Catholic University of Avila, Spain, & Catholic University of Santiago de Guayaquil, Ecuador)
Business Science Reference • © 2022 • 454pp • H/C (ISBN: 9781799876892) • US $275.00

Digital Transformation and Internationalization Strategies in Organizations
Orkun Yildiz (Izmir Democracy University, Turkey)
Business Science Reference • © 2022 • 326pp • H/C (ISBN: 9781799881698) • US $195.00

IGI Global
PUBLISHER of TIMELY KNOWLEDGE

701 East Chocolate Avenue, Hershey, PA 17033, USA
Tel: 717-533-8845 x100 • Fax: 717-533-8661
E-Mail: cust@igi-global.com • www.igi-global.com

Table of Contents

Preface xv

Chapter 1
Issues and Strategies in Reconciling the Malaysia-EU Palm Oil Discord 1
Ratnaria Wahid, Universiti Utara Malaysia, Malaysia
Norafidah Ismail, Universiti Utara Malaysia, Malaysia

Chapter 2
Branding Through Online Social Networks: Impacts on Export Markets 15
Sana Arshad, Universiti Utara Malaysia, Malaysia
Asmat-Nizam Abdul-Talib, Universiti Utara Malaysia, Malaysia
Fahad Manzoor, Emirates NBD, UAE

Chapter 3
South Korea Film-Induced Tourism: The K-Drama Determinant for Malaysian Tourists 27
Mazni Saad, International Islamic University Malaysia, Malaysia
Nor Azilah Husin, Universiti Selangor, Malaysia
Nur Zafirah Ramlee, International Islamic University Malaysia, Malaysia

Chapter 4
Early Internationalizing of Small-Medium Firms: A Conceptualization on Internationalisation of International New Ventures (INVs) 46
Afifah Alwani Ramlee, Universiti Utara Malaysia, Malaysia

Chapter 5
Self-Initiated Expatriates: A Case of Academic Expatriates in Malaysia 64
Subramaniam Sri Ramalu, Universiti Utara Malaysia, Malaysia
Nida Malik, Universiti Utara Malaysia, Malaysia

Chapter 6
The Impact of Terrorism on Trade in Nigeria and Chad 76
Isaac Terungwa Terwase, Federal University of Kashere, Nigeria
Muhammad Yusuf, Federal University of Kashere, Nigeria
Abubakar Sambo Mohammed, Federal University of Kashere, Nigeria
Safwan Mikaila Sani, Federal University of Kashere, Nigeria

Chapter 7
Antecedents and Consequences of International Joint Venture Knowledge Acquisition: Evidence From Algeria 92
Tamma Elhachemi, University of Echahid Hamma Lakhdar, Eloued, Algeria

Chapter 8
The Spread of Cross-Border High-Tech Manufacturing Component Goods in International Trade Integration 112
Dyah Wulan Sari, Airlangga Universty, Indonesia
Haura Azzahra Tarbiyah Islamiya, Airlangga University, Indonesia
Wenny Restikasari, Airlangga University, Indonesia

Chapter 9
Sustainability Analysis of Sino-Brazilian Bilateral Trade: A Case Study of the 2020 Global Epidemic Event 132
Poshan Yu, Soochow University, China
Jiayi He, Independent Researcher, China
Michael Sampat, Independent Researcher, Canada

Chapter 10
Portfolio Investment in Malaysia and Saudi Arabia: Effect of Graham Stock Selection on Return on Investment 155
Fariza Hashim, University Kuala Lumpur, Malaysia
Nadisah Zakaria, UCSI University, Malaysia
Abdul Rahim Abu Bakar, Prince Sultan University, Saudi Arabia
Kamilah Kamaludin, Prince Sultan University, Saudi Arabia

Chapter 11
International Trade Fairs and Initial Impacts of COVID-19 on International Fairs: The Case of Dubai 176
Muharrem Can, Turkish Ministry of Trade, Turkey
Ahmet Canlı, Turkish Consulate in Dubai, UAE

Chapter 12
Skill Acquisition: A Panacea for Economic Development in Nigeria 191
Bolaji Comfort Adeniyi, Bamidele Olumilua University of Education, Science, and Technology, Nigeria

Chapter 13
The Impact of Market Orientation, Entrepreneurial Orientation, and Relationship Orientation on the International Performance of SMEs 203
Kabiru Sa'ad Sa'id, Federal University, Dutse, Nigeria

Chapter 14
Iron Silk Road Trans-Caspian East-West-Middle Corridor Initiative and Baku-Tbilisi-Kars Railway Line: Impact on International Trade 222
Özlem Karadağ Albayrak, Kafkas University, Turkey
Başak Çelik, Kafkas University, Turkey

Chapter 15
Exploring Cultural Factors Impacting Female Digital Entrepreneurs in Underdeveloped Countries: A Comparative Analysis 237
Areeba Waseem Shaikh, University of Wollongong in Dubai, UAE
Norhayati Zakaria, University of Wollongong in Dubai, UAE

Chapter 16
COVID-19's Impact on Tertiary Institutions in Nigeria and Its Effects on the Economy 252
Temitope Teniola Onileowo, Universiti Teknologi Malaysia, Malaysia & Ekiti State University, Nigeria
Farrah Merlinda Muharam, Universiti Teknologi Malaysia, Malaysia
Mohd Khairuddin Ramliy, Universiti Teknologi Malaysia, Malaysia

Chapter 17
Reflections and Future Directions for the Green Maritime Supply Chain in Malaysia 270
Muhamad Fairuz Ahmad Jasmi, Universiti Utara Malaysia, Malaysia
Yudi Fernando, Universiti Malaysia Pahang, Malaysia
Rusdi Omar, Universiti Utara Malaysia, Malaysia
Muhammad Shabir Shaharudin, Universiti Sains Malaysia

Chapter 18
Travel Motivations and Travel Careers of Malaysian Backpackers 290
Samshul Amry Abdul Latif, International Islamic University Malaysia, Malaysia
Mazni Saad, International Islamic University Malaysia, Malaysia
Nuraini Ismail, International Islamic University Malaysia, Malaysia
Murodjon Matniyozov, Urgench State University, Uzbekistan
Mona Fairuz Ramli, Kolej Universiti Islam Perlis, Malaysia

Compilation of References 308

About the Contributors 365

Index 372

Detailed Table of Contents

Preface xv

Chapter 1
Issues and Strategies in Reconciling the Malaysia-EU Palm Oil Discord 1
Ratnaria Wahid, Universiti Utara Malaysia, Malaysia
Norafidah Ismail, Universiti Utara Malaysia, Malaysia

The EU has decided to phase out imports of palm oil used in biofuels in the EU by 2030. This affects people in Malaysia who rely on the palm oil business for their livelihood. This chapter examines the events leading up to the EU's anti-palm oil actions and the many ways in which Malaysia has responded to defend its palm oil sector. This includes 1) countering EU's allegation through scientific research, 2) demonstrating its commitment to transform the palm oil industry toward sustainability through certification standards, 3) fostering the commitment to grow palm oil sustainably, 4) garnering support from ASEAN and the international community, 5) expressing its opposition and warnings for retaliatory measures against the EU, and 6) requesting consultation under the WTO dispute settlement mechanism. It presents the political processes that generate policy interventions aimed at defending palm oil trade with the EU alerting that economic decoupling and direct conflict may exacerbate the problem, weaken bilateral relations, and elude good improvements in the palm oil business.

Chapter 2
Branding Through Online Social Networks: Impacts on Export Markets 15
Sana Arshad, Universiti Utara Malaysia, Malaysia
Asmat-Nizam Abdul-Talib, Universiti Utara Malaysia, Malaysia
Fahad Manzoor, Emirates NBD, UAE

The hurdles to entering a foreign market have been dismantled by greater internet connectivity. As a result, there is virtually endless potential to expand a company abroad. In growing abroad, it's crucial to keep the brand at the forefront of the approach. When enterprises enter foreign markets, they confront several problems such as a lack of market intelligence, buyer expectations, severe rivalry from global brands, and a lack of trending awareness. Most exporters focus on the short product-focused and sales-driven methods, such as producing that which is simple to create, finding a contract, fulfilling the request, and closing sales. This method just forces an exporter into a pricing competition in a globalized world, leaving the limited possibility to continuous production, product innovation, and credibility. Every company that wishes to export should aim towards market-driven, long-term, and sustainable exporting.

Chapter 3
South Korea Film-Induced Tourism: The K-Drama Determinant for Malaysian Tourists 27
Mazni Saad, International Islamic University Malaysia, Malaysia
Nor Azilah Husin, Universiti Selangor, Malaysia
Nur Zafirah Ramlee, International Islamic University Malaysia, Malaysia

This study surveyed 150 Malaysian tourists regarding the South Korean drama (K-drama) factors that drew them back to South Korea. The analyses revealed that K-drama was highly successful in enticing the young generation and discovered a clear scenario for Malaysians' response for a repeat visit. The results show that collaboration for the development of heritage tourism should be linked to the national identity and replicated through dramas similar to K-dramas. Universities should work closely with other stakeholders to produce high-quality films for international distribution.

Chapter 4
Early Internationalizing of Small-Medium Firms: A Conceptualization on Internationalisation of International New Ventures (INVs) 46
Afifah Alwani Ramlee, Universiti Utara Malaysia, Malaysia

Internationalization is not an odd term in business, and increasing numbers in the business world show this phenomenon as a vital element that must be emphasized and practiced by an organization to become the top company in international markets. Born global has become a new entity entering the global market and rapidly evolved to catch up and maintain its pace with international new ventures. Gaining the upper hand in the international market has motivated the born global entity to compete with other giant companies in the same markets. This chapter's findings enlighten the crucial parts of the definition between these two terms supported with previous studies that encompass gaps, conventional and new ventures, and the advantages versus liabilities that existed in the new venture firms. In addition, this chapter's discussions would offer better justification and views in global market perspectives.

Chapter 5
Self-Initiated Expatriates: A Case of Academic Expatriates in Malaysia 64
Subramaniam Sri Ramalu, Universiti Utara Malaysia, Malaysia
Nida Malik, Universiti Utara Malaysia, Malaysia

This chapter discusses the emergence of a new category of expatriates, namely self-initiated expatriates. In particular, the demand for self-initiated academic expatriates has increased tremendously over the years in tandem with the globalization of the higher education sector across the globe. Hence, this chapter aims to provide greater understanding about the nature and motivation for expatriation among this group of expatriates which will have significant impact on the international human resource management policies and practices. This chapter begins with explanation about the concept of expatriation and expatriate. This is followed by comparison between organizational expatriates and self-initiated expatriates. The underlying motivation behind self-initiated expatriation is discussed as well. Definitions of academic self-initiated expatriates and their motivation to expatriate were included as well in this chapter. This chapter conclude with findings of one case study conducted among 152 academic self-initiated expatriates employed in 20 public universities in Malaysia.

Chapter 6
The Impact of Terrorism on Trade in Nigeria and Chad 76
Isaac Terungwa Terwase, Federal University of Kashere, Nigeria
Muhammad Yusuf, Federal University of Kashere, Nigeria
Abubakar Sambo Mohammed, Federal University of Kashere, Nigeria
Safwan Mikaila Sani, Federal University of Kashere, Nigeria

The Boko Haram conflict started in Nigeria from a city in the north-eastern part of the country known as Maiduguri in 2009 during the administration of President Umaru Musa Yar'Adua. It was a new thing to Nigeria considering the fact that the country was yet to witness terrorism and its activities. Boko Haram later continued after the death of President Yar'Adua, and they became stronger during the President Jonathan's administration. Boko Haram later transformed from an insurgent group into a terrorist group where they spread from Nigeria to other parts of African countries such as Chad, Niger, and Cameroon. This has it effects, impacts, and consequences on trade in Africa. The objective of this chapter is to draw the impact of terrorism on trade with specific attention to Nigeria and Chad.

Chapter 7
Antecedents and Consequences of International Joint Venture Knowledge Acquisition: Evidence From Algeria 92
Tamma Elhachemi, University of Echahid Hamma Lakhdar, Eloued, Algeria

Studies on the establishment of international joint ventures (IJVs) in open-oriented markets as a vehicle for knowledge acquisition have been increasing of late. Drawing on the transaction cost economics theory and the knowledge-based view, the chapter examines the impact of absorptive capacity, transfer mechanisms, knowledge management practices, and environmental uncertainty on knowledge acquisition of IJVs from foreign partners. Further, the author examines IJV innovativeness as a consequence of knowledge acquisition. The author tested the model with data from 122 IJVs in Algeria. By analyzing the data using SPSSv25 and smart PLS 3.0, the findings show that absorptive capacity and transfer mechanisms are positively and significantly related to knowledge acquisition of the IJVs. However, knowledge management practices and environmental uncertainty are not significant. In addition, the relationship between IJV knowledge acquisition and innovativeness is significant.

Chapter 8
The Spread of Cross-Border High-Tech Manufacturing Component Goods in International Trade Integration 112
Dyah Wulan Sari, Airlangga Universty, Indonesia
Haura Azzahra Tarbiyah Islamiya, Airlangga University, Indonesia
Wenny Restikasari, Airlangga University, Indonesia

The objective of this study is to examine the spread of cross-border trading in determining the firm's production in high-technology manufacturing industries in Indonesia. The spread of cross-border trading in the model is measured by export intensity and alternatively is measured by vertical trade integration. The firm-level data of high-tech industries are implemented in this study. A panel data regression procedure is applied to estimate the model. The estimation results elucidate that vertical trade integration is a significant determinant on affecting firm's production while export intensity is not. This evidence proves that the pattern of cross-border international trade of high-technology industries shifted from exporting finished goods to exporting fragmented products. The export intensity variable is no longer representing the international trade when the firms break-down their production process. The usage of export intensity variable in firms undertaking the vertical trade integration would lead to a misleading conclusion.

Chapter 9
Sustainability Analysis of Sino-Brazilian Bilateral Trade: A Case Study of the 2020 Global Epidemic Event 132
Poshan Yu, Soochow University, China
Jiayi He, Independent Researcher, China
Michael Sampat, Independent Researcher, Canada

The large-scale health crisis caused by COVID-19 that appeared in late 2019 has undoubtedly had a huge influence on the global economy. This chapter takes the interruption of international trade in the context of epidemics as the main research subject, using the change in Sino-Brazilian trade as a case study. From the international management perspective, this chapter will investigate how this epidemic affects Sino-Brazilian cross-border trade and business practices. The interlinked relationship between both countries' cross-border trade will be examined. Recommendations will be provided for further enhancing both countries' economic growth and trade practices.

Chapter 10
Portfolio Investment in Malaysia and Saudi Arabia: Effect of Graham Stock Selection on Return on Investment 155
Fariza Hashim, University Kuala Lumpur, Malaysia
Nadisah Zakaria, UCSI University, Malaysia
Abdul Rahim Abu Bakar, Prince Sultan University, Saudi Arabia
Kamilah Kamaludin, Prince Sultan University, Saudi Arabia

Several strategies are adopted by investors in lowering the risk of investment while maximising its return. Graham's stock selection criteria are noted as one of the best strategies in selecting portfolios by investors. Although the model is universally accepted, it is less commonly practised and examined in emerging markets. Considering the growth of these emerging countries' financial markets, it is worthwhile to investigate the doctrine's effect on investment in these countries. This study endeavours to review the consequence of Graham's stock selection criteria on portfolio returns in the Malaysian and Saudi Arabian stock markets. Each country represents the fastest growing market in their region which justifies this study. The study found that the Malaysian stock market is capable of proffering abnormal returns to investors while the Saudi stock market is capable to offer abnormal returns to investors despite being an undeveloped and immature stock market. The study concludes that the model of stock selection remains beneficial and indeed valuable to regional investments.

Chapter 11
International Trade Fairs and Initial Impacts of COVID-19 on International Fairs: The Case of Dubai 176
Muharrem Can, Turkish Ministry of Trade, Turkey
Ahmet Canlı, Turkish Consulate in Dubai, UAE

In ITFs, participating companies introduce their products to potential buyers, perceive their reactions, communicate face-to-face with them, and closely observe their competitors. Moreover, there are other benefits of ITFs such as export and market share increase effect, problem-solving effect with the costumers, so it is one of the critical tasks of commercial diplomacy. The COVID-19 pandemic in 2020 affected the exhibition sector. So the number of fairs held in Dubai decreased dramatically compared to the previous years and also the number of participators and visitors in the fairs, including Turkish companies. Nevertheless, fair activities have adapted quickly and started to be organized in the virtual world. This study examined the literature and analyzed the Dubai exhibitions' statistics thoroughly both before and after COVID-19. The authors' goal is to find out if physical exhibitions maintain their importance despite technological developments.

Chapter 12
Skill Acquisition: A Panacea for Economic Development in Nigeria 191
Bolaji Comfort Adeniyi, Bamidele Olumilua University of Education, Science, and Technology, Nigeria

The purpose of the study was to examine the extent to which skill acquisition would influence economic development in Nigeria. The descriptive research design of the survey type was adopted in the study. The population of this study comprised all the students of government technical colleges in Southwest Nigeria. The reliability of the instrument was estimated using Chronbach's Alpha reliability method. The data collected for this study was analyzed using both descriptive and inferential statistics. The result of the study revealed that skill acquisition program has a positive and significant effect on the ability of students of technical colleges in Southwest Nigeria to be self-reliant at graduation; skill acquisition program has a positive and significant effect on the ability of students of technical colleges in Southwest Nigeria to produce goods for local consumption. It was also recommended based on the study that the various government parastatals should review, standardize, and expand the curricula of all skill acquisition schemes in Nigeria among others.

Chapter 13
The Impact of Market Orientation, Entrepreneurial Orientation, and Relationship Orientation on the International Performance of SMEs.. 203
Kabiru Sa'ad Sa'id, Federal University, Dutse, Nigeria

The relationship between strategic orientation and SME international performance is empirically inadequate, specifically in a developing country. This study focuses on the effect of three dimensions of strategic orientation, namely market orientation, entrepreneurial orientation, and relationship orientation on the international performance of SMEs applying the theory of resource-based view. The study is quantitative and uses the data collected from 296 managers of SMEs operating an international business in Nigeria. The authors revealed that entrepreneurial orientation, relationship orientation have a positive effect on firm international performance. On the other hand, market orientation has no significant impact on a firm international performance. The authors explain the managerial contribution of study findings and provide future research suggestions.

Chapter 14
Iron Silk Road Trans-Caspian East-West-Middle Corridor Initiative and Baku-Tbilisi-Kars Railway Line: Impact on International Trade 222
Özlem Karadağ Albayrak, Kafkas University, Turkey
Başak Çelik, Kafkas University, Turkey

The East-West Middle Corridor (Middle Corridor) with the Caspian Transit, which starts from Turkey with the Baku Tbilisi Kars Railway line, reaches the Caucasus region. From here it travels over the Caspian Sea through Turkmenistan and Kazakhstan to Central Asia and China and is one of the most important components of historical silk road resuscitation project. With this study, the contribution of Baku Tbilisi Kars railway line and Kars Logistics Center, which is the European and Turkish gateway of the middle corridor, to the silk railway in terms of international leasing is explored.

Chapter 15
Exploring Cultural Factors Impacting Female Digital Entrepreneurs in Underdeveloped Countries: A Comparative Analysis 237
Areeba Waseem Shaikh, University of Wollongong in Dubai, UAE
Norhayati Zakaria, University of Wollongong in Dubai, UAE

This chapter aims at understanding the cultural influence on female digital entrepreneurs in underdeveloped countries and the possible effects of cyberostracism by integrating the significance of culture and its influence on females providing a holistic view of how women with entrepreneurial desires experience challenges due to the identified existing gaps in underdeveloped countries. Besides sociocultural dynamics, education is a factor observed to be extremely impactful. Basic and digital literacy are considered essential to progress in conducting businesses across borders. From a digital perspective, "cyberostracism" is identified as a potential issue women could encounter due to lack of education. In this study, a comparative analysis on female digital entrepreneurs of the Asian and European region is conducted based on the view of a collectivistic and individualistic society concluded by providing a framework to minimize gaps and establish an environment for women to pursue digital entrepreneurship in their societies, mitigating the possible effects of cyberostracism.

Chapter 16
COVID-19's Impact on Tertiary Institutions in Nigeria and Its Effects on the Economy 252
Temitope Teniola Onileowo, Universiti Teknologi Malaysia, Malaysia & Ekiti State University, Nigeria
Farrah Merlinda Muharam, Universiti Teknologi Malaysia, Malaysia
Mohd Khairuddin Ramliy, Universiti Teknologi Malaysia, Malaysia

This chapter addressed Coronavirus disease 2019 (COVID-19) impact on tertiary institutions in Nigeria, its effect on the economy, and possible coping strategies in a time of global pandemic and national disaster. COVID-19 was reported as a pandemic by the World Health Organization (WHO) on March 11, 2020, discovered in Wuhan, China, in December 2019, spread to several nations, forcing the closure of tertiary institutions all over the world. The effect has also disrupted the school academic calendar at tertiary institutions, decreased international education, Suspension of local and international conferences, etc. And the economy, leading to job losses, revenue loss in the informal sector, business closure, agricultural production and food insecurity, a sharp drop in oil revenues, and economic uncertainties. Which, thus, harms the economy. This chapter makes recommendations to assist Nigeria's government and the educational institutions in coping with the effect of the outbreak and similar pandemics soon.

Chapter 17
Reflections and Future Directions for the Green Maritime Supply Chain in Malaysia 270
Muhamad Fairuz Ahmad Jasmi, Universiti Utara Malaysia, Malaysia
Yudi Fernando, Universiti Malaysia Pahang, Malaysia
Rusdi Omar, Universiti Utara Malaysia, Malaysia
Muhammad Shabir Shaharudin, Universiti Sains Malaysia

The maritime sector and shipping industry have been argued to be effective drivers of international trade. Internationalization has become a strategic business plan by entrepreneurs and industry players to expand the business, especially when their business was already established in the domestic market. However, current international laws began to be tightened by requiring each exporting and shipping firms to implement green sea transport practices and documentations. A limited number of empirical-based evidence has forced the maritime practitioners to conduct business without clear green concepts knowledge and availability of best business practices to be benchmarked. With this in mind, the aim of this chapter is to examine current issues, differences, and dilemmas confronting practitioners, governments, stakeholders, and scholars. This chapter has developed a green maritime supply chain concept based on practitioners' reflections and provides future direction to scholars interested in studying green logistics and supplying chain management in the maritime sector.

Chapter 18
Travel Motivations and Travel Careers of Malaysian Backpackers 290
Samshul Amry Abdul Latif, International Islamic University Malaysia, Malaysia
Mazni Saad, International Islamic University Malaysia, Malaysia
Nuraini Ismail, International Islamic University Malaysia, Malaysia
Murodjon Matniyozov, Urgench State University, Uzbekistan
Mona Fairuz Ramli, Kolej Universiti Islam Perlis, Malaysia

The study's two primary goals are to determine the main travel motives of Malaysian backpackers and to examine the variations in travel motivations across three categories of backpackers: first-time, repeat, and serial. The results were collected using a self-administered online survey adopting a convenience sample technique. The non-normally distributed data were examined using exploratory factor analysis, median score assessment, and Kruskal-Wallis H tests on a sample of 249. Stimulation is the most crucial factor motivating backpackers, while recognition is the least important. The study also found that backpackers' motivation varied with travel experience. Due to limited research on Asian motivational travel determinants, notably among Malaysian backpackers, this study's motivational features are drawn from other countries. Future research should focus on non-Western motivators impacting backpackers. There is a need for more research on Asian tourism, notably Malaysian backpackers at various stages of their travel careers.

Compilation of References 308

About the Contributors 365

Index 372

Preface

INTRODUCTION

Cross border business transactions have become increasingly important due to new norms of doing business. Cross border business has led to the emergence of multiply business opportunities and challenges to various stakeholders. Such global reality cannot simply be ignored, thus business entities that operate across national borders need to fully employ global strategies in order to compete and survive in the dynamic global environment. In fact, businesses need to have a wider world view when conducting business across the border. The future growth of global businesses depends on many crucial aspects such as managing and recruiting global workforces, developing effective international marketing strategies, coordinating global supply chains and operations, introducing innovative sales tactics, utilizing information technology, and many others. In this light, businesses need to employ a synergistic approach to manage cross border transactions -- mainly comprising of internal and external elements. Additionally, businesses are also required to engage with state and non-state actors whenever they design their business policies and strategies to deal with the turbulent global business challenges lying ahead of them.

OBJECTIVE

The book aims to capture the multi-faceted outlook on international business phenomena particularly when cross border businesses were severely affected by the worldwide pandemic. The book brings the perspectives of the communities, consumers, employees, businesses, producers and many other stakeholders regardless of their home country. The investigation includes both developed and developing countries. From here on, there are new economic, socio-cultural, health-related, well-being and many more challenges which have emerged when operating under the new norms. This publication could provide comprehensive coverage within these areas.

TARGET AUDIENCE

The book aims at a general readership as well as scholars with profound interest in cross-border and international business disciplines. This book is an excellent resource for entrepreneurs, executives, managers, and businesses intending to expand into cross-border markets. The materials offered in this book are ideal for academics and undergraduate/postgraduate students who requires a complementary book and resources to debate relevant concerns and challenges faced by global business entities based on the vast range of themes covered here.

The book is also appropriate for class discussions since it is customized to issues covered in courses such as international politics, international business, and so on. Furthermore, we provide this book as a resource for scholars and business executives as practitioners who require both theoretical and practical elements in studying the subject matter relevant to business and political viewpoints in addressing globalisation concerns and challenges.

We present this book as a resource for business executives seeking a practical understanding of the subject matter in three areas relevant to enabling and attaining sustainable global business operations. This will serve as a guide for multinational organisations with a transnational structure comprised of heterogeneous teams and a diversified workforce from any sector or industry. The book is primarily focused on managing multicultural environments in the context of international business and management practises.

OVERVIEW OF THE BOOK

This book consists of 18 chapters that encompass a wide range of topics involving myriad perspectives that affect business across the globe. The selected authors come from ten countries and are affiliated to multidisciplinary faculties such as business and management, international studies, international business, marketing, tourism, entrepreneurship, political science, economic, commercial and management, engineering, and industrial management. A brief synopsis of each chapter is presented accordingly as the following.

In Chapter 1, Wahid and Ismail discusses on the pertinent issues and strategies in reconciling the Malaysia-Eu palm oil discord. The EU has decided to phase out imports of palm oil used in biofuels into the EU by 2030. This affects people in Malaysia who rely on the palm oil business for their livelihood. Thus, their chapter presents the political processes that generate policy interventions aimed at defending palm oil trade with the EU alerting that economic decoupling and direct conflict may exacerbate the problem, weaken bilateral relations, and elude good improvements in the palm oil business. Next, in Chapter 2, Arshad and colleagues began to look at branding through online social networks, and how impacts on export market. They noted that the hurdles to entering a foreign market have been dismantled by greater internet connectivity. As a result, there is virtually endless potential to expand a company abroad. Every company that wishes to export should aim towards market-driven, long-term, and sustainable exporting.

In Chapter 3, Saad and team looked at the South Korea Film-Induced Tourism and how the K-Drama becomes a determinant factor for Malaysian tourists. Their results show that collaboration for the development of heritage tourism should be linked to the national identity and replicated through dramas similar to K-dramas. universities should work closely with other stakeholders to produce high-quality films for international distribution. Given such understanding, under Chapter 4, Ramlee looks further into the early internationalizing of small medium firms and how they aim at conceptualization the concept of internationalisation for new ventures (IJVs). Such nature of international new ventures (INJVs) and born global has become a new entity entering the global market and rapidly evolved to catch up and maintain its pace with international new ventures.

Apart from business, human resource is equally an important asset to be considered. Thus, under Chapter 5, Ramalu and Malik looks further into the case of academic expatriates in Malaysia. The chapter discusses and aims to provide greater understanding about the nature and motivation for expatriation which will have significant implication on the international human resource management policies and practices. This chapter begins with explanation about the concept of expatriation and expatriate. This is followed by comparison between organizational expatriates and self-initiated expatriates. Another aspect is on the impact of terrorism on trade in Nigeria and Chad, thus the subsequent Chapter 6 is written by Terwase and colleagues who look into *The Boko Haram* conflict started in Nigeria from a city in the north-eastern part of the country known as Maiduguri in 2009 during the administration of President Umaru Musa Yar'adua. It was a new thing to Nigeria considering the fact that the country was yet to witnessed terrorism and its activities. The objective of the chapter is to draw the impact of terrorism on trade with specific attention to Nigeria and Chad.

Chapter 7 elaborate antecedents and consequences of international joint ventures' knowledge acquisition: Under this chapter, Elhachemi studied on the establishment of international joint ventures (IJVs) in open-oriented markets as a vehicle for knowledge acquisition. Our findings show that absorptive capacity and transfer mechanisms are positively and significantly related to knowledge acquisition of the IJVs. however, knowledge management practices and environmental uncertainty are not significant. in addition, the relationship between IJVs knowledge acquisition and innovativeness is significant. Thus, this bring into discussion of the spread of cross-border high-tech manufacturing component goods in international trade integration.

Chapter 8, Sari, Islamiya and Restikasari examine the spread of cross-border trading in determining the firm's production in high-technology manufacturing industries in Indonesia. The spread of cross-border trading in the model is measured by export intensity and alternatively is measured by vertical trade integration. his evidence proves that the pattern of cross-border international trade of high-technology industries shifted from exporting finished goods to exporting fragmented products. The export intensity variable is no longer representing the international trade when the firms break-down their production process. The usage of export intensity variable in firms undertaking the vertical trade integration would lead to a misleading conclusion.

For Chapter 9, the research team look into the study based on the sustainability analysis of Sino-Brazilian bilateral trade. Yu, He and Sampat apply - a case study of the 2020 global epidemic event that disrupt business in late 2019 has undoubtedly had a huge influence on the global economy. This chapter takes the interruption of international trade in the context of epidemics as the main research subject, using the change in Sino-Brazilian trade as a case study. From the international management perspective, this chapter will investigate how this epidemic affects Sino-Brazilian cross-border trade and business practices. Likewise, for Chapter 10, Hashim and colleagues looked into other geographical markets to cross-examine: Portfolio Investment in Malaysia and Saudi Arabia: Effect of graham stock selection on return on investment. Their study discussed the strategies that investors took to lower the risk of investment while maximising its return. The study concludes that the model of stock selection remains beneficial and indeed valuable to regional investments.

Amidst of the condition on international trade fairs and initial impacts of Covid19 on international cases in Dubai, under Chapter 11, Can and Canli mentioned that participating companies introduce their products to potential buyers, perceive their reactions, communicate face-to-face with them, and closely observe their competitors. It seemed that the Covid19 pandemic in 2020 affected the exhibition sector where only fair activities have adapted quickly and started to be organized in the virtual world. This study examined the literature and analyzed the Dubai's exhibitions' statistics thoroughly both before and after Covid19. The authors' goal is to find out if physical exhibitions maintain their importance despite technological developments.

Different context and culture introduced different skills acquisitions. For example, Adeniyi and colleagues concurred that skill acquisition acts as a panacea for economic development in Nigeria. Following up to the discussion, under Chapter 12, Adeniyi examine the extent to which skill acquisition would influence economic development in Nigeria. The aim was followed through till one incident. The result of the study revealed that skill acquisition program has a positive and significant effect on the ability of students of technical colleges in southwest, Nigeria to be self-reliant at graduation; skill acquisition program has a positive and significant effect on the ability of students of technical colleges in southwest, Nigeria to produce goods for local consumption. Now that we understand about knowledge exchanges, sharing and ownership, as such: the more we are trusting each other, business could be leverage on other account/aspects.

Under Chapter 13, Sa'id express his thoughts on the impact of market orientation, entrepreneurial orientation and relationship orientation on international performance of SMEs. It is expected that the relationship between strategic orientation and SMEs international performance is empirically inadequate, specifically in a developing country. this study focuses on the effect of three dimensions of strategic orientation, namely market orientation, entrepreneurial orientation, and relationship orientation on the international performance of SMEs applying the theory of resource-based view. The study is quantitative and using the data collected from 296 managers of SMEs operating an international business in Nigeria. The authors revealed that entrepreneurial orientation, relationship orientation have a positive effect on firm international performance. on the other hand, market orientation has no significant impact on a firm international performance. the authors explain the managerial contribution of study finding and provide future research suggestion.

Interestingly, under Chapter 14, we have witnessed the growing population and scientific communities which looked into the issue of Silk Road Trans-Caspian East-West-Middle Corridor Initiative and Baku-Tbilisi-Kars Railway Line: Impact On International Trade. Albayrak and Celik mentioned that the east-west middle corridor (middle corridor) with the caspian transit, which starts from turkey with the Baku Tbilisi Kars railway line, reaches the caucasus region, from here over the Caspian Sea through Turkmenistan and Kazakhstan, to Central Asia and China is one of the most important components of historical silk road resuscitation project. with this study, the contribution of Baku Tbilisi Kars railway line and kars logistics center, which is the european and turkish gateway of the middle corridor, to the silk railway in terms of international leasing.

Under Chapter 15, Shaikh and Zakaria explores cultural factors impacting female digital entrepreneurs in underdeveloped countries through a comparative analysis. This chapter aims at understanding the cultural influence on female digital entrepreneurs in underdeveloped countries. Besides, the possible effects of cyberostracism by integrating the significance of culture and its influence on females providing a holistic view of how women with entrepreneurial desires experience challenges due to the identified existing gaps in underdeveloped countries. besides sociocultural dynamics, education is a factor observed to be extremely impactful. basic and digital literacy, both are considered essential to progress in conducting businesses across borders. In this study, a comparative analysis on female digital entrepreneurs of the Asian and European region is conducted, based on the view of a collectivistic and individualistic society, concluded by providing a framework to minimize gaps and establish an environment for women to pursue digital entrepreneurship in their societies, mitigating the possible effects of cyberostracism.

Notably, that Covid-19's impact on tertiary institutions in Nigeria and its effect on internally generated revenue challenges and opportunities. In Chapter 16, Onileowo, Muharam and Ramliy addressed COVID19 impact on tertiary institutions in/Nigeria and its effect on internally generated revenue. They highlight the importance of e-learning in a time of global pandemic and national disaster, its challenges, and opportunities. Covid-19 has a peculiar but unprecedented impact on the education sector, affecting over 1.5 billion students worldwide, resulting in revenue loss to institutions, especially those relying on tuitions and using typical face-to-face teaching methods. Nigerian students and those from other West African countries were marginalised. There is a critical need for reflections and future directions for green maritime supply chain in Malaysia.

In Chapter 17, Jasmi and his other three different scholars came on board to discuss on the maritime sector and shipping industry that have been argued to be effective drivers of international trade. Internationalization has become a strategic business plan by entrepreneurs and industry players to expand the business, especially when their business was already established in the domestic market. however, current international laws began to be tightened by requiring each exporting and shipping firms to implement green sea transport practices and documentations. a limited number of empirical-based evidence has forced the maritime practitioners to conduct business without clear green concepts knowledge and availability of best business practices to be benchmarked.

Finally, under Chapter 18, the study's two primary goals are to determine the main travel motives of Malaysian backpackers and to examine the variations in travel motivations across three categories of backpackers: first-time, repeat, and serial. The results were collected using a self-administered online survey adopting a convenience sample technique. Stimulation is the most crucial factor motivating backpackers, while recognition is the least important. the study also found that backpackers' motivation varied with travel experience. The authors concluded that future research should focus on non-western motivators impacting backpackers. there is a need for more research on Asian tourism, notably Malaysian backpackers at various stages of their travel careers.

EDITORS

Asmat-Nizam Abdul-Talib
Universiti Utara Malaysia, Malaysia

Norhayati Zakaria
University of Wollongong in Dubai, UAE

Samshul-Amry Abdul-Latif
International Islamic University Malaysia, Malaysia

REFERENCES

Hofstede Insights. (2020). *Country Comparison - Hofstede Insights*. Available at: https://www.hofstede-insights.com/country-comparison/

Morais, F., & Ferreira, J. J. (2020). SME internationalisation process: Key issues and contributions, existing gaps and the future research agenda. *European Management Journal*, *38*(1), 62–77. doi:10.1016/j.emj.2019.08.001

Zakaria, N., Abdul-Talib, A. N., & Amelinckx, A. (Eds.). (2020). *Transcending cultural frontiers: practices, challenges, and strategy for international business*. Springer. doi:10.1007/978-981-15-4454-5

Zakaria, N., Abdul-Talib, A. N., & Othman, N. (Eds.). (2016). *Handbook of research on impacts of international business and political affairs on the global economy*. IGI Global. doi:10.4018/978-1-4666-9806-2

Zhou, N., & Guillén, M. F. (2015). From home country to home base: A dynamic approach to the liability of foreignness. *Strategic Management Journal*, *36*(6), 907–917. doi:10.1002mj.2242

Chapter 1
Issues and Strategies in Reconciling the Malaysia–EU Palm Oil Discord

Ratnaria Wahid
https://orcid.org/0000-0001-9424-9285
Universiti Utara Malaysia, Malaysia

Norafidah Ismail
Universiti Utara Malaysia, Malaysia

ABSTRACT

The EU has decided to phase out imports of palm oil used in biofuels in the EU by 2030. This affects people in Malaysia who rely on the palm oil business for their livelihood. This chapter examines the events leading up to the EU's anti-palm oil actions and the many ways in which Malaysia has responded to defend its palm oil sector. This includes 1) countering EU's allegation through scientific research, 2) demonstrating its commitment to transform the palm oil industry toward sustainability through certification standards, 3) fostering the commitment to grow palm oil sustainably, 4) garnering support from ASEAN and the international community, 5) expressing its opposition and warnings for retaliatory measures against the EU, and 6) requesting consultation under the WTO dispute settlement mechanism. It presents the political processes that generate policy interventions aimed at defending palm oil trade with the EU alerting that economic decoupling and direct conflict may exacerbate the problem, weaken bilateral relations, and elude good improvements in the palm oil business.

INTRODUCTION

Since 1985, palm oil has surpassed soyabean oil as the world's second most consumed oil. Palm oil is used in nearly every consumer retail food and snack product, personal care and cosmetics, biofuel and energy, animal feed, pharmaceuticals, industrial and food service industries. Palm oil is deemed as a versatile, efficient source, cheap and it presents opportunities for economic development, employment

DOI: 10.4018/978-1-7998-9071-3.ch001

and smallholder livelihoods. Palm oil is framed as a "driver of development" or 'development engine' and provides mutual benefits for both exporting and importing countries (Hinkes, 2019).

According to critics, expanding industrial palm oil production has negative environmental and socioeconomic consequences. Critics stated that by establishing oil palm monoculture plantations, forest areas are destroyed, resulting in biodiversity loss, soil erosion, waste, and decreased air and water quality (Hinkes, 2019). Additionally, it endangers biological systems and numerous species by triggering forest fires and the emission of carbon dioxide into the atmosphere, which contributes to climate change. Moreover, the resultant smog exacerbated respiratory and other human health concerns (Varkkey, 2013). Additionally, there are negative social consequences, such as exploitation and forced labour, conflicts over land and resources, and the influence on local economies and food sovereignty (White et al., 2012). Despite the various benefits of palm oil, these adverse consequences frequently became a point of contention (Pye & Bhattacharya, 2013).

Malaysia has an important role to play in fulfilling the growing global need for oils and fats sustainability. The Malaysia Palm Oil Council (2021a) reported that Malaysia accounted for 25.8 percent of global palm oil production and 34.3 percent of global palm oil exports making it the second largest producer of palm oil in 2020. Specifically, after India and China, the European Union (EU) remained Malaysia's third-largest palm oil export market. In 2020, Malaysia exported approximately 1.8 million metric tonnes of palm oil to the European Union (Hirschmann, 2021).

However, as a result of the 2018 EU Resolution, the European Commission's plans to phase out the use of palm oil in transportation fuel by 2030, which may threaten to reduce the market for Malaysian palm oil in the future. This is due to the report that identified palm oil as the leading cause of rainforest deforestation, contributing to climate change and aggravating social and economic issues. Palm oil accounted for roughly 38% of the value of Malaysia's agricultural output in 2020, and it contributed 3% to the country's gross domestic product (Chang, 2021). Palm-oil plantations cover around 18 percent of the country's territory, employ 441,000 people directly (more than half of them are tiny landholders), and indirectly employ at least that many in a country with a population of 32 million (Chang, 2021). Understandably, Malaysia would pursue a foreign policy that seeks to advance and protect its country's palm-oil industry, particularly if it believes that industry is under threat.

Several studies have looked into different aspects of the Malaysia-EU palm oil discord. Mayr, Hollaus & Madner (2021) examines the compatibility of the EU's contentious measures that freeze and phase-out certain biofuels introduced in the Renewable Energy Directive with WTO law, casting doubt on their justification due to the deliberate targeting of palm oil. According to Arief et al. (2020), the EU renewable energy directive policy is influenced by market forces. Oosterveer (2020) conducted an assessment of the EU's disputes over the use of palm oil for biofuels and other applications. The study viewed that interaction with producing countries is unlikely to have a significant impact on the EU's biofuels strategy. Nonetheless, a focus on the legitimacy and accountability of producing countries' engagement would increase market opportunities for food and other commodities (Oosterveer, 2020). Hinkes (2019) provided a classification of relevant political discourses and concluded that both the EU and palm oil exporters Indonesia and Malaysia are biased due to factual misinterpretation. Limenta (2020) further examines whether the EU violates WTO anti-discrimination regulations. Dauvergne (2018) advances further understanding of business strategies that navigate weak governance rules and certification loopholes to meet palm oil demands while promoting the protection of rain forests. Yet there is a lack of literature that investigates the strategies to promote palm oil through state narratives, foreign policies, or governmental measures.

This chapter looks into the development leading to the EU anti palm oil measures affecting Malaysia's palm oil industry. This chapter showed various ways Malaysia has responded to protect the Malaysian palm oil industry. These include scientific-backed arguments, framing positive viewpoints through certification standards, negotiations, mobilizing support from ASEAN and appeals at the international forum, voicing criticism and warnings, as well as bringing the matter to the World Trade Organization. This chapter further offers insights into the political processes that shape policy interventions with respect to protecting palm oil trade to the EU.

EUROPEAN UNION RESTRICTIONS TOWARDS PALM OIL

The EU's staunch opposition to palm oil may have been impacted by the establishment of numerous international treaties post-2014 (Hinkes, 2019). The 2015 New York Declaration on Forests, being the outcome of the 2014 UN Climate Summit, has aimed for the ending of global deforestation by 2030, explicitly naming deforestation for palm oil production as one of its focus. Similarly, the 2015 Paris Agreement legally bound member countries to undertake efforts to stop climate change. Several Sustainable Development Goals set up in 2015, also affect palm oil supply chains, particularly "Responsible Consumption and Production" (Goal 12); "Climate Action" (Goal 13) and "Life on Land" (Goal 15). Consequently, the EU has made a number of efforts to discourage people from purchasing palm oil goods. As of 2014, EU law started requiring palm oil to be clearly identified on the ingredients' labels (not merely as "vegetable oil"). Six EU countries—Denmark, France, the United Kingdom, Germany, the Netherlands, and Norway—signed the Amsterdam Declaration Partnership in 2015, declaring their support for only 100% sustainable palm oil and their intention to end illegal logging and deforestation by 2020.

A report by the Committee on the Environment, Public Health and Food Safety (2017) on Palm Oil and Deforestation of Rainforest was delivered to the Members of the European Parliament, highlighting palm oil as the primary source of rainforest deforestation, which contributes to climate change and exacerbates social and economic concerns. The Report received widespread support, and its recommendations were subsequently adopted as EU Resolution 2017, which paved the way for several contentious initiatives to halt deforestation. By 2020, one of the goals is to phase out the use of non-sustainable vegetable oils in biofuels. Additionally, they suggest that after 2020, only sustainable palm oil verified by a single EU-wide sustainability certification process be permitted to enter the EU. The European Parliament agreed to prohibit the use of palm oil in the production of biofuels in the EU by 2020, pledging to put an end to the devastation of rainforests in primarily Indonesia and Malaysia (Klepper, 2018).

In 2018, the revised EU Renewable Energy Directorate II (RED II), covered within the EU Resolution, paved the way for Directive (EU) 2018/2001 which limits the contribution of palm oil as a biofuel usage in transport onwards to the EU's Union 2030 renewable energy target. RED II classifies palm oil as a high indirect land use change product that raises its greenhouse gas emissions to unacceptable levels and so will be gradually phased out of the EU renewable energy mix by 2030. As a result of the EU Directive, the use of palm oil as a biofuel in the EU will be excluded from the calculation of renewable energy targets. This will result in unjustified trade restrictions on Malaysia's palm oil industry. In particular, given that shipments of biofuel-designated palm oil from Southeast Asia to Europe roughly quadrupled between 2008 and 2018, surpassing imports of palm oil for food and cosmetics. Furthermore, a record-high 65 percent of all palm oil imported into the EU in 2018 was expected to be used as biofuel for automobiles or electricity generation. Two important policies, namely a) the European Parliament resolution on palm oil and the deforestation of rainforests, and b) the revised Renewable Energy Directive II (RED II) of the European Union, have mainly brought about discourses that strongly influence environmental policy and induce change in production, consumption, and trade relations.

The implication of the EU Resolution on Malaysia is significant. Since the EU is one of the largest importers of Malaysian palm oil, it is likely that the palm oil exports to Europe will decrease. This will affect approximately 3 million people in Malaysia who depend upon the palm oil industry as their means of livelihood. 40% of the palm oil growers in Malaysia are small holders, numbering 650,000. The EU directive, which Malaysia and Indonesia call a 'ban' would also have a long-term impact which could be damaging to the Malaysian reputation and economy.

MALAYSIA'S STRATEGIES FOR PROTECTING THE PALM OIL INDUSTRY

The European Union's new palm oil policy has elicited negative or critical reactions, generating heated political debate and fury among not only the palm oil business, but also policymakers in Southeast Asian oil-producing countries. Malaysia and Indonesia have both denounced the European Parliament's decision to phase out imports of palm oil used in biofuels into the EU by 2030. Prime Minister, Tun Mahathir and Indonesian President, Joko Widodo wrote letters opposing the EU's intention to phase out palm oil from biofuels (Reuters, 2019). Malaysia and Indonesia have both characterised the policy change as a "ban on palm oil," "crop apartheid," and the beginning of a potential "trade war" (Hinkes, 2019). Tun Mahathir cites the European Union's proposed prohibition on the import of palm oil as a textbook example of a rejection of free trade (Mohamad, 2019). Tun asserted that the EU's inability to maintain the competitiveness of its own edible oils prompted them to launch a campaign to prohibit palm oil (Mohamad, 2019).

The palm oil industry is very important to Malaysia's economy and has brought a lot of positive impacts. This starts from a humble beginning when Malaysia first established its palm oil plantations in 1917. In 1966, Malaysia and Indonesia began to dominate world trade in palm oil, taking over Nigeria and Zaire (Sheil et al, 2009). By 1998, palm oil contributed over 5% of Malaysia's gross domestic product. Malaysia is now the second largest producer and exporter of palm oil in the world, after being overtaken by Indonesia in 2006. The palm oil industry contributed in terms of export earnings, employment, improved access to social services, research and development, and innovation. It plays a significant role in alleviating poverty and providing a better standard of living to many rural communities (Dayang Norwana et. al, 2011). Palm oil's enormous contribution to the Malaysian economy is all the more reason for Malaysia to adopt different measures that aim to safeguard the country's palm-oil sector.

1. Scientifically Refuting Palm Oil Allegations

Both Malaysia and Indonesia contend that palm oil is unfairly targeted in order to benefit other vegetable oils, particularly those produced in Europe. Malaysia and Indonesia claimed that the EU resolution was based on the ENVI Report, which was biased and lacked verified references such as EU-commissioned studies and several sceptical NGOs such as Amnesty International, FERN, and Rainforest Action Network, with the exception of the WWF, which collaborates with the RSPO. This increases the danger of data tampering, misinterpretation, and the emergence of palm oil's 'alternative facts.'

Malaysia proved its stance against the EU's claims through investigations and scientific studies. The Malaysian Palm Oil Council (MPOC) is critical to the assumption that palm oil contributes significantly to forest loss. The MPOC cited research by the Union of Concerned Scientists, reported by Anair & Mahmassani (2013) that found beef is the leading driver of deforestation, accounting for up to 71.2 percent of the world's 5 billion hectares of agricultural land, while palm oil accounts for just 0.31 percent (Malaysian Palm Oil Council, 2021a). Furthermore, substituting soybean or coconut oil for palm oil would need four to ten times the amount of land, merely moving the problem elsewhere (World Wildlife Fund, n.d.).

Several studies questioned the EU policy, stating that singling out palm oil does not actually help the environment. The EU resolution only focuses on palm oil although the European Commission (2013) has previously reported that imported beef and soy have contributed more to deforestation than imported palm oil. In addition, Meijaard et al. (2020) found that the alternatives to palm oil, such as sunflower and soybean oil actually require more land, water and fertiliser, lower productivity, shorter lifespans and store less CO2 emissions. The study confirmed years of previous research from the University of Oxford and the International Union for the Conservation of Nature. This is confirmed by the study by European Parliamentary Research Service (EPRS) that contends that the EU's approach is unsustainable.

2. Framing a Positive Viewpoint Through Certification Standards

Malaysia asserted that by adopting the Malaysian Sustainable Palm Oil (MSPO) standard for achieving sustainable palm oil output, it exhibited a strong commitment to transforming the palm oil industry toward sustainability. This is in conjunction with the 2015 Sustainable Development Goals, formally titled Transforming our World: the 2030 Agenda for Sustainable Development (Abdul Majid et al., 2021).

The MSPO are Malaysian government initiatives based on Malaysian domestic laws and regulations and adopted in accordance with Malaysia's interpretation of the RSPO (Ivancic & Koh, 2016). MSPO certification entails legal compliance, as well as safety and health requirements, all of which contribute indirectly to the achievement of several SDGs. This is in addition to the Roundtable on Sustainable Palm Oil's (RSPO) voluntary 2004 international sustainable certification criteria, which aim to promote the growth and use of sustainable palm oil products. The MSPO certification scheme is being launched as a complement to the RSPO certification in order to give an option for smallholders and outgrowers who cannot afford the fees associated with third-party audits of their processes and plantations (Abdul Majid et al., 2021).

The MSPO's national certification scheme for palm oil sustainability serves as a road map for reversing deforestation. According to the Malaysian Palm Oil Board (MPOB), as of June 2021, about 96% of the total comprising 4.06 million hectares have obtained the MSPO certification (Malaysian Palm Oil Council, 2021b). The Malaysia Palm Oil Board (MPOB) commits to the safe and healthy production of palm oil-based products whilst reducing its impact on environmental ecosystems (Yatim 2017). This is despite criticism that producers that are certified by a credible system that avoids deforestation are losing out to other oils (soy, canola, rapeseed) that are still exported despite their threat to deforestation (Wong & Nanoo, 2020). Nonetheless, the EU asserted that existing voluntary certification procedures are insufficient to ensure a sustainable and deforested palm oil output.

3. Promoting Cooperation and commitment in Enhancing Palm Oil Sustainability

Malaysia has made a pledge to improve the sustainability of its palm oil industry, which includes limiting its deforestation and staying true to it. Malaysia has voluntarily vowed to preserve 50% of its land area for forest since the 1992 United Nations Conference on Environment and Development, during the Rio Earth Summit (Nossal & Stubbs, 1997). This commitment has significantly decreased deforestation in Malaysia. Between 1999 and 2004, approximately 300,000 hectares of old rubber plantations were converted to oil palm crop (Varkkey, Tyson & Choiruzzad, 2018). This means that, palm oil plantations make use of easily available land and do not result in significant deforestation of natural rainforests. (Varkkey, Tyson & Choiruzzad, 2018). Malaysia is still the world's major producer and exporter of palm oil, focusing on local intensification and expanding into Indonesia while adhering to its vow.

Malaysia's government has repeatedly reaffirmed its commitment to the 50% pledge both domestically and internationally, most recently at the 2009 Copenhagen Climate Conference and the 2012 United Nations Conference on Sustainable Development. (Embas, 2012). The Malaysian former Prime Minister, Tun Mahathir (2019), reiterated during the United Nation General Assembly that Malaysia had lived up to and exceeded its goal, with forest cover presently at 55.3 percent, exceeding the 1992 Rio pledge. Similarly, during the 2019 WTO Committee on Trade and Environment meeting, when members expressed worry about the sustainability of palm oil, Malaysia emphasised its commitment to conserving more than half of its land mass as forest and its well-regulated palm oil industry.

Ministers under Mahathir's leadership were also audacious in arguing Malaysia's position. Teresa Kok, the former Malaysian Minister of Primary Industries, slammed the EU Directive as being founded on a 'policy of protectionism' that is not backed by research and is based on erroneous and discriminatory reasons. Teresa explained that the Malaysian government has decided to cap the expansion of oil palm plantations at 65,000 square kilometres by 2023. Malaysia is also now focusing in utilising higher-yielding planting materials and increasing productivity without needing to expand into new forests or peatlands. There is also prohibition on cultivating on peatland the tightening of regulations on existing plantations on peat. In addition, mapping of oil palm plantations will be carried out throughout the country for public access to enhance transparency. Teresa further explained that Malaysia have taken efforts in protecting its wildlife, for instance, Malaysia has contributed funds for wildlife conservation in Sabah to protect iconic species such as orangutan, Borneo, pygmy elephants, sun bears and others (Jong 2019). She claims that this move reflects EU's insincerity in implementing the UN SDGs.

Malaysia also opined that it is possible to produce palm oil in a sustainable way as the efficiency of palm oil production may be improved to meet the global palm oil demand (Noor et al., 2017). EU decisions have also failed to consider various efforts undertaken by palm oil producers, including commitment to reforestation, conservation, research, and also stricter certification. For instance, Malaysia, is expanding its oil palm plantations not at the expense of the tropical forest, but rather by converting lands previously used for other crops.

Malaysia has made various efforts to cooperate, through bilateral arrangements and also multilateral forums. Several economic and technical missions were sent to Europe to give feedback on the implementation of RED II, which had not been taken into account.

4. Mobilizing Regional and International Support

Malaysia also mobilized intra-regional support from the Association of Southeast Asian Nations (ASEAN) and its members against the EU policy to stop recognizing palm oil as a biofuel (Jong, 2019). This being the fact that palm oil is an important sector in Southeast Asia. Singapore, for instance, is home to the headquarters of some of the world's biggest palm oil companies and its banks are financing the expansion of the palm oil industry. Philippines, Thailand, Vietnam, and Cambodia also invested in the palm oil sector and have been blamed for deforestation, environmental degradation, land disputes, social conflicts, food sovereignty, and livelihood insecurity, as well as human rights violations (Colchester et al., 2011). The palm oil discord have not only caused tensions between the EU and Malaysia-Indonesia but have also become a point of contention with other Southeast Asian countries (Maier-Knapp, 2020).

The former Malaysian Minister of Primary Industry, Teresa Kok, has called on ASEAN to fight against unfair and discriminatory judgments targeted by a global network of campaigns which she viewed as an external threat to the Southeast Asian region's important industry, during the Singapore Dialogue on Sustainable World Resources in May 2019 (Jong, 2019). Critics also viewed that EU has failed to recognize ASEAN's efforts to address environmental issues. For example, the 2002 Agreement on Transboundary Haze Pollution and the 2014 Haze Agreement compel ASEAN member states to establish and enforce rules that promote sustainable palm oil cultivation (Wong & Nanoo, 2020). Southeast Asian states have also demonstrated a political commitment to restraining hazardous practises and establishing local agencies to mitigate the negative effects of palm oil cultivation (Wong & Nanoo, 2020). However, none of these efforts to solve the underlying issue received assistance from the EU; rather, the commodity was sanctioned (Wong & Nanoo, 2020).

Moreover, the EU appears to be pursuing a serious climate change policy inside ASEAN but is hesitant to apply environmental trade restrictions while establishing strategic ties with major Asian nations such as Japan, China, and South Korea. This demonstrates the EU's double standard in imposing a contentious and dubious policy on comparatively weak states by using its market power (Wong & Nanoo, 2020).

Within EU-ASEAN diplomacy, these changes affecting palm oil imports and sustainability standards have created new bilateral bargaining realities for Southeast Asian palm oil exporting countries engaged in ongoing free trade negotiations with the EU. In the 22nd ASEAN-EU Ministerial meeting in January 2019 in Brussels, the effort to upgrade the relationship to an EU-ASEAN inter-regional strategic partnership becomes a challenge in light of the palm oil conundrum. These FTA talks are overseeing that political issues are set as bargaining tools for the promotion of the economic agendas, pointing towards a difficult time ahead for EU-ASEAN diplomacy (Maier-Knapp, 2020).

During the General Debate of the United Nations General Assembly's 74th session, Mahathir (2019) also made an appeal to wealthy countries. stating as followed:

Palm oil is still a big contributor to our economy. There is no evidence that it is poisonous. We appeal to the good sense of the rich not to impoverish us, not to deprive hundreds of thousands of our workers from earning a living. You will be doing a good deed by consuming palm oil.

Mahathir expressly called for dialogue and engagement to achieve joint solutions, including better regulation and stronger certification standards. Malaysia continues to extend a hand of friendship to the EU in the hope of reviving a fair, honest, and mutual trading partnership. Malaysia is relying on the EU to follow the advice of various environmental experts and incentivize sustainable palm oil production rather than pursuing boycotts and protectionism (Mahathir, 2019).

5. Issuing Tough Criticisms and Warnings

Responding to EU policies geared towards decreasing the use of palm oil, Mahathir alleged that the EU policies were "grossly unfair" and an example of "rich people... trying to impoverish poor people" and that this may risk starting a trade war with Malaysia (Ananthalakshmi, Sipalan & Brock, 2019). Mahathir previously expressed his disappointment with European food producers labelling products with 'No Palm Oil' as a propaganda attempt to protect their markets (Bernama, 2019). The 'palm oil-free' labels on products are discriminatory or even illegal since they give the perception that palm oil is harmful to consumers. Such labels would bring about negative perceptions without educating the consumers of different modes of production (Mohamad, 2019). According to Mahathir, "This blatant hypocrisy is a form of modern colonialism that has no place in today's world. By using trade as a weapon, the EU is in effect bullying poorer regions of the world" (Mohamad, 2019).

The CEO of the Malaysian Palm Oil Council similarly adds that requiring developing countries to conserve the environment while Europe itself fails to comply, particularly on the issue of timber, is simply an act of hypocrisy (Hinkes, 2019). Europe's own practise of exploitation on forests and peatlands centuries ago (Chapman et al., 2003) was reminded of. The Malaysian Minister of Plantation Industries and Commodities further described the policy development as a form of 'crop apartheid' (Spross, 2018).

Mahathir even warned the EU that if it maintained its ban on Malaysian palm oil, Malaysia would retaliate by switching to China for its fighter jets as well as boycotts against European products (Tan 2019, Reuters 2018a). In July 2019, Malaysia had warned to take action against the EU Renewable Energy Directive II (Reuters, 2021) should it violate international law regulating world trade. Malaysia was never hesitant to take countermeasures or bring the EU to the international court.

6. Instituting Legal Actions

Malaysia's seriousness in safeguarding the country's palm oil industry against the policy implemented by the EU is evident when Malaysia institutes legal actions against the EU. On January, 2021, the Malaysian Plantation Industries and Commodities Ministry, with the cooperation of the Attorney General's Chambers and the International Trade and Industry Ministry, filed a request for consultations under the WTO Dispute Settlement Mechanism (DSM) regarding measures adopted by the EU and its member states affecting palm oil and palm crop-based biofuels (World Trade Organization, 2021a).

Malaysia regards the EU renewable-energy directive as "discriminatory action." Minister Mohd Khairuddin Aman Razali stated that the EU went ahead with implementing the directive despite Malaysia's commitment, views, feedback and effort of sending economic and technical missions to Europe (Reuters, 2021). This creates an unreasonable trade barrier against Malaysia and is incompatible with the WTO's free trade principle.

In addition, Malaysia also challenged that the measures were inconsistent with the WTO most-favoured-nation principle that requires WTO members to treat each other the same without preference to another (World Trade Organization, 2021b). This is stipulated under the three WTO agreements, namely the first article of the General Agreement on Tariffs and Trade (GATT), Article 2 of the General Agreement of

Trade in Services (GATS) and Article 4 of the Trade-Related Aspects of Intellectual Property Rights Agreement (TRIPS), as well as the Agreement on Subsidies and Countervailing Measures.

Malaysia contended that EU and EU member state measures, specifically those taken by France and Lithuania, violate EU and WTO principles of non-discrimination, as enshrined in the WTO's Agreement on Technical Barriers to Trade, which aims to provide secure and fair trading conditions. Under the national-treatment principle, imported and locally-produced goods should be treated equally. This is also found in Article 3 of GATT, Article 17 of GATS and Article 3 of TRIPS.

Through the consultation request, parties have the chance to discuss the subject and reach an agreement without resorting to litigation. Malaysia, on the other hand, may seek adjudication by a panel if the matter cannot be resolved. This legal action reflects the government's commitment to defending the country's palm oil economy against the EU's agenda.

DISCUSSION

The discord over palm oil is not a new problem. The sustainability of palm oil has been contested between palm oil producing and palm oil consuming countries for decades. For instance, Malaysia has faced negative campaigns against palm oil since the late 1990s, but Malaysia has consistently defended the palm oil industry. The haze problem in 1997, which led to criticism of the practise of forest burning, has tarnished palm oil's image even further. To protect the palm oil industry, information and funds were aggressively used through discourse, science, networking, and widespread distribution.

The high demand for palm oil has put other vegetable oil producers at risk, including France, which produces rapeseed oil, and the United States, which produces soybean oil. In retrospect, Malaysia's government was effective in lobbying against anti-palm oil sentiments in the 1980s, when the United States began an anti-palm oil campaign backed by the Soybean Association and the Heart Disease Prevention Association (Masaaki, 2018). Malaysia has scientifically debunked the harmful palm oil hypothesis by actively spreading palm oil-positive campaigns, fostering collaboration, and engaging in public relations efforts highlighting palm oil's health advantages and flexibility (Masaaki, 2018). Additionally, Malaysia used promotion funding to counter unfavourable campaigns and engage in public relations operations.

The MPO Promotion Committee was created in the 1990s to increase the effectiveness of palm oil promotion. Government officials undertake worldwide marketing through industry-government partnership. Seminars, workshops, exhibitions, and conferences were conducted by the MPO Promotion Committee, as well as exchanges with media. The organization's name has been changed to MPO Council, and it continues to promote public relations aggressively. Malaysian Palm Oil Research Institute and Palm Oil Licensing Agency combined to establish the Malaysian Palm Oil Board, which finances research in Malaysia, the United States, and major European institutions in attempt to persuade Western customers. Additionally, the MPOC has avoided open confrontations with other oil and fat sectors, even pushing for the use of palm oil in conjunction with other oils. All efforts, from the discourse on palm farming and healthy palm oil to scientific reasoning and partnership with Western nations, are directed toward boosting the income of impoverished farmers. All of these examples demonstrate Malaysia's proactive approach to tackle the threat posed by its palm oil sector.

Despite Malaysia's numerous tactics for lobbying the EU, either through dialogue or even forcefully, to avoid implementing the palm oil embargo, Malaysia has also made several attempts to come to terms with the consequences. Malaysia has pursued a range of economic measures in response to the

EU Directive's economic effects. Domestic demand for biodiesel as a green alternative to aviation and shipping fuel has been increased, as have exports to India and China, with APAC and African markets identified as important export targets. Malaysia also used research and technology to create new product uses in the food and beverage industries, expanding and boosting the value of palm oil products beyond crude palm oil exports.

CONCLUSION

Palm oil is positioned as a "development driver" or "development engine" that benefits both exporting and importing countries. Tensions between the EU and palm oil-producing countries have existed for many years, but recent European policy developments, particularly from 2014 to 2019, have directly or indirectly exacerbated political disputes over palm oil production, consumption, and trade (Hinkes, 2019). The European Union (EU) remained as Malaysia's third largest palm oil export market, behind India and China. However, in response to multiple international treaties aimed at halting global deforestation, reversing climate change, and achieving Sustainable Development Goals, the EU has taken steps to discourage consumers from purchasing palm oil. Specifically, the EU Directive 2018/2001 has set a cap on the contribution of palm oil as a biofuel to the EU's 2030 renewable energy target. Palm oil is classified by RED II as a high-indirect land use change product that significantly increases greenhouse gas emissions, and hence will be phased out of the EU's renewable energy mix by 2030.

Malaysia has not remained silent in the face of this barrage of criticism. It has become far more proactive, engaging and reshaping criticisms, as well as channelling discourses, policies, and governing institutions toward a dichotomy of unsustainable and sustainable palm oil (Dauvergne, 2018). Malaysia and Indonesia have both described the policy shift as a "ban on palm oil," "crop apartheid," and the start of a potential "trade war." This decision has threatened to significantly limit the amount of this prospective market for Malaysian palm oil. This in turn will have a negative impact on around 3 million people in Malaysia who rely on the palm oil business for their livelihood, 40% of which Malaysia's oil palm growers are smallholders.

This chapter examines the events leading up to the EU's anti-palm oil actions, which have a negative impact on Malaysia's palm oil business. This chapter discussed the many ways in which Malaysia has responded to defend its palm oil sector. Numerous government efforts have been made to cooperate with the EU. To begin with, Malaysia counters the EU's allegation through investigations and scientific research that questions the EU's approach, which does not help the environment. Second, Malaysia demonstrated its unwavering commitment to transform the palm oil industry toward sustainability by instituting MSPO certification standards on top of the voluntary RSPO international certification. Thirdly, Malaysia fosters cooperation and dedication to grow palm oil sustainably. As EU renewable energy directives highly influenced Indonesia's strategy towards the reduction of emissions and sustainability of palm oil (Kartika et al., 2020), Malaysia continued to commit to legal and environmental best practices to foster a sustainable palm oil industry, develop engagement with other countries and even put on ongoing pressure despite EU punitive measures. Fourthly, Malaysia has forged closer diplomatic engagement in order to garner support from ASEAN member states as well as making appeals to international forums. Unfortunately, the EU determined that Malaysia's certification procedures are insufficient, and various attempts to cooperate through bilateral arrangements, multilateral forums as well as economic and technical missions to provide feedback were unsuccessful and ignored. Fifthly, Malaysia exerted pressure, boldly expressing its opposition and warnings of retaliatory measures against the EU. Finally, Malaysia escalated the dispute to the World Trade Organization by requesting consultation under the WTO Dispute Settlement Mechanism. Malaysia alleged that the EU had breached the WTO's non-discrimination principles and imposing trade barriers to safeguard its own interests.

Additionally, this chapter sheds light on Malaysia's previous experience when threatened by the US anti-palm oil campaign that would be useful to learn from. The chapter presents the political processes that generate policy interventions aimed at defending palm oil trade with the EU. This raises concerns that pursuing economic decoupling and direct conflict may exacerbate the problem. Punitive measures and the EU's lack of sensitivity will aggravate the reaction and weaken bilateral relations between Malaysia and the EU, far from bringing about good improvements in the palm oil business.

REFERENCES

Abdul Majid, N., Ramli, Z., Md Sum, S., & Awang, A. H. (2021). Sustainable palm oil certification scheme frameworks and impacts: A systematic literature review. *Sustainability*, *13*(6), 3263. doi:10.3390u13063263

Agreement on Subsidies and Countervailing Measures, Apr. 15, 1994, Marrakesh Agreement Establishing the World Trade Organization, Annex 1A, 1869 U.N.T.S. 14.

Anair, D., & Mahmassani, A. (2013). Cattle, Cleared Forests, and Climate Change. Academic Press.

Ananthalakshmi, A., Sipalan, J., & Brock, J. (2019)., *Exclusive: EU risks 'trade war' with Malaysia over palm oil – Mahathir*. Reuters. Retrieved September 23, 2021, from Reuters at https://www.reuters.com/article/us-malaysia-politics-mahathir-exclusive-idUSKCN1R917W

Arief, R. A., Cangara, A. R., Badu, M. N., Baharuddin, A., & Apriliani, A. (2020, October). The impact of the European Union (EU) renewable energy directive policy on the management of Indonesian palm oil industry. *IOP Conference Series. Earth and Environmental Science*, *575*(1), 012230. doi:10.1088/1755-1315/575/1/012230

Bernama. (2019). M'sia to switch to Chinese fighter jets if palm oil ban continues: Mahathir. *The Sun Daily*. Retrieved September 25, 2021, from https://www.thesundaily.my/local/m-sia-to-switch-to-chinese-fighter-jets-if-palm-oil-ban-continues-mahathir-DM718306

Chang, F. K. (2021). *Palm oil: Malaysian economic interests and foreign relations*. Foreign Policy Research Institute. https://www.fpri.org/article/2021/04/palm-oil-malaysian-economic-interests-and-foreign-relations/

Chapman, S., Buttler, A., Francez, A. J., Laggoun-Défarge, F., Vasander, H., Schloter, M., Combe, J., Grosvernier, P., Harms, H., Epron, D., Mitchell, E., & Gilbert, D. (2003). Exploitation of northern peatlands and biodiversity maintenance: A conflict between economy and ecology. *Frontiers in Ecology and the Environment*, *1*(10), 525–532. doi:10.1890/1540-9295(2003)001[0525:EONPAB]2.0.CO;2

Colchester, M., Chao, S., Dan, V. T., & Villanueva, J. (2011). Oil palm expansion in south East Asia. *Bogor, Moreton-in-Marsh: Forest People Programme and Perkumpulan Sawit Watch.*

Committee on the Environment, Public Health and Food Safety. (2017). *On Palm Oil and Deforestation of Rainforest* (2016/2222(INI)). European Parliament. https://www.europarl.europa.eu/doceo/document/A-8-2017-0066_EN.html

Dauvergne, P. (2018). The global politics of the business of "sustainable" palm oil. *Global Environmental Politics*, *18*(2), 34–52. doi:10.1162/glep_a_00455

Dayang Norwana, A. A. B., Kanjappan, R., Chin, M., Schoneveld, G. C., Potter, L., & Andriani, R. (2011). The local impacts of oil palm expansion in malaysia; an assessment based on a case study in Sabah state. *Center for International Forestry Research (CIFOR) Working Paper, 78*, 1-17.

Embas, D. U. (2012). Statement by The Honourable Dato' Sri Douglas Unggah Embas, Minister of Natural Resources and Environment, *Malaysia. The United Nations Conference on Sustainable Development*, Rio De Janeiro.

GATS. General Agreement on Trade in Services, Apr. 15, 1994, Marrakesh Agreement Establishing the World Trade Organization, Annex 1B, 1869 U.N.T.S. 183, 33 I.L.M. 1167 (1994)

GATT 1994:General Agreement on Tariffs and Trade 1994, Apr. 15, 1994, Marrakesh Agreement Establishing the World Trade Organization, Annex 1A, 1867 U.N.T.S. 187, 33 I.L.M. 1153 (1994)

Hinkes, C. (2019). Adding (bio) fuel to the fire: Discourses on palm oil sustainability in the context of European policy development. *Environment, Development and Sustainability*, *22*(8), 7661–7682. doi:10.100710668-019-00541-y

Hirschmann, R. (2021). *Export volume of palm oil from Malaysia to the EU 2011-2020*. Statista. Retrieved September 23, 2021, from https://www.statista.com/statistics/1091983/export-volume-palm-oil-malaysia-eu/#:~:text=In%202020%2C%20Malaysia%20exported%20around,oil%2C%20after%20India%20and%20China

Ivancic, H., & Koh, L. P. (2016). Evolution of sustainable palm oil policy in Southeast Asia. *Cogent Environmental Science*, *2*(1), 1195032. doi:10.1080/23311843.2016.1195032

Jong, H. N. (2019). *Malaysia calls on Southeast Asia to back palm oil against EU's 'unfair' claims*. Eco-Business. Retrieved September 23, 2021, from https://www.eco-business.com/news/malaysia-calls-on-southeast-asia-to-back-palm-oil-against-eus-unfair-claims/

Kartika, I. T., Cangara, A. R., Nasrun, M., & Marifat, I. D. N. (2020, October). Interaction between the European Union's renewable energy directives and Indonesia's sustainable palm oil policy. *IOP Conference Series. Earth and Environmental Science*, *575*(1), 012228. doi:10.1088/1755-1315/575/1/012228

Klepper, G. (2018)., *Winners and losers from the proposed ban on palm oil*. EcoBusiness. Retrieved September 23, 2021, from https://www.iscc-system.org/eco-business-winners-and-losers-from-the-proposed-ban-on-palm-oil/

Kunene, N., & Chung, Y. C. (2020). Sustainable production policy impact on palm oil firms' performance: Empirical analysis from Indonesia. *Sustainability*, *12*(20), 8750. doi:10.3390u12208750

Limenta, M. (2020). Palm oil for fuels: WTO rules and environmental protection. *Global Trade and Customs Journal, 15*(7).

Maier-Knapp, N. (2020). *The European Commission's palm oil conundrum*. East Asia Forum. Australia at https://www.eastasiaforum.org/2020/02/28/the-european-commissions-palm-oil-conundrum/?utm_source=rss&utm_medium=rss&utm_campaign=the-european-commissions-palm-oil-conundrum

Malaysian Palm Oil Council. (2021a). *The implications of EU resolution to the Malaysian palm oil industry*. http://mpoc.org.my/the-implications-of-eu-resolution-to-the-malaysian-palm-oil-industry/

Malaysian Palm Oil Council. (2021b)., *96.04% of Oil Palm Estates have achieved MSPO Certification* – MPOB. http://mpoc.org.my/96-04-of-oil-palm-estates-have-achieved-mspo-certification-mpob/

Masaaki, O. (2018). Another "oil war": the birth and development of unhealthy palm oil and its counter discourse; 岡本正明. (2018). もう一つの油戦争—不健康なパーム油という言説, その対抗言説の誕生と発展—. 東南アジア研究, *55*(2), 217-239.

Mayr, S., Hollaus, B., & Madner, V. (2021). Palm oil, the RED II and WTO law: EU sustainable biofuel policy tangled up in green? *Review of European, Comparative & International Environmental Law, 30*(2), 233–248. doi:10.1111/reel.12386

Meijaard, E., Brooks, T. M., Carlson, K. M., Slade, E. M., Garcia-Ulloa, J., Gaveau, D., Lee, J. S. H., Santika, T., Juffe-Bignoli, D., Struebig, M. J., Wich, S. A., Ancrenaz, M., Koh, L. P., Zamira, N., Abrams, J. F., Prins, H. H. T., Sendashonga, C. N., Murdiyarso, D., Furumo, P. R., ... Sheil, D. (2020). The environmental impacts of palm oil in context. *Nature Plants*, *6*(12), 1418–1426. doi:10.103841477-020-00813-w PMID:33299148

Mohamad, M. (2019). Dr. Mahathir: Britain should break with Europe on palm oil. *New Straits Times*. Retrieved September 23, 2021, from, August 19, https://www.nst.com.my/news/nation/2019/08/514041/dr-mahathir-britain-should-break-europe-palm-oil

Mohamad, M. (2019, September 27). *Statement by the General Debate of the 74th session of the United Nation General Assembly, New York*. https://www.nst.com.my/news/nation/2019/09/525269/dr-ms-full-speech-text-74th-unga

Noor, F. M. M., Gassner, A., Terheggen, A., & Dobie, P. (2017). Beyond sustainability criteria and principles in palm oil production: Addressing consumer concerns through in setting. *Ecology and Society*, *22*(2), 1–5. PMID:29780429

Nossal, K. R., & Stubbs, R. (1997). Mahathir's Malaysia: an emerging middle power? In Niche diplomacy (pp. 147-163). Palgrave Macmillan. doi:10.1007/978-1-349-25902-1_8

Oosterveer, P. (2020). Sustainability of palm oil and its acceptance in the EU. *Journal of Oil Palm Research*, *32*(3), 365–376.

Pye, O., & Bhattacharya, J. (Eds.). (2013). *The palm oil controversy in Southeast Asia: A transnational perspective*. Institute of Southeast Asian Studies.

Reuters. (2018a). *European move to ban palm oil from biofuels is 'crop apartheid'—Malaysia*. Retrieved September 23, 2021, from https://www.reuters.com/article/malaysia-palmoil-eu-idUSL3N1PD1NJ

Reuters. (2019). *Malaysia, Indonesia send protest letter to EU on palm o il curbs.*, Malaysiakini. Retrieved September 23, 2021, from https://www.malaysiakini.com/news/471322

Reuters. (2021). *Malaysia takes WTO legal action against EU over palm biofuel curbs.* Retrieved January 23, 2021 from https://www.reuters.com/article/us-malaysia-palmoil-eu-idUSKBN29L054

Sheil, D., Casson, A., Meijaard, E., Van Noordwijk, M., Gaskell, J., Sunderland-Groves, J., Wertz, K., & Kanninen, M. (2009). *The impacts and opportunities of oil palm in Southeast Asia: What do we know and what do we need to know?* (Vol. 51). Center for International Forestry Research.

Spross, H. (2018). *Does EU biofuel deal compromise the environment for trade with Southeast Asia?* Deutsche Welle. Retrieved September 23, 2021, from, https://p.dw.com/p/305XJ

Tan, T. (2019). Stop palm oil discrimination. *The Star.* Retrieved September 25, 2021, from https://www.thest ar.com.my/news/nation/2019/03/21/stop-palm-oil-discrimination/

TRIPS. Agreement on Trade-Related Aspects of Intellectual Property Rights, Apr. 15, 1994, Marrakesh Agreement Establishing the World Trade Organization, Annex 1C, 1869 U.N.T.S. 299, 33 I.L.M. 1197 (1994)

Varkkey, H. (2013). Patronage politics, plantation fires and transboundary haze. *Environmental Hazards, 12*(3-4), 200–217. doi:10.1080/17477891.2012.759524

Varkkey, H., Tyson, A., & Choiruzzad, S. A. B. (2018). Palm oil intensification and expansion in Indonesia and Malaysia: Environmental and socio-political factors influencing policy. *Forest Policy and Economics, 92*, 148–159. doi:10.1016/j.forpol.2018.05.002

White, B., Borras, S. M. Jr, Hall, R., Scoones, I., & Wolford, W. (2012). The new enclosures: Critical perspectives on corporate land deals. *The Journal of Peasant Studies, 39*(3-4), 619–647. doi:10.1080/03066150.2012.691879

Wong, R., & Nanoo, A. (2020). Palm Oil: A Case for Conciliation over Confrontation. *Asia Global Online Journal.* https://www.asiaglobalonline.hku.hk/palm-oil-case-conciliation-over-confrontation

World Trade Organization. (2021a). *European Union and certain Member states – certain measures concerning palm oil and oil palm crop-based biofuels – Request for consultations by Malaysia* (G/L/1384; G/SCM/D131/1; G/TBT/D/54; WT/DS600/1). https://docs.wto.org/dol2fe/Pages/FE_Search/FE_S_S006.aspx?Query=(%20@Symbol=%20(wt/ds600/1%20))&Language=ENGLISH&Context=FomerScriptedSearch&languageUIChanged=true#

World Trade Organization. (2021b). *Understanding the WTO Basics, Principles of the trading system.* https://www.wto.org/english/thewto_e/whatis_e/tif_e/fact2_e.htm

World Wildlife Fund. (n.d.). *8 things to know about palm oil.* Retrieved September 23, 2021, from https://www.wwf.org.uk/updates/8-things-know-about-palm-oil

Yatim, P. (2017). CSR in a controversial industry: The case of Malaysian oil palm companies. *International Journal of Sustainable Society, 9*(4), 327–345. doi:10.1504/IJSSOC.2017.090521

Zakaria, N., Abdul-Talib, A. N., & Amelinckx, A. (Eds.). (2020). *Transcending Cultural Frontiers: Practices, Challenges, and Strategy for International Business.* Springer. doi:10.1007/978-981-15-4454-5

Zakaria, N., Abdul-Talib, A. N., & Othman, N. (Eds.). (2016). *Handbook of research on impacts of international business and political affairs on the global economy.* IGI Global. doi:10.4018/978-1-4666-9806-2

Chapter 2
Branding Through Online Social Networks:
Impacts on Export Markets

Sana Arshad
Universiti Utara Malaysia, Malaysia

Asmat-Nizam Abdul-Talib
https://orcid.org/0000-0001-6820-2918
Universiti Utara Malaysia, Malaysia

Fahad Manzoor
Emirates NBD, UAE

ABSTRACT

The hurdles to entering a foreign market have been dismantled by greater internet connectivity. As a result, there is virtually endless potential to expand a company abroad. In growing abroad, it's crucial to keep the brand at the forefront of the approach. When enterprises enter foreign markets, they confront several problems such as a lack of market intelligence, buyer expectations, severe rivalry from global brands, and a lack of trending awareness. Most exporters focus on the short product-focused and sales-driven methods, such as producing that which is simple to create, finding a contract, fulfilling the request, and closing sales. This method just forces an exporter into a pricing competition in a globalized world, leaving the limited possibility to continuous production, product innovation, and credibility. Every company that wishes to export should aim towards market-driven, long-term, and sustainable exporting.

INTRODUCTION

The subject of branding has currently remained challenged by way of a key subject of research in the marketing arena (Moore, Karl, Reid & Susan, 2008), yet it is just about as ancient as civilizations. As early as the Mesopotamian or Greek civilizations, they utilized signs and labels to distinguish the offer-

DOI: 10.4018/978-1-7998-9071-3.ch002

ings which consisted typically of drinks, gels, and ointments (Sarkar & Singh, 2005). The term brand is originated out from the Norse Mythology word brandr, meaning signifies "to burn" (an identification scar burnt on cows with a heating iron), subsequently brands have been and continue to be used by herders to recognize their herds.

However, market segmentation and product differentiation strategies lead to the creation of the brand. When it comes to branding, it's more than just providing an organization's imprint and impression of a good or service. Branding implies changing a line of products; it requires longer company participation and also a high level of skills and competencies (Kapferer, 2004). According to Moore et al. (2008), a significant percentage of brand studies is focused on improving the concept of brand selection (or preference), brand knowledge, brand recognition, and line extension. Surprisingly, just a handful of the research has attempted to answer the question: "What is a brand?" As people try to conceptualize the brand, the challenge arises: The value of a brand is evaluated. What metrics (factors) can we use to assess brand equity (Kapferer, 2004).

Also, a company's brand is considered to be a key intangible asset (Paul, 2018). Rapid innovations in branding have centered on investigating the emotional aspect of branding. The study also indicates that, in addition to personality variables, the customer's behavior is affected by his or her affections about a brand (Sniehotta, Presseau & Araujo-Soares, 2014). As a result, those perceptions play a vital role in determining the brand's status at national and international levels. Consequently, consumer–brand connections have taken center stage in the relationship marketing literature. These have an important part in the development of a brand towards exports too (Wang, Sarkar & Sarkar, 2018). Also, the value-driven purpose is at the heart of any great, successful brand and it guides everything it does. This is evident for some well-established brands like Apple, IKEA, and Sony, as well as for positive effects on organizational enterprises that have managed to break free from generic offering and generate higher benefits to their own branded items (International Trade Centers, 2019).

Likewise, new transport and telecommunications technologies, on the other hand, enable even the tiniest businesses to form partnerships with foreign competitors to benefit from their experience, cost reductions, and access to new markets. The capacity to quickly discover international partners and manage complex business relationships across ethnic and language divides is a scarce resource in this different world (Saxenian, 1999). Exporting to international markets can frequently cut per-unit costs by boosting processes to meet increased demand. Furthermore, companies that expand to emerging markets gain access to new statistics and skills that can help them spot emerging technologies, develop marketing strategies, and obtain competitive advantages (Investopedia, 2021).

Moreover, one of the most popular telecommunication technologies is using social networks. Nearly 3.6 billion people worldwide used digital platforms in 2020, with that number is predicted to grow to approximately 4.41 billion by 2025 (Statista, 2021). These Online Social Networks (OSNs) provide novel opportunities for businesses because of their excellent interactive and communication capabilities (Sigala, 2012; Yoon, Choi & Sohn, 2008). OSNs are widely used as an impact of awareness and communication channels by organizations. On the other hand, OSNs can aid in brand awareness (Barwise & Meehan, 2010). Brand awareness affects customer purchases (Lin, 2013; Hoyer & Brown, 1990). As a result, it is a crucial notion across both behavior research. Tourism marketing can benefit from OSNs because they help businesses improve their digital marketing activities (Gretzel, 2006). Unidentified brands are considerably less likely to be considered, and so chosen, than well-known brands. The very well a brand is known, more than likely it is that people will want to buy and suggest positively (Horng,

Liu, Chou & Tsai, 2011). As a result, developing great brand awareness among OSN users impacts users' willingness to recommend and consider lifetime purchasing (Oh, 2000).

Similarly, the economies that had previously been cut off from one another due to geographical distances and socioeconomic divisions have begun to interact more with one another. The World Trade Organization (WTO) and policies undertaken by different governments across the globe have also played an important role in the growing exchanges and business links across states. Global commerce in products and services is expected to expand in the coming years. The Trade Facilitation Agreement (TFA), which was established in 2013 and went into effect in early 2017, has the potential to boost global GDP by $1 trillion per year (GDP). This agreement requires members of the (WTO) to modernize customs procedures and reduce regulatory red tape, allowing products and services to move more quickly across borders while lowering prices. The US government has created an "open door" system that provides some of the same perks and advantages as the WTO plan (WTO, Trade Facilitation Agreement Database, 2019, 2013, 2001).

Due to these reasons, many developing countries have taken advantage of the high expansion in international consumption of resources, increasing export profits, and foreign direct investment in some circumstances (Acosta & Brand, 2018). However, the internationalization literature, on the other hand, is brimming with suggestions for how companies might use different pathways to overcome obstacles to globalization. The main point in networking literature is that connections develop knowledge and transmit significant information that enterprises may use to find overseas potential markets (Johanson & Vahlne, 2009), but also pick locations and entering modalities (Chetty & Blankenburg-Holm, 2000; Coviello & Munro, 1997). Strong domestic competitiveness (Ramaseshan & Soutar, 1996), procedures for exporting from one's home nation (da Silva & da Rocha, 2001), and scarcity of exporting aid from the respective governments are all examples of extrinsic hurdles that have received considerable research (Okpara & Kombiadis, 2009). Additional extrinsic hurdles include tax barriers (Arteaga-Ortiz & Fernandez-Ortiz, 2010; Korneliussen & Blasius, 2008), as well as a regional and cognitive barrier among domestic and international markets (Hanson & Xiang, 2011; Arteaga-Ortiz & Fernandez-Ortiz, 2010; Korneliussen & Blasius, 2008).

The majority of studies on internationalization have focused on how views of barriers change as they progress through the stages of export engagement (Suerez-Ortega, 2003). Different research has revealed that export barriers differ according to these stages, with higher-stage enterprises experiencing fewer barriers than lower-stage firms. "As for distinguishing elements, various experts have added modifications on the issue of the brand's appealing essentials (Koch, 1994). Brands, on the other hand, are just like cognitive associations; good brands seem to have a genuine connection (Kapferer, 2004). Should customers usually make decisions based on a brand's name as a simple solution? Besides the time, so what are the limitations? Howard and Seth's (1969) consumer behavior theory contributes toward a basic awareness of such issues. Heritage, individuality, self-projection, appearance, ability to reflect, and interaction are all linked aspects of a brand, according to Kapferer (1992). In which external aspect reflects product attributes, signs, and qualities; individuality represents personality and values; correlation symbolizes beliefs and relationships; heritage encompasses a series of virtues; reflective thinking represents the consumer's perception of the brand, and ability to reflect represents the user's intrinsic rearview as a brand user.

However, these rapid innovations in branding have centered on investigating the emotional aspect of branding through internationalization and frequent communication via OSNs. The study also indicates that, in addition to personality variables, the customer's behavior is affected by his or her affections about a brand (Sniehotta, Presseau, & Araujo-Soares, 2014). As a result, those perceptions play a vital role in determining the brand's status. As a result, consumer–brand connections have taken center stage in the relationship marketing literature. These have an important part in the development of a brand at global levels as well (Wang, Sarkar & Sarkar, 2018).

BRAND AWARENESS AND WHAT IT MEANS?

Consumers' brand awareness pertains to their memorizing or market offering, or basically if they are familiar with it (Keller, 2008). Brand equity develops after brand awareness. In users' minds, the brand tag provisions memory nodes (Aaker,1991), and clients associate brand information to the brand term, consequential in brand equity (Keller, 1993; Aaker, 1991). As an outcome, brand recognition gives the brand a knowledge opportunity (Keller, 2008) and influences purchasing. Customers are convinced to expand their core group to include brands they are familiar with (MacDonald & Sharp, 2000; Hoyer & Brown, 1990). When making purchasing decisions, consumers may utilize brand awareness as a factor. In a conclusion, brand awareness is capable of boosting brand performance in the marketplace.

Moreover, Online Social Networks (OSNs) can, nevertheless, help to raise brand recognition (Barwise & Meehan, 2010). Consumer preferences are influenced by brand awareness (Lin, 2013; Hoyer & Brown, 1990). As a result, it is a crucial notion across both behavior research and marketing. But when comes to making decisions, consumers rely on online environments more than anything. The impact of these initiatives on customer perceptions of activities is yet unclear (Hutter, Hautz, Dennhardt & Fuller, 2013; Nusair, Bilgihan, Okumus & Cobanoglu, 2013; Nusair, Bilgihan, Okumus & Cobanoglu, 2013). Because of their widespread use, these networks have matured into forums that may promote brand awareness. On major OSNs like Facebook, every person's contribution has been seen by a minimum of 35% of their followers (Bernstein, Bakshy, Burke & Karrer, 2013). As a result, it's critical to nail the principles of branding in OSNs (Barwise & Meehan, 2010). Brand awareness is defined as when provided a stimulus, a client's capacity is to analyze and remember a brand (Bilgihan, Peng & Kandampully, 2014; Lin, 2013; Berry, 2000). Originally referred to as decision-ability makers to recognize a brand in the B2C scenario (Homburg, Klarmann & Schmitt, 2010). For communication to be effective, brand awareness is essential (Jakeli & Tchumburidze, 2012).

THE IMPORTANCE OF BRAND AWARENESS IN EXPORT INDUSTRY

Users' purchasing decisions are influenced by their brand awareness. Individual identification, expertise supremacy, and brand recall are all part of it (Kim, Kim, Kim, Kim & Kang, 2008). Correspondingly, consumers utilize brand awareness as a choice rationale, as it has a meaningful effect on their decision-making. A renowned brand is significantly more likely to be selected over a new one by consumers (Hoyer & Brown, 1990). This renowned brand outperforms in the industry when equated to the brand that isn't well-known. According to a study conducted of individuals' unintentional brand encounters in their everyday routines, the recurrence of brand exposure considerably increases the likelihood of the brand being preferred, even if people are unaware of this kind of experience (Ferraro, Bettman & Chartrand, 2009).

According to research, known brands retrieve information faster in brain regions then-new brands as individuals are familiarized with your brand and are likely to develop trust (Esch, Moll, Schmitt, Elger, Neuhaus & Weber, 2012). Though, previous research has considered brand awareness and brand associations as a single measurement, making it impossible to distinguish between their effects based on brands value and credibility (Gil, Andres & Salinas, 2007; Yoo, Donthu & Lee, 2000). But then again, over the last two decades, there has been a flow in academic interest in business-to-business (B2B) branding (Seyedghorban, Matanda & LaPlaca, 2016). This is in line with the rising understanding that B2B brands are significant in today's worldwide markets (Wang & Hao, 2018) and that the monetary value of B2B transactions is equivalent to that of B2C transactions (Wang & Hao, 2018; Lilien, 2016). Therefore, branding is equally important in B2B and B2C export markets. However, to increase the brand awareness, the exporting enterprises wanting to be involved alongside the local competitors must show solid, persuasive proof on issues such as after-sales servicing, guarantees, reliability, security, and other variables that affect the buyer's opinion of quality product (Sweeney & Soutar 2001; Sheth, Newman & Gross, 1991).

LACK OF BRANDING IN EXPORT MARKETS

Exporting is a growing source of profit. The value of global commerce in commodities is expected to reach US$ 6.6 trillion in 2021, representing a year-over-year increase of roughly 31% from the low point in 2020 and around 3% from pre-pandemic levels in 2019 (Global Trade Statistics 2021). Global export trade has expected to increase from 20% of global GDP (International Monetary Fund, 2007; World Bank, 2007). Exporting is crucial because of the numerous benefits it provides to both governments and businesses. By supplying foreign cash, job openings, economic linkages, and spillover effectiveness from the export industry to non-export businesses, exporting can help public officials handle expanding trade imbalances and slow economic growth (Czinkota & Ronkainen, 2004; Marin, 1992; Madsen, 1989).

Moreover, an examination of the literature finds that empirical research on the importance of branding benefit in export marketing, a core type of export competitive advantage, is woefully lacking. There is a shortage of study on the antecedents of branding added benefit and its future results repercussions in the export marketing arena, except Zou, Fang and Zhao (2003) work on the implications of core competencies on presentation in the context of Chinese exporters. Astonishingly, this is true even though the significance of branding in differentiating basic consumables based on their social position as well as their emotional features and subjectivity traits is well-phrased, with the progress of positive brands equity (Morgan & Rego, 2009; Keller, 2003; Fournier, 1998; Shocker, Srivastava & Ruekert,1994; Aaker, 1991).

Furthermore, global competition, as a result of globalization, and the integration of markets, current research reveals that branding on a global scale has never been more necessary for the sustainability, development, and prosperity of businesses today (Townsend, Yeniyurt & Talay, 2009; Ozsomer & Altaras, 2008; Strizhakova, Coulter & Price, 2008; Fastoso & Whitelock, 2007). Assumed that the growing occurrence of the internationalization concept and the resulting proliferation of exporting organizations, as well as the huge concentration in branding, equally in academic and industrial sectors, the inadequate study on export branding obvious benefit is an essential omission in the literature, impeding the progress of philosophy in the practical world. Internal and external limitations that limit a company's capacity to start, maintain and retain exporting operations are known as export barriers (Leonidou, 2004). Intrinsic obstacles occur as a result of a scarcity of funds and competencies within the company. Extrinsic factors arise from outside of the company's ecosystem, mostly as a result of the governmental, vendor, client, and competitive moves.

However, businesses export goods and services for a variety of reasons. These exports can boost revenues and profits by expanding into new markets or growing current ones, and they can even enable the company to gain a major part of the worldwide market. Exporting businesses diversify their risk by selling to a wide variety of sectors (Investopedia, 2021). Likewise, emerging an exporting venture branding benefit should be well-thought-out as the product of a range of factors and variables that are mostly internal to the organization. Although circumstances beyond the firm's control (like rivals, government entities, or other special interests) impact a brand's positioning, it should be perceived as the outcome of a wide range of factors and elements that are primarily core to the organization (De Chernatony & Cottam, 2006; Keller & Lehmann, 2006; Boulding, Lee & Staelin, 1994). Also, brand marketing services are the core components that may contribute to a product's higher value (Nordas, 2010). When it comes to environmental resources and consumables, wherein distinction is difficult, the ability to create value through these types of services is dependent on the ability to tell consumers about the commodities' special attributes and their connection to their geographical origin (Neilson, Wright & Aklimawati, 2018; Rawat, 2017). This concludes to be an important aspect of branding in export markets.

Earlier research paradigms have emphasized the status of recognizing possessions and qualities which are uniquely similar to the modern research setting (Newbert, 2008; Morgan et al., 2006; Kaleka, 2002; Ling-Yee & Ogunmokun, 2001). The necessity of substantial operating capital, expertise and efficient marketing strategies in supporting an export endeavor to build a distinctive edge and stay competitive in the intended export market was stressed in researchers' earlier discussions. One of the executives questioned, for example, stated, "The aim is to increase the brand equity and boost bottom-line performance." "It is not a contest of commodities; it is a struggle of perceptions," said another executive. "Defining the brand's essence is difficult. " One export manager added. "We have to comprehend consumers' perspectives, observe when people engage with goods, how they are using it, you have to live out their lives." "Deprived of acceptable funding and skills, a concept, even if it is brilliant, it will not succeed, and a brand cannot be developed," remarked another export manager. "Experience is the only way to gain a certain kind of understanding," one export manager added. "We now understand whatever succeeds what doesn't succeed, we comprehend that industry or researchers realize where and how to acquire information about it." Even though several core competencies have been acknowledged in the literature (Morgan et al., 2004; Zou et al., 2003; Kaleka, 2002; Ling-Yee & Ogunmokun, 2001), we emphasize exporting venture in the financing, experience-based assets, and interconnection in enhancing export venture branding and output.

There has been researching in the area of export promotion that has shown that monetary resources may contribute in assisting export ventures to strive magnificently in the chosen export markets (Morgan et al., 2006; Ling-Yee & Ogunmokun, 2001; Yaprak, 1985). Marketing benefit relates to the extent to which a company's marketing position amongst export consumers is superior to its competitors (Zou et al., 2003).

A good brand can be built, not created, and its building is a very complicated task; the brand is typically considered as something the consumer considers (Brakus, Schmitt & Zarantonello, 2009; De Chernatony & Cottam, 2006; Chattopadhyay & Laborie, 2005). Export market knowledge is a critical factor in developing and executing an efficient export marketing plan, according to the international marketing research literature, such as Souchon (an examination of Branding Advantage 915 NYU,

Kogut & Zander, 2003; Cadogan, Diamantopoulos & Siguaw, 2002; Autio, Sapienza & Almeida, 2000; Diamantopoulos, 1996).

A product or service's brand is the first step in creating client awareness by naming it and distinguishing it from comparable ones inside a market (Kay, 2006). As a result of consumer perspective (Aaker, 1991; Keller, 2003; Rust and colleagues, 2004), brand equity can be defined as the additional worth that a brand has in the minds and behavior of customers (Kumar, Lemon & Parasuraman, 2006; Leone, Rao, Keller, Man Luo, McAlister & Srivastava, 2006; Pappu, Quester & Cooksey, 2006; Netemeyer, Krishnan, Pullig, Wang, Yagci, Dean, Ricks & Wirth, 2004; Yoo & Donthu, 2001). As a result of a company's communication operations (Duncan 2002; Naik & Raman, 2003), a brand's core brand associations are shaped, and the brand is differentiated (Naik & Raman, 2003; Duncan, 2002) and (to a feasible extent) competition supremacy is established (Keller, Sternthal & Tybout, 2002; Kapferer, 1997). Current research considers branding as a "holistic" experience that takes into account economic, sociopolitical factors (Brakus et al., 2009; Rindfleisch, Burroughs & Wong, 2009; Cova, Pace & Park, 2007; De Chernatony & Cottam, 2006; Chattopadhyay & Laborie, 2005). If you want your brand to be effective internationally, you need to retain its core (a single clear value that is loved and accepted by foreign clients) (Park & Rabolt, 2009; Pappu et al., 2006; De Chernatony, Halliburton & Bernath, 1995). As a result, exporting venture leaders must not only use a growing variety of social media channels such as multiple sorts of broadcasting, printing, and integrating digital, direct challenge, sponsors, and media affairs; the brand must also be more than just a slogan (De Chernatony & Cottam, 2006). In terms of developing distinctive methods of providing superior customer value and thus accomplish a favorable exportation venture branding position (Christensen et al., 2008; O'Cass & Ngo, 2007; Keller & Lehmann, 2006; Naik & Raman, 2003;), export managers must expertly facilitate these operations and start encouraging creativity and innovation.

HOW TO INCREASE BRAND AWARENESS AMONG FOREIGN BUYERS

Pleasure is the favorable attitude that a customer acquires as a result of analyzing his consuming encounter with a specific item (Erci, Unal, Candan & Yildirim, 2012). Consumer expectations and experiences are developed over the period, and this shapes brand satisfaction. It frequently results in recurring purchases of the brands (Zeithaml & Berry, 1996), which ultimately enhances brand loyalty. Similarly, by introducing brands to consumers, marketing generates and boosts brand recognition (Yoo et al. 2000; Batra, Lehmann, Burke, & Pae, 1995; Keller 1993; Aaker 1991; Rossiter & Percy 1987).

Marketing by boosting the visibility correspondingly enhances the possibility of a brand's existence used in a consumer's reference group, enhancing the brand's market presentation (Krishnan & Chakravarti, 1993). Brand awareness is positively related to the amount of money spent on advertising for the brand which may include social media ads, search ads, and display ads (Yoo et al., 2000). People are encouraged to switch brands and try new items by promotions. Such products help to increase brand awareness (Keller, 2008). Although previous research has found a link among terms of price-quality (Yoo et al., 2000; Tellis & Wernerfelt, 1987), the link involving price and brand awareness has yet to be investigated. The consequences of a venture's actions in the focused export industry are referred to as exporting innovation performance (Katsikeas, Leonidou & Morgan, 2000; Shoham, 1998). They focus on the economy's key metrics such as exporters, the satisfaction of customers, and profits (Styles, Patterson & Ahmed, 2008; Diamantopoulos & Kakkos, 2007; Cadogan et al., 2002). In the existing literature, there is indeed a common link connecting the influence of brand equity to buyer value and lifetime worth (Seno & Lukas, 2007; Kumar et al., 2006; Leone et al., 2006; Pappu et al., 2006; Netemeyer et al., 2004). As a result, an export venture with a branding gain can reap multiple benefits in terms of efficiency. Consumers utilize brands as consumption indicators; thus, brand image has a great potentiality to generate cashflows (Holt, 2002; Srivastava et al., 1998; Shocker et al., 1994; Keller, 1993).

In short, brands allow brand extensions; within and without the core product line – well-known and recognized brands require fewer product - development costs that can more easily obtain widespread reach (Kay, 2006; Keller & Lehmann, 2006; Tauber, 1988). In addition, having a brand edge in the export marketplace might help you build a loyal international consumer base (Zou et al., 2003; Ling-Yee & Ogunmokun, 2001). Persistent individuals are much less receptive to prices (Kay, 2006; Keller, 2003) and much more responsive to opponents' approaches (Kay, 2006; Keller, 2003). (Wong & Merrilees, 2007; Dick & Basu, 1994). Which allows to get a large share in the market and demand a higher pricing policy in export business (Morgan et al., 2004; Zou et al., 2003). However, increased organic visibility in the new export market should be a priority.

SOCIAL MEDIA STRATEGIES TO BUILD BRAND AWARENESS

Traditionally, businesses attempt to raise brand awareness through restricted one-way communication. OSNs, on the other hand, allows for two-way discussions with people who are responsible for developing a destination's brand identification (Lim, Chung & Weaver, 2012). Moreover, there seems to be an ongoing dispute about brands' activity in OSNs (Laroche, Habibi & Richard, 2013). The process by which individuals are mindful of a brand term, as well as recall and recognize it, is known as brand awareness (Gursoy, Chen & Chi, 2014; Lin, 2013; Jakeli & Tchumburidze, 2012). WOM is critical to a business's accomplishment, who know how to use word of mouth for marketing are more successful than those that don't (Mason, 2008).

SOLUTIONS AND RECOMMENDATIONS

OSNs profiles and pages are a logical extension of the brands' platforms. They are strong and operative methods for attracting target visitors, increasing consumer engagement, converting leads, and even closing purchases. They're also great for increasing brand recognition. For marketers, establishing strong brand recognition is a vital goal. Creating Search engine Optimization (SEO-friendly) content such that people may find your social media and site whenever they're seeking the item or brand you provide.

FUTURE RESEARCH DIRECTIONS

Online Social Networks (OSNs) enable locations and businesses to raise brand recognition through their excellent interactive and communicative capabilities. In the export sectors, several tourist locations and hospitality businesses are looking into using OSNs to raise brand recognition and generate positive word-of-mouth. International expansion activities have become progressively significant for the existence, development, besides profitability of contemporary businesses as a result of internationalization. This makes it easier for customers to distinguish your product. Exports benefit from branding because customers associate it with high quality and excellent customer service. As result clients from other countries are willing to pay a greater price for it. Customers are more likely to trust a branded name, which gives the organization more legitimacy and promotes new business. It attracts talent, instills confidence in your firm, and eventually raises brand awareness. Brands' chances of developing significant brand recognition using OSNs are thus boosted. When consumers are aware of the brand, they spread the word and purchase it. This research investigates brand awareness in-depth, a topic that has received little attention, and provides significant contributions. Originally, it investigates the link between brand awareness and attractive marketplace outputs like sales volume and discovers a favorable correlation. Ongoing research into the aspects that contribute to an export venture's branding gain from the standpoint of a foreigner buyer is actively urged. Several types of resources and competencies can also be highlighted as possibly aiding in the development and establishment of a branding advantage. Other sets of determinants, such as natural, social, and cultural features, as well as the whole range of advertising competencies (product, price, distribution, and service) and also creative thinking (Newbert, 2007), could therefore be investigated in upcoming studies. In a comparable theme, greater research into the role of various categories of marketing edge in export is a key area to pursue. Pricing, product, service, and distribution advantages are all potentially fundamental dimensions of export competitive benefit.

REFERENCES

Abdul-Latif, S.-A., & Abdul-Talib, A. N. (2017). Consumer Racism: A Scale Modification. *Asia Pacific Journal of Marketing and Logistics*, *29*(3), 616–633. doi:10.1108/APJML-02-2016-0026

Abdul Talib, A., & Teong, N. (2019). Internet Sales Channel and Manufacturers' Brand: A Transaction Cost Analysis. *International Journal of Supply Chain Management*, *8*(5), 1130–1340.

Abdul-Talib, A. N., & Adnan, M. M. (2017). Determinants of consumer's willingness to boycott surrogate products. *Journal of Islamic Marketing*, *8*(3), 345–360. doi:10.1108/JIMA-08-2015-0065

Abdul-Talib, A. N., & Arshad, S. (2021). Searching the effects of viral marketing via customer-based brand equity on purchase intentions. Handbook of Research on Technology Applications for Effective Customer Engagement, 66–75. doi:10.4018/978-1-7998-4772-4.ch005

Abdul-Talib, A. N., & Japeri, N. (2020). Brand consciousness and brand loyalty. *Economic, Educational, and Touristic Development in Asia*, 106–126. doi:10.4018/978-1-7998-2239-4.ch006

Abdul-Talib, A. N., & Yusof, M. (2020). Antecedents of global brands preference among generation y in malaysia. *Leveraging Consumer Behavior and Psychology in the Digital Economy*, 153–171. doi:10.4018/978-1-7998-3042-9.ch009

Arshad, S., Shahid, M., Laeeq, M., & Ashfaq, M. Which school of thought better measure the concept of market orientation. *International Journal of Research, 2*(12), 1178-1180.

Barreda, A. A., Bilgihan, A., Nusair, K., & Okumus, F. (2015). Generating brand awareness in online social networks. *Computers in Human Behavior*, *50*, 600–609. doi:10.1016/j.chb.2015.03.023

Bernstein, M. S., Bakshy, E., Burke, M., & Karrer, B. (2013, April). Quantifying the invisible audience in social networks. In *Proceedings of the SIGCHI conference on human factors in computing systems* (pp. 21–30). ACM 10.1145/2470654.2470658

Bustamante, J. C. (2019). Intellectual property rights as branding services for exports value-adding: An analysis of Chile-s-Sello de Origen-programme. *International Journal of Intellectual Property Management, 9*(3-4), 315–341. doi:10.1504/IJIPM.2019.103044

da Silva, P. A., & da Rocha, A. (2001). Perception of export barriers to Mercosur by Brazilian firms. *International Marketing Review, 18*(6), 589–610. doi:10.1108/EUM0000000006296

De Chernatony, L., & Dall'Olmo Riley, F. (1998). Defining a" brand": Beyond the literature with experts' interpretations. *Journal of Marketing Management, 14*(5), 417–443. doi:10.1362/026725798784867798

Dibb, S., Simkin, L., Pride, W. M., & Ferrell, O. C. (1994). *Marketing: Concepts and strategies* (2nd ed.). Houghton Mifflin.

Esch, F.-R., Moll, T., Schmitt, B., Elger, C. E., Neuhaus, C., & Weber, B. (2012). Brands on the brain: Do consumers use declarative information or experienced emotions to evaluate brands. *Journal of Consumer Psychology, 22*(1), 75–85. doi:10.1016/j.jcps.2010.08.004

Falko, F., Presseau, S. J., & Vera, A. S. (2014). Time to retire the theory of planned behavior. *Health Psychology Review, 8*(1), 1–7. doi:10.1080/17437199.2013.869710 PMID:25053004

Ferraro, R., Bettman, J. R., & Chartrand, T. L. (2009). The power of strangers: The effect of incidental consumer brand encounters on brand choice. *The Journal of Consumer Research, 35*(5), 729–741. doi:10.1086/592944

Gil, R. B., Andres, E. F., & Salinas, E. M. (2007). Family as a source of consumer-based brand equity. *Journal of Product and Brand Management, 16*(3), 188–199. doi:10.1108/10610420710751564

Hasan, A., & Ramzan, M. (2018). Exploring effect of challenge on employee engagement. *Merit Research Journal of Education and Review, 6*(6), 92–100.

Hashim, F., Bakar, A. R. A., & Abdul-Talib, A. N. (2010). *International Business* (2nd ed.). Oxford Fajar Press.

Hassan, S. S., & Craft, S. (2012). Examining world market segmentation and brand positioning strategies. *Journal of Consumer Marketing, 29*(5), 344–356. doi:10.1108/07363761211247460

Homburg, C., Klarmann, M., & Schmitt, J. (2010). Brand awareness in business markets: When is it related to firm performance? *International Journal of Research in Marketing, 27*(3), 201–212. doi:10.1016/j.ijresmar.2010.03.004

Horner, S., & Swarbrooke, J. (2012). *Leisure marketing*. Routledge. doi:10.4324/9780080478937

Huang, R., & Sarigollu, E. (2014). How brand awareness relates to market outcome, brand equity, and the marketing mix. In *Fashion branding and consumer behaviors* (pp. 113–132). Springer. doi:10.1007/978-1-4939-0277-4_8

Joshi, R., & Garg, P. (2021). Role of brand experience in shaping brand love. *International Journal of Consumer Studies*, *45*(2), 259–272. doi:10.1111/ijcs.12618

Kim, K. H., Kim, K. S., Kim, D. Y., Kim, J. H., & Kang, S. H. (2008). Brand equity in hospital marketing. *Journal of Business Research*, *1*(61), 75–82. doi:10.1016/j.jbusres.2006.05.010

Maurya, U. K., & Mishra, P. (2012). What is a brand? A Perspective on Brand Meaning. *European Journal of Business and Management*, *4*(3), 122–133.

Mehar, M. R., Naeem, M., Nazeer, M., & Arshad, S. (2018). Relationship of Economic and Financial variables with behavior of Stock Prices: A case of Pakistan Stock Exchange. *Merit Research Journal of Education and Review*, *6*(6), 92-100.

Milanzi, M. A. (2012). Export barrier perceptions in Tanzania: The influence of social networks. *Journal of African Business*, *13*(1), 29–39. doi:10.1080/15228916.2012.657941

Moore, K., & Reid, S. (2008). The Birth of Brand: 4000 Years of Branding History. *Business History*, *50*(4), 419–432. doi:10.1080/00076790802106299

Pyper, K., Doherty, A. M., Gounaris, S., & Wilson, A. (2019). Investigating international strategic brand management and export performance outcomes in the B2B context. *International Marketing Review*, *37*(1), 98–129. doi:10.1108/IMR-02-2019-0087

Pyper, K. L., Gounaris, S., & Doherty, A. M. (2015). *Export to expand: A conceptual examination of branding as a deterministic parameter in export performance*. Academic Press.

Rauch, J. E. (2001). Business and social networks in international trade. *Journal of Economic Literature*, *39*(4), 1177–1203. doi:10.1257/jel.39.4.1177

Santos, I. M. (2020). The effect of exports on a wealth of a country: A comment on the role of natural capital in the Amazon basin. *PRACS: Revista Eletrônica de Humanidades do Curso de Ciências Sociais da UNIFAP*, *13*(2), 17–30. doi:10.18468/pracs.2020v13n2.p17-30

Seyedghorban, Z., Matanda, M. J., & LaPlaca, P. (2016). Advancing theory and knowledge in the business-to-business branding literature. *Journal of Business Research*, *69*(8), 2664–2677. doi:10.1016/j.jbusres.2015.11.002

Spyropoulou, S., Skarmeas, D., & Katsikeas, C. S. (2011). An examination of branding advantage in export ventures. *European Journal of Marketing*, *45*(6), 910–935. doi:10.1108/03090561111119967

Stylidis, K., Hoffenson, S., Rossi, M., Wickman, C., Soderman, M., & Soderberg, R. (2020). Transforming brand core values into perceived quality: A Volvo case study. *International Journal of Product Development*, *24*(1), 43–67. doi:10.1504/IJPD.2020.106448

Tybout, A. M., & Sternthal, B. (2012). Developing a compelling brand positioning. *Kellogg on Marketing*, 73-91.

Waheed, A., Khan, S. Z., Arshad, S., Rafique, K., & Laeeq, M. (2018). How Market Orientation Helps to Gain Competitive Advantages in New Product Offering. *IJAMEE*, *3*(3), 1-7.

Wang, C. L., Sarkar, A., & Sarkar, J. G. (2018). Building the holy brand: Towards a theoretical model of brand religiosity. *International Journal of Consumer Studies*, *42*(6), 736–743. doi:10.1111/ijcs.12430

Yoo, B., Donthu, N., & Lee, S. (2000). An examination of selected marketing mix elements and brand equity. *Journal of the Academy of Marketing Science*, *28*(2), 195–211. doi:10.1177/0092070300282002

Zakaria, N., Abdul-Talib, A. N., & Amelinckx, A. (Eds.). (2020). *Transcending Cultural Frontiers: Practices, Challenges, and Strategy for International Business*. Springer. doi:10.1007/978-981-15-4454-5

Zakaria, N., Abdul-Talib, A. N., & Amelinckx, A. (2020). Advancing cultural frontiers to champion global business in emerging markets. In *Transcending Cultural Frontiers* (pp. 1–10). Springer. doi:10.1007/978-981-15-4454-5_1

Zakaria, N., Abdul-Talib, A. N., & Othman, N. (Eds.). (2016). *Handbook of research on impacts of international business and political affairs on the global economy*. IGI Global. doi:10.4018/978-1-4666-9806-2

Zakaria, N., Wan-Ismail, W.-N. A., & Abdul-Talib, A. N. (2021). Seriously, Conspicuous Consumption? The Impact of Culture, Materialism and Religiosity on Malaysian Generation Y Consumers' Purchasing of Foreign Brands. *Asia Pacific Journal of Marketing and Logistics*, *33*(2), 526–560. doi:10.1108/APJML-07-2018-0283

KEY TERMS AND DEFINITIONS

Brand Awareness: Customers' awareness of the features or image of a specific brand of goods or services.

Brand Loyalty: Consumers' positive association with a product or service provided by the brand.

Brand Satisfaction: Customers repeat purchases due to the positive experience with the product or services.

Branding: When a product or service stands out from the competitors, it is branded.

Competitive Advantage: A condition to have an edge on your competitors.

Customer Equity: Lifetime worth provided by the company to the customer

Export: Goods and services created in one country can be distributed worldwide.

Export Performance: An organization can sell domestically produced goods and services in other countries.

Globalization: When a company begins to operate on a global scale or develops influence on the world stage.

International Marketing: It relates to any advertising strategy that takes place outside of one's own country.

Perceived Quality: It is, first and foremost, a customer perspective.

Purchase Intentions: Purchase intention refers to a customer's willingness to buy a specific product or service.

WOM: Whenever a customer's interest is mirrored in their regular conversation, this is known as word-of-mouth marketing.

Chapter 3
South Korea Film-Induced Tourism:
The K-Drama Determinant for Malaysian Tourists

Mazni Saad
International Islamic University Malaysia, Malaysia

Nor Azilah Husin
Universiti Selangor, Malaysia

Nur Zafirah Ramlee
International Islamic University Malaysia, Malaysia

ABSTRACT

This study surveyed 150 Malaysian tourists regarding the South Korean drama (K-drama) factors that drew them back to South Korea. The analyses revealed that K-drama was highly successful in enticing the young generation and discovered a clear scenario for Malaysians' response for a repeat visit. The results show that collaboration for the development of heritage tourism should be linked to the national identity and replicated through dramas similar to K-dramas. Universities should work closely with other stakeholders to produce high-quality films for international distribution.

INTRODUCTION

South Korea as a Tourism Destination

From an economic standpoint, cultural heritage has benefited from residents' willingness to support tourism development (Wei et al., 2021). Culture is a multifaceted concept that encompasses man's acquired knowledge, beliefs, customs, morals, and other abilities and habits as a member of society (Spencer-Oatey, 2015). Nowadays, people love to travel to gain new knowledge from other cultures. Tourism that

DOI: 10.4018/978-1-7998-9071-3.ch003

involves culture is known as cultural tourism. Cultural tourism is when people travel away from their familiar environment because of cultural attractions. They aim to integrate information and experiences from the new culture (Petroman et al., 2013). Korean popular culture has become famous, especially their music, K-pop. Many people get inspired by K-pop idols due to their stunning dance steps on the stage and their perfect vocals that can attract a huge audience worldwide, especially teenagers. Besides the Korean Wave, South Korea has become a tourism destination that attracts many Muslims to visit the country due to the Muslim-friendly hospitality services offered.

According to the Korea Institute of Halal Industry (KIHI), South Korea has been witnessing an increasing number of Muslim travellers (Malay Mail, 22 May 2019). One million people arrived in the country in 2016, a 33% increase from 2015. Thus, KIHI has sought Malaysia's expertise and accreditation to strengthen the halal sector in the country in order to expand the offerings of Muslim-friendly services to Muslim travellers. The article also stated that the promotion of South Korea as a Muslim-friendly destination has resulted in a rapid growth of halal restaurants across the country. Currently, there are 130 Muslim-friendly restaurants, including 14 Halal certified restaurants, and one halal ski resort in South Korea to cater to the demand of Muslim tourists. Thus, the increasing demand for Muslim-friendly services can help Malaysian expertise grow outside Malaysia to contribute to the halal industry.

TOURISM MARKETING

Tourism marketing is one of the major elements that affect the effectiveness of any tourism product promotion. The marketing involves social media in ensuring the success of tourism strategies. Digital marketing is a crucial element of marketing. Without digital marketing, it would be challenging to attract tourists to visit the tourist spots.

Literature works have demonstrated the role of social media in promoting the tourism industry. Jang and Park (2020) documented the transformation of a traditional residential neighbourhood, Ihwa in Seoul, into a tourist attraction through personal blogs and news articles. The text analytics performed in the study suggest that texts that appear in blogs play a unique role in promoting tourist attractions. Shared experiences from a trip to a small place can influence other travellers to visit the place. Texts in blogs that show a strongly positive view of the place can create new tourist demand. Studying the cultural determinants of K-dramas can help in the efforts of promoting Malaysia as a tourism destination in the region. Thus, the objective of this study is to identify the cultural determinants that influence Malaysians to travel to South Korea.

FILM-INDUCED TOURISM

K-drama tourism, according to Raj (2018), is film-induced tourism. It can be defined as a person's visit to a destination or attraction because the place was featured on television, video, or the cinema screen. K-drama is the Korean Wave (*hallyu*) that has reached many countries, including Malaysia, to position cultural goods (Chen, 2016; Kim et al., 2016). The love story of *Winter Sonata* resulted in an increase in foreign tourist arrivals to South Korea to 1.3 million in 2017 from 707,000 in 2016. Due to the success of the series, tourists flocked to South Korea, especially Nami Island. The audience enjoyed the storyline, and the scenery pictured in the K-drama delivered an extraordinary experience to them. As a result, they were drawn to re-enact and take photographs at the tourism locations featured in the series. *Winter Sonata* has captured immense attention among tourism researchers, with Google Scholar listing 35,300 results for the search word "Winter Sonata." *Goblin*, a drama series aired in December 2016, managed to capture a huge audience worldwide. Later, its filming locations such as Jumunjin Beach, Hagwon Farm, and Mirinae Holy Site became tourist spots for photography sessions. The drama has a positive impact on the site development; for example, a street in Incheon where an old bookstore called Hanmija was located has been revived due to an increase in the number of visitors after the bookstore was featured in the drama (The Jakarta Post, 2017). *Goblin* became a hit K-drama and boosted a tourism honeypot at the scene where the on-screen couple met and talked for the first time.

Ordoyo et al. (2021) reviewed K-dramas from 2017 to 2019 by examining popular blogs. Of place, personality, and performance, the researchers revealed that the personality and popularity of the actors and actresses have contributed to the growth of tourism in South Korea. Recent reviews of *Empress Ki* on YouTube indicate that the actors' good looks and personalities add to the values of the singing, dancing, costumes, calligraphy, and fighting arts shown in the K-drama.

TOURISTS' TRAVELLING MOTIVATION

Malaysia's outbound travel statistics have been showing an increasing trend annually, particularly in South Korea (see Figure 1). Malaysia is one of the countries affected by the Korean popular culture or Korean Wave, which has spread to Malaysia in various ways, including music, drama, food, and fashion. According to Ramli (2016), 10,000 fans, most of whom were young people, were going to attend the South Korean boy band, Big Bang, MADE World Tour in Kuala Lumpur. Consequently, this scenario led to tremendous interest in the Korean society and culture among Malaysians, influencing them to learn the Korean language and travel to South Korea. This phenomenon will contribute to the growth of Korea's economy through the rapid development of the country's tourism industry. Teh and Goh (2018) also found that South Korea has received many tourists, and the country has been increasingly gaining popularity as an outbound destination in recent years.

As Figure 1 shows, approximately 311,000 visitors in 2016 from Malaysia travelled to South Korea, an increase of 223,000 from 2015. Based on the statistics, Malaysians are travelling to Korea to experience the culture itself. Bae et al. (2017) found that many people travel to South Korea due to their interest and the influence of the Korean Wave, which has led to an increasing number of foreigners visiting South Korea.

Furthermore, many Malaysians, especially adolescents, follow various trends and fashions from South Korea, such as their skincare products (Anh, 2016). Examples of popular Korean cosmetic brands in Malaysia include Laneige, Innisfree, Clio, and Etude House. Korean cosmetic brands are well-known not only in Asia but also throughout the world. As a result, many companies from South Korea have opened their business in Malaysia to attract more Malaysian customers. Lafaurie (2018) stated that South Korea is viewed as a cultural powerhouse that provides influence or inspiration, similar to Japan and the United States, and the government of South Korea has leveraged the Korean Wave phenomenon to enhance its image and attract more tourists to the country. For the past decade, the Korean Wave has been credited for exporting South Korean culture and the arrival of Asian tourists to South Korea to visit the locations featured in dramas and music videos from the country (Lafaurie, 2018).

Figure 1. The trend of Malaysian travelling to South Korea from 2012 to 2016
Note. Source: Statista (2019)

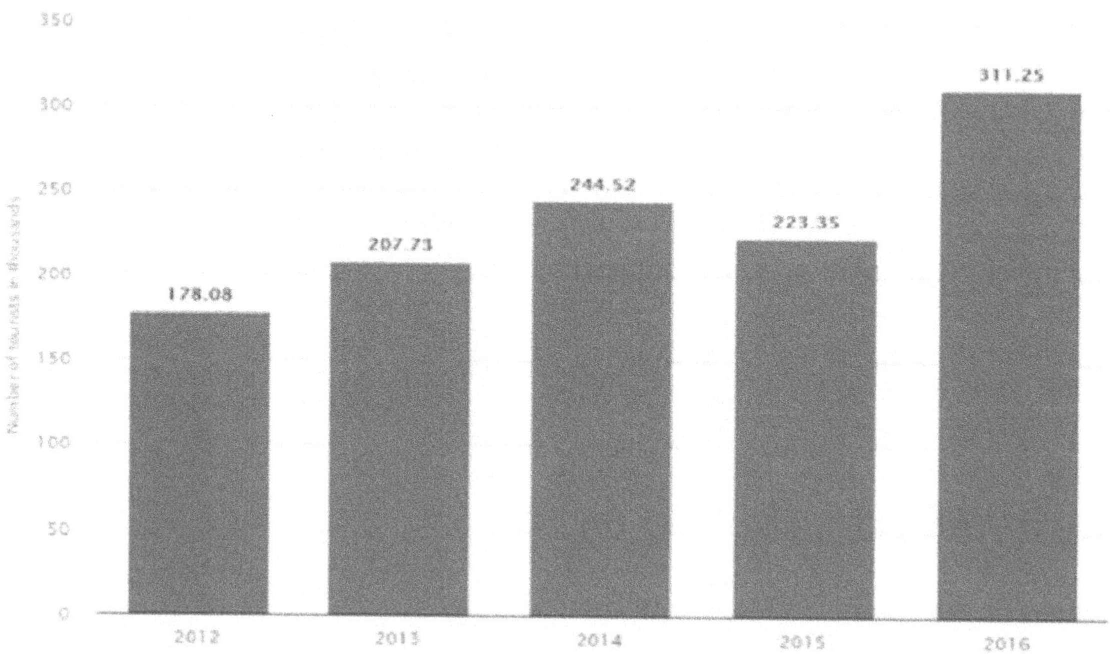

K-DRAMA FACTORS AND REVISIT INTENTION

Although the entertainment industry in most parts of the world is suffering from production problems and delays due to Covid-19, the South K-drama machine seems to continue to operate. Currently, people are mostly staying at home due to the lockdown forced by the pandemic. As a result, many dramas have attracted a large number of audiences, particularly those broadcasted on streaming platforms such as Netflix and Viu.

Ching (2000), Ju (2010), and Vu (2011) previously linked the success of K-dramas and Korean Wave (the increasing global popularity of South Korean culture) with culture. Most of the researchers also acknowledged the role of South Korean culture in contributing to the success of K-dramas. Thus, it is crucial to understand what makes the South Korean culture attract substantial interest and attention among the people in other Asian countries, including Malaysia. The Korean Wave started to penetrate Malaysia in 2002 with the airing of the Korean hit drama *Winter Sonata* on a terrestrial channel, TV3 (The Edge Markets, 2011). *Winter Sonata* is a cultural hit that has become a classic, making it a must-see series for all K-drama enthusiasts globally. It started the proliferation of the Korean Wave all over the world. *Winter Sonata* was followed by *Jewel in the Palace*, which was aired in Malaysia on 8TV from November 2004 to February 2005 with subtitles in Mandarin. It was replayed on TV Alhijrah with Korean and Bahasa Melayu subtitles in 2011. *Autumn in My Heart* is another hugely popular K-drama that trailed on the success of *Winter Sonata* and *Jewel in the Palace*.

Malaysian television stations began to subscribe to and incorporate K-dramas into the local programmes, which gradually increased the popularity of K-dramas in Malaysia. The growing popularity of

K-dramas can also be attributed to the emergence of another exciting digital media technology, Internet Television, which allows audiences to access TV series through the internet. Internet Television is rising significantly (Arango, 2009), offering free online viewing of television programmes. Today, many websites offer streaming services with subtitles. Online forums and message boards allow Malaysians to chat about Korean popular culture with each other in the online communities. For instance, Drama Fever is one of the websites that allow viewers to watch any K-drama for free, and viewers can write reviews and rate their favourite dramas on the website. Other similar sites include Dramacool, Dramacrazy, Mysoju, and KimchiDrama.

Many K-dramas are well-known among Malaysians. Due to the high interest of the Malaysian audience in K-dramas, Dimsum, a video-on-demand (VOD) service in Malaysia, set forth the idea of partnering with Oh! K, a Turner Asia Pacific channel, to expand their Korean entertainment content offerings to subscribers from Malaysia and Brunei (Rao, 2017). The contents are to be offered with multiple language subtitles. According to Dimsum Marketing Manager, Lam Swee Kim, the partnership can increase the variety of K-drama genres offered on Dimsum (Rao, 2017). With Dimsum subscriptions, viewers can watch K-dramas and dramas from other countries at any time as long as they have a mobile device and an internet connection. Malaysian audiences are now strongly attracted to K-dramas compared to local Malaysian dramas. K-dramas have gradually influenced the perception and lifestyle of Korean theatre lovers without them even realising it.

Figure 2. Popularity of South Korean dramas in Malaysia in 2019

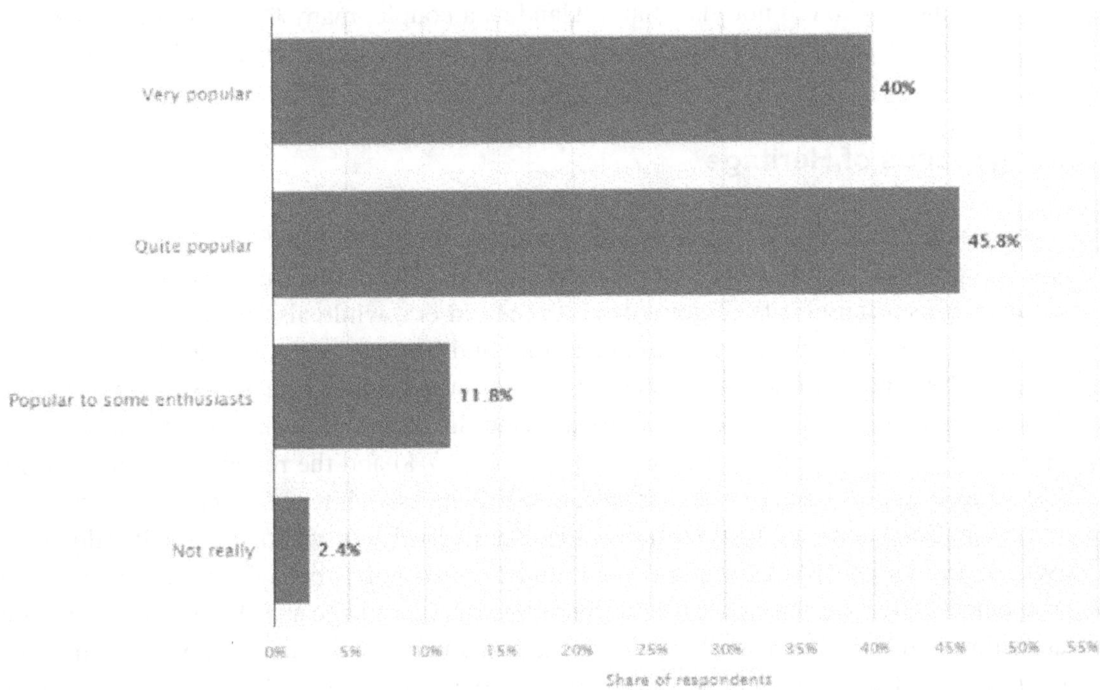

As shown in Figure 2, the survey was on 500 people in Malaysia aged 15 to 59 on the South Korean cultural content (Statista, 2019). The survey shows that 40% of the respondents considered K-dramas as very popular in Malaysia. A further 46% thought them to be quite popular. Through forums and streaming websites and other social media services like Facebook and Instagram, viewers share their passion and experience of touring Korea with other *hallyu* (Korean Wave) theatre fans worldwide. The question that arises is, what contributes to the immense popularity of K-dramas? Why is this success not happening with the enchanting American soap operas? The possible reasons for the popularity and fame of K-dramas are discussed below.

1. Romantic Places

South Korea is well-known for its "couple culture", making it a favourite destination for romantic get-aways not only on Valentine's Day but also throughout the year. Inspired by the *hallyu* wave and the widespread popularity of Korean romantic dramas, ideal locations surround the city for couples from around the globe to renew their love. In *hallyu* tourism, tourists somewhat understand the reminisce of being romantic by recreating the scenes from the drama that inspired them to travel to South Korea. For example, Sang Kyun Kim (2010) chronicled how couples visiting South Korea re-enacted scenes from the sensational drama *Winter Sonata* to relive the ideal love story portrayed in the series. The researcher discovered that the couples tried to realise their wish to be the hero and heroine of the *Winter Sonata* series by visiting Nami Island (where the series was filmed) and acting out the scenes involving the hero and heroine. They aspired to attain the same level of romance as depicted by the actors in the drama series. Even among those who did not visit Nami Island as a couple, many female tourists queued in front of the movie poster located on the island to take pictures, reliving their romantic fantasies inspired by the drama.

2. Interesting Places of Heritage

One of the major reasons behind the successes of K-dramas is their manifestation of picturesque land-scapes, palace conspiracies, vibrating costumes, and love stories. The dramas have the right ingredients to make a drama with special effects of going back to the old era, while also providing an overview to culture enthusiasts about South Korea's vibrant culture and history. Lee et al. (2021) surveyed the impact of Hanok experience on tourists' attitude and behavioural intention. The results revealed that educational, entertainment, and escape experiences affected the functional value significantly, but not aesthetic experience. Most respondents were regular visitors (67%) and the remaining were first-time visitors (33%), reflecting the popularity of Jeonju Hanok Village as an interesting place of heritage.

In the same vein, Song and Kim (2018) studied the characteristics of visitors to a cultural place of heritage based on an assessment of the place value and corresponding behaviour for better tourism heritage management. They discovered that Hwaseong Fortress (a heritage site) has physical and envi-ronmental attraction values, including landscapes, vegetation, and the environment, as well as emotional and cognitive factors such as culture and history, which are the factors for the formation of place value proposed by previous scholars. This UNESCO World Heritage site, located in Suwon, can be a tourist destination for foreigners and a place of leisure activities for the residents of Suwon. This study is a dual-perspective approach of foreigners and residents and aims to integrate recreation and tourism sites by segregating visitors according to the place value and examining group differences in the assessment of the World Heritage site. The results show that this place adds value to K-drama spectators, enticing them to revisit South Korea.

3. A Modern Nation

Through the consumption of K-dramas, transnational viewers reframe their perceptions of South Korea as orientalist images of the nation (Lee, 2020). Li et al. (2013) studied the striking similarity between two eras: the ancient and modern. Understanding modern women's consumption and criticism can provide a historical context of their experiences in 21st-century Korean consumer culture. Their study utilised secondary data from the literature published in English and Korean from Korean newspapers, magazines, and print advertisements from the 1920s and 1930s. They found that for the sake of modernity, cosmetic surgery has become a tool for constructing both local (Korean) and global consumers' desired identities.

4. Beautiful Korean Ladies

Beautiful Korean ladies never cease to mesmerise the K-drama audience. The Korean entertainment industry is booming with dramas depicting actresses blessed with beautiful, flawless, and porcelain white skin. The movie *Parasite* earned an Oscar for best picture category. K-pop has dominated the world, and K-beauty has become a global phenomenon. The insatiable appetite for all things "K" continues with Netflix and the dozens of favourite K-dramas they stream for endless enjoyment. Korean female stars are well-known for their beauty and youthful face. Most of them follow strict skincare and exercise regimes to maintain their inner and outer beauty (Lee et al., 2017). Fans are still hoping that the *Legend of the Blue Sea* actress Jun Jihyun could star in the *Kingdom* prequel since the appearance of her warrior character, Ah Sin. The audience, in an instant, immersed in the character of the drama. Jun Jihyun's beauty, glowing skin, and blood-stained lips can defeat any bloodthirsty zombie as she quickly becomes the queen of the K-drama dynasty. Undoubtedly, beautiful ladies of K-drama are the major factors attracting viewers to watch K-dramas and revisit Korea.

5. Good Looking Men

Korean actors tend to be taller, younger, and possibly prettier than their Japanese and Chinese counterparts (Parc & Moon, 2013). Korean men tend to have good looks, and in terms of character, they have to be chivalrous, gentle, cute, handsome, and show affection, just like drama heroes (Lee, 2020). Viewers covet Korea's dating culture and Korean men in a way that seeks alternative forms of intimacy. This desire for closeness is supported by the transnational emotive communities of K-drama fans (Lee, 2020). Viewers, repeatedly watching their favourite dramas (mostly comedies or romantic musicals) and communicating with other fans through touching "timed comments", develop imaginations of Korea, especially Korean male celebrities and the dating culture. *Hallyu* fans' deep desire for Korean flirting and dating, as portrayed in K-dramas, and even for Korean men themselves, evokes dynamic emotions. They long for an ideal they cannot find in real life but have seen in K-dramas. They create new forms of transnational closeness with the Korean culture, specifically the Korean dating culture, making them want to experience the feelings of love and intimate immersion with the Korean men shown in the dramas. Thus, good-looking men in K-dramas serve as a pull factor for tourists to revisit Korea to see their favourite actors.

6. Fashionable Korean People

Koo et al. (2016) looked at the role of the media as a cultural influencer for the intention of experienced and inexperienced travellers to visit South Korea. Viewers of the Korea Tourism Organization (KTO) website were significantly satisfied with the cultural exposure obtained from the website, in which fashionable design was identified as among the creativities that reflect the lifestyle of a cultural city. The incredible fashion design of K-pop has also attracted potential travellers to visit South Korea. Indeed, the K-pop industry has tremendously influenced musical and fashion trends in China, Taiwan, Japan, and Southeast Asia (Chen, 2014).

7. Unique Traditional Costumes

Hwang et al. (2018) studied the success factors for Korean food that affected customer satisfaction, revisit intention, and a change in South Korea's image. The researchers highlighted those traditional Korean costumes such as Hanbok, turned into staff uniforms at some restaurants, have become a cultural heritage fashion branding and impacted the management of product placement in marketing promotions. Unique traditional costumes like Hanbok are typical in Damyeon shows and promoted in movies such as *Untold Scandal* (2003). Damyeon presented Hanbok in movies and dramas, including *Hanbando* (2005), *The Last Empress* (2005), and *Ssanghwajum* (2008). While the marketing helped increase the general awareness of Hanbok as a cultural archetype and of the brand itself, the restaurant staff's uniforms could attract customers' interest when enjoying the cuisines at the restaurants. Other than in Korea, unique traditional costumes are also highly regarded as cultural heritage fashion branding in Japan and China, emphasising traditional fabric and preservation of traditional craftsmanship (Ko & Lee, 2011).

8. Filming Locations

K-dramas are known for their filming locations. Kim and O'Connor (2011) made a cross-cultural analysis of international tourists by nationalities associated with the hallyu phenomenon. The investigation revealed that repeat visitors consisted of 40% Japanese, 17% Taiwanese, and 13% Chinese and Thai, respectively. The results suggest that the most visited Daejanggeum filmed locations are in Seoul and its suburban areas, including Daejanggeum Theme Park, Changdeokgung Palace, Korean Folk Village, and Hwaseong Haenggung Palace. As a result of watching K-dramas, the filming locations increased foreign audiences' general interest in South Korea and its culture and influenced the perception and behaviour of potential tourists towards Korea as a tourism destination. The hotspots were recently filmed in a music video of the popular Korean boy band BTS, which further attracted their fans to visit the filming locations. The filming locations of Ihwa Mural Village have also increased the numbers of tourists visiting South Korea.

9. A Curiosity About Korea

Chen (2014) examined the modes of entry and positioning strategies used by media producers of the South Korean music industry through historical analysis of archived documents such as news articles. The researcher identified that South Korean organisations regularly invite singing celebrities to promote tourism through the influence of K-pop. Trolan (2017) analysed the influence of hallyu on Korea's image and the government's role in promoting the social impact of hallyu as a policy of cultural tourism. The content analysis revealed the overall impact of the Korean Wave and the government's strategies of using prominent actors and actresses, including in the regional marketing of Samsung, LG, KIA, and Hyundai. The South Korean government has viewed the Korean Wave through the popularity of K-dramas, and K-pop has eventually given South Korea a positive image.

10. Aspiring Country

South Korea has aspired people through medical tourism. Li et al. (2019) collected annual reports, press releases, media reports, and industry analyses of Korean medical tourism (cosmetic surgery tourism in particular) to explore the link between the corporatisation of K-beauty and Korea's national branding. Through the investigation of the transformation of Korea's beauty industry, the authors highlighted that the medical tourism service is to provide "happiness" to customers through an aspiring language, such as "pride", "smile", or "wish", to connect Korea's medical tourism to consumers' desire for life transformation. The ability of Korean surgeons to transform patients' lives is a powerful message that is often used in medical tourism promotional materials. Modern medical advances now make it possible to fulfil modern Asian consumers' wish lists and influence the global marketplace. Besides, South Korea also aspires pro-environmental education. Kim and Stepchenkova (2019) discovered that environmental knowledge had strengthened the link between pro-environmental attitudes and behaviour, which are the factors impacting tourist education. Jeju Island was chosen by South Korea's tourism authorities as an aspiration to educate tourists about the environmental issues Jeju faces and how tourists can be part of the solution.

11. Rare Images

Some tourists seek a rare image. Kang (1999), cited in Radzuan et al. (2014), found that the Korean clan villages have unique spatial structures and patterns that cannot be found elsewhere, including in China or Japan, although they share the same oriental culture boundary. The historic villages reflect a unique combination of urban and suburban fabrics' natural, cultural, and social characteristics. Bukchon Hanok village has the largest cluster of traditional Korean houses, called Hanok. These traditional urban houses were built during the 1920s and 1930s. Many tourists sit in the narrow alleys characterised by unique traditional Korean wood-framed design and construction detailing. Another rare image in Korea could be from experience in gastro tourism. Choi and Jeon (2020) said that some tourists might prefer to try new food that is tied to a culture or is unique and memorable at the visited destinations. The researchers found that the new experience contributed to the feelings of satisfaction and loyalty among tourists. In the research, tourists stated that the Chinese food culture is unique, different from Korea, in the cooking methods and ingredients used as well as serving principles and table manners, but both cultures are considered rare experiences for international tourists. Travelling for gastronomy due to the epistemic values associated with foods is a commitment reflected through tourists' behaviour (Saad et al., 2021). Based on the discussion as mentioned earlier, this study conjectured the following hypothesis:
H1: K-dramas determinants have influenced the revisit intention of Malaysian tourists to South Korea.

(a): Romantic places have influenced the revisit intention of Malaysian tourists to South Korea
(b): Interesting places of heritage have influenced the revisit intention of Malaysian tourists to South Korea
(c): A modern nation has influenced the revisit intention of Malaysian tourists to South Korea

(d): Beautiful Korean ladies have influenced the revisit intention of Malaysian tourists to South Korea
(e): Good looking men have influenced the revisit intention of Malaysian tourists to South Korea
(f): Fashionable Korean people have influenced the revisit intention of Malaysian tourists to South Korea
(g): Unique traditional costumes have influenced the revisit intention of Malaysian tourists to South Korea
(h): Film locations have influenced the revisit intention of Malaysian tourists to South Korea
(i): A curiosity about Korea have influenced the revisit intention of Malaysian tourists to South Korea
(j): Aspiring country has influenced the revisit intention of Malaysian tourists to South Korea
(k): Rare image has influenced the revisit intention of Malaysian tourists to South Korea

RESEARCH METHODOLOGY

Research Design, Population, And Sampling

This study chose the quantitative approach as it was identified as the best method due to its emphasis on numbers and figures in data collection and analysis (Daniel, 2016). The population of this study consisted of Malaysians who visited Korea. The KTO stated that approximately 354,948 Malaysians travelled to South Korea in 2018. Thus, based on the given population, the proposed sample size is 384 (Krejcie & Morgan, 1970).

Research Instrument, Data Collection, And Data Analyses

The research instrument of this study is a survey questionnaire using a 6-point *Likert* scale. This study adopted and adapted the questions on K-dramas from Teh (2016) and Teh and Goh (2016). For the revisit intention, this study adopted and adapted the items from Puad et al. (2012) and Tan (2017). According to Hung and Yang (2017), an instrument's validity denotes the degree to which the evidence supports the correct interpretation. The pretesting involves collecting and analysing data to assess the instrument's accuracy. This study also piloted the instrument and made necessary adjustments to the questionnaire items.

Data for this study were collected by snowballing a questionnaire form through social media platforms such as WhatsApp, Facebook, and Twitter to the people who had visited Korea. Besides that, the questionnaire was also distributed in hard copies. The questionnaire was snowballed in October 2019 for one month. This study performed the statistical analyses using IBM-SPSS version 24. The analyses consisted of descriptive analysis, reliability tests, and regression analysis.

RESULTS

Demographic Profile

This study obtained a response rate of 39%. Table 1 summarises the profiles of the 150 respondents participating in the study. The majority were young, in the 18–24 years old (67%) age group, and most were still single (84%). The respondents were mostly females (86%), and most studied up the first-degree level (70%). Information on South Korea was obtained from K-dramas (59%), and mostly, the respondents liked the natural landscape portrayed in the dramas. As Figure 3 shows, 70% of the respondents had visited South Korea at least once.

Table 1.

Items		Frequency	Valid Percent
Age	18-24	100	66.7
	25-35	38	25.3
	36-45	6	4.0
	46-55	6	4.0
Marital status	Single	126	84.0
	Married	24	16.0
Highest education level	SPM	16	10.7
	Diploma	20	13.3
	Degree	105	70.0
	Master	8	5.3
	PHD	1	.7
Gender	Male	20	13.6
	Female	127	86.4
	Missing	999	2.0
Source of Information about South Korea	Newspaper/magazines/article	21	14.0
	Korea tourism advertisement	5	3.3
	Korean drama	89	59.3
	Travel fairs	3	2.0
	Friends	32	21.3
Factors attract you the most?	Natural landscape	73	49.3
	Fashion	5	3.4
	Korean pop music	34	23.0
	Korean cuisine	18	12.2
	Filming location	18	12.2
	Missing	2	
n=150			

Figure 3. Visit Frequency

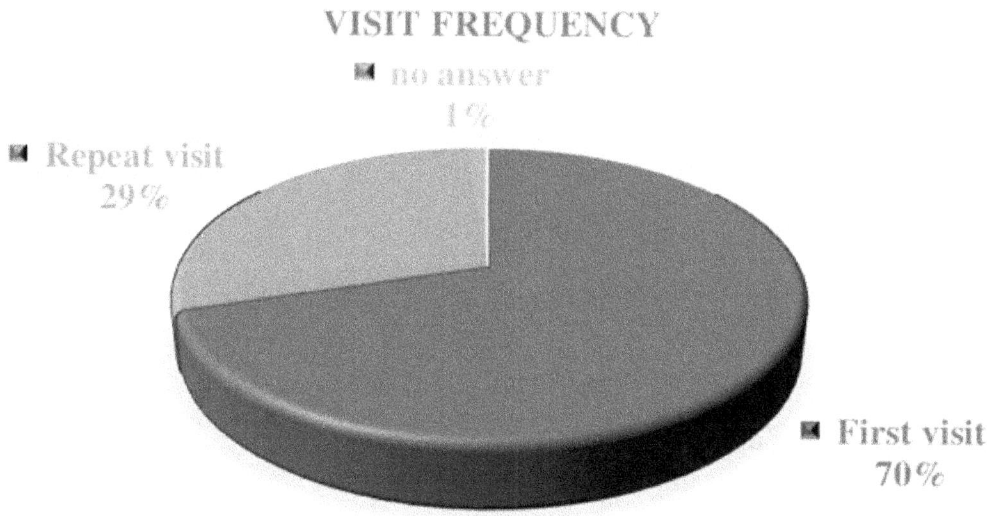

Table 2 presents the frequency statistics for each K-drama pulling factor. Based on a 6-point *Likert* scale, the statistic shows that K-drama influenced the respondents' interest in places of heritage, which reported the highest score (*m* = 5.26, *SD* = 0.88), followed by traditional costumes (*m* = 5.21, *SD* = 0.86), and the modern nation (*m* = 5.12, *SD* = 0.88). For the 11 items on K-drama, the average mean score was 4.2 (SD = 0.62), and the four items on revisit intention reported a mean score of 5.2 (*SD* = 0.74), indicating substantial agreement towards the K-drama and revisit intention items.

Table 2.

Statistics

		Seems like a romantic place	Many places of heritage	A modern nation	Korean ladies are beautiful	Korean men are good-looking	Korean people are fashionable	The traditional costume is unique	To visit filming locations	To fulfil the curiosity of the "Korea" that	Korean drama gives Korea an image of
N	Valid	150	150	150	150	150	150	150	150	150	150
	Missing	0	0	0	0	0	0	0	0	0	0
Mean		4.67	5.26	5.12	4.29	4.29	5.07	5.21	4.67	4.42	4.61
Std. Deviation		1.145	.878	.882	1.307	1.369	1.024	.862	1.173	1.357	1.433
Skewness		-.948	-1.500	-.952	-.547	-.545	-1.365	-1.307	-.526	-.702	-.932
Std. Error of Skewness		.198	.198	.198	.198	.198	.198	.198	.198	.198	.198
Kurtosis		.716	2.792	.661	-.224	-.521	2.427	3.001	-.637	-.231	.037
Std. Error of Kurtosis		.394	.394	.394	.394	.394	.394	.394	.394	.394	.394

Both the independent and dependent variables were checked for Cronbach's alpha values. Internal consistency was .89 for the 11-item K-drama subscale and .94 for the 5-item revisit intention subscale. Internal consistency values were between .8 and .9, indicating that they were satisfactory to excellent. The value for revisit intention was slightly greater than .9, but this does not always imply redundancy

(Ursachi et al., 2015). Additionally, the skewness and kurtosis distributions were confirmed to be normal and within the acceptable range (see Table 2).

HYPOTHESIS TESTING RESULTS

The main hypothesis of this study is to examine the positive influence of K-dramas on the revisiting intention of Malaysian tourists to South Korea. The model summary in Table 3 shows that the K-dramas model is a fit model in significantly predicting Malaysian tourists' revisit intention. However, a closer look at Table 4 identifies only heritage places as statistically influencing Malaysian tourists' intention to revisit South Korea. The findings are aligned with Chen (2016) and Kim et al. (2016), which found culture and heritage to be a significant pulling factor for South Korea's inbound tourism.

Table 3.

Model Summary[b]

Model	R	R Square	Adjusted R Square	Std. Error of the Estimate	Durbin-Watson
1	.707[a]	.499	.459	.77068	1.739

a. Predictors: (Constant), Rare Korean image, A modern nation, A romantic place, Worth visit filming locations, Unique traditional costume, Fashionable people, Interesting places of heritage, Beautiful Korean ladies, Curiosity of the "Korea", Aspired country, Good-looking Korean men
b. Dependent Variable: Mean_Intention_to_Revisit

ANOVA[a]

Model		Sum of Squares	df	Mean Square	F	Sig.
1	Regression	81.695	11	7.427	12.504	.000[b]
	Residual	81.965	138	.594		
	Total	163.660	149			

a. Dependent Variable: Mean_Intention_to_Revisit
b. Predictors: (Constant), Rare Korean image, A modern nation, A romantic place, Worth visit filming locations, Unique traditional costume, Fashionable Korean people, Interesting places of heritage, Beautiful Korean ladies, Curiosity of the "Korea," Aspired country, Good-looking Korean men

Table 4.

Model	Unstandardised Coefficients		Standardised Coefficients	t	Sig.
	B	Std. Error	Beta		
(Constant)	.636	.496		1.281	.202
A romantic place	.139	.073	.152	1.899	.060
Interesting places of heritage	**.237**	**.094**	**.199**	**2.516**	**.013**
A modern nation	.051	.085	.043	.604	.547
Beautiful Korean ladies	-.096	.086	-.119	-1.112	.268
Good-looking Korean men	.158	.091	.207	1.740	.084
Fashionable Korean people	.141	.087	.138	1.613	.109
Unique traditional costume	.026	.093	.022	.283	.778
Worth filming locations	.072	.069	.081	1.048	.297
Curiosity of "Korea"	.085	.082	.110	1.040	.300
Aspired country	.065	.087	.081	.745	.458
Rare image	.054	.068	.074	.789	.432

Coefficients[a]

a. Dependent Variable: Mean_Intention_to_Revisit

DISCUSSION AND CONCLUSION

Literature works show that technology, cultural content, collaborations with local talent, and joint ventures with local markets are the successful factors in promoting South Korea through K-dramas. The SPSS results show that K-dramas contribute almost 50% to the revisit intention among the respondents. The possible reason is that most of the respondents have watched K-dramas and want to experience the culture shown in the dramas. K-dramas also have sophisticated cinematography and unpredictable scripts that attract the respondents' interest in the dramas and the country. Most of the respondents also agreed that K-dramas did influence their intention to revisit South Korea.

This study's findings are consistent with Poh (2017), who mentioned that K-dramas have the most significant influence on Gen Y for visiting South Korea. K-dramas are among the TV programmes with many influences that are watched by the majority of Malaysians. Good-looking actors and actresses play an essential role in increasing the popularity of K-dramas. Dramas that feature famous actors or actresses will attract more K-drama lovers. Also, K-dramas project the image of South Korea. Malaysian tourists agreed that the places in the country seem romantic, such as Namsan Seoul Tower, and Han River Cruise. They watch K-dramas due to the romance theme featured in the dramas, such as My Girl, Boys over Flowers, and Why Secretary Kim. The drama directors usually play with lighting and editing to make the places look romantic.

From the dramas, people learn about the Korean language. More than one-third of the respondents stated that the Korean language is polite. The results also show that K-dramas entice people to explore South Korea to visit the filming locations featured in their favourite series such as *Winter Sonata*, *Goblin*, and *Descendant of the Sun*. The hypothesis that K-dramas positively influences tourists' revisit intention is supported by Ha et al. (2018) and Lee et al. (2019). The authors stated that K-dramas project a good image to tourists, leading to satisfaction. Then, the satisfaction will lead to revisiting intention. It is crucial to have repeat tourists because it shows that the place is exciting and attractive. As in the case of *Goblin*, the memorable scene in the series attracted 61 respondents that watched the series to travel to the place where the scene was filmed to experience it. Thus, it can be concluded that K-dramas could be utilised to promote tourism destinations by influencing tourists to visit a filming location that they have watched in their favourite series.

Interestingly, as Chen (2016), Kim et al. (2016), Lee et al. (2021), Song and Kim (2018), and Wei et al. (2021) discovered, the heritage factor also had a significant effect on Malaysian tourists who travelled to South Korea in this study. Malaysians returned to South Korea because of the heritage value of the filming scenes, implying that the country should continue to preserve its historic sites, buildings, monuments, and artefacts for future generations. Additionally, this study demonstrates that Malaysians value heritage. Hence, Malaysian policymakers, particularly Tourism Malaysia and tourism business operators, can investigate domestic heritage tourism in order to promote this sector. The collaboration in developing heritage tourism should be linked to the national identity and replicated through dramas similar to K-dramas. In terms of broadcasting Malaysia's multiracial culture, the Korean broadcasting system (KBS) may serve as a model for RTM, TV3, and Astro in Malaysia. Malaysian broadcasting agencies may consider establishing a channel dedicated to diverse perspectives on heritage values. Institutions of higher learning that offer courses in film, broadcasting, and cinematic arts should collaborate with the national broadcaster and the government. Many institutions, including Universiti Teknologi MARA, Multimedia University, Taylor's University, and the University of Wollongong Malaysia (UOWM) KDU, offer such study programmes. Film producers and Seniman Malaysia (SENIMAN) should collaborate with the National Film Development Corporation Malaysia (FINAS) and National Academy of Arts Culture and Heritage (ASWARA) to produce quality films that could be sold internationally.

LIMITATIONS

Two apparent limitations were discovered in this study. Firstly, the findings are primarily from millennials, demonstrating K-dramas' influences on this generation. Second, snowballing the Google form has its limitations, as the coverage is highly dependent on the survey's distribution. Nonetheless, future studies may replicate this study's questionnaire items on K-dramas and intend to revisit domestic tourism in Malaysia for further research.

REFERENCES

Abdul-Talib, A. N., & Abd-Razak, I. S. (2012). Export market oriented behaviours within the medical tourism industry: A case study. *International Journal of Tourism Policy*, *4*(4), 289–301. doi:10.1504/IJTP.2012.052546

Anh, D. T. (2016). *The causes and effects of Korean pop culture on Vietnamese consumer behavior the causes and effects of Korean pop* (Unpublished Master's thesis). College of Interdisciplinary Studies Thammasat University.

Arango, T. (2009, June 23). Cable TV's big worry: Taming the web. *The New York Times*. Retrieved from https://www.nytimes.com/2009/06/24/business/media/24pay.html?_r=1

Bae, E., Chang, M., Park, E., & Kim, D. (2017). The effect of Hallyu on tourism in Korea. *Journal of Open Innovation, 3*(22), 2–12. doi:10.118640852-017-0075-y

Chen, S. (2016). Cultural technology: A framework for marketing cultural exports – analysis of Hallyu (the Korean wave). *International Marketing Review, 33*(1), 25–50. doi:10.1108/IMR-07-2014-0219

Ching, L. (2000, Winter). Globalising the Regional, Regionalising the Global: Mass Culture and Asianism in the Age of Late Capital. *Public Culture, 12*(1), 233–257. doi:10.1215/08992363-12-1-233

Choi, J., & Jeon, H. H. (2020). Are all Asian tourists the same? Chinese versus Japanese dining satisfaction. *British Food Journal, 122*(11), 3529–3545. doi:10.1108/BFJ-06-2019-0454

Daniel, E. (2016). The usefulness of qualitative and quantitative approaches and methods in researching problem-solving ability in science education curriculum. *Journal of Education and Practice, 7*(15), 91–100.

Ha, S., Chan, G., & Lee, A. (2018). A Phenomenological study on the effects of Korean TV dramas on Chinese. *Journal of Tourism & Hospitality (Los Angeles, Calif.), 2018*(02), 1–7. doi:10.29011/THOA

Han, P. M. (2016). *Influences of Korean Wave on the Intention of Visiting Korea in Generation Y Malaysia*. http://eprints.intimal.edu.my/id/eprint/914

Hashim, F., Bakar, A. R. A., & Abdul-Talib, A. N. (2010). *International Business* (2nd ed.). Oxford Fajar Press.

Hung, J.-L., & Yang, D. (2017). The validation of an instrument for evaluating the effectiveness of professional development program on teaching online. *Journal of Educational Technology Development and Exchange, 8*(1). Advance online publication. doi:10.18785/jetde.0801.02

Hwang, J., Kim, S. S., Choe, J. Y. J., & Chung, C. H. (2018). Exploration of the successful glocalisation of ethnic food: A case of Korean food. *International Journal of Contemporary Hospitality Management, 30*(12), 3656–3676. doi:10.1108/IJCHM-07-2017-0452

HWU. (2015). Cultural guide to Malaysia. *HWU Malaysia Cultural Awareness*, (March), 1–9. Retrieved from https://www.hw.ac.uk/documents/HWU_Malaysia_Cultural_awareness_document_190315(1).pdf

Jang, H., & Park, M. (2020). Social media, media and urban transformation in the context of overtourism. *International Journal of Tourism Cities, 6*(1), 233–260. doi:10.1108/IJTC-08-2019-0145

Ju, H. (2010). *Glocalization of the Korean popular culture in East Asia: Theorising the Korean wave*. The University of Oklahoma.

Kim, D., Cho, S.-D., & Jung, G. O. (2016). Wave of home culture and MNC performance: The Korean Wave (Hallyu). *International Marketing in Rapidly Changing Environments, 24*, 193–216. doi:10.1108/S1474-7979(2013)0000024012

Kim, M. S., & Stepchenkova, S. (2019). Altruistic values and environmental knowledge as triggers of pro-environmental behavior among tourists. *Current Issues in Tourism, 23*(13), 1575–1580. doi:10.1080/13683500.2019.1628188

Kim, S. (2010). Extraordinary experience: Re-enacting and photographing at screen tourism locations. *Tourism and Hospitality Planning & Development, 7*(1), 59–75. doi:10.1080/14790530903522630

Kim, S., & O'Connor, N. (2011). A cross-cultural study of screen-tourists' profiles. *Worldwide Hospitality and Tourism Themes*, *3*(2), 141–158. doi:10.1108/17554211111123005

Ko, E., & Lee, S. (2011). Cultural heritage fashion branding in Asia. *Tourism Sensemaking: Strategies to Give Meaning to Experience*, 89–109. doi:10.1108/S1871-3173(2011)0000005008

Koo, C., Chung, N., Kim, D. J., & Hlee, S. (2016). The impact of destination websites and cultural exposure: A comparison study of experienced and inexperienced travelers. *International Journal of Tourism Cities*, *2*(1), 1–16. doi:10.1108/IJTC-04-2015-0009

Krejcie, R. V., & Morgan, D. W. (1970). Determining sample size for research activities. *Educational and Psychological Measurement*, *30*(3), 607–610. doi:10.1177/001316447003000308

Lafaurie, J. (2018). Deux monnaiesmérovingiennestrouvées à Reculver (Kent). *Bulletin de la Société Nationale des Antiquaires de France*, *1971*(1), 209–219. doi:10.3406/bsnaf.1973.8048

Lee, C.-K., Reisinger, Y., Ahmad, M. S., Park, Y.-N., & Kang, C.-W. (2021). The influence of Hanok experience on tourists' attitude and behavioral intention: An interplay between experiences and a Value-Attitude-Behavior model. *Journal of Vacation Marketing*, *27*(4), 449–465. doi:10.1177/13567667211011761

Lee, M. J. (2020). Touring the land of romance: Transnational Korean television drama consumption from online desires to offline intimacy. *Journal of Tourism and Cultural Change*, *18*(1), 67–80. doi:10.1080/14766825.2020.1707467

Lee, S., Lee, K., Kwak, G., & Kim, H. (2017). The effect of the Korean wave on Malaysian university students' perception. *Culinary Science & Hospitality Research*, *23*(1), 79–83. doi:10.20878/cshr.2017.23.1.009009009

Li, E. P. H., Min, H. J., & Lee, S. (2020). Soft power and nation rebranding. *International Marketing Review*, *38*(1), 141–162. doi:10.1108/IMR-01-2019-0053

Min, H. J. (2013). New women and modern girls: Consuming foreign goods in colonial Seoul. *Journal of Historical Research in Marketing*, *5*(4), 494–520. doi:10.1108/JHRM-01-2013-0004

Oh, Y. (2020). *From concrete walls to digital walls: Transmedia construction of place myth in Ihwa Mural Village, South Korea*. doi:10.1177/0163443720916410

Ordoyo, A. F. P., Menor, J. C., & Felecia, M. L. D. (2021). A case study on the effect of K-Drama in choosing South Korea as a Travel Destination. *International Journal of Sciences, Basic and Applied Research*, *58*(2).

Parc, J., & Moon, H. (2013). *Korean dramas and films: Key factors for their international competitiveness*. doi:10.1163/15685314-12341295

Petroman, I., Petroman, C., Marin, D., Ciolac, R., Vaduva, L., & Pandur, I. (2013). Types of cultural tourism. *Lucrari Stiintifice. Zootehnie si Biotehnologii*, *46*(1), 385–388.http://search.ebscohost.com/login.aspx?direct=true&db=a9h&AN=90641216&site=ehost

Raj, M. P. M. (2018). Film induced tourism Model-A qualitative research study. *Asian Journal of Research in Marketing*, *7*(2), 28. doi:10.5958/2277-6621.2018.00005.1

Radzuan, M. I. S., Inho, S., & Ahmad, Y. (2015). A rethink of the incentives programme in the conservation of South Korea's historic villages. *Journal of Cultural Heritage Management and Sustainable Development*, *5*(2), 176–201. doi:10.1108/JCHMSD-02-2014-0006

Ramli, B. N. (2016, October 10). *Big Bang entertains over 10,000 fans in KL with music, fun, and games*. Retrieved from New Straits Times: Retrieved from https://www.nst.com.my/news/2016/10/179225/bigbang-entertains-over-10000-fans-kl-musicfun-and-games

Rao, M. (2017, May 1). *Dimsum brings more Korean drama content to Malaysia*. Retrieved May 7, 2017, from Marketing Interactive: https://www.marketing-interactive.com/dimsum-bringsmore-korean-dramas-to-malaysia/

S. Korea seeks Malaysia's expertise for its Muslim-Friendly Hospitality. (2019, May 22). *Malay mail*. Retrieved from https://www.malaymail.com/news/malaysia/2019/05/22/s.-korea-seeksmalaysias-expertise-for-its-muslim-friendly-hospitality/1755357

Saad, M., Kamarizzaman, N. A., Ishak, N., & Pratt, T. J. (2021). The influence of Pahang heritage food on behavioral intentions among Malaysian domestic tourists. *Environment-Behaviour Proceedings Journal*, *6*(16), 163–169. doi:10.21834/ebpj.v6i16.2680

Som, A. P. M., Marzuki, A., & Yousefi, M. (2012). Factors influencing visitors' revisit behavioral intentions: A case study of Sabah, Malaysia. *International Journal of Marketing Studies*, *4*(4), 39–50.

Song, H., & Kim, H. (2019). *Value-Based Profiles of Visitors to a World Heritage Site: The Case of Suwon Hwaseong Fortress (in South Korea)*. doi:10.3390/su11010132

Statista. (2016). Retrieved August 30, 2021, from https://www.statista.com/statistics/898274/south-korea-inbound-tourists-from-malaysia/

Statista. (2019). Retrieved August 30, 2021, from https://www.statista.com/statistics/1017835/south-korea-korean-drama-popularity-malaysia/

Spencer-Oatey, H. (2015). *What is Culture? A Compilation of Quotations*. Retrieved from http://www.warwick.ac.uk/globalpadintercultural

Tan, W.-K. (2017). Repeat visitation: A study from the perspective of leisure constraint, tourist experience, destination images, and experiential familiarity. *Journal of Destination Marketing & Management*, *6*(3), 233–242. doi:10.1016/j.jdmm.2016.04.003

Teh, P. Y. (2016). *The role of Korean drama promoting tourism among Malaysians* (PhD thesis). University of Malaya.

Teh, P. Y., & Goh, H. C. (2018). Does Korean drama have a real influence? An analysis of Malaysia outbound tourists to South Korea. *Tourism, Culture & Communication*, *16*, 147–160.

Tourists flock to Korean drama 'Goblin" filming sites. (2017, January 12). Retrieved from The Jakarta Post: https://www.thejakartapost.com/travel/2017/01/12/tourists-flock-to-korean-drama-goblin-filming-sites

Trolan, J. (2017). A look into Korean popular culture and its tourism benefits. *International Journal of Educational Policy Research and Review*, *4*(9), 203–209. doi:10.15739/ijeprr.17.022

Ursachi, G., Horodnic, I. A., & Zait, A. (2015). How reliable are measurement scales? External factors with indirect influence on reliability estimators. *Procedia Economics and Finance*, *20*, 679–686. doi:10.1016/S2212-5671(15)00123-9

Vu, H. T., & Lee, T.-T. (2013). Soap operas as a matchmaker: A cultivation analysis of the effects of South Korean TV dramas on Vietnamese women's marital intentions. *Journalism & Mass Communication Quarterly*, *90*(2), 308–330. doi:10.1177/1077699013482912

Wei, Y., Liu, H., & Park, K.-S. (2021). Examining the structural relationships among heritage proximity, perceived impacts, attitude and residents' support in intangible cultural heritage tourism. *Sustainability*, *13*(15), 8358. doi:10.3390u13158358

Zakaria, N., Abdul-Talib, A. N., & Amelinckx, A. (Eds.). (2020). *Transcending Cultural Frontiers: Practices, Challenges, and Strategy for International Business*. Springer. doi:10.1007/978-981-15-4454-5

Zakaria, N., Abdul-Talib, A. N., & Amelinckx, A. (2020). Advancing cultural frontiers to champion global business in emerging markets. In *Transcending Cultural Frontiers* (pp. 1–10). Springer. doi:10.1007/978-981-15-4454-5_1

Zakaria, N., Abdul-Talib, A. N., & Othman, N. (Eds.). (2016). *Handbook of research on impacts of international business and political affairs on the global economy*. IGI Global. doi:10.4018/978-1-4666-9806-2

Chapter 4
Early Internationalizing of Small-Medium Firms:
A Conceptualization on Internationalisation of International New Ventures (INVs)

Afifah Alwani Ramlee
Universiti Utara Malaysia, Malaysia

ABSTRACT

Internationalization is not an odd term in business, and increasing numbers in the business world show this phenomenon as a vital element that must be emphasized and practiced by an organization to become the top company in international markets. Born global has become a new entity entering the global market and rapidly evolved to catch up and maintain its pace with international new ventures. Gaining the upper hand in the international market has motivated the born global entity to compete with other giant companies in the same markets. This chapter's findings enlighten the crucial parts of the definition between these two terms supported with previous studies that encompass gaps, conventional and new ventures, and the advantages versus liabilities that existed in the new venture firms. In addition, this chapter's discussions would offer better justification and views in global market perspectives.

INTRODUCTION

The phenomenon of internationalization is becoming crucial as the business operates shows better performance, especially in international business (Morais & Ferreira, 2020). The internationalization of firms and the emergence of International New Ventures (INVs) have been among the most exciting topics in business research during the last few decades because they have acknowledged and addressed the link between international business and entrepreneurship more explicitly (Oviatt & McDougall, 1994; Autio, 2005). Moreover, globalization and internationalization literature has put considerable emphasis on promoting the theoretical understanding of the internationalization process of large firms, but Fillis

DOI: 10.4018/978-1-7998-9071-3.ch004

(2001) demonstrates that smaller firms are becoming involved in international activities as well. Previous studies on internationalization stressed the international and global market influence, especially on the firm's background, networking, experiences, and strategic orientation, which could steer company growth (Morais & Ferreira, 2020; Andresen & Bergdolt, 2017). This claim supported by a study commissioned by the Organization for Economic Cooperation and Development (OECD) (2009) on the globalization of SMEs, provided evidence from 18 member countries, suggest the number of crucial motivation factors for SMEs to internationalize, including growth motives, knowledge-related motives, network and also domestic/regional market factor. Not only that, new businesses have evolved due to ICT growth and challenges in the global economic environment beyond traditional-stage company models, such as global new businesses and born global businesses (Park, Lee & Jeong, 2018). Based on Pukall and Calabro (2014), this phenomenon is viewed as a dynamic process that can be clarified through two variables; "state" and "change" variables, and these two elements work on each other continuously.

Furthermore, Mladenović, Mladenović, and Ranđelović (2020) scrutinized that entering the foreign market is a critical advantage for businesses to invest in due to the possibility of high success rate and adapting to internationalization, which reflects the organization reputation and characteristics of employees (Cuzovic et al., 2019). However, Oviatt and McDougall (1997) added that cultural homogeneity, social change, and firm strategy are essential factors that lead to this phenomenon. Not only that, but there is also finding of the firms rapid internationalization among the small and young firms. Thus, it is proved that small firms which involve with international business activities are almost from their inception and are known as 'international new ventures' is emerging.

Therefore, this chapter aims to bridge the gap in the literature on the understanding of the central concept of International New Venture (INV) and Born Global (BG). In addition, this chapter will highlight discussions on the approach between traditional and new ventures, strategic orientation, learning advantages of newness, and INV applied in the resource-based view. Although there are still gaps in previous studies related to these two entities, it is hoped that this chapter will provide a clear explanation and justification of the direction of these two entities. The following section will begin with an examination of INV definitions and classifications.

INTERNATIONAL NEW VENTURES (INVS): DEFINITION AND CATEGORIZATION

Oviatt and McDougall first introduced the term International New Ventures (INVs) in their 1994 Journal of International Business Studies (JIBS) article. Oviatt and McDougal (1994) define INVs as a firm that seeks a significant competitive advantage from using their resources in pursuing international sales in multiple countries from the early stages of their operation. According to them, these firms are global from inception or internationalize within 2 years of establishment. Other authors defined the timescale as within 3 years from their start-up (Knudsen & Servais, 2007), to six years (Zahra, Ireland, & Hitt 2000; Knight & Cavusgil, 1996), to seven years (Jolly, Alahuhta, & Jeannet 1992) and up to eight years (Coviello & Yli-Renko, 2016). Zahra (2006) argues that it is difficult to determine the exact launch time of firms; instead, the firm's goal, resources, or connection with others (networking) are essential in determining the time to start internationalize. To be consistent, this research define International New Venture as suggested by Knight and Cavusgil (2004), they mentioned that INVs is a "business organization that, from or near their founding, seeks superior international business performance from applying knowledge-based resources to the sale of outputs in multiple countries."

Furthermore, different terms could describe INVs; few scholars have used the term 'Born Global' (BG) firms (Madsen & Servais, 1997; Knight & Cavusgil, 1996), while others have called them "instant internationals" (Preece et al.,1999), or early internationalizing firms (Rialp, Rialp & Knight, 2005). Fundamentally, international new venture is synonymous with 'born global' and global start-up'. Although different terms are used to describe the phenomenon of INVs, most literature contends to use them interchangeably (Jones et al., 2011). The definitions of INVs/BG are shown in Table 1:

Table 1. Definitions of International New Ventures

Authors	Vision	Time before starting export	Export Vs. Global growth
Oviatt and McDougall (1994)	A business that strives to positively impact productivity by utilizing resources and selling outputs in various nations from the start.	-	-
McKinsey and Co (1993) and Rennie (1993)	Management sees the world as their marketplace.	With an average age of 14 years, they achieved 76 percent of their total revenues through exports.	At the age of 14, they achieved 76 percent of their total sales through exporting.
Knight and Cavusgil (1996) Knight (1997)	Management sees the world as their marketplace.	Within two years of starting, start exporting one or more products. Within the first three years of their existence, they have become a household name.	Approximately a quarter of overall production is usually exported. Companies that sell at least 25% of their products in other countries
Chetty and Campbell-Hunt (2004)	-	Within two years of the company's founding.	Outside of New Zealand, 80% of sales are made; marketplaces are found worldwide.
Luostarinen and Gabrielsson (2006)	At a global economic growth path and with a global vision.	At the onset, they entered global markets.	Make more than half of business sales outside of their continent. After 1985, the company was founded.
Knudsen and Servais (2007)	-	Within three years after its inception.	More than a quarter of all foreign sales or sourcing takes place outside of the native continent.
Nowinski and Rialp (2013)		Operationalize from 6 years	
Ismail and Kuivalainen (2015)	Absorptive and adaptive capabilities are crucial aspects in expanding INV		
Devinney, Markman, Pedersen and Tihanyi (2016)	Internationalization age determine INV's characteristics		
Coviello and Yli-Renko (2016)		Operationalize from 8 years	
Ferencikova and Ferencikova (2016)	The concept is the firm's age, not the size		
Baranowska-prokop and Sikora (2017)	Crucial in new products, innovation, and developing business models		
Paul and Rosado (2019)	Distances between physical and cultural also facilitate human capital mobility		

Additionally, the previous study on INV's scope showed that scholars focused less on identifying factors that lead to the scopes (Morais & Ferreira, 2020). Bembom and Schwens (2018) and Paul and Rosado-Serrano (2019) stressed distinguishing processes in the initial internationalization of firms and scarce works on INV's network dynamic that might penetrate global markets (Morais & Ferreira, 2020).

Thus, it is crucial to explore INV, especially decision-making on internationalization towards foreign markets (Paul & Rosado-Serrano, 2019). Past studies by Ismail and Kuivalainen (2015), Cavusgil and Knight (2015), and Knight and Liesch (2016) highlighted two crucial elements in expanding INV; adaptive and absorptive capabilities in order to justify INV pathways. In addition, some previous studies also highlighted developing vital capabilities in penetrating the global market through the geographical scope (Liu, Chang, & Fang, 2020).

All in all, this diversity of the definitions indicates that there is, in fact, no precise, universally accepted definition of what an INVs/ BG firm is (Rasmussen & Madsen, 2002). Following Oviatt and McDougall (1994) line, the primary critical dimensions in their study of INVs are the scale (e.g., export intensity), scope (possible indicators include market distance and some markets), and time (speed) of internationalization (as cited in Kuivalainen et al., 2012). Therefore, to make relevant characteristics of INVs, researchers suggest that future researchers adopt the least ambiguous definition to identify this INVs firm (Chetty & Campbell, 2004). In this research, INVs firms are consequently defined as:

Firms that undertake international operations from within two (2) years of inception (Oviatt & McDougall, 1994) and up to eight (8) years (McDougall, Shane & Oviatt 1994 cited in Chetty and Campbell, 2004) after inception. The researcher decides to be more flexible in terms of the age of having international activities and the period because exporting is not a straightforward process, especially for the start-up companies with limited international exposure (Gabrielsson et al., 2014).

1. They should be independent firms (Gabrielsson et al., 2014)
2. Generate at least 25% of its revenue from international business (Knight & Cavusgil, 1996)
3. Possibly enter multiple foreign markets (Oviatt & McDougall, 1994) that are psychically distant from the home country using one of several types of entry modes, including exporting, licensing, joint ventures, and even foreign direct investment.

Another argument in the literature is that INVs are often involved in advanced, specialist technologies or knowledge-intensive sectors (Autio et al., 2000). Research corroborates this by Stray, Bridgewater, and Murray (2001), which indicated that technology-based enterprises have differing rates of internationalization, with the period among establishing and first global market entry estimated to be shorter than for other firms. To advocate for this literature, comparing and contrasting the traditional stages and global new ventures approaches is necessary to identify their distinguishing qualities.

TRADITIONAL VERSUS NEW VENTURES APPROACH

At present, there is a confrontation between the traditional stage theory and the whole model of born global businesses (Love et al., 2016). Unlike more traditional internationalizing and domestic enterprises, INVs and BGs face distinct circumstances, necessitating various strategies to navigate foreign market conditions. INVs and BGs are frequently oriented toward international markets from the start, have limited funds, and engage in highly dynamic and competitive combination activities with a high level of inventive complexity (Evers, Gliga & Rialp-Criado 2019). INVs and BGs frequently use hybrid strategies to gain resources to aid their early and rapid international activities. Additionally, as many experts believe, INVs pose a unique challenge to the classic stage internationalization theory, which holds that corporations follow a step theory of gradual internationalization before being global.

According to Johanson and Vahlne (1990), firms are more likely to pursue internationalization when they have a sufficiently significant resource base, when global economic fundamentals are stable and consistent, and when the enterprises are familiar with the target market. In contrast to the stage theory of internationalization, INVs show a faster growth rate in their internationalization processes, often skipping multiple stages to internationalize their corporate operations and activities from the start. When compared to enterprises that internationalize in the typical stage approach, INVs are less concerned with creating a global market base in this situation.

Nevertheless, the well-known Uppsala Theory of business internationalization (Johanson & Vahlne, 1990) is the most appropriate and applicable theory to describe firms that gradually internationalize, according to Oviatt and McDougal (2005) in their retrospective essay. Because they still lack experiential expertise and the commitment to internationalizing is regarded as dangerous, corporations move to the nearby regions with similar cultures to their local markets. It is not essential to be physically close at this point (Johanson & Vahlne, 1977). Johanson and Vahlne (1977) coined the phrase "psychic distance" to explain the disparities between the home nation and the dominant culture in language, culture, political systems, commercial practice, industrial growth, and educational systems. As a result, as the enterprises understood the industry, they would eventually expand into other sectors further away from a psychic distance (Johanson & Wiedersheim-Paul, 1975). The phenomena result from driving forces such as transforming corporate environments into more dynamic environments and company entrepreneurial innovation. Oviatt and McDougal (1995) are prominent supporters of this viewpoint. Some argue that the managers' experience and exposure and having a good business network before starting a new venture play a role in going international early (Madsen & Servais, 1997).

On the other hand, others argue that the rapid education of these energy sources, technology-oriented firms allow them to go international early (Madsen & Servais, 1997). In other words, the founders' prior foreign experience or the firms' inherent learning ability lessens hesitation about internationalization at a young age. They discovered that none of the 24 INVs studied by McDougall et al. (1994) followed the gradual steps of internationalization. In fact, during the first year of operation, one of their case study sample, Oxford Instruments, received more than half of its revenue from the worldwide market. For similar reasons, McDougall et al. (1994) reject Vernon (1966) International Product Life Cycle theory and the oligopolistic reaction theory, which they believe fails to explain why enterprises choose to go global at a young age. Table 2 shows further specific contrasts between traditional and new ventures concepts, as Chetty and Campbell (2004) described in their journal of International Marketing.

Table 2. Traditional stages versus new ventures

Internationalization Attributes	Traditional Stages View	New Ventures /Born Global View
Home market	A domestic market developed first	The domestic market is largely irrelevant (this study requires 75% export ratios)
Prior internationalization experience	None expected	The founder has extensive experience in relevant international markets
Extent of internationalization	International markets developed serially	Many international markets developed at the same time
Pace of internationalization	Gradual	Rapid
Psychic distance	In order of psychic distance	Psychic distance irrelevant
Learning to internationalize	At a pace governed by the ability to learn from (slowly) accumulated experience	Learning occurs more rapidly because of superior internationalization knowledge
Firm strategy	Not central to the firm's motivation to internationalize	Realization of competitive advantage requires rapid, full internationalization; product-market scope is focused/niche
Use of information and communications technology	Not central to internationalization	Critical role as an enabler of the global market reach and learning
Networks of business partners	Used in early stages of internationalization and gradually replaced with the firm's resources	The rapid development of global reach requires rapid, comprehensive network of partners
Time to internationalize	Not crucial to a firm success; slow	Crucial to firm success within a few years of inception (e.g., two years)

Sources: Chetty and Campbell-Hunt(2004), Journal of International Marketing

Furthermore, previous research has aims to demonstrate INVs as a type of entrepreneurial behavior. For example, entrepreneurial managers' views toward foreign markets are characterized by their inventive, proactive, and risk-taking behavior, linked to the firm's internationalization behavior and, eventually, its indicator of success (McDougall & Oviatt, 2000). This viewpoint is confirmed by relevant research, which reveals that entrepreneurial orientation (or inclination) is crucial for the initiation and future performance outcomes (Knight & Cavusgil, 2004). The following discussion is born global or born regional, which is crucial to differentiate between these two terms and international new ventures (INV) as every term comes with different meanings and perceptive.

BORN GLOBAL OR BORN REGIONAL?

In recent decades, the born global phenomenon and technical improvements have changed the purpose and companies' expansion frequency globally (Cavusgil & Knight, 2015). The transformation was more swift, especially for small dan newly-established organizations (Fan & Phan, 2018). This indicates that small entities could survive and succeed globally (Jafari-Sadeghi, Nkongolo-Bakenda, Dana, Anderson & Biancone, 2020). To be precise, the rapid internalization process has triggered this born global as it adopted a global vision at the beginning of operations (Fan & Phan, 2018). However, born global still lacks practices and theory, which is still evolving compared to international new venture companies (Buckley & Casson, 2021). On top of that, there is no specific and consensus on the born global definition, which also causes more difficulties in making valid comparisons (Stocker, Abib, Jhunior & Irigaray, 2021). On the other hand, some of the adopted definitions defined this entity as an organization that has the intention to compete in the international market, although it will face challenges due to geographical, billing, and internationalization percentage (Reuber, Knight, Liesch & Zhou, 2018).

In addition, their internationalization development processes are not believed to be driven by the psychic distance logic neither by the founders' and partners' previous international experience or networks (Rialp et al., 2005). However, some scholars argued that previous international experience of founders and employees has also been proposed as playing a mediating role in early internationalization (Bengtsson, 2004). Interestingly, Lopez et al. (2009) have raised whether the firm is born global or regional? The finding from their work tested among firms in developing and small economies proved that only a few born global firms emerged, and most companies are generally evolved from the gradual internationalization. Their empirical work demonstrates that most of the firms that they had analyzed are born regional. Even though they are exporting at an early age after inception, they focus more on the neighboring countries in their cultural traits and business practices. This finding is similar to the empirical evidence explored by Rugman and Brain (2003), where they found that foreign sales activities and total sales for 500 multinational enterprises were regionally based.

Therefore, we can see that small gaps can be filled by studying the phenomenon of internationalization in such small open economies. Another critical area of research that surrounds with this phenomenon of INV and born global is the discussion on Learning Advantage of Newness (LAN). This concept offers better potential in developing and modernizing the new enterprises efficiently and helps them respond to economic and business realities.

CRITICAL AREAS OF RESEARCH: LEARNING ADVANTAGE OF NEWNESS AND THE RAPID GROWTH OF INVS

According to Autio et al. (2011), if the new venture's management team has fewer previously everyday experiences, it will search and test the market more broadly because past and possibly contradictory experiences will not influence its responses. New initiatives, on the other hand, with the effect of earlier shared experiences, had the effect of slowing down the development of capacities. They are unwilling to develop alternative solutions based on current international market feedback, preferring instead to stick to action schemas and justify them thru narrative and myths (Lounsbury & Glynn, 2001).

As a result, the putative "learning advantage of newness" (LAN) of INVs has arisen as a continuous necessity to share that has evolved to explain their rapid expansion (Autio et al., 2000). The start-up businesses unable to understand the current market and structure of foreign markets, the LAN claims that their potential to develop different and modern perspectives to launch international new enterprises further efficiently is not limited by their lack of prior information or experience. Because fledgling businesses lack prior information and experience, the LAN was created to help them better comprehend their economic and business realities.

As a result, they can understand more innovative information and respond with more innovative actions. As a result of their existing expertise and knowledge, incumbent enterprises are less able to discover innovative means-end linkages and, as a result, operate more conservatively. The newness advantage states company penetrates a global market in its cycle, the better its international performance will be due to the increasing opportunities for novel learning that are not hampered by legacies and artifacts from previous experience and expertise (Autio et al., 2000).

Despite the learning value of newness theory, INVs face liabilities and problems in addition to the many benefits of being global at such a young age. Some of these affect the INV simply due to its large and age, as they do any fresh start-up or inexperienced firm, while others are unique to its setting. Inadequate resources and competencies in general cause these liabilities and challenges. Cazura et al. (2007) can be described as a shortage of complementary resources that will lead to critical firm-specific challenges. The liability of newness is one of the strategic assets that INV enterprises lack. This is when firms require specific additional resources that they cannot move across nations or have not created to participate in a new paradigm.

LIABILITIES OF NEWNESS AND FOREIGNNESS: DOUBLE WHAMMY OR DOUBLE ADVANTAGE?

There are abundant of factors that impact performance in organizations. These factors become more intensify as a firm becomes international since they are subject to the liability of foreignness (as cited in Chinta et. al., 2015). It is because, the interaction of newness and foreignness is critical to international firms' success. There are assumptions that foreignness and newness can work together in order to reduce the disadvantages associates with each factor came about from the large body of research on both the advantages and disadvantages of both factors.

Liability of Newness

Several organizational ecologists studied the link between corporate performance and age, with various findings supporting the liability of newness (Le Mens, Hannan, & Pólos, 2014). The first few years of a firm's existence are risky and volatile, with failure rates decreasing as the business expands older (Henderson, 1999). Stinchcombe's (1965) initial concentration on start-up companies in new major sectors has been represented in early LON research. Freeman et al. (1983) found scientific data from semiconductor manufacturers and labor organizations in Henderson's (1999) empirical sample. Henderson's (1999) scientific sampling frame is that personal computers are factories and unions, contributing to the same study.

Additionally, Thornhill and Amit (2003) defines the liability of newness as a tendency in organizational performance as a dependent. Studies have been directed at LON as a character trait of a global company, regardless of if the new firm is in an emerging, soaring, sophisticated, or shrinking market

(Wiklund, Baker, & Shepherd, 2010). Instead of being reflective of an economic sector of the economy (industry) developmental stage, researchers have looked at LON as a firm no matter whether the new firm is developing, rising, advanced. Even though some of the sources of LON recommended by Stinchcombe and listed above may be more severe in the arising economy due to the company's overall apparent lack of legitimation, new businesses in all areas of the economy are likely to be subject to the company's strategic plan may be diverse (Le Men's et al., 2014).

Liability of Foreignness

Firm globalization is a broad notion that outlines how environmental and organizational resources are divided between foreign and local activities (Sullivan, 1994). To be precise, globalization alludes to a business's decision to expand its operations beyond its home market. Internationalization typically starts with foreign assets, calculated as a percentage of total overseas trade, and involves expenditures in other nations' assets, employees, and operations (Sullivan, 1994). The company's main incentive for starting any business is financial: it wants to increase earnings. Operating internationally can help in this area because it gives you access to a broader range of markets and possibly lower-cost resources. An internationalizing corporation anticipates that income from overseas markets will more than pay the costs of selling globally, which are the expenses that make up the foreignness liability.

As per Hymer (1976), businesses that expand their operations outside of their home country pay expenditures that they would not incur if they stayed in their home country. Foreign competitors have less information regarding their competitors in the market. As a result, a company faces a competitive disadvantage compared to a domestic company in the same country (Kindleberger, 1969). According to Zaheer and Mosakowski (1997), the origins of LOF focused on a business's lack of understanding and local cultural context resulting from the environment (internal and external) and the findings showed many international business researchers have adopted the LOF notion (Zhou & Guillén, 2015).

The core of empirical research on LOF has emphasized how multinational corporations (MNEs) might mitigate the risk of doing business in another country. MNEs have been lauded for their scale economies, more significant technological innovation, brand awareness, and organizational and administrative capabilities (Zaheer & Mosawksi, 1997). The LOF approach, on the other hand, is equally suitable for internationalizing new and small firms.

In general, there is little research on how new enterprises may overcome LOF (Autio, Sapienza, & Arenius, 2005). Emerging enterprises, unlike MNEs, some of which have enormous resource endowments, frequently suffer resource constraints. Young enterprises typically have the brand image or cost advantages (size or scope economies) that have been touted as strategies for MNEs to tackle LOF.

Transition from Liabilities to Advantages and Buffers of Inv

LOF explains the performance discrepancies in firms while LON examines survival dissimilarities. On the other hand, it can assist us to understand why it takes a new company so long to globalize. The dependant design of the claims we present below is immediately essential for this line of inquiry because international activities' launch is crucial for a strong market (Rialp et al., 2005). Organizational learning refers to developing new knowledge or discoveries in an enterprise that can influence the firm's behavior. Both the LOF literature explain on-stage models of globalization that created persuasive arguments.

Early internationalization considers market knowledge gained via education to be a vital facilitating resource for globalization.

The learning approach suggests that the predecessors of early globalization can be located in the act of acquisition instead of in the institution's reservoir of knowledge. This may explain why, in some circumstances, increased knowledge is correlated to internationalization success (Autio et al., 2000). Due to their foreignness liability, which stems from the need to understand other markets, foreign businesses should be at a deficit in host nation marketplaces (Zaheer, 1995).

A new venture that represents LON would be one in which people's roles are built from the bottom up, connections, and flexible and minimized restrictions. Also, informal interaction as the information moves swiftly, silly inquiries are permitted and even fostered, and unusual concepts from other industries and organizations are accepted. A learning organization can benefit from the diversity of cultures encountered, service providers served, and political institutions observed to widen its quest for a global market. A study by Sipila (2021) stressed on LOF which it is related to cost and difficulties when they penetrate the foreign market. According to a study by Kang, Kumar and Ku (2021), their finding on corporation showed LOF risk large foreign corporations as the magnitude of the risks are greater than local company in US firms and this type of liabilities states that foreign corporation easily get discriminate by formal institutions (Hengeveld, 2021).

Some businesses, such as those involved in internationalization, must unlearn old methods before implementing new ones. As per Sapienza, Autio, George, and Zahra (2006), lack of inertia and limited routines can aid globalization in three ways. First, organizations with fewer procedures and inertial constraints are better able to spot and pursue opportunities in international markets. Second, new organizations are more receptive to new information and prospects.

Third, because young enterprises have not formed strong bonds with domestic partners, they are more vulnerable to international partners' influence. Furthermore, Bingham and Davis (2012) stated that the benefits of newness acquisition extend beyond enterprises to individual entrepreneurs: Entrepreneurs who had less foreign experience before beginning their contemporary international trade seem to possess more. While existing experience, relationships, and information can assist some established companies in exploring emerging global growth opportunities trajectory (Johanson & Vahlne, 2009), they can also limit the user from exploring truly novel options outside of the chosen path. Small businesses face a lot of LON because they start from scratch, but they do not have to cope with acknowledging thought traditions and possibly obsolete information in exploring new fields.

Even if all new firms learn, the extent to which they learn varies, even if the reasons for these disparities are not well understood. Some entrepreneurs are known for their fanatical beliefs, while others are known for being individualists who find it challenging to listen to opposing viewpoints. These business owners are hesitant to support exchanging information and convergence tools to help INVs maintain their organizational effectiveness (Zahra, 2005). Start-up companies have a diverse set of skills and a strong desire to learn. It is believed that learning skills associated with newness can enable the initial growth of internationalization in existing businesses, where continuous improvement is critical to firms' effectiveness (Zahra & Hayton, 2008).

RESOURCE BASED VIEW (RBV) AND INTERNATIONAL NEW VENTURES (INVS)

The resources that enable the generation of capabilities are primary theoretical supports for the INVs phenomenon (Kocak & Abimbola, 2009). As a result, a resource-based view (RBV) is the best-suited theoretical model for the INV concept, as RBV explains how enterprising firms develop and leverage resources and capabilities (Knight & Cavusgil, 2004). In general, resources serve as a firm's foundation and the foundation for its capabilities. RBV, in particular, implies that firms can be conceptualized as bundles of resources that are heterogeneously distributed across the firm.

Based on that assertion, Barney (1991) contends that when businesses have important, rare, inimitable, and non-substitutable assets, they can maximize profits (SCA) that rival firms find difficult to duplicate. This logic appears to apply to INVs that can leverage proposed LAN to catalyze the growth of unique core competencies. To enter global markets, Bloodgood et al. (1996) believe that modern ventures must acquire physical and intellectual resource stocks, valuable, unique, and non-substitutable.

As a result, firms with distinctive bundles and more extensive resource stocks may be more inclined to internationalize. Furthermore, in today's volatile and uncertain atmosphere, small and new businesses must start engaging in cross-border activities and ensure their performance and sustainability. As a result, Autio et al. (2011) discovered in their formative research that resource centralization (ability to transfer them to represent different uses) is one of the various significant variables in order to increase the uniqueness of possible process configurations and also act as a factor in the firm's formation of new abilities, particularly in 'situational uncertain' environments. The term "situational uncertainty" refers to the combination of firm-specific, perspective ambiguity, variability, and complexity of the structural, product, and market trends in which the appropriate course of action for the new venture is not immediately apparent.

Human resources and technological resources are examples of fungible resources (Autio et al., 2011). The resource centralization of human capital endowments, in particular, played a critical role in the frequency with which new processes are generated or modified. Entry into multiple foreign markets was made possible in several firms due to the ease with which employees could be moved between markets or if employees possessed skills to operate in very different markets (Autio et al., 2011)

Given that new ventures frequently face resource constraints, it stands to reason that centralization in resource exploitation has a strong relationship with the firm's capability initiation and growth (Autio et al., 2011). They also claimed that resource fungibility could increase the likelihood of experimentation, experience transfer, and learning through adaptation by lowering the cost of deploying the same resource for different purposes.

CONCLUSION

Discussion on the above has made some contribution to the literature regarding international new ventures and born global. First of all, the rising of born global companies originated from developing countries as most of the born global are small and medium enterprises and with some weaknesses due to some unstable political and economic has led to internationalization among this entity. The evolution of born global from developing countries to internationalization has shown the increasing numbers of this entity in the international market. However, born global must be aware of facing greater risk due to international market exposure, and they must strategize an excellent plan to face high competitiveness among them.

This study contributes to the international new ventures literature and definition of this term. This chapter offers essential insight for decision-makers in understanding the INV itself, and they also require considering the degree of liabilities (newness and foreignness) before executing any plan regarding penetrating the market. This insight is crucial in emerging markets in which it would affect the whole operation of companies. Thus, entrepreneurs shall observe the movements of global markets, and this venture helps generate new wealth and allows the entrepreneur to penetrate the market easily; also, a good business plan would aid in focusing on specific steps to achieve short-term and long-term objectives. Future study might consider liability of foreigness effect on positive sides which would aid corporation in securing their survival for long terms and it is crucial to grasp advantage of liability also turning it into an assets (Lee, Paik, Horak & Yang, 2021). Another recommendation for future study is considering additional case-study or survey-data which would enhance the findings of the study and generalizability of the results (Kowalik, Danik & Francioni, 2020).

REFERENCES

Andresen, M., & Bergdolt, F. (2017). A systematic literature review on the definitions of global mind-set and cultural intelligence – Merging two different research streams. *International Journal of Human Resource Management, 28*(1), 170–195. doi:10.1080/09585192.2016.1243568

Autio, E. (2005). Creative tension: The significance of Ben Oviatt's and Patricia McDougall's article 'toward a theory of international new ventures'. *Journal of International Business Studies, 36*(1), 9–19. doi:10.1057/palgrave.jibs.8400117

Autio, E., George, G., & Alexy, O. (2011). International entrepreneurship and capability development: Qualitative evidence and future research directions. *Entrepreneurship Theory and Practice, 3*(1), 11–37. doi:10.1111/j.1540-6520.2010.00421.x

Autio, E., Sapienza, H. J., & Almeida, J. G. (2000). Effects of age at entry, knowledge intensity, and imitability on international growth. *Academy of Management Journal, 43*(5), 909–924.

Autio, E., Sapienza, H. J., & Arenius, P. (2005). International social capital, technology sharing, and foreign market learning in internationalizing entrepreneurial firms. *Advances in Entrepreneurship, Firm, Emergence, and Growth, 8*, 9–42. doi:10.1016/S1074-7540(05)08002-5

Baranowska-Prokop, E., & Sikora, T. (2017). Competitiveness of polish international new ventures from managerial perspective. In A. Vlachvei (Ed.), *ABSCA) book series. Factors affecting firm competitiveness and performance in the modern business world, Business Science Reference* (pp. 83–107). doi:10.4018/978-1-5225-0843-4.ch003

Barney, J. B. (1991). Firm resources and sustained competitive advantage. *Journal of Management, 17*(1), 99–120. doi:10.1177/014920639101700108

Bembom, M., & Schwens, C. (2018). The role of networks in early internationalizing firms: A systematic review and future research agenda. *European Management Journal, 36*(6), 679–694. doi:10.1016/j.emj.2018.03.003

Bengtsson, L. (2004). Explaining born globals: An organisational learning perspective on the internationalisation process. *International Journal of Globalisation and Small Business, 1*(1), 28–41. doi:10.1504/IJGSB.2004.005616

Bingham, C. B., & Davis, J. P. (2012). Learning sequences: Their existence, effect, and evolution. *Academy of Management Journal, 55*(3), 611–641. doi:10.5465/amj.2009.0331

Bloodgood, J. M., Sapienza, H. J., & Almeida, J. G. (1996). The internationalization of new high potential U.S. ventures: Antecedents and outcomes. *Entrepreneurship Theory and Practice, 20*(4), 61–76. doi:10.1177/104225879602000405

Buckley, P. J., & Casson, M. (2021). Thirty years of International Business Review and international business research. *International Business Review, 30*(2), 101795. doi:10.1016/j.ibusrev.2021.101795

Cavusgil, S. T., & Knight, G. (2015). The born global firm: An entrepreneurial and capabilities perspective on early and rapid internationalization. *Journal of International Business Studies, 46*(1), 3–16. doi:10.1057/jibs.2014.62

Cazura, A. C., Mary, M. M., & Manrakhan, S. (2007). Causes of the difficulties in internationalization. *Journal of International Business Studies, 38*(5), 709–725. doi:10.1057/palgrave.jibs.8400295

Chetty, S., & Campbell-Hunt, C. (2004). A strategic approach to internationalization: A traditional versus a "born-global" approach. *Journal of International Marketing, 12*(1), 57–81. doi:10.1509/jimk.12.1.57.25651

Chinta, R., Cheung, M.-S., & Capar, N. (2015). Double whammy or double advantage: "Foreignness" and "newness" as determinants of success in international business. *Journal of Management and Strategy, 6*(1), 76–87. doi:10.5430/jms.v6n1p76

Coviello, N., & Yli-Renko, H. (2016). *Handbook of measures for international entrepreneurship research: multi-item scales crossing disciplines and contexts*. Edward Elgar Publishing. doi:10.4337/9781784711405

Ćuzović, S., Sokolov Mladenović, S., & Ćuzović, Đ. (2019). The impact of social and cultural factors on success of trade internationalization. *Poslovna Izvrsnost, 13*(1), 57–76. doi:10.22598/pi-be/2019.13.1.57

Devinney, T. M., Markman, G., Pedersen, T., & Tihanyi, L. (2016). *Global Entrepreneurship: Past, Present & Future*. Emerald Group Publishing. doi:10.1108/S1571-5027201629

Evers, N., Gliga, G., & Rialp-Criado, A. (2019). Strategic orientation pathways in international new ventures and born global firms—Towards a research agenda. *Journal of International Entrepreneurship, 17*(3), 287–304. doi:10.100710843-019-00259-y

Fan, T., & Phan, P. (2018). International new ventures: revisiting the influences behind the 'bornGlobal' firm. *International Entrepreneurship: The Pursuit of Opportunities across National Borders*, 131–172.

Ferencikova, S., & Ferencikova, S. (2016). The International New Ventures: Applicability of the Theory on the Slovak Innovative Start-Ups. In *Internet of Things. IoT Infrastructures. IoT360*. Springer. doi:10.1007/978-3-319-47075-7_16

Fillis, I. (2001). Small firm internationalization: An investigate survey and future research direction. *Management Decision, 39*(9), 767–783. doi:10.1108/00251740110408683

Freeman, J., Carroll, G. R., & Hannan, M. T. (1983). The liability of newness: Age dependence in organizational death rates. *American Sociological Review, 48*(5), 692–710. doi:10.2307/2094928

Henderson, A. D. (1999). Firm strategy and age dependence: A contingent view of the liabilities of newness, adolescence, and obsolescence. *Administrative Science Quarterly, 44*(2), 281–314. doi:10.2307/2666997

Hengeveld, J. (2021). *Using CSR within emerging markets to gain legitimacy* [Master dissertation]. University of Southampton.

Hymer, S. H. (1976). *The international operations of national firms: A study in direct foreign investment*. MIT Press.

Ismail, N. A., & Kuivalainen, O. (2015). The effect of internal capabilities and external environment on small-and medium-sized enterprises' international performance and the role of the foreign market scope: The case of the Malaysian halal food industry. *Journal of International Entrepreneurship, 13*(4), 418–451. doi:10.100710843-015-0160-x

Jafari-Sadeghi, V., Nkongolo-Bakenda, J. M., Dana, L. P., Anderson, R. B., & Biancone, P. P. (2020). Home country institutional context and entrepreneurial internationalization: The significance of human capital attributes. *Journal of International Entrepreneurship, 18*(2), 165–195. doi:10.100710843-019-00264-1

Johanson, J., & Vahlne, J.-E. (1977). The internationalization process of the firm. *Journal of International Business Studies, 8*(1), 23–32. doi:10.1057/palgrave.jibs.8490676

Johanson, J., & Vahlne, J.-E. (1990). The mechanism of internationalization. *International Marketing Review, 7*(4), 11–24. doi:10.1108/02651339010137414

Johanson, J., & Vahlne, J. E. (2009). The Uppsala internationalization process model revisited: From liability of foreignness to liability of outsidership. *Journal of International Business Studies, 40*(9), 1411–1431. doi:10.1057/jibs.2009.24

Johanson, J., & Wiedersheim-Paul, F. (1975). The internationalization of the firm—Four Swedish cases. *Journal of Management Studies, 12*(3), 305–322. doi:10.1111/j.1467-6486.1975.tb00514.x

Jolly, V. K., Alahuhta, M., & Jeannet, J. P. (1992). Challenging the incumbents: How high technology start-ups compete globally. *Strategic Change, 1*(2), 71–82. doi:10.1002/jsc.4240010203

Jones, M. V., Coviello, N. E., & Tang, Y. K. (2011). International entrepreneurship research (1989–2009): A domain ontology and thematic analysis. *Journal of Business Venturing, 26*(6), 632–659. doi:10.1016/j.jbusvent.2011.04.001

Kang, S., Kumar, S. S., & Ku, B. (2021). The liability of foreignness in early-stage corporate venture capital investment. *Humanities and Social Sciences Letters, 9*(1), 72–85. doi:10.18488/journal.73.2021.91.72.85

Kindleberger, C. P. (1969). *American business abroad: Six lectures on direct investment*. Yale University Press.

Knight, G. A., & Cavusgil, S. T. (1996). The born global firm: A challenge to traditional internationalization theory. *Advances in Intemational Marketing*, *8*, 11–26.

Knight, G. A., & Cavusgil, S. T. (2004). Innovation, organizational capabilities, and the born global firm. *Journal of International Business Studies*, *35*(2), 124–141. doi:10.1057/palgrave.jibs.8400071

Knight, G. A., & Liesch, P. W. (2016). Internationalization: From incremental to born global. *Journal of World Business*, *51*(1), 93–102. doi:10.1016/j.jwb.2015.08.011

Knight, J. (1997). A shared vision? Stakeholders' perspectives on the internationalization of higher education in Canada. *Journal of Studies in International Education*, *1*(1), 27–44. doi:10.1177/102831539700100105

Knudsen, M. P., & Servais, P. (2007). Analyzing internationalization configurations of SME's: The purchaser's perspective. *Journal of Purchasing and Supply Management*, *13*(2), 137–151. doi:10.1016/j.pursup.2007.06.002

Kocak, A., & Abimbola, T. (2009). The effects of entrepreneurial marketing on born global performance. *Journal of International Marketing Review*, *26*(4/5), 439–452. doi:10.1108/02651330910971977

Kuivalainen, O., Saarenketo, S., & Puumalainen, K. (2012). Start-up patterns of internationalization: A framework and its application in the context of knowledge intensive SMEs. *European Management Journal*, *30*(4), 372–385. doi:10.1016/j.emj.2012.01.001

Le Mens, G., Hannan, M. T., & Pólos, L. (2014). Organizational obsolescence, drifting tastes, and age dependence in organizational life chances. *Organization Science*, *26*(2), 550–570. doi:10.1287/orsc.2014.0910

Lee, J. M., Paik, Y., Horak, S., & Yang, I. (2021). Turning a liability into an asset of foreignness: Managing informal networks in Korea. *Business Horizons*. Advance online publication. doi:10.1016/j.bushor.2021.04.002

Li, X. (2021, April). FDI and International Trade: A Review. In *2021 6th International Conference on Social Sciences and Economic Development (ICSSED 2021)* (pp. 904-909). Atlantis Press. 10.2991/assehr.k.210407.171

Liu, C. H., Chang, A. Y. P., & Fang, Y. P. (2020). Network activities as critical sources of creating capability and competitive advantage. *Management Decision*, *58*(3), 544–568. doi:10.1108/MD-08-2017-0733

Lopez, C., & Fan, Y. (2009). Internationalisation of the Spanish fashion brand Zara. *Journal of Fashion Marketing and Management*, *13*(2), 279–296. doi:10.1108/13612020910957770

Lounsbury, M., & Glynn, M. A. (2001). Cultural entrepreneurship: Stories, legitimacy, and the acquisition of resources. *Strategic Management Journal*, *22*(6/7), 545–564. doi:10.1002mj.188

Love, J. H., Roper, S., & Zhou, Y. (2016). Experience, age and exporting performance in UK SMEs. *International Business Review*, *25*(4), 806–819. doi:10.1016/j.ibusrev.2015.10.001

Luostarinen, R., & Gabrielsson, M. (2006). Globalization and marketing strategies of born globals in SMOPECs. *Thunderbird International Business Review*, *48*(6), 773–801. doi:10.1002/tie.20122

Madsen, T. K., & Servais, P. (1997). The internationalization of born globals: An evolutionary process? *International Business Review*, *6*(6), 561–583. doi:10.1016/S0969-5931(97)00032-2

McDougal, P. P., & Oviatt, B. M. (2000). International entrepreneurship: The intersection of two research paths. *Academy of Management Journal*, *43*, 902–908.

McDougal, P. P., Shane, S., & Oviatt, B. M. (1994). Explaining the Formation of International New Ventures: The limits of theories from international business research. *Journal of Business Venturing*, *9*(6), 469–487. doi:10.1016/0883-9026(94)90017-5

McKinsey & Co. (1993). *Emerging Exporters*. Australian Manufacturing Council.

Mladenović, S. S., Mladenović, I., & Ranđelović, M. P. (2020). Emerging Markets And Internationalization Of Retail: The Case Of Bric Countries. *Economic Themes*, *58*(4), 479–500. doi:10.2478/ethemes-2020-0027

Mohamed, M. A., Abdul-Talib, A. N., & Ramlee, A. (2022). Determinants of the firm performance of returnee entrepreneurs in Somalia: the effects of external environmental conditions. *Journal of Enterprising Communities: People and Places in the Global Economy*.

Morais, F., & Ferreira, J. J. (2020). SME internationalisation process: Key issues and contributions, existing gaps and the future research agenda. *European Management Journal*, *38*(1), 62–77. doi:10.1016/j.emj.2019.08.001

Nowiński, W., & Rialp, A. (2013). Drivers and strategies of international new ventures from a Central European transition economy. *Journal for East European Management Studies*, *18*(2), 191–231. doi:10.5771/0949-6181-2013-2-191

OECD. (2009). *Top Barriers and Drivers to SME Internationalisation. Report by the OECD Working Party on SMEs and Entrepreneurship*. OECD.

Oviatt, B. M., & McDougal, P. (1994). Toward a theory of international new ventures. *Journal of International Business Studies*, *25*(1), 45–64. doi:10.1057/palgrave.jibs.8490193

Oviatt, B. M., & McDougal, P. (1997). Challenges for Internationalization Process Theory: The Case of International New Ventures. *Management International Review*, *37*(2), 85–99.

Oviatt, B. M., & McDougall, P. P. (2005). The internationalization of entrepreneurship. *Journal of International Business Studies*, *36*(1), 2–8. doi:10.1057/palgrave.jibs.8400119

Park, J. M., Lee, J. E., & Jeong, Y. H. (2018). The effect of strategic orientation on the speed of internationalization in small and medium-sized enterprises in South Korea. *Muyeog Yeon'gu*, *14*(5), 21–42.

Paul, J., & Rosado-Serrano, A. (2019). Gradual internationalization vs born-global. International new venture models. *International Marketing Review*, *36*(6), 830–858. doi:10.1108/IMR-10-2018-0280

Preece, S. B., Miles, G., & Baetz, M. C. (1999). Explaining the international intensity and global diversity of early-stage technology-based firms. *Journal of Business Venturing*, *14*(3), 259–281. doi:10.1016/S0883-9026(97)00105-5

Pukall, T. J., & Calabro, A. (2014). The internationalization of family firms: A critical review and integrative model. *Family Business Review, 27*(2), 103–125. doi:10.1177/0894486513491423

Rasmussen, E. S., & Madsen, T. K. (2002). The born global concept. *Proceedings of the 28th EIBA 2002 Conference*, 1-26.

Rennie, M. W. (1993). Global competitiveness: Born global. *The McKinsey Quarterly, 4*, 45–52.

Reuber, A. R., Knight, G. A., Liesch, P. W., & Zhou, L. (2018). International entrepreneurship: The pursuit of entrepreneurial opportunities across national borders. *Journal of International Business Studies, 49*(4), 395–406. doi:10.105741267-018-0149-5

Rialp, A., Rialp, J., & Knight, G. A. (2005). The phenomenon of early internationalizing firms: What do we know after a decade (1993-2003) of scientific inquiry? *International Business Review, 14*(2), 147–166. doi:10.1016/j.ibusrev.2004.04.006

Rialp, A., Rialp, J., Urbano, D., & Vaillant, Y. (2005). The born-global phenomenon: A comparative case study research. *Journal of International Entrepreneurship, 3*(2), 133–171. doi:10.100710843-005-4202-7

Rugman, A., & Brain, C. (2003). Multinational enterprises are regional, not global. *Multinational Business Review, 11*(1), 3–12. doi:10.1108/1525383X200300001

Sapienza, H. J., Autio, E., George, G., & Zahra, S. A. (2006). A capabilities perspective on the effects of early internationalization on firm survival and growth. *Academy of Management Review, 31*(4), 917–933. doi:10.5465/amr.2006.22527465

Sipilä, K. (2021). *Finnish SMEs' manifestation of agility in the uncertain US business environment* [Master Dissertation]. University of Vaasa.

Stinchcombe, A. L. (1965). Social structure and organizations. In J. G. March (Ed.), *Handbook of organizations*. Rand McNally.

Stocker, F., Abib, G., Jhunior, R. D. O. S., & Irigaray, H. A. R. (2021). Brazilian craft breweries and internationalization in the born global perspective. *Revista de Gestão, 28*(2), 163–178. doi:10.1108/REGE-01-2021-0014

Stray, S., Bridgewater, S., & Murray, G. (2001). The internationalisation process of small, technology-based firms: Market selection, mode choice and degree of internationalisation. *Journal of Global Marketing, 15*(1), 7–29. doi:10.1300/J042v15n01_02

Sullivan, D. (1994). Measuring the degree of internationalization of a firm. *Journal of International Business Studies, 25*(2), 325–342. doi:10.1057/palgrave.jibs.8490203

Thornhill, S., & Amit, R. (2003). Learning about failure: Bankruptcy, firm age, and the resource based view. *Organization Science, 14*(5), 497–509. doi:10.1287/orsc.14.5.497.16761

Vernon, R. (1966). International investment and international trade in the product cycle. *The Quarterly Journal of Economics, 80*(2), 190–207. doi:10.2307/1880689

Wiklund, J. (1999). The sustainability of the entrepreneurial orientation–performance relationship. *Entrepreneurship Theory and Practice, 24*(1), 37–48. doi:10.1177/104225879902400103

Wiklund, J., Baker, T., & Shepherd, D. A. (2010). The age-effect of financial indicators as buffers against the liability of newness. *Journal of Business Venturing*, *25*(4), 423–437. doi:10.1016/j.jbusvent.2008.10.011

Zaheer, S. (1995). Overcoming the liability of foreignness. *Academy of Management Journal*, *38*, 341–363.

Zaheer, S., & Mosakowski, E. (1997). The dynamics of the liability of foreignness: A global study of survival in financial services. *Strategic Management Journal*, *18*(6), 439–446. doi:10.1002/(SICI)1097-0266(199706)18:6<439::AID-SMJ884>3.0.CO;2-Y

Zahra, A. S., Sapienza, H. J., & Davidsson, P. (2006). Entreprenuership and Dynamic Capabilities: A review model and research agenda. *Journal of Management Studies*, *43*(4), 917–955. doi:10.1111/j.1467-6486.2006.00616.x

Zahra, S. A. (2005). A theory of international new ventures: A decade of research. *Journal of International Business Studies*, *36*(1), 20–28. doi:10.1057/palgrave.jibs.8400118

Zahra, S. A. (2006). A theory of international new ventures: A decade of research. *Journal of International Business Studies*, *36*(1), 20–28. doi:10.1057/palgrave.jibs.8400118

Zahra, S. A., & Hayton, J. C. (2008). The effect of international venturing on firm performance: The moderating influence of absorptive capacity. *Journal of Business Venturing*, *23*(2), 195–220. doi:10.1016/j.jbusvent.2007.01.001

Zahra, S. A., Ireland, R. D., & Hitt, M. A. (2000). International expansion by new venture firms: International diversity, mode of market entry, technological learning and performance. *Academy of Management Journal*, *43*(5), 925–950.

Zakaria, N., Abdul-Talib, A. N., & Amelinckx, A. (Eds.). (2020). *Transcending Cultural Frontiers: Practices, Challenges, and Strategy for International Business*. Springer. doi:10.1007/978-981-15-4454-5

Zakaria, N., Abdul-Talib, A. N., & Othman, N. (Eds.). (2016). *Handbook of research on impacts of international business and political affairs on the global economy*. IGI Global. doi:10.4018/978-1-4666-9806-2

Zhou, N., & Guillén, M. F. (2015). From home country to home base: A dynamic approach to the liability of foreignness. *Strategic Management Journal*, *36*(6), 907–917. doi:10.1002mj.2242

Chapter 5
Self-Initiated Expatriates:
A Case of Academic Expatriates in Malaysia

Subramaniam Sri Ramalu
Universiti Utara Malaysia, Malaysia

Nida Malik
Universiti Utara Malaysia, Malaysia

ABSTRACT

This chapter discusses the emergence of a new category of expatriates, namely self-initiated expatriates. In particular, the demand for self-initiated academic expatriates has increased tremendously over the years in tandem with the globalization of the higher education sector across the globe. Hence, this chapter aims to provide greater understanding about the nature and motivation for expatriation among this group of expatriates which will have significant impact on the international human resource management policies and practices. This chapter begins with explanation about the concept of expatriation and expatriate. This is followed by comparison between organizational expatriates and self-initiated expatriates. The underlying motivation behind self-initiated expatriation is discussed as well. Definitions of academic self-initiated expatriates and their motivation to expatriate were included as well in this chapter. This chapter conclude with findings of one case study conducted among 152 academic self-initiated expatriates employed in 20 public universities in Malaysia.

CONCEPT OF EXPATRIATION AND EXPATRIATE

Globalization has led to changes in political, economic, cultural, technology, and educational environments (Altman & Shortland, 2008). Accordingly, has opened the doors for many multinational companies to set up their businesses in foreign countries to remain competitive in global market (Srivastava & Pandey, 2012). As a result of this, there is increasing demands for expatriates globally since organizations believe that expatriates will enhance the subsidiary's performance by transferring technology, knowledge, and skills (Cerdin & Selmer, 2014; Chang & Peng, 2012).

DOI: 10.4018/978-1-7998-9071-3.ch005

According to Shaffer, Harrison & Gilley, (1999) the utilization of expatriates leads to many advantages for organizations such as technical skills, rich experience of products, accountability, control improvement, and improved employees' effectiveness. Expatriates sent to foreign subsidiaries generally assume strategic roles among the others as controllers, coordinators, and transferors (Edstrom & Galbraith, 1977; Harzing, 2001; Paik & Sohn, 2004; Torbiörn, 1994) These strategic tasks are important to achieve the competitive advantage of the organizations (Gregersen & Black, 1990;Selmer & Lauring, 2010).

Expatriation is a phenomenon where people move across their country's borders to live and work in another country for a certain period (Richardson & McKenna, 2006; Che Rose et al., 2010). The term expatriate is derived from the Latin word 'ex patria', which refers to moving away out of the country of origin to another country for better work and life conditions (Suutari, Brewster, Mäkelä, Dickmann, & Tornikoski., 2018). Thus, an expatriate is an individual who intends to remain in a different country or different culture to work and live for a particular period (Holopainen & Björkman, 2005).

COMPARISON BETWEEN ORGANIZATIONAL EXPATRIATES AND SELF-INITIATED EXPATRIATES

There are two different categories of expatriates seeking jobs abroad namely organizational expatriates (OEs) or also known as traditional expatriates and the other category is the self-initiated expatriates (SIEs) (Howe-Walsh & Schyns, 2010). Organizational expatriates are those professional and skilled employees who are sent by their home organizations to fill positions in the host country subsidiaries for an identified contractual period, usually from three to five years (Mckenna & Richardson, 2007). Besides, SIEs are those individuals who initiate their move seeking for opportunity and work in a foreign country by themselves without any support from the home country organizations (Selmer & Lauring, 2010; Tharenou & Caulfield, 2010). Comparatively, OEs are given preparation and skills before the host country subsidiary assignment before they move, whereas SIEs on the other hand take charge of their expatriation decisions (Howe-Walsh & Schyns, 2010).

SELF-INITIATED EXPATRIATES AND THEIR MOTIVATION TO EXPATRIATE

The term self-initiated expatriation has historically evolved many times in different ways. The notion of SIEs was first introduced by Inkson, Arthur, Pringles, & Barry (1997) as an "overseas experience" to describe those individuals who are motivated and encouraged by career-related and personal factors to live and work abroad without support from the home country organizations. SIEs also characterized such as self-initiated foreign experiences (Myers & Pringle, 2005; Suutari & Brewster, 2000), overseas experience (Inkson et al., 1997) self-initiated international work opportunities (Tharenou, 2003), self-selecting expatriates (Richardson & McKenna, 2003), self-made expatriates and self-expatriates (Tharenou & Caulfield, 2010), and international self-initiated mobility and self-initiated movers (Thorn, 2009).

Existing literature revealed that SIEs are more common and popular than OEs and the number of SIEs is remarkably higher than OEs (Biemann & Andresen, 2010; Swim et al., 2011). This is because SIEs are free to initiate their movement abroad and not committed to serving in specific organizations like OEs who are restricted to following the roles of their organizations in terms of serving back in their organization once the international assignment is completed. Findings showed that 65 percent of professional employees are classified as SIEs (Doherty, 2013). In addition, surveys also revealed that about 50-70 percent of the expatriates are classified as SIEs (Swim et al., 2011; Jokinen et al., 2008; Peltokorpi & Froese, 2009).

Research has found that SIEs are motivated to go overseas for many reasons for example, in a qualitative study based on British academics, it was found that SIEs are motivated and encouraged to go abroad for four major reasons namely 1). exploration, to escape from issues in their home country, 2). financial issues, 3). building an international experience and 4). career development purposes (Richardson & McKenna, 2006). In a related study, Doherty & Dickmann, (2012) revealed six key motivational factors driving them to move abroad. The key influences on the decision to move overseas were associated with career development considerations, concerns about family members and friends, individual interests such as a desire for adventure, the assessment of monetary and non-monetary organizational incentives, host country environments such as history, nature, security, and climate) and specific host country location.

When concentrating on the motivating elements that push SIEs to relocate overseas, it is crucial to remember that SIEs are a diverse group, and the driving factors differ (Suutari & Brewster, 2000). For example, studies in the existing literature on SIEs indicated that the major reasons for deciding on accepting overseas jobs were excitement, growth, international experiences, meeting different people from different cultures, and future career opportunities (Tharenou, 2003). Jackson, (2005) in their study found five factors that motivated skilled employees to work abroad. In their study, lifestyle and family concerns were found to be pull factors motivating individuals to move to the host country, whereas culture, career, and economic factors were found to be home country push factors leading and forcing one to move abroad. Howe-Walsh et al. (2010) found that SIEs could be motivated to travel abroad for personal desires such as following a partner or working in a specific country and for career development such as starting a new job or building a career development.

Furthermore, Richardson et al. (2006) in his qualitative study among British employees working in certain universities in Singapore, Turkey, New Zealand, and UAE found that family-related reasons, particularly spouse and children well-being are important key factors considered in decisions related to expatriation. Therefore, the motivational factors in the host countries play an important role in the decision of individuals and SIEs in specifically to accept the international assignment.

In line with this, the motivation for SIEs to work and live overseas may vary depending on the context as suggested by (Jackson, 2005; Doherty & Dickmann, 2012). Previous studies discovered that context one of the essential motivational variables that attract and pull the expatriates to work in a specific country (Doherty & Dickmann, 2012; Hippler, 2009; Tharenou et al. 2010). Research studies showed that SIEs attracted and encouraged to accept the international assignment in developed countries due to promising stability, security, and better lifestyle (Al Ariss & Özbilgin, 2010; Tharenou, 2010). (Swim et al., 2011) in their study found that 14 out of 34 valuable motivational factors related to the host country location attractions such as host country reputation and the acceptance of foreign employees. Therefore, the host location is considered one of the most important motivational (Doherty & Dickmann, 2012) factors that attract and motivate SIEs to accept working and living in a different country and is also considered a key determinants factor that drives the willingness of individuals to accept the international assignment.

DEFINITION OF ACADEMIC SELF-INITIATED EXPATRIATES AND THEIR MOTIVATION TO EXPATRIATE

Academic expatriates are categorized as self-initiated expatriates who intend to move abroad seeking better job opportunities on their initiative (Richardson, 2006; Selmer & Lauring, 2010). Lately, there is an increase in number of academic SIEs seeking new working experience outside their country of derivation (Howe-Walsh & Schyns, 2010; Trembath, 2016). Academic SIEs are more transient, working outside their home countries, than at any other time in the history of academics (Romanowski & Nasser, 2015).

The globalization of higher education has led to increasing interest among academic SIEs to move abroad (Richardson & Mallon, 2005; Selmer & Lauring, 2010). These academics are encouraged by three main dominant motivations namely, adventure, financial reasons, and life change and family (Richardson & Mallon, 2005). In this regard, academic SIEs are highly employable in the global marketplace due to their skills and knowledge on specific subject matters (Selmer & Lauring, 2010). This is because of the increased demand for talented academics who are needed globally by the universities and other educational institutions such as colleges and universities as part of their internationalization effort to become world-class universities (Dessoff, 2011).

The motivational factors for academic SIEs to move abroad vary but could be divided into four possible metaphors namely, architect, mercenary, explorer, and refugee (Froese, 2012; Richardson & Mckenna, 2002; Selmer & Lauring, 2013). The architect refers to those academics who are motivated by job opportunities and development. The mercenary refers to those academics who are motivated to work abroad in terms of financial incentives. The explorer refers to those academics who are motivated to explore the other side of the world. Finally, the refugee refers to those academics who are motivated to seek a better career and life outside the county of residence.

Howe-Walsh & Schyns, (2010) in their study found that academic SIEs are motivated and encouraged to expatriate due to reasons related to personal concerns in following a partner or a relationship, having and joining a different career in a different country especially when the reality of life and career conditions in the home country was not satisfied, and also because of their desires and interests to migrate to a particular country about to explore different kinds of experiences in a different culture.

Besides the motives for career advancement (Selmer & Lauring, 2010), the financial motive is also considered as one of the most influential motivational factors in expatriation decisions (Richardson & McKenna, 2003) (Richardson & McKenna, 2006). A financial incentive is considered as one of the strongest predictors that motivate academic SIEs to accept the international assignment (Carr, 2005; Selmer & Lauring, 2010). The motivational factors that influenced academic SIEs to work in developed countries have been widely addressed and studied (Andresen et al., 2015; Inkson et al., 1997; Richardson, 2006; Richardson & McKenna, 2006)).

A CASE EXAMPLE IN MALAYSIA: CULTURAL INTELLIGENCE AND WORK ENGAGEMENT OF EXPATRIATE ACADEMICS: THE ROLE OF PSYCHOLOGICAL NEEDS SATISFACTION

Introduction

In the era of globalization, the self-relocation of expatriate academics to universities all over the world has become a common phenomenon. This is partly because of the liberalization and globalization of the higher education sector in many parts of the world, creating job opportunities for expatriate academics to explore the possibility of global relocation. Furthermore, the inclusion of internationalization component as one of the criteria for ranking universities by several universities ranking agencies has help to accelerate the recruitment of expatriate academics. This has been the case in Malaysia as well. Intending to become a regional education hub by 2020, the Ministry of Higher Education Malaysia encourages Malaysian public universities to increase their visibility and competitive advantage in the ever-changing higher education market. Heeding the call by the Ministry, several Malaysian public universities have successfully obtained reputable international accreditations, such as the Association of MBAs and the Association to Advance Collegiate Schools of Business, to name a few, which apply to academic programs and even the university as a whole. Some of the Malaysian universities also have been ranked by the Times Higher Education World University Rankings and QS World University Rankings in their annual world university rankings exercises. All these internationalization efforts have resulted in an increasing number of expatriate academics taking up faculty positions in Malaysian universities. The growing number of expatriate academics taking up faculty positions in universities in an upper-middle-income economy, like Malaysia, which is known for its complex cultural, racial, and religious diversity, has posed greater challenges to human resource managers of the respective universities. This study aims to examine the direct and indirect effects of Cultural Intelligence (CQ) on work engagement (WE) with the presence of psychological needs satisfaction (PNS) as a mediating factor.

Literature Review

Predictors of expatriate effectiveness has been well documented in international human resource management literature. One such predictor that has received considerable research attention is the concept of cultural intelligence (CQ), which refers to a person's capability to function effectively in culturally diverse contexts ((Ng et al., 2009). In other words, it reflects one's capability to successfully navigate through a new cultural environment (Ang, Van Dyne, et al., 2015). CQ may represent a valuable cross-cultural skill leading to positive outcomes among expatriates (Barakat et al., 2015). Despite this development, most of the studies regarding CQ have been conducted on organizational expatriates and self-initiated expatriates in non-academic settings. With a few exceptions, the predictive ability of CQ on expatriate academics' work outcomes remains unclear in countries, like Malaysia, which is known for its complex cultural, racial, and religious diversity (Kaboudarahangi et al., 2013).

Furthermore, the understanding of the direct and indirect effects of CQ on workplace outcomes may not be comprehensive enough, without assessing one important effective outcome, namely psychological needs satisfaction (PNS) attained during international assignments in a diverse cultural environment, like Malaysia. Drawing from the self-determination theory (SDT) of Deci & Ryan (2000), and (Ryan & Deci, 2000), it is believed that all expatriate academics, regardless of their culture and experience, have a set of innate basic psychological needs (competence, autonomy, and relatedness) that must be satisfied for their overall positive growth, development, and well-being (Chen et al., 2015; Deci & Ryan 2000; Ryan & Deci, 2000). Studies have found dissatisfaction with psychological needs undermines motivation and leads to reduced adjustment and well-being (Chen et al., 2015; Church et al., 2012; Van Den Broeck et al., 2008; Vansteenkiste et al., 2006).

In the domestic setting, work engagement (WE) have been associated with positive organizational behaviour, such as in-role and extra-role performance (Halbesleben & Wheeler, 2008) job satisfaction (Lopes et al., 2017) and negatively related to withdrawal behaviour (Schaufeli et al., 2009). Unlike literature in the domestic context, research regarding WE among expatriate academics is scarce. Researchers, such as Selmer & Lauring (2015), and Selmer & Lauring (2016) have studied the outcomes of work engagement on various workplace behaviors among expatriate academics. Selmer & Lauring (2016), for example, in their study of expatriate academics residing in China, found that the dimension of work engagement has a positive relationship with a job, interaction, and general adjustment, suggesting the importance of work attitude, like WE, in predicting affective outcomes among expatriate academics. Lauring and Selmer (2015), on the other hand, found physical engagement predicts the work performance of academic expatriates in their study among 102 expatriate academics residing in Singapore.

Methodology

Data were obtained from expatriate academics employed in 20 public universities in Malaysia using a self-administered questionnaire. Both the mail and online survey methods were employed in this study. A total of 477 questionnaires were distributed. The data collection yielded 152 usable questionnaires for the analysis of the 477 questionnaires distributed which resulted in a 32 percent response rate. The hypotheses of the study were formally tested with multiple regression and mediation analysis to assess each component of the proposed model using PROCESS Macro (Hayes, 2013) and SPSS 23. PROCESS is a conditional process modelling program developed by Preacher and Hayes that utilizes an ordinary least squares-based path analytical framework to test for both direct and indirect effects (Hayes, 2013).

Findings

The positive association between CQ and WE suggest that CQ, as a form of personal intercultural capability, helps individuals to effectively deal with cultural barriers encountered in new cultural environments and as a result of this, they develop a positive, fulfilling, work-related state of mind. In other words, they engage in their work. The JD-R model of WE also suggest personal resources, like CQ, which is associated with qualities, like optimism, self-efficacy, self-esteem, resilience, and active coping style, is a key determinant of WE (Bakker & Demerouti, 2007). The findings of this study also suggest that CQ, a malleable cross-cultural capability, can predict attitudinal outcomes such as WE at the workplace. WE have been associated with employees' performance in the domestic setting.

The positive association between CQ and PNS indicates that CQ capability works in unison to help individuals to fulfil their basic psychological needs of competence, autonomy, and relatedness when navigating through a new cultural environment. Basic psychological needs could be at stake when being an expatriate academic in a foreign university requires the expatriate to cope with uncertainties and demands of moving, working, and living in a foreign culture. Hence, one needs to have a high level of CQ to meet these basic psychological needs for global well-being and adjustment (Vansteenkiste &

Ryan, 2013). The finding is consistent with the premise of the SDT (Deci & Ryan 2000; Ryan & Deci, 2000) (Vallerand, 2000) that posits that individuals, regardless of their cultural differences, will have three basic psychological needs as indicated above.

The positive association between PNS and WE, on the other hand, is consistent with previous research findings that have linked PNS with employees' work-related outcomes, such as job satisfaction, WE, and lower burnout (Deci, 2005; Ilardi et al., 1993), (Marylene & Edward, 2005) employees' performance (Baard et al., 2004); and turnover intentions (Vansteenkiste et al., 2007). In other words, basic psychological needs will stimulate intrinsic motivation that provides energy to engage actively in more needs-fulfilling activities (Howell et al., 2011; Vansteenkiste et al., 2007). The desire to fulfil basic psychological needs in a new culture is more crucial given the need to maintain overall well-being and life satisfaction during the expatriates' stay in the host country (Chen et al., 2015).

The evidence of partial mediation suggests that CQ, as a personal resource, should energize individuals to engage in their work that is much needed to fulfil their basic satisfaction needs of competence, autonomy, and relatedness. The partial mediation effect of PNS found in this study also suggests that CQ passes directly to WE. The finding is consistent with the premise of the spill over theory (Wilensky, 1960) that posits affective reactions like PNS as a result of one's capability in a social setting (CQ) will be manifested in positive attitudinal outcomes, such as WE.

Implications

Theoretically, this study is the first to examine the effects of CQ on PNS and WE among expatriate academics. Previous studies on CQ which have focused on outcomes commonly studied among business expatriates, for example, cultural adjustment, cultural judgment and decision-making, job performance, and turnover intention. Findings of this study evince that CQ is also capable of predicting workplace outcomes that have received considerable research attention in the domestic setting. WE, in particular, is a very important attitudinal outcome that is relevant in both domestic and across cultures since it has been associated with workplace outcomes, such as in-role and extra-role performance (Halbesleben and Wheeler, 2008; Lauring and Selmer, 2015), job satisfaction (Ramos and Almeida, 2017), and cultural adjustment (Selmer and Lauring, 2016). Similarly, the predictive ability of CQ on PNS is another important theoretical implication of this study. It should be noted that dissatisfaction with basic psychological needs undermines motivation and reduces adjustment and well-being of individuals working in cross-cultural environments (Chen et al., 2015; Deci et al., 2001). This study provides support that CQ works in unison to influence expatriate academics' PNS attained through perceived competence, relatedness, and autonomy when working and living abroad. The mediating role of PNS is another important theoretical contribution of this study. Consistent with findings in domestic studies (Kovjanic et al., 2013; Van den Broeck et al., 2008), PNS is also found to serve as an important underlying mechanism for explaining individual attitude in the quest for well-being in an inter-cultural setting. PNS is another important effective outcome in the intercultural setting that can be studied as the mediator in future research in addition to commonly studied enablers, such as cross-cultural adjustment.

In practical terms, it is important to note that CQ is capable of predicting both PNS and WE among expatriate academics. Specifically, it is found that CQ accounts for greater variance in WE than PNS. First, this observation suggests that universities must have a greater understanding of the set of expected behavior that are needed if the universities want to improve the work outcome of expatriate academics. WE should be included in the performance appraisal of expatriate academics. In this regard, CQ capability development can be treated as an effective intervention to promote WE. Secondly, universities may need to incorporate the assessment on CQ capability in their selection and recruitment process when sourcing for foreign faculty. In the case of expatriate academics, the assessment process should not just focus on traditional recruitment criteria currently used to recruit academics regardless of their background. Different assessment methods should be used for expatriate academics, which focus on intercultural capabilities, like CQ. Self-assessment and later the 360-Degree Feedback using CQS developed by Ang et al. (2007) can be used for this purpose. Thirdly, universities should focus on providing necessary support to expatriate academics to fulfil their basic psychological needs of perceived competence, relatedness, and autonomy. New faculty orientation programs should be made mandatory for newcomers, including foreign faculty, to introduce them to the university community and serve as a platform to provide relevant information, resources, and support for teaching, research, publication, and so on. Finally, the potential applicants themselves should be able to do self-assessment on their perceived job-fit and environment-fit before accepting the job offer. The findings of this study will provide a better understanding of what is required of them to enable them to make the necessary arrangements before their arrival.

CONCLUSION

The key conclusion of this study is that PNS partially mediates the relationship between CQ and WE. In other words, the relationship between CQ and WE is both direct and indirect in direction, mediated through PNS. The current study enhances the cross-cultural management literature, particularly on the management of expatriate academics by incorporating the mediation effect of PNS between the CQ and WE relationship. The evidence on the indirect influence of PNS on the relationship between CQ and WE prove that PNS has a major contribution in the promotion of a positive workplace attitude, like WE. Future researchers are encouraged to further study the overview of the present research findings to other types of global employees.

REFERENCES

Al Ariss, A., & Özbilgin, M. (2010). Understanding self- initiated expatriates: Career experiences of Lebanese self-initiated expatriates in France. *Thunderbird International Business Review*, *52*(4), 275–285. doi:10.1002/tie.20355

Altman, Y., & Shortland, S. (2008). Women and international assignments: Taking stock—A 25-year review. *Human Resource Management*, *47*(2), 199–216. doi:10.1002/hrm.20208

Andresen, M., Biemann, T., & Pattie, M. W. (2015). What makes them move abroad? Reviewing and exploring differences between self-initiated and assigned expatriation. *International Journal of Human Resource Management*, *26*(7), 932–947. doi:10.1080/09585192.2012.669780

Baard, P. P., Deci, E. L., & Ryan, R. M. (2004). A motivational basis of performance and weil-being in two work settings. *Journal of Applied Social Psychology*, *34*(10), 2045–2068. doi:10.1111/j.1559-1816.2004.tb02690.x

Bakker, A. B., & Demerouti, E. (2007). The job demands-resources model: State of the art. *Journal of Managerial Psychology*, *22*(3), 309–328. doi:10.1108/02683940710733115

Biemann, T., & Andresen, M. (2010). Self-initiated foreign expatriates versus assigned expatriates: Two distinct types of international careers? *Journal of Managerial Psychology*, *25*(4), 430–448. doi:10.1108/02683941011035313

Carr, J. E. (2005). Multiple-Baseline Designs Across Participants. *Behavioral Interventions*, *20*(3), 219–224. doi:10.1002/bin.191

Cerdin, J. L., & Selmer, J. (2014). Who is a self-initiated expatriate? Towards conceptual clarity of a common notion. *International Journal of Human Resource Management*, *25*(9), 1281–1301. doi:10.1080/09585192.2013.863793

Chang, Y., & Peng, M. W. (2012). Expatriate knowledge transfer, subsidiary absorptive capacity, and subsidiary performance. National Taiwan University of Science and Technology Hong Kong University of Science and Technology. *Academy of Management Journal*, *55*(4), 927–948. doi:10.5465/amj.2010.0985

Che Rose, R., Sri Ramalu, S., Uli, J., & Kumar, N. (2010). Expatriate Performance in International Assignments: The Role of Cultural Intelligence as Dynamic Intercultural Competency. *International Journal of Business and Management*, *5*(8), 76–85. doi:10.5539/ijbm.v5n8p76

Deci, E. L., & Ryan, R. M. (2000). The "what" and "why" of goal pursuits: Human needs and the self-determination of behavior. *Psychological Inquiry*, *11*(4), 227–268. doi:10.1207/S15327965PLI1104_01

Doherty, N. T. (2013). Understanding the self-initiated expatriate. A review and directions for future research. *International Journal of Management Reviews*, *15*, 447–469. doi:10.1111/ijmr.12005

Doherty, N. T., & Dickmann, M. (2012). Measuring the return on investment in international assignments: An action research approach. *International Journal of Human Resource Management*, *23*(16), 3434–3454. doi:10.1080/09585192.2011.637062

Edstrom, A., & Galbraith, J. R. (1977). Transfer of Managers as a Coordination and Control Strategy in Multinational Organizations. *Cornell Univers.*, *22*(2), 248–263.

Froese, F. J. (2012). Motivation and adjustment of self-initiated expatriates: The case of expatriate academics in South Korea. *International Journal of Human Resource Management*, *23*(6), 1095–1112. doi:10.1080/09585192.2011.561220

Gregersen, H. B., & Black, J. S. (1990). A multifaceted approach to expatriate retention in international assignments. *Group & Organization Management*, *15*(4), 461–485. doi:10.1177/105960119001500409

Halbesleben, J. R. B., & Wheeler, A. R. (2008). The relative roles of engagement and embeddedness in predicting job performance and intention to leave. *Work and Stress*, *22*(3), 242–256. doi:10.1080/02678370802383962

Harzing, A. (2001). Spiders : The Role of Expatriates in Controlling Foreign. *Journal of World Business*, *36*(4), 366–379. doi:10.1016/S1090-9516(01)00061-X

Hippler, T. (2009). Why do they go? Empirical evidence of employees' motives for seeking or accepting relocation. *International Journal of Human Resource Management*, *20*(6), 1381–1401. doi:10.1080/09585190902909889

Holopainen, J., & Björkman, I. (2005). The personal characteristics of the successful expatriate: A critical review of the literature and an empirical investigation. *Personnel Review*, *34*(1), 37–50. doi:10.1108/00483480510578476

Howe-Walsh, L., & Schyns, B. (2010). Self-initiated expatriation: Implications for hrm. *International Journal of Human Resource Management*, *21*(2), 260–273. doi:10.1080/09585190903509571

Ilardi, B. C., Leone, D., Kasser, T., & Ryan, R. M. (1993). Richard m. ryan. *Journal of Applied Social Psychology*, *23*(21), 1789–1805. doi:10.1111/j.1559-1816.1993.tb01066.x

Inkson, K., Arthur, M. B., Pringle, J., & Barry, S. (1997). Expatriate assignment versus overseas experience: Contrasting models of international human resource development. *Journal of World Business*, *32*(4), 351–368. doi:10.1016/S1090-9516(97)90017-1

Jackson, M. O. (2005). The economics of social networks, based on a lecture. *Proceedings of the 9th World Congress of the Econometric Society*, 1–86. http://scholar.google.com/scholar?q=related:fmyMXEu64lQJ:scholar.google.com/&hl=en&num=30&as_sdt=0,5%5Cnpapers2://publication/uuid/C2505DB7-3CD1-410F-BF91-B71C3B22812E

Jokinen, T., Brewster, C., & Suutari, V. (2008). Career capital during international work experiences: Contrasting self-initiated expatriate experiences and assigned expatriation. *International Journal of Human Resource Management*, *19*(6), 979–998. doi:10.1080/09585190802051279

Kaboudarahangi, M., Tahir, O. M., & Kamal, M. (2013). Malaysia's three major ethnic group preferences in creating a malaysian garden identity. *The Australian Geographer*, *44*(2), 197–213. doi:10.1080/00049182.2013.789588

Kovjanic, S., Schuh, S. C., & Jonas, K. (2013). Transformational leadership and performance: An experimental investigation of the mediating effects of basic needs satisfaction and work engagement. *Journal of Occupational and Organizational Psychology*, *86*(4), 543–555. doi:10.1111/joop.12022

Lopes, S. de F., Ramos, M. B., & de Almeida, G. R. (2017). The role of mountains as refugia for biodiversity in Brazilian Caatinga: Conservationist implications. *Tropical Conservation Science*, *10*. Advance online publication. doi:10.1177/1940082917702651

Marylene, G., & Edward, D. (2005). Self-determination theory and work motivation. *Journal of Organizational Behavior*, *26*(4).

Mckenna, S., & Richardson, J. (2007). The increasing complexity of the internationally mobile professional: Issues for research and practice. *Cross Cultural Management*, *14*(4), 307–320. doi:10.1108/13527600710830331

Myers, B., & Pringle, J. K. (2005). Self-initiated foreign experience as accelerated development: Influences of gender. *Journal of World Business*, *40*(4), 421–431. doi:10.1016/j.jwb.2005.08.009

Ng, K. Y., Van Dyne, L., & Ang, S. (2009). From experience to experiential learning: Cultural intelligence as a learning capability for global leader development. *Academy of Management Learning & Education*, *8*(4), 511–526. doi:10.5465/amle.8.4.zqr511

Paik, Y., & Sohn, J. D. (2004). Expatriate managers and MNC's ability to control international subsidiaries: The case of Japanese MNCs. *Journal of World Business*, *39*(1), 61–71. doi:10.1016/j.jwb.2003.08.003

Peltokorpi, V., & Froese, F. J. (2009). Organizational expatriates and self-initiated expatriates: Who adjusts better to work and life in Japan? *International Journal of Human Resource Management*, *20*(5), 1096–1112. doi:10.1080/09585190902850299

Richardson, J., & Mallon, M. (2005). Career interrupted? The case of the self-directed expatriate. *Journal of World Business*, *40*(4), 409–420. doi:10.1016/j.jwb.2005.08.008

Richardson, J., & Mckenna, S. (2002). Leaving and experiencing: Why academics expatriate and how they experience expatriation. *Career Development International*, *7*(2), 67–78. doi:10.1108/13620430210421614

Richardson, J., & McKenna, S. (2003). International experience and academic careers: What do academics have to say? *Personnel Review*, *32*(6), 774-795+802. doi:10.1108/00483480310498710

Richardson, J., & McKenna, S. (2006). Exploring relationships with home and host countries: A study of self-directed expatriates. *Cross Cultural Management*, *13*(1), 6–22. doi:10.1108/13527600610643448

Romanowski, M. H., & Nasser, R. (2015). Identity issues: Expatriate professors teaching and researching in Qatar. *Higher Education*, *69*(4), 653–671. doi:10.100710734-014-9795-0

Ryan, R. M., & Deci, E. L. (2000). Intrinsic and extrinsic motivations: Classic definitions and new directions. *Contemporary Educational Psychology*, *25*(1), 54–67. doi:10.1006/ceps.1999.1020 PMID:10620381

Selmer, J., & Lauring, J. (2010). Self-initiated academic expatriates: Inherent demographics and reasons to expatriate. *European Management Review*, *7*(3), 169–179. doi:10.1057/emr.2010.15

Selmer, J., & Lauring, J. (2013). Cognitive and affective reasons to expatriate and work adjustment of expatriate academics. *International Journal of Cross Cultural Management*, *13*(2), 175–191. doi:10.1177/1470595813485382

Selmer, J., & Lauring, J. (2015). Host country language ability and expatriate adjustment: The moderating effect of language difficulty. *International Journal of Human Resource Management*, *26*(3), 401–420. doi:10.1080/09585192.2011.561238

Selmer, J., Lauring, J., Eleanor, L., & Charlotte, Z. (2016). *Global Talent Management and Staffing in MNEs*. doi:10.1108/S1876-066X20160000032018

Shaffer, M. A., Harrison, D. A., & Matthew Gilley, K. (1999). Dimensions, determinants, and differences in the expatriate adjustment process sixteen to forty percent of assignments. *Journal of International Business Studies*, *30*(3), 557–581. doi:10.1057/palgrave.jibs.8490083

Srivastava, V., & Pandey, P. M. (2012). Effect of process parameters on the performance of EDM process with ultrasonic assisted cryogenically cooled electrode. *Journal of Manufacturing Processes*, *14*(3), 393–402. doi:10.1016/j.jmapro.2012.05.001

Suutari, V., & Brewster, C. (2000). Making their own way: International experience through self-initiated foreign assignments. *Journal of World Business, 35*(4), 417–436. doi:10.1016/S1090-9516(00)00046-8

Suutari, V., Brewster, C., Mäkelä, L., Dickmann, M., & Tornikoski, C. (2018). The effect of international work experience on the career success of expatriates: A comparison of assigned and self-initiated expatriates. *Human Resource Management, 57*(1), 37–54. doi:10.1002/hrm.21827

Swim, J. K., Stern, P. C., Doherty, T. J., Clayton, S., Reser, J. P., Weber, E. U., Gifford, R., & Howard, G. S. (2011). Psychology's contributions to understanding and addressing global climate change. *The American Psychologist, 66*(4), 241–250. doi:10.1037/a0023220 PMID:21553950

Tharenou, P. (2003). The initial development of receptivity to working abroad: Self-initiated international work opportunities in young graduate employees. *Journal of Occupational and Organizational Psychology, 76*(4), 489–515. doi:10.1348/096317903322591604

Tharenou, P., & Caulfield, N. (2010). Will i stay or will i go? Explaining repatriation by self-initiated expatriates. *Academy of Management Journal, 53*(5), 1009–1028. doi:10.5465/amj.2010.54533183

Thorn, K. (2009). The relative importance of motives for international self-initiated mobility. *Career Development International, 14*(5), 441–464. doi:10.1108/13620430910989843

Torbiörn, I. (1994). Operative and strategic use of expatriates in new organizations and market structures. *International Studies of Management & Organization, 24*(3), 5–17. doi:10.1080/00208825.1994.11656634

Trembath, J. L. (2016). The professional lives of expatriate academics: Construct clarity and implications for expatriate management in higher education. *Journal of Global Mobility, 4*(2), 112–130. doi:10.1108/JGM-04-2015-0012

Vallerand, R. J. (2000). Deci and Ryan's self-determination theory: A view from the hierarchical model of intrinsic and extrinsic motivation. *Psychological Inquiry, 11*(4), 312–318.

Van Den Broeck, A., Vansteenkiste, M., De Witte, H., & Lens, W. (2008). Explaining the relationships between job characteristics, burnout, and engagement: The role of basic psychological need satisfaction. *Work and Stress, 22*(3), 277–294. doi:10.1080/02678370802393672

Vansteenkiste, M., Neyrinck, B., Niemiec, C. P., Soenens, B., De Witte, H., & Van Den Broeck, A. (2007). On the relations among work value orientations, psychological need satisfaction and job outcomes: A self-determination theory approach. *Journal of Occupational and Organizational Psychology, 80*(2), 251–277. doi:10.1348/096317906X111024

Yusuf, B. N. M., Zakaria, N., & Abdul-Talib, A. N. (2021). Using social network tools to facilitate cultural adjustment of self-initiated Malaysian female expatriate nurses in Saudi Arabia. *Journal of Infection and Public Health, 14*(3), 380–384. doi:10.1016/j.jiph.2020.11.008 PMID:33621801

Zakaria, N., Abdul-Talib, A. N., & Amelinckx, A. (Eds.). (2020). *Transcending cultural frontiers: practices, challenges, and strategy for international business*. Springer. doi:10.1007/978-981-15-4454-5

Zakaria, N., Abdul-Talib, A. N., & Othman, N. (Eds.). (2016). *Handbook of research on impacts of international business and political affairs on the global economy*. IGI Global. doi:10.4018/978-1-4666-9806-2

Chapter 6
The Impact of Terrorism on Trade in Nigeria and Chad

Isaac Terungwa Terwase
https://orcid.org/0000-0002-9231-8707
Federal University of Kashere, Nigeria

Muhammad Yusuf
Federal University of Kashere, Nigeria

Abubakar Sambo Mohammed
Federal University of Kashere, Nigeria

Safwan Mikaila Sani
Federal University of Kashere, Nigeria

ABSTRACT

The Boko Haram conflict started in Nigeria from a city in the north-eastern part of the country known as Maiduguri in 2009 during the administration of President Umaru Musa Yar'Adua. It was a new thing to Nigeria considering the fact that the country was yet to witness terrorism and its activities. Boko Haram later continued after the death of President Yar'Adua, and they became stronger during the President Jonathan's administration. Boko Haram later transformed from an insurgent group into a terrorist group where they spread from Nigeria to other parts of African countries such as Chad, Niger, and Cameroon. This has it effects, impacts, and consequences on trade in Africa. The objective of this chapter is to draw the impact of terrorism on trade with specific attention to Nigeria and Chad.

INTRODUCTION

Nigeria, indeed, has the largest population in Africa and her population of 201 million stands as the major market for trade and investment in Africa. Several multinational corporations such as the oil and gas sector of the African economy, civil and structural engineering, and automobile companies such as Toyota, Honda, Hyundai, Mercedes Benz, Ford, and Peugeot have their investment in Nigeria and in-

DOI: 10.4018/978-1-7998-9071-3.ch006

deed, Africa. Nigeria has the capacity for the production oil which serves as a yardstick for multinational companies such as Shell, Mobil, Total, and Schlumberger to do business in Nigeria as Africa' largest economy (Terwase, Abdul-Talib & Zengeni, 2014). Nigeria, again serves as a place for cheap labour in as much as the country's resources are sold right from within and equally exported to other countries. In view of the above, terrorism and general insecurity in the country causes panic among the people and foreigners who visit Nigeria and Chad.

The attempt to curtail Boko Haram could not work and it spread to these countries mentioned above. To this regards, Boko Haram equally spread to Chad and the then President of Chad, Idris Debey fought Boko Haram over the years. This chapter therefore, tends to focus on Nigeria and Chad in order to draw it impacts and consequences on trade in the said countries. Many people have lost their lives as a result of the Boko Haram conflict which has bedevilled socio-economic development as well as political development where many international investors fear to invest in the two countries. It is worthy to note that many Nigerians especially in the north-east were forced to leave the country as refugees in Cameroon, Chad and Niger (Okunade, Faluyi & Matambo, 2021). The United Nations department in charge of refugees has data on the number of Nigerians who are staying outside the country as refugees.

The state of insecurity causes fear, psychological trauma, material and human losses, environment degradation, conflict between one group and another, and a state of political and economic instability within a given country or geographical entity. All these mentioned therein, has impact on both local and international trade. Thus, that informed the reason behind this chapter and to foster ways of resolving the said conflict which has lingered for more than a decade now. Maiduguri, the capital city of Borno State, Nigeria cannot be forgotten in history over the thousands of souls that have been lost as a result of the Boko Haram conflict and its effects on cross border conflict to other countries. In the Republic of Chad, the country equally lost hundreds of lives due to the conflict. The Government of Chad fought the terrorist group over her occupation of the Lake Chad and their activities around the Lake Chad basin. The Boko Haram occupied the Lake Chad for economic gains; this is as a result of fishing activities in the Lake Chad which serves as a means of survival for the terrorist group (Ukhuegbe & Fenemigho, 2021).

Nigeria equally benefits from the Lake Chad since it is sharing borders between Nigeria, Cameroon, Chad and Niger. Multi-billion Naira trade activities are usually carried out in the Lake Chad and that also forms a part of interest for the Boko Haram and the Nigerian State. The conflict has thus, affected the businesses within the areas as a result of the activities of the Boko Haram (Onuche & Ogbe, 2021). This has also necessitated the reason behind this chapter since conflict between the Boko Haram and the Nigerian State has spread across borders and it has proven majorly its impact on trade within the coverage area.

This work therefore, has used both primary and secondary data as sources of information for the conduct of this chapter. The work has conducted interviews electronically to source for data. The secondary data has been drawn from books, journals and proceedings, as well as any other available material that served as relevant for the conduct of this chapter. The result has formed part of this chapter and it shall equally contribute to knowledge. This chapter shall bring to the fore, all relevant information that will enhance the resolution to this on-going conflict which has lingered for more than one decade. It is believed that, if both governments of Nigeria and Chad shall come together in truthful desire to end the conflict, its root causes shall be addressed.

The chapter attempts to look into the roots causes of the said conflict, the challenges to the roots factors and the contemporary issues surrounding the on-going conflict. In the past, Nigeria has demonstrated military power in the West African sub-region where she serves as a big brother and was known as giant of Africa militarily. The Nigerian military in the past engaged in peace keeping operations in African countries such as Liberia and Sierra Leon where conflict was resolved in those countries and political stability was restored. These are the issues that triggered the conduct of this chapter believing that, the return of peaceful co-existence in Nigeria and Chad shall contribute to both local and international trade. It shall also contribute to socioeconomic, cultural and political development of these two countries. The chapter shall equally outline areas where terrorism has affected the both countries and it shall draw it consequences to trade especially international trade where much attention shall be focused on. It will therefore open the eyes of the audience where other scholars have not touched in their previous works.

THE ISSUES AND IT IMPACT ON TRADE IN NIGERIA AND CHAD

The Dynamics of Conflict in Africa And Its Impact on Nigeria

The Work of Mayaki (2013) argued that, for African States to move forward, the government of African States needs to showcase transparency in meeting the demands of their people. Governance and State building is a combination of all other actors through partnership with regional, continental and the global communities. On this note, Michailof (2013) assert the need to move out of conflict within the African Continent with the notion that, Africa countries have undergone a series of fragility and conflict which has brought down the progress as well as the growth of the said Africa States. The work posed to see how Africa by 2050 can be placed on the desired level where issues that bedevilled the development of African States can be wiped out in order to achieve the desired good for the people.

In addition, the issue of conflict within the context of this chapter, Yusuf (2013) argued that, the government's inability to bridge the gap between rich and the poor has promoted an environment for the youths to be recruited into the membership of terrorist groups such the Boko Haram since some of these members are poor, and driven within the breeds of poverty. The work also found out that, poverty breeds violence and political corruption which in turn creates conflict. Carl-LeVan (2013) asserts that, the prosecution of the former leader of the Boko Haram, Mohammed Yusuf's killers would pave way for the resolution of the conflict. That the government of Nigeria spent nearly a quarter of her budget on security yet without success since the issue could not be resolved by the Jonathan's led government.

As a matter of fact, the work of Hill (2013) focused on the religious extremism in relation to the study on Boko Haram; it was revealed in the work that, the Boko Haram is allegedly linked to other organizations such as Al Qaeda, and Al Shabaab which operates in Somalia. The work also asserts that the Boko Haram had a sanctuary in Nigeria's bordering countries of Niger and the Republic of Chad. Carl-LeVan (2013) again argued that the Niger Delta rebels were granted Amnesty by the federal government of Nigeria in order to call for peace within the region and that became a tool in resolving the conflict in the Niger Delta. As such, the same Amnesty should be given to the Boko Haram members for cease-fire as called by the politicians especially from the North.

By and large, the Nigerian State is heterogeneous society as a result of different ethnic nationalities both from the North and Southern part of the country. The Southern part of the country especially the Niger-Delta sought for the control of state power and resources. In this regards, Chambers (2013) connotes the views of Chinua Achebe's work; There was A Country: which reviews on how the Igbo people have been marginalized in Nigeria since after the civil war 1967-1970 when the Nigerian leader, General Yakubu Gowon sought to integrate the Igbo people into one Nigeria as an entity. The Nigerian government under the leadership of Gowon pronounced "No victor and No vanquished" after the civil war but yet the Igbo seems to be marginalized without having control of Nigeria's leadership as President after the end of the civil war in 1970.

On the whole, Ekwe-Ekwe (2013) on the other hand, in another book review of Chinua Achebe's work; The Achebean Restoration: concurred that, the Igbo people are the most affected by the Boko Haram attacks in the Northern part of the country. The work also assert that Jonathan's government had sympathizers of the Boko Haram in all the arms of the government functionary such as the Legislative, Executive, and Judiciary arm as well as the Security Forces. The quest for power in Nigeria has neglected the usage of ethnic differences in relation to unity in diversity as source of strength for the country. Hansen and Musa (2013) on this view of ethno-religious difference argued that, Nigerian national identity suffers as a result of ethno-religious weakness which ought to have been used as strong national identity to promote unity in diversity which could be deemed fit for the progress of the country.

In another development, the work of Agbiboa (2013) argued that religion is the major tool that is used in dividing the people through the quest for national identity, as such; past leaders like General Ibrahim Babangida also used religion as a tool in as much as the country is multi-religious in nature. Babangida during his rule in office as the country's Head of State, he registered Nigeria under the Organization of Islamic Country (OIC) and placed the country under a single religious nation, thus undermined the fact that Nigeria is a multi-religious country. Agbiboa and Maiangwa (2013) in their work on Boko Haram, religion and violence, seek to study the non-killing approach and resolving the trend of violence in the Northern part of the country, they found out that Boko Haram attacks goes beyond killing and bombing of worship centers such as the case of St. Theresa's Catholic Church in Madala, Suleja Local Government of Niger State and they extended their attacks to International Institutions such as the bombing of United Nations building in Abuja.

Given these points, Agbiboa and Maiangwa (2013) noted that, many diplomats and Nigerian citizens were killed in the bombing of the UN building, in August, 2011, as they were affected. The work of Bartusevicius (2013) observed that, some of the issues that motivate people in carrying arms against the government or a particular society is as a result of the feeling that they are unequal with other people of the same society due to lack of access to education, health facilities, and as well as social services. To some, there is no opportunity for them to participate in politics and as such they become available in participating or taking arms against the government.

Equally important, Ndlovu-Gatsheni (2012) examined the issues that relates to violence in African countries and the work found that, violence in African countries are derived from the differences in races, ethnicities, tribes and religion with the understanding that, such issues are traced to colonial, post-colonial and the understanding of violence between separates ideologies such as capitalist and socialist ideological background. On the other hand, Salaam (2012) posits that, issues such as poverty, mass illiteracy, unemployment, endemic corruption, and social-political marginalization are the factors which facilitates the availability of youths to engage in the insurgency activities against the people and the government in power.

As shown above, the work of Solomon (2012) on Counter Terrorism in Nigeria: portrays that, the deep problems and difficulties in countering the Boko Haram attacks in Nigeria remains difficult as the group found her sympathizers right within the President Jonathan's led government whom some are in the executive arm of government, some in the legislative arm of government and as well as in the judiciary thus, becoming so difficult to counter the group. The work also noted that, the armed forces and as well as the police force is also infiltrated by the Boko Haram since their sympathizers are within these government agencies. This shows that, even some who are employed by the government and working for the government are sympathizers of the Boko Haram group and they could be passing information to them.

Under those circumstances, Onapajo, Uzodike and Whetho (2012) argued that, the Boko Haram has their members not only from Nigeria but also outside the Nigerian State to countries such as Cameroon, Niger, Sudan and Chad. Their work also connotes the Boko Haram to be worse than the Nigerian civil war of 1967-1970. The work of Isumonah (2012) examined the paper titled: Armed Society in Niger Delta; in his study, the work found out that, lack of development of the Niger Delta led to the carrying of arms against the Nigerian State by the Niger Delta militants. Findings from the work also revealed that, the Niger Delta leaders preferred paying the strongmen, the youths in that region to protect their personal interest instead of the leaders using the available public resources to developed the Niger Delta region.

In addition, Isumonah (2012) further suggest that, social and political issues that led to the demand for arms should be tackled by the government in order to have an environment or region that is free of militants and secured. The work also noted the fact that, a wasteful of resources in the name of securing the Niger Delta region became the order of the day during the attack against the government and the communities located within the region. Other issues that are needed to be taken care of and should not be underestimated include the use social media work, it was found that there is security implication to the usage of social media network as it portrait potential security threat to the Nigerian polity such as the Biafra online discourses which is aimed at disintegrating from the Nigerian State to form or established another entity to be called the Republic of Biafra through their advocacy on social media network (Chiluwa, 2012).

Consequently, Magbadelo (2012) argued that, the transformation of the Nigerian defence would help the country. In this regard, the work posits for a repositioning of the Nigerian military to meet up the current challenges in securing the country and that would require re-equipping of the military institution and implementing the set goals to transform the military force. That would help in safe-guarding the polity. Aghedo (2012) observed that, militancy and the case of the Niger Delta crisis was fuelled by environmental insecurity in the region where those areas that were affected by oil spillage from the activities of the oil industries within the region and that spoilt their land which farming became difficult. The work also found that, lack of development of the region and issues such as human rights violation in as much as the region is strategic to the growth of Nigeria's economy since it is the oil producing area for the country. Such issues led to the carrying of arms against the Federal Government of Nigeria by the youths from the Niger Delta region.

All things considered, a review on inter-religious conflict as argued in the work of Rakodi (2012) indicates that, inter-religious conflict occurs as a result of the different religious belief. It is then motivated and used as a tool in the quest for power and resource control. Some politicians thus, found religion as a tool for fighting political gains and that may lead to the destruction of properties and killing of people. Religion can serve as a tool to separate the masses along that line since people with different identities stay together in a complex society or environment.

In addition, the work of Waldek and Jayasekara (2011) sought for redress on the issue of ethnicity and religion in relation to the Boko Haram group whom are known as Islamist extremist. Their work found out that, the members of the Boko Haram got their weapons through the Nigerian bordering States of Chad, Cameroon and Niger. They use the weapons in engaging in activities such as bombing, usage of suicide bombers who then engage in using explosive detonation.

By and large, Terwase, Abdul-Talib & Zengeni (2015), Terwase, Abdul-Talib, Siben, Puldu & Adesina (2017) in their work argued that, ECOWAS countries suffer as a result of poor governance and weak institutions. On the other hand, Mayaki (2010) observed that, African countries can drive forward through innovations and exchange of knowledge. However, the work of Jackson (2007) also pointed out that, ECOWAS countries and indeed the Nigerian State, suffer as result of poor governance, security challenges which are factored in the context of poverty, corruption, unemployment, government's failure to deliver basic services to the people, weak institution and religious crisis between the Christians and the Muslims and that serve a threat to national security.

In the same way, the work of Pham (2012) attributes the factors that led to the re-emergence of Boko Haram in late 2010 due to the support of some Northern Nigeria's marginalized Muslims, these factors revolts around social, economic, religious and political issues concerning Northern Nigeria. There is a great concern on the issue of the Boko Haram since their attacks increased from 2011 with brutal killings of innocent souls across board in the Northern part of the country where men and women, young and old, children both in schools and out of school have been victims of the Boko Haram's attacks. Their attacks are not limited to the public alone but it cut across private and public institutions, they may have equally extended their links to other parts of Africa in a reach to other terrorist groups.

In addition, Anyadike (2013) observed that, Boko Haram has constituted not only threat to security in the Northern part of the country but their formation serves as threat to national security since their attacks represents breaking out of a harmonious co-existence of the Nigerian State. The work further explained that, socio-economic, religious issues and political factors are what fuelled the conflict in the Northern part of the country where the Boko Haram attacks has been explained as problems that led to their emergence. The work also explained, President Jonathan had noted that, Boko Haram infiltrated the Nigerian government as well as the Nigerian security agencies, the military inclusive which becomes very difficult in defeating the group.

It is also noted that, the Boko Haram seek to take control of the political machinery of the Nigerian state in order to Islamized the country through imposture of sharia legal code, however, on her membership, the Boko Haram draws her followership and supporters amongst the unemployed graduates, the youths living in poverty driven environments from the Northern part of the country (Agbiboa, 2013). The continuous attacks on the people also suggest the deep-seated socioeconomic and political grievances on the part of the Boko Haram members against the government which are rooted in poor governance and corruption.

Generally speaking, Agbiboa (2013) also argued that, the Boko Haram before launching her attacks and waging war against the government in 2009, the introduction of a new law for all motorcyclists in Nigeria to wear crash-helmets which was rejected by the Boko Haram members later became the beginning of a crash between the Boko Haram and the Nigerian security agencies as it started in Bauchi State. This development became the beginning of insurgency in 2009 as related to the Boko Haram group whom their leader was later killed by the security force in Maiduguri, Borno State. The work also noted that, Boko Haram membership cut across bankers, the unemployed graduates, political elites, university lecturers, and migrants from the bordering countries with Nigeria.

As a matter of fact, the work of Suleiman and Karim (2015) on the other hand focused on bad governance and corruption as a triggered tool that led to the rise of the Boko Haram in the Northern part of the country. Their work raised issues such as poverty, relating to 75% of the population of the people who are living the Northern part of the country as those living in abject poverty and as such, cited the former National Chairman of the then ruling political party, the People's Democratic Party (PDP), Bamanga Tukur, who related the Boko Haram spring in the North as a people whom out of hunger, became aggrieved and angered against government's inability to solve the prevailing issues raised.

Consequently, some of the issues that also triggered the rise of Boko Haram membership include poor infrastructure in the Northern of the country such as poor electricity supply, poor supply of health care facilities within the region, inadequate number of Medical Doctors to work in the hospitals in the Northern states compared to the Southern states in Nigeria. Issues such as youth's unemployment in the Northern part of the country, while on the part of the leaderships in some part of the Northern states were alleged of corrupt charges and were waiting trials under charges by the Economic and Financial Crimes Commission (Suleiman and Karim, 2015).

By and large, Uzodike and Maiangwa (2012) argued that, state failure on the part of the government led to the rise of the Boko Haram in the Northern part of the country citing issues such as poverty, unproductive government agencies which mostly known as weak institutions, the high level of under-development of the Northern region as contribution to the rise of the insurgency in the North. Their work further explained the deepening issue that divide the country which are lined within the context of ethnicity, religion, and regional divides. This notwithstanding, the work also focused on the notion that, the rise of the Boko Haram insurgency is derived from the context that of endemic corruption and the government failure to address the said issues raised above which pervasive poverty, youths who are unemployed and the underdevelopment of the Northern region are part of. The works of Zakaria, Abdul-Talib & Amelinckx (2020), Zakaria, Abdul-Talib & Othman (2016), Hashim, Bakar & Abdul-Talib (2010) all illustrated how challenges of transcending cultural frontiers can affect International Business irrespective of the country involved.

As shown above, on the formation of the Boko Haram group, Uzodike and Maiangwa (2012) further cited the work of Gusau (2009) who argued that, the group was formed as an evangelic group by some of the Muslim students from the University of Maiduguri, these were students who felt dissatisfied with Western Education and its culture in totality of which their ideology also defers from the context of Western Education. The work also explains as citing one of the leaders of Boko Haram, Mallam Sanni Umaru who defers on what Western Education is, referring to it as forbidden and as such, their belief is centred on Islamic culture as supreme.

In the same way, as relating to the political divide between the North and South, Uzodike and Maiangwa (2012) also reveals the dividing factor as dated back to the colonial rule where the colonials masters had taken their time to developed the Southern part of the country unlike the Northern part was left undeveloped. The argued in their work as referring to the vested resources in developing the Southern part of the country through establishing schools, as well as promotion the industrial base through construction of light industries in the South. Such level of development in the South led to the North staging behind and undeveloped. Another dimension is that of the Christians and Muslims divide which is characterized under religious divide where the majority of those in the North are Muslims and that of the South, Christians.

On the whole, this divide is what has been expressed in the context of Nigeria's leadership during the return to democratic government in 1999. Again, Uzodike and Maiangwa (2012) viewed this as a turning point to religious violence as in the case of the electoral violence that greeted the elections that brought in President Jonathan in 2011 as the winner of the presidential elections as opposed by some Northern youths of Muslim faith who took to the street in protest against the election of Jonathan into power to rule from 2011-2015.

Given these points, Uzodike and Maiangwa (2012) again cited another work in giving more light to the Boko Haram uprising in the North after the presidential elections that was won by President Jonathan as citing Vanguard Newspaper (February 13, 2012) in relation to political sponsorship of the

Boko Haram group to expand and to serve as a tool in fighting against the Nigerian state and making the country ungovernable.

In the past, the Nigerian state suffered disintegration when some South-easterners were demanding for the soul of the country and that led Nigeria through a civil war. Agbiboa (2013) connotes that, the former Nigeria President, Goodluck Jonathan had described the attacks lunched by the Boko Haram during his tenure as the worst attack on the Nigerian State and even worse than the dreaded civil war 1967-1970. It was a period when the country was set in division through the secession of the present South-East from the Nigerian State.

Under those circumstances, in the case of the Boko Haram, it is more than the three years of civil war 1967-1970 since their attacks started from 2009 to date (2021) and even still on-going which one does not have a cruel of when the conflict would be resolved. Literature have it that, many attempts have been made on the part of the government to resolve the crisis yet, the attacks continues which serves as the most dreaded attacks on the soul of the Nigerian State and as well as threat to national security.

Consequently, Agbiboa (2013) further argued in his work on understanding the religious terrorism that, the Nigerian State is predominantly divided into two along religious lines. As such, the Muslims are predominantly in the Northern part of the country as against the number of Christian Northerners who less in number from the North. The Christians on the other hand, dominates the Southern part of the country and this shows that they are much more in number from the Southern part as against the Muslims within that region. This division is sharply created and it toes the political line in another dimension. The Boko Haram from the angle of religious terrorist group, forged attacks on the country since their inception in 2009 following series of fighting against the government of Nigeria, their attacks are more than any other armed group from the time of Nigeria's independence to date under study.

On the whole, this has called for a serious concern since their attacks are not limited to the shows of Nigeria alone and even if it were only Nigeria, the country serves as a strategic state in Africa with her population of more than 170 million people and having the largest population in Africa (Gerland, Raftery, Sevcikova, Li, Gu, Spoorenberg, Alkema, Fosdick, Chunn, Lalic, Bay, Buettner, Heilig and Wilmoth, 2014). It is no longer news that they country is under attacks. There have been multiple attacks and fight in terms of counter-terrorism which also a times result into crossfire between the Boko Haram group and the Nigerian security agencies on their part to restore peace (Agbiboa, 2013).

By and large, religion again has a way of being used as a tool in even appointing political officers in power as to the case of Nigeria, Agbiboa and Maiangwa (2013) argued in their work on towards a non-killing approach as how the case of religion is also a determinant factor even in contesting for political positions in the country. This type of divide is seen when periods of elections draws nearer and it becomes real when such positions are being contested by two or more people whom the factor comes into play of what religion is he or she? The dividing line here is the notion of either he or she is a Christian or Muslim.

Given these points, Terwase, Adesina, Puldu & Abdul-Talib (2018) argued that, Unity of the African people can only be sustained when the interest of the people is protected by the government. The chapter has therefore, discussed clearly the issues that led to the continuous attacks by the Boko Haram against the Nigerian State (Terwase, Abdul-Talib & Zengeni, 2015). The chapter, thus, relates as the Boko Haram further spread to under countries such as Chad, Niger and Cameroon. In view of these, the activities of Boko Haram have negative impact on Trade in Nigeria and Chad under study.

INTERNALLY DISPLACED PERSONS CAMPS

The issue of internally displaced persons (IDP) came in the northern part of the country as a result of Boko Haram terrorists' attacks which particularly started in 2009 even though they were in existence through their formation in 2002 (Terwase, Abdul-Talib, Zengeni, & Terwase, 2015). The Boko Haram has destroyed many properties belonging to the government of Nigeria especially the security agencies where the bombed the Nigeria Police Headquarters in Abuja and several attacks that were focused on military formations in different parts of the North. They attacked military barracks in different locations in the North and they equally attacked so many communities in the North as well.

These actions by the Boko Haram led to the displacement of many Nigerians especially those in the rural communities. According to United Nations High Commissioner for Refugees (2021) through the NEMA, there are about 2,191,193 Nigerians who are currently living in the IDP's camps in different part of the country. This number of displaced persons shows the magnitude of the conflict between the Boko Haram and the Nigerian State. In view of that, a respondent reveals:

We are truly suffering from the attacks by the Boko Haram terrorists whose activities have crippled our economic well-being since they started their attacks in 2009. Most of us from the rural communities are displaced especially from Borno State, Yobe State and Adamawa State. They killed many people in the villages and the rural communities which were not protected by the Nigerian security agencies. As a result, we left our farmlands and as well as our crops alongside our animals that we were keeping. It is quite unfortunates that we lost our businesses to Boko Haram terrorism.

On the other hand, in respect to the challenges and impact of Boko Haram conflict between the Nigerian government on how it affects the trade in Nigeria and the Republic of Chad since the attacks escalated from Nigeria to Niger, Chad and Cameroon, another respondent concurred that:

We were buying and selling fishes from the Lake Chad which was our major sources of revenue. Fishing business from the Lake Chad created a wide of market for us since people were coming from Maiduguri, Kano, Abuja, Makurdi, Enugu and other parts of the country to buy fish from us. In some instances, the countries that shares border along the Lake Chad such as Chad, Niger and Cameroon, all engaged in the fishing business but today, Baga town which was known for fishing business has been deserted because of the Boko Haram activities.

It is indeed, not just the issue of internally displaced persons, but other issues such as job losses, human killings, destruction of properties, issues related to refugees staying in Cameroon and Niger as well as Chad remains as factors impacting negatively on trade in Nigeria and Chad. To this note, another respondent opined that:

Nigeria and Chad are sharing boundary alongside Cameroon and Niger where they necked at the Lake Chad at the Northern parts of Nigeria and Cameroon, while on the Southern parts of Niger and Chad. This whole environment which is demarcated by the Lake Chad basin is an active business environment which was known for international trade before the arrival of Boko Haram terrorism. Many Nigerians and Chadians as well as Cameroonians were known to be active partners in respect to fishing business. It was form of international trade but today, terrorism has created a vacuum in the business since many business men and women are afraid of doing business in the said environment. This has absolutely affected trade but the two countries of Nigeria and Chad. Many people are internally displaced in Nigeria and Chad. We also have refugees from Nigeria living in Chad, Cameroon and Niger.

Table 1. IDP population by country

Country of origin	Source	Data date	Population
Nigeria	*IOM, NEMA*	3 Aug 2021	**2,191,193**
Chad	*IOM*	31 Jul 2021	**401,511**
Cameroon	*IOM*	31 Jul 2021	**321,886**
Niger	*Government*	30 Jun 2021	**121,850**

Source: UNHCR, Government (2021)

REFUGEE CAMPS

According to the United Nations High Commissioner for Refugees (2021) there are 317,773 Nigerians who are refugees in Chad, Cameroon and Niger. These Nigerians are victims of Boko Haram terrorists who attacked different villages and communities in Nigeria. The Boko Haram terrorist has waged war on the Nigerian state since 2009 and they are still attacking the country up to date (2021) and that has truly created a sense of fear in the affected areas in Nigeria and its environs. This chapter thus, present a picture of the population of Nigerians who are still outside Nigeria as refugees in Niger with a total population of 182,730 Nigerians, those living in Cameroon to a population of 118,409 Nigerians and those camping in Chad to a population of 16,634 Nigerians as seen the table 2 below. The United Nations High Commissioner for Refugees (UNHCR) has worked in conjunction with the Nigerian Government, the Cameroonian Government, the Republic of Niger and Republic of Chad for many years in respect to the Boko Haram attacks which started since 2009 in Nigeria.

Thus, they have been keeping data on both refugees and Internally Displaced Persons (UNHCR, 2021). The table 2 shows the number of Nigerians living in Chad, Cameroon and Niger to a total number of 317,773 of whom they were displaced from their various homes and places of origin. According to Terwase, Terwase, Puldu & Abdul-Talib (2018) connotes that some of these people who are displaced are equally traumatize by the event of things ranging from killing of their loved family members, friends and associates, kidnapping of school girls out of secondary school, destruction of properties and destruction of agricultural products, as well as displacement of farmers from different parts of Nigeria.

Table 2. Nigerian refugees in Chad, Cameroon and Niger

Location name	Source	Data date	Percentage	Population
Niger	*UNHCR, Government*	30 Jun 2021	57.5%	**182,730**
Cameroon	*UNHCR, Government*	31 Jul 2021	37.3%	**118,409**
Chad	*UNHCR, Government*	31 Jul 2021	5.2%	**16,634**

Source: UNHCR, Government (2021).
Total Population of 317,773
Refugees by country of asylum

In respect to the various attacks on the Nigerian state and Chad which are the focus point of this chapter, different respondents opined that:

We have suffered several attacks by the Boko Haram since the conflict started in 2009 and many Nigerians today are in Cameroon, Chad and Niger as a result of the conflict. We are pleading with both the Nigerian government and the international community to come to our aid and resolve the conflict between the Boko Haram and the Nigerian government since the conflict started in Nigeria and not in Chad, Niger or Cameroon. We want to return back to Nigeria peacefully and we do not want war in Nigeria. Let the Nigerian government resolve the conflict just as she did during the President Yar'Adua's administration where the government was able to resolve the conflict between the government and the Niger-Delta militants.

Another respondent also reveals that:

We have lost our businesses as a result of the conflict since many of us could not go back to the businesses that we were doing. Some of us were selling goods and products that were derived from the farm. We totally lost it because no one wants to die as a result of the attacks by the Boko Haram. Indeed, many people have been killed by the Boko Haram and they are gone into the eternity. They won't come back again to life. That is how painful it is but we do not have power to stop these attacks on our own. The government on her part needs the political will to do so. Human lives are precious and the country benefits more when her citizens are living in peace. How can we do business when the country is in crisis? It is not possible because we need political stability in Nigeria and Chad to do business.

A picture of Nigerians as refugees' to attend a meeting in Dar es Salam camp, Chad, January 2019.

Figure 1.
Source: UNHCR /Aristophane Ngargoune (2019)

HUMAN KILLINGS

There are many Nigerians and Chadians who have lost their lives because of the activities of the Boko Haram since its inception in 2009 when they started their attacks on the Nigerian State. Boko haram has killed so many Nigerians both the military and the civilians in different parts of the country. So many communities are affected and that has really created the scenario where some people who survived became refugees in other countries and to some, they are in Nigeria as internally displaced persons (Terwase, Abdul-Talib, Zengeni & Terwase, 2015). Several scholars have written on the issue of these killings but the conflict is still on-going. Hence, it still necessitates more researches on its impact Boko Haram terrorism on trade in Nigeria and Chad. There is no amount of money that can be paid for the lives of human beings who are killed deliberately by a group of insurgents or terrorists. We cannot pay any family any money and it will be enough.

Trade cannot survive in a crisis zone and that is to say, doing business internationally across borders is equally important to have a peaceful environment. Therefore, political stability is very important and Nigeria needs such for foreign investors to come do business in Nigeria. During the administration of President Jonathan, many Nigerians were killed especially before the 2015 general elections in Nigeria. President Jonathan made it clearly that his ambition is not worth the blood of any Nigerian and his quest to hand over power before the announcement of the outcome of the presidential elections by the then INEC Chairman Professor Attahiru Jega was a formidable achievement by President Jonathan in order to avoid bloodshed in Nigeria.

There was serious tension in the country considering the fact that the North wanted a shift in power from the South to the North since President Jonathan is from the Southern part of the country. Boko Haram in most of their messages that were released through videos never wanted President Jonathan in power. The power tussle was on the bases that power had remained in the southern part of the country since 1999 during the return to civilian administration. The then President Obasanjo ruled from 1999 to 2007 as a Southerner. President Yar'Adua stayed in power from 2007 to 2010 and he died, that brought about power shift back to the southern part of the country under President Jonathan who stayed till 2015 (Mohammed, 2021). During the said period of President Jonathan's administration, so many Nigerians and other nationals were killed by the Boko Haram in many communities across the Northern Nigeria. In respect to the killings, a respondent from the field connotes that:

It is very sad to mention that Nigeria has become what it is today. When we were growing up, towns like Maiduguri, Bama and Baga were populated with many people in such a way that we felt nothing evil will befall these areas. Borno State was known as home of peace but today there is no peace in Borno State especially our rural areas. Many people in Borno and Yobe have been killed by Boko Haram even people from Adamawa communities. We lost so many families to Boko Haram terrorism. We are actually helpless when we think of the lives that we have lost to Boko Haram.

IMPACT ON FOOD SECURITY

The issue of food security is very important to any given country because of her citizens. Some countries do import food just to make sure her citizens won't suffer. It's actually the responsibility of the government to protect her citizens and the country in generally to avoid both internal and external attacks (Terwase,

Terwase, Puldu & Abdul-Talib, 2018). As such, Boko Haram terrorism has made so many farmers in the Northeast especially in Yobe State, Abamawa State and Borno State to abandon their respective farms as a result of the fear of the unknown. Thus, many people in the villages are no longer farming. They are mostly in different Internally Displaced Person's camps. It's very challenging for them as a people. The situation is also applicable to the Republic of Chad in those communities where the conflict has affected the rural dwellers and it serves as an obstacle for the farmers who could no longer return back to their farms.

You can see on the media how the conflict between the Boko Haram and the Nigerian State has affected us negatively and that has led us to the camp where we are now. We are no longer farming on our farmlands. Some of our families are refugees in Chad and Cameroon because of the conflict. How do we trade between the Chadians and Nigerians when we are scattered all over in different camps? Sincerely, we are saddled with the present situation Nigeria. People no longer come from Chad to buy our farm products because of the conflict and no one wants to be killed by the Boko Haram.

On the other hand, some of the farmers who were interviewed on the subject of food security responded that:

How can Nigeria survive without food? Food is the major source of human survival and without it many people have lost their lives even as a result of hunger. When you do not have food to eat it becomes a problem. Hunger is no respecter of any man or woman. When you are hungry, you must eat food. Nigeria as a nation needs to feed her citizens and that is why the issue of food security is very paramount to the country. Indeed, Nigeria must protect her people and those who are professional farmers must go back to the farm so that Nigeria can have sufficient food security. When we have enough, we can equally export to other countries and that will serves as another source of foreign exchange earnings for the country at large.

When a state of insecurity continues, it is difficult to trade between one group and another, one country and another, and that is exactly the situation between Nigeria and Chad in those areas that are affected by insecurity. Everyone wants to survive and none wants to be killed by terrorist group either in Nigeria or Chad.

CONCLUSION

This chapter has contributed to knowledge on the various issues that led to Boko Haram attacks in Nigeria and how the attacks later spread to other countries like Chad, Niger and Cameroon. It further established that, the conflict has affected the well-being of the people in Nigeria and Chad especially in the area of trade which is the main focused of the chapter. The work therefore, employs the use of dialogue in resolving the conflict between the Boko Haram and the Nigerian government.

REFERENCES

Agbiboa, D. E. (2013). No retreat, no surrender: Understanding the religious terrorism of Boko Haram in Nigeria. *African Study Monographs*, *34*(2), 65–84.

Agbiboa, D. E. (2013). Why Boko Haram exists: The relative deprivation perspective. *African Conflict and Peacebuilding Review*, *3*(1), 144–157. doi:10.2979/africonfpeacrevi.3.1.144

Agbiboa, D. E., & Maiangwa, B. (2013). Boko Haram, religious violence, and the crisis of national identity in Nigeria: Towards a non-killing approach. *Journal of Developing Societies*, *29*(4), 379–403. doi:10.1177/0169796X13503198

Aghedo, I. (2012). Winning the war, losing the peace: Amnesty and the challenges of post- conflict peace-building in the Niger delta, Nigeria. *Journal of Asian and African Studies*, *48*(3), 267–280. doi:10.1177/0021909612453987

Anyadike, N. O. (2013). Boko Haram and national security challenges in Nigeria: Causes and solutions. *Journal of Economics and Sustainable Development*, *4*(5).

Bartusevicius, H. (2013). The inequality-conflict nexus re-examined: Income, education and popular rebellions. *Journal of Peace Research*, *51*(1), 35–50. doi:10.1177/0022343313503179

Carl-LeVan, A. (2013). Sectarian rebellions in post-transition Nigeria compared. *Journal of Intervention and Statebuilding*, *7*(3), 335–352. doi:10.1080/17502977.2013.783999

Chambers, D. B. (2013). *There* was a country: Achebe's final work. *Journal of Asian and African Studies*, *48*(6), 752–759. doi:10.1177/0021909613506454

Chiluwa, I. (2012). Social media networks and the discourse of resistance: A sociolinguistic CDA of Biafra Online discourses. *Discourse & Society*, *23*(3), 217–244. doi:10.1177/0957926511433478

Ekwe-Ekwe, H. (2013). The Achebean restoration. *Journal of Asian and African Studies*, *48*(6), 698–709. doi:10.1177/0021909613506485

Hansen, W. W., & Musa, U. A. (2013). Fanon, the wretched and Boko Haram. *Journal of Asian and African Studies*, *48*(3), 281–296. doi:10.1177/0021909612467277

Hashim, F., Bakar, A. R. A., & Abdul-Talib, A. N. (2010). *International Business* (2nd ed.). Oxford Fajar Press.

Hill, J. N. C. (2013). Religious extremism in northern Nigeria past and present: Parallels between the Pseudo-Tijanis and Boko Haram. *The Round Table: The Commonwealth Journal of International Affairs*, *102*(3), 235–244. doi:10.1080/00358533.2013.796146

Isumonah, V. A. (2012). Armed society in the Niger Delta. *Armed Forces and Society*, *39*(2), 331–358. doi:10.1177/0095327X12446925

Jackson, A. (2007). Nigeria: A security overview. *The Round Table: The Commonwealth Journal of International Affairs*, *96*(392), 587–603. doi:10.1080/00358530701626040

Magbadelo, J. O. (2012). Defence transformation in Nigeria: A critical issue for national security concerns. *India Quarterly. Journal of International Affairs, 68*(3), 251–266. doi:10.1177/0974928412454603

Mayaki, I. A. (2010). *South-South mutual learning: A priority for national capacity development in Africa.* Retrieved from /WBI/Resources/213798-1286217829056/mayaki.pdf

Michailof, S. (2013). Africa 2050: Jobs and prosperity in a multipolar global economy moving out of fragility and conflict. *Global Journal of Emerging Market Economies, 5*(2), 117–149. doi:10.1177/0974910113494537

Mohammed, K. (2021). The state and the fight against Boko Haram insurgency in Nigeria. In *The Routledge Handbook of Counterterrorism and Counterinsurgency in Africa* (pp. 395–407). Routledge. doi:10.4324/9781351271929-26

Ndlovu-Gatsheni, S. J. (2012). Beyond the equator there are no sins: Coloniality and violence in Africa. *Journal of Developing Societies, 28*(419), 419–440. Advance online publication. doi:10.1177/0169796X12463143

Okunade, S. K., Faluyi, O. T., & Matambo, E. (2021). Evolving patterns of insurgency in Southern and West Africa: Refocusing the Boko Haram lens on Mozambique. *African Security Review*, •••, 1–17. doi:10.1080/10246029.2021.1959360

Onapajo, H., Uzodike, U. O., & Whetho, A. (2012). Boko Haram terrorism in Nigeria: The international dimension. *South African Journal of International Affairs, 19*(3), 337–357. doi:10.1080/10220461.2012.740319

Onuche, U., & Ogbe, F. G. (2021). Comparative analysis of Nigeria's aquaculture and capture fisheries development across different policy regimes from 1960 to 2016: A case for an inclusive and sustainable fisheries development. *University-Led Knowledge and Innovation for Sustainable Development*, 143.

Pham, J. P. (2012, April). *Boko Haram's evolving threat, African security briefs.* Retrieved https://www.questia.com/read/1P3-2711932791/boko-haram-s-evolving-threat

Rakodi, C. (2012). Inter-religious violence and its aftermath: Insights from Indian and Nigerian cities. *Journal of Asian and African Studies, 48*(5), 557-576. DOI: 10.1177/0021909612464339

Salaam, A. O. (2012). Boko Haram: Beyond religious fanaticism. *Journal of Policing, Intelligence and Counter Terrorism, 7*(2), 147-162. DOI: .2012.719096 doi:10.1080/18335330

Solomon, H. (2012). Counter-terrorism in Nigeria. *RUSI Journal, 157*(4), 6–11. doi:10.1080/03071847.2012.714183

Suleiman, M. N., & Karim, M. A. (2015). Cycle of bad governance and corruption: The rise of Boko Haram in Nigeria. *SAGE Open, 5*(1), 1–11. doi:10.1177/2158244015576053

Terwase, I. T., Abdul-Talib, A. N., Siben, N. E., Puldu, G. S., & Adesina, O. S. (2017). The AU/Nepad peace and security governance in Africa. *Otoritas: Jurnal Ilmu Pemerintahan, 7*(2), 93–99. doi:10.26618/ojip.v7i2.825

Terwase, I. T., Abdul-Talib, A. N., & Zengeni, K. T. (2014). Nigeria, Africa's largest economy: International business perspective. *International Journal of Management Sciences*, *3*(7), 534–543.

Terwase, I. T., Abdul-Talib, A. N., & Zengeni, K. T. (2015). The role of ECOWAS on economic governance, peace and security perspectives in West Africa. *Mediterranean Journal of Social Sciences*, *6*(3), 257. doi:10.5901/mjss.2015.v6n3p257

Terwase, I. T., Abdul-Talib, A. N., Zengeni, K. T., & Terwase, J. M. (2015). The psychological trauma on Boko Haram victims in Nigeria: Conflict resolution perspective. *Mediterranean Journal of Social Sciences*, *6*(S4), 519-519.

Terwase, I. T., Adesina, O. S., Puldu, G. S., & Abdul-Talib, A. N. (2018). The role of ecowas on peace and conflict resolution in Nigeria and Gambia. *IRA-. International Journal of Management and Social Sciences*, *12*(3), 55–61.

Terwase, J. M., Terwase, I. T., Puldu, G. S., & Abdul Talib, A. N. (2018). Unemployment, psychological trauma, militancy and Boko Haram conflict in Nigeria. IRA. *International Journal of Education and Multidisciplinary Studies*, *13*(3), 27–40. doi:10.21013/jems.v13.n3.p1

Ukhuegbe, S., & Fenemigho, A. I. (2021). Determining the termination of a non-international armed conflict: an analysis of the Boko Haram insurgency in northern Nigeria. In *Nigerian Yearbook of International Law 2018/2019* (pp. 299–327). Springer. doi:10.1007/978-3-030-69594-1_14

UNHCR. (2021). *Nigeria Emergency*. Retrieved from https://www.unhcr.org/afr/nigeria-emergency.html

Uzodike, U. O., & Maiangwa, B. (2012). Boko Haram terrorism in Nigeria: Causal factors and central problematic. *African Renaissance*, *9*(1), 91–118.

Waldek, L., & Jayasekara, S. (2011). Boko Haram: The evolution of Islamist extremism in Nigeria. *Journal of Policing. Intelligence and Counter Terrorism*, *6*(2), 168–178. doi:10.1080/18335330.2011.605217

Yakubu, M. J., & Falode, A. J. (2021). Analyzing Nigerian army-Boko Haram's conflict through the prisms of Marx's theory of economic determinism. *Društvene i humanističke studije*, *6*(3), 299-320.

Yusuf, H. O. (2013). Harvest of violence: The neglect of basic rights and the Boko Haram insurgency in Nigeria. *Critical Studies on Terrorism*, *6*(3), 371–391. doi:10.1080/17539153.2013.835528

Zakaria, N., Abdul-Talib, A. N., & Amelinckx, A. (Eds.). (2020). *Transcending Cultural Frontiers: Practices, Challenges, and Strategy for International Business*. Springer. doi:10.1007/978-981-15-4454-5

Zakaria, N., Abdul-Talib, A. N., & Amelinckx, A. (2020). Advancing Cultural Frontiers to Champion Global Business in Emerging Markets. *Transcending Cultural Frontiers*, 1–10.

Zakaria, N., Abdul-Talib, A. N., & Othman, N. (Eds.). (2016). *Handbook of research on impacts of international business and political affairs on the global economy*. IGI Global. doi:10.4018/978-1-4666-9806-2

Chapter 7
Antecedents and Consequences of International Joint Venture Knowledge Acquisition:
Evidence From Algeria

Tamma Elhachemi
https://orcid.org/0000-0001-9983-159X
University of Echahid Hamma Lakhdar, Eloued, Algeria

ABSTRACT

Studies on the establishment of international joint ventures (IJVs) in open-oriented markets as a vehicle for knowledge acquisition have been increasing of late. Drawing on the transaction cost economics theory and the knowledge-based view, the chapter examines the impact of absorptive capacity, transfer mechanisms, knowledge management practices, and environmental uncertainty on knowledge acquisition of IJVs from foreign partners. Further, the author examines IJV innovativeness as a consequence of knowledge acquisition. The author tested the model with data from 122 IJVs in Algeria. By analyzing the data using SPSSv25 and smart PLS 3.0, the findings show that absorptive capacity and transfer mechanisms are positively and significantly related to knowledge acquisition of the IJVs. However, knowledge management practices and environmental uncertainty are not significant. In addition, the relationship between IJV knowledge acquisition and innovativeness is significant.

INTRODUCTION

Forming international joint ventures (IJVs) with more sophisticated foreign firms has long been touted as a vital means for IJVs to get access to, acquire, share, and utilize knowledge resources that would otherwise be unavailable locally (Anh, Baughn, Hang, & Neupert, 2006; Lee, Park, & Vertinsky, 2012). In addition, in order to function effectively, IJVs get resources and assistance from both parties (for example, sophisticated technology and managerial expertise from international partners, and government, local business, and labor relationships from local partners) (Chen, Chen, & Zhou, 2014). According to

DOI: 10.4018/978-1-7998-9071-3.ch007

Nguyen and Aoyama (2015), an IJV's knowledge acquisition can be defined as new information obtained from its foreign partners, digested, and applied by the IJV to create the same management approaches and production activities, as well as to achieve the original economic organization's learning objectives.

Nevertheless, once the IJVs are formed and knowledge transmission by foreign partners is possible, these IJVs may not always be successful in acquiring foreign partners' knowledge and skills (Ado, Su, & Wanjiru, 2017). In addition, given the rise in the reported frequency of failed IJVs, more research on the innovativeness of IJVs is needed. Two out of every five IJVs are perpetual strugglers or complete failures, according to Beamish and Delios (1997).

From the literature review on IJVs' knowledge acquisition from foreign partners, since the pioneering work by Lyles and Salk (1996), a few empirical investigations (e.g., Anh & Baughn, 2013; Dhanaraj, Lyles, Steensma, & Tihanyi, 2004; Lane, Salk, & Lyles, 2001; Minbaeva, Park, Vertinsky, & Cho, 2018; Park, Vertinsky, & Minbaeva, 2013; Rotsios, Sklavounos, & Hajidimitriou, 2018), have been undertaken, which have mostly indicated absorptive capacity and social capital elements as factors that enhance IJVs' knowledge acquisition. However, there is lack of studies that have examined the combined role of absorptive capacity and different factors. As a result, having a fine-grained understanding of the underlying causes and conditions through which an IJV could take advantage of knowledge transfer benefits is important. It will be impossible for IJVs to really benefit from knowledge transferred from their foreign partner(s) unless they have a thorough understanding of this.

Consequently, in order to fill the gap, the researcher proposes absorptive capacity (Okonkwo, 2018; Thi Thuc Anh, 2017); transfer mechanisms (Chen, Hsiao, & Chu, 2014; Williams, 2007); environmental uncertainties (Battistella et al., 2016); and knowledge management practices (Evangelista, 2009; Nguyen & Aoyama, 2015). These antecedents, with the exception of IJVs' absorptive capacity, are mostly lacking in the literature on IJVs' knowledge acquisition from foreign partners. These proposed antecedents are derived from several empirical studies on knowledge transfer in different contexts, such as knowledge transfer through inter-firm collaborations, suppliers and purchasers; between partner firms in strategic alliances; and between multinational corporations.

Therefore, this paper presents a two-part paradigm that takes absorptive capability, transfer mechanisms, knowledge management practices, and environmental uncertainty into account as antecedents; and IJVs' innovativeness as a result of knowledge acquisition. On the basis of this theoretical framework (Figure 1), we posit the following research questions: a) Do absorptive capacity, transfer mechanisms, knowledge management pactices, and environmental uncertainty influence IJVs' knowledge acquisition? and b) Is an IJV's innovativeness a consequence of its knowledge acquisition? In addition to the research questions, the study has the following research objectives: a) To determine the effect of IJVs' absorptive capacity, transfer mechanisms, knowledge management practices, and environmental uncertainty on IJVs' knowledge acquisition; and b) To study the effect of IJVs' knowledge acquisition on its innovativeness.

This article is organized as follows: following the introduction, the theoretical framework and hypotheses are presented, after which the investigation of 122 Algerian oil and gas IJVs is displayed. The findings are reported next, followed by a discussion and conclusion. Limitations and potential directions are discussed in the final part.

Figure 1. Framework of the Paper

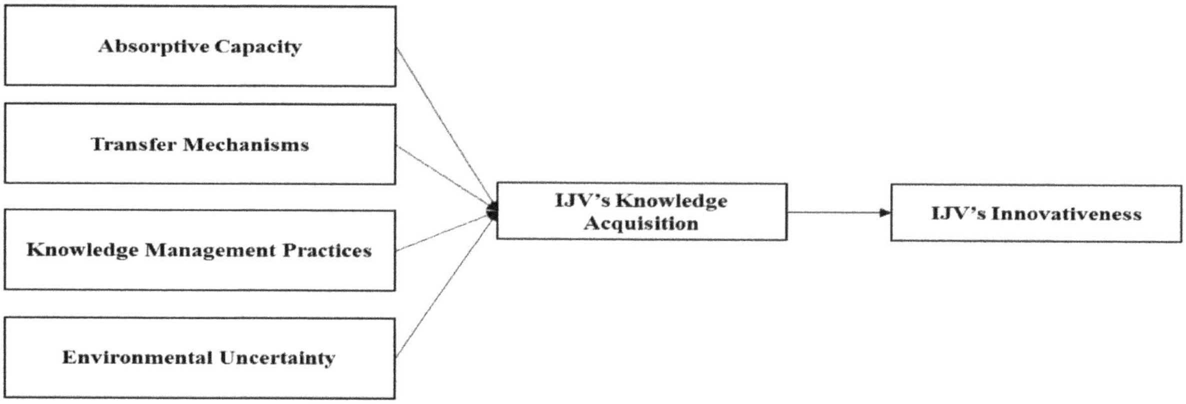

REVIEW OF LITERATURE

Knowledge Acquisition and Innovativeness

Innovation is a critical component of a company's strategy (Gunday, Ulusoy, Kilic, & Alpkan, 2011); an important part of internationalization (Berry, 2014); and a main player to enhance competitiveness (Singh, 2009). According to Hult, Hurley, and Knight (2004), innovativeness relates to an organization's ability to offer new methods, products, or ideas. In terms of knowledge acquisition and its importance to IJVs, researchers have defined knowledge acquisition in IJVs as new information obtained from foreign partners, absorbed, and practiced in order to create the same management approaches and production activities as the original economic organization, as well as to fulfill the original economic organization's learning aims and success to the same extent as the foreign partner's learning goals (Sazali & Raduan, 2011). Previous research on a firm's knowledge-based view (Grant, 1996; Nonaka & Takeuchi, 1995; Spender, 1996), has developed the concept that a firm's competitive strength is based on its ability to access information, produce knowledge, and increase its innovation capabilities. As a result, businesses must continually expand and disseminate knowledge to their staff in order to keep up with new goods and technology (Hung, Lien, Yang, Wu, & Kuo, 2011; Jaguli, Malek, & Palil, 2014). Achieving learning objectives is the process of improving an organization's performance and creativity; one of the learning goals that is a crucial component of organizational strategy is innovativeness (Gunday, Ulusoy, Kilic, & Alpkan, 2011); and a roadmap to competitiveness (Singh, 2009). Therefore, knowledge is an essential resource of a company, according to the knowledge-based theory, since it generates, mixes, recombines, and exploits knowledge, which is critical for an organization's capacity to innovate (Grant, 1996; Szulanski, Ringov, & Jensen, 2016; Wang, 2013).

A number of empirical studies have demonstrated the positive knowledge-innovations link. For example, scholars (Urgal, Quintás, & Arévalo-Tomé, 2013), have discovered in their research that knowledge resources have a direct and positive impact on innovation performance as well as an indirect and positive impact on improving the firm's innovation capabilities. Another study (Al-Sa'di, Abdallah, & Dahiyat, 2017) has revealed that information exchange has substantial benefits for product and process innovations, as well as organizational performance, in a sample of 207 manufacturing businesses operating in

Amman, Jordan. As a result, I expect to see a positive relationship between knowledge acquisition and IJVs' innovativeness. Stated more formally, I hypothesize that:

Hypothesis One: IJV's knowledge acquisition has a significantly positive effect on IJVs' innovativeness. In the following sections, I discuss an IJV's knowledge acquisition antecedents.

Absorptive Capacity and Knowledge Acquisition

The main authors on absorptive capacity have emphasized the importance of absorptive capacity in the workplace as a prerequisite for learning from others (Cohen & Levinthal, 1990). According to these authors, an IJV's ability to create new information, as well as its ability to absorb that knowledge, is dependent on its resources, which must be accumulated through time. As a result, absorptive capacity is crucial for defining the course of an IJV's growth (Park, 2010). Because absorptive capacity refers to a company's ability to detect, evaluate, and use relevant external knowledge, this is the case (Cohen & Levinthal, 1990). Besides, when it comes to an organization's internal resources, increasing organizational capacities, and obtaining new information for commercial objectives, absorptive capacity is a crucial facilitator of learning. Thus, an organization's capacity to acquire new information, technology, and learning aptitude are crucial in order to achieve efficient and effective knowledge acquisition. The capacity to gather fresh data that is not available internally can aid in the development of a successful client network and the discovery of routine organizational activities that support services (Cohen & Levinthal, 1990). Additionally, absorptive capacity is reliant on prior information. Educational background, expertise, and experiences possessed by staff are all examples of existing knowledge.

Absorptive capacity is particularly essential when the IJV's parent business has a lower level of development than the receiver, such as when the sender is from a developing nation and the recipient is from a developed one. Algeria is categorized as a developing economy, with the majority of foreign investment coming from industrialized nations, like from Europe and the United States. This shows that partners in the same industry have a substantial knowledge gap. Because the transmitting and receiving parties' ability to absorb and receive a specific piece of knowledge differs, such an IJV is doomed to fail. As a result, the knowledge gap between both parties narrows as the recipient's ability to learn improves and the IJV can gather data. Many studies have looked at IJVs in developing and transitional economies, and they have demonstrated that if the local absorptive capacity is weak, local employees may be unable to acquire and integrate new knowledge. As a result, the receiving party may be motivated by the giver's acceptable knowledge giving in order to overcome the learning barrier (Anh et al., 2006; Park, Giroud, & Mirza, 2007). Thus, it is hypothesized that:

Hypothesis Two: absorptive capacity has a significantly positive effect on IJVs' knowledge acquisition.

Transfer Mechanisms and Knowledge Acquisition

Researchers have studied transfer mechanisms as the means by which organizations carry out knowledge transfer operations (Mason & Leek, 2008), by which the receivers must reproduce or change the obtained information based on the situation. According to Björkman, Barner-Rasmussen, and Li (2004), knowledge transfer is a socially collaborative construct, and management experts have long recognized its contextual aspect. Transfer mechanisms are the methods used by an acquiring firm to replicate and adapt the given knowledge of a parent firm (Easterby-Smith, Lyles, & Tsang, 2008; Mason & Leek, 2008). Consequently, in order to establish wide transfer channels needed to embed foreign knowledge in the local environment, an IJV must first determine the nature of the knowledge transfer practice. Transfer mechanisms are strategies used by acquiring organizations to replicate and adapt the expertise imparted by their parent company. Due to the inherent causal ambiguity of complex production processes (Lippman & Rumelt, 1982), replication of knowledge is critical, to the point where enterprises are unable to identify fundamental operating know-how. Furthermore, it is a condition for knowledge sharing adaptation when knowledge is compatible with the new situation.

Williams (2007) developed an important model that shows the effects of information replication and adaptation. The theory claims that ambiguous and contextual information is responsible for a firm's replication and flexibility. Firms prefer replication when information is discrete, and prefer adaptation when knowledge is shared, according to the model. Successful knowledge transfer is facilitated by knowledge replication and flexibility, both of which increase a company's performance. As a result, businesses not only aid in the accurate replication of data, but also emphasize the difficult and time-consuming embodied adaptation of information.

Chen et al. (2014) empirically discovered that through adaptation and replication (transfer mechanisms), knowledge transfer performance can be enhanced through the mediating role of cooperative competency in their study that was performed in China with a sample of 120 inter-actor knowledge transfer firms. Another study (Pak, Ra, & Lee, 2015) has found that knowledge adaptation moves at a rapid rate in the process of knowledge management and in making the most of transferred information to fit the new culture and environment of IJVs. Balboni, Marchi, and Vignola (2017) discovered that both formal and informal information transfer channels favorably affect knowledge acquisition in a study with 105 consumers from a medium-sized Italian producer's client portfolio. Based on the above, the next hypothesis is:

Hypothesis Three: Transfer mechanisms has a significantly positive effect on knowledge acquisition.

Knowledge Management Practices and Knowledge Acquisition

Knowledge management practices, according to Schiuma, Andreeva, and Kianto (2012), refer to a set of management methods employed by the IJV to improve the efficiency and effectiveness of the organization's knowledge resources. Knowledge management techniques are organizational and administrative processes that aim to achieve corporate goals by effectively and efficiently managing the firm's knowledge resources (Inkinen & Inkinen, 2016; Kianto, Ritala, Spender, & Vanhala, 2014). Knowledge management practices are defined in this paper as IJVs' managerial practices aimed at achieving the company's goals (e.g., obtaining new technological knowledge) through effective and efficient management of the company's knowledge resources.

Scholars have explained that the core of management commitment is to enhance an organization's learning approaches and goals (Senge, 1990). Enterprises should strive to achieve these goals, and their dedication will allow them to realize their vision of greatness. If one is committed to learning, it may be easier to develop a learning agenda, methods, and routines to help achieve the specified goals (Simonin, 2004). These benefits, however, can be obtained only if the company's executives are committed to encouraging learning behavior and attitude among firm employees (Pham & Swierczek, 2006). According to Lee, Gon Kim, and Kim, (2012), top management assistance is critical because it aids in predicting corporate dangers in order to survive and adapt to changing market information, as well as in supporting knowledge processes toward improved organizational learning, resulting in higher-quality services and commodities. Managers can also encourage a learning culture by instilling values, such as

risk-taking, boldness, effective communication, and empowerment, all geared towards improving performance (Teare, 1998). Therefore, knowledge management methods may be seen of as a key enabler of corporate learning orientation and results. Others have discovered that commitment from leaders is critical for learning and performance (Thuy Pham & Swierczek, 2006). In the context of IJVs, a Vietnamese study has found that having clearly defined goals might help with information acquisition (Lyles & Salk, 1996). Another study on IJVs in Vietnam has found that managerial commitment can minimize conflict, which can improve learning (Tsang, Nguyen, & Erramilli, 2004). Another factor to consider is that the beneficial impact of managerial commitment varies depending on whether the information is explicit or implicit (Evangelista, 2009). Finally, the outcomes of the studies mentioned above show that managerial commitment improves knowledge acquisition. Thus, it is hypothesized that:
Hypothesis Four: Knowledge management practices has a significantly positive effect on IJV's knowledge acquisition.

Environmental Uncertainty and Knowledge Acquisition

The degree or variety of instability in environmental circumstances is characterized by Wong et al. (2011) as environmental uncertainty. Environmental uncertainty is defined as the degree of turbulence and its impact on products, services, technology, and market demand for products and services (Dess & Davis, 1984). Knowledge acquisition has been a common subject of previous research in the context of an IJV. One of an organization's most important tasks is to develop and execute solutions to address external environmental challenges that might cause turbulence. Strategic partnerships, such as IJVs, have long been stressed upon to obtain external expertise (Cassiman & Veugelers, 2006). In their critical literature review, Battistella et al. (2015) clarified that knowledge transfers across companies are frequently framed in a contextual reference. The environment in which external knowledge is acquired and processed has a major influence on an organization's demand for it (Cohen & Levinthal, 1990). Another essential element to consider while looking for external data is the company's operational environment (Lichtenthaler, 2009).

Legal concerns and the state of the financial infrastructure, which has a significant shortfall, produce environmental uncertainty. This includes extremely unpredictable markets and consumer needs, unfriendly competition, and rapid changes in legal, political, and economic structures, which in turn, result in environmental uncertainty in developing and transitional economies (Li & Atuahene-Gima, 2001). Also, environmental restrictions impact the success of a collaborative strategy (Holweg, Disney, Holmström, & Smros, 2005). This has a knock-on effect.

Environmental uncertainty in the light of the transaction cost economics theory, has a significantly negative influence on external search breadth. Transaction costs may be split into three categories based on this approach: searching, negotiating, and contract supervision (Macher & Richman, 2008). As a result, participating businesses must develop and maintain strong connections with their relevant and useful information sources in order to get access to crucial external information sources. However, under chaotic situations, the cost of finding and obtaining acceptable external sources of information, particularly commercially viable information, is likely to increase. Hence, in highly unpredictable conditions, businesses are more likely to restrict the scope of their external knowledge search in order to save transaction costs. According to empirical studies, environmental uncertainty may hinder the activities of acquiring and sharing knowledge in particular conditions (Levine & Prietula, 2012; Prasad & Junni, 2017; Urbany, Dickson, & Wilkie, 1989; Li, Long, Li, & You, 2014). The next hypothesis is:

Hypothesis Five: Environmental uncertainty has a significantly negative effect on IJV's knowledge acquisition.

METHOD

Data Collection

To test the preceding hypotheses, a study of IJVs' operations in Algeria was undertaken. Algeria is a recent example of a transitioning economy. The information was gathered from oil and gas joint ventures. The rationale for this decision is because Algeria's oil and gas industry is the country's economic backbone. According to a study by Investment Climate Statements on Algeria (2020), the hydrocarbon industry is a significant element of the Algerian economy, accounting for roughly 60% of budget revenue, 45% of gross domestic product (GDP), and over 94% of export revenue. Therefore, the oil and gas sector is vital for the country's economy and particular emphasis is placed on acquiring knowledge in the industry to sustain its competitiveness.

Based on data by the National Center of Trade Register, the foreign partners of the IJVs in this study are primarily from more developed countries: the United States, France, Italy, China, Turkey, and so on (2020). Over 80% of the businesses are concentrated in four cities: Algiers, Boumardes, Hassi Masoud, and Ouarigla, all of which are located inside the Algiers, Boumardes, Hassi Masoud, and Ouarigla industrial zones. The top managers, such as the CEO, were the responders, and if they were unavailable, the next highest manager was requested to participate in the survey. These respondents were chosen because they would be knowledgeable about organizational learning as well as their IJV's overall success. In order to distribute the questionnaire, a meeting was scheduled with these respondents to deliver the questionnaire in person at their offices. A polite reminder was given to the responders via phone call after a week to check that the questionnaires had been completed and were ready for collection. A total of 126 questionnaires were collected, with four of them being incomplete. As a consequence, a total of 122 valid questionnaires were collected and were ready to be analyzed (37.42% of the distributed survey). An independent sample t-test (Lambert and Harrington, 1990) revealed no changes in the mean scores of all research variables between these two groups, indicating that the survey procedure had no impact on the outcomes. I also looked at non-response bias by comparing early and late respondents' replies. A t-test on these two groups revealed no statistically significant differences, demonstrating that non-response bias is not an issue.

MEASURES

Knowledge Acquisition

Knowledge acquisition was measured using Lin (2007) and Nguyen & Aoyama's (2015) questionnaire. It comprised seven items regarding the extent of staff acquiring exclusive knowledge; improvement of technical information; increase in operating skills ability to manufacture quality products; increase in the local staff's motivation for further study; ability to improve product quality; existence of trained and more knowledgeable staff in the IJV; and the cooperation and sharing of ideas between local and foreign staff (e.g., Every local technical staff member has fully learned exclusive knowledge; The technical information and knowledge of the local technical staff has improved significantly). All items were assessed on a seven-point Likert scale, with 1 indicating strong disagreement and 7 indicating strong agreement.

ABSORPTIVE CAPACITY

The instrument used to measure absorptive capacity was adopted from Roberts (2015), who adapted it from Pavlou & El Sawy (2006). This study assessed absorptive capacity with eight items using a Likert-type scale.

Transfer Mechanisms

Transfer mechanisms were measured using two subscales, i.e., adaptation and replication. According to Williams' (2007) scale, adaptation focuses on altering operations to integrate them with the new context, whereas replication refers to modifying the receiving unit's operations to be more similar to its partner's. The questionnaire had been validated by previous studies and a good internal consistency found. Adaptation was measured using four items, indicating the extent to which firms have implemented the modified practices from the IJV partner into their own firm. For example, "We usually combine ideas from our foreign partners with other ideas when we adopt them". Replication refers to the extent that firms try to manage their business exactly like their partner using four items, e.g. "We spend substantial time making sure practices we adopt from our foreign partners work just as they do there". All items were measured using a seven-point Likert scale, ranging from 1= strongly disagree to 7= strongly agree. Previous studies have found the scale to be internally consistent.

Knowledge Management Practices

Knowledge management practices were assessed through management commitment, adopted from prior studies (Evangelista, 2009; Sinkula, Baker, & Noordewier, 1997), and measured on a six-point Likert scale. These items discuss the policy of the management towards knowledge transfer in IJVs.

Environmental Uncertainty

The current study measured environmental uncertainty in terms of technological and market uncertainties. Technological uncertainty explains the complications of technology, making it problematic for organizations to make precise forecasts (Song & Montoya-Weiss, 2001). Market uncertainty alludes to the unpredictability of business areas, alterations in the structure of the market or in the level of rivalry (Chen et al., 2005). The measurement of environmental uncertainty used a 10-point Likert-scale, adopted from previous studies (DeSarbo, Anthony Di Benedetto, & Sinha, 2005).

Ijv's Innovativeness

IJV's innovativeness was assessed through a six-point Likert scale. These measurements were adopted from previous studies (Wang & Ahmed, 2004). The items of IJV's innovativeness are the degree of agreement on IJV's novelty of products and services, changes of products and services, cutting edge technology, improvement of business processes, management of problems and solutions, updated technology and machinery, tolerance of individual work style differences, solving of problems with new methods, as well as adopting new ways of doing things.

DATA ANALYSIS

For analyzing and reporting PLS-SEM results, I used a two-step procedure (Henseler, Ringle, & Sinkovics, 2009). The measurement model and the structural model were both evaluated as part of the two-step procedure. Hypotheses testing followed the review of measurement and structural models.

A. Measurement Model Evaluation

Before evaluating the study model's assumptions, internal consistency reliability, convergent validity, and discriminant validity, were examined.

Internal consistency reliability: Cronbach's alpha and composite reliability coefficients are the most generally used estimators of a scale's internal consistency dependability (e.g., Bacon, Sauer, & Young, 1995; Peterson & Kim, 2013). Because Cronbach's alpha is sensitive to a number of items in the measures, it tends to underestimate the measures' internal consistency dependability. Thus, it may be used to assess internal consistency dependability in a cautious manner (Hair et al., 2016). Due to the fact that it finally assumes all elements contributing equally to its construct with no consideration of individual loadings, the composite reliability coefficient produces a significantly lower biased estimate of reliability than Cronbach's alpha coefficient (Barclay, Higgins, & Thompson, 1995; Götz, Liehr-Gobbers, & Krafft, 2010). The threshold values of both Cronbach's alpha and composite reliability values should be higher than 0.70, which is regarded as satisfactorily sufficient for the model; meanwhile, a value less than 0.60 indicates a lack of reliability (Hair, Ringle, & Sarstedt, 2011; Tenenhaus, Vinzi, Chatelin, & Lauro, 2005). From the findings, Cronbach's alpha values of all constructs range between 0.852 and 0.918 as shown in Table 1. Further, the composite reliability of all constructs are acceptable, where their values range from 0.890 to 0.933. In addition, the outer loading values are all above 0.60, which are above the lowest requirement. Thus, it can be summed up that the internal consistency reliability of the measures is verified and confirmed.

Convergent Validity: convergent validity is the extent to which measurements (items) truthfully represent the intended latent variable and correlate with other measures of the same latent variable (Hair, Black, Babin, Anderson, & Tatham, 2006). They further explained that factor loadings, composite reliability, and average variance extracted (AVE) are used to assess convergent validity. Table 1 lists the indicator loadings, weights, and AVE for all the items listed in the model. The loadings of all indicators surpass the required cut-off level of 0.50 as suggested by Hair et al. (2006). AVE values for all constructs are above the recommended value of 0.50 as suggested (Fornell & Larcker, 1981), where the values range from 0.596 to 0.724. In other words, convergent validity is established. Therefore, the study demonstrates acceptable convergent validity.

Table 1. Internal Consistency Reliability

Items	Alpha	Loading	CR	AVE
IJV's Knowledge Acquisition (KWA)	0.910		0.929	0.653
KWA1		0.799		
KWA2		0.851		
KWA3		0.872		
KWA4		0.846		
KWA5		0.784		
KWA6		0.753		
KWA7		0.741		
Absorptive Capacity (AC)	**0.918**		**0.933**	**0.636**
AC1		0.710		
AC2		0.823		
AC3		0.773		
AC4		0.834		
AC5		0.839		
AC6		0.796		
AC7		0.800		
AC8		0.795		
Transfer Mechanisms (TM)	**0.891**		**0.913**	**0.569**
TM1		0.805		
TM2		0.823		
TM3		0.685		
TM4		0.684		
TM5		0.723		
TM6		0.830		
TM7		0.739		
TM8		0.729		
Knowledge Management Practices (KMP)	**0.883**		**0.911**	**0.632**
KMP1		0.747		
KMP2		0.831		
KMP3		0.836		
KMP4		0.769		
KMP5		0.825		
KMP6		0.758		
Environmental Uncertainty (EU)	**0.890**		**0.909**	**0.502**
EU1		0.627		
EU2		0.648		
EU3		0.700		
EU4		0.690		

Continued on following page

Table 1. Continued

Items	Alpha	Loading	CR	AVE
EU5		0.790		
EU6		0.760		
EU7		0.678		
EU8		0.792		
EU9		0.715		
EU10		0.661		
IJV's Innovativeness (INNO)	**0.852**		**0.890**	**0.575**
INNO1		0.729		
INNO2		0.727		
INNO3		0.828		
INNO4		0.789		
INNO5		0.742		
INNO6		0.729		

Discriminant Validity: Discriminant validity is characterized by researchers as the degree to which a latent construct differs from other latent constructs (Duarte & Raposo, 2010). The Fornell-Larcker criterion and the cross-loadings of the items, can be used to assess discriminant validity (Hair et al., 2014). Fornell and Larcker's (1981) criterion for discriminant validity was used. To attain discriminant validity, they advocate comparing the square root of AVE values to the correlations of each latent component. Furthermore, the square root of each latent construct's AVE must be greater than its greatest correlation with any other latent construct (Hair et al., 2014). The square root of the AVE is more than the correlations among the latent variables, as seen in Table 2. Consequently, all of the measures used in this study have appropriate discriminant validity, according to Fornell and Larcker's criterion (1981).

Table 2. Discriminant Validity

	AC	EU	INNO	KMP	TM	KWA
AC	**0.797**					
EU	0.620	**0.708**				
INNO	0.565	0.590	**0.758**			
KMP	0.659	0.559	0.618	**0.795**		
TM	0.720	0.597	0.686	0.736	**0.754**	
KWA	0.644	0.535	0.659	0.635	0.688	**0.808**
Note: Diagonals represent the square root of the AVE while the off-diagonal entries represent the correlations between constructs.						

B. Structural Model Evaluation

After ascertaining the measurement model, the next step in the PLS path modeling analysis was to test the structural model. To do so, based on researchers' suggestions, the evaluation of the structural model was investigated through several requirements, including structural model specification (R^2), effect size (f^2), and predictive relevance *(Q^2)* (Hair Jr., Hult, Ringle, & Sarstedt, 2016; Henseler, Ringle, & Sinkovics, 2009; Straub, Boudreau, & Gefen, 2004). Tenenhaus et al. (2005) proposed goodness-of-fit (GoF) to be included in the structural model evaluation for diagnostic purposes. Finally, to test the significance of the hypotheses in the research model, bootstrapping was performed.

Structural model specification (R^2): According to Hair et al. (2006), the R-squared value represents the fraction of variance in the dependent variable that can be explained by one or more predictor factors. Chin (1998) proposed that R-squared values of 0.67, 0.33, and 0.19 in PLS-SEM can be regarded considerable, moderate, and weak, respectively, for the significance level of R2. From the findings (Table 3), R-squared values of IJV's knowledge acquisition (KWA) and IJV's innovativeness (COMP) are 0.542 and 0.434, respectively. Table 3 below shows the R-squared values for KWA and COMP.

Table 3. R-Squared (R^2)

INNO	0.434
KWA	0.542

Effect Size (f^2): Finding the effect size of certain latent variables' influence on the dependent variable using f2 analysis, which is supplementary to R2 analysis, is one of the most significant tasks in testing the structural model (Chin, 2010). The increase in the R-squared value of the latent variable to which the path is related, relative to the latent variable's fraction of unexplained variance, is computed as effect size (Chin, 1998). Cohen (1988) suggested that f2 values of 0.02, 0.15, and 0.35 in the structural model, imply modest, medium, and large effects, respectively. Therefore, as demonstrated in Table 4, f^2 values for absorptive capacity, transfer mechanisms, and knowledge management practices are 0.043, 0.084, and 0.035, respectively (large). Furthermore, environmental uncertainty value is 0.010 which means that it has a small f^2.

Table 4. f square (f^2)

		KWA
AC		0.043
EU		**0.010**
KMP		0.035
TM		0.084

Predictive relevance (Q^2): according to Chin (2010), 'predictive relevance is a measure of how successfully the model and its parameter estimates reproduce observed values. As a result of the blindfolding technique, the Stone-Geisser test was used in the current study to determine the predictive significance of the research model (Geisser, 1974; Stone, 1974). Based on the recommendation by Hair et al. (2016), I used the cross-validated redundancy construct, which comprises both the structural and measurement models for data prediction. Further, with regards to the assessment of the Q-squared values (Fornell & Larcker, 1994; Hair et al., 2011, 2016), a research model with a cross-redundancy value (Q^2) higher than zero has predictive relevance; otherwise, the predictive relevance of the model cannot be confirmed. As shown in Table 5, the Q-squared values of knowledge acquisition and IJV's innovativeness range from 0.319 to 0.228. Therefore, these values show the predictive relevance of the model.

Table 5. Construct Cross-validated Redundancy (Q^2)

	SSO	SSE	Q^2 (=1-SSE/SSO)
INNO	732.000	564.909	0.228
KWA	854.000	581.180	0.319

Goodness-of-Fit (GoF): it is used to evaluate the overall model. Researchers have described GoF for PLS as the geometric mean of the average communality and the average R-squared for the endogenous constructs (Tenenhaus et al., 2005). In this regard, the GoF measure accounts for the variance extracted by both inner and outer models. According to the suggestion of Wetzels et al. (2009), the standard values of GoF are small (0.1), medium (0.25), and large (0.36). After calculation, the GoF value is 0.538 (large), which indicates a satisfactory level of PLS model validity.

FINDINGS

After confirming the reliability and validity of the study's measurement and structural models, the subsequent stage was to test the hypothesized relationships. The tests were run in order to verify the hypotheses of this paper, simultaneously answering its research questions. To conclude whether or not the hypotheses are statistically significant, I applied the bootstrapping technique together with the Smart-PLS 3.0. Moreover, with the intention of obtaining the statistical t-value and the standard error, bootstrapping was performed with 5,000 samples and 122 cases. Subsequently, a p-value at the 0.05 significance level was obtained (Hair et al., 2016; Henseler et al., 2009). Table 6 below shows the summary of hypotheses testing.

From the findings, of the four knowledge acquisition determinants, only two hypotheses, (H1) - absorptive capacity, and (H2) - transfer mechanisms, are significant (B= 0.220, T= 2.209; and B= 0.331, T= 2.870), respectively. However, the other two IJV's knowledge acquisition determinants, i.e., (H3) - knowledge management practices, and (H4) -environmental uncertainty (*B*= 0.195, T= 1.210; and *B*= 0.091, T= 0.874), respectively, are insignificant. Finally, (H5) - the relationship between IJV's knowledge acquisition and IJV's innovativeness is significant (*B*= 0.659, T= 10.547). Table 6 below shows the results of the structural model.

Table 6. Results of the Structural Model

Hypotheses	Relationship	Coefficient	T value	Result
H1	AC -> KWA	0.220	2.209	Supported
H2	TM -> KWA	0.331	2.870	Supported
H3	KMP -> KWA	0.195	1.210	Not Supported
H4	EU -> KWA	0.091	0.874	Not Supported
H4	KWA -> INNO	0.659	10.547	Supported

DISCUSSION AND CONCLUSION

IJVs' ability to acquire knowledge is becoming increasingly reliant on the successful combination of several factors. The majority of prior theoretical and empirical investigations in transitional economics have concentrated on understanding the extent to which IJVs acquire knowledge. Effective acquisition has also been proposed to be determined by IJVs' absorptive capacity and social capital perspectives (e.g., Minbaeva et al., 2018; Simonin, 2004; Thi Thuc Anh, 2017). This paper presents a two-fold framework that includes absorptive capacity, transfer mechanisms, knowledge management practices, and environmental uncertainty as determinants of IJVs' innovativeness and knowledge acquisition outcomes, based on the findings and integrating insights from knowledge-based and transaction cost economics theories. This is in response to existing studies' recommendations for future research on the determinants and outcomes of knowledge acquisition (Van Wijik et al., 2008), in order to gain a better understanding of the learning process, especially during the post-knowledge exchange stage between the actors involved.

Therefore, this study maintains the role of absorptive capacity of IJVs to increase the absorption of external knowledge from foreign partners. When an IJV has high absorptive capacity, it refers to the IJV's capacity to perceive the value of the parent firm's knowledge, which may entail a sense-making process in which the IJV connects new knowledge to existing knowledge and disseminates activities to develop new knowledge from it. As a result, the bigger the IJV's absorption capacity, the more information it can absorb from its parent companies. Moreover, knowledge management practices are found to be the key support to learning and knowledge transfer; by this means, leaders' dedication may be demonstrated via the formulation of strategies and the dissemination of information through formal practices and processes. They might also create learning frameworks and tactics to assist in the learning process. The result of the study also demonstrates that transfer mechanisms are crucial to IJVs, as long as knowledge is not taken in its crude form. Successful internalizing of acquired knowledge from foreign partners can be achieved through the process of recognizing the contextual nature of the knowledge, and by practicing replications and adaptation of knowledge. The findings demonstrate that IJVs' absorptive capacity, transfer mechanisms, and knowledge management practices have a significantly positive impact on IJVs' knowledge acquisition; however, environmental uncertainty has an insignificant impact on IJV's knowledge acquisition.

The findings offer several important practical implications in relation to knowledge acquisition of IJVs in the context of Algeria. First of all, the study findings would be important to the policymakers, such as the authorities in the Algerian Ministry of Industry and Mines, the Algerian National Agency for Investment Development, Sonatrach (the biggest oil company in Algeria), and finally the managers of IJVs in the oil & gas industry, particularly in the designing of policies and entrepreneurship programs in the country. This study contributes to the understanding of knowledge acquisition and the way to effectively transfer it by enhancing the learning capacity of IJVs; this study also may inspire practitioners, such as managers, to implement the necessary organizational practices in terms of the IJVs' commitment to learning. Further, this study offers valuable insights into IJVs' knowledge management, especially in uncertain business environments. Finally, the findings can help policymakers to formulate better policies for IJVs. Such understanding and awareness may be valuable for policymakers to make the right decisions to prevent the failure of IJVs.

LIMITATIONS AND FUTURE DIRECTIONS

Obviously, this study is not without limitations and directions for future research, which emanate from its quantitative nature, while offering new avenues for future studies. First, the findings of this study are based on IJVs located in Algeria and are limited in their generalizability to other developing and transitional economies. Future research should examine knowledge acquisition of IJVs located in other new transition economies other than China, Vietnam and Hungry, which have been studied before. Secondly, this study is conducted in the oil and gas industry; future research should examine IJVs in different industries so as to provide more generalizable insights. Thirdly, the framework of this paper is limited to studying absorptive capacity, transfer mechanisms, knowledge management practices, and environmental uncertainty, as IJVs' knowledge acquisition antecedents. Future researchers can study other potential factors that may increase the knowledge acquisition of IJVs.

REFERENCES

Ado, A., Su, Z., & Wanjiru, R. (2017). Learning and knowledge transfer in Africa-China JVs: Interplay between informalities, culture, and social capital. *Journal of International Management*, *23*(2), 166–179. doi:10.1016/j.intman.2016.11.003

Al-Sa'di, A. F., Abdallah, A. B., & Dahiyat, S. E. (2017). The mediating role of product and process innovations on the relationship between knowledge management and operational performance in manufacturing companies in Jordan. *Business Process Management Journal*, *23*(2), 349–376. doi:10.1108/BPMJ-03-2016-0047

Anh, C. P. T. T., & Baughn, C. (2013). Antecedents and consequence of International Joint Venture Learning: The case of Vietnam. *Journal of Economic Development*, *13*(3), 58–71.

Anh, P. T. T., Baughn, C. C., Hang, N. T. M., & Neupert, K. E. (2006). Knowledge acquisition from foreign parents in international joint ventures: An empirical study in Vietnam. *International Business Review*, *15*(5), 463–487. doi:10.1016/j.ibusrev.2006.05.004

Barclay, D., Higgins, C., & Thompson, R. (1995). *The Partial Least Squares (PLS) approach to casual modeling: personal computer adoption ans use as an illustration*. Academic Press.

Battistella, C., De Toni, A. F., & Pillon, R. (2016). Inter-organisational technology/knowledge transfer: A framework from critical literature review. *The Journal of Technology Transfer, 41*(5), 1195–1234. doi:10.100710961-015-9418-7

Cassiman, B., & Veugelers, R. (2006). In search of complementarity in innovation strategy: Internal R&D and external knowledge acquisition. *Management Science, 52*(1), 68–82. doi:10.1287/mnsc.1050.0470

Chen, C.-J., Hsiao, Y.-C., & Chu, M.-A. (2014). Transfer mechanisms and knowledge transfer: The cooperative competency perspective. *Journal of Business Research, 67*(12), 2531–2541. doi:10.1016/j.jbusres.2014.03.011

Chin, W. W. (2010). *How to write up and report PLS analyses. In Handbook of partial least squares.* Springer.

DeSarbo, W. S., Anthony Di Benedetto, C., & Sinha, I. (2005). Revisiting the Miles and Snow strategic framework: Uncovering interrelationships between strategic types, capabilities, environmental uncertainty, and firm performance. *Strategic Management Journal, 26*(1), 47–74. doi:10.1002mj.431

Dhanaraj, C., Lyles, M. A., Steensma, H. K., & Tihanyi, L. (2004). Managing tacit and explicit knowledge transfer in IJVs: The role of relational embeddedness and the impact on performance. *Journal of International Business Studies, 35*(5), 428–442. doi:10.1057/palgrave.jibs.8400098

Easterby-Smith, M., Lyles, M. A., & Tsang, E. W. (2008). Inter-organizational knowledge transfer: Current themes and future prospects. *Journal of Management Studies, 45*(4), 677–690. doi:10.1111/j.1467-6486.2008.00773.x

Evangelista, F., & Hau, L. N. (2009). Organizational context and knowledge acquisition in IJVs: An empirical study. *Journal of World Business, 44*(1), 63–73. doi:10.1016/j.jwb.2008.03.016

Fornell, C., & Larcker, D. F. (1981). Evaluating structural equation models with unobservable variables and measurement error. *JMR, Journal of Marketing Research, 18*(1), 39–50. doi:10.1177/002224378101800104

Fornell, C., & Larcker, D. J. (1994). Partial Least Squares. Cambridge, MA: Blackwell Publishers.

Geisser, S. (1974). A predictive approach to the random effect model. *Biometrika, 61*(1), 101–107. doi:10.1093/biomet/61.1.101

Götz, O., Liehr-Gobbers, K., & Krafft, M. (2010). *Evaluation of structural equation models using the partial least squares (PLS) approach. In Handbook of partial least squares.* Springer.

Grant, R. M. (1996). Toward a knowledge-based theory of the firm. *Strategic Management Journal, 17*(S2), 109–122. doi:10.1002mj.4250171110

Gunday, G., Ulusoy, G., Kilic, K., & Alpkan, L. (2011). Effects of innovation types on firm performance. *International Journal of Production Economics, 133*(2), 662–676. doi:10.1016/j.ijpe.2011.05.014

Hair, J. F., Black, W. C., Babin, B. J., Anderson, R. E., & Tatham, R. L. (2006). *Multivariate data analysis* (Vol. 6). Pearson Prentice Hall.

Hair, J. F. Jr, Hult, G. T. M., Ringle, C., & Sarstedt, M. (2016). *A primer on partial least squares structural equation modeling (PLS-SEM).* Sage Publications.

Hair, J. F., Ringle, C. M., & Sarstedt, M. (2011). PLS-SEM: Indeed a silver bullet. *Journal of Marketing Theory and Practice*, *19*(2), 139–152. doi:10.2753/MTP1069-6679190202

Hashim, F., Bakar, A. R. A., & Talib, A. N. (2010). *International Business* (2nd ed.). Oxford Fajar Press.

Henseler, J., Ringle, C. M., & Sinkovics, R. R. (2009). *The use of partial least squares path modeling in international marketing. In New challenges to international marketing*. Emerald Group Publishing Limited.

Ho, M. H.-W., & Wang, F. (2015). Unpacking knowledge transfer and learning paradoxes in international strategic alliances: Contextual differences matter. *International Business Review*, *24*(2), 287–297. doi:10.1016/j.ibusrev.2014.08.002

Hult, G. T. M., Hurley, R. F., & Knight, G. A. (2004). Innovativeness: Its antecedents and impact on business performance. *Industrial Marketing Management*, *33*(5), 429–438. doi:10.1016/j.indmarman.2003.08.015

Hung, R. Y. Y., Lien, B. Y.-H., Yang, B., Wu, C.-M., & Kuo, Y.-M. (2011). Impact of TQM and organizational learning on innovation performance in the high-tech industry. *International Business Review*, *20*(2), 213–225. doi:10.1016/j.ibusrev.2010.07.001

Inkinen, H., & Inkinen, H. (2016). Review of empirical research on knowledge management practices and firm performance. *Journal of Knowledge Management*, *20*(2), 230–257. doi:10.1108/JKM-09-2015-0336

Inkpen, A. (1998). Learning, knowledge acquisition, and strategic alliances. *European Management Journal*, *16*(2), 223–229. doi:10.1016/S0263-2373(97)00090-X

Jaguli, A. R., Malek, M. M., & Palil, M. R. (2014). Do MNCS'high quality and standard requirements matter? A channel for vertical spillovers. *International Journal of Business and Society*, *15*(1), 127.

Jaworski, B. J., & Kohli, A. K. (1993). Market orientation: Antecedents and consequences. *Journal of Marketing*, *57*(3), 53–70. doi:10.1177/002224299305700304

Kianto, A., Ritala, P., Spender, J.-C., & Vanhala, M. (2014). The interaction of intellectual capital assets and knowledge management practices in organizational value creation. *Journal of Intellectual Capital*, *15*(3), 362–375. doi:10.1108/JIC-05-2014-0059

Lane, P. J., Salk, J. E., & Lyles, M. A. (2001). Absorptive capacity, learning, and performance in international joint ventures. *Strategic Management Journal*, *22*(12), 1139–1161. doi:10.1002mj.206

Lee, C., Park, C.-S., & Vertinsky, I. (2012). *Relational Capital, Knowledge Transfer and Performance in International Joint Ventures (IJVs) in Korea. In Korean Science and Technology in an International Perspective*. Springer.

Levine, S. S., & Prietula, M. J. (2012). How knowledge transfer impacts performance: A multilevel model of benefits and liabilities. *Organization Science*, *23*(6), 1748–1766. doi:10.1287/orsc.1110.0697

Li, H., & Atuahene-Gima, K. (2001). Product innovation strategy and the performance of new technology ventures in China. *Academy of Management Journal*, *44*(6), 1123–1134.

Lichtenthaler, U. (2009). Absorptive capacity, environmental turbulence, and the complementarity of organizational learning processes. *Academy of Management Journal, 52*(4), 822–846. doi:10.5465/amj.2009.43670902

Lin, W. B. (2007). Factors affecting the correlation between interactive mechanism of strategic alliance and technological knowledge transfer performance. *The Journal of High Technology Management Research, 17*(2), 139–155. doi:10.1016/j.hitech.2006.11.003

Long, Y., Li, P., & You, B. (2014). Knowledge transfer, governance mechanisms in alliance and environmental uncertainty: An empirical study. *Chinese Management Studies, 8*(3), 438–472. doi:10.1108/CMS-07-2013-0129

Lyles, M. A., & Salk, J. E. (1996). Knowledge acquisition from foreign parents in international joint ventures: An empirical examination in the Hungarian context. *Journal of International Business Studies, 27*(5), 877–903. doi:10.1057/palgrave.jibs.8490155

Mason, K. J., & Leek, S. (2008). Learning to build a supply network: An exploration of dynamic business models. *Journal of Management Studies, 45*(4), 774–799. doi:10.1111/j.1467-6486.2008.00769.x

Minbaeva, D., Park, C., Vertinsky, I., & Cho, Y. S. (2018). Disseminative capacity and knowledge acquisition from foreign partners in international joint ventures. *Journal of World Business, 53*(5), 712–724. doi:10.1016/j.jwb.2018.03.011

Nguyen, N. T. D., & Aoyama, A. (2014). Achieving efficient technology transfer through a specific corporate culture facilitated by management practices. *The Journal of High Technology Management Research, 25*(2), 108–122. doi:10.1016/j.hitech.2014.07.001

Nguyen, N. T. D., & Aoyama, A. (2015). The impact of cultural differences on technology transfer: Management practice moderation. *Journal of Manufacturing Technology Management, 26*(7), 926–954. doi:10.1108/JMTM-09-2013-0130

Nonaka, I., & Takeuchi, H. (1995). *The knowledge-creating company: How Japanese companies create the dynamics of innovation*. Oxford University Press.

Pak, Y. S., Ra, W., & Lee, J. M. (2015). An integrated multi-stage model of knowledge management in international joint ventures: Identifying a trigger for knowledge exploration and knowledge harvest. *Journal of World Business, 50*(1), 180–191. doi:10.1016/j.jwb.2014.02.006

Park, B. I. (2011). Knowledge transfer capacity of multinational enterprises and technology acquisition in international joint ventures. *International Business Review, 20*(1), 75–87. doi:10.1016/j.ibusrev.2010.06.002

Park, C., Vertinsky, I., & Minbaeva, D. (2013). *The influence of foreign partners' disseminative capacities on knowledge transfers to international joint ventures*. Academic Press.

Pavlou, P. A., & El Sawy, O. A. (2006). From IT leveraging competence to competitive advantage in turbulent environments: The case of new product development. *Information Systems Research, 17*(3), 198–227. doi:10.1287/isre.1060.0094

Penrose, E. T. (2009). *The Theory of the Growth of the Firm*. Oxford University Press.

Prasad, B., & Junni, P. (2017). Understanding top management team conflict, environmental uncertainty and firm innovativeness: Empirical evidence from India. *International Journal of Conflict Management, 28*(1), 122–143. doi:10.1108/IJCMA-02-2016-0006

Roberts, N. (2015). Absorptive capacity, organizational antecedents, and environmental dynamism. *Journal of Business Research, 68*(11), 2426–2433. doi:10.1016/j.jbusres.2015.02.019

Rotsios, K., Sklavounos, N., & Hajidimitriou, Y. (2018). *Knowledge Transfer and Trust Among Partners: The Case of Greek IJVs. In Economy, Finance and Business in Southeastern and Central Europe*. Springer.

Schiuma, G., Andreeva, T., & Kianto, A. (2012). Does knowledge management really matter? Linking knowledge management practices, competitiveness and economic performance. *Journal of Knowledge Management, 16*(4), 617–636. doi:10.1108/13673271211246185

Seng, T. L., & Taha, A. Z. (2017). Interpartner relation fit, knowledge transfer, and IJVs innovativeness: The Malaysian context. *International Journal of Advanced and Applied Sciences, 4*(1), 47–54. doi:10.21833/ijaas.2017.01.007

Simonin, B. L. (2004). An empirical investigation of the process of knowledge transfer in international strategic alliances. *Journal of International Business Studies, 35*(5), 407–427. doi:10.1057/palgrave.jibs.8400091

Singh, D. A. (2009). Export performance of emerging market firms. *International Business Review, 18*(4), 321–330. doi:10.1016/j.ibusrev.2009.03.002

Sinkula, J. M., Baker, W. E., & Noordewier, T. (1997). A framework for market-based organizational learning: Linking values, knowledge, and behavior. *Journal of the Academy of Marketing Science, 25*(4), 305–318. doi:10.1177/0092070397254003

Song, M., & Montoya-Weiss, M. M. (2001). The effect of perceived technological uncertainty on Japanese new product development. *Academy of Management Journal, 44*(1), 61–80.

Spender, J.-C. (1996). Organizational knowledge, learning and memory: Three concepts in search of a theory. *Journal of Organizational Change Management, 9*(1), 63–78. doi:10.1108/09534819610156813

Stone, M. (1974). Cross-validatory choice and assessment of statistical predictions. *Journal of the Royal Statistical Society. Series B. Methodological, 36*(2), 111–147. doi:10.1111/j.2517-6161.1974.tb00994.x

Straub, D., Boudreau, M.-C., & Gefen, D. (2004). Validation guidelines for IS positivist research. *Communications of the Association for Information Systems, 13*(1), 1–63.

Szulanski, G., Ringov, D., & Jensen, R. J. (2016). Overcoming stickiness: How the timing of knowledge transfer methods affects transfer difficulty. *Organization Science, 27*(2), 304–322. doi:10.1287/orsc.2016.1049

Tenenhaus, M., Vinzi, V. E., Chatelin, Y.-M., & Lauro, C. (2005). PLS path modeling. *Computational Statistics & Data Analysis, 48*(1), 159–205. doi:10.1016/j.csda.2004.03.005

Thi Thuc Anh, P. (2017). Toward A Comprehensive Model of International Joint Venture Learning. *Journal of Economic Development, 19*(1), 51.

Thuy Pham, N., & Swierczek, F. W. (2006). Facilitators of organizational learning in design. *The Learning Organization, 13*(2), 186–201. doi:10.1108/09696470610645502

Tsang, E. W., Nguyen, D. T., & Erramilli, M. K. (2004). Knowledge acquisition and performance of international joint ventures in the transition economy of Vietnam. *Journal of International Marketing, 12*(2), 82–103. doi:10.1509/jimk.12.2.82.32901

Urbany, J. E., Dickson, P. R., & Wilkie, W. L. (1989). Buyer uncertainty and information search. *The Journal of Consumer Research, 16*(2), 208–215. doi:10.1086/209209

Urgal, B., Quintás, M. A., & Arévalo-Tomé, R. (2013). Knowledge resources and innovation performance: The mediation of innovation capability moderated by management commitment. *Technology Analysis and Strategic Management, 25*(5), 543–565. doi:10.1080/09537325.2013.785514

Wang, C. L., & Ahmed, P. K. (2004). The development and validation of the organisational innovativeness construct using confirmatory factor analysis. *European Journal of Innovation Management, 7*(4), 303–313. doi:10.1108/14601060410565056

Wang, X. (2013). Forming mechanisms and structures of a knowledge transfer network: Theoretical and simulation research. *Journal of Knowledge Management, 17*(2), 278–289. doi:10.1108/13673271311315213

Williams, C. (2007). Transfer in context: Replication and adaptation in knowledge transfer relationships. *Strategic Management Journal, 28*(9), 867–889. doi:10.1002mj.614

Ya. Li, E., Long, Y., Li, P., & You, B. (2014). Knowledge transfer, governance mechanisms in alliance and environmental uncertainty: An empirical study. *Chinese Management Studies, 8*(3), 438–472. doi:10.1108/CMS-07-2013-0129

Zakaria, N., Abdul-Talib, A. N., & Amelinckx, A. (Eds.). (2020). *Transcending Cultural Frontiers: Practices, Challenges, and Strategy for International Business*. Springer. doi:10.1007/978-981-15-4454-5

Zakaria, N., Abdul-Talib, A. N., & Othman, N. (Eds.). (2016). *Handbook of research on impacts of international business and political affairs on the global economy*. IGI Global. doi:10.4018/978-1-4666-9806-2

Chapter 8
The Spread of Cross-Border High-Tech Manufacturing Component Goods in International Trade Integration

Dyah Wulan Sari
Airlangga Universty, Indonesia

Haura Azzahra Tarbiyah Islamiya
Airlangga University, Indonesia

Wenny Restikasari
Airlangga University, Indonesia

ABSTRACT

The objective of this study is to examine the spread of cross-border trading in determining the firm's production in high-technology manufacturing industries in Indonesia. The spread of cross-border trading in the model is measured by export intensity and alternatively is measured by vertical trade integration. The firm-level data of high-tech industries are implemented in this study. A panel data regression procedure is applied to estimate the model. The estimation results elucidate that vertical trade integration is a significant determinant on affecting firm's production while export intensity is not. This evidence proves that the pattern of cross-border international trade of high-technology industries shifted from exporting finished goods to exporting fragmented products. The export intensity variable is no longer representing the international trade when the firms break-down their production process. The usage of export intensity variable in firms undertaking the vertical trade integration would lead to a misleading conclusion.

DOI: 10.4018/978-1-7998-9071-3.ch008

INTRODUCTION

The spread of cross-border manufacturing component goods in international trade integration has become a growing phenomenon in global transaction. Most multinational companies (MNCs) prefer to break down their production processes. It allows foreign affiliation to unbundle stages of production so that each stage can be relocated in some countries. Most of MNCs have been headquartered in the United States, Western Europe, and Japan. These MNCs locate their plants in some different developing countries. The share of global foreign direct investment (FDI) in developing countries upsurged to 54% in 2019, the highest, with an 11% increase in Africa, 4% in Asia, and 2% in other developing economies as a whole (World Benchmarking Alliance, 2020).

There are some incentives for MNCs to branch out their production to other countries with different levels of development and income. They have placed some plants in the developing countries due to location advantages that stem from different factor endowments, such as labor price. There is a vast number of people who do not have jobs, leading to lower labor price in the developing countries (Athukorala & Yamashita, 2006). Ford Motor Company from United States employs over 81,000 people in 7 developing countries. Ericsson from Sweden employs over 34,000 people in 11 developing countries. Samsung Electronics owned by Japanese company is operationally active in 28 developing countries (World Benchmarking Alliance, 2020). According to Amador & Cabral (2016), the MNCs allow to unbundle their production process or outsource into developing economies because it cuts the production chain in the component parts of a particular good, reduces transportation and communication costs. In addition, Sari & Restikasari (2021) also said that trade liberalization, free trade zones, and reduced tariffs were the driving factors for the existence of foreign companies in the developing countries.

MNCs are no longer focused on exporting finished goods, but they change the focus on exporting fragmented products. They prefer to sub-contract into other countries that have low-cost inputs or to produce components of a particular good for later re-exported. Some studies have empirically evaluated the phenomenon of the international fragmentation of production and show that the components product trading is expanding more rapidly than conventional final goods trading. This rapid growth of components trade is a natural consequence and mainly associated with the activities of MNCs. This trading pattern is known as vertical trade integration (Athukorola & Yamashita, 2006; Kimura, et al., 2007; Jones, et al., 2005; Shimbov, et al., 2013).

The vertical trade integration refers to the usage of imported inputs to produce goods that are afterwards exported. Using export intensity to measure international trade will cause misleading if the firms export component goods. It is usually measured by exported goods divided by the total goods produced and this commonly reflects as a key indicator of competitiveness. Furthermore, most of the components product trading in this situation is high-tech products. Srholec (2007) stated that a large proportion of high-tech exports sourced from developing countries are closely related to their participation in fragmented global production networks. Xing (2014) also highlighted that the high-tech exports from developing countries are based on assembled high-tech products and indifferent from other labor-intensive products in terms of technological intensity.

The high-tech manufacturing industries have a very important role in national development. These industries not only have contributions to the international markets but also to the domestic markets. In Table 1 shows that the value of import (Rp150,939 billion) is greater than the value of export (Rp131,209 billion). The high-tech manufacturing industries export around 33.23% of their products and import 15.50% of their inputs. On the other hand, they hire a workforce around 551,057 people and generate value added approximately Rp392,057 billion. This condition causing the high-tech manufacturing sector has the largest contribution on the fluctuations of Indonesia's economic growth. By comparing the high-tech manufacturing industry in Indonesia, the chemical & chemical product industry (ISIC 20) is a sector that has a potential in absorbing the most workers (186,228 people) and in generating a largest value added (Rp200,835 billion). Moreover, the computers, electronic product & optic industry (ISIC 26) has a biggest export, that is around Rp62,890 billion or 41.12% of its products is exported.

Table 1. The Production of of High-Tech Manufacturing Industries in Indonesia

ISIC	Labor	Value Added	Output	Export		Input	Impor	
	(Persons)	(Billion Rp)	(Billion Rp)	(Billion Rp)	(%)	(Billion Rp)	(Billion Rp)	(%)
20	186,228	200,835	461,442	40,994	8.88	260,607	72,399	27.78
21	55,077	14,845	32,322	4,463	13.81	17,477	3,859	22.08
26	149,152	61,704	152,935	62,890	41.12	91,231	48,621	53.30
27	97,165	67,746	131,830	22,594	17.14	64,084	20,942	32.68
28	63,435	46,945	67,794	268	0.40	20,848	5,117	24.54
Total	551,057	392,075	846,322	131,209	15.50	454,247	150,939	33.23

Source: BPS (2015)

Note: ISIC 20 (chemicals & chemicals product industry), ISIC 21 (pharmacy industry), ISIC 26 (computers, electronic product & optics), ISIC 27 (electrical equipment industry) and ISIC 28 (machinery & equipment industry).

Table 2. The Number and Percentage of Indonesia High-Tech Manufacturing Industries

1SIC	Foreign Firms										Domestic Firms										Total Firms
	International Trading						Domestic Trading		Total		International Trading						Domestic Trading		Total		
	VT		OEx		Total						VT		OEx		Total						
20	74	72%	29	28%	103	51%	98	49%	201	20%	42	36%	75	64%	117	14%	698	86%	815	80%	1016
21	13	93%	1	7%	14	52%	13	48%	27	11%	14	64%	8	36%	22	10%	192	90%	214	89%	241
26	69	81%	16	19%	85	52%	79	48%	164	48%	13	68%	6	32%	19	10%	162	90%	181	52%	345
27	41	75%	14	25%	55	57%	41	43%	96	29%	19	76%	6	24%	25	11%	205	89%	230	71%	326
28	34	67%	17	33%	51	53%	45	47%	96	25%	14	56%	11	44%	25	9%	263	91%	288	75%	384
Total	231		77		308		276		584		102		106		208		1520		1728		2312
Avarege		77%		23%		53%		47%		27%		60%		40%		11%		89%		73%	

Source: BPS (2015)

Note: VT is vertical trading; OEx is ordinary trading.

Based on Table 2, the number of foreign firms is around 584 firms. It is only 27% of high-tech manufacturing industries in Indonesia. However, 53% of foreign firms (232 firms) conduct global trading in which 77% of them are doing vertical trading and the rest (around 23%) are doing ordinary trading. Additionally, most of the product exported by pharmacy industry (ISIC 21) is component goods. The foreign pharmacy firms which conduct vertical trading were around 93%. On the other side, the number of domestic firms is about 1728 firms and most of them (1520 firms or 89%) conduct domestic trading. It is only 11% or 208 firms export their product and most of them (60%) conduct vertical trading.

Therefore, the purpose of this book chapter would develop a cross-border trade model. We examine the model using Indonesian firm level data, focusing on high-tech manufacturing industry. The next section in this book chapter will consist of developing the cross-border trade model and discuss the data and estimation method followed by empirical results. Finally, we provide a concluding remark.

THE CROSS-BORDER INTERNATIONAL TRADE MODEL

The cross-border transaction is a common feature of global component trading. It is some enlightenments of the effect of global transaction on firm's production. The foreign affiliations are expected to be more productive than local companies. They deal with high technology through their global activity. The foreign companies might receive technology spillovers through their global experience. It is likely that they get more access and develop advance technology. This circumstance raises technological capacity, which in turn increases their production. It also argues that only more productive company self-select into worldwide markets (Yasar & Paul, 2007; Keller, 2010; Pham, et al., 2013 Kiendrebeogo, 2020; Dawu, 2021).

In the recent decade, the pattern of global trade of high-tech companies especially for foreign affiliations has changed. Most of them prefer to break down their production process into several stages and each stage is usually located in a different country. Each component of the goods is produced in the different stages from the basic upstream production to the final completion at the downstream stage. Every stage can be placed in a country which offers low price of inputs. Relocating stages of their production process to another country can be revealed as a way to attain cost reduction that is not available in the home country. The companies are no longer focused on exporting finished goods, but the companies focus on exporting components of unfinished good. They produce components of a particular good and resell the components in the world market. Trading of unfinished goods is growing more rapidly than finished goods. This situation is known as vertical trade integration and might increase firms' production capacities (Athukorala, 2005; Constantinescu, et al., 2017; Sari, et al., 2020).

The objective of reallocating each production process in a different country is not only to get low input costs, but also by cutting the production chain in certain component parts may expect a different possible effect. Firms outsource their intermediary inputs internationally, which may be available at higher quality than those available in the domestic. This may be important especially for firms operating far away from the international technological frontiers in their industry. Home productions could then focus on those activities in which they can produce more efficient or more productive, and outsource the intermediate goods produced abroad. Therefore, an increase in the use of internationally traded inputs may yield in a direct improvement in production capacity and moving its production function upward (Görg, et al., 2008; Okafor, 2020).

In the context of vertical trade integration, high-tech manufactures use imported intermediate materials to produce goods that are afterwards exported. Measuring variable of cross-border trading for high-tech manufactures in determining their production capability using export intensity can be misleading. Hence, it will be measured at the firm level following Khalifah (2013). Applying the overlap of exports and imported intermediate materials to output, the vertical trade integration is defined as follows:

$$Vti_{it} = 2\min\left(Ex_{it}, Im_{it}\right)xQ_{it} \tag{1}$$

where, Vti_{it} is vertical trade integration. Ex_{it} and Im_{it} are exports and imported inputs respectively. Q_{it} refers to gross output. The subscript i indicates firm while the subscript t is time period.

On the other side, the indigenous firms that carry out export activities are usually more productive than those that do not export. The local firms which have international trading partners will gain in the form of advanced technology through their export experiences. Generally, foreign customers need a higher standard of product quality than local customers. By participating in the global market, they learn and get ideas for fulfill the standard of their products. The export process makes exporting firms have a better average production capacity than non-exporting firms. It is not uncommon for trading partners abroad to provide information on how to fulfill the required product qualifications. These products are usually produced with certain production standards using the new technology which is quite sophisticated. This condition makes them get a technology spillover from their export experience. They get in touch with the latest modern technology and get more access to apply this technology into their production process. Thus, the firms will increase their technological capacity quickly that in return will increase their production capabilities (De Loecker, 2007; Wagner, 2007; Najafi-Tavani, et al., 2018). These kinds of export activities will be measured by export intensity. It can be formulated as follows:

$$ExI_{it} = \frac{Ex_{it}}{Q_{it}} \tag{2}$$

where ExI_{it} is export intensity.

Furthermore, there are several important determinants that may affect firms' production capability. The determinants can be related to the external and internal environment of firms. The external variables can be related to the surrounding environment, such as the level of market competition and the presence of foreign affiliates. Meanwhile, the internal conditions of the firm itself such as the type of ownership and firm size can also have an influence on its production capabilities.

The level of market competition is believed to affect the firms' production capability. There are two hypotheses which can explain the relationship between the level of market competition and the firms' production capabilities. On the one hand, a high level of market concentration can be the result of dynamic competition from firms with better production capabilities. Dynamic competition is driven by changes in external conditions. Any substantial change in the market structure will lead to a relocation of output among the most productive firms. The existence of innovation in the production process, improvement of product quality in the market, and new business models in the external environment have made the companies managing their resources efficiently. In addition, productive companies also have greater intensity of technological innovation to carry out research and development (R&D) activities. Companies that have greater production capabilities will be more profitable and can expand market share so that the market concentration increases. Therefore, high market concentration or low level of business competition is very likely to occur for companies that make rapid technological changes and ultimately increase their production capabilities (Sidak & Teece, 2009; Teece, 2011; Alvarez & Gonzalez, 2020).

On the other hand, a high degree of market concentration also obtained from the results of the static competition which can protect less productive companies. An increase in production capacity can be also stimulated in more competitive environment. The level of business competition can affect the ability of managers and the skills of their workers. The remuneration provided to managers and workers in a monopolistic competition market will affect the ability of managers to manage the company and the skills of employees at work. The pressure of intense competition can improve the ability of managers to run their businesses to get bigger and require their workers to work with more skills. This must be balanced by providing more remuneration so that employees can work more active and productive. Thus, it can be said that a low level of market concentration or a high level of business competition can lead to an increase in the production capability (Ahn, 2002; Bajgar, et al., 2019). The market concentration of industry j at time t can be calculated as follows:

$$MC_{jt} = \sum_{i=1}^{n} s_{it}^2, \qquad i \in j \tag{3}$$

where s_{it} is market share of each firm i in period t.

The existence of MNCs might create spillovers and affect the production capabilities of other companies. Spillover is defined as an externality that comes from the presence of foreign companies which are beneficial or detrimental to other companies. The presence of new products with high quality from foreign companies definitely will bother the goods produced by other companies. This spillover will be beneficial if the presence of foreign companies causes other companies to learn the ways to produce these new products. Therefore, there is transfer of technology and, as a result, the company's managerial capabilities are better, which eventually can increase production capabilities. These spillovers are considered as intra-industry spillovers or horizontal spillovers when the presence of foreign firms generates positive impact on domestic firms in the same industry (Moralles & Moreno, 2020; Negash, et al. 2020). It can be formulated as follows:

$$HorS_{jt} = \frac{\sum_{i \in j} FOS_{it} * Q_{it}}{\sum_{i \in j} Q_{it}} \tag{4}$$

where $HorS$ represents horizontal spillover, FOS measures the share of firm's total equity owned by foreign investors. Q expresses output, the subscript i symbolizes the i-th firm, j describes the j-th industry, $i \in j$ indicates a firm in a given industry, and t denotes time.

In addition, there is a fairly suspicion about the possible negative effects of incoming foreign affiliates. Incoming foreign affiliates could attract the best employees from local companies by offering the lure of high salaries. Competition with MNCs may result in negative spillovers to domestic companies. The entry of foreign companies into domestic market might reduce the sales and decrease the market power of domestic companies. This condition can force the domestic companies to operate with less production or even lead to the exit of some domestic companies from the market (Sari et al., 2016; Rojec & Knell, 2018; Li & Luo, 2019).

The type of ownership can also influence a firm's production capability. The larger the percentage of foreign ownership in a company, the greater the production capacity of the company is in comparison to domestic firms. By the presence of a foreign party in the company, the company will require to make improvements in the production process, distribution, and marketing. It is also possible for foreign parties to transfer technology to their companies in the host country. For this reason, companies that involve foreign parties will have much better production capabilities than those that do not involve (Nguyen, et al., 2020). Based on many studies, the definition of foreign equity capital varies. They use different foreign ownership thresholds. Haddad and Harrison (1993) in their study define a foreign enterprise as a legal enterprise in which a foreign investor possesses 5% or more of equity assets. The IMF (2004) and OECD (2009) depict that foreign companies are at least 10% equity capital owned by foreigners. This 10% threshold is usually used as an internationally standard definition of foreign company. Another study conducted by Djankov and Hoekman (2000) consider a relevant threshold, which is to be more than 20%. Our study attempts to implement IMF and OECD thresholds. All joint-venture companies with more than or equal to 10 percent of foreign ownership will be included as foreign ownership in the models.

Firm size is depiction of a small or large production of the firm and it can affect the firm's ability to produce. A firm with large production usually has a research and development (R&D) department. The firm can benefit from research and development activities carried out. Hence, the firm has a better access to high technology and has the ability to bear a greater risk than a firm that has a smaller size. To become a larger firm, the firm must be more productive and has a lower cost structure, which in turn allows the firm to reduce prices and to expand its production (Sari, 2019; Vinh, 2019). The study conducted by Kohpaiboon (2009) also said that the firm size in the models could control the industry effects, especially when employed a sample covering some industries and used the aggregation. In this study, the firm size is calculated using output of the firm i divided by output of the industry j at time t.

Furthermore, it is also convenient to describe the productive capabilities of an establishment through a production function. It specifies the relationship between the amount of product attained with the quantities of productive factors (e.g., labor and capital stock or fixed assets). This function expresses the amount of product that can be produced from every combination of input factors, assuming that technology used is static. The production capability can be increased by adding more productive factors (Dornbusch, et al., 2011; Nicholson & Snyder, 2012; Samuelson, & Nordhaus, 2019).

Besides the input factors, cross-border international trade variables as well as external and internal environment factors which have been discussed above can also boost firms' production capabilities. In model (5a), the production function is augmented with cross-border international trade variables as well as external and internal environment variables. The cross-border international trade variables are treated as main variables and all environment variables are preserved as control variables. The independent variables (X_i) in the production function will consist of input factor variables (X_1), cross-border international trade variables (X_2), external environment variables (X_3) and internal environment variables (X_4). Hence, the cross-border international trade model can be formulated as follows:

$$q_{it} = \alpha_0 + \beta_i \sum X_{1it} + \gamma_i \sum X_{2it} + \delta_i \sum X_{3it} + \eta_i \sum X_{4it} + \varepsilon_{it} \quad (5a)$$

$$\varepsilon_{it} = \lambda_i + u_{it} \quad (5b)$$

$$q_{it} = \alpha_0 + +_1 k_{it} +_2 l_{it} + \gamma_1 Vti_{it} + \gamma_2 ExI_{it} + \delta_1 MC_{jt} + \delta_2 HorS_{jt} + \eta_1 FOS_{it} + \eta_2 FirmS_{it} + \lambda_i + u_{it} \quad (5c)$$

where q is natural logarithm of gross output, k_{it} is natural logarithm of capital stock, l_{it} is natural logarithm of labor, ExI_{it} is export intensity, Vti_{it} is vertical trade integration, MC_{it} is the degree of market concentration, $HorS_{it}$ is horizontal spillover from foreign affiliations within industry, FOS_{it} is foreign ownership, $FirmS_{it}$ is firm size, α_0 is intercept, β_i is the coefficient of production variables, γ_i is the coefficient of global trading variables, δ_i is the coefficient of external variables, η_i is the coefficient of internal variables, ε_i is error component which consist of individual specific effect (λ_i) and disturbance (u_{it}), while subscript $i, j,$ and t represent individual firm, industry, and year respectively.

DATA AND ESTIMATION METHOD

The data are sourced from the Indonesian Central Board of Statistics (BPS), namely an annual survey of medium and large manufacturing industries. The survey is designed for all manufacturing establishments engaging with at least 20 workers. A medium establishment employs with 20 to 99 workers, while large establishment employs more than 99 workers. The capital stock is calculated using replacement values of fixed assets. The values of fixed assets consist of three asset types: lands and buildings, machinery, equipment and other capital goods and vehicles.

The periods of data used are covered from 2010 to 2014. Based on the international standard industrial classification (ISIC), the high-tech manufacturing industries in this study are divided into 5 classifications with 2-digit ISIC level. The ISIC codes used in this study are ISIC 20 (chemicals & chemicals product industry), ISIC 21 (pharmacy industry), ISIC 26 (computers, electronic product & optics), ISIC 27 (electrical equipment industry), and ISIC 28 (machinery & equipment industry). Furthermore, wholesale price index (WPI) is a supplementary data. It is also obtained from BPS. The WPI data are used to deflate the output and all input values into real values.

The original dataset are minimized from the noises, such as misreporting and obvious typing mistakes in inputs. The methodology for adjustment process of cleaning dataset will follow Sari et al. (2016). After the adjustment process for constructing a balanced panel data, the total number of observation becomes 4,627 firms in chemicals & chemicals product industry, 1,215 firms in pharmacy industry, 1,589 firms in computers, electronic product & optics, 1,554 firms in electrical equipment industry, and 1,704 firms in machinery & equipment industry. The summary statistics of the data is presented in Table 3.

Table 3. Summary Statistics of Variables

Variables	Unit		Chemicals & Chemicals Product (ISIC 20)	Pharmacy (ISIC 21)	Computers, Electronic Product & Optics (ISIC 26)	Electrical Equipment (ISIC 27)	Machinery & Equipment (ISIC 28)
Output (Q)	Billion Rupiah	Mean	337.2512	175.5471	230.4451	325.9402	105.9754
		SD	2570.3670	1692.6090	640.2982	1106.6620	377.2294
		Min	0.0400	0.1211	0.2564	0.0478	0.0921
		Max	90499.9500	44950.0000	10360.0000	16358.1600	7691.4610
Capital Stock (K)	Billion Rupiah	Mean	44.1587	44.1587	12.9333	64.8574	15.7095
		SD	401.3463	401.3461	84.3538	514.8917	87.1545
		Min	0.0006	0.0012	0.0027	0.0008	0.0018
		Max	14333.7100	2005.9942	3557.9166	14803.7500	1157.5190
Labor (L)	Workers	Mean	190.9758	257.1243	490.5828	356.2284	159.3509
		SD	566.6648	423.3973	942.4774	742.5589	306.2469
		Min	20	20	20	20	20
		Max	13890	3578	8125	7552	2833
Vertical Trade Integration (Vti)	Ratio	Mean	0.0381	0.0294	0.1392	0.0749	0.0480
		SD	0.1467	0.1242	0.3295	0.2274	0.1720
		Min	0	0	0	0	0
		Max	1.6409	1.2963	1.2963	1.6601	1.4462
Export Intensity (ExI)	Ratio	Mean	0.1105	0.0425	0.2511	0.1435	0.0930
		SD	0.2578	0.1407	0.4027	0.3012	0.2401
		Min	0	0	0	0	0
		Max	1	1	1	1	1
Market Concentration (MC)	Ratio	Mean	0.2414	0.2015	0.1782	0.2447	0.2739
		SD	0.2264	0.1660	0.1825	0.1642	0.1758
		Min	0.0270	0.0304	0.0291	0.0451	0.0769
		Max	1.0000	0.6472	1.0000	0.9591	1.0000
Horizontal Spillovers ($HorS$)	Ratio	Mean	0.3175	0.0998	0.4117	0.4225	0.3775
		SD	0.2263	0.2852	0.4790	0.2544	0.2596
		Min	0	0	0	0	0
		Max	1	1	1	0.9926	1
Foreign Ownership (FOS)	Ratio	Mean	0.1520	0.0165	0.0497	0.2314	0.2043
		SD	0.3366	0.0690	0.1341	0.3992	0.3872
		Min	0	0.2978	0	0	0
		Max	1	0.7982	1	1	1
Firm Size ($FirmS$)	Ratio	Mean	0.0337	44.1587	12.9333	0.0515	0.0781
		SD	0.1038	401.3461	84.3538	0.1205	0.1516
		Min	0.0000	0.0012	0.0027	0.0000	0.0000
		Max	1	0.7982	1	0.9791	1
Number of Observation			4,627	1,215	1,589	1,554	1,704

Note: Mean is arithmetic mean; SD is standard deviation; Min is Minimum Value; Max is Maximum value.

A regression of static panel data method will be implemented to estimate the equation (5c). There are three alternative models in the panel data regression, namely pooled ordinary least square (PLS), fixed effect (FE) model, and random effect (RE) model. The PLS uses all information, but it is the most restrictive in which the errors are assumed to be independent and identically distributed and uncorrelated with the regressors (Hill, et al., 2018; Wooldridge, 2015). When the individual effect (λ_i) is correlated with regressors (X_i), we have a FE model. The FE model uses within variation in the data only, but it is the most flexible which allows for the endogeneity of regressors. However, when λ_i is uncorrelated with regressors X_i, we have a RE model. The RE model uses a weighted average of the between and within variation (not exactly all information) but RE can accommodate within unit serial correlation. In order to choose the correct model, the Breuch-Pagan or Lagrangian Multiplier (LM) test is done. It aims to determine between the PLS Model and the RE model. The null hypothesis is (H_0)$:\sigma^2_\lambda = 0$. When rejecting H_0, the RE model is the most appropriate, otherwise the OLS would be BLUE (best unbiased linear estimator). The second test is the Hausman specification test. It is commonly used in applied panel data analysis to determine which one is more appropriate RE model or FE model. The null hypothesis is $H_0 : Cov\left(\lambda_i, X_{it}\right) = 0$, rejection of the null hypothesis favors the FE model.

After conducting LM and Hausman tests to select an appropriate model whether PLS, FEM or REM, then we perform various diagnostic checks such as multicollinearity, heteroskedasticity and autocorrelation. Multicollinearity refers to linear relationship among some or all explanatory variables of a regression model. It violates no regression assumptions. It does not destroy the property of minimum variance and it is still efficient. If multicollinearity is very high, the estimators still retain the property of BLUE. However, it is hard to get estimated coefficient with small standard error (Gujarati & Porter, 2009).

The standard error component specified in equations (5) assumes that the disturbances have homoscedastic variances and no serial correlation through the random individual effects. This may be a limiting assumption for panel data regression, where the cross-sectional units may vary in size and as a result may show different variations. Even though, assuming homoscedastic disturbances when heteroskedasticity is present will still result in consistent estimates of the regression coefficients, but these estimates will not be efficient. Also, the standard errors of these estimates will be biased. Hence, it is computed robust standard errors correcting for the possible presence of heteroskedasticity (Baltagi, 2021).

Furthermore, there are occasions where the effects of unobserved variables vary systematically over time, such as the effects of omitted variables that are serially correlated or the effects of transient variables whose effects last more than one period. The presence of these variables is not well designated by the error term being constant or independently distributed over a period of time. To overwhelm a more general autocorrelation problem, Hsiao (2014) relaxes the restriction that u_{it} are serially uncorrelated. And, Hoechle (2007) gives selected treatment to produce robust standard error estimates for linier panel models like robust to avoid heteroskedastic, and cluster to ignore heteroskedastic and autocorrelation problem in regression.

RESULTS

We have applied a panel data regression procedure to estimate the cross-border trade models in high-tech manufacturing industries. As explained earlier, there are 5 classifications of high-tech manufacturing industries. The models of each high-tech manufacturing industry are regressed separately. Furthermore, the LM and Hausman tests are performed to select the appropriate panel data model. Then to get best linear unbiased estimator, all assumptions have been relaxed and statistical diagnoses have been checked, such as multicollinearity, heteroscedasticity, and autocorrelation. Since the problems of heteroscedasticity and autocorrelation appear in the models, it will be solved by using either cross-section clustering or robust standard error estimations. This means that all relevant variables are involved in the models or no superfluous variables included in the model. The probability distribution of the error term is correctly specified and there are no errors of measurement in the regressand and regressors. The estimation results of each high-tech manufacturing industry are provided in Table 4 and 5.

Table 4. The Estimation Results of Cross-Border Trade Models on High-Tech Manufacturing Industries of ISIC (20), (ISIC 21)and ISIC (26)

	Coefficients					
Variables	**Chemicals & Chemicals Product (ISIC 20)**		**Pharmacy (ISIC 21)**		**Computers, Electronic Product & Optics (ISIC 26)**	
	Model 1A	**Model B1**	**Model 2A**	**Model 2B**	**Model 3A**	**Model 3B**
$Constant$	5.991*	5.999*	5.248*	5.289*	5.671*	5.780*
	(0.244)	(0.243)	(0.224)	(0.224)	(0.324)	(0.322)
k	0.236*	0.232*	0.244*	0.242*	0.261*	0.255*
	(0.008)	(0.008)	(0.018)	(0.018)	(0.013)	(0.013)
l	0.574*	0.580*	0.617***	0.620*	0.604*	0.603*
	(0.055)	(0.055)	(0.046)	(0.046)	(0.063)	(0.063)
Vti	0.671*	-	0.702**	-	0.363*	-
	(0.182)	-	(0.337)	-	(0.103)	-
ExI	-	0.132	-	-0.405	-	0.005
	-	(0.168)	-	(0.264)	-	(0.147)
MC	-0.006	-0.005	0.574*	0.559*	-1.658*	-1.708*
	(0.084)	(0.084)	(0.165)	(0.164)	(0.316)	(0.322)
$HorS$	0.180**	0.184***	0.443*	0.445*	-0.184*	-0.156*
	(0.073)	(0.073)	(0.076)	(0.076)	(0.081)	(0.080)
FOS	-0.032	-0.037	-0.370*	-0.363*	0.232*	0.216*
	(0.068)	(0.068)	(0.111)	(0.111)	(0.084)	(0.090)
$FirmS$	3.476*	3.484*	1.809*	1.870**	2.524*	2.479*
	(0.477)	(0.478)	(0.786)	(0.803)	(0.435)	0.448
R^2	0.75	0.744	0.840	0.827	0.852	0.852
F_{Stat}	156.38	157.09	73.91	73.58	95.38	95.38
N	4,627	4,627	1,215	1,215	1,589	1,589

Note: * denotes significance at 1%, ** denotes significance at 5%, and *** indicates significance at 10%. Values in parentheses are the standard errors. R^2 is coefficient determination. F_{Stat} is value of F statistic. N is number of observation.

Table 5. The Estimation Results of Cross-Border Trade Models on High-Tech Manufacturing Industries of ISIS (27) and ISIC (28)

Variables	Coefficients			
	Electrical Equipment (ISIC 27)		**Machinery & Equipment (ISIC 28)**	
	Model 4A	**Model 4B**	**Model 5A**	**Model 5B**
$Constant$	6.325*	6.374*	6.025*	6.047*
	(0.298)	(0.303)	(0.316)	(0.317)
k	0.261*	0.257*	0.211*	0.207*
	(0.013)	(0.013)	(0.012)	(0.012)
l	0.414*	0.422*	0.517*	0.521*
	(0.058)	(0.058)	(0.071)	(0.071)
Vti	0.510*	-	0.614*	-
	(0.126)	-	(0.168)	-
ExI	-	-0.071	-	0.220
	-	(0.245)	-	(0.258)
MC	0.284	0.271	-0.686*	-0.675*
	(0.243)	(0.243)	(0.15)	(0.151)
$HorS$	0.319*	0.322*	0.211**	0.208**
	(0.091)	(0.091)	(0.088)	(0.088)
FOS	-0.004	-0.026	-0.122	-0.128
	(0.116)	(0.116)	(0.091)	(0.093)
$FirmS$	4.273*	4.183*	2.613*	2.588*
	(0.499)	(0.482)	(0.449)	(0.452)
R^2	0.815	0.811	0.731	0.724
F_{Stat}	99.87	100.43	62.7	62.95
N	1,554	1,554	1,704	1,704

Note: * denotes significance at 1%, ** denotes significance at 5%, and *** indicates significance at 10%. Values in parentheses are the standard errors. R^2 is coefficient determination. F_{Stat} is value of *F* statistic. N is number of observation.

The particular interest of this study is on the estimated coefficients of two different global trade variables, which are vertical trade integration variables and export intensity. We examine those two different coefficients in order to compare relative performance between export of final goods and component goods. See Table 4A and 4B, we include a vertical trade integration variable in all models A, while in all models B, we replace the vertical trade variable using an export intensity variable. The estimation results show that the coefficients of vertical trade integration variables (Vti) in all models A are statistically significant and have positive signs. This means that the cross-border trade of component goods in high-tech manufacturing industries has significant effect on firms' production capacities assuming other variables constant. The result is consistent with the research from Constantinescu, et al., (2017). On the other hands, the coefficients of export intensity variables (ExI) in all models B are not statistically significant. The high-tech manufacturers are no longer focused on exporting finished goods, but they are focused on exporting components of unfinished good. The usage of measurement of export intensity is no longer representing the cross-border global trade when the manufacturers break-down their production process. The result is consistent with previous studies conducted by Khalifah, et al., (2013), Rei, et al., (2019), Ozsov, et al., (2021), and Sari, et al., (2020). Therefore, including export intensity variable in the model when the companies carry out the vertical trade integration would lead to a misleading measurement.

According to Table 4A and 4B, the estimated coefficients of production variables such as capital (k) and labor (l) in all models are different from zero and have positive signs. These indicate when percentage of capital and labor increase, then the percentage of production also increases, assuming the other variables are constant. Comparing both capital coefficients and labor coefficients, the coefficients of labor show a larger number than the coefficients of capital. This specifies that there is higher labor intensity in Indonesian high-tech manufacturing industry. This is because the number of workers in Indonesia is very abundant so the wages are low. Therefore, high-tech companies prefer to choose labor-intensive in their production process because production costs will still be cheaper than using capital-intensive.

The market concentration variable tends to possess a different result. The coefficients of market concentration (MC) in the Model 1 and Model 4 are not statistically significant. This means that the degree of market concertation in chemicals & chemicals product industry and electrical equipment industry do not have an impact on production capacity. In contrast, the coefficients of market concentration in the Model 2, Model 3 and Model 5 are different from zero. The coefficients of market concentration in Model 3 and Model 5 have negative signs but it has a positive sign in Model 2. As discussed earlier, a firm's higher production can emerge as a result of a lower or higher degree of market competition. A negative sign indicates that the market is high competition (Sari, 2019), while a positive sign is less competition (Esquivias & Harianto, 2020). The lower market concentration in computers, electronic product & optics industry (ISIC 26) as well as in machinery & equipment industry (ISIC 28) indicate that their production could be stimulated by more competitive environment. The high degree of market concentration represents the less competitive in the market. In such circumstances, the lower the competition in pharmacy industry (ISIC 21), the more it will encourage companies to increase their production capacity. This result is consistent with the result of research on Indian drugs and pharmaceutical industry conducted by Arora & Lohani (2017).

The horizontal spillover ($HorS$) coefficients in all models in Table 4A and 4B are statistically different from zero and have positive signs, except for Model 3A and 3B. These results show that the existence of foreign competitors brings impact instantaneously on all high-tech manufacturing firms (firms in chemicals & chemicals product industry; pharmacy industry; electrical equipment industry, and machinery & equipment industry, except for computers, electronic product & optics industry). The existence of foreign companies has created a high competitive pressure in the same industries.This pressure is an incentive for other companies with similar product to exploit their resources efficiently. Therefore, this condition have force those companies to preserve their market share by increasing their productivity

(Brournstkid, 2021; Lensert & Mervade, 2018). On the other hand, the competitive pressure from foreign firms may restrict the market power of computers, electronic product & optics industry. The entrance of foreign partnerships may reduce the sales of other companies in the computers, electronic product & optics industry, cause some other companies to leave, and give back the sales of the remaining companies to zero profit level. The finding of negative horizontal spillovers in this study is consistent with the findings from previous researches, which are Orlic, et al., (2018) and Van, et al., (2019).

By evaluating in Table 4A and 4B, the foreign ownership (FOS) coefficients in Model 1, Model 4 dan Model 5 are not different from zero. This means that the degree of foreign ownership in establishment does not seem to have a significant effect on production. This specifies that the production capacity of foreign companies is the same with the production capacity of domestic companies in chemicals & chemicals product industry, electrical equipment industry as well as machinery & equipment industry, regardless the share of ownership. This insignificant result is consistent with the research of Chen & Tang (1987), Sterner (1990), and Soderbom & Teal (2001). However, the foreign ownership (◆) coefficients in the Model 2 dan Model 3 are statistically different from zero. The coefficient sign in the Model 2 is negative, but in the Model 3 is positive. The positive sign in the Model 3 confirms that the larger the share of foreign ownership in computers, electronic product & optics industry, the more the goods can be produced. The result from research conducted by Guadalupe, et al., (2012) exhibits the same positive magnitude. On the other side, the negative sign in the Model 2 designates that the larger the share of domestic ownership in pharmacy industry, the more the goods can be produced. This is supported by the result of reseacrch conducted by Sari, et al., (2016).

Examining the remaining regressors, the firm size (FOS) coefficients in all models in Table 4A and 4B appear to be positive and statistically significant. The positive impact of firm size is consistent with the results of research conducted by Toma (2020). This evidence may not be a astonishment. A bigger company tends to own advanced technology and modern capital equipment compared to a smaller company. Hence, the greater size of the firm in all high-tech manufacturing industries point out a greater effect on increasing production.

Those findings suggest that the Indonesia government should support cross-border international trade activities and promote the entry of multinational corporations, especially in high-tech manufacturing sectors. The government should consider not only the export of final goods but also export of component goods. This is because of higher level of vertical integration positively related with the firm's production capacity. Hence, the policy makers should stimulate the entrance of multinational corporations as long as they bring benefits to high-tech manufacturing industries and assure that the potential weaknesses of foreign firms do not outweigh the advantages. In this situation where there are potential advantages and disadvantages from the foreign affiliations, policy makers should at least guarantee that the negative effects on domestic companies do not outweigh the overall benefits of the presence of foreign companies. In contrast, when there are potential gains from multinational companies for local companies, policy makers should offer incentives to encourage the existence of multinational corporations.

CONCLUDING REMARK

The empirical results show that the higher global trade on component goods is positively related to the firm's production on high-tech manufacturing industry such as chemicals & chemicals product industry, electrical industry and machinery & equipment industry. However, when we measure the cross-border global trade on high-tech manufacturing companies using export intensity, the empirical results show that export intensity has no impact on the firm's production. This study proves that the pattern of cross-border global trade on high-tech manufacturing companies has changed. The cross-border trade on high-tech manufacturing companies is no longer export the final goods, but more focuses exporting on the component goods. Therefore, when we use export intensity to measure global trading for component goods in high-tech manufacturing industry can be misleading measurement.

Furthermore, the results of core variables explain that the capital and labor positively influence the firm's production performance. When the percentage of capital and labor upsurge, the percentage of production also upsurges. The coefficients of capitals in all models of high-tech manufacturing industries are less than the coefficient of labor. This designates that the high-tech manufacturing industries in Indonesia are more labor intensive. The results of control variables show that not all environment variables have impacts on firms' production performance.

An external environment variable, such as market concentration which is defined the degree of market competition does not influence production capacity in chemicals & chemicals product industry and in electrical equipment industry. However, the degree of market competition really affects production capacity in pharmacy industry, in computers, electronic product & optics industry as well as in machinery & equipment industry. Another external environmental variable is horizontal spillover, which is described as an externality created by the attendance of foreign affiliations that benefits other companies. The results of horizontal spillovers variable show that the presence of foreign competitors bring positive impacts to all high-tech manufacturing firms, except for computers, electronic product & optics industry.

Not all foreign ownership as an internal environment variable in the models seems to have influences the production performance. This means that both foreign and domestic ownership do not affect the firm's production. Only foreign ownership in pharmacy industry as well as in computers, electronic product & optics industry has significant effect on the production capacity. A remaining internal environment variable which is the firm size also confirms to be positively affecting the firm's production. The larger the firms, the larger the firm's production is.

The policy implication based on this study is that the Indonesian government should consider a cross-border global trade in the context of component goods trading. This is because of higher degree of vertical integration positively related to the firm's production performance. Hence, the policy makers should stimulate the entrance of foreign affiliates as long as they bring benefits to high-tech manufacturing industry and assures that the potential weaknesses of foreign firms do not outweigh the advantages.

REFERENCES

Abdul-Talib, A. N., Salleh, M. F. M., Shamsuddin, F. M., & Ashari, H. (2011). The effects of firm size and international business experience on export attitudes. *Journal of Competitiveness Studies*, *19*(1&2), 4–14.

Álvarez Espinoza, R., & González Tissinetti, A. (2020). *Competition, selection, and productivity growth in the Chilean manufacturing industry*. Universidad de Chile.

Amador, J., & Cabral, S. (2016). Global value chains: A survey of drivers and measures. *Journal of Economic Surveys*, *30*(2), 278–301. doi:10.1111/joes.12097

Arora, N., & Lohani, P. (2017). Does foreign direct investment spillover total factor productivity growth? A study of Indian drugs and pharmaceutical industry. *Benchmarking*, *24*(7), 1937–1955. doi:10.1108/BIJ-09-2016-0148

Athukorala, P. C., & Yamashita, N. (2006). Production fragmentation and trade integration: East Asia in a global context. *The North American Journal of Economics and Finance*, *17*(3), 233–256. doi:10.1016/j.najef.2006.07.002

Bajgar, M., Berlingieri, G., Calligaris, S., Criscuolo, C., & Timmis, J. (2019). *Industry concentration in Europe and North America*. London School of Economics and Political Science.

Baltagi, B. H. (2021). *Econometric analysis of panel data*. Springer Nature. doi:10.1007/978-3-030-53953-5

Bournakis, I. (2021). Spillovers and productivity: Revisiting the puzzle with EU firm level data. *Economics Letters*, *201*, 109804. doi:10.1016/j.econlet.2021.109804

BPS (Badan Pusat Statistik). (2015). *Annual Manufactuirng Survey*. Badan Pusat Statistik Republik Indonesia.

Chen, T. J., & Tang, D. P. (1987). Comparing technical efficiency between import-substitution-oriented and export-oriented foreign firms in a developing economy. *Journal of Development Economics*, *26*(2), 277–289. doi:10.1016/0304-3878(87)90030-7

Constantinescu, C., Mattoo, A., & Ruta, M. (2019). Does vertical specialisation increase productivity? *World Economy*, *42*(8), 2385–2402. doi:10.1111/twec.12801

Dawu, S. (2021). *Export participation and productivity: Evidence from the Ghana manufacturing industry* [Master Theses]. UMEA University.

De Loecker, J. (2007). Do exports generate higher productivity? Evidence from Slovenia. *Journal of International Economics, 73*(1), 69-98. doi: .2007.03.003 doi:10.1016/j.jinteco

Djankov, S., & Hoekman, B. (2000). Foreign investment and productivity growth in Czech enterprises. *The World Bank Economic Review*, *14*(1), 49–64. doi:10.1093/wber/14.1.49

Dornbusch, R., Fischer, S., & Startz, R. (2011). *Macroeconomics* (11th ed.). The McGraw-Hill Companies.

Esquivias, M. A., & Harianto, S. K. (2020). Does competition and foreign investment spur industrial efficiency?: Firm-level evidence from Indonesia. *Heliyon*, *6*(8), 1–10. doi:10.1016/j.heliyon.2020.e04494 PMID:32904310

Gnizy, I., Cadogan, J. W., Oliveira, J. S., Abdul-Talib, A. N., & Nizam, A. (2017). National Regional Diversification Strategy and Export Performance: An Extended Abstract. *2016 Academy of Marketing Science (AMS) World Marketing Congress*, 29–33. 10.1007/978-3-319-47331-4_5

Guadalupe, M., Kuzmina, O., & Thomas, C. (2012). Innovation and Foreign Ownership. *The American Economic Review*, *102*(7), 3594–3627. doi:10.1257/aer.102.7.3594

Gujarati, D. N., & Porter, D. C. (2009). *Basic econometrics (international edition)*. McGraw-Hills Inc.

Haddad, M., & Harrison, A. (1993). Are there positive spillovers from direct foreign investment?: Evidence from panel data for Morocco. *Journal of Development Economics*, *42*(1), 51–74. doi:10.1016/0304-3878(93)90072-U

Hashim, F., Bakar, A. R. A., & Abdul-Talib, A. N. (2010). *International Business* (2nd ed.). Oxford Fajar Press.

Hill, R. C., Griffiths, W. E., & Lim, G. C. (2018). *Principles of econometrics*. John Wiley & Sons.

Hoechle, D. (2007). Robust standard errors for panel regressions with cross-sectional dependence. *The Stata Journal*, *7*(3), 281–312. doi:10.1177/1536867X0700700301

Hsiao, C. (2014). *Analysis of panel data*. Cambridge university press. doi:10.1017/CBO9781139839327

IMF. (2004) Definition of foreign direct investment (FDI) terms, IMF committee on balance of payments statistics and OECD. In *Workshop on International Investment Statistics, Direct Investment Technical Expert Group (DITEG)*. Issues Paper (DITEG) #20, Statistics Canada.

Jones, R., Kierzkowski, H., & Lurong, C. (2005). What does evidence tell us about fragmentation and outsourcing? *International Review of Economics & Finance*, *14*(3), 305–316. doi:10.1016/j.iref.2004.12.010

Keller, W. (2010). International trade, foreign direct investment, and technology spillovers. In *Handbook of the Economics of Innovation* (Vol. 2, pp. 793–829). North-Holland. doi:10.1016/S0169-7218(10)02003-4

Khalifah, N. A., & Jafaar, Z. (2017). Technical efficiency of establishments in Malaysia's electrical electronics industries: Exporting or vertical trade? *Jurnal Ekonomi Malaysia*, *51*(1), 15–30.

Kiendrebeogo, Y. (2020). Learning by exporting or self-selection into exporting? *Middle East Development Journal*, *12*(2), 304–325. doi:10.1080/17938120.2020.1756105

Kimura, F., Takahashi, Y., & Hayakawa, K. (2007). Fragmentation and parts and components trade: Comparison between East Asia and Europe. *The North American Journal of Economics and Finance*, *18*(1), 23–40. doi:10.1016/j.najef.2006.12.002

Kohpaiboon, A. (2009). Vertical and horizontal FDI technology spillovers: evidence from Thai manufacturing. *ERIA Discussion Paper, 8*.

Lenaerts, K., & Merlevede, B. (2018). Indirect productivity effects from foreign direct investment and multinational firm heterogeneity. *Review of World Economics*, *154*(2), 377–400. doi:10.100710290-017-0298-9

Li, C., & Luo, Y. (2019). Spillover effects of foreign direct investment: Evidence from the west midlands of England. *Economic Issues, 24*(Part 1).

Moralles, H. F., & Moreno, R. (2020). FDI productivity spillovers and absorptive capacity in Brazilian firms: A threshold regression analysis. *International Review of Economics & Finance, 70*, 257–272. doi:10.1016/j.iref.2020.07.005

Najafi-Tavani, S., Najafi-Tavani, Z., Naudé, P., Oghazi, P., & Zeynaloo, E. (2018). How collaborative innovation networks affect new product performance: Product innovation capability, process innovation capability, and absorptive capacity. *Industrial Marketing Management, 73*, 193–205. doi:10.1016/j.indmarman.2018.02.009

Natsuda, K., & Thoburn, J. (2020). *Automotive Industrialisation: Industrial Policy and Development in Southeast Asia*. Routledge. doi:10.4324/9780429445354

Negash, E. S., Zhu, W., Lu, Y., & Wang, Z. (2020). Does chinese inward foreign direct investment improve the productivity of domestic firms? Horizontal linkages and absorptive capacities: Firm-level evidence from Ethiopia. *Sustainability, 12*(7), 3000–3023. doi:10.3390u12073023

Nguyen, T. X. H., Pham, T. H., Dao, T. N., Nguyen, T. N., & Tran, T. K. N. (2020). the impact of foreign ownership and management on firm performance in Vietnam. *The Journal of Asian Finance, Economics, and Business, 7*(9), 409–418. doi:10.13106/jafeb.2020.vol7.no9.409

Nicholson, W., & Snyder, C. M. (2012). *Microeconomic theory: Basic principles and extensions* (11th ed.). Nelson Education.

OECD. (2009). *OECD benchmark definition of foreign direct investment 2008*. Organisation for Economic Co-operation and Development Publishing.

Okafor, L. E. (2021). Export market destinations, imported intermediates, and productivity: Firm-level evidence from Ghana. *The International Trade Journal, 35*(4), 383–410. doi:10.1080/08853908.2020.1718567

Orlic, E., Hashi, I., & Hisarciklilar, M. (2018). Cross sectoral FDI spillovers and their impact on manufacturing productivity. *International Business Review, 27*(4), 777–796. doi:10.1016/j.ibusrev.2018.01.002

Özsoy, S., Ergüzel, O. Ş., Ersoy, A. Y., & Saygılı, M. (2021). The impact of digitalization on export of high technology products: A panel data approach. *The Journal of International Trade & Economic Development*, 1–22. doi:10.1080/09638199.2021.1965645

Pham, T. T. T., Hoang, T. A. N., Pham, H. H., & Ngo, M. T. (2014). *Does exporting spur firm productivity and promote inclusive growth? Evidence from Vietnam.* https://idl-bnc-idrc.dspacedirect.org/bitstream/handle/10625/54699/IDL-54699.pdf?sequence=1&isAllowed=y

Raei, M. F., Ignatenko, A., & Mircheva, M. (2019). *Global Value Chains: What are the Benefits and Why Do Countries Participate?* International Monetary Fund.

Rojec, M., & Knell, M. (2018). Why is there a lack of evidence on knowledge spillovers from foreign direct investment? *Journal of Economic Surveys, 32*(3), 579–612. doi:10.1111/joes.12207

Samuelson, P. A., & Nordhaus, W. D. (2019) Economics (19th ed.). New York: McGraw-Hill Education.

Sari, D. W. (2019). The potential horizontal and vertical spillovers from foreign direct investment on Indonesian manufacturing industries. *Economic Papers: A Journal of Applied Economics and Policy, 38*(4), 299-310.

Sari, D. W., Khalifah, N. A., & Suyanto, S. (2016). The spillover effects of foreign direct investment on the firms' productivity performances. *Journal of Productivity Analysis*, *46*(2), 199–233. doi:10.100711123-016-0484-0

Sari, D. W., & Restikasari, W. (2021). Global Trade Pattern on High-Tech Firms. *Jurnal Ekonomi dan Pembangunan Indonesia, 21*(1), 77-94. doi:10.21002/jepi.v21i1.1342

Sari, D. W., Restikasari, W., & Haryanto, T. (2020). Global Trading of Electronic Component in Indonesia Manufacturing Industry. *Elementary Education Online*, *19*(4), 639–646. doi:10.17051/ilkonline.2020.04.167

Shimbov, B., Alguacil, M., & Suárez, C. (2013). Fragmentation and parts and components trade in the Western Balkan countries. *Post-Communist Economies*, *25*(3), 371–391. doi:10.1080/14631377.2013.813142

Söderbom, M., & Teal, F. (2001). *Are African manufacturing firms really inefficient?: Evidence from firm-level panel data*. UNIDO.

Srholec, M. (2007). High-tech exports from developing countries: A symptom of technology spurts or statistical illusion? *Review of World Economics*, *143*(2), 227–255. doi:10.100710290-007-0106-z

Sterner, T. (1990). Ownership, technology, and efficiency: An empirical study of cooperatives, multinationals, and domestic enterprises in the Mexican cement industry. *Journal of Comparative Economics*, *14*(2), 286–300. doi:10.1016/0147-5967(90)90073-I

Toma, P. (2020). Size and productivity: A conditional approach for Italian pharmaceutical sector. *Journal of Productivity Analysis*, *54*(1), 1–12. doi:10.100711123-020-00580-y

Torsekar, M. P., & VerWey, J. (2019). East Asia-Pacific's participation in the global value chain for electronic products. *Journal of International Commerce Economics*, *1*, 1–21.

Tsougkou, E., Cadogan, J. W., Hodgkinson, I. R., Oliveira, J. S., Abdul-Talib, A. N., Story, V. M., & Lioliou, E. (2019). *Achieving export competitive advantage: can global orientation and export product adaptation be reconciled.* In *2019 AMA Global Marketing SIG Conference*, Buenos Aires, Argentina.

Van Ha, Holmes, & Hassan. (2019). Does foreign investment benefit the exporting activities of Vietnamese firms? *The World Economy*. doi:10.1111/twec.12912

Vinh, V. X. (2019). Foreign Ownership and Firm Performance-Evidence in Vietnam. *Journal of Economic Development*, 85–104.

Wagner, J. (2007). Exports and productivity: A survey of the evidence from firm-level data. *The World Economy, 30*(1), 60-82. DOI: .00872.x doi:10.1111/j.1467-9701.2007

Wooldridge, J. M. (2015). *Introductory econometrics: A modern approach*. Cengage Learning.

World Benchmarking Alliance. (2020). *The impact of multinationals in developing countries: A framework of Benchmarking*. worldbenchmarkingalliance.org

Xing, Y. (2014). China's high-tech exports: The myth and reality. *Asian Economic Papers*, *13*(1), 109–123. doi:10.1162/ASEP_a_00256

Yasar, M., & Paul, C. J. M. (2007). International linkages and productivity at the plant level: Foreign direct investment, exports, imports and licensing. *Journal of International Economics*, *71*(1), 373–388. doi:10.1016/j.jinteco.2006.03.004

Zakaria, N., Abdul-Talib, A. N., & Amelinckx, A. (Eds.). (2020). *Transcending Cultural Frontiers: Practices, Challenges, and Strategy for International Business*. Springer. doi:10.1007/978-981-15-4454-5

Zakaria, N., Abdul-Talib, A. N., & Othman, N. (Eds.). (2016). *Handbook of research on impacts of international business and political affairs on the global economy*. IGI Global. doi:10.4018/978-1-4666-9806-2

Chapter 9
Sustainability Analysis of Sino-Brazilian Bilateral Trade:
A Case Study of the 2020 Global Epidemic Event

Poshan Yu
https://orcid.org/0000-0003-1069-3675
Soochow University, China

Jiayi He
Independent Researcher, China

Michael Sampat
Independent Researcher, Canada

ABSTRACT

The large-scale health crisis caused by COVID-19 that appeared in late 2019 has undoubtedly had a huge influence on the global economy. This chapter takes the interruption of international trade in the context of epidemics as the main research subject, using the change in Sino-Brazilian trade as a case study. From the international management perspective, this chapter will investigate how this epidemic affects Sino-Brazilian cross-border trade and business practices. The interlinked relationship between both countries' cross-border trade will be examined. Recommendations will be provided for further enhancing both countries' economic growth and trade practices.

INTRODUCTION

Pearce believes that "sustainable development is that today's use should not reduce future real income", "when development can maintain the current people's welfare increase, it will not reduce the welfare of future generations as well ("Sustainable development", n.d.). With the rapid growth of the world economy and the intensifying development of economic globalization, the growth of international trade has been

DOI: 10.4018/978-1-7998-9071-3.ch009

significantly accelerated. International trade has become one of the important pillars for an increasing number of developing and even developed countries, playing an increasingly important role in the tide of economic globalization and liberalization (Li, 2010).

Sudden developments in the current affairs of the world are undoubtedly a major threat to the sustainable development of international trade. Since the end of 2019, COVID-19 has first spread at an unprecedented rate in China. In this respect, the occurrence of international public health emergencies will have a negative impact on international trade (Bai, 2019).

With the outbreak of COVID-19, international epidemic prevention and control has seriously affected global economic and trade exchanges and international economic cooperation. Considering the delay in the withdrawal of epidemic prevention and control measures and the carry-over effect of the epidemic, the impact on the global economy and trade will be far-reaching. The outbreak of COVID-19 is fast, long-lasting and has a wide-ranging impact. It not only interferes with the establishment of foreign trade enterprises, increases foreign trade costs, and reduces international demand, it also causes the restructuring of the global industrial chain and supply chain, creating uncertainties in global policy forecasts, thus producing a serious negative impact on international trade (Shen, 2020). Particularly for some developing countries, the low standard of medical technology and inadequate national infrastructure lead to an uncontrolled number of patients, leading to huge losses for these countries in all aspects of civil society, the economy, and politics.

The epidemic has caused huge losses to relevant industries and international trade. It also has fueled protectionism, prompted some countries to review their industrial layout and opening-up policies, and accelerated the localization and diversification of global supply chains. Globalization in the post-pandemic era will undergo profound adjustments. (Yuan, 2020). Not only that, but the impact of COVID-19 on international financial management has been enormous. The pandemic is likely to wreak havoc on fragile states, cause massive destruction and severely test crisis management systems (Zizek, 2020).

To this end, this paper aims to select specific and relatively representative bilateral international trade cases in the context of the epidemic to prove the threat to the sustainable development of the global economy and the new vitality of the global economy after the epidemic from a small perspective. As China and Brazil are important emerging economies in the world, China is the world's second largest economy and largest trading nation. Brazil is the largest economy in Latin America, the second largest economy in the Americas, and China's largest trading partner in the region. Bilateral trade relations are of great significance to the economic development of both countries (Chen et al., 2018).

In addition, it can be found from literature collection that although scholars have always discussed Sino-Brazilian trade from various angles, there are relatively few comparative studies on Sino-Brazilian trade before and after the background of global epidemic emergencies. Therefore, this paper further selects the bilateral trade between China and Brazil as a case study. This paper hopes to analyze the view that international trade can bring economic win-win results for both countries by describing the cases of China and Brazil recovering trade and strengthening international cooperation from the disruption of international trade in the context of the epidemic.

Outbreak of research under the status of the trade between China and Brazil, is not only with the aid of the outbreak of this incident to study inspection of bilateral trade between China and Brazil development sustainability, especially from the angle of the theory of market integration and the trade efficiency theory to analyze the bilateral trade between China and Brazil. In addition, this paper emphasizes once again the benefits of the healthy development of international trade for all participants by studying and analyzing the relatively extreme event that China and Brazil cooperated together to overcome the epidemic. In addition, this chapter also identifies the success factors and future challenges related to the coronavirus outbreak in bilateral trade cooperation.

THEORETICAL BASIS AND LITERATURE BACKGROUND

This paper discusses the impact on Sino-Brazilian trade of the COVID-19 pandemic, a situation that poses a major threat to international finance (Holmes et al., 2020). Due to COVID-19, most organizations face many strategic challenges in managing their supply chains with respect to the delivery of products and services and maintain customer satisfaction. If organizations fail to live up to such expectations, society will suffer huge consequences. Catastrophic scenarios clearly demonstrate the need for resilience (Mafabi et al., 2012). Supply chain resilience refers to "the adaptability of supply chain to cope with and recover from disruptions by maintaining continuity of operations and control of structure and function" (Ponomarov & Holcomb, 2009, pp. 131).

This paper refers to the concept of international management. International management is the management of business operations in organizations that exist in more than one country (Kogut, 2002). This definition emphasizes the need for more advanced skills than border management, including a broad understanding of local conditions and adaptations (Chi-Koffi & Wang, 2021). With the continuous growth of international trade, the higher the degree of integration of international enterprises, the greater the demand for international management of enterprises. International finance is not only about maximising shareholders, but also about maximising stakeholders. The company is no longer limited to producing and selling its products and services in the domestic market (Calvet, 1983). Economic shocks or financial instability may hinder international financial management, making it difficult for stakeholders to fully participate in international trade (Bekaert & Hodrick, 2017).

Apart from that, this paper will mainly use the trade efficiency theory and market integration theory as the theoretical basis of the analysis of Sino-Brazilian bilateral trade research. Trade efficiency is defined as the distance between the actual trade flow and the maximum trade volume. The closer the actual trade flow is to the maximum trade volume, the higher the trade efficiency will be. Trade efficiency is an important index to measure international trade. The more efficient a country is at maximizing trade, the smaller the gap between the actual volume of trade and the maximum value of trade at a given level of technology. Trade efficiency is influenced by the overall domestic and international trade environment (Shuai et al., 2018). Market integration, on the other hand, means that in the case of perfect market competition, the prices of the same kind of goods in different markets keep synchronous changes, which reflects the reasonable flow of economic resources and reflects the efficiency of market operation. Market integration has further improved trade efficiency among trading partners (Sheng et al., 2014).

As a small country compared with China, Brazil has improved its trade efficiency through bilateral trade with China, while China has further improved its trade efficiency due to the continuous development of trade potential between the two countries, and finally reached a win-win situation in trade and promoted the sustainable development of trade. An important benefit of market integration between China and Brazil in commodities such as iron ore and oil -- trade economists have long used gravity models to examine the relationship between bilateral trade flows and their determinants. In the literature, an important argument is made that market integration can improve trade efficiency, thereby improving the welfare of all trading partners by providing additional trade creation (Anderson, 1979; Anderson & Winkop, 2003; Costient & Rodriguez, 2013).

The theoretical analysis of this paper is based on many previous researches on market integration and trade efficiency. Among them, Chen Lin et al. (2018) used the Stochastic frontier model (SFA) to measure China's trade efficiency, trade potential and factor input scale efficiency of 153 countries and regions in the world from 1980 to 2015, and conducted a comparative analysis between OECD countries and non-OECD countries and regions. Through the research, it is found that China's trade efficiency with other countries and regions in the world is on the rise. At the same time, through data analysis, the study judged Brazil as a country with an important trade partnership with China and a country with "huge trade potential" in 2018, suggesting that there is a broad space for the development of Sino-Brazilian trade and a great space for the growth of bilateral trade. The study also suggests that China should focus on expanding trade with Brazil in the future, improving trade market conditions, deepening trade development, giving full play to trade potential with these countries and regions, maximizing trade volume, and promoting the economic development of the two countries. The forecast is in line with a development trend of Sino-Brazilian trade cooperation.

Li Hongbin and Zou Jiayu (2019) selected panel data related to trade between China and Brazil from 2006 to 2016 to construct a time-varying stochastic frontier gravity model to estimate the efficiency of bilateral trade and export trade between China and Brazil. The results show that the export efficiency between China and Brazil is between 0.79 and 0.87, and the bilateral trade efficiency between China and Brazil is between 0.44 and 0.80, and the bilateral trade efficiency is lower than the export efficiency. The potential of Sino-Brazilian bilateral trade is greater than that of Sino-Brazilian export trade. China will become an important export trading country for Brazil, and China's trade deficit with Brazil is further widening (Li & Zou, 2019). This prediction is also supported by basic data after the epidemic today, which has very important reference significance.

In addition, this paper also draws on the study of market integration and energy trade efficiency by Sheng, Y. et al. (2014), which used balanced panel data from 40 countries from 1995 to 2008 to show that market integration will increase trade by improving trade efficiency among trading partners.

CHARACTERISTICS OF INTERNATIONAL TRADE BETWEEN CHINA AND BRAZIL BEFORE THE EPIDEMIC

Brazil's Participation in International Trade

The largest country in South America, Brazil is also one of the most resource-rich countries in the world. It has the world's second-largest forest, one of the world's largest ranches, and ranks fifth in the world for arable land. In addition, Brazil is rich in iron ore and oil resources. Vale of Brazil is the world's largest producer and exporter of iron ore and the largest mining company in the Americas, known as the "crown jewel" of Brazil and the "engine of the Amazon" (Anonymous, 2018). Vale of Brazil has 5 international offices around the world, including the office set up in China in 1994. Vale has business operations and mineral exploitation activities in 15 countries and regions. With Vale's investment projects in China, the two countries are conducting feasibility studies. ("Companhia Vale do Rio Doce", n.d.).

Globally Brazil is a supplier of intermediate inputs and regionally it is a major production center (Araújo et al., 2021). Although Brazil's overall participation in international trade is not particularly significant, and it is often considered one of the most closed countries in the world (in 2019 Brazil's import to GDP ratio was 12.1%, less than one-third of Mexico's), foreign trade still plays an important role in Brazil's economy. Before World War II, Brazil was one of the world's leading exporters of primary products such as agricultural goods. After the war, with the acceleration of Brazil's industrialization, a large number of advanced technologies and equipment needed to be introduced. The active development of foreign trade has become an important means of accelerating economic development. Before the 1960s, however, Brazil's foreign trade stagnated as the economy turned inward (Anonymous, 2015). After the mid-1960s, the Brazilian economy was transformed from inward to outward, and the strategic slogan of "export and outlet" was put forward, which promoted the development of foreign trade (Schmitz, 1999). Brazil's exports soared in items such as footwear, from a small amount in the late 1960s to 150 million pairs in the late 1980s (Abaex, 1992).

In 2018, the total value of Brazil's exports reached \$239.5 billion, an increase of 9.6% over the previous year. The top five export destination countries were China, the United States, Argentina, the Netherlands and Chile, and the proportion of exports to the top five export destination countries was 26.8%, 12%, 6.3%, 5.5% and 2.7%, respectively. Other major export destinations include Chile, Mexico, Germany, Spain and Korea.

Figure 1. Top 15 Countries and regions of Brazil's goods exports in 2018(10 million dollars)
Source: Brazilian Foreign Trade Secretariat, 2018

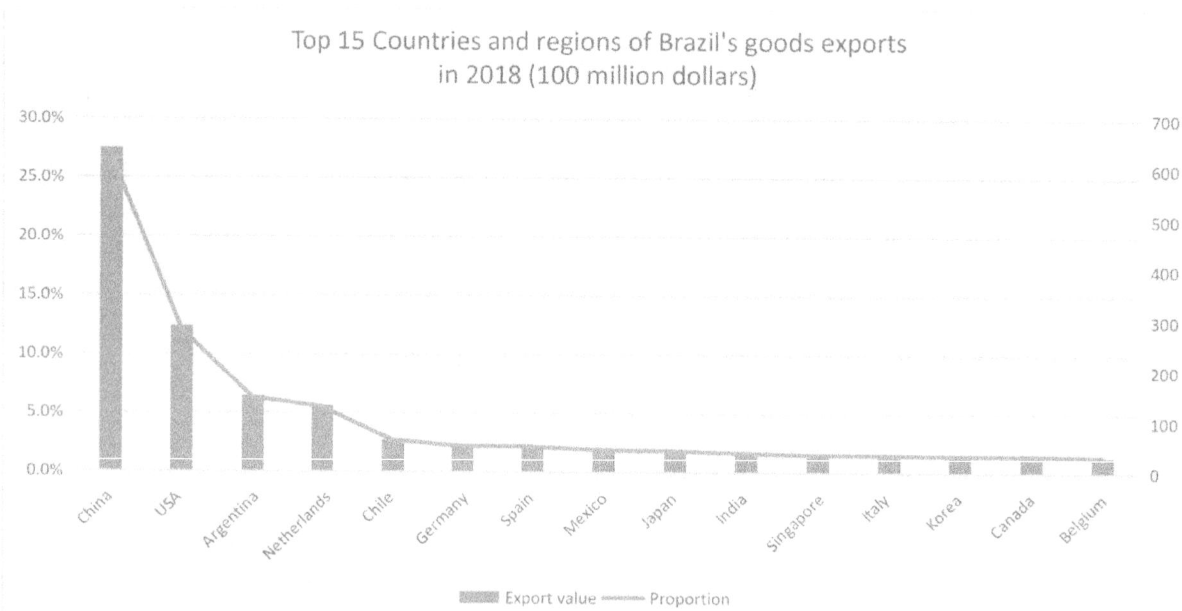

In addition, Brazil has contributed to the mitigation of global climate change by promoting the implementation of global energy sustainable development plans through its international trade. Brazil's energy matrix is three times the global average in size, with renewables accounting for 47.5% of total energy. The national energy footprint is 267.4 million barrels of oil, of which 61.7 percent comes from domestic sources and 38.3 percent from imports. Imports add to Brazil's non-renewable carbon footprint, as only 3.8% of the emissions from imported goods and services come from renewable energy sources.

By contrast, Brazil's exports contribute to the world's cleaner carbon footprint, as 39.4% of its export emissions come from renewable energy (Montoya, 2021).

China's Participation in International Trade

Since its admission to the WTO, China has developed into the world's second-largest economy and has become an indispensable part of world economic development. International trade not only drives China's economic development but also brings it challenges and opportunities (Chen, 2020).

With the rapid development of China's economy over the 30 years since reform and opening up, its economic status has improved significantly and its proportion and role in the international economy has become more and more prominent. Overall, however, China's economy is still in the stage of exploration and development. China has not yet established a systematic and complete socialist economy market structure, and the level of economic development needs further improvement (Chen, 2020). Although China's economic power and influence on the international economy are gradually increasing, its economic development is still focused on its extensive economy. While the lion's share of China's labour is still in agriculture, the US and EU have captured that share in the tertiary sector by outsourcing much of their agriculture, mining and industry; about half of their working hours are consumed (Laura et al., 2021). At the same time, because China's economic expansion is still in the exploratory stage, there remains a great deal of room for China's economic development. Presently the development trend of international economic integration points out a new direction for China's development going forward.

At the same time, China has also optimized its energy trade relations with border countries through the "Belt and Road Initiative," occupying an advantageous position (Shuai et al., 2020). Belt and Road Initiative countries rely more on China as a source of exports than China relies on them as a source of imports. In particular, the influence of the Organization of Petroleum Exporting Countries (OPEC) on China's energy security has declined due to the diversification of Chinese oil import suppliers (He & Guo, 2021).

Research by the International Energy Agency (IEA) also suggests that Belt and Road Initiative countries will install 1.94 gigawatts of new renewable energy capacity by 2030 and another 2.6 gigawatts over the next decade. Under the Paris Agreement's carbon reduction targets, Belt and Road Initiative countries are expected to add 3.5 trillion kilowatt-hours of renewable energy capacity in 2030 (Tang, 2018). Therefore, there is no doubt that China and the Belt and Road Initiative countries have great potential in the development and utilization of renewable energy and international trade (Fang et al., 2020).

A SUMMARY OF BILATERAL TRADE BETWEEN BRAZIL AND CHINA

From the establishment of diplomatic relations between China and Brazil on August 15, 1974, to the establishment of a strategic partnership between the two countries in 1993 and a comprehensive strategic partnership in 2012, the trade between China and Brazil was officially started. China and Brazil have signed several cooperation agreements, including the general framework of the implementation plan between the two governments for the period 2015-2021, covering infrastructure, production capacity cooperation, energy, agriculture, science and technology, aerospace, and more (Foresight Industrial Research Institute, 2019).

According to the statistics of the Brazilian Foreign Trade Secretariat, the trade between China and Brazil began to pick up in 2017. By 2018, bilateral imports and exports of goods between Brazil and China reach US $98.94 billion, an increase of 32.3%. By 2019, China becomes Brazil's largest exporter and importer and China has been Brazil's largest trading partner for 11 consecutive years. The trade between the two countries is highly complementary (Foresight Industrial Research Institute, 2019).

Figure 2. Sino-Brazilian bilateral trade volume and growth from 2013 to 2019 (100 million dollars)
Source: Brazilian Foreign Trade Secretariat, 2019

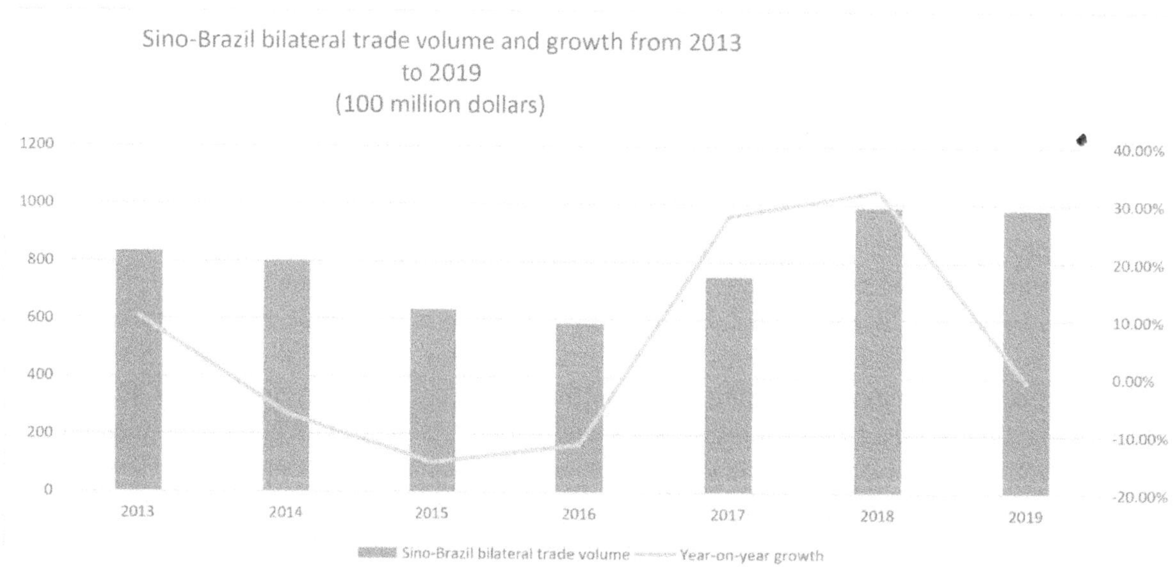

On the one hand, Brazil is rich in iron ore and oil. On the other hand, China is now the world's largest importer of food, the largest importer of iron ore and the largest importer of oil. Thus, the two countries have natural complementarities in agricultural products (including soybeans and pork), iron ore and oil. In addition, for Brazil, China's large quantity of mechanical and electrical output and chemical products are highly competitive, the main products that Brazil imports from China (Anonymous, 2018). For China, Brazil's iron ore, soybeans, pork, oil and so on are important to the Chinese market. At the same time, because of China's emphasis in recent years on closer ties with Latin American countries, it has become increasingly dependent on Brazilian exports (He & Guo, 2021).

In the bilateral trade between China and Brazil, although some products compete with each other, they are more often mutually beneficial, interdependent and inseparable. It is believed that with the continuous economic development of the two countries, the trade complementarity between China and Brazil will continue to deepen and the bilateral trade will continue its trend of steady improvement (Anonymous, 2018).

BILATERAL TRADE IN MINERALS BEFORE THE EPIDEMIC

With the rapid development of China's iron and steel industry and the rapid growth of steel output, the consumption of iron ore has been rising sharply year by year and China has become the world's largest iron ore consumer country (Zhang et al., 2018). As domestic iron ore is far from meeting the requirements of the rapidly developing steel industry, China needs to import large quantities of iron ore from countries with rich iron resources, such as Brazil and Australia, to ease the scarcity of ore at home. In order to compete for the Chinese market, Brazil's Vale, one of the world's three mining giants, began to expand its role from a simple ore trader to an industrial investor. However, Vale of Brazil has been at a disadvantage compared with the other two Australian mining giants and Indian mining companies in terms of the construction of large ships to reduce freight costs and travel farther from China. Therefore, Vale has ordered a large iron ore carrier with a capacity of 400,000 tons, greatly reducing iron ore transport costs (Companhia Vale do Rio Doce, n.d.). In terms of trade, bilateral trade products between China and Brazil are relatively concentrated. Brazil's main exports to China are iron ore and other products (Duan, 2011).

Table 1 shows that from 2005 to 2020, China's annual imports of iron ore from Brazil accounted for about 20% of China's total imports, which was still relatively large, and China was relatively dependent on Brazil's iron ore exports. As can be seen from Table 2, although Brazil is rich in iron ore resources, iron ore exported from Brazil to China accounts for a high proportion of the total export of Brazil, indicating that Brazil's iron ore is very dependent on the export to the Chinese market. According to the analysis of the data from 2005 to 2020, the amount of Brazilian iron ore imported by China accounted for 21.45%, 21.46%, 25.56%, 22.68%, 25%, 21.14%, 20.85%,17.8%, 24.27%, 18.11%, 20.04%, 15.92%, 21.46%, 19.75%, 21.33% and 20.15% of China's total imports in these sixteen years. The amount of Brazil's iron ore exports to China accounts for 26.36%, 29%, 39%, 35.46%, 60.16%, 42.1%, 43.2%, 43.2%,40.37%, 60.61%, 49.13%, 52.33%, 43.58%, 52.33%, 43.58%, 58.85%, 52.56%, 64.96% and 71.42% of Brazil's total exports. Brazil exports to China at a much faster rate than China imports.

Table 1. China's iron ore imports from Brazil from 2005 to 2020 (100 million tons)

China's iron ore imports from Brazil from 2005 to 2020 (100 million tons)																
Iron ore	2005	2006	2007	2008	2009	2010	2011	2012	2013	2014	2015	2016	2017	2018	2019	2020
China's total imports	2.75	3.26	3.84	4.44	5.68	6.19	6.86	7.44	8.24	9.33	9.53	10.24	10.53	10.38	10.69	11.70
China's imports from Brazil	0.59	0.70	0.98	1.05	1.42	1.31	1.43	1.32	2.00	1.69	1.91	1.63	2.26	2.05	2.28	2.36
Proportion	21.45%	21.46%	25.56%	22.68%	25%	21.14%	20.85%	17.74%	24.27%	18.11%	20.04%	15.92%	21.46%	19.75%	21.33%	20.15%

Source: Ministry of Commerce of China and China Customs statistics

Table 2. Brazilian iron ore exports to China from 2005 to 2020 (100 million tons)

Brazilian iron ore exports to China from 2005 to 2020 (100 million tons)																
Iron ore	2005	2006	2007	2008	2009	2010	2011	2012	2013	2014	2015	2016	2017	2018	2019	2020
Brazil's total iron ore exports	2.24	2.41	2.69	2.82	2.36	3.11	3.31	3.27	3.30	3.44	3.65	3.74	3.84	3.90	3.51	3.30
Brazil's iron ore exports to China	0.59	0.70	1.05	1.00	1.42	1.31	1.43	1.32	2.00	1.69	1.91	1.63	2.26	2.05	2.28	2.36
Proportion	26.36%	29%	39%	35.46%	60.16%	42.10%	43.20%	40.37%	60.61%	49.13%	52.33%	43.58%	58.85%	52.56%	64.96%	71.42%

Source: Ministry of Commerce of China and China Customs statistics

Brazil exported $28.5 billion worth of iron ore in 2010, according to the country's foreign trade association. Strong global demand has pushed Brazil's iron ore exports past the $20 billion mark, the first time six percent of a single commodity has been exported that amount.

Brazil's Vale, for example, exported 17.4 percent of its iron ore to China in 2009, and the share is growing (Wang, 2011). In general, the import ratio of iron ore and other resource products shows a trend of steady increase year by year, while the import of other products is very small and fluctuates greatly.

THE EFFICIENCY AND MARKET INTEGRATION OF BILATERAL TRADE BETWEEN CHINA AND BRAZIL ARE THREATENED

The Impact of The Epidemic on Sino-Brazilian Trade

Cases of COVID-19 are increasing every day in Brazil, with 18,909,037 positive cases as of July 8, 2021. At the time of writing, the number of COVID-19 deaths in Brazil has risen to 528,611. The southeastern region of Brazil includes the states of Minas Gerais, Espirito Santo, Sao Paulo, and Rio de Janeiro. The region is also the most populous in Brazil, contributing significantly to the country's economic growth, and has the highest number of cases of COVID-19. About 16 percent of Brazil's urban population in the area lives in shantytowns, known in Brazil as favelas. These poorer communities lack access to decent housing and quality health services. The backdrop of inadequate health care and economic inequality, coupled with winter which brings the flu season, adds to the uncertainty and unpredictability of the future impact of the COVID-19 pandemic on Brazil (Cesar, 2021).

As Table 3 shows, Brazil's overall exports were hit hard during the epidemic. Until recently, there was a degree of recovery and rebuilding, which cannot be separated from the turnaround of COVID-19, the policy adjustment of Brazil's government, and the assistance of some countries in the world.

Table 3. Monthly Brazil Export

Month	Export volume (millon dollars)	Growth rate
November'19	17736.72	4.20%
December'19	18502.98	4.32%
January'20	14498.03	-21.64%
February'20	15581.31	7.47%
March'20	18347.83	17.76%
April'20	17593.15	-4.11%
May'20	17526.90	-0.38%
June'20	17498.86	-0.16%
July'20	19453.60	11.17%
August'20	17564.24	-9.71%
September'20	18459.48	5.10%
October'20	17855.40	-3.27%

Source: Trading Economics, 2020

Figure 3. Brazilian unemployment rate
Source: Bank World, 2020

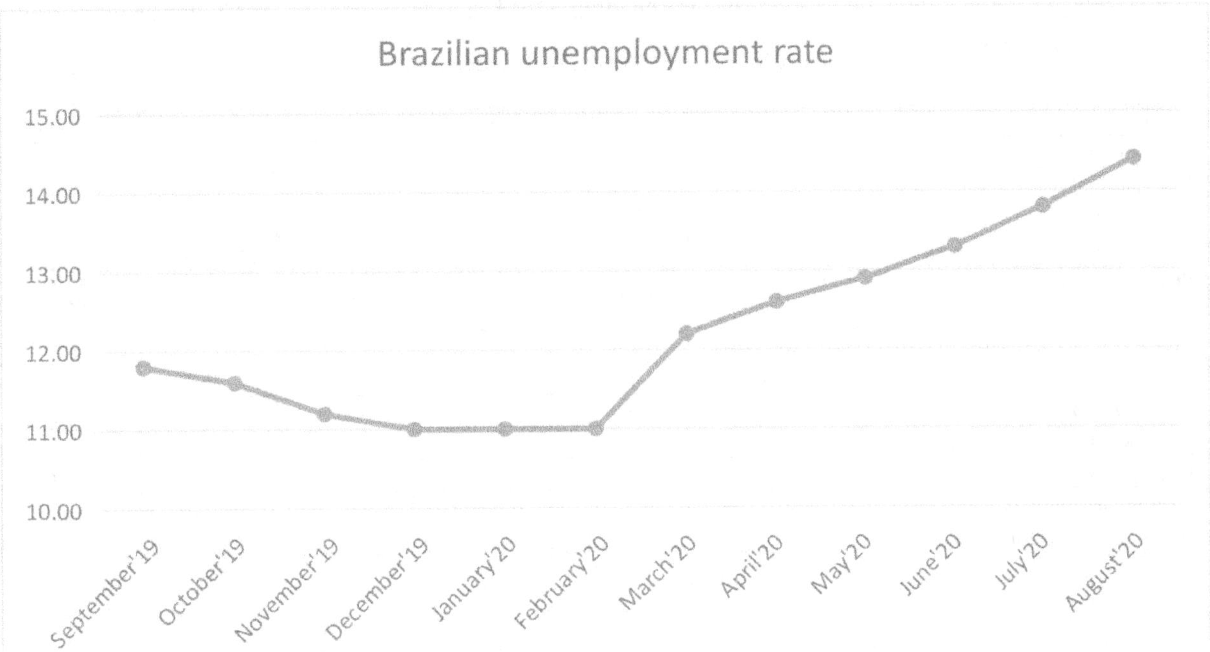

According to the website of El Pais newspaper on June 22, iron ore prices have started to climb amid fears of a supply shortage. The price rise comes after Brazil, the world's second-largest producer, was forced to close a major iron-ore mining district in the country after 188 workers were infected with novel Coronavirus. This is no small matter, as the metal is a key factor in economic development (China Trade News Net, 2020). Thus, unemployment in Brazil has begun to rise because of the outbreak.

In early June, a Brazilian court ordered Vale, the world's largest iron ore miner, to halt operations at the Itabira complex. Experts believe the shutdown could cut the company's output by as much as 10 percent, a loss that has yet to be made up. "The supply in Brazil was already severely affected by the monsoon rains earlier this year, and the recent closure of a mine following the novel Coronavirus is a wake-up call," commented Julian Hall, Head of Asian metals prices at Platts. "Any change will have a direct impact on prices," said Lucas Carvalho, an analyst (China Social Science Network, 2020).

In the meantime, for China, shipping embargoes were imposed by the world's major economies during the pandemic, which hindered effective exporting from China and imports from Europe and the United States. Other economies have also responded to the outbreak with trade restrictions. Combined with the impact of trade protectionism and the long-term weakness of global trade activities, along with the impact of various other factors, global trade has stalled in the short term. Market participants face difficulties fulfilling contracts, delayed delivery of goods, and longer clearance times, which could lead to a number of trade disputes between global companies. China's total RMB import and export to "Belt and Road Initiative" countries reached 2.76 trillion yuan, up 0.9%, accounting for 30.4% of China's total foreign trade, as shown in Table 4:

Table 4. The total value of China's imports and exports from January to April 2020

Trade way	From January to April			Year-on-year		
	Import and export	Export	Import	Import and export	Export	Import
Total value	1,298,330.9	678,283.4	620,047.5	-7.5	-9.0	-5.9
General trade	776,851.3	396,454.4	380,396.9	-7.2	-8.9	-5.4
International organizations provide free assistance and gifts of materials	244.4	242.3	2.1	6.7	6.3	81.7
Other donated materials	548.2	177.4	370.8	7,973.3	59,164.3	5,612.3
Processing and assembling trade with supplied materials	47,348.4	21,387.8	25,960.7	-10.7	-12.5	-9.2
Import processing trade	264,840.8	171,431.3	93,409.4	-11.1	-13.4	-6.3
Border petty trade	9,436.3	6,877.0	2,559.3	-23.8	-25.2	-19.9
Processing trade import equipment	90.9	—	90.9	-23.8	—	-23.3
Contracted projects to export goods	3,770.1	3,770.1	—	-20.4	-20.4	—
Leasing trade	307.7	54.2	253.5	-87.6	2.5	-89.6
Equipment and goods imported by enterprises with foreign investment	1,266.7	—	1,266.7	-40.0	—	-40.0
Material processing trade	195.8	112.4	83.4	3.6	43.3	-24.6
Customs special supervision area logistics goods	100,407.8	35,522.7	64,885.0	0.2	-5.9	3.8
Import equipment in special customs supervision area	3,524.5	—	3,524.5	22.0	—	22.0
Other	30,944.4	26,391.4	4,553.0	12.1	22.9	-25.8

Source: Bureau of Customs Statistics of China, 2020

Second, the proportion of import and export in general trade has been increasing, reaching about 60%. In the first four months of this year, the total value of foreign trade was about US $0.777 trillion, down 7.5 percent from 2019 and accounting for 59.8 percent of China's total foreign trade. That's an increase of about 0.2 percent from the same period in 2019, as shown in Table 5.

According to statistics from the Ministry of Commerce, China's total import and export value in 2019 was 315, 44.6 billion yuan, up 3.4%. Of which, export is 17.22298 billion yuan, up 5%; Imports were 14.3148 billion yuan, up 1.6%; The trade surplus was 2.915 billion yuan, up 25.4%.

Thirdly, viral outbreaks pose serious challenges to the world economy, including cross-border foreign direct investment (FDI). China's inward foreign direct investment (IFDI) and outward foreign direct investment (OFDI) also face unprecedented risks and challenges.

Fourth, the COVID-19 outbreak's influence on overseas mining trade policy risk is mainly manifested in three aspects. The first of these is personnel for immigration control measures, namely business negotiation, project management personnel, or service personnel affected by quarantines or immigration control. Also problematic are delays or incapacity to reach the project host country engaged in labor services or management activities. Second, the control of trade for the import of mining machinery and equipment or raw materials, including port customs clearance control, inspection and quarantine requirements, and compulsory goods collection or elimination; Thirdly, ore shipment restrictions. The outbreak has begun to affect the supply chain. When shippers go to China looking for work, some projects in host countries are delayed by the closure of border crossings. When the product is blocked from shipping to project host-countries by the outbreak, Chinese traders and smelters downstream in the procurement process can experience high contract-default risk (Shanghai Municipal Commission of Commerce, 2020).

Table 5. The total value of China's imports and exports from January to April 2020 in major countries (regions)

Import country of origin export country of final destination	Import and export	Export	Import	January-April period %		
	From January to April	From January to April	From January to April	Import and export	Export	Import
Total value	90,713	47,435	43,278	-4.9	-6.4	-3.2
The European Union	12,345.7	7,190.1	5,155.6	-6.5	6.6	-6.4
The United States	9,584.6	7,022.8	2,074.5	-12.8	-15.9	-3
Association of Southeast Asian Nations	13,494.1	7,409	6,085.1	5.7	3.9	8
Japan	6,656.8	3,028.6	3,628.2	-2.1	-2.2	-2
Hong Kong, China	5,163.1	5,019.9	143.3	-10.6	-9.8	-30.3
South Korea	5,967.5	2,327.9	3,639.7	-4.6	-3.4	-5.4
Taiwan, China	5,016.4	1,229.9	3,786.5	8.6	10.2	8.1
Australia	3,601.5	961.1	2,640.4	1.8	-1.7	3.1
Russian Federation	2,344.6	919.6	1,425	2.9	-6.5	10.1
India	1,658.4	1,304.4	353.9	-14.9	-14.8	-15.6
Britain	1,477.4	1,025.1	452.3	-17	-19.6	-10.6
Canada	1,095	650.4	444.6	-25.3	-14.6	-36.8
New Zealand	421.9	110.7	331.2	2.1	-4.7	4.7
Brazil	2,290.5	670.4	1,620.1	-3.2	-1.1	-4
South Africa	720.6	282	438.6	-23.9	-18.2	-27.2

Source: China Customs, 2020

Fifth, with regard to mining equity investment, the pandemic has had an impact on deal certainty and workers. On the one hand, many cross-border M&A transactions are conducted through competitive bidding or public bidding. In such transactions, in addition to price, transaction certainty is an important consideration for sellers to select suitable buyers. According to China's regulations on overseas investment, overseas investment enterprises are required to complete a series of filing and approval procedures in China. As the epidemic has seriously affected the pace of work, many government agencies have spent a lot of energy on epidemic prevention and control, which may cause a certain delay in the approval work, which will further increase the seller's concern about the uncertainty of approval. On the other hand, due to the complexity of cross-border investment, enterprises usually need to form a large business negotiation team and hire professional intermediary agencies to participate in the project. Affected by the epidemic, many places in China have adopted traffic control or quarantine measures, which will inevitably affect the personnel in place. In addition, the epidemic will also have an impact on project due diligence, especially for high-risk projects such as mining, where on-site due diligence becomes more important (Shanghai Municipal Commission of Commerce, 2020).

Affected by the epidemic, bilateral trade between China and Brazil has declined. Consistent with the downward trend of Brazil's foreign trade, bilateral imports and exports of goods between Brazil and

China in 2019 were US $98.14 billion, down 0.8%. According to the statistics of China's Ministry of Commerce, the bilateral trade value between China and Brazil in 2020 was 17.49 billion US dollars, down 2.7% year on the year. Among them, China's export to Brazil was US $15.37 billion, down 4.9%. Imports from Brazil were $2.12 billion, up 17.5% year over year. As a result, the bilateral trade deficit shrank 7.73 percent to $13.25 billion (Anonymous, 2020). Trade efficiency in China and Brazil has declined significantly.

As the supply side affected by the epidemic reduced shipments, iron ore prices rose sharply. According to Boil GTA data, on the supply side, Australia and Brazil delivered 2.506 million tons, down 690,000 tons from last week, and the average weekly shipment of the two countries in the year was 21.8 million tons. Port arrival value was 22.53 million tons, 1.39 million tons more than last week, and the average weekly arrival value of the year was 22.17 million tons. Australia and Brazil shipments are generally stable, the value of shipments indicated that the impact of the early cyclone gradually subsided (China Money Network, 2020). On Feb. 11, VALE.US said its fourth-quarter iron ore production fell 22.4 percent from a year earlier to 78.34 million metric tons, while its quarterly iron ore sales fell 3.2 percent to 77.91 million metric tons (Vale, 2020).

Despite the response measures taken by other countries, so far, Brazil's restrictions are not severe enough to have a major impact on mining operations, transportation, and exports. However, they are all still essential for efficiency of delivery and the risk of disruption is much higher (Anonymous, 2020).

Sino-Brazilian International Management Strategies After the Epidemic

Affected by the epidemic, 141 countries and regions have imposed entry control, visa suspension and quarantine measures on Chinese citizens. It is difficult for Chinese buyers to send Chinese personnel to work in the project area. At the same time, the online meeting method has also been greatly popularized and applied, which may help to offset problems created by restrictions on movement (Shanghai Municipal Commission of Commerce, 2020).

On November 4, 2020, with the outbreak's impact on economics and trade in the background, China held the third annual import expo, continuing to expand imports, and adhering to its goals to open the Chinese market. The aim was to speed up the global economy recovery. The construction of the open market plays an important role in the world economy. In light of the COVID crisis and demand of the global economy, a special exhibition area for public health and epidemic prevention has been set up (Zhonghong National Research Institute, 2020). Through this exhibition, Vale of Brazil further strengthened its partnership with China and shared high-quality technology with Chinese partners in the early stages of development (Vale, 2020). In response to the epidemic, Brazil has increased the flexibility of foreign exchange management in import and export trade, and the Central bank of Brazil has relaxed these regulatory requirements as well (Xie & Zhang, 2020).

In the post-COVID-19 era, China Baowu Steel and Vale of Brazil, the world's largest iron ore supplier, completed the cross-border settlement of some imported iron ore under the long-term agreement in RMB, with a total settlement amount of about 330 million YUAN (nearly 50 million US dollars). This move marks a new breakthrough for China Baowu to adopt RMB cross-border settlement with the world's major mining companies in iron ore import procurement. It is also represents important progress for China Baowu in fulfilling its responsibility as a central enterprise to promote the process of RMB internationalization. Carrying out RMB cross-border settlement of imported iron ore, allows domestic buyers to effectively avoid risks caused by exchange rate fluctuations. As for overseas mining enterprises, with the increasingly close business relationship with China, they can also reduce the risk of exchange rate fluctuations caused by accidents in their trade in China (Lian, 2020). Vale of Brazil announced that it will continue to strengthen cooperation with China in the future, and it is ready to ship 400,000 tons of iron ore resources to China (McMahon, 2021).

DISCUSSION AND ANALYSIS

Key Factors for the Successful Response of China and Brazil to the Epidemic

With no vaccine or antiviral drugs available, China, the epicenter of the outbreak, moved quickly to deal with it. Typical measures include the use of existing, traditional strategies of detection, isolation, physical distance, and community containment of public health epidemics, which have had an immediate positive effect in containing the virus (Olufadewa et al., 2020). The findings of Muhammad (2020) suggest that a combination of measures including cordon, strict control of social distance, investigation of common symptoms, transportation restrictions, and quarantine policy are the main factors in controlling the spread of the COVID-19 virus in China. Through its innovation and practice, China developed effective measures to deal with the pandemic and immediately shared them with the world (Guo, 2020).

Brazilian Ambassador to China Paulo Valle said that when China was hit by the first wave of the COVID-19 pandemic, the Brazilian government and people offered encouragement and help to the Chinese government and people (Anonymous, 2020). While the epidemic in China has been getting better and Brazil is facing a grim situation, the Chinese government and people have also expressed sincere sympathy and offered firm support to the Brazilian government and people in their fight against the epidemic, actively providing Brazil with anti-epidemic resources. At the same time, relevant departments and professionals of the two countries held video conferences, which provided great help to Brazil in its fight against the epidemic. Valle greatly appreciated the exchange mechanism between the two countries and hoped that it would continue and help find a way to defeat COVID-19 once and for all (Guo, 2020). Ronnie Linse, director of the Center for Chinese Studies in Brazil, said that Chinese government departments at all levels, including medical workers, community workers, and countless ordinary workers, have shouldered their responsibilities and made important contributions to epidemic prevention and control. Related enterprises in the fields of health and epidemic prevention, medical equipment, food and medicine have stepped up production to ensure the supply of medical supplies and basic necessities. Complete transportation and logistics network ensures the transportation and timely delivery of materials. After the epidemic was basically stabilized, China began to steadily promote the resumption of work and production, adopted a series of incentive policies to improve the business environment, and provided greater financial support to small and medium-sized enterprises. As a result, the international trade between China and Brazil soon returned to normal (Zhao, 2020).

As a result, Brazil's exports to China have increased this year despite the COVID-19 pandemic, making China the biggest bright spot in Brazil's foreign trade this year. Some Brazilian experts and scholars believe that trade with China brings Brazil a large amount of foreign exchange income, which prevents the Brazilian economy from facing a very severe situation.

OPPORTUNITIES AND FUTURE CHALLENGES

Brazil's iron ore exports reached 33.68m tones in June, the highest level in nine months, up 12.2 percent from a year earlier and 26.3 percent from the previous month, according to official government data. This is because major producers such as Vale have increased shipments in response to higher international prices. Global commodity prices have been rising and iron ore prices have been supported by strong demand from China (Hong, 2021).

The Brazil's Folha De Sao Paulo newspaper (2021) reported that the growth in Brazil's trade surplus is being driven by the recovery of the world economy as countries begin to recover from the epidemic. In addition to the continued growth of exports to China, most countries and regions increased their purchases of Brazilian products in the first half of the year. Imports to China rose 37.8 percent year on year, and exports to China rose to 35.3 percent of Brazil's total exports from 34.9 percent a year earlier, cementing China's position as the biggest buyer of goods. In addition, exports to the United States, the European Union and South American countries increased by 33.2 percent, 25.9 percent and 50.5 percent, respectively (Hong, 2021).

In recent years, Brazil's iron ore production, recovery, and export growth trend show that, even though it cannot shake Australia's position as a major exporter of iron ore in the world, it is conducive to promoting the diversification of China's imported iron ore and reducing China's dependence on imported Australian iron ore. In addition, as China vigorously promotes the construction of "The Belt and Road Initiative" and encourages enterprises to go global, the human resource management mode of overseas companies is constantly innovating and corporate culture is constantly integrated. Brazilian companies attach great importance to cultivating talents with global vision and open thinking, paying attention to talent training and development, and improving the ability of international operation and cross-cultural communication. Since the outbreak, Brazilian companies have arranged online exchange and learning sessions for their employees in China mainly through international video conferences to enhance their understanding and integration of Chinese culture and corporate culture (Zheng, 2019). The pandemic has given a strong boost to telecommuting in Brazil by changing people's behaviour.

In general, Sino-Brazilian relations have developed by leaps and bounds in the past decade and more, and have become an important link in the relations between major powers in the global context. Economic and trade relations between China and Brazil are naturally complementary and this economic and trade partnership is important to both countries. Economic and trade cooperation is the most efficient area of bilateral relations. Although the global macroeconomic situation and trade environment are facing challenges and uncertainties, Sino-Brazilian economic and trade cooperation still enjoys strong resilience and great potential in the post-epidemic period (Zhou, 2020).

The successful containment of the epidemic has enhanced the risk resistance and resilience of China-Brazil international trade cooperation, and strengthened the expansion and sustainability of future cooperation. In the opinion of this paper, since China's financial system is generally regarded as an international financial system. While the four main headings of international financial management include foreign exchange, market imperfections, enhanced opportunity sets (foreign direct investment) and political risk (Eun & Resnick, 2010). Therefore, in a sense, It is through relatively successful international financial management that China has helped Brazil maintain the normal operation of the supply chain of iron ore, oil and other commodities in bilateral trade, jointly resisted the huge impact of the epidemic on bilateral trade, and maintained the efficiency and sustainable development of bilateral trade.

Nevertheless, Brazil's gross domestic product fell 9.7 percent in the second quarter from the previous quarter and 11.4 percent from the same period last year, according to data released by the country's geographical statistics office on September 1. Although Brazil has seen some relief in the last two months, it will take some time for the economy to recover (Zhu, 2020). Diego Davila Trinidad, an international relations expert at the Brazilian Center for Global Studies, said China's large purchases of Brazilian agricultural products have kept the Brazilian economic problems from becoming too serious and given the government enough money to fight the epidemic. Luo Zhiming, Commercial Consul of the Brazilian Consulate General in Shanghai, said that this year's trade figures have surpassed last year's in many areas, so it is difficult to categorize as a recovery (Chen, 2020). This shows that the impact of the epidemic on Sino-Brazilian bilateral trade has yet to be fully recovered. Continued international coordination is essential to support fragile states, restore market confidence and reduce risks to financial stability (Chi-Koffi & Wang, 2021).

In this case, the continued spread of COVID-19 poses a major challenge to public health and economic recovery. Governments must play an active role in designing and implementing economic policies to address problems that pure market forces cannot address, such as externalities and the lack of risk markets. In addition to providing fiscal stimulus, the government needs to take a range of other steps to fill the gap in the market and promote a strong recovery. In addition to ensuring full employment, these measures include regulating externalities, promoting strong competition, preventing exploitation, limiting market forces and providing social protection. In countries that have been most successful in dealing with COVID-19, governments have played these roles effectively (Stiglitz, 2021).

Especially for China and Brazil, the government should increase fiscal and financial support, expand domestic demand and upgrade infrastructure, tap internal potential, and promote high-quality economic development. At present, China's external demand is shrinking and the external driving force of economic growth is weakening. The government must step up fiscal stimulus and tax cuts and exemptions to stimulate domestic demand. For example, the government could promote the construction of new infrastructure and speed up the digital upgrading of Chinese enterprises and industrial chains. Second, the government should earnestly optimize the business environment, promote market-oriented reform at home and deepen economic opening abroad. In the face of efforts by the international conservative forces to "de-sinify" and de-link themselves from China, China needs to firmly uphold the vision of a community with a shared future for mankind, promoting common global development, sharing opportunities, achieving mutually beneficial relationships, and supporting international efforts to stop the epidemic (Xu, 2020).

In view of the ongoing epidemic situation, it is still a huge challenge for both countries to realize further development and breakthrough in the trade relationship between China and Brazil. Research toward this end also requires the continuous tracking of the trade status of the two countries by scholars.

LIMITATIONS AND FUTURE PROSPECTS

Despite this article's repeated emphasis on the global economic impact of the COVID-19 pandemic, containment measures have had some positive impacts for stakeholders in international financial management. Central banks have played a key role in maintaining stability in global financial markets and keeping credit flowing among other benefits. Financial, monetary and fiscal policies aimed at reducing the impact of COVID-19 have also been put in place to ensure a stable and sustainable economic recovery once the outbreak is contained (Chi-Koffi & Wang, 2021).

Similarly, the pandemic has prompted countries to improve their governance capacity. One area is crisis management ability. The pandemic is a test of the ability of governments to make accurate judgments, make decisions quickly and act decisively in a short period of time when information is scarce and the situation is highly uncertain. Another area is the ability to integrate resources. With the rapid spread of the epidemic in a short period of time, the unified deployment, coordination and efficient allocation of resources by the government directly affects the epidemic prevention and control process. A third area is social management ability. Effectively stopping the spread of the virus requires the active response of the public, households and enterprises and the coordination of the government's prevention and control deployment. The pandemic has boosted the social mobilization and management capacity of governments (Yuan, 2020).

This paper also has some limitations in the study of the bilateral trade between China and Brazil before and after the epidemic. The most important point is that the epidemic has not ended by the time of writing this paper, and the trade status forecast between China and Brazil after the epidemic has not been supported by a large number of specific literature and data. Therefore, the bilateral trade status of the iron ore market between China and Brazil in the post-epidemic era still needs further and longer follow-up and research by scholars.

In must be said, the logic of this paper's argument is based on the theoretical benefits of trade efficiency and market integration, mainly starting from a perspective surveying the damage done to the sustainability of international trade and international management by the pandemic. However, this paper is mainly a conceptual paper on the selected topics, without establishing concrete or substantive model.

CONCLUSION AND RECOMMENDATIONS

In recent years, with the continuous development of economic globalization, economic exchanges between countries have become increasingly close and international trade has developed rapidly (Shahbaz et al., 2017). In the context of the global COVID-19 pandemic, sustainable development is considered a key concept and solution for creating a hopeful and prosperous future for human society (Pirouz et al., 2020). Sustainable consumption must become a global policy (Cohen, 2020), because the conservation of natural resources must be sustainable to meet the needs of the next generation (Severo et al., 2021).

While much research has focused on the global ecological, economic, and energy transformation brought about by COVID-19, most research has focused on the insides of a country or group, effectively ignoring the interconnections between countries. However, in the context of economic globalization, a country is no longer an island (Olmo et al., 2020).

Based on the theory of trade efficiency and market integration, research and analysis before and after the outbreak of bilateral trade between the two countries, especially in the trade of iron ore market conditions change, the data clearly shows, before the outbreak on the iron ore trade between China and Brazil have begun in earnest, and outbreak appears directly at the source of destroyed the supply chain and demand chain, resulting in the trade volume of the inevitable decline. This paper also analyzes the characteristics of China and Brazil's participation in international trade, the severe impact of the pandemic on their respective economies, and, in particular, the key factors that have enabled China and Brazil to successfully resist the negative impact of the pandemic on trade from the perspective of international governance and the international financial system. The full and effective international management of health risks caused by the epidemic in China and Brazil has enhanced post-epidemic trade efficiency, thus achieving sustainable market integration and maintaining the sustainable development of trade. At the same time, this paper points out the challenges that Bilateral trade between China and Brazil will continue to face in the post-COVID-19 era.

Nevertheless, this paper inevitably contains some weaknesses and research limitations. The viewpoints expressed need to be confirmed and revised by follow-up research on this topic in all aspects.

REFERENCES

Abaex, B. (1992). *Brazilian Footwear.* Brazilian Association of Export Agents.

Analysis of the impact of the epidemic on China's metal mineral imports. (2020, March 28). My steel.com.

Anderson, J. (1979). A theoretical foundation for the gravity equation. *The American Economic Review, 69*(1), 106–116.

Anderson, J., & Wincoop, E. (2003). Gravity with gravitas: A solution to the border puzzle. *The American Economic Review, 93*(1), 170–192. doi:10.1257/000282803321455214

Araújo, I. F., Perobelli, F. S., & Faria, W. R. (2021). Regional and global patterns of participation in value chains: Evidence from Brazil. *Inter Economics, I*(165), 154–171. doi:10.1016/j.inteco.2020.12.009

Bai, S. (2019). Study on the impact of international public health emergency response measures on international trade and countermeasures. *Port Health Control*, (4), 1–3.

Bekaert, G., & Hodrick, R. (2017). *International Financial Management.* Cambridge University Press. doi:10.1017/9781316282274

Brazil exported 33.68m tonnes of iron ore in June, the highest level in nearly nine months. (2021). *Economic and trade information.* https://www.tjgportnet.com/m/news-33899.aspx

Calvet, A. L. (1983). A synthesis of foreign directinvestment theories and theories of the multinational firm. *International Accounting and Transnational Decisions,* 315-334.

Cesar, A. S. S. J. (in press). Brazil and the COVID-19 pandemic. *Kidney International Reports.*

Chen, L., Xie, X. Z., & Liu, L. (2018). China's export trade efficiency and trade potential: 1980~2015. *International Economic and Trade Exploration, 34*(1), 33–50.

Chen, N. (2017). China's economic and trade development under the international economic and trade situation. University of International Business and Economics, (4).

Chen, W. H. (2020). *Bilateral trade between China and Brazil has bucked the trend.* Gwangmyong Net. https://www.sohu.com/a/433634676_162758

Chi-Koffi, L. C. Y., & Wang, W. D. (2021). Effects of Covid-19 Pandemic on International Financial Management. *International Journal of Trend in Scientific Research and Development, 5*(3), 321–323.

China imports iron ore and soybeans from Brazil, while Brazil imports mechanical, electrical and chemical products from China. (2018). https://www.sohu.com/a/256885828_100110525

China Money Network. (2020, April 15). *Forecast of large market trend of various varieties.* Qishun Investment.

China Social Science Network. (2020). *The price of iron ore in Brazil has risen after the closure of a mine because of the outbreak.* http://ex.cssn.cn/hqxx/ywhg/202006/t20200625_5147651.shtml?ivk_sa=1023197a

China Trade News Net. (2020). http://www.guangrunwuliu.com/xwzx/xydt/102375.shtml; https://baijiahao. baidu. com/s?id=1669830382126371019&wfr=spider&for=pc

Cohen, M. J. (2020). Does the COVID-19 outbreak mark the onset of a sustainable consumption transition? *Sustainability: Science, Practice, and Policy, 16*(1), 1–3. doi:10.1080/15487733.2020.1740472

Companhia Vale do Rio Doce. (n.d.). In *Baidupedia.* https://baike.baidu.com/item/%E5%B7%B4%E8%A5%BF%E6%B7%A1%E6%B0%B4%E6%B2%B3%E8%B0%B7%E5%85%AC%E5%8F%B8/3372019?fr=aladdin

Costinot, A., & Rodriguez-Clare, A. (2013). Trade Theory with Numbers: Quantifying the Consequences of Globalization. Handbook of International Economics, 4.

Ding, J. (2020). Three essential problems of the spread of COVID-19 and the acceleration of globalization. *Xinhua Finance.* http://news.xinhua08.com/a/20200623/1943879.shtml

Duan, B. L. (2011). *Research on Iron Ore Trade and Investment between China and Brazil* [Unpublished master dissertation]. University of International Business and Economics, Chaoyang District, Beijing, China.

Economic development in Brazil. (2015). https://wenku.baidu.com/view/695b0014680203d8cf2f245c.html

Eun, C. S., & Resnick, B. G. (2010). *International Financial Mgmt* (4th ed.). Tata McGraw-Hill Education.

Fang, J., Collins, A., & Yao, S. (2021). On the global COVID-19 pandemic and China's FDI. *Journal of Asian Economics, 1*(74), 101300. doi:10.1016/j.asieco.2021.101300

Foresight Industrial Research Institute. (2019). *Report on in-depth interpretation of bilateral trade between China and major countries in the Americas in 2019.* Author.

Guo, H. (2020, June 12). *The COVID-19 epidemic will not affect the broad prospects of Sino-Brazilian economic and trade cooperation, said Brazilian Ambassador to China.* China Radio International Online. http://www.cri.cn/

Hashim, F., Bakar, A. R. A., & Talib, A. N. (2010). *International Business* (2nd ed.). Oxford Fajar Press.

He, S., & Guo, K. (2021). What factors contribute to the mutual dependence degree of China in its crude oil trading relationship with oil-exporting countries? *Energy, 228,* 120–547. doi:10.1016/j.energy.2021.120547

Holmes, O'Connor, R. C., Perry, V. H., Tracey, I., Wessely, S., Arseneault, L., Ballard, C., Christensen, H., Cohen Silver, R., Everall, I., Ford, T., John, A., Kabir, T., King, K., Madan, I., Michie, S., Przybylski, A. K., Shafran, R., Sweeney, A., ... Bullmore, E. (2020). Multidisciplinary research priorities for the COVID-19 pandemic: A call for action for mental health science. *The Lancet. Psychiatry*, *7*(6), 547–560. doi:10.1016/S2215-0366(20)30168-1 PMID:32304649

Hong, X. T. (2021). Latest official data from Brazil: Iron ore exports reached 33.68 million tons in June, the highest level in nearly 9 months. *Sina Finance.* https://baijiahao.baidu.com/s?id=1682950467157288988&wfr=spider&for=pc

Kogut, B. (2002). International management and strategy. Handbook of strategy management, 261-278.

Laura, P. S., Raúl, V. F., & Giampietro, M. (2021). The international division of labor and embodied working time in trade for the US, the EU and China. *Ecological Economics*, (180), 106909.

Li, B. D. (2020). *The Epidemic and the Changing World.* Boao Forum for Asia.

Li, H. (2010). Sustainable Development of International Trade. *Modern Economy*, (3).

Li, H. B., & Zou, J. Y. (2019). Research on the Potential and Efficiency of Trade between China and Brazil-Based on the Analysis of Stochastic Frontier Gravity Model. *Economic Research Guide*, (10), 184–189.

Lian, Z. (2020). *China Baowu and Brazil's Vale realize RMB cross-border settlement.* Observer Network.

Mafabi, S., Munene, J., & Ntayi, J. (2012). Knowledge management and organisational resilience: Organisational innovation as a mediator in Uganda. *Parastatals. J. Strateg. Manag*, *5*(1), 57–80. doi:10.1108/17554251211200455

McMahon, D. (2021). As Australia loses its trump card, China and Brazil strike a trade deal. *Global Times.* https://new.qq.com/rain/a/20210707A070PD00

Montoya, M. A., Allegretti, G., Sleimann Bertussi, L. A., & Talamini, E. (2021). Renewable and Non-renewable in the energy-emissions-climate nexus: Brazilian contributions to climate change via international trade. *Journal of Cleaner Production*, *312*, 127700. doi:10.1016/j.jclepro.2021.127700

Muhammad, H., Pasha, M. F., & Ghani, I. (2020). Combined measures to control the COVID-19 pandemic in Wuhan, Hubei, China: A narrative review. *Journal of Biosafety and Biosecurity*, *2*(2), 51–57. doi:10.1016/j.jobb.2020.10.001 PMID:33521592

Olmo, J. C., Hassoun, S. S., & Fernández, P. M. (2020). Spatial relationship between economic growth and renewable energy consumption in 26 European countries. *Energy Econ*, *92*, 104962. doi:10.1016/j.eneco.2020.104962

Olufadewa, I. J., Adesina, M. A., Ekpo, M. D., Akinloye, S. J., Iyanda, T. O., Nwachukwu, P., & Kodzo, L. D. (2020). Lessons from the coronavirus disease 2019 (COVID-19) pandemic response in China, Italy, and the U.S.: A guide for Africa and low- and middle-income countries. *Global Health Journal*, *5*(1), 56–61. doi:10.1016/j.glohj.2021.02.003 PMID:33585052

Pirouz, B., Shaffiee Haghshenas, S., Pirouz, B., Shaffiee Haghshenas, S., & Piro, P. (2020). Development of an assessment method for investigating the impact of climate and urban parameters in confirmed cases of Covid-19: A new challenge in sustainable development. *International Journal of Environmental Research and Public Health, 17*(8), 2801. doi:10.3390/ijerph17082801 PMID:32325763

Ponomarov, S. Y., & Holcomb, M. C. (2009). Understanding the concept of supply chain resilience. *International Journal of Logistics Management, 20*(1), 124–143. doi:10.1108/09574090910954873

Research on the situation, strategy and policy of mineral resources in China. (2020). In *Baidu Encyclopaedia online*. https://baike.baidu.com/item/Researchonthesituation,strategyandpolicyofmineralresourcesinChina/56513210?fr=aladdin

Schmidheiny, S., & Zorraquin, F. J. (1998). *Financing change: the financial community, eco-efficiency, and sustainable development*. MIT Press.

Schmitz, H. (1999). *Global Competition and Local Cooperation: Success and Failure in the Sinos Valley, Brazil* [Unpublished doctoral dissertation]. University of Sussex, Brighton, UK.

Severo, E. A., Guimaraes, J. C. F. D., & Dellarmelin, M. L. (2021). Impact of the COVID-19 pandemic on environmental awareness, sustainable consumption and social responsibility: Evidence from generations in Brazil and Portugal. *Journal of Cleaner Production, 286*, 124947. doi:10.1016/j.jclepro.2020.124947 PMID:33173257

Shahbaz, M., Nasreen, S., Ahmed, K., & Hammoudeh, S. (2017). Trade openness-carbon emissions nexus: The importance of turning points of trade openness for country panels. *Energy Econ, 61*, 221–232. doi:10.1016/j.eneco.2016.11.008

Shanghai Municipal Commission of Commerce. (2020). *What is the impact of the epidemic on China's overseas mining investment, out of service port.* Author.

Shen, G. (2020). Impact of the global spread of COVID-19 on international trade and mitigation measures. *People's Forum Academic Frontiers, 2*, 2–7.

Sheng, Y., Wu, Y., Shi, X., & Zhang, D. (2014). Market Integration and Energy Trade Efficiency: An Application of Malmqvist Index to Analyse Multi-Product Trade. Energy Market Integration in East Asia: Energy Trade, Cross Border Electricity, and Price Mechanism, 29, 135-161.

Shuai, J., Chen, J. H., Leng, Z. H., Wang, Z. H., & Shi, Z. Y. (2018). Research on the International Competitiveness of Chinese Renewable Energy Products under the Background of "One Belt And One Road". *China Soft Science, 7*.

Shuai, J., Leng, Z., Cheng, J., & Shi, Z. (2020). China's renewable energy trade potential in the "Belt-and-Road" countries: A gravity model analysis. *Renewable Energy, 161*, 1025–1035. doi:10.1016/j.renene.2020.06.134

Sino-Brazilian economic and trade cooperation in 2020. (2020). *Information on CPEC.* Author.

Stiglitz, J. E. (2021). The proper role of government in the market economy: The case of the post-COVID recovery. *Journal of Government and Economics, 1*, 100004. doi:10.1016/j.jge.2021.100004

Sustainable Development. (n.d.). In *Baidu Encyclopaedia online*. https://baike.baidu.com/item/sustainabledevelopment/360491?fr=aladdin

Tang, F. Y. (2018). *Countries along the "One Belt And One Road" should increase the use of renewable energy*. China Economic Times.

The OECD predicts the global economic losses caused by the new crown epidemic by the end of 2021. (2020, September 17). Kommersant.

Vale. (2020, February 11). In the fourth quarter, iron ore production fell 22.4% year-on-year, and sales fell 3.2% year-on-year. *U.S. Stock News.*

Vale looks forward to meeting you at the 4th CIIE. (2021, October 11). *Vale.*

Wang, H. L. (2019). Analysis on the relationship between international trade and the ecological environment under the background of sustainable development. *Science Technology and Industry, 8.*

Wang, J. (2011). Vale accounts for 80% of Brazil's $20 billion worth of iron ore exports. *China Finance and Economics.* http://news.xinhua08.com/

World Bank. (2019). *Belt & Road Economics: Opportunities and Risks of Transport Corridors*. World Bank.

Xie, F., & Zhang, G. (2020). Brazil's countermeasures and enlightenment to deal with the impact of the epidemic and stabilize the economic and financial system. *Contemporary Financial Research, 4*, 54-61.

Xu, F. B. (2020, April 28). Expert: How does the world epidemic affect China's economy. *China International Import Expo.*

Yuan, Y. (2020, June 5). *The epidemic has profoundly affected the prospects of global economic development.* China Economic Net.

Zakaria, N., Abdul-Talib, A. N., & Amelinckx, A. (Eds.). (2020). *Transcending Cultural Frontiers: Practices, Challenges, and Strategy for International Business*. Springer. doi:10.1007/978-981-15-4454-5

Zakaria, N., Abdul-Talib, A. N., & Amelinckx, A. (2020). Advancing cultural frontiers to champion global business in emerging markets. In *Transcending Cultural Frontiers* (pp. 1–10). Springer. doi:10.1007/978-981-15-4454-5_1

Zakaria, N., Abdul-Talib, A. N., & Othman, N. (Eds.). (2016). *Handbook of research on impacts of international business and political affairs on the global economy*. IGI Global. doi:10.4018/978-1-4666-9806-2

Zhang, Z., Zhao, J., & Liu, L. (2018). Analysis of iron ore trade between China and Brazil, China Economic and Trade Guide I. *Foreign Investment Economic and Trade*, 26.

Zhao, Y. (2020, December 8). *Brazilian Expert: Adhering to the people-centered approach is the key to China's success in fighting the epidemic.* International Online Report.

Zheng, S. Y. (2019). *Research on Innovative Human Resource Management Model—Taking Brazilian companies as an example.* Academic Press.

Zhonghong National Research Institute. (2020, May 8). *Affected by the epidemic How are the preparations for the 3rd China International Import Expo.* Zhonghong State Research Institute of Information Technology. http://www.china-cer.com.cn/guwen/202005185134.html

Zhou, Z. (2020). Prospects of Sino-Brazilian economic and trade cooperation in post-epidemic era. *Maritime China, 1*(9).

Zhu, D. J. (2020). Many Latin American countries are actively promoting economic recovery. *City Financial Newspaper.* https://baijiahao.baidu.com/s?id=1677520127105244128&wfr=spider&for=pc

Zizek, S. (2020). *PANDEMIC!: Covid-19 Shakes the World.* John Wiley & Sons. doi:10.2307/j.ctv16t6n4q

Chapter 10
Portfolio Investment in Malaysia and Saudi Arabia: Effect of Graham Stock Selection on Return on Investment

Fariza Hashim
University Kuala Lumpur, Malaysia

Nadisah Zakaria
UCSI University, Malaysia

Abdul Rahim Abu Bakar
Prince Sultan University, Saudi Arabia

Kamilah Kamaludin
Prince Sultan University, Saudi Arabia

ABSTRACT

Several strategies are adopted by investors in lowering the risk of investment while maximising its return. Graham's stock selection criteria are noted as one of the best strategies in selecting portfolios by investors. Although the model is universally accepted, it is less commonly practised and examined in emerging markets. Considering the growth of these emerging countries' financial markets, it is worthwhile to investigate the doctrine's effect on investment in these countries. This study endeavours to review the consequence of Graham's stock selection criteria on portfolio returns in the Malaysian and Saudi Arabian stock markets. Each country represents the fastest growing market in their region which justifies this study. The study found that the Malaysian stock market is capable of proffering abnormal returns to investors while the Saudi stock market is capable to offer abnormal returns to investors despite being an undeveloped and immature stock market. The study concludes that the model of stock selection remains beneficial and indeed valuable to regional investments.

DOI: 10.4018/978-1-7998-9071-3.ch010

INTRODUCTION

There are many strategies adopted by investors in maximising their return on investment whilst lowering the risk involved. The issue of investing strategies has undergone substantial study including Barberis and Shleifer (2003). Value investing is one of the enduring investing strategies as it is based on a long-term view which believes that long run investments offer greater returns (Rani, 2019). There are numerous value stocks alternative methods, and many studies were conducted on value investing in the past. Benjamin Graham, known as father of value investing, manifested the ideas of investing from his trading experience in the stock market. He sets criteria for selecting undervalued stocks and emphasised that the stocks which go through the criteria were yielding average returns above than the market returns (Graham, 1934). Graham's method remains practical on time-tested value investing strategies used by more recent super investors such as Walter Schloss, and Warren Buffett (Pragmatic Investor, 2020). In fact, the pragmatic investment approach is essentially derived from Graham's value investing method.

Most investment strategies could be categorised based on the type of predictors used in calculating future performance. A significant amount of work regarding such predictors has been conducted in early studies of value investing and the most well-known scholars in this subject matter are Fama and French (1995). Value investing is one of the most prevalent investment strategies and investors apply different predictors to anticipate the future behaviour of the related stock price. It should be highlighted that though historical performance does not necessarily transform into future investment opportunities, there could be some lessons learned from analysing previous patterns. In this circumstance, there is a risk of oversimplifying by assuming that the techniques that have worked in some countries, such as value investing, are appropriate for other countries. The differences among countries might be rather significant even in the current globalised work. These differences might be even more extreme when comparing results in Western and Asian as well as Middle Eastern countries due to considerably diverse economic and social conditions, levels of development, as well as several other chronological reasons.

The evolution of value investing is commonly drawn from Graham and Dodd (1934) who believed that buying stocks that are trading at a significant discount to their intrinsic value is crucial. Graham (1949) alleged that the intrinsic, or central, the value of any asset would be revealed by quantitative elements and that prices tend to fluctuate around this true value. However, he emphasised that security analysis usually cannot precisely confirm the intrinsic value of a given security. The analysis can only contribute to determining that the value is either acceptable as to protect a bond or to justify a stock purchase, or else that the value is significantly higher or significantly lower than the market price. Nonetheless, this undefined and imprecise assessment of intrinsic value could be sufficient for such purposes. Value investing has gone through numerous cycles of acceptance over the period since the first writings of Graham and Dodd (1934). However, it is only in the last three decades that the success or otherwise of value investing has been subjected to deeper theoretical analysis. Basu (1977) evaluated earnings-to-price as a value measure; Rosenberg, Reid, and Lanstein (1984) investigated price-to-book; while Chan, Hamao, and Lakonishok (1991) studied price-to-cash flow. A number of scholars evaluated several measures both individually and in combination (Lakonishok, Schleifer, & Vishny, 1994; Dreman & Berry, 1995; Bernard, Thomas, & Whalen, 1997). They confirmed that value investing is a lucrative investment strategy not only in the US but also in other major countries (Doukas et al., 1998; Rouwenhorst, 1999). This leads to a concern on the excess returns, i.e. do the excess returns associated with a value strategy represent a market anomaly (Lakonishok, Schliefer, & Vishny, 1994) or whether they simply represent a premium for taking on extra risk (Fama & French, 1992).

The fundamental idea of value investing is that the price earnings ratio (P/E) of a company is a predictor of the future performance of the stock. Companies with low P/E are predicted to outperform companies with high P/E ratios. The concept of value investing has been often stated as an argument contrary to the efficient market hypothesis. In its most stringent version, the market hypothesis requires that all information, both public and non-public, be confined in security prices; therefore, there is no way for an investor to constantly outperform the market. Value investing suggests that the P/E of a stock can be used as a predictor of future performance, potentially allowing a skilled investor to outperform. Graham bestowed an entire chapter of his book (Graham, 1949) to distinguishing between investment and speculation with the author considering that investing requires following a set of rules (value investment rules) and considering most other methods of investment as speculation. This is possibly one of the oldest systematic approaches to investment for modern capital markets. Despite many criticisms, this investing strategy remains one of the investment techniques with stronger theoretical and empirical backing. Some relatively recent articles such as (Bird & Gerlach, 2003) show empirical support for value investing in the US, UK, and Australia.

Several recent studies provide convincing evidence that historical financial data are informative and beneficial in fundamental investing. The quality composite featured in Asness et al. (2013) are all variables constructed from historical financial statements. Cautious fundamental analysis can help investors to derive performance measures that help predict the future profitability and growth of firms. As valuation theory shows, both elements are useful in evaluating the present value of a firm's future growth opportunities. In fact, the key predictions from valuation theory unite nicely not only with recent empirical findings in academia but also with the age-old wisdom advocated by many experience investors (Lee, 2014).

The success of value investing is evident not only in the US but also in other countries such as Canada (Athanassakos, 2009), New Zealand (Truong, 2009), and United Kingdom (UK) (Bird & Gerlach, 2003), pointing towards the same type of event. Gharghori et al. (2012) affirmed that in the Australian market, the book to market value is a good predictor of stock performance, giving some support to the value investment approach. Truong (2009) reached a similar conclusion when analysing the New Zealand market; he used P/E values as a predictor of future performance and concluded that stocks with low P/E will outperform the market, predominantly those who have reasonably high expected growth rates. In addition, several researches on Graham's share selection criteria investigated developed markets such as the US, UK, and other European capital markets (Oppenheimer & Schlarbaum, 1981; Oppenheimer, 1984; Vu, 1988; Lauterbach & Vu, 1993; Bildersee, Cheh, & Zutshi, 1993; Klerck & Maritz, 1997; Xiao & Arnold, 2008; Balik & Mehran, 2008; Chee, Sloan, & Uysal, 2013).

Today emerging markets have become the preferred destinations for global portfolio investments. Though these markets have high volatility, low liquidity, macroeconomic and policy uncertainties, and market micro-structural frictions, they also provide higher returns and serve as the means of diversification for international investors (Ferson and Harvey, 1994). The importance of these markets also reflected in the current composition of the MSCI all-country index. The weight of emerging markets has increased from 1% in 1988 to almost 20% in 2020. This growth has come mainly from equity issuance in these countries (Ali & Badhani, 2020).

As previously mentioned, there are fewer research regarding value investing in developing and Asian countries than in developed markets such the UK or US. Nevertheless, what appears to be clear from the existing literature is that every country has their own circumstances and conditions which would seem to favour an individualised analysis rather than reaching conclusions across different markets.

When comparing the developed and developing countries, obviously the circumstances and conditions in these countries are different; therefore, conclusions that apply to developed countries cannot be generalised for the developing countries. The lack of evidence on value investing in developing countries has motivated this study to examine its performance in different circumstances and market conditions. It is worthwhile to investigate the stock market performance in countries that are less developed economically and socially as well as those with smaller market capitalisation compared with the well-studied markets mentioned above.

This study endeavours to provide some evidence and cover the gap in the value investing literature by examining the effect of Graham's share selection criteria on portfolio returns in selected developing countries, such as Malaysia and the Kingdom of Saudi Arabia. Both countries are rapidly developing and share similar market growth. Therefore, they could provide some insights into Graham value investing and market performance. The work also aims to unfold the performance of investment in both countries and highlight the possible differences between them. The research questions of this study are: First, do the shares listed in emerging countries fulfil Graham's primary and secondary selection criteria, even though they are relatively young companies? Second, if they satisfy Graham's selection criteria, would they create abnormal returns to investors? The study will throw light on Graham's selection criteria and its influence on the value of investment in the developing markets. This study examines time series data spanning from 2000 to 2011 for the shares listed on both Bursa Malaysia, the stock exchange of Malaysia and Tadawul, the stock exchange of Saudi Arabia.

LITERATURE REVIEW

Value Investing Theories

In understanding share prices and value investing, two theories are notable in predicting security prices: the (1) Efficient Market Hypothesis (EMH) and Random Walk Theory (RWT). According to the EMH, the price of a security reflects all the available information. In an efficient market all investors are assumed to be rational, profit maximisers who are actively competing which causes any new information to be reflected and adjusted in the security price (Malkiel, 2003; Arnold, 2008; Norli, Annuar, & Taufik, 2010; Fama, 1970). Subject to the different levels of available information, Fama (1970) identified three forms of market efficiency: the weak form, semi strong form, and strong form. In the weak form, only historical information about the share price is available. No new information which is unrelated to the earlier information is incorporated in the share price. In the semi strong form, both the historical and current public information are available and incorporated in the share price. Any emerging new publicly available information will be acted upon, moving the price to a new equilibrium. In other words, any new information will be quickly reflected in the market price and as such investors who act upon this new information cannot consistently earn abnormal returns (Yalcin, 2010). Lastly, in its strongest form, all information relevant to the share value, that is historical, current public and private information (from insider trading) are quickly and accurately reflected in the market price (Fama, 1970; Kondak, 1997; Lim & Brook, 2006; Yalcin, 2010), leaving no investors, including the technical analysts and fundamentalists from earning any abnormal returns. For example, with the availability of private information, rational investors would buy shares to exploit the pricing anomaly to a point where that information has completely driven up the share price to the value of their private information. Beyond this point, investors have no incentive to continue buying causing the price to be stabilised at the new equilibrium level. The EMH argues that in its efficient form, immediate price correction renders prediction models worthless. In contrast, the Random Walk Theory (RWT) posits those changes in stock prices have the same distribution and are independent of each other. RWT somewhat corroborates the arguments of the semi-strong EMH model which suggests all information has been incorporated and reflected in the current price and cannot be used to predict any future price movement (Malkiel, 2003; Yalçin, 2010). Because short-term share price movements are unpredictable and random (Malkiel, 1973), any methods of predictions are futile as it is impossible to outperform the market consistently.

Fama and French (2017) examine the five-factor model for developed stock markets including North America (U.S. and Canada), Europe, Asia Pacific, and Japan. The study is essentially an out of sample test of the U.S. results of Fama and French (2015). They acknowledge that the five-factor model largely absorbs the patterns in average returns, in global perspective. The model is also tested for other major developed markets, such as: Australian market by Elliot et al. (2018) and Huynh (2018) and Japanese market by Kubota and Takehara (2018). They found that different regions have different kinds of anomalies, and the significance of a specific factor is diverse among different regions (Jacobs, 2016). For instance, the value factor is reported redundant for the U.S., whereas the investment factor is reported redundant for China (Guo et al. 2017). Likewise, the profitability and investment effects are strong in Europe and Asia Pacific. But for Japan, profitability and investment effects have a weaker relationship with the average returns. With respect to momentum factor, it is less pronounced in many emerging Asian markets including China and Korea (Chui, Wei, and Titman 2010; and Lin 2017), but well performed in developed markets (Asness, Moskowitz, and Pedersen 2013), except for Japan (Asness 2011; Fama and French 2012). Fama and French (2017) assert that the global version of the model performs poorly, and the local version plausibly can give a better explanation of the anomalies. A huge number of asset pricing studies examine anomalies in the U.S. market. Karolyi (2016) highlights a U.S. "home bias" in the field of empirical finance because most of these studies cover U.S. markets only, and some other non-U.S. countries that are covered more often than other countries "foreign bias". These countries are either developed markets or major emerging economies. Since the advanced markets are well integrated, the same phenomena and risk measures should apply to these markets, which yield similar findings. Therefore, out-of-sample test to understand the applicability of the model, particularly in the context of emerging markets, is critical. This is because these markets care for different characteristics and dynamics than the developed markets. Empirical evidence for emerging markets is still very limited. However, Zaremba and Czapkiewicz (2017), Zaremba et al. (2019), Foye (2018), Hanauer and Lauterbach (2019), and Zaremba and Maydybura (2019) noted inconclusive evidence about the application of three-, four-, five-, and six factor models. It is also discussed that the five-factor model is unable to explain the low average returns on small stocks, whose returns are like those of firms with low profitability that invested aggressively (Fama and French 2015, 2017). Elliot et al. (2018) discuss that such stocks are only a small fraction of the U.S. market, but the case is different across global markets.

Several anomalies, suggesting pockets of inefficiencies, have been detected in share price patterns that undermine EMH arguments, most notably in developing countries. Some of the common market anomalies include: (1) the size effect, where companies with smaller market capitalisation outperform those with large market capitalisation (Drew & Veeraraghanan, 2002; Nathrah, 2006; Fan Fah, Shamsher, & Annuar, 2008; Yalçin, 2010); (2) valuation effect that indicates companies with low price-to-earnings ratio, high book-to-market ratio, and high dividend yield ratio deliver higher return (Ebrahim, Hudson, Iqbal, & Shah, 2016). As such, this study will use the low price-to-earnings ratio as one of the criteria in share selection consistent with the Benjamin Graham share selection approach. Although the importance of emerging stock markets is consistently rising, only a few studies have investigated anomalous stock return patterns for emerging markets (Ali & Badhani, 2020). Given the existence of these anomalies, it is in our interest to ascertain whether by using the Benjamin Graham selection criteria, individual and institutional investors will earn abnormal returns in the long term in these two stocks exchanges: Bursa Malaysia and Tadawul.

Many studies have examined investment strategies involving value investing (Basu, 1977; Chan, Hamao, & Lakonishok, 1991; Shleifer & Vishny, 1994; Chan & Lakonishok, 2004). Basu (1977) found the value effect in his study hence rejecting the semi-strong EMH arguments. His findings indicated the P/E ratio information was not fully reflected in security prices as posited by the semi-strong EMH arguments. As such, disequilibria persisted during the period studied where earning an abnormal return was possible (Basu, 1977). His finding indicated low P/E portfolios on a risk-adjusted basis earned superior returns. Additionally, other studies also found that value shares (shares with low P/E ratio or low price-to-book ratio) generally outperformed growth shares (high P/E ratio and high price-to-book ratio) in the US and global markets (Oppenheimer, 1986; Chan, Hamao, & Lakonishok, 1991; Fama & French, 1992, 1993, 1998; Lakonishok, Shleifer, & Vishny, 1994; Chan & Lakonishok, 2004). These studies also confirmed that overperformance of value shares as compared to growth shares exist despite market volatility, economic conditions, and speculations. Ergo, it is safe to say that value investing engenders abnormal returns without the additional risks. Consistent results have been observed outside the United States. Investing in net current asset value to market value (NCAV/MC) portfolios produced significant abnormal returns relative to market benchmarks (Bildersee, Cheh, & Zutshi, 1993; Chan, Hamao, & Lakonishok, 1991; Xiao & Arnold, 2008). Xiao and Arnold (2008) in their study of the London Stock Exchange between the period of 1981 to 2005 found that shares with NCAV/MV greater than 1.5 earned significant positive market-adjusted returns (up to 19.7% per year) over its 5 holding years; this premium still exists even after adjusting for the size effect. Sareewiwathana and Janin (2017) examine the Graham and Greenblatt"s investing strategy by using Sharpe ratio and resulted that both the strategies out-perform the market. Palazzo et al. (2018) reaffirm the validity of the Value investing technique at the Brazilian stock exchange by getting higher adjusted returns during the sample time frame from May 2005 to April 2015.

The traditional view on the value investing that it is a largely statistical approach for building a portfolio of securities with a low price-to-earnings ratio (P/E) or a price-to book ratio (P/B) relative to the market (Hanson & Fraser, 2013). However, such a narrow definition as investing in undervalued securities hardly reflects the essence of value investing (Damodaran, 2012). As time passed, the term "value investing" has become quite general and is often used to name any strategies that are opposed to "growth investing" (Eyland, 2020). As a result, the widespread use of the term "value investing" indicates an inability to distinguish between the "value effect" on stock returns, which is the issue of the academic finance, and the role of fundamental analysis in generating higher than market returns, which underlies the investing philosophy of Graham and Dodd. The academic approach to value investing based on the P/E and P/B ratio analysis is limited by deliberate neglect of the company's fundamentals, such as balance sheet quality, as these ratios do not provide any information about the risks and the costs of financial distress (Hanson & Fraser, 2013). The approach of Graham and Dodd described in their books "Security Analysis" and "The Intelligent Investors" focuses solely on investing in listed stocks from the perspective of external minority shareholders (Eyland, 2020). They developed a research methodology that allows identifying and buying securities whose prices are much lower than their true values, thereby providing a rational basis for investment decisions. This methodology is based on the following key concepts of intrinsic value of a security whereby the value that is based solely on the internal company's factors: asset value, profit, dividends, future outcomes. An investor will buy a security only when its market price is significantly lower than its calculated intrinsic value, to manage risks.

Chang (2012) employed the Graham share selection criteria and studied the Malaysian share market for the period of 2000 to 2009. He used the following screening rules in his share selections: (1) price-to-earnings ratio of not more than 15; (2) price-to-book value of not more than 1; (3) price-to-earnings ratio of not more than 15, price-to-book ratio of not more than 1 and current ratio of at least 2; (4) price-to-earnings ratio of not more than 15, price-to-book value of not more than 1 and dividend yield of at least the risk-free rate; and (5) price-to-earnings ratio of not more than 15, price-to-book value of not more than 1, current ratio of at least 2 and dividend yield of at least the risk-free rate. Chang's period of study included the subprime crisis that happened in 2008 and 2009. Despite that, he found that the shares chosen by the above selection criteria outperformed the value-weighted market index (Kuala Lumpur Composite Index) by between 4.23% and 81.18%. In particular, Chang (2012) argued that criteria (4) above produced the highest one-year returns, implying that investing based on the screening rules provided greater returns than the value-weighted market index. However, Chang (2012) did not use the equal-weighted market index in his analysis.

Malaysian Stock Market

The Malaysian stock market has experienced a major development as the number of Malaysian public-listed companies that transform into multinationals is escalating. By 31st December 2013, FBM KLCI companies generated 45% of their revenues overseas and provided one of the highest dividend yields in the ASEAN region at 3.3% (Bursa Malaysia, 2013). By 17th May 2014, the FBM KLCI was expected to trend even higher after rising to a record-closing-high (1,879.83 points on May 15, 2014). Fundamentally, the market was supported by a strong domestic buying momentum, an inflow of defensive funds, and the positive tone of global central banks. Technically, the index looked set to test the psychological 1,900 points support on high volume and rising oscillators. Any decisive break above the 1,880 level would trigger the next breakout price target with more buying up to 1,900 points (Murugiah, 2014).

Both EMH and behavioural finance prevail in the Malaysian equity market. This is because both rational and irrational investors exist in the market. The rational investors represent the market participants who have mature trading psychology and pursue a longer-term investment strategy. The irrational investors also unavoidably exist since it is part of human nature. Institutional investors would be in a better position to exploit inside information before it is released to the public. Nonetheless, the rapid change of technology has sped up the information dissemination. The enhancement of capital market structure and regulations by Bursa Malaysia also contributes to the rise of individual investors in stock investing. The level of informational efficiency of the Malaysian stock market will be upgraded over time as technology advances and capital market regulations improve. This situation would encourage individuals to identify effective stock market investing strategies.

Many studies in the literature highlight the empirical evidence for efficiency in the Malaysian stock market. Lim (1980) employed the monthly closing prices of 30 actively traded stocks and six indices of the Kuala Lumpur Stock Exchange running from June 1974 to June 1980 and verified that the Malaysian stock market was weak form efficient for active stocks. For the same period, Lanjong (1983) achieved the same result by examining the monthly data of 104 actively traded stocks in the market. Annuar,

Ariff, and Shamser (1992) analysed the monthly closing prices of all stocks traded for the period of January 1975 to December 1989, concluding that the Malaysian stock market was a semi-strong efficient market. Yakob (2001) investigated monthly data for the period of January 1989 to March 2001 and confirmed that the findings supported EMH since the past information did not seem to affect the current stock prices. Worthington and Higgs (2005) stated the existence of a weak form of market efficiency in Asian emerging and developed equity markets, including the Malaysian equity market. Othman (1989) analysed the weekly closing prices of 30 randomly selected stocks for the period of January 1977 to June 1988 and asserted that the Malaysian stock market was in the weak-form inefficient. Habibullah (1998) investigated the relationship between money supply and stock prices, inferring that Malaysia's stock market was inefficient since the market participants would be able to use the information on broad money supply to predict the share prices. Balkiz (2003) also verified that the Malaysian stock market was predictable and was not informational in the weak sense by observing the daily composite index for the period of January 1977 to May 2002.

Lian and Leng (1994) noted that the market efficiency changed in different periods of time as the Malaysian stock market changed from the weak-form inefficient market in the mid-1980s to a weak-form efficient market by the late 1980s and early 1990s. Various studies have revealed inconclusive results of EMH in the Malaysian stock market. This is perhaps due to the advancement of technology in message dissemination. The existence of market inefficiency in Bursa Malaysia in the context of behavioural finance was discovered by Neoh (1986), Annuar et al. (1994) and Ibrahim and Yong (1994). Annuar and Shamsher (1987) noted the existence of the 'January effect' phenomenon in the Malaysian market. The 'January effect' refers to a phenomenon where January returns are the highest among the calendar months, which could represent the evidence of behavioural finance in the market. In addition, Annuar, Shamsher, and Ali (1988) revealed that the daily average return of Malaysia's stock market was negative on Monday and Tuesday but positive on Friday. Albaity and Rahman (2012) observed that gender, religion, and ethnic differences influenced the key determinants of individual behaviour. The gender difference was shown to be statistically significant and associated with risk taking behaviour, maximisation, and overconfidence. Religious beliefs and ethnic origins significantly affect life time income risk, regret, maximisation, happiness, confidence, and trust. Hence, the influence of behavioural finance on financial decisions is obvious in Malaysia.

Saudi Stock Market

In comparison with other stock markets such as the London Stock Exchange (LSE), New York Stock Exchange (NYSE), and Istanbul Stock Exchange (ISE), the Saudi Stock Exchange (Tadawul) is considerably young; it was formally established in 1984 (SAMA, 1997).

Ever since its beginning, the Saudi stock market has received a great deal of attention from the government because of its vital role in lessening Saudi Arabia's dependence on oil. Notably, in 1986, there were only 46 listed companies in the market; by the year 2020, the number had dramatically increased to 203 (Tadawul Annual Statistic Report, 2020). The remarkable increase during the last 35 years suggests that the Capital Market Authority (CMA), the regulator and supervisor of the Tadawul, has succeeded in deepening the stock market by increasing the number of listed companies.

Along with the growing number of listed companies in Tadawul, the number of shares traded also experienced an extraordinary volume surge, suggesting that investors are confident with the Saudi Stock Exchange. The Saudi stock market expanded significantly from the early period of 2003, where the

Tadawul All-Share Index (TASI) closed at 4437.6 points in December, as compared with the 2518.1 points recorded at the end of 2002 (SAMA 40th Annual Report, 2004). The performance of TASI continuously increased until the end of 2005, when it closed at 16,712.64 points (SAMA 42nd Annual Report, 2006).

According to Al-Tuwaijri (2007), the main reason for the dramatic rise was the huge supply and demand by investors, both institutional and individual. During this boom period, share trading was largely unsupervised, easy credit was made available by banks to investors, insider trading flourished, and a huge amount of both legal and illegal speculations were created by companies (Bader AbdulAziz, 2015).

Given that situation, the Saudi stock market experienced a 'bubble burst' in February 2006. By the end of 2006, TASI had declined by 52.53% from the previous year and stood at 7,933.29 points (Al-Tuwaijri, 2007). Bader AbdulAziz (2015) pointed out some factors that contributed to the said unique event; one of them was the lack of transparency and disclosure by the companies, banks, and some governmental agencies. Ironically, over four million Saudis had invested money in the stock market; many of these investors were inexperienced, and most of them were widowed, retirees, and lower-income investors who had liquidated their assets and savings (Bader AbdulAziz, 2015). Several measures were undertaken following the unprecedented event, and government agencies including the Saudi Arabian Monetary Agency (SAMA), CMA, and Tadawul announced new rulings and mechanisms related to listing rules, transparency and disclosure, and manipulation or misleading transactions, including allowing non-Saudi residents to invest in the Saudi stock market beginning March 25, 2006 (Bader AbdulAziz, 2015).

At present, the total value of shares traded has reached SAR2,087.80 billion, with 76.69 million transactions executed during the year 2020 (Tadawul Annual Statistic Report, 2020). In a 2019 comparison between Tadawul and other Arab stock exchanges, evidence indicated that the market capitalisation of Tadawul demonstrated the highest value of USD2,407.0 billion, representing 80.2% of the total market capitalisation of Arab stock exchanges (SAMA 56th Annual Report, 2020). These exponential increases demonstrate the CMA commitment in elevating the position of the Saudi stock market as the main market in the Middle East and North Africa. Several efforts had been undertaken by the CMA, among others, the listing of new companies and the increase in trading activities and values, strengthening procedures to reduce risks related to security transactions, protecting investors from unfair practices, ensuring fairness and transparency in security transactions, and including several initiatives under the Financial Leadership (FLP) and the Financial Sector Development Program (FSDP) (SAMA Annual Report, 2020).

Despite being the largest and most important stock market in the Middle East, the evidence put forward by Lamouchi (2020) indicated there was a long memory dependence process in stock returns over the period of October 2000 until February 2019, indicating that the Saudi stock market is inefficient, allowing investors to exploit the abnormal returns. This is because the market is considered as an emerging market, and the market prices are influenced and conducted by speculative trading behaviours, particularly from retail investors with excess liquidity and limited investment opportunities (Lerner, Limen, & Dew, 2017). In addition, evidence also suggested that, for an oil-dependent country like Saudi Arabia, the market activities are very much correlated to oil, implying that the pattern of oil prices may affect the fluctuations of the stock prices (Khamis, Hanasweh, & Hamdan, 2018; Lamouchi & Alawi, 2020). Earlier studies (Butler, Kirt, & Malaikah, 1992; Al-Razen, 1997; AlKolifey, 2000; Saudi Chamber of Commerce, 2005) also indicated that the Saudi stock market was inefficient, in the weak-form, due to several reasons including high transaction cost, lack of information, inadequate infrastructure, lack of transparency, small firm effect, and several other factors. Given such a situation, we can hypothetically deduce that both institutional and individual investors in Saudi Arabia, can exploit higher abnormal returns due to its weak efficiency as compared with the Malaysian stock market.

METHODOLOGY

Though value investing is theorised on recognizing stocks whose prices understate their intrinsic value, there is no commonly accepted way of executing the value strategy. Hence, multiple value measures are used in practice and academic research. For example, in addition to the book-to-market ratio, Lakonishok et al. (1994) studied cash flow and earnings to market value. Piotroski (2000) and Mohanram (2005) advanced value strategies that add the 'quality' variable to the book-to-price (B/P) ratio. We did not scrutinise all the value indicators used by researchers and investors; instead, we focused on examining the common value indicator which is the price-earnings ratio.

The Net Current Asset Value (NCAV) was derived from the balance sheet items of the companies listed on Bursa Malaysia (Malaysian stock exchange) and Tadawul (Saudi stock exchange). Specifically, financial information that encompass the companies' current assets, current liabilities, long-term debt, and preferred shares were obtained from the Bloomberg Professional Services database. We excluded all companies in the financial sectors as they followed a different disclosure listing rules and regulations. The NCAV/MV portfolios were constructed according to Graham's share selection approach, as follows: (1) initial selection of companies on Bursa Malaysia and Tadawul using the primary criteria; (2) further reiteration was done using the secondary criteria. The primary criteria identified companies with net current asset value per share greater than 1.5 times the current asset share price. Then, the buy-and-hold portfolios were constructed for 1, 2 and 3 years, beginning in July 2000 and ending in July 2011. Table 1 below lists the number of companies that have been selected based on the primary and secondary criteria.

According to Benjamin Graham investment philosophy, stocks which have intrinsic value far exceeds their prices are best for investment. The indicators which show that intrinsic value of stock is exceeds their prices include Price to Earnings (P/E) ratio; Price to Book value (P/B) ratio and Dividend Yield ratio.

Table 1. Number of companies in the NCAV/MV portfolio in each year

Year	Number of companies (Bursa Malaysia)	Number of companies (Tadawul)
2000	25	23
2001	23	21
2002	22	20
2003	19	18
2004	18	17
2005	17	16
2006	16	15
2007	18	8
2008	12	6
2009	11	5
2010	10	5
2011	8	4

Source: Bloomberg 2015

Note: NCAV: net current asset value; MV: market value

Companies that fulfilled the primary criteria would further be evaluated and selected based on the secondary criteria. The secondary criteria have the following requirements as depicted in Table 2.

Table 2. Secondary criteria for sample selection

No.	Criteria	Explanation
1.	Satisfactory earnings	Earnings growth should be at least 5% annual compound rate (Singh & Kaur, 2014) Positive earnings per share from continuing operations for the past 10 years where price to earnings ratio < 15 (Chang, 2012) Price-to-book ratios < 1 (Chang, 2012) Low price to earnings ratios (Chang, 2012)
2.	Financial strength	Total liabilities are less than 50% of the net current asset value (NCAV) Holding these companies in the NCAV/MV portfolios is less likely to fail than holding those that do not qualify (Graham & Dodd, 1934).
3.	Current ratio	To ensure that a sizeable working capital is available, current asset value should be at least double the current liabilities, i.e., current ratio > 2 (Graham & Dodd, 1934).
4.	Additional filter	The financial sectors, as their financial statements are not directly comparable to other industries (Xiao & Arnold, 2008).

We employed two novel market indices: the Malaysia All-Shares Equal Weight Index (MAS-EWI) and the Malaysia All-Shares Value Weight Index (MAS-VWI). Both benchmarks are more comprehensive than any used in previous Malaysian event studies, which commonly adopted two popular market indices, namely the FTSE Kuala Lumpur Composite Index (KLCI) and the FTSE Bursa Malaysia EMAS Index, which fail to represent the broader Malaysian market. We used the Buy-and-Hold Abnormal Returns (BHARs) approach as it is the most comprehensive accepted methodology in modern event studies. As such, this study employed a similar method to evaluate the share return performance of NCAV portfolios over the long-run period. According to Ritter (1991), in order to reduce problems related to measuring portfolio performance, benchmarking of these portfolios is vital. Therefore, this study benchmarked against two market indices: equal-weight index (EWI) and value weight index (VWI).

The three-year holding period return was evaluated by computing the compounded monthly buy-and-hold return for net current asset value companies for time t as follows:

$$BHR_{jT} = \left[\prod_{t=1}^{T}(1 + r_{jt})\right] - 1 \qquad (1)$$

Where r_{jt} is the actual monthly return on the security *j* in event period *t*. T is designated as the number of months in event period *t*. The condition measures the total return from a buy-and-hold strategy where a share is purchased at the closing market price and held until 12, 24 or 36 months following the NCAV/MV portfolio's formation.

The buy-and-hold returns, BHR_{mT} for the market benchmarks, represented by the EWI and VWI for Bursa Malaysia and Tadawul are:

$$BHR_{mT}\left[\prod_{t=1}^{T}(1+r_{mt})\right]-1 \tag{2}$$

Where r_{mt} is the corresponding monthly index level of market indices in event period t. The market-adjusted buy-and-hold abnormal returns for each security or company in the NCAV portfolio in event period t are computed as:

$$BHAR_{jt}=\left[\prod_{t=1}^{T}(1+r_{jt})-1\right]-\left[\prod_{t=1}^{T}(1+r_{mt})-1\right] \tag{3}$$

where $BHAR_{jt}$ is the buy-and-hold abnormal return of security j in event period t. This measures the market-adjusted buy-and-hold abnormal returns earned by investors over the 12, 24 or 36 months following the NCAV/MV portfolio's formation. The test statistic for the market-adjusted monthly buy-and-hold abnormal returns, $BHAR_{(t_1,t_2)}$, during the clustering period from t_1 to t_2, is calculated as:

$$t=\frac{\overline{BHAR_{(t1,t2)}}}{\sigma(BHAR_t)\,/\,\sqrt{T}} \tag{4}$$

where $\overline{BHAR_{(t_1,t_2)}}$ is the market-adjusted monthly average buy-and-hold abnormal return from period t_1 to period t_2, $\sigma(BHAR_t)$ is the standard deviation of market-adjusted monthly buy-and-hold abnormal return in event period t, and T is the total number of companies in the NCAV portfolios.

RESULTS AND DISCUSSION

Table 3 below summarises the results of the study, showing the monthly percentage of market-adjusted buy-and-hold abnormal returns for the full sample of NCAV/MV portfolios for both Bursa Malaysia and Tadawul over the three-year period against the equal-weighted and value-weighted market indexes.

Panel A presents the results of market-adjusted BHAR for value investing companies which are traded on Bursa Malaysia. The results for the t-tests for the share portfolios from the EWI against buy-and-hold abnormal return were as follows. For the 12-month (one-year) period, the t-test result was 0.30 (not significant at $p = 0.1$), and BHAR was 7.82%. For the 24-month (two-year) period, the t-test result was 0.43 (not significant at $p = 0.1$), and BHAR was 11.70%. For the 36-month (three-year) period, the t-test result was 5.59 ($p = 0.01$), and BHAR was 51.40%. These results suggest that the longer investors hold the portfolios, the higher the abnormal return.

Our study finds that investors in Saudi Arabia could earn significantly superior market-adjusted BHAR than investors in Malaysia. Panel B shows the results of market-adjusted BHAR for NCAV/MV companies which are traded on Tadawul. The results for the t-tests for the share portfolios from the EWI against buy-and-hold abnormal return were as follows. For the 12-month (one-year) period, the t-test result was 2.90 ($p = 0.05$), and BHAR was 20.17%. For the 24-month (two-year) period, the t-test result was 4.87 (p = 0.01), and BHAR was 46.70%. For the 36-month (three-year) period, the t-test result was 6.10 (p = 0.01), and BHAR was 83.47%. These results suggest that the highest abnormal returns are obtained from the three-year holding period, confirming that the longer the investors hold their portfolios, the greater their return.

Table 3. Average market-adjusted buy-and-hold returns for NCAV/MV portfolios

Panel A: Average market-adjusted buy-and-hold test period returns in Bursa Malaysia						
Market indices	**MAS-EWI**			**MAS-VWI**		
	Months after portfolio formation					
	12	24	36	12	24	36
Market-adjusted ABHARs	7.82%	11.70%	51.40%	-3.34%	-5.84%	57.21%
T-stat	0.30	0.43	5.59***	-0.12	-0.20**	4.08***
	SAS-EWI			**SAS-VWI**		
Panel B: Average market-adjusted buy-and-hold test period returns in Tadawul						
	Months after portfolio formation					
	12	24	36	12	24	36
Market-adjusted ABHARs	20.17%	46.70%	83.47%	8.62%	27.69%	49.02%
T-stat	2.90*	4.87**	6.10**	1.34	3.28**	3.31**

Note: Shares are allocated to the NCAV portfolios if their NCAV/MV ratios are higher than 1.5 at the beginning of July 2000 and after July 2011. Market-adjusted buy-and-hold abnormal returns for shares within a portfolio are calculated for periods of one, two- and three-years post-formation. Table 3 indicates the market-adjusted average buy-and-hold abnormal returns (ABHARs) for all the Malaysian companies against the MAS-EWI and MAS-VWI benchmarks. MAS-EWI denotes the Malaysia all-shares equal weight index; MAS-VWI denotes the Malaysia all-shares value weight index. SAS-EWI denotes the Kingdom of Saudi Arabia all shares–equal weight index, while SAS-VWI denotes the Saudi Arabia all shares-value weight index. Asterisks indicate statistical significance at the 5% (*) and 1% (**), respectively using a two-tailed test. Asterisks indicate statistical significance at the 5% (**) and 1% (***) level, respectively, using a two-tailed test.

Despite the results above, the share portfolio results from VWI in both markets demonstrated a moderately different situation. The t-test results for the share portfolios from the MAS-VWI against buy-and-hold abnormal return were as follows: For the 12-month (one-year) period, the t-test result was -0.12 (not significant at p = 0.1), and BHAR was -3.34%. For the 24-month (two-year) period, the t-test result was -0.20 (not significant at p = 0.2), and BHAR was -5.84%. For the 36-month (three-year) period, the t-test result was 4.08 (p = 0.01), and BHAR was 57.21%. These results reflect that those Malaysian investors gained positive abnormal returns only after 24 months (two years) of investment, which implies that the abnormal return is assured, though it requires a longer period of holding the portfolios.

Nevertheless, the results of stock portfolios from SAS-VWI demonstrated a different scenario, showing an immensely significant market-adjusted BHAR, particularly over the second and third-year periods. The t-test results for the stock portfolios from the VWI against buy-and-hold abnormal return were as follows: For the 12-month (one-year) period, the t-test result was 1.34 (not significant at p = 0.1), and BHAR was 8.62%. For the 24-month (two-year) period, the t-test result was 3.28 (p = 0.01), and BHAR was 27.69%. For the 36-month (three-year) period, the t-test result was 3.31 (p = 0.01), and BHAR was 49.02%. Unlike in the Malaysian stock market, we find that Saudi investors gained abnormal returns only after a year of investment.

Unlike Saudi Arabia, Malaysia had experienced several financial crises which occurred within the period of the study. Among them are the recovery period from the Asian financial crisis (2000–2001), the 9/11 attack and technology slump (2001–2002), the SARS epidemic (2002–2003), and the subprime crisis (2008–2009). These crises could be among the causes of the negative market-adjusted buy-and-hold abnormal returns experienced by investors over the 12- and 24-month (one- and two-year) periods.

The result of the study indicates that value shares, as defined by a low price-to-earnings ratio—one of the criteria used in Benjamin Graham's approach—seem to have provided profitable trading opportunities that can be exploited by both individual and institutional investors in both countries over the long-run period of investment. Notably, the finding is inconsistent with the efficient market hypothesis. Therefore, the present study adds to the extant literature that both share markets are inefficient in pricing shares. As mentioned earlier in the literature, there is evidence of value-effect anomalies in the Malaysian share market alone. Bodie, Kane and Marcus (2007) pointed out that there are mounting numbers of anomalies in the empirical evidence to justify the under-pricing of shares, even though these anomalies have remained one of the most puzzling phenomena in the finance literature.

CONCLUSION

In the Malaysian context, this study finds that the NCAV/MV portfolios measured against two market benchmarks, MAS-VWI and MAS-EWI significantly outperform investors' expectations, on average by +57.21% and 51.40%, respectively, in the 36-month (three-year) holding period. The outcome from this study also supports the reverse-size effect. Evidently, larger companies on Bursa Malaysia yield a higher return than smaller companies during the period of study. Arguably, larger companies are more stable and financially sound. These companies have greater capacity and productivity and can leverage on the basis of economies of scale, which as a result, enable them to outperform smaller sized companies.

The Saudi Arabian market indicates a consistent pattern. The NCAV/MV selection criteria portfolio outperform investors' expectations. The NCAV/MV portfolios when measured against the market benchmarks, SAS-EWI and SAS-VWI perform significantly exceeding expectations by +83.47% and 49.02%, respectively, in the 36-month (three-year) holding period. In contrast to the Malaysian market, the Saudi stock market is still inefficient based on the extant evidence put forward in the literature. It can be noticed that, the evidence of small firm effect still exists in the Saudi stock market, one of the market anomalies which goes against the efficient market hypothesis.

This study also indicates that the Malaysian equity market comprises more rational investors who are sensible and responsible in investing than irrational investors. The rational investors quest after long-run returns and investment strategy. They are willing to buy and hold the stocks for several years though the market seems volatile and in turmoil due to various economic and financial crises throughout the period of investing. The significant performance of the stock markets also signifies the improvement in market efficiency as argued by EMH. This could also be a contribution of the enhancement of the Malaysian capital market structure in terms of its technology and regulations. This study also supports the Random Walk Theory which argues that in a less rigorous or semi-efficient market, investors can outperform the market and earn abnormal returns. This study confirms that size is an important element in value investing that contributes to excess returns.

Our study points out that over the long-run period of investment, share selection using Benjamin Graham's criteria yields abnormal returns on both Bursa Malaysia and Tadawul. As such, exploiting this knowledge may give investors an edge over their peers. Additionally, this study is also beneficial to both fund and hedge fund managers as it further reaffirms the reliability of Benjamin Graham's selection criteria in value investing. On the one hand, the fund managers may choose similar selection criteria when creating their equity-based mutual fund portfolios. On the other hand, the hedge fund managers can incorporate this knowledge in their risk management analysis. The limitation of this study is that it only examined value investing in the Malaysian and Saudi Arabian context. As such, a similar study can be extended to include other emerging markets in the ASEAN and MENA regions to further corroborate our findings and validate Graham's selection theory. Expanding the scope of the study will also help investigate value investing in less mature economies, work which clearly has been scarce.

REFERENCES

Al-Razeen, A. M. (1997). *The Weak-Form Efficiency of the Saudi Stock Market* [Ph.D. Thesis]. University of Leicester.

Al-Twaijry, A. A. (2007). Saudi stock market historical view and crisis effect: Graphical and statistical analysis. *Journal of Human Sciences*, *34*(1), 80–95.

Albaity, M., & Rahman, M. (2012). Behavioral finance and Malaysian culture. *International Business Research*, *5*(11), 65–76. doi:10.5539/ibr.v5n11p65

Ali, A., & Badhani, K. N. (2020). Beta-anomaly: Evidence from the Indian equity market. *Asia-Pacific Financial Markets*, *8*, 1–24.

Alkholifey, A. (2000). *The Saudi Arabian Stock Market: Efficient Market Hypothesis and Investors Behavior* [PhD Thesis]. Colorado State University.

Annuar, M., Shamsher, M., & Ali, M. (1988). Stock Returns and the Weekend Effect: The Malaysian Experience. *Pertanika*, *11*(1), 107–114.

Annuar, M., Shamsher, M., & Zainal, M. (1987). An empirical study of the treasury bill in malaysia: Part 1 – using treasury bills as predictor of inflation. *Pertanika*, *10*(3), 349–355.

Annuar, M. N., Ariff, M., & Shamsher, M. (1992). A test of semi-strong efficiency of the KLSE. *Malaysian Journal of Economic Studies*, *22*(2), 1–18.

Arnold, G. C. (2008). *Corporate Financial Management* (4th ed.). Pearson Education Limited.

Asness, C. S., Frazzini, A., & Pedersen, L. H. (2013). *Quality Minus Junk. Working Paper*. AQR Capital Management and New York University.

Asness. (2011). Momentum in Japan. The exception that proves the rule. *The Journal of Portfolio Management. Summer*, *37*(4), 67-75.

Athanassakos, G. (2009). Value versus growth stock returns and the value premium: The Canadian experience 1985-2005. *Canadian Journal of Administrative Sciences / Revue Canadienne des Sciences de Administration*, *26*(2), 109 - 121.

Bader Abdulaziz Alkhaldi, J. D. (2015). The Saudi capital market: The crash of 2006 and lessons to be learned. *International Journal of Business, Economics and Law*, *8*(4), 235–250.

Balik, R., & Mehran, J. (2008). *Benjamin Graham revisited.* Available from: http://www. academy financial. org/09Conference/09Proceedings/(5D)% 0Balik,% 0Mehran.pdf

Balkiz, O. (2003). Testing informational market efficiency on Kuala Lumpur stock exchange. *Jurnal Ekonomi Malaysia*, *37*(3), 3–20.

Barberis, N., & Shleifer, A. (2003). Style investing. *Journal of Financial Economics*, *68*(2), 161–199. doi:10.1016/S0304-405X(03)00064-3

Basu, S. (1977). Investment performance of common stocks in relation to their price-earnings ratios: A test of the efficient market hypothesis. *The Journal of Finance*, *32*(3), 663–682. doi:10.1111/j.1540-6261.1977.tb01979.x

Bernard, V., Thomas, J., & Wahlen, J. (1997). Accounting-based stock price anomalies: Separating market inefficiencies from risk. *Contemporary Accounting Research*, *14*(2), 89–136. doi:10.1111/j.1911-3846.1997.tb00529.x

Bildersee, J. S., Cheh, J. J., & Zutshi, A. (1993). The performance of Japanese common stocks in relation to their net current asset values. *Japan and the World Economy*, *5*(3), 197–215. doi:10.1016/0922-1425(93)90011-R

BirdR. G.GerlachR. H. (2013). *The Good and the Bad of Value Investing: Applying a Bayesian Approach to Develop Enhancement Models*. https://ssrn.com/abstract=391686 doi:10.2139/ssrn.391686

Bloomberg, L.P. (2015). *Net current asset value and market value*. Author.

Bodie, Z., Kane, A., & Marcus, A. (2007). *Essentials of investments* (6th ed.). McGraw-Hill/Irwin.

Butler, K., & Malaikah, S. J. (1992). Efficiency and inefficiency in thinly traded stock markets: Kuwait and Saudi Arabia. *Journal of Banking & Finance*, *16*(197), 108–209. doi:10.1016/0378-4266(92)90085-E

Chan, L. K., Hamao, Y., & Lakonishok, J. (1991). Fundamentals and stock returns in Japan. *The Journal of Finance*, *46*(5), 1739–1764. doi:10.1111/j.1540-6261.1991.tb04642.x

Chan, L. K., & Lakonishok, J. (2004). Value and growth investing: Review and update. *Financial Analysts Journal*, *3*(2), 71–86. doi:10.2469/faj.v60.n1.2593

Chang, D. (2012). Testing some of Benjamin Graham's stock selection criteria: A case of the FTSE Bursa Malaysia Emas Index from year 2000 to 2009. *Jurnal Manajemen Dan Kewirausahaan/Journal of Management and Entrepreneurship*, *13*(2), 99-106.

Chee, S., Sloan, R., & Uysal, A. (2013). A framework for value investing. *Australian Journal of Management*, *38*(3), 599–633. doi:10.1177/0312896213510715

Chui, A., Wei, J., & Titman, S. (2010). Individualism and momentum around the world. *The Journal of Finance*, *65*(1), 361–392. doi:10.1111/j.1540-6261.2009.01532.x

Damodoran. (2012). *Investment valuation: Tools and technique for determining the value of any asset.* Wiley Finance.

David, N. (1995). Analyst forecasting errors and their implications for security analysis. *Financial Analysts Journal, 51*(3), 30–41. doi:10.2469/faj.v51.n3.1903

DoukasJ. A.BalaA.CogginT. D. (1998). Multifactor Asset Pricing Analysis of International Value Investment Strategies. https://ssrn.com/abstract=54002 doi:10.2139/ssrn.54002

Drew, M. E., & Veeraraghanan, M. (2002). A closer look at the size and value premium in emerging markets: Evidence from the Kuala Lumpur Stock Exchange. *Asian Economic Journal, 16*(4), 337–351. doi:10.1111/1467-8381.00156

Ebrahim, S., Hudson, R., Iqbal, A., & Shah, E. (2016). Dispelling the myth of value premium: Contrary evidence of Malaysian crony capitalism. *International Journal of Banking, Accounting and Finance, 7*(1), 1–33.

Elliot, B., Docherty, P., Easton, S., & Lee, D. (2018). Profitability and investment-based factor pricing models. *Accounting and Finance, 58*(2), 397–421. doi:10.1111/acfi.12217

Eyland, G. (2020). *A Brief History of Value Investing. Fundamental Finance Playbook.* Available: https://fundamentalfinanceplaybook.com/histories/what-is-value-investing/

Fama, E. (1970). Efficient capital markets: A review of theory and empirical work. *The Journal of Finance, 25*(2), 383–417. doi:10.2307/2325486

Fama, E. F. (1998). Market efficiency, long-term returns, and behavioral finance. *Journal of Financial Economics, 49*(3), 283–306. doi:10.1016/S0304-405X(98)00026-9

Fama, E. F., & French, K. R. (1992). The cross-section of expected stock returns. *The Journal of Finance, 47*(2), 427–465. doi:10.1111/j.1540-6261.1992.tb04398.x

Fama, E. F., & French, K. R. (1993). Common risk factors in the returns on stocks and bonds. *Journal of Financial Economics, 33*(1), 3–56. doi:10.1016/0304-405X(93)90023-5

Fama, E. F., & French, K. R. (1995). Size and Book-to-Market Factors in Earnings and Returns. *The Journal of Finance, 50*(1), 131–155. doi:10.1111/j.1540-6261.1995.tb05169.x

Fama, E. F., & French, K. R. (1998). Value versus growth: The international evidence. *The Journal of Finance, 53*(6), 1975–1999. doi:10.1111/0022-1082.00080

Fama, E.F., & French, K.R. (2012). *Size, value and momentum in international stock returns.* Academic Press.

Fama, E. F., & French, K. R. (2015). A five-factor asset pricing model. *Journal of Financial Economics, 105*(3), 457–472. doi:10.1016/j.jfineco.2012.05.011

Fama, E. F., & French, K. R. (2017). International tests of a five-factor asset pricing model. *Journal of Financial Economics, 123*(3), 441–463. doi:10.1016/j.jfineco.2016.11.004

Fan Fah, C., Shamsher, M., & Annuar, M. N. (2008). Earning announcements: The impact of firm size on share prices. *Journal of Money. Investment and Banking*, *3*(3), 36–46.

Ferson, W. E., & Harvey, C. R. (1994). Sources of risk and expected returns in global equity markets. *Journal of Banking & Finance*, *18*(4), 775–803. doi:10.1016/0378-4266(93)00020-P

Foye, J. (2018). A comprehensive test of the Fama-French five-factor model in emerging markets. *Emerging Markets Review*, *37*(1), 199–222. doi:10.1016/j.ememar.2018.09.002

Gharghori, P., Sebastian, S., & Madhu, V. (2012). Value versus growth: Australian evidence. *Accounting and Finance*, *53*(1), 393–417.

Graham, B. (1949). The Intelligent Investor. Harper & Brothers.

Graham, B. (1976). A conversation with Benjamin Graham. *Financial Analysts Journal*, *2*(1), 20–23. doi:10.2469/faj.v32.n5.20

Graham, B. (2003). *The intelligent investor* (Revised ed.). Harper Collins.

Graham, B., & Dodd, D. L. (1934). *Security analysis: principles and technique*. McGraw-Hill.

Guo, B., Zhang, W., Zhang, Y., & Zhang, H. (2017). The five-factor asset pricing model tests for the Chinese stock market. *Pacific-Basin Finance Journal*, *43*(2), 84–106. doi:10.1016/j.pacfin.2017.02.001

Hanauer, M. X., & Lauterbach, J. G. (2019). The cross-section of emerging market stock returns. *Emerging Markets Review*, *38*(1), 265–286. doi:10.1016/j.ememar.2018.11.009

Hanson, D., & Fraser, J. (2013). ESG Investing in Graham & Doddsville. *Journal of Applied Corporate Finance, 25*(3), 20–31. Available: https://us.jflglobal.com/media/uploads/news/2015-09/Hanson-2013

Hashim, F., Bakar, A. R. A., & Talib, A. N. (2010). *International Business* (2nd ed.). Oxford Fajar Press.

Huynh, T. D. (2018). Explaining anomalies in Australia with a five-factor asset pricing model. *International Review of Finance*, *18*(1), 123–135. doi:10.1111/irfi.12125

Ibrahim, I., & Yong, O. (1994). *The Behavior of Far Eastern Stocks*. Leeds Publication.

InvestorP. (2020). *Home*. Available: http://pragmaticinvestor.com/

Jacobs, H. (2016). Market maturity and mispricing. *Journal of Financial Economics*, *122*(2), 270–287. doi:10.1016/j.jfineco.2016.01.030

Karolyi. (2016). Home bias, an academic puzzle. *Review of Finance*, *20*(6), 2049-2078.

Khamis, R., Anasweh, M., & Hamdan, A. (2018). Oil prices and stock market returns in oil-exporting countries: Evidence from Saudi Arabia. *International Journal of Energy Economics and Policy*, *8*(3), 301–306.

Klerck, W. G., & Maritz, A. C. (1997). A test of Graham's stock selection criteria on industrial shares traded on the JSE. *The Investment Analysts Journal*, *26*(45), 25–33. doi:10.1080/10293523.1997.11082374

Kondak, N. E. (1997). The efficient market hypothesis revisited: Some evidence from the Istanbul Stock Exchange. *Capital Board of Turkey*, *83*(1), 23–35.

Kubota, K., & Takehara, H. (2017). Does the Fama and French Five-Factor Model Work Well in Japan? *International Review of Finance*, *18*(1), 137–146. doi:10.1111/irfi.12126

Lakonishok, J., Shleifer, A., & Vishny, R. W. (1994). Contrarian investment, extrapolation, and risk. *The Journal of Finance*, *49*(5), 1541–1578. doi:10.1111/j.1540-6261.1994.tb04772.x

Lamouchi, R. A. (2020). Long Memory and Stock Market Efficiency: Case of Saudi Arabia. *International Journal of Economics and Financial Issues*, *10*(3), 29–34. doi:10.32479/ijefi.9568

Lamouchi, R. A., & Alawi, S. M. (2020). Dynamic linkages between the oil spot, oil futures, and stock markets: Evidence from Dubai. *International Journal of Energy Economics and Policy*, *10*(1), 377–383. doi:10.32479/ijeep.8705

Lanjong, M. N. (1983). *A study of market efficiency and risk return relationship in the Malaysian stock market* [Unpublished Ph.D Thesis]. Katholieke Universitiet Te Leuven, Belgium.

Lauterbach, B., & Vu, J. D. (1993). Ben Graham's net current asset value rule revisited: The size-adjusted returns. *Quarterly Journal of Business and Economics*, *3*(2), 82–108.

Lee, C. M. C. (2014). Value Investing: Bridging Theory and Practice. *China Accounting and Finance Review*, *16*(2), 10–38. doi:10.760340570-014-0005-3

Lerner, J. O. S., Leamon, A., & Dew, S. T. E. (2017). *The CMA and the Saudi Stock Market Crash of 2006*. BELLA Research Group, Saudi Capital Market Authority.

Lian, K. K., & Leng, K. G. (1994). Weak Form Efficiency in the KLSE: New Evidence. *Capital Market Review*, *2*(1), 45–58.

LimK. P.BrooksR. D. (2006). The evolving and relative efficiencies of stock markets: empirical evidence from rolling bi-correlation test statistics. *Social Science Research Network*. Available from: http://ssrn.com/abstract=931071

Lim, T. L. (1980). *The Efficient Market Hypothesis and Weak Form Test on the KLSE* [Unpublished dissertation (MBA)]. University of Sheffield.

Lin, Q. (2017). Noisy prices and the Fama–French five-factor asset pricing model in China. *Emerging Markets Review*, *31*, 141–163. doi:10.1016/j.ememar.2017.04.002

Malaysia, B. (2013). Bursa Malaysia Annual Report 2012. Kuala Lumpur, Malaysia: Bursa Malaysia

Malkiel, B. G. (1973). *A random walk down Wall Street*. W.W. Norton and Co.

Malkiel, B. G. (2003). The efficient market hypothesis and its critic. *The Journal of Economic Perspectives*, *17*(3), 59–82. doi:10.1257/089533003321164958

Mohanram, P. (2005). Separating winners from losers among low book-to-market stocks using financial statement analysis. *Review of Accounting Studies*, *10*(2), 133–170. doi:10.100711142-005-1526-4

Murugiah, S. (2014). KLCI Week Ahead – KLCI to trend higher, support seen at 1,870. *The Edge Malaysia*. Available at: http://www.theedgemalaysia.com/business news/289984-klci-week-ahead-klci-to-trend-higher-support-seen-at-1870.html

Nathrah, Y. (2006). *The evidence of size effect during bull and bear markets* [Unpublished MSc thesis]. Universiti Putra Malaysia.

Neoh, H. K. (1986). *An Examination of the Efficiency of the Malaysian Stock Market* [PhD Dissertation]. University of Edinburg.

Norli, A., Annuar, M. N., Taufik, H., & Sazali, Z. A. (2010). Short-run stock overreaction: Evidence from Bursa Malaysia. *International Journal of Economics and Management*, *4*(2), 319–333.

Oppenheimer, H. R. (1984). A test of Benjamin Graham's stock selection criteria. *Financial Analysts Journal*, *40*(5), 68–74. doi:10.2469/faj.v40.n5.68

Oppenheimer, H. R. (1986). Ben Graham's net current asset values: A performance update. *Financial Analysts Journal*, *8*(1), 40–47. doi:10.2469/faj.v42.n6.40

Oppenheimer, H. R., & Schlarbaum, G. G. (1981). Investing with Benjamin Graham: An ex ante test of the efficient markets hypothesis. *Journal of Financial and Quantitative Analysis*, *16*(3), 341–360. doi:10.2307/2330242

Palazzo, V., Savoia, J. R., Securato, J. R., & Bergmann, D. R. (2018). Análise de carteiras de valor no mercado brasileiro. *Revista Contabilidade & Finanças*, *29*(78), 452–468. doi:10.1590/1808-057x201804810

Piotroski, J. (2000). Value investing: The use of historical financial statement information to separate winners from losers. *Journal of Accounting Research*, *38*, 1–41. doi:10.2307/2672906

Ritter, J. R. (1991). The long-run performance of initial public offerings. *The Journal of Finance*, *46*(1), 3–27. doi:10.1111/j.1540-6261.1991.tb03743.x

Rosenberg, B., Reid, K., & Lanstein, R. (1984). Persuasive evidence of market inefficiency. *Journal of Portfolio Management*, *11*(2), 9–17.

SAMA. (n.d.). *Annual Report 1997-2013*. SAMA Press.

Sareewiwatthana, P., & Janin, P. (2017). Test of Quantitative Investing Strategies of Famous Investors: Case of Thailand. *Journal of Investment Management & Financial Innovation*, *12*(2), 13–25. doi:10.21511/imfi.14(3-1).2017.06

Saudi Arabian Monetary Agency. (2004). 40th Annual Report. Author.

Saudi Arabian Monetary Agency. (2006). 42nd Annual Report. Author.

Saudi Arabian Monetary Agency. (2020). 56th Annual Report. Author.

Saudi Chamber of Commerce in Riyadh. (2005). *Explore to What Extend the Efficiency of the Local Stock Market and its Role in Supporting the National Economy*. In the 15th Annual Meeting of Saudi Economic Association, Riyadh, Saudi Arabia.

Singh, J., & Kaur, K. (2014). Testing Benjamin Graham's stock selection criteria in Indian stock market. *Management and Labor Studies*, *39*(1), 43–62. doi:10.1177/0258042X14535156

Tadawul, A. S. R. (2020). Annual Report. Academic Press.

Tala, A., Ahmad, A., & Amjad, A. (2016). Do behavioral finance factors influence stock investment decisions of individual investors? Evidence from Saudi stock market. *American International Journal of Contemporary Research*, *6*(3), 234–250.

Truong, C. (2009). Value investing using price earnings ratio in New Zealand. *University of Auckland Business Review*, *12*(1), 1–7.

Vu, J. D. (1988). An empirical analysis of Benjamin Graham's net current asset value. *Financial Review*, *23*(2), 215–225. doi:10.1111/j.1540-6288.1988.tb00787.x

World Federation Exchanges. (2014). *Monthly Report February 2014*. https://www.world-exchanges.org/statistics/monthly-reports

Worthington, A., & Higgs, H. (2005). *Weak-form Market Efficiency in Asian Emerging and Developed Equity Markets: Comparative Tests of Random Walk Behavior*. University of Wollongong, School of Accounting and Finance Working Paper Series, No. 05/03.

Xiao, Y., & Arnold, G. C. (2008). Testing Benjamin Graham's net current asset value strategy in London. *Journal of Investing*, *17*(4), 11–19. doi:10.3905/JOI.2008.17.4.011

Yakob, N. (2001). *Monetary Uncertainty and Stock Prices: The Case of Malaysia. Department of Finance*. Universiti Kebangsaan Malaysia.

Yalσin, K. C. (2010). Market rationality: Efficient market hypothesis versus market anomalies. *European Journal of Economic and Political Studies*, *2*(1), 23–38.

Zakaria, N., Abdul-Talib, A. N., & Amelinckx, A. (Eds.). (2020). *Transcending Cultural Frontiers: Practices, Challenges, and Strategy for International Business*. Springer. doi:10.1007/978-981-15-4454-5

Zakaria, N., Abdul-Talib, A. N., & Othman, N. (Eds.). (2016). *Handbook of research on impacts of international business and political affairs on the global economy*. IGI Global. doi:10.4018/978-1-4666-9806-2

Zaremba, A., & Czapkiewicz, A. (2017). Digesting anomalies in emerging European markets: A comparison of factor pricing models. *Emerging Markets Review*, *31*(3), 1–15. doi:10.1016/j.ememar.2016.12.002

Zaremba, A., Maydybura, A., Czapkiewicz, A., & Arnaut, M. (2019). Explaining equity anomalies in frontier markets: A horserace of factor pricing models. *Emerging Markets Review*, *35*(3), 211–230.

Chapter 11
International Trade Fairs and Initial Impacts of COVID-19 on International Fairs:
The Case of Dubai

Muharrem Can
Turkish Ministry of Trade, Turkey

Ahmet Canlı
https://orcid.org/0000-0002-1204-9819
Turkish Consulate in Dubai, UAE

ABSTRACT

In ITFs, participating companies introduce their products to potential buyers, perceive their reactions, communicate face-to-face with them, and closely observe their competitors. Moreover, there are other benefits of ITFs such as export and market share increase effect, problem-solving effect with the costumers, so it is one of the critical tasks of commercial diplomacy. The COVID-19 pandemic in 2020 affected the exhibition sector. So the number of fairs held in Dubai decreased dramatically compared to the previous years and also the number of participators and visitors in the fairs, including Turkish companies. Nevertheless, fair activities have adapted quickly and started to be organized in the virtual world. This study examined the literature and analyzed the Dubai exhibitions' statistics thoroughly both before and after COVID-19. The authors' goal is to find out if physical exhibitions maintain their importance despite technological developments.

INTRODUCTION

The Covid-19 pandemic in 2020 adversely affected the fairs held in Dubai, an important regional exhibition hub, and the number of fairs held numerically decreased to 30 percent. At the same time, the

DOI: 10.4018/978-1-7998-9071-3.ch011

number of participating companies decreased. Therefore, due to the cancellation of significant fairs in Dubai, Turkish companies have also been negatively affected.

The main reasons for the companies to attend to International Trade Fairs (ITFs), bring together buyers and sellers from different places, within specific periods, while reducing their costs, including visitors search costs and saving time. ITFs are an important international economic activity with many apparent purposes, such as increasing exports, increasing market share, as well as unseen goals. Among these goals are the exchange of information between companies, the solution of existing problems, and, most importantly, the spread of information and technology. However, the Covid-19 outbreak that started in 2020 has significantly affected IFTs. Many of these fairs have been canceled, and some of them have been realized virtually.

In this study, the authors did a critical literature review and obtained statistical information from the Dubai Fair Authority and the Turkish Ministry of Trade. In addition, the authors discussed the effects of technological development on International Trade Fairs (ITFs) and their essential invisible functions. The level of success of the new generation fairs in achieving these goals is discussed.

DEFINITION OF INTERNATIONAL TRADE FAIR AND ITS FUNCTIONS

It is undoubtedly clear that certain size companies can reach their marketing goals properly, only if they penetrate external markets. In order to grow, these companies need to develop linkages to knowledge that is not available in their countries and local ecosystems (Owen-Smith & Powell, 2004; Scott, 1998). Therefore, they need to keep in touch with other regional and national economies to track the latest technological and marketing developments and avoid potentially harmful regional lock-in processes (Grabher, 1993; Uzzi, 1997; Rinallo et al., 2017, p. 96). The 1980s and 1990s concentrated on localized synergies and the network effects of regional industry clusters. The buzz and pipelines model suggested that cluster success depends on connecting internal and external cycles of knowledge generation and opening networks to the other region in the world. This argument caused questions about how firms in clusters systematically acquire knowledge about global market opportunities and technology developments and establish connections with companies in other countries. Questions such as these directed the economic geography (EG) research to become more interested in the effects of ITFs (Rinallo et al., 2017, p. 96).

The industry trend is towards vertical ITFs, as organizers respond to buyer and seller preferences for contact and transaction efficiency. The literature covers both vertical and horizontal ITFs. Thus, buyers are an obvious requirement for the success of any ITF, but the literature primarily does not take the exhibitor's perspective enough (Rossen and Seringhause, 1994: 313). Whereas, in an ITF, organizer companies perform activities according to the calendar that is a specific day and time, such as arranging the physical space (Pinchera & Rinallo, 2017, p. 5). Organizer companies provide basic needs of the companies such as communication, lighting and promoting the fair through traditional and digital media. According to the work of the French proximity school (Boschma, 2005; Rallet & Torre,1999), ITFs are viewed as events that companies get together an organizational field, display their latest products and technological developments, and have the opportunity to connect with firms from other regions and countries (Norcliffe & Rendace, 2003; Power & Jansson, 2008), (Rinallo et al., 2017, p. 96). Due to these reasons, up-to-date IFTs[1] organizers also (in addition to other functions, such as designing, producing, and marketing these events) have received scant attention in the industrial marketing (IM) literature (Rinallo et al., 2017, p. 94).

Participants worldwide are invited to ITFs, and business representatives from many countries take part as both manufacturers and potential customers. Thus, thanks to the fairs, companies have the opportunity to communicate with important customers. On the other hand, the countries and cities where the fairs are held can provide a significant financial return. Again, trade fairs can play an active role in promoting cities and countries (Bilgen, 2019, p. 228). There are different ITFs types that fulfill different purposes and involve different forms of interaction among the sellers and buyers. A fundamental way of distinguishing between ITFs is to compare the levels of international participation on the exhibitor-supplier and visitor-buyer sides with each other (Bathelt et al., 2014; Rinallo & Golfetto, 2011). *Import shows*, which their participants are mainly international suppliers-exhibitors and mainly local buyers as visitors, offer exhibitors the opportunity to learn more about local (producers, trade channels and customers, etc.) and better understand their international competitors and their customers' strategies on the local market. Typically, consumer shows belong in this category. When devoted to professional buyers, these trade shows are especially important for the companies in emerging economies that national manufacturing industries do not achieve a sufficient level of development (see Li, 2014). In *export shows*, there are many international visitors and mainly local suppliers-exhibitors offer exhibitor companies initial contacts with foreign markets and opportunities to learn more about local competitors and their international strategies. *Hub shows,* which their exhibitors and visitors are mainly foreigners, combine many of the elements of the previously mentioned trade show types. So, they offer many opportunities to learn about global industries, markets, innovations, and marketing strategies and practices. They represent an advanced stage of trade show development and usually take place in cities with high international or intercontinental accessibility, in the center of larger manufacturing areas (Rinallo et al., 2017, p. 97-98).

ADVANTAGES AND THE MAIN GOALS OF THE INTERNATIONAL TRADE FAIRS FOR PARTICIPATING COMPANIES

Until recently, since ITFs had been collective events, they provided an opportunity to contact a large number of potential buyers at a relatively low cost, due to the fact that part of the overall organizing and advertising expenses were shared among many participants. Thus, ITFs were a particularly effective communication tool for European companies, which were typically small- and medium-sized. But in recent years, all this has changed because the events market has become much larger and more fragmented, characterized by the development of an extensive array of formats (Golfetto & Rinallo, 2014, p. 2). This literature considers ITFs to be crucial events that enable local producers to link with non-local partners to gain access to new markets and acquire important information about technologies and production conditions in distant regional/national contexts (Rinallo et al., 2017, p. 17).

i-Export Increase and Trade Fairs

ITFs provide some valuable benefits for participating companies. During ITFs activities, they find the opportunity to meet with the market leaders and other companies trying to enter the market for the first time.

One of the main other objectives for the participating companies is to increase their export. The companies carry out structural market access and establishing distribution channels through agents or importers/distributors in the target market (Gębarowski & Wiażewicz, 2014, p. 320). Because trade fairs offer ideal cooperation opportunities to find agents and distributors.Thus, various studies focused on the increase in exports of participating companies in trade fairs. Three surveys examined on ITFs effect on the exports in follow-up studies. Some 64 percent of respondents had purchased one or more products within seven months of the World of Concrete '86 Show. Moreover, 72 percent of these indicated that their purchases were influenced by what they saw at their visited ITFs (Seringhause & Rossen 1995, p. 86). ITFs also provide the participating companies with the opportunity to maintain the continuity of relations with existing customers and the visibility of their company and products. Actually, the participating companies follow some strategies during the IFTs.

Table 1. Aims targets and strategies

Aims	Target Groups
Gain market share with new products	Old and new customer
Protect market share with existing products	Old users (Assurance, appeal to security, needs, and relationship, Treat old customers as friends
Market development with new product	potential users (Create awareness of problem/solution)

Source: Gębarowski & Wiażewicz, 2012, p. 317.

Trade fairs are very beneficial in terms of cooperation, especially for small and medium-sized companies, which have limited experience in foreign markets. Creating a positive nation brand and attracting foreign buyers, IFTs are especially beneficial to the survival and growth of smaller industrial firms. In this context, Asia, and to a lesser extent South America and Eastern Europe, are characterized by smaller but high-growth ITFs trade show markets (Rinallo et al., 2017, p. 201).

ii-Some Other Goals for Exhibitors Companies

The participating companies have some other goals to attend ITFs other than export, access new markets, and contact customers and suppliers. During the events, they engage in intensive interaction with all these actors their day-to-day interactions and problem-solving processes, they develop and maintain networks, scan other markets, watch their competitors, and use the events as a benchmark to evaluate developments in the industry (Bathelt & Schuldt, 2008, 2010). Based on such interactions and knowledge acquisition patterns during ITFs, firms further existing networks and promote trans-local linkages over time. (Rinallo et al., 2017, p. 97). They see and get to know their competitors and their products closely and evaluate their relative position in the market.

One of the factors that determine how information-related advantages of the ITFs shows is used is the diversity of information sources. The post-show period is also very significant. By utilizing trade show information, the organization will realize good benefits (Bettis-Outland et al., 2012, p. 386). These are:

- new customers,
- increased sales from current customers, and/or,
- purchase of new products, services, technical training, and updates to enhance customer support.

Disseminated ITFs information is also used by the organization to produce intangible benefits. Some of these benefits are (Bettis-Outland et al., 2012, p. 386):

- improvements in strategic planning,
- improvements in policy development,
- new product development ideas, and
- improved corporate image (Gębarowski, Wiażewiczi 2014: 337)

The companies participating in ITFs offer also have other important goals that they aimed to achieve. For example, these showed exhibitor's presence and position on the market and presented the offer face-to-face (Gębarowski & Wiażewicz, 2014, p. 343). ITFs also enable companies to introduce their products by contacting potential customers, communicating with them face-to-face, observing their reactions to the product,

ITFs provide a suitable venue for working on such relationships, whether they are vertical (with suppliers, intermediaries, or customers) or horizontal (with associations, partners, or regulators. The main intangible goals of the exhibitors are the latest offer (58,1 percent), creation of experience, as well as making the customers remember the brand (48,8 percent), and gathering information about the latest trends in the industry (45,3 percent). Less than 30 percent declared that they intend to monitor the behaviors of the competitors. Nearly every fourth respondent claimed that ITFs give an excellent opportunity to recognize customers' demands. A similar group of 26,7 percent declared that they establish and maintain social and business contacts during ITFs (Gębarowski & Wiażewicz, 2014, p. 340). Industry associations and other industry actors sometimes benefit from ITFs as collaborative promotional platforms. This happens mainly in the case of export-oriented shows, which trade associations tend to organize or strongly support. Bathelt et al. (2014) report several empirical cases indicating how Italian ITFs in various industries have helped local manufacturers, through the mediation of trade associations, to promote their competencies and create a collective nation brand (Rinallo et al., 2017, p. 201).

MAIN GOALS OF THE VISITING COMPANIES TO PARTICIPATE IN THE INTERNATIONAL TRADE FAIRS

Although there is some limited information on the reasons that lead managers not to attend ITFs. One of the controversial reasons not to attend is the time and cost pressures. Because for the majority of the companies, ITFs are too great a distance. Another reason for non-attendance is their negative experience and booth personnel knowledge (Rossen & Seringhause, 1995, p. 84). In ITFs, visiting companies have the chance to see and taste product samples, get first-hand information about the producers and products from the experts and establish face-to-face relations with the suppliers (Rinallo et al., 2017, p. 97). Moreover, trade fairs offer visitors the opportunity to see new goods and services as well as observe current trends.

One another reason for the visitors to attend the ITFs is to reduce search costs. Because the ITFs gather companies in the same place and simultaneously, it is argued that exhibitors provide visitors with the possibility to collect a significant amount of important purchase data at a minimal cost and also in a short time. Many studies suggest that visitors attending in ITFs are motivated by more than just information search. For most of the attendants, the reasons are not mainly for planned, economic reasoning.

On the contrary, they said many times, "If you are in this business, you have to be here". In the ITFs, there are ritualized, standard appointments in the life of an industry. The attendance of the ITFs is taken for granted is significantly insulated from competing events because of visitor (and exhibitor) loyalty (Rinallo et al., 2010, p. 256). Because ITFs are built on a knowledge-based view of the firm and of territorial agglomeration, they provide platforms for observation and interaction that accelerate learning and innovation during these activities (Pinchera & Rinallo, 2017, p. 5).

Information search processes for ITFs by doing physical activities are quite different from browsing a website or glancing through the pages of a magazine. Because of these differences, ITFs visits should be described as personnel experiences. Consequently, the information-processing situations faced by visitors are radically different from those regarding other communication instruments, as they are characterized by:

- sensorial overwhelming;
- information over-load; and
- physical fatigue.

Nevertheless, the ITFs environment is rich in sensorial stimuli, sounds, noises, odors, colors, signs, physical objects, and the crowd, all of which carry information and help attract visitors' attention (Rinallo et al., 2010, pp. 251-252). ITFs provide "premium quality information" because they gather thousands of specialists and experts devoted to a particular branch or area of activity in one place and time. Moreover, ITFs usually enable to exhibit the latest offer to the market. Modern ITFs have an opportunity for many information-gathering channels. In this context, the primary sources of information are the following:

- face-to-face conversations with visitors at the stands,
- demonstrations of their produces on exhibitions,
- printed advertising materials (leaflets, brochures, catalogs, folders, etc.),
- promotional materials on electronic devices (promotional films and presentations of a company on CD or pen drives).
- especially ITFs' catalogs issued by organizers of the events (containing detailed information about all exhibitors and their products and handed out or sold to visitors),
- trade fair website (in particular pages on relevant branch and exhibitors and their products),
- that additional events prepared by organizers during the ITFs, such as contests, seminars, and conferences, also offer unique opportunities for attendances and visitors (Gebarowski & Wiazewicz, 2014, p. 336-337).

In the 1980s, executives in technology-based industries appear to have almost no clear idea about their preference for ITFs over other methods of seeing the latest developments and knowledge of how to do this work for their companies. Although ITF scores were reasonably well, other information sources were not (Hough, 1986, 1988; Trade Show Bureau, 1992b). It was almost clear that the best source of information on technology, suppliers, and products in these years were industry press and news, ITFs and conferences, vendor presentations, salespersons, directories, executive seminars, and permanent exhibit centers (Seringhause &, Rossen, 1995, p. 86). Today the information channels have not been changes. Especially interaction with competent stand personnel is a valuable experience for the visitors. Because these activities make opportunities for social exchange, information sharing, dialogues with different issues. They reduce the distance to the supplier and optimize problem-solving measures. For the buyers' side, speaking to the supplier's technical personnel is in itself a good return on the investment to visit the supplier. For many exhibitors, the interaction with visitors offers many learning opportunities; that is, ITFs participations feed the R&D staff with exciting ideas for months (Rinallo et al., 2010, p. 255).

Depending on the nature of the fairs, the participating companies cooperate with other companies for different purposes. ITFs provide such vertical cooperation refers to sales-oriented activities in final products. IFTs are also temporary clusters and multidimensional relational spaces where firms have the opportunity to learn through interaction processes with peers, existing or potential value-chain partners, and third parties. For their vertical dimension, firms have a unique overview of competition during ITFs, especially at large international hub events. They create opportunities for horizontal learning by showing what is going on relating to the new products, competitors, and new product trends in the field. ITFs also offer firms such feedback that generates benchmarks for industrial production and innovation (Rinallo et al., 2017, p. 97). For participating companies, horizontal cooperation refers to cooperation for intermediate goods and input supply other than final products. Besides cognitive elements, ITFs permit visitors to establish or maintain social bonds with key actors in their business and occupational networks. For many visitors, ITFs provide an opportunity to meet members of the suppliers' staff with whom they rarely interact. For example, they can ask technical help from the very competent engineer who designed the machine that is creating problems at the customer's plant, or have an informal conversation on future fashion trends with a creative designer, or simply "shake hands with an entrepreneur esteem" or a manager who is a good position (Rinallo et al., 2010, p. 254).

SOCIAL PLACES AND INTERACTING FUNCTION OF THE INTERNATIONAL TRADE FAIRS

ITFs are not just places where products are exhibited. It enables participants and visitors to come together in cafes, restaurants, and cocktail venues. In fact, the areas reserved for this purpose in some fairs may reach a significant proportion of the total areas. In addition, organizations such as dinner parties and cocktail hours in the evening allow people to socialize more and get to know each other better.

For the reasons above mentioned, many stands in ITFs have socialization areas of various kinds, including bars (65 percent), restaurants (10 percent), and relaxation corners (24 percent). On average, approximately 6 percent of the total space is dedicated to this kind of activity (Rinallo et al., 2010, p. 251). Table 2 illustrates the average stand space distribution at textile-apparel fairs.

Table 2. Stand space distribution at textile-apparel fairs by exhibited products

Space function on the stand	Consumer products	Products Exhibited at the ITFs		
		Intermediate products	Capital goods	Average
Product exhibition	73	44	61	60
Professional interaction	20	53	30	34
Relaxation and socialisation	7	3	34	6

Source: Rinallo et all, 2010: 252

According to ITFs attendances, the social interaction opportunities offered by suppliers, for example, cocktail hours, invitations to dinners, social events, provide pleasant relief from the weariness of the fair activities and, most of all, bring about and reinforce social ties with the supplier's staff. Furthermore, these kinds of activities events may also very useful interactions with other buyers, an additional benefit of which exhibitors are not always aware of. An exhibitor who gathers many customers in a friendly and pleasant environment is seen as a good partner and a social facilitator. Moreover, by inviting speakers who are experts in their fields, the participants are given the opportunity to have in-depth knowledge of the product and sector. The Florentine Fashion Show, which is an export-oriented trade fair, not only provided Italian couturiers with an opportunity to promote themselves to foreign markets and buyers but also to learn about market needs. This outcome happened by means of countless informal interactions with buyers and journalists (Pinchera & Rinallo, 2017, p. 14). On the other hand, interaction among visitors is a phenomenon that has not been highlighted in the literature on ITFs. For individuals holding positions of responsibility within firms, the possibility to interact with people in similar positions in other companies (e.g., other technicians, buyers, designers) is very valuable. ITFs provide interaction among the occupational communities. Other visitors are also important sources of knowledge through informal conversations that contribute to disseminating knowledge about products and suppliers, even through rumors and gossip. However, unlike exhibitors, other visitors are difficult to locate at trade shows. Therefore, cocktail hours at the exhibitor stands and technical seminars or social events arranged by the trade show organizers give a change for the individual visitors. Thus, ITFs are important appointments in the professional lives of individuals as well as companies and industries (Rinallo et al., 2010, p. 254).

COMMERCIAL DIPLOMACY AND INTERNATIONAL TRADE FAIRS

Since ITFs have an important effect on foreign trade, especially in the increase of exports, they are among the top agendas of commercial diplomacy. ITFs, and procurement committees (buying missions) are important promotional activities of interest to commercial diplomats. While ITFs are individual promotional activities, others provide an opportunity to increase their effectiveness (ITC, 1987, p. 142). On the other hand, fair incentives are among the most common export support programs provided by governments. However, participation in ITFs gives results in the long term (ITC, 1987, p.156).

It is widely accepted that supporting fair and trade mission events, developing economic intelligence, and improving networking are the primary duties of commercial diplomats (Ruël & Zuidema, 2012, p. 5). Thus, the main activities of the commercial diplomats are primarily commercial promotional activities. An experienced commercial diplomat from New Zeland defines his duties as managing the sellers' and buyers' relationships. It covers topics such as participation in trade fairs, exhibitions, procurement committees, conferences/seminars, and "made in" campaigns. In addition to these, commercial diplomats are involved in tourism promotion activities (Kostecki & Naray, 2007, p. 7). These kinds of activities comprise a significant share of commercial diplomatic activities. For example, trade fairs make up 60 percent of total activities for the USA diplomats. In comparison, it is 30 percent for Canadian diplomats, 20 percent for Japanese diplomats, 30 percent for South Korean diplomats, and 25 percent for Sweden and Austria diplomats (Kostecki & Naray, 2007, p. 12).

Commercial diplomats can obtain necessary market data and forecasts for exporters in their countries by contacting importers, visiting fairs, and communicating with major store chains and mail-order companies based on their assigned countries (Rana, 2016, p. 83). For this reason, among the duties of

British business diplomats are the promotion of British-origin goods in the host market through seminars, trade fairs, and direct lobbying activities (Lee, 2004, p. 51). Commercial diplomats provide support for visits of the home country businesspeople and politicians to host countries and encourage the participation of businesspeople in various fairs, exhibitions, and call for tenders, and so on (Kostecki & Naray, 2007, p. 15). Since specialized trade fairs, which take place in certain cities, may also require commercial diplomats' presence there. Paris, Milan, and London are the center of numerous clothing and textile promotion activities. So, the commercial diplomats from textiles exporting countries must operate in these countries, even in these cities (Kostecki & Naray, 2007, p. 13). Additionally, trade fairs have an important effect on foreign trade, especially in the increase of exports. They are among the top agendas of commercial diplomacy. It is one of the primary duties of commercial diplomats to help the companies and suppliers of the host country participate in those organized in their home country as well.

DIGITAL AND VISUAL FAIRS

In order to organize successful fairs that attract related participants and visitors to come together, the organizers utilize numerous marketing and advertisement tools. These tools help participants and visitors choose the most appropriate exhibitions for their time, effort, and budget. Since the cost of attending fairs comprises a big part of firms' marketing budget, they have to choose the best events for their marketing goals. Marketing and advertisement are more crucial for ITFs since the companies are distantly scattered in other countries (Rinallo et al., 2017, p. 94; Golfetto & Rinallo, 2014, p. 4). In the last several decades, technological developments have also affected communication and advertisement methods. Advertisement is carried out via social media and the websites of fairs and, as well as traditional promotional methods However, innovative methods such as films and CDs can be used (Gebarowski & Wiażewicz, 2014). More recently, tools such as Google and Facebook have been used widely for promotional and advertising purposes. Organizers utilize social media to publicize their events by communicating event information, reaching relevant actors, attracting influencers, creating databases, and distributing special offers. The promotion's success can be calculated by various methods such as how many likes the advertisement and promotion received or how many people visited these mediums. By using social media and getting feedback from their targeted groups, organizers took the opportunity to add more value to the content of fairs, which was primarily limited to the physical space only (Golfetto & Rinallo, 2014, pp. 15-17).

Similarly, companies have been increasingly using social media and web pages to promote their products and find new customers outside of fairs. For example, international companies have been meeting remotely via teleconferencing for a long time. Due to the improvements in the technology of video teleconference tools, companies have the chance to inspect the color of the textile or sewing of the garments online (Viotti & Kauppi, 2014, p. 151). Although virtual events and video teleconferencing might help companies meet with their counterparts and promote their products more efficiently, they caused doubts about whether they pose more threats or opportunities over physical events. Both types of events experience structural and functional changes in recent years. Physical events have been evolving from a "promotion-information" to a "promotion-relationship-experience" model, which attracts the attention of the participants, as well as the media. Initially thought to replace live events, virtual events have not been successful enough and become more complementary to physical events (Golfetto & Rinallo, 2014, pp. 17-19). In addition to digital materials and website promotions, advertising activities of trade fairs have started to occur on the internet, such as Google and Facebook. Depending on the increasing use of technology in commercial life, some assert that physical fairs will be replaced by virtual fairs in the future, while others believe that this transition will not be possible in the short term.While discussing the importance of virtual events and the prospect of fairs Covid-19 pandemic hit the sector at the beginning of 2020. Developments after the pandemic have also significantly changed the way fairs are performed and were primarily realized in the form of virtual exhibitions. All the physical events were canceled or postponed. According to the Union des Foires Internationales (UFI) Global Exhibition Barometer, when companies were also asked if they believed exhibitions would open again in their city, more than half of these companies declared "no activities" between April and August 2020 (UFI Global Exhibition Barometer, 2021, p. 5).

According to the Dubai World Trade Center (DWTC) website, all the significant events and exhibitions were canceled or postponed in Dubai between March and December.. Promotions of these virtual exhibitions are also carried out on platforms such as Facebook and Google. The effectiveness of promotions and exhibitions is measured by the number of virtual visitors. However, although these fairs bring together buyers and sellers to a certain extent in digital media, they are deprived of the opportunities brought by the experiential marketing relationship, such as one-to-one promotion and seeing product samples. Likewise, virtual exhibitions cannot offer companies and visitors opportunities such as spreading the knowledge and innovation brought by the social aspect of the fairs, evaluating their relative place among other competitors since face-to-face meetings and leisure activities are not possible.

Having left with no other alternative and within the unfavorable circumstances of the pandemic, organizers had to organize virtual events that would ultimately replace physical ones or hybrid models. However, despite all the developments in digital technology and the way of using it, physical trade fairs have not lost their importance. According to UFI, as of 2021, the proportion of companies that expected the "normalization of activities" grew from 10 percent for January to 37 percent for June. Although 64 percent of companies believe that the pandemic confirmed the value of physical events and express their confidence that the sector will recover rapidly, 63 percent consider that there will be fewer international physical exhibitions and therefore fewer participants. Eighty percent of companies agree that there will be more push towards hybrid events and more digital elements at events. Only 14 percent of companies believe virtual events will replace physical events (UFI Global Exhibition Barometer, 2021, p. 5). UFI Global Recovery Insights 2020 Report surveyed visitors of the exhibitions as well as exhibitors who participated at the digital events in more than 30 countries. The report reflects the expectations of visitors and exhibitors separately. According to this report, while both visitors and exhibitors showed a strong preference for physical events, visitors accept that digital exhibitions have more time and cost advantages over live events, effectively delivering the content. Still, visitors believe that digital events offer less quality of networking and enjoyable experience. Exhibiting companies believe that live events provide a better return on investment by offering better networking opportunities, representing their brands, and generating more sales (UFI Global Recovery Insights, 2020, pp. 5-14; Ngoni et al. 2021, pp. 4-7). These survey results clearly show that companies have begun to demand more experiential interaction, which requires face-to-face communication.As explained above, trade fairs have essential functions other than increasing sales and finding new customers. Therefore, with the control of Covid-19 and reducing certain social risks, it is expected that trade fairs will take place physically again.

FAIR CENTERS IN THE WORLD AND DUBAI

Globally, ITFs take place mainly in Western European and North American countries. First of all, these countries are important markets for national companies and foreign exporters who would like to penetrate. Secondly, their exhibition infrastructures are more developed compared to other regions of the world. Thirdly, their logistic and transportation facilities are developed. Especially Germany, France, and Italy are highly developed countries in fair organizing, and they host the most important fairs internationally. Recently, however, countries in Asia, Australia, and Latin America have started to host important trade fairs. Trade fairs can be organized according to the needs of the city, country, and region (Seringhaus & Rosson, 1994, pp. 311-313). Some of them have the characteristics of hubs as they receive exhibitors and visitors from regional countries. Dubai, one of the leading "regional hubs", hosts international trade fairs where exhibitors and visitors from the Gulf countries, the Middle East, Southeast Asia, and African countries show great interest.

PARTICIPATION OF TURKISH COMPANIES IN THE FAIRS IN DUBAI

Due to the pandemic, the number of ITFs held in Turkey and abroad, where Turkish companies participated, has decreased significantly in 2020. The number of fairs attended by Turkish companies abroad was 279 in 2018 and 2019, while it was only 60 in 2020 (Ministry of Trade, Republic of Turkey). Dubai is an important location for Turkish companies to expand to Africa, Gulf countries, and Southeast Asian countries. For this reason, the fairs held in the United Arab Emirates are essential for Turkish companies. Out of 49, the authors analyzed 20 major international exhibitions that a significant number of Turkish companies participated in regularly for the past several years. Turkish companies either have not participated in a significant number or have not participated at all. That is why the authors chose these fairs for comparison to understand the effects of the pandemic. These exhibitions, covering main sectors in the economy, such as food, health, technology, leisure, and construction, also attracted other countries as well as Turkey. According to the DWTC, the number of fairs held in Dubai in 2020 was only 49 due to the restrictions brought by the pandemic, declining from 159 in 2018 and 150 in 2019. These figures show that the number of fairs held in the country in 2020 has decreased by more than two-thirds compared to previous years.

Table 3 shows that the number of prominent international fairs decreased significantly in 2020. Due to the pandemic, 12 fairs out of 20 were canceled or postponed just after the pandemic. In parallel to the decline in the fairs, the number of companies participating in these fairs also decreased significantly compared to 2019. While the number of participating companies was 33,084 in 2018 and 33,948 in 2019, this number decreased to 15,097 in 2020, reflecting a decline of 55 percent. Considering the importance of fair industry and its spillover effects on Dubai's economy, the cancelation of the fairs caused a significant financial loss for several businesses. For example, according to the Dubai Statistics Center, the average occupancy rate of 5-star-hotels was 45 percent in 2020, showing a considerable decrease from 85 percent in 2019. Similarly, the transportation industry contracted nearly 30 percent in the half of 2020, partly due to the cancelation of business trips (Dubai Statistics Center, 2021).

Table 3. Prominent international fairs in Dubai

	2018				2019				2020			
	Turk. Comp.	Countries	Total Comp.	Share	Turk. Comp.	Countries	Total Comp	Share	Turk. Comp.	Countries	Total Comp.	Share
GITEX TECHNIOLOGY WEEK	17	100	4,500	0.4%	9	97	4,500	0.2%	-	60	363	-
GULFOOD & GULFHOST	161	120	5,000	3.2%	169	120	5,000	3.4%	182	120	5,000	3.6%
DUBAI WOOD SHOW / DIFAC	26	20	120	21.7%	25	20	120	20.8%		canceled		
MIDDLE EAST ENERGY	139	61	1,604	8.7%	128	61	1,359	9.4%	103	65	1,400	7.4%
ARAB HEALTH	171	69	4,176	4.1%	175	66	4,262	4.1%	150	64	4,250	3.5%
MEDLAB ME & AEEDC	28	46	3,162	0.9%	35	50	3,142	1.1%	47	50	3,000	1.6%
BEAUTYWORLD MIDDLE EAST	120	62	1,738	6.9%	108	62	1,790	6.0%		canceled		
INDEX & FUTURE INTERIORS	48	64	1,000	4.8%	33	61	1,175	2.8%		canceled		
THE HOTEL SHOW	18	50	790	2.3%	109	55	950	11.5%		canceled		
THE BIG 5 & MIDDLE EAST STONE	284	66	2,501	11.4%	219	65	2,533	8.6%		canceled		
ARAB PLAST		Biannual			33	29	1,202	2.7%		Biannual		
AUTOMECHANIKA DUBAI	53	61	1,801	2.9%	74	63	1,880	3.9%		canceled		
INTERSEC	33	59	1,337	2.5%	31	54	1,202	2.6%	28	56	1,084	2.6%
WINDOWS DOORS&FACADES	16	14	127	12.6%	14	16	160	8.8%		canceled		
CITYSCAPE GLOBAL DUBAI	23	10	276	8.3%	12	19	100	12.0%		canceled		
WETEX & SOLAR SHOW	13	53	2,016	0.6%	10	55	2,350	0.4%		canceled		
YUMMEX	43	43	283	15.2%	30	60	300	10.0%		canceled		
GULFOOD MANUFACTURING & INGREDIENTS MIDDLE EAST	135	54	1,544	8.7%	131	60	1,600	8.2%		canceled		
INTERNATIONAL APPAREL & TEXTILE FAIR	14	17	147	9.5%	7	18	151	4.6%		canceled		
MIDDLE EAST NATURAL & ORGANIC PRODUCTS EXPO	29	95	962	3.0%	16	55	172	9.3%	-	8	NA	
Total	**1,371**		**33,084**	**4.1%**	**1,368**		**33,948**	**4.0%**	**482**		**15,097**	**3.2%**

Source: Dubai World Trade Center

According to the Table 3, Turkey has been one of the major participants of these exhibitions. Although, the average share of Turkish companies participating in the selected fairs was four percent in 2019, the participation rate in specific sectors has been much higher. For instance, the share of Turkish companies for the Wood Show event was 21.7 percent in 2018 and 20.8 percent in 2019. While the participation rate for the Hotel Show event was 2.3 percent in 2018, it increased significantly in 2019 and reached 11.5 percent. Similarly, the share for CityScape Global Dubai was 8.3 percent in 2018, it grew to 12 percent in 2019, reflecting a noteworthy increase. Although, the number of Turkish companies attending the Middle East Energy fair decreased in 2019, the participation rate increased to 9.4 percent in 2019, from 8.7 percent in the previous year.

For some fairs, the participation rate of Turkish companies declined slightly in 2019, while it still remained at significant rates. For example, the share of Turkish companies to the Golfood Manufacturing & Ingredients Middle East fair was 8.5 percent in 2018, it realized as 8.2 percent in 2019; for the Beauty World Middle East fair, it was 6.0 percent in 2019, declining from 6.9 percent in 2018. While the share for the Yummex fair was 15.2 percent in 2018, this rate decreased to 10 percent in 2018; for The Big 5 & Middle East Stone fair, Turkish companies' share declined to 8.6 percent in 2019 from 11.4 percent in the previous year; for the Windows & Doors Facades fair the rate decreased to 8.8 percent in 2019, while it was 12.6 percent in 2018.

Unfortunately, all of these important fairs, where Turkish companies have a significant presence, were canceled in 2020, except for the Middle East Energy fair. However, the rate of Turkish companies in the existing fairs did not decrease significantly in 2020 and realized an average of 3.2 percent. In 2020, the total number of Turkish companies attending these fairs was only 482, representing a decrease of 65 percent.

On the other hand, it is evident that the negative trend in 2020 continues in 2021 when the epidemic's effect is still going on. However, the declining number of participants and visitors to the fairs reflects that Dubai faces a severe financial loss. The Dubai government is carrying out an intensive vaccination program to compensate for these losses in the exhibition sector, among other sectors. Having reached a specific rate in vaccination, Dubai intends to increase the number of fairs that will take place physically in the country in the coming months and bring millions of company representatives together on the occasion of Expo2020. To be able to that, they need to convince the participants and visitors that vaccination has reached a level that would protect everyone.

CONCLUSION

The COVID-19 pandemic in 2020 had a significant negative impact on international economic activities. In this study, the authors carried out intensive literature research and employed the Turkish Ministry of Trade data, which shows the numerical view of the ITFs attended by Turkish companies between 2018 and 2020. The authors also analyzed and compared the numbers of trade fairs held in Dubai in 2020 and the number of participants and visitors attending these fairs with previous years, using the data of the Dubai World Trade Center LLC. Due to COVID-19 pandemic, the number of international fairs attended by Turkish companies decreased significantly in 2020. It is also true for Dubai, an important regional exhibition hub. Virtual fairs took place instead of physical fairs. Despite the technological development, physical fairs seem to continue to maintain their importance for a long time. Especially after the intensive vaccination in Dubai, it is expected that the fairs held in the country will be organized physically again. Depending on the normalization in the countries, a similar trend is expected for the ITFs where Turkish companies participate outside of Dubai.

REFERENCES

Abdul-Talib, A. N., & Teong, N. (2019). Internet sales channel and manufacturers' brand: A transaction cost analysis. *International Journal of Supply Chain Management*, *8*(5), 1130–1340.

Bilgen, İ. (2019). Fuarcılıkta Bugünün Geleneği: Sanal Fuarlar. In Pazarlama Düşüncesiyle Sürdürüleblir Fuarcılık ve istihdam (pp. 227-238). Sokak Yayın Grubu.

Bondarouk, E., & Ruël, H. (2012). Lobbying of commercial diplomats: institutional setting as a determining factor. In H. Ruël (Ed.), *Commercial diplomacy and international business: A conceptual and empirical exploration, Advanced Series in Management* (Vol. 9, pp. 251–291). Emerald Group Publishing Limited. doi:10.1108/S1877-6361(2012)0000009013

Dubai Statistics Center. (n.d.). *Dubai Socioeconomic Statistics*. Retrieved from https://www.dsc.gov.ae/en-us/Themes/Pages/National-Accounts.aspx?Theme=24

GębarowskiM.WiażewiczJ. (2014). Trade shows as a place of knowledge sharing about tourism Products. In *Human Capital without Borders: Knowledge and Learning for Quality of Life, Proceedings of the Management, Knowledge and Learning International Conference 2014, 25-27 June 2014, Portorož.* https://ssrn.com/abstract=2706205

Global Exhibition Barometer, U. F. I. (2021). *Report based on the results of a survey concluded in January 2021* (26th ed.). The Global Association of the Exhibition Industry.

Global Recovery Insights, U. F. I. (2020). *Part 2: The future of digital and hybrid events*. The Global Association of the Exhibition Industry.

Golfetto, F., & Rinallo, D. (2014). Trade show events, from live to digital: towards the development of new competencies. *Spatial Aspects Concerning Economic Structure, 12*(3), 1-24.

Hashim, F., Bakar, A. R. A., & Talib, A. N. (2010). *International Business* (2nd ed.). Oxford Fajar Press.

ITC. (1987). *Commercial representation: Handbook for official trade representatives*. International Trade Center UNCTAD/GATT.

Koctecky, M., & Naray, O. (2007). Commercial Diplomacy and International Business, Clingendael Discussion Papers in Diplomacy. *Clingendael Institute, 107.*

Lee, D. (2004). The growing influence of business in UK diplomacy. *International Studies Perspectives, 5*(1), 50–54. doi:10.1111/j.1528-3577.2004.00154.x

Ministry of Trade, Republic of Turkey. (n.d.). https://ticaret.gov.tr/ihracat/fuarlar

Ngoni, C. S., Felicity, N. N., & Precious, M. (2021). Exhibitors' preference at trade fairs: The case of Zimbabwe International Trade Fair (ZITF). *Journal of Convention & Event Tourism*, 1–21. Advance online publication. doi:10.1080/15470148.2021.1893241

Pinchera, V., & Rinallo, D. (2017). The emergence of Italy as a fashion country: Nation branding and collective meaning creation at Florence's fashion shows (1951–1965). *Business History*, 1–29.

Rana, K. S. (2016). *Bilateral Diplomacy*. Manas Publication.

Rinallo, D., Bathelt, H., & Golfetto, F. (2017). Economic geography and industrial marketing views on trade shows: Collective marketing and knowledge circulation. *Industrial Marketing Management, 61*, 93–103. doi:10.1016/j.indmarman.2016.06.012

Rinallo, D., Borghini, S., & Golfetto, F. (2010). Exploring visitor experiences at trade shows. *Journal of Business and Industrial Marketing, 25*(4), 249–258. doi:10.1108/08858621011038207

Ruël, H. J. M., & Zuidema, L. (2012). *The effectiveness of commercial diplomacy; a survey among Dutch embassies and consulates.* Discussion Papers in Diplomacy, Clingendael Institute, March 2012(123), 1-54. http://www.clingendael.nl/cdsp/publications/discussion-papers/archive.html

Seringhaus, F. H. R., & Rosson, P. J. (1994). International trade fairs and foreign market involvement: Review and research directions. *International Business Review, 3*(3), 311–329. doi:10.1016/0969-5931(94)90008-6

Seringhaus, F. H. R., & Rosson, P. J. (1995). Visitor and exhibitor industrial trade fairs interaction. *Journal of Business Research, 32*, 81–90. doi:10.1016/0148-2963(94)00012-4

Viotti, P. R., & Kauppi, M. V. (2014). *Uluslararası ilişkiler ve dünya siyaseti* [International relations and world politics]. Nobel.

What's On. (2021, May 30). *Dubai World Trade Center.* https://www.dwtc.com/en/events

Zakaria, N., Abdul-Talib, A. N., & Amelinckx, A. (Eds.). (2020). *Transcending cultural frontiers: practices, challenges, and strategy for international business.* Springer. doi:10.1007/978-981-15-4454-5

Zakaria, N., Abdul-Talib, A. N., & Amelinckx, A. (2020). Advancing cultural frontiers to champion global business in emerging markets. In *Transcending Cultural Frontiers* (pp. 1–10). Springer. doi:10.1007/978-981-15-4454-5_1

Zakaria, N., Abdul-Talib, A. N., & Othman, N. (Eds.). (2016). *Handbook of research on impacts of international business and political affairs on the global economy*. IGI Global. doi:10.4018/978-1-4666-9806-2

ENDNOTE

1 Since they fulfill similar functions, the concept of "international trade fairs" has been used to include the concepts of "trade show" and "fasion show" for the sake of literature compatibility in our study.

Chapter 12
Skill Acquisition:
A Panacea for Economic Development in Nigeria

Bolaji Comfort Adeniyi
Bamidele Olumilua University of Education, Science, and Technology, Nigeria

ABSTRACT

The purpose of the study was to examine the extent to which skill acquisition would influence economic development in Nigeria. The descriptive research design of the survey type was adopted in the study. The population of this study comprised all the students of government technical colleges in Southwest Nigeria. The reliability of the instrument was estimated using Chronbach's Alpha reliability method. The data collected for this study was analyzed using both descriptive and inferential statistics. The result of the study revealed that skill acquisition program has a positive and significant effect on the ability of students of technical colleges in Southwest Nigeria to be self-reliant at graduation; skill acquisition program has a positive and significant effect on the ability of students of technical colleges in Southwest Nigeria to produce goods for local consumption. It was also recommended based on the study that the various government parastatals should review, standardize, and expand the curricula of all skill acquisition schemes in Nigeria among others.

INTRODUCTION

One of the noted ways in which Nigeria can achieve some of its main national educational goals of building a united, strong and self-reliant nations; a great & dynamic economy and a land full of bright opportunities for all citizens is the development of the informal education sector which will lead to the attainment of skills by the citizens, especially, the young ones. It appears that the major challenges associated with developing countries especially in Africa, in recent times, is the alarming unemployment rate which has rendered some of its able youths idle and has further degenerated to social vices like kidnappings, highway robbery and all sorts of cybercrimes.

It was observed that countries like Nigeria keep building and laying too much emphasis on the formal sector by establishing tertiary institutions, producing graduate without a proving for their em-

DOI: 10.4018/978-1-7998-9071-3.ch012

ployment. Unlike the formal sector, informal activities are often characterized by low levels of capital, skills, access to organized markets and technology; low and unstable incomes and poor and unpredictable working conditions. In the words of ILO (2000), Informal activities are often outside the scope of official statistical enumeration and government regulations, and beyond formal systems of labour and social protection. Some studies suggest that the smallest enterprises are the most likely to be informal (Anand, 1999). It might be interesting to note that as unorganised as the informal education appears, it could be intertwined with the formal education system to mean that attendants of schools will acquire a skill of their choice and be able to work and be self-employed after graduation. Perhaps this is what the government seeks to achieve by approving as at today, 123 technical colleges across the country with the sole mission of promoting the production of skilled technical and professional manpower for the development and sustenance of the National Economy.

STATEMENT OF THE PROBLEM

Without minding all the obvious contributions of skills, technical and vocational education in our nation, Nigeria is yet to accord this type of education the attention and support it deserves. This perhaps one of the major reasons for the rising unemployment, poverty and unabated crimes in the society today. The nation's poverty level has increased to about 70%, the per capital income has become so poor and many Nigerians now live on less than one dollar a day. Also, it appears that too much emphasis on university education in Nigeria has drastically reduced the economic opportunities of those who are more work oriented than academics. It is against this backdrop that this study is set to examine the influence of skill acquisition on the development of the economic sector.

PURPOSE OF THE STUDY

The study examines the extent to which Skill Acquisition would influence Economic Development in Nigeria. Specifically, the study intends to:

1. Examine the extent of Implementation of Skill Acquisition programs by Technical Colleges in Southwest, Nigeria;
2. identify the challenges of Skill Acquisition programs in Technical Colleges in Southwest, Nigeria;
3. examine the effectiveness of Skill Acquisition programs on the ability of students of Technical Colleges in Southwest, Nigeria to be self-reliant at graduation;
4. investigate the effectiveness of Skill Acquisition programs on the ability of students of Technical Colleges in Southwest, Nigeria to produce goods for local consumption;
5. examine the effectiveness of Skill Acquisition programs on the ability of students of Technical Colleges in Southwest, Nigeria to export.

RESEARCH QUESTIONS

The following Research Questions were raised to guide the study;

1. What is the extent of Implementation of Skill Acquisition programs by Technical Colleges in Southwest, Nigeria?
2. What are the challenges of Skill Acquisition programs in Technical Colleges in Southwest, Nigeria?

RESEARCH HYPOTHESES

The following hypotheses were formulated and tested at 0.05 level of significance:

1. Skill Acquisition programs does not have any significant influence on the ability of students of Technical Colleges in Southwest, Nigeria to be self-reliant at graduation;
2. Skill Acquisition programs does not have any significant influence on the ability of students of Technical Colleges in Southwest, Nigeria to produce goods for local consumption;
3. Skill Acquisition programs does not have any significant influence on the ability of students of Technical Colleges in Southwest, Nigeria to produce goods for exportation.

LITERATURE

Different views have emerged on the definition of technical education. Technical and vocational education is used as a comprehensive term in the educational process involving, in addition to general education, the study of technologies and related sciences and acquisition of practical skills, attitudes, understanding and knowledge relating to occupations in various sectors of economic and social life (FRN, 2004). Momoh (2012) defines vocational education as a form of education whose primary purpose is to prepare persons for employment in recognized occupation. He also defines technical education as a post-secondary vocational training programme whose major purpose is the production of technicians.

The terms technical education and vocational education are often used interchangeably especially for the purpose of this study, the paper focuses on the end result which is the acquisition of skills which is the center and focus of both terms. Vocational education refers to skill-based programmes which are designed for skill acquisition at lower level of education. Vocational education programmes focus on specific vocations for entry into defined workplace. Technical education, is not usually designed for any particular vocation but provides general technical knowledge. Technical and vocational education is usually a merger of technical education and vocational education i.e. the inclusion of basic technical and scientific knowledge with the skill based vocational programme. According to Uwaifo (2009), technical education is the training of technically oriented personnel who are to be the initiators, facilitators and implementers of technologically development of a nation. In his own opinion, this training of its citizens on the need to be technologically literate would eventually lead to self-reliance and sustainability.

Skill acquisition could be seen as is a designed way to offer people the opportunity of improving themselves in their general proficiency, especially in relation to their present or future occupation, which can be achieved through technical and vocational education. Nuru (2007) opined that changes in any nation's economy is required to prepare young people for the jobs of the future of which technical and vocational education have crucial roles to play. This cut across garments making, sowing, electrical and electronics technology, metal work technology, mechanical/automobile technology, building technology, woodwork technology among others. It seems that skill acquisition has direct impact on the development of the country. It is a practical oriented education which is unique in its content and approach thereby demanding special attention. May (2007) observed that technical and vocational education are very much still neglected in the aspect of adequate funding, personnel, modern facilities, staff motivation which consequently are robbing the country of the economic development to be contributed by graduates of technical/vocational education. Asogwa and Diogu (2007) maintained that there is an urgent need for the Nigeria's attention to be redirected towards self-reliant and sustainable means of livelihood which technical education provides. Most analysts agree that employers of labour today demand more skills than they did in the past (Yang, 2008). Oranu (2010) also observed that there are many factors that have contributed to the ever rising demand for skills in the labour market which include the following; technological and organizational change, trade, deregulation of key industries and the decline of unions.

Skill Acquisition at the technical schools appears to have been handicapped over the years due to some factors which according to Oranu (2004) range from inadequate funding of technical & vocational education, inadequate facilities, brain drain, staff training & retention to curriculum of technical education. No matter how beautiful a programme is, bottlenecks like the ones mentioned above are like going to choke it up, thereby hampering the achievement of its goals. It appears that skill acquisition could foster self-reliance on students especially after graduation. In line with this, Bolt-Lee and Foster (2003) see skills as the art of possessing the ability to have power, authority or competency to do the task required of an individual on the job. Also, Ezeani (2012) stated that skills are not a person's fundamental, innate capacities but must be developed through training, practice and experience. Skill acquisition is the process of acquiring or gaining effective and ready knowledge in developing one's aptitude and ability in a particular field (Kikechi, Owano, Ayodo and Ejakait, 2013). The preparation of students for skill acquisition in order to be self-reliant is dependent on the acquisition of basic knowledge about employment opportunities, requirements and trends as well as the possession of marketable skills. According to Ogundele, Oluwolara and Adegbemi (2011) skills acquired by students would aid job creation, youth empowerment and poverty alleviation, which in turn has the capacity to solve various social problems. Mbionwu (2008) in his work, avers that students who acquire adequate work-skills have better options to become entrepreneurs after graduation. It was noted that skill acquisition leads to capacity building that could yield the ability and potentials to produce consumable goods by the students. According to Okeke and Egbuonu (2008) capacity building is given individuals training to enable them perform entrepreneurial tasks. It enables the individuals become more creative and thus sees opportunities where none seems to exist (Okeke 2007). Capacity building could mean an integration of both entrepreneurial and occupational skills. In the words of Olutoyin (2009), while occupational skills are scientific production skills or process skills that lead to the manufacturing of goods like paints, candle, laboratory chemicals among others, entrepreneurial skills are business managing skills like creative thinking, decision making, marketing among others. Possibly, skill acquisition could help a country in achieving export opportunities. This is achievable through the production of goods to export to other countries. Weaving of baskets, clothes making at the textile industries, bags, belts, production of furniture, plastics and mats making are one of the items that could be produced in Nigeria because of the availability of their respective raw materials.

METHODOLOGY

The descriptive research design of the survey type is adopted in the study. The population of this study comprised all the students of Government Technical Colleges in Southwest, Nigeria. The sample of the study consisted of 150 respondents which was achieved through stratified random sampling and simple random sampling techniques.

The study adapted an instrument tagged 'Skill Acquisition and Economic Development in Nigeria (SAEDN). The questionnaire is structured on a five-point likert scale as follows: Strongly Agreed (SA), Agreed (A), Strongly Disagreed (SD) Disagreed (DA) and Neutral (N). The reliability of the instrument was estimated using Chronbach's Alpha reliability method. The data collected for this study was analyzed using both descriptive and inferential statistics. The study was delimited to all the public technical colleges in Southwest, Nigeria.

RESULT AND DISCUSSION

Analysis of the Items on the Questionnaire

Table 1.

Gender	Frequency	Percentage
Male	120	80
Female	30	20
Total	150	100.0
Age	**Frequency**	**Percentage**
21-25	80	53.3
26-30	30	20
31-35	25	16.7
36-40	15	10
Total	150	100.0
Marital Status	**Frequency**	**Percentage**
Single	107	71.3
Married	43	28.7
Total	150	100.0
Religion	**Frequency**	**Percentage**
Christian	115	76.7
Muslim	35	23.3
Total	150	100.0

Source: Author's Computation, 2021

Table 1 shows that 120(80%) of the respondents are male, while 30(20%) of the respondents are female. This infers that most of the respondents were male. The table also discloses that 80(53.3%) of the respondents were between the age range of 21-25, 30(20%) of the respondents were between the age range of 26-30, 25(16.7%) of the respondents were between the age range of 31-35, while 15(10%) of the respondents were between the age range of 36-40. This shows that most of the respondents were between the age range of 21-25. The table also reveals that 107(71.3%) of the respondents were single, while 43(28.7%) of the respondents were married. This shows that most of the respondents were single. The table unveils that 115(76.7%) of the respondents were Christian, while 25(23.3%) of the respondents were Muslim. This shows that most of the respondents were Christian.

DESCRIPTIVE ANALYSIS

Mean and standard deviation were used to analyze the research questions. Mean scores was used to check the average responses of the respondents while Standard deviation was used to find out the spread of the respondents' opinions around the mean. The mean of each item was determined based on boundary limits. The boundary limits were as follows:

Table 2. Decision Rules

<table>
<tr><td>Response mode</td><td>Rating</td><td>Scale value</td><td>Cut off point</td><td>Decisions</td></tr>
<tr><td>Strongly Agreed/Highly Implemented</td><td>4</td><td>3.50-4.49</td><td rowspan="4">2.50</td><td rowspan="2">Agreed/ Implemented 2.50-4.49</td></tr>
<tr><td>Agreed/Moderately Implemented</td><td>3</td><td>2.50-3.49</td></tr>
<tr><td>Disagreed/Sparingly Implemented</td><td>2</td><td>1.50-2.49</td><td rowspan="2">Disagreed/Not Implemented 0.50-2.49</td></tr>
<tr><td>Strongly Disagreed/Not Implemented</td><td>1</td><td>0.50-1.50</td></tr>
</table>

Research Question 1: What is the extent of Implementation of Skill Acquisition programs by Technical Colleges in Southwest, Nigeria?

Table 3. Responses of the respondents on the extent of implementation of skill acquisition programs by Technical Colleges in Southwest, Nigeria

S/N	Items	Mean	Std. Deviation	Remarks
1	Skill Acquisition and Entrepreneurship Development Scheme (SAED)	3.30	0.668	Implemented
2	National Directorate of Employment (NDE)	3.23	0.522	Implemented
3	State Economic Empowerment and Development Strategy (SEEDS)	2.45	0.325	Not Implemented
4	National Poverty Alleviation Program (NAPEP)	3.11	0.754	Implemented
5	Youth Enterprise with New Innovation in Nigeria (YOUWIN)	3.45	0.961	Implemented

Source: Author's Computation, 2021.

Table 3 above reported that Skill Acquisition and Entrepreneurship Development Scheme (SAED), National Directorate of Employment (NDE), National Poverty Alleviation Program (NAPEP) and Youth Enterprise with New Innovation in Nigeria (YOUWIN) are implemented by the technical colleges across the Southwest states in Nigeria with mean and standard deviation scores of 3.30 (0.668), 3.23 (0.522), 3.11 (0.754) and 3.45 (0.961) respectively. Also, the respondents the State Economic Empowerment and Development Strategy (SEEDS) with mean and standard deviation of 2.45 (0.325) is not implemented by the technical colleges across the Southwest states in Nigeria.

Research Question 2: What are the challenges of Skill Acquisition programs in Technical Colleges in Southwest, Nigeria?

Table 4. Responses of the respondents on the challenges of Skill Acquisition programs in Technical Colleges in Southwest, Nigeria

S/N	Items	Mean	Std. Deviation	Remarks
1	Lack of funds for the training programs	3.72	0.899	Agreed
2	Poor trainees' attitude towards skills acquisition	3.78	0.961	Agreed
3	Poor recognition of acquired certificate by the society	3.13	0.499	Agreed
4	Insufficient number of instructors	3.16	0.321	Agreed
5	Insufficient availability of facilities for training	2.78	0.481	Agreed

Source: Author's Computation, 2021.

Table 4 above reported that the respondents agreed that the challenges of Skill Acquisition programs in Technical Colleges in Southwest, Nigeria include lack of funds for the training programs, poor trainees' attitude towards stills acquisition, poor recognition of acquired certificate by the society, insufficient number of instructors and insufficient availability of facilities for training with mean and standard deviation scores of 3.72 (0.899), 3.78 (0.961), 3.13 (0.499), 3.16 (0.321) and 2.78 (0.481) respectively.

TEST OF HYPOTHESIS

Hypothesis 1: Skill Acquisition Programs does not have any significant influence on the ability of students of Technical Colleges in Southwest, Nigeria to be self-reliant at graduation

Table 5. Regression Analysis

Variables	Coefficient	Std Error	T-Statistic	Prob.
C	8.308	1.676	4.957	.000
Skill Acquisition Programs	0.493	0.101	4.875	.000

R=0.457, R-square=0.209, F-statistics=23.769, Prob (F-stat) =0.000 (*) connotes significance at 5% level of significance
Source: Author's Computation (2021).

Table 5 shows that correlation coefficient (R) given to be 0.457 implies that there is a moderate relationship between skill acquisition programs and the ability of students of Technical Colleges in Southwest, Nigeria to be self-reliant at graduation. The coefficient of determination R^2 value stood at 0.209. This indicates that 21% of the systematic variation on the ability of students of Technical Colleges in Southwest, Nigeria to be self-reliant at graduation can be explained by skill acquisition programs. An explanation of the remaining 79% variation on the ability of students of Technical Colleges in Southwest, Nigeria to be self-reliant at graduation can be given by other factors not in this model. Skill acquisition program has a positive and significant effect on the ability of students of Technical Colleges in Southwest, Nigeria to be self-reliant at graduation to the tune of 0.493 (0.000 < 0.05). Therefore, the null hypothesis is rejected while the alternative hypothesis is accepted. The size of the coefficient shows that 1% increase in Skill Acquisition program will cause 49% increase on the ability of students of Technical Colleges in Southwest, Nigeria to be self-reliant at graduation. This is further emphasized by the probability of the f-statistic given to be 0.0001 which shows that the regression result is statistically significant because this is less than 5%, the level of significance adopted for this study.

Hypothesis 2: Skill Acquisition programs does not have any significant influence on the ability of students of Technical Colleges in Southwest, Nigeria to produce goods for local consumption

Table 6. Regression Analysis

Variables	Coefficient	Std Error	T-Statistic	Prob.
C	7.320	0.958	7.643	0.000
Skill Acquisition Programs	0.574	0.060	9.645	0.000

R=0.713, R-square=0.508, F-statistics=93.031, Prob (F-stat) =0.0001 (*) connotes significance at 5% level of significance
Source: Author's Computation (2021).

Table 6 shows that correlation coefficient (R) given to be 0.713 implies that there is a moderate relationship between skill acquisition programs and the ability of students of Technical Colleges in Southwest, Nigeria to produce goods for local consumption. The coefficient of determination R^2 value stood at 0.508. This indicates that 51% of the systematic variation on the ability of students of Technical Colleges in Southwest, Nigeria to produce goods for local consumption can be explained by skill acquisition programs. An explanation of the remaining 49% variation on the ability of students of Technical Colleges in Southwest, Nigeria to produce goods for local consumption can be given by other factors not in this model. Skill acquisition program has a positive and significant effect on the ability of students of Technical Colleges in Southwest, Nigeria to produce goods for local consumption to the tune of 0.574 (0.000 < 0.05). Therefore, the null hypothesis is rejected while the alternative hypothesis is accepted. The size of the coefficient shows that 1% increase in Skill Acquisition program will cause 57% increase on the ability of students of Technical Colleges in Southwest, Nigeria to produce goods for local consumption. This is further emphasized by the probability of the f-statistic given to be 0.0001 which shows that the regression result is statistically significant because this is less than 5%, the level of significance adopted for this study.

Hypothesis 3: Skill Acquisition programs does not have any significant influence on the ability of students of Technical Colleges in Southwest, Nigeria to produce goods for exportation.

Table 7. Regression Analysis

Variables	Coefficient	Std Error	T-Statistic	Prob.
C	7.118	1.314	5.418	0.000
Skill Acquisition Programs	0.568	0.079	7.153	0.000

R=0.602, R-square=0.362, F-statistics=51.167, Prob (F-stat) =0.0001 (*) connotes significance at 5% level of significance
Source: Author's Computation (2021).

Table 7 shows that correlation coefficient (R) given to be 0.602 implies that there is a moderate relationship between skill acquisition programs and the ability of students of Technical Colleges in Southwest, Nigeria to produce goods for exportation. The coefficient of determination R^2 value stood at 0.362. This indicates that 36% of the systematic variation on the ability of students of Technical Colleges in Southwest, Nigeria to produce goods for exportation can be explained by skill acquisition programs. An explanation of the remaining 64% variation on the ability of students of Technical Colleges in Southwest, Nigeria to produce goods for exportation can be given by other factors not in this model. Skill acquisition program has a positive and significant effect on the ability of students of Technical Colleges in Southwest, Nigeria to produce goods for exportation to the tune of 0.568 (0.000 < 0.05). Therefore, the null hypothesis is rejected while the alternative hypothesis is accepted. The size of the coefficient shows that 1% increase in Skill Acquisition program will cause 57% increase on the ability of students of Technical Colleges in Southwest, Nigeria to produce goods for exportation. This is further emphasized by the probability of the f-statistic given to be 0.0001 which shows that the regression result is statistically significant because this is less than 5%, the level of significance adopted for this study.

DISCUSSION OF FINDINGS

An attempt has been made to examine the extent to which Skill Acquisition would influence Economic Development in Nigeria. The discussion of this study is based on the simple linear regression analysis results for the study. It was discovered that skill acquisition program has a positive and significant effect on the ability of students of Technical Colleges in Southwest, Nigeria to be self-reliant at graduation to the tune of 0.493 (0.000 < 0.05). This implies that 1% increase in Skill Acquisition program will cause 49% increase on the ability of students of Technical Colleges in Southwest, Nigeria to be self-reliant at graduation. This could be attributed to the fact that skill acquisition program aims at empowering the youth most especially students of technical colleges in Nigeria with several productive skills to enhance their level of independency after graduation from the college. This finding is in-line with the conclusion of Oladeji (2019) that the several skill acquisition programs enhance the empowerment of jobless youths across the federation.

Also, it was revealed that skill acquisition program has a positive and significant effect on the ability of students of Technical Colleges in Southwest, Nigeria to produce goods for local consumption to the tune of 0.574 (0.000 < 0.05). The coefficient shows that any increase in Skill Acquisition program will also cause increase on the ability of students of Technical Colleges in Southwest, Nigeria to produce goods for local consumption. This implies that implementation of skill acquisition programs could independently enhance the ability of students of Technical Colleges in Southwest, Nigeria to produce goods for local consumption. Basically, several skills are acquired such as soap making, catering, welding, hair dressing, tie and dye, fashion design among others. The end products could be consumed locally to improve the standard of living of the populace. This finding is in agreement with the conclusion of Onah and Okwuosa (2016) that there exists a significant relationship between Skill Acquisition Program and production of goods and services for consumption.

Finally, it was discovered that skill acquisition program has a positive and significant effect on the ability of students of Technical Colleges in Southwest, Nigeria to produce goods for export to the tune of 0.568 (0.000 < 0.05). The corollary of this result implies that any increase in Skill Acquisition program will lead to an increase on the ability of students of Technical Colleges in Southwest, Nigeria to produce goods for export. Also, the output of the skill acquisition programs implementation in forms of goods and services could be export to neighbouring countries. The finding is in tandem with the findings of Solaja and Adenuga (2016).

CONCLUSION AND RECOMMENDATIONS

Over the years, it appeared that the contributions of skills, technical and vocational education in Nigeria are not significant to poverty eradication and unemployment among graduates in the society today. Day in day out, the tertiary institutions across the federation keep producing graduates, hence the level of unemployment and poverty keep rising. This could be attributed to the fact that many graduates fail to utilize the various skill acquisition programs put in place across the nation. The study concluded that an increase in Skill Acquisition program will engender a rise in the ability of students of Technical Colleges in Southwest, Nigeria to be self-reliant at graduation; increase in Skill Acquisition program will cause an increase in the ability of students to produce goods for local consumption and exportation. Based on these discoveries, it was therefore recommended that the various government parastatals should review, standardize and expand the curricula of all skill acquisition schemes in Nigeria; federal ministries of education and information communication in collaboration with agencies and professional associations, should enlighten and sensitize the public with the importance of Technical, Vocational Education And Training (TVET) as a veritable tool for national development and the need for individuals to acquire employable skills. Also, ITF should collaborate with regulatory agencies such as National Board for Technical Education (NBTE) with a view to making certificate issued by Skills Acquisition Schemes recognized for career development.

REFERENCES

Anand, V. K. (1999). Informal sector and its role in employment creation in developing countries. *Journal of the Indian Institute of Economics*, *41*(3), 542–556.

Bolt-Lee, C., & Foster, S. (2003). The core competency framework: A new element in continuing call for accounting education change in the United States. *Accounting Education*, *12*(1), 33–47. doi:10.1080/0963928031000074486

Ezeani, N. S. (2012). The teacher and skills acquisition at business education: From the perspective of accounting skills. *Arabian Journal of Business and Management Review*, *2*(4), 25–36.

Fafunwa, A. B. (2002). *History of Education in Nigeria*. NPS Educational Publishers Ltd.

Federal Republic of Nigeria. (2013). *National Policy on Education*. NERDC Press.

FRN. (2004). *National Policy on Education Lagos*. NERDC Press.

Hashim, F., Bakar, A. R. A., & Talib, A. N. (2010). *International Business* (2nd ed.). Oxford Fajar Press.

Ibrahim, M. B., Abdul-Talib, A. N., & Jedin, M. H. (2018). Determinants of knowledge sharing among banks employees and its effect on service innovation: A conceptual framework. *Journal of Business and Management, 20*(5), 39–45.

ILO. (2000). *InFocus Programme on Skills, Knowledge and Employability*. Series on the Informal Economy.

Kikechi, W., Owano, A., Ayodo, T. M. O., & Ejakait, E. (2013). Do entrepreneurial skills acquired from technical subjects help secondary school graduates in self employment in kenya. *International Journal of Education and Research, 1*(8), 1–12.

May, I. A., Arogundadade, B.B., & Ekundayo, H.T. (2007). Assessing realities and challenges of technical education in imo state secondary school education system. *Nigeria Journal of Educational Administration and Planning, 7*.

Mbionwu, U. (2008). *School Administration in a Dwindling Economy: Nigeria Case*. Awka: Erudite Printers.

Momoh, O. A. (2012). Revitalization of technical education in Nigeria as a vehicle for transformation. *Proceedings of COREN 21st Engineering Assembly*, 53 – 81.

Nuru, A. (2007). *The Relevance of National Vocational Education Qualification (NVQS) in TVE in Nigeria*. Unpublished Conference Paper.

Ogundele, M.O., Oluwolara, F.K., & Adegbemi, F.O. (2011). *Fundamentals of Organizational Behaviors*. Ilorin: Ramfik Concepts.

Okeke, B. C. (2007). Vocational and technical education: Meeting goals, objectives and visions of national economic empowerment development strategies (NEEDS) and MDGS. *Journal of Science Education, 9*(1), 11–20.

Okeke, S. O. C., Egbuonu, R. N., & Ugbaja, J. N. (2009). Entrepreneurship skills acquisition of biology education students through design project. *50th STAN Annual Conference Proceedings*, 106 – 108.

Oladeji, O. F. (2019). The skills acquisition programme and youth empowerment in ondo state of Nigeria. *Global Journal of Human Social Science: A Arts and Humanity Psychology, 19*(6).

Olutoyin, D. S. (2009). Developing entrepreneurial skills through chemistry education. *50th STAN Annual Conference Proceedings*, 190 – 194.

Onah, N., & Okwuosa, L. (2016). Youth employment and peace in Nigerian society. *Mediterranean Journal of Social Sciences, 7*(1), 52–58.

Oranu, R. N. (2004). *Vocational and technical education in Nigeria*. Academic Press.

Solaja, O. M., & Adenuga, O. A. (2016). Investigating the impact of skill acquisition programmes on graduates unemployment dilemma in Lagos state, Nigeria. St. Theresa. *Journal of the Humanities and Social Sciences*, *2*(2), 16–39.

Terwase, I. T., Abdul-Talib, A. N., & Zengeni, K. T. (2014). Nigeria, Africa's largest economy: International business perspective. *International Journal of Management Sciences*, *3*(7), 534–543.

Uwaifo, V. O. (2009). Technical Education and its Challenges in Nigeria in the 21st Century. *International NGO Journal*, *5*(2), 40–44.

Yang, J. (2008). General or vocational? The tough choice in the Chinese education policy. *International Journal of Educational Development*, *18*(4), 289–304. doi:10.1016/S0738-0593(98)00026-1

Zakaria, N., Abdul-Talib, A. N., & Amelinckx, A. (Eds.). (2020). *Transcending Cultural Frontiers: Practices, Challenges, and Strategy for International Business*. Springer. doi:10.1007/978-981-15-4454-5

Zakaria, N., Abdul-Talib, A. N., & Amelinckx, A. (2020). Advancing cultural frontiers to champion global business in emerging markets. In *Transcending Cultural Frontiers* (pp. 1–10). Springer. doi:10.1007/978-981-15-4454-5_1

Zakaria, N., Abdul-Talib, A. N., & Othman, N. (Eds.). (2016). *Handbook of research on impacts of international business and political affairs on the global economy*. IGI Global. doi:10.4018/978-1-4666-9806-2

Chapter 13
The Impact of Market Orientation, Entrepreneurial Orientation, and Relationship Orientation on the International Performance of SMEs

Kabiru Sa'ad Sa'id
Federal University, Dutse, Nigeria

ABSTRACT

The relationship between strategic orientation and SME international performance is empirically inadequate, specifically in a developing country. This study focuses on the effect of three dimensions of strategic orientation, namely market orientation, entrepreneurial orientation, and relationship orientation on the international performance of SMEs applying the theory of resource-based view. The study is quantitative and uses the data collected from 296 managers of SMEs operating an international business in Nigeria. The authors revealed that entrepreneurial orientation, relationship orientation have a positive effect on firm international performance. On the other hand, market orientation has no significant impact on a firm international performance. The authors explain the managerial contribution of study findings and provide future research suggestions.

INTRODUCTION

The small and medium enterprise (SMEs) contribution to economic development is related to their international performance (Nakos et, 2019; Dimitratos & Elbanna 2019). It has been proved that SMEs international activities enhance export earning, reduce poverty, provide employment and ultimately increases the survival rate of many businesses due to non-dependent on the domestic market (Karami & Tang, 2019; Solano Acosta et al., 2018; Zakaria, Abdul-Talib, & Othman 2016). However, SMEs usually lack resources and strategic orientations to operate in the international market (Keskin, 2006; Solano

DOI: 10.4018/978-1-7998-9071-3.ch013

Acosta et al., 2018). Strategic orientations are responsible for defining the outline of the enterprise's strategy, determining its decisions, and carrying out enterprise/organisational efforts and investments (Zamani, Abdul-Talib, & Ashari, 2016). Moreover, strategic orientation is an enterprise culture that represents intangible enterprise resources that enhance managerial decision making and resource allocation (Barney, 1991). However, there are limited studies that investigated the relationship between SMEs international performance and strategic orientation. The majority of previous studies have focused on international experience, innovation capacity and export commitment (Keskin, 2006; Solano Acosta et al., 2018). In addition, past studies usually concentrated on large enterprise in the developed nation with little consideration to other emerging countries like Nigeria.

Table 1. Nigeria Foreign Trade Indicators

Foreign Trade Indicators	2015	2016	2017	2018	2019
Foreign Trade *(in % of GDP)*	21.3	20.7	26.3	33.0	n/a
Trade Balance *(million USD)*	-6,447	-536	13,148	20,467	2,868
Trade Balance (Including Service) *(million USD)*	-22,900	-8,551	-86	-5,599	-30,893
Imports of Goods and Services *(Annual % Change)*	-26.8	-9.0	4.8	49.2	n/a
Exports of Goods and Services *(Annual % Change)*	0.1	11.5	8.7	-1.4	n/a
Imports of Goods and Services *(in % of GDP)*	10.7	11.5	13.2	17.5	n/a
Exports of Goods and Services *(in % of GDP)*	10.7	9.2	13.2	15.5	n/a

Source: https://www.nordeatrade.com/en/explore-new-market/nigeria/trade-profile

On the other hand, in Nigeria different administrations come up with many programmes and implemented many policies in struggles to develop a lively SME sector that will contribute hugely to the national economic development at the international market but most of these policies/programmes are yet to show any substantial results (Chinedu, Titus, & Thaddeus, 2010; Mohamed & Abdul-Talib. 2020). Concerning this, Mambula (2002), states that since 1960 of the Nigerian Independence Day, the country has been spending a large amount of money on SMEs development programmes, but the results are unsatisfactory mostly. Recently the Federal Government came up with a new policy named Economic

Recovery and Growth Plan, 2017. The aim of the policy to achieve industrialization and increase international performance among SMEs in Nigeria before the year 2025. However, this lack of international performance among SMEs in Nigeria has become an issue of great concern especially, to stakeholders due to the contribution of SMEs to economic growth and development. Chima (2017) reported that the current governor of the Central Bank of Nigeria (CBN) admitted that most SMEs in Nigeria are not performing in the international market. Similarly, the director-strategic partnership, of SMEDAN disclosed that SMEs international performance in Nigeria is almost at zero levels. According to SMEDAN (2013), SMEs poor international performance in Nigeria is a result of such as poor marketing skill, lack of entrepreneurship, inadequate knowledge of managing an enterprise, lack of relationship orientation. Table 1 indicates the trade figure in Nigeria.

From the above table, it is obvious that the Nigerian SMEs contribution to international trade is insignificant considering the appearance of a negative figure in the balance of trade likewise importation figures is greater than the exportation figures this highlighted there are some issues which affected their productivity and ability to generate export earnings.

In this regard, and in line with the approach recommended by Solano Acosta, Crespo and Agudo (2019), this study determine to investigate the impact of strategic orientation on the international performance of SMEs, in the view of the methods of Resources Base Theory: More specifically, the aim of this research is to determine how market orientation, entrepreneurial orientation and relationship orientation which have been recognized as intangible resources in past literature, affect performance of SMEs in the international markets.

Consequently, conducting empirical research on SMEs international performance is motivated due to the lack of empirical evidence on the role of strategic orientations and SMEs internal performance in emerging countries particularly, Nigeria (Mahmoud, 2011; Nakos et al., 2019; Ra'ed et al., 2018; Shehu & Mahmood, 2014). And this might affect policy formulation and execution in the SMEs sector considering the aim of the country to be among the 20 nations of the world big economy by the year 2025 (Economic Recovery & Growth Plan [ERGP] 2017).

THEORETICAL BACKGROUND AND HYPOTHESES

According, to Resources Based View (RBV) the firm's competitive benefits develop from the assembly of resources that a company possesses (Penrose, 1959). A company's competitive advantage is achievable if it owns resources that are valuable, inimitable, rare and non-substituted (Barney, 1991). A company may achieve a competitive benefit from various types of resources, either tangible or intangible. For instance, the firm's physical assets and brand name are inimitable assets that could offer it a competitive edge, likewise intangible resources such as managerial skill and relationships. Thus, RBV provides an elucidation of why a firm with an extensive strategic orientation such as market, entrepreneurial and relationship orientation may succeed in the international market. This is because engaging in a foreign market requires knowledge and resources that are very difficult to duplicate. Knowledge of customer and competitor action could be achieved through market orientation (Zakaria & Abdul-Talib 2010; Hashim, Bakar, & Abdul-Talib 2010). Equally operating in the international market, a company must be a risk-taker in order to efficiently accumulate innovative knowledge and pro-active idea which will be difficult to imitate. In addition, international markets may constitute informal and formal trade barrier that in some instances are difficult for an international firm to address by itself. The most effective way to access resources and overcome this trade barrier is through relationship orientation. Thus, the capabilities of a firm to complement these strategic orientations and accumulate knowledge and resources will possibly result in a greater overall international performance as advocated by RBV.

The performance of SMEs has significant implication for the growth and socio-economic wellbeing of a nation (Abor & Quartey, 2010; Kanibir et al., 2014). Despite the important roles of SMEs in emerging countries, they are unstable and many of them do not survive more than five years (Acquaah & Agyapong, 2015). Nevertheless, several issues have been recognised as constraints to the success and international performance of SMEs and those problems are more evident in Africa (Wang, 2016; Zakaria, Abdul-Talib, & Amelinckx 2020). These comprise of lack of entrepreneurial skill, restricted market information, lack of relational abilities and low level of managerial skill (Muddaha et al., 2018; SMEDAN, 2013). What is normally missing from these issues expected to be constraining the success and performance of SMEs is their ability to focus on strategic orientation (Acquaah & Agyapong, 2015; Mahmoud, 2011; Solano Acosta et al., 2018).

Strategic orientation is SMEs belief or culture that guides its decision-making practice and strategic implementation through the use of scarce resources to higher international performance (Kohli & Jaworski, 1990; Lonial & Carter, 2015; Narver & Slater, 1990; Ra'ed, Al-Henzab, Tarhini, & Obeidat, 2018; Rauch, Wiklund, Lumpkin, & Frese, 2009; Sinkula, Baker, & Noordewier, 1997).

Furthermore, for SMEs to survive in a global market environment they require to build multiple strategic orientations (Kajalo & Lindblom, 2015; Lonial & Carter, 2015; Ra'ed et al., 2018; Solano Acosta et al., 2018). Though some researchers opined that market orientation, entrepreneurial orientation and relationship orientation individually improve performance the potential of these orientations should not be in isolation because it is better to research the integrated impact of strategic orientation rather than a divided approach of single orientation (Gruber-Muecke & Hofer, 2015; Kropp, Lindsay, & Shoham, 2006; Nasir et al., 2017; Solano Acosta et al., 2018). This is because it has been argued that the combined effect of multiple strategic orientations is more beneficial to the enterprise (Atuahene-Gima & Ko, 2001; Nasir et al., 2017; Slater & Narver, 1995). This study, therefore, focused on market orientation, entrepreneurial orientation and relationship orientation because they have been identified in the literature as the most relevant strategic orientation recently.

MARKET ORIENTATION AND SMES INTERNATIONAL PERFORMANCE

Market orientation (MO) is described as strategic action that focuses on customer orientation, competitive orientation and inter-functional coordination (Han, Kim, & Srivastava, 1998; Ho, et al., 2017; Li et al., 2008). Sa'id, Talib and Hassan, (2019); Gruber-Muecke and Hofer (2015) viewed market orientation as an essential component of strategic orientation that has a significant effect on the international performance of a firm. Scholars have recognized three main component of market orientation, namely customer orientation, competitive orientation and inter-functional coordination (Narver & Slater, 1990). Company that have higher customer orientation usually is customer centric, constantly try to improve their knowledge about what is essential for their clients and put interest of customer more than anything else. They always attempt to know their clients, to assess customer happiness, and give better products. Inter-functional coordination concentrates on the matching of all resources of the firm to harmonise its tactics to build a company that successfully counter to market instability. The firm has to successfully gather information outside its environment and convert it into meaningful information that will be spread throughout the firm. Finally, a company that is competitor centric has a complete knowledge of the threat and the weakness of the strong competitors in the industry. An understanding of competitor's capacity will assist a firm to efficiently forecast and react to their future action (Narver & Slater, 1990).

Although theoretically it has been projected there is strong relationship between market orientation and international performance, wonderfully very few studies have investigated this association empirically (Lee, Kim, Seo, & Hight, 2015; Abdul-Talib & Abd-Razak, 2012). This is not surprising because market orientation activities provide a firm with crucial information about the business environment, either competitor or customer environment and the inter-functional coordination needed to effectively allocate the assets of the firm to an international target market (Ashari et al., 2018; Hassim et al., 2011; Abdul-Talib & Abd-Razak 2020). Deploying these activities enable a firm to build up an organizational knowledge to modify its internal structures that will enable it to better react to environmental challenges and enhance its international performance. Further, a successful market orientation system may enable a firm to identify its knowledge and resource constraint for effectively operating in an international target market (Sa'id, Talib, & Hassan, 2019a). This consciousness is possibly to lead a company to seek alliance or relationships that will assist to acquire the needed resources and knowledge.

The limited studies that have investigated the association between market orientation and performance have indicated that a serial connection occur both for multinationals companies and small companies (Sa'id, Talib, & Hassan, 2019b). For instance, Lee et al. (2015) investigated 253 firms in Spain and revealed a direct relationship between market orientation and firm non financial and financial performance there is corresponding of increase in performance with increase in market orientation. However, some scholars have reported MO has an insignificant relationship with performance (Chao & Spillan, 2010; Keskin, 2006; Pinho, 2008; Polat & Mutlu, 2012; Voss & Voss, 2000). Specifically, study by Solano Acosta et al., (2018), conducted on 161 SMEs in Mexico. The finding obtained from the analysis revealed that the SMEs International Performance is positively influenced by their network capability and international entrepreneurial orientation, but not by international market orientation. Precisely finding discovered that market orientation has no significant impact on SMEs international performance. SMEs can only achieve superior performance through good networking with international partners. Similarly, Pinho (2008), conducted a study on 135 SMEs in Portugal which explored the influence of market orientation, total quality management (TQM) on innovation and performance. The study revealed that there is no empirical evidence that market orientation influence performance. Moreover, the study argued to achieve performance marketing-oriented firm have to innovate products and services through their market orientation. Consequently this highlighted the need for more study that will integrate market orientation, entrepreneurial orientation and relationship orientation on SMEs international performance in another context. According to Nakos et al. (2019), the impact of market orientation on SMEs should be investigated on international performance rather than domestic performance. Also, suggested that in emerging countries there is a lack of empirical studies on the relationship between market orientation and SMEs international performance. Thus the first hypothesis is

H1: Market orientation has significant positive effect on SMEs international performance in Nigeria

ENTREPRENEURIAL ORIENTATION AND SMES INTERNATIONAL PERFORMANCE

According to Miller (1983), entrepreneurial orientation (EO) is the simultaneous exhibition of innovativeness, pro-activeness, and risk-taking (Engelen et al., 2015; Palmer et al., 2017). Entrepreneurial firm pro-actively identifies novel opportunities, undertake some risky project, and innovate higher customer's value from the existing products which subsequently increase firm performance (Aktan & Bulut, 2008; Brouthers et al., 2015; Covin & Slevin, 1989; Engelen et al., 2015; Gupta & Batra, 2016). The key aspect of entrepreneurial firm are innovativeness, proactiveness, and risk-taking (Aloulou, 2019; Mamun et al., 2018). Innovativeness is viewed as the firm's willingness to support invention of new ideas, or experimentation that lead to the design and formation of new goods and services as well as technological advancement (Irwin et al., 2018). Pro-activeness is firm's ability to anticipate any possible market change and turn such change to potential opportunities in the markets and get first mover advantage (Lechner & Gudmundsson, 2012). Risk-taking is described as an extent to which an firm is willing to go into a venture with an uncertain outcome or disbursement of huge resources into a risky project (Buli, 2017). It is also described as a strategic decision to tap opportunities even in the presence of uncertainty (Covin & Miller, 2013). The firms' ability to exploit potential opportunities and achieve higher international performance is depended upon how they galvanised innovativeness, risk-taking and pro-activeness (Aloulou, 2019). However, some studies discovered that a positive relationship between entrepreneurial orientation and firm performance is predominantly conducted on domestic performance, not international firm performance. Further, there are limited studies in developing countries, regarding SMEs international performance. Given this, scholars have suggested more research on the relationship between entrepreneurial orientation and SMEs international performance.

Entrepreneurial company is perhaps taking risks, and risk-taking businesses are eager to invest and commit huge capital to ventures that have uncertain results (Zahra & Garvis, 2000). In the foreign context, risk-taking is usually associated with both pro-activeness and innovativeness. In order to overcome some limitation of a foreign market, company need to be ready to initiate and evolve innovative tactics and structures thereby establish novel capabilities that would help a firm to be victorious in a specialized international market (Zahra & Garvis 2000). Additionally, pro-activeness in a global market requires identification and pursuit of new markets or customer through the dedication of time and resources commitment without assurance of an increase in sales. Taking this bold decision without assured success could be important for obtaining legitimacy, alleviating liabilities of a foreign market, and building a competitive benefit in an international market. Thus, to operate in the international market, a firm must be a risk-taker in order to effectively exploit innovative and proactive idea to help eliminate foreign liabilities and generate international performance. Thus, the first hypothesis

H2: Entrepreneurial orientation has significant positive effect on SMEs international performance in Nigeria

RELATIONSHIP ORIENTATION AND SMES INTERNATIONAL PERFORMANCE

Relationship orientation (RO) has been described in many different contexts and is one of the types of orientation underlying strategic orientation therefore,-; there is no single accepted definition of the construct (Panayides, (2007). According to Balboni, Bortoluzzi and Vianelli (2014). RO is the skills to take benefit of business to a business relationship and obtain access to resources possessed by business partners (Jiang & Liu, 2018). Equally, relationship orientations are the ability to gain timely customer information through an alliance with customers, competitor and suppliers (Bai, Holmström-Lind, & Johanson, 2018; Lorenzoni & Lipparini, 1999; Tehseen et al., 2019; Weerawardena & O'Cass, 2004). RO describes that partner involved in the business relationship would better obtain relationship-specific knowledge and utilize the benefit of collaboration thereby attain superior performance (Karami & Tang, 2019; Smirnova & Kushch, 2006). As such RO have been described in the literature the company skill to govern, communicate and coordinate business with other company (Dyer & Singh, 1998; Jacob, 2006; Paulraj, Lado, & Chen, 2008).

RO could guide the firm to understand that it lacks the critical resources needed for operating in the international market (Bai et al., 2018; Tehseen et al., 2019). Some of these resources are external knowledge that may be difficult to develop internally (Espino-Rdriguez et al. 2008). For instance, particular distribution pattern and knowledge of complex foreign policy can be unattainable to understand in a limited period (Karami & Tang, 2019). While a multinational company has the capacity to obtain this particular knowledge or resources by recruiting local workers who have the expertise or by acquiring a domestic firm, an SME generally does not have the resources to adopt this tactic (Karami & Tang, 2019). To address this shortage of resources and liability of foreign knowledge, SMEs could overcome this through relationship orientation with other companies (Balboni et al. 2014). Consequently, it will enable SMEs to obtain resources and the specific knowledge possess by these partners (Smirnova et al. 2011). Thus the third hypothesis is

H3: Relationship orientation has significant positive effect on SMEs international performance in Nigeria

METHODOLOGY

Respondents

In this study, the target respondents are the owner or managers of the SMEs operating in the international market in Kano. This is because the owner or managers are the people who know the trend of the company and have all the necessary information about the success or failure of the business (Sekeran & Bougie, 2013). The owner or managers are assumed to have accurate, reliable, dependable information that is needed which is available in their respective enterprise. However, these owners or managers who are representative of the sampled SMEs (i.e., unit of analysis) may confidently and objectively fill that structured questionnaires if given to them. Alternatively, a manager can assign any other office personnel to answer the questionnaire issue to their enterprise, provided that the person has the required knowledge and information needed.

Data Collection nd Procedure

The population of the study includes 2,686 SMEs operating in the international market registered by the Small and Medium Development Association of Nigeria. The sampling technique employed a systematic sample and collected 296 questionnaires from managers. The survey was conducted personally with owners or managers from each export SME, using the hand delivery method for collecting data (Peltier & Naidu, 2012).

Measuring Instrument

In this research, market orientation (MO) is defined as an organizational culture that focuses on creating superior value for customers through the activities of customer orientation, competitor orientation, and inter-functional coordination (Narver & Slater, 1990).

To measure MO, 13 items adapted from the work of Farrell et al. (2008), a measurement scale was employed. Similarly, entrepreneurial orientation is described as the overall enterprise abilities to deliver goods and services in the market through innovation, pro-activeness and risk-taking (Hakala & Kohtamäki 2011). To measure EO, 12 items adapted from work of Hakala and Kohtamäki (2011) was employed. Additionally, relationship orientation (RO) is defined as the enterprise's ability to communicate, coordinate and govern business interaction with business partners (Smirnova et al., 2011). To measure RO 4 items adopted from Smirnova et al. (2011). International Performance was measured by adapting the measure developed by Spillan and Parnell (2006). Six indicators were used (EP01 to EP06). (the measurement of a construct is subject upon the method it is being operationalised), A seven-point Likert scale (ranging from "1"' 'strongly disagree' to "7" 'strongly agree' was used and measured all items.

RESULTS

The main analysis comprises an outer model and an inner model. The outer model established satisfactory requirement. Data was estimated by employing the partial least square (PLS), a structural equation modelling (SEM) method which enables simultaneous assessment of theory and measures. PLS is useful for investigating the association between latent constructs and for elucidation variance in international firm performance. The selection method is dependent upon the research objective. The PLS-SEM has been employed in this study according to Chin, Marcolin and Newsted (2003), the research carried out in two-step to estimate and report smart PLS finding (Chin, 1998) (1) assessment measurement model, and (2) estimate of the structural model The PLS-SEM which is a two-step approach for model validation.

The first stage in PLS-SEM allows evaluation of the outer model followed by evaluation of the inner model. In the outer model an evaluation of the reliability and validity of the constructs is conducted (Hair, Hult, Ringle and Sarstedt 2017). Inner model validation estimates the association between the latent constructs.

OUTER MODEL EVALUATION

Table 2 indicates that all the indicators loading for construct MO, EO, RO and FP have adequate [greater than the minimum value of 0.5 as recommended by Chin (1998)], Hence, indicators reliability are affirmed. Determining composite reliability (CR) and convergent validity of the entire constructs under this study, shows that CR and average variance extracted (AVE) have greater than the criterion value of 0.7 and 0.5 respectively (Hair Jr. et al., 2017). Therefore, it is confirmed that the latent constructs achieved reliability and convergent validity.

Table 2. Measurement Model

Constructs	Dimension	Items	Loading	CR	AVE
Market Orientation	Customer Orientation	MO01	0.638	0.80	0.51
		MO02	0.748		
		MO04	0.689		
		MO05	0.783		
	Competitive Orientation	MO06	0.774	0.86	0.60
		MO07	0.794		
		MO08	0.809		
		MO09	0.713		
	Inter-functional Coordination	MO10	0.785	0.88	0.65
		MO11	0.847		
		MO12	0.855		
		MO13	0.721		
Entrepreneurial Orientation	Innovativeness	EO01	0.784	0.88	0.65
		EO02	0.834		
		EO03	0.854		
		EO04	0.738		
	Risk-Taking	EO05	0.741	0.84	0.57
		EO06	0.751		
		EO07	0.789		
		EO08	0.732		
	Pro-activeness	EO09	0.763	0.86	0.60
		EO10	0.822		
		EO11	0.780		
		EO12	0.720		
Relationship Orientation	-	RC01	0.734	0.85	0.60
		RC02	0.817		
		RC03	0.775		
		RC04	0.755		
Intl Firm Performance	-	EP01	0.764	0.86	0.51
		EP02	0.800		
		EP03	0.702		
		EP04	0.711		
		EP05	0.700		
		EP06	0.708		

DISCRIMINANT VALIDITY

In order to estimate the discriminant validity of the measures, we computed the square root of the AVE (as indicated in Table 3). All figures are above the scores in related rows and columns, representing acceptable fit of discriminant validity of all the measures (Fornell & Larcker 1981)

Table 3. Discriminant Validity

Constructs	1	2	3	4	5	6	7	8
Competitive Orientation	**0.774**	-	-	-	-	-	-	-
Customer Orientation	0.588	**0.717**	-	-	-	-	-	-
Innovativeness	0.580	0.563	**0.804**	-	-	-	-	-
Inter-functional Coordination	0.582	0.562	1.000	**0.804**	-	-	-	-
International Performance	0.497	0.516	0.547	0.544	**0.717**	-	-	-
Pro-activeness	0.586	0.621	0.642	0.639	0.628	**0.772**	-	-
Relationship Orientation	0.566	0.564	0.622	0.618	0.713	0.745	**0.771**	-
Risk-Taking	0.560	0.611	0.694	0.690	0.606	0.761	0.684	**0.754**

STRUCTURAL MODEL EVALUATION

The first step for assessing inner model is the estimation of robustness of each structural path coefficient and the combined productiveness (R2) of its latent construct(s) (Chin 1998). According to Falk and Miller (1992) recommended that R2 for latent construct should be above the 0.1. As showed in (Table 3. 1) R2 for the model EO-SMEs Intl-P and RO- SMEs Intl P are 0.54 and 0.21 respectively. Hence, the tested model fits the analysed data. After calculation of path coefficient, this research employed a bootstrap approach to establish the statistical relevance of structural paths. As indicated in Table 3, it portray clearly that there is direct influence of path coefficients for EO-SMEs Intl P and RO-SMEs Intl P which have higher positive t. value (1.891 and 7.805) and highly significant ($p < 0.029$ and 0.001). Thus, it can be concluded that EO and RO significantly and positively predict SMEs Intl performance. Whereas path coefficients from MO to SMEs Intl P it has lower positive t value (1. 110) and is insignificant ($p < 0.134$). Equally, disclose the values of Q2 are higher than 0, hence the model present predictive relevance (Geisser, 1975; Stone, 1974).

Table 4. Path coefficients and Hypothesis Testing

Path	Mean	STDEV	T Stat	P Values	Decision	R^2	F^2	Q^2
EO -> SMEs Intl P	0.200	0.109	1.891	0.029	Supported	0.54	0.018	0.258
MO -> SMEs Intl P	0.102	0.090	1.110	0.134	Not Supported		0.005	
RO -> SMEs Intl P	0.494	0.062	7.805	0.001	Supported	0.21	0.214	

EO=Entrepreneurial Orientation, MO= Market Orientation, RO= Relationship Orientation
SMEs Intl P= Small and Medium Enterprise International Performance

Figure 1. Result of Path Analysis

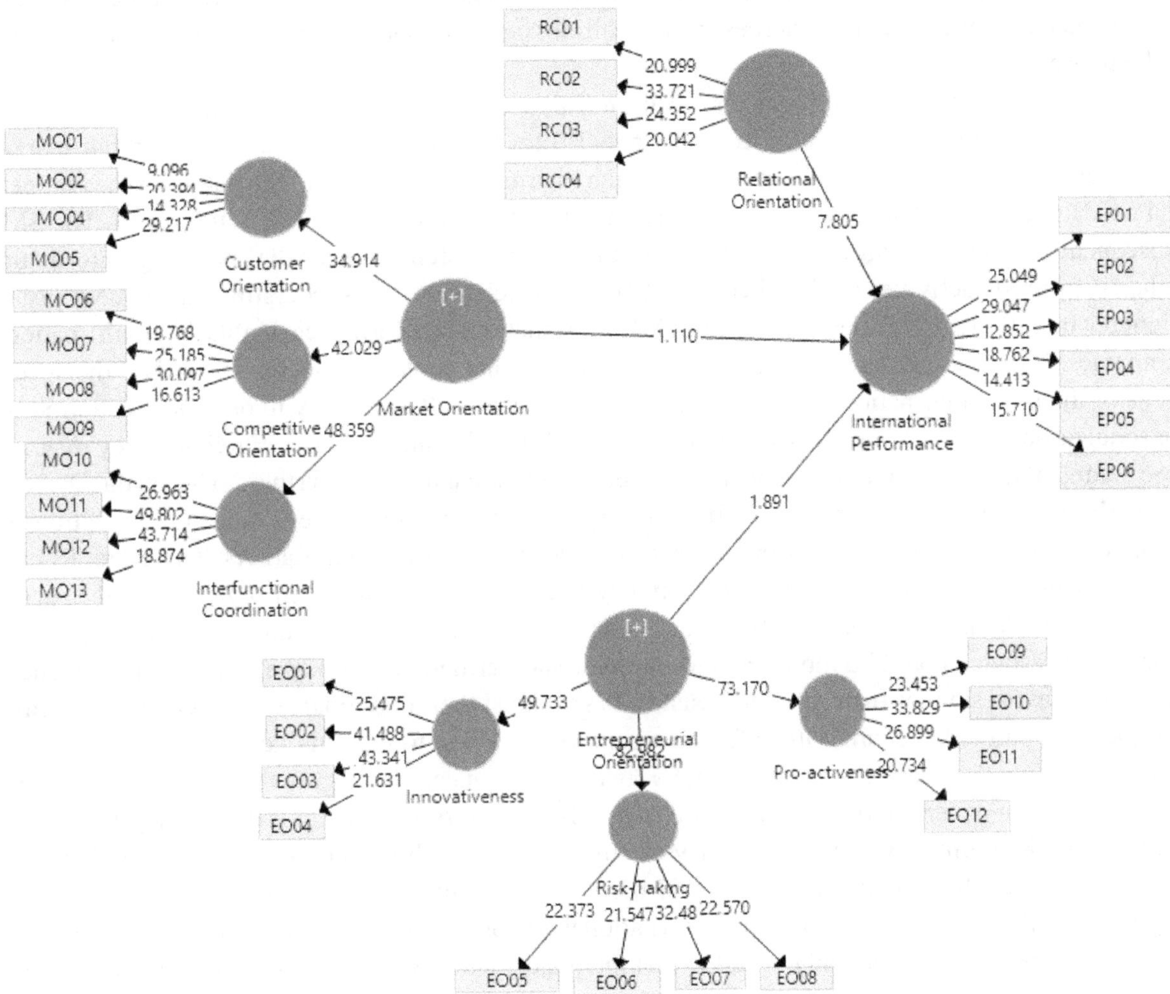

STUDY IMPLICATION

The research findings expand the investigation on the association of strategic orientation such as market orientation, entrepreneurial orientation, relationship orientation that focus on the international performance of SMEs. The direct and positive influence of both EO and RO on the SME's international performance attends to the current need for more researches on how various dimensions of the strategic orientation influence the performance of SMEs in the international market (Brouthers et al. 2015). The present study serves as evidence for the importance of adopting a complementary method concerning various dimensions of strategic orientations and specifically investing in EO and RO to maintain the SME's international performance (Boso et al. 2013). Therefore, the business practitioners should develop a passionate strategy and focus more on EO and RO to attain higher levels of international performance.

Contrary to what this study proposed, the relationship between market orientation and international SMEs performance was insignificant. This is not surprising because most SMEs do not have the resources and technological capabilities to study customer need and monitor competitor activity in the international market and achieve performance (Abdul Talib 2005). Hence, international managers and marketer need to develop more resources and capabilities before adopting market orientation as a strategy in the international market.

This study also provides an important recommendation for SMEs' managers that have the plan to operate in international markets. A RO is essential for a business that operates in a foreign market. Knowledge of the environmental requirement of the international market and the nature of the competition needs to be studied and understood before embarking globally (Karami & Tang, 2019). The SME consequently require aligning and reorganising its managerial system based on the knowledge information gathered from RO activities (Balboni et al. 2013). Nevertheless, even a successful management system might not be sufficient to achieve maximum SME's international performance. Unlike big multi-national companies, SMEs do not have enough internal resources that could be allocated to satisfy the special needs of the target international markets. They also not possess the capacity to buy these resources by the acquisition of some companies, a simple strategy of their business partner. Foreign policy may also pose a threat that is hard or unattainable to conquer without local business partners. The available choice for SMEs is to try to obtain resources by building relationships with other companies. Relationship orientation can offer SMEs with needed asset to succeed in international markets. Therefore, RO and EO are significant for SMEs not for the reason they direct them to modify their organizational structure but since it guides them to identify their limitations. A firm that has the self-understanding to admit its shortage of resource could be more open to international partnership. Policymaker and other agencies that want to assist smaller firms need to assist SMEs to boost their relational activities and help them to find the right partners that are critical for successful operation in foreign markets.

Since it has been accepted, generally, SMEs are the driver of economic growth, job creation and serve an instrument for poverty reduction (Hassim, Asmat-Nizam, & Addul Rahim 2011). Policy-maker such as Small and Medium Development Agency of Nigeria (SMEDAN) should understand that their policies have a direct effect on the activities of SMEs. It is pertinent to know what policies or programme may be formulated that can improve the international performance of SMEs in Nigeria. Based on the literature review, the present study revealed that the majority of SMEs faced insufficient resources and operates a business with a lack of institutional support.

Regarding the insufficient resources or some critical resources for international business operation, the policy-maker need to influence SMEs to use their strategic orientation (MO, EO, RO) to create viable business relationship with foreign firm since one of the possible reason for SMEs failure at international market is because of the high risk associated foreign market due cost of entering. Therefore having a good relationship with other business partners may reduce the risk associated in the international market. As such, it is recommended that government should encourage SMEs to adopt strategic orientations (MO, EO, RO) in order to improve their relational capabilities thereby achieve better performance.

LIMITATION AND FURTHER RESEARCH SUGGESTIONS

This research paper was conducted under some constraints. Firstly, limited data were collected; secondly, the sampling technique has its limitation and constraints; thirdly, the sample was collected from Kano, and is not big enough in a broader sense. Therefore, an attempt to generalize apart from Kano must be made with carefulness. Apart from limitation, this study contributes to the literature of entrepreneurship and marketing by empirically estimating the association between MO, EO and RO to SMEs international performance and presents the basis for SMEs at the international level to focus on more EO and RO. It also established that MO in the context of international performance for SMEs in the emerging country could not be achievable due to resources constraints. Future research could investigate these problems in specific industries, with large samples, employing dyadic survey. Another study could carry out a longitudinal research approach to establish the proposed dependence associations.

CONCLUSION

The findings of the present study established that the three research objectives are to determine the positive relationship between strategic orientations such as MO, EO, RO and international performance of SMEs in Nigeria. The result of smartPLS3.0 illustrated that the relationship between entrepreneurial orientation, relationship orientation, and SMEs international performance is supported and market orientation and International performance is not supported. Hence there is a need for owners/managers of SMEs to put more emphasis on entrepreneurial orientation and also emphasise relationship orientation with a view of having a competitive advantage.

To academic researcher, governments, and practitioners in the area of entrepreneurship and marketing have given much concern to the SMEs international performance and several variables that influence the performance of SMEs. Based on the result of this study, some important contributions were acknowledged especially in terms of SMEs international performance in Nigeria. The outcomes of the present study come up with theoretical contributions. These important contributions are explained in the subsequent part of the study.

Furthermore, the study finding provides some important managerial contributions to owners/managers of SMEs. Limitation and future research direction were recommended from this study. The study has contributed to the managerial and theoretical contributions for the body of knowledge in marketing and entrepreneurship field.

Lastly, the theoretical framework of the present study was established based on the reviewed literature. The variable investigated in the study includes market orientation, entrepreneurial orientation, relationship orientation, and SMEs international performance based on the study result a conclusion can be reached that all research question and research objective were answered. However, the theoretical framework is in line with the underpinning theory (Resources based view) which is used to explain the framework of this study success.

REFERENCES

Abd-Razak, I. S., & Abdul-Talib, A. N. (2009). Explorative study of proactive and responsive export market orientation: an in-depth interview. In *Australian and New Zealand Marketing Academy (ANZMAC) Conference*. Retrieved from www. duplication. net. au/ANZMAC09/papers/ANZMAC2009-288. pdf

Abdul Talib, A. N. (2005). *Differences in market-oriented behaviour levels accross firms' domestic and export marketing operation: A study of antecedents and consequences*. Aston University.

Abdul-Talib, A. N., & Abd-Razak, I. S. (2012). Export market oriented behaviours within the medical tourism industry: A case study. *International Journal of Tourism*, *4*(4), 289–301.

Abdul-Talib, A. N., & Abd-Razak, I.-S. (2020). Proactive and responsive export market orientation behaviours, antecedents, and firm performance. *Leveraging Consumer Behavior and Psychology in the Digital Economy*, 191–204.

Abdul-Talib, A. N., & Keung, C. W. (2021). Impact of Organisational Capabilities on R&D Project Innovation Performance of E&E Manufacturing Firms in Malaysia. *International Journal of Business Innovation and Research.*, *1*(1), 10042101. doi:10.1504/IJBIR.2021.10042101

Abor, J., & Quartey, P. (2010). Issues in SME development in Ghana and South Africa. *International Research Journal of Finance and Economics*, *39*(6), 215–228.

Acquaah, M., & Agyapong, A. (2015). The relationship between competitive strategy and firm performance in micro and small businesses in Ghana: The moderating role of managerial and marketing capabilities. *Africa Journal of Management*, *1*(2), 172–193. doi:10.1080/23322373.2015.1025684

Aloulou, W. J. (2019). Impacts of strategic orientations on new product development and firm performances: Insights from Saudi industrial firms. *European Journal of Innovation*, *22*(2), 257–280. doi:10.1108/EJIM-05-2018-0092

Altuntaş, G., Semerciöz, F., & Eregez, H. (2013). Linking strategic and market orientations to organizational performance: The role of innovation in private healthcare organizations. *Procedia: Social and Behavioral Sciences*, *99*, 413–419. doi:10.1016/j.sbspro.2013.10.509

Ashari, H., Yusof, Y., Zamani, M., Norhashmaedayu, S., Talib, A., & Nizam, A. (2018). A study of effect of market orientation on Malaysian automotive industry supply chain performance. *International Journal of Technology*, *9*(8), 1651–1657. doi:10.14716/ijtech.v9i8.2749

Bai, W., Holmström-Lind, C., & Johanson, M. (2018). Leveraging networks, capabilities and opportunities for international success: A study on returnee entrepreneurial ventures. *Scandinavian Journal of Management*, *34*(1), 51–62. doi:10.1016/j.scaman.2017.12.001

Barney, J. B. (1991). Firm resources and sustained competitive advantage. *Journal of Management*, *17*(1), 99–120. Advance online publication. doi:10.1177/014920639101700108

Boso, N., Story, V., & Cadogan, J. (2013). Entrepreneurial orientation, market orientation, networks ties and performance: Study of entrepreneurial firms in a developing economy. *Journal of Business Venturing*, *28*(6), 708–727. doi:10.1016/j.jbusvent.2013.04.001

Brouthers, K. D., Nakos, G., & Dimitratos, P. (2015). SME entrepreneurial orientation, international performance, and the moderating role of strategic alliances. *Entrepreneurship Theory and Practice*, *39*(5), 1161–1187. doi:10.1111/etap.12101

Buli, B. M. (2017). Entrepreneurial orientation, market orientation and performance of SMEs in the manufactiuring industry: Evidence from Ethiopian entreprises. *Management Research Review*, *40*(3), 292–309. doi:10.1108/MRR-07-2016-0173

Chao, M. C., & Spillan, J. E. (2010). The journey from market orientation to firm performance: A comparative study of US and Taiwanese SMEs. *Management Research Review, 33*(5), 472–483. doi:10.1108/01409171011041901

Chima, O. (2017, September 27). New Vista for MSMEs. *Thisday*. Retrieved from https://www.pressreader.com/nigeria/thisday/20170927/281724089743223

Chin, W. W., Marcolin, B. L., & Newsted, P. R. (2003). A partial least squares latent variable modeling approach for measuring interaction effects: Results from a monte carlo simulation study and an electronic-mail emotion/ adoption study. *Information Systems Research, 14*(2), 1–18. Retrieved from file:///F:/Mendeley/2003/Material/Material - 2003 - Moderators 82-95.pdf

Chinedu, E. A., Titus, O. C., & Thaddeus, E. O. (2010). Achieving vision 2020 in Nigeria: A review of the economic and market-oriented business reforms. *Journal of Sustainable Development in Africa, 12*(4), 58–71.

Day, G. S. (1994). The capabilities of market-driven organisation. *Journal of Marketing, 58*(4), 37–52. doi:10.1177/002224299405800404

Engelen, A., Gupta, V., Strenger, L., & Brettel, M. (2015). Entrepreneurial orientation, firm performance, and the moderating role of transformational leadership behaviors. *Journal of Management, 41*(4), 1069–1097. doi:10.1177/0149206312455244

Espino-Rdriguez, T. F., & Rodriguez-Diaz, M. (2008). Effect of internal and relational capabilities on outsourcing: An intergrated model. *Industrial Management & Data Systems, 108*(3), 328–345. doi:10.1108/02635570810858750

Falk, R. F., & Miller, N. B. (1992). *A primer for soft modeling*. University of Akron Press.

Fornell, C., & Larcker, D. F. (1981). *Structural equation models with unobservable variables and measurement error: Algebra and statistics*. Academic Press.

Gruber-Muecke, T., & Hofer, K. M. (2015). Market orientation, entrepreneurial orientation and performance in emerging markets. *International Journal of Emerging Market, 10*(3), 560–571. doi:10.1108/IJoEM-05-2013-0076

Hair, J. F., Black, W. C., Babin, B. J., Anderson, R. E., & Tatham, R. L. (2010). *Multivariate data analysis: A global perspective.*

Hair, J. F., Hult, G. T. M., Ringle, C. M., & Sarsteddt, M. (2017). *A primer on partial least square structural equation modeling (PLS-SEM)* (2nd ed.). Sage.

Hair, J. F. Jr, Sarstedt, M., Hopkins, L., & Kuppelwieser, V. (2014). Partial least squares structural equation modeling (PLS-SEM). *European Business Review, 26*(2), 106–121. doi:10.1108/EBR-10-2013-0128

Hakala, H., & Kohtamäki, M. (2011). Configurations of entrepreneurial- customer- and technology orientation: Differences in learning and performance of software companies. *International Journal of Entrepreneurial Behaviour & Research, 17*(1), 64–81. doi:10.1108/13552551111107516

Hashim, F., Bakar, A. R. A., & Abdul-Talib, A. N. (2010). *International Business* (2nd ed.). Oxford Fajar Press.

Hashim, F., Bakar, A. R. A., & Talib, A. N. (2010). *International Business* (2nd ed.). Oxford Fajar Press.

Hassan, M. G., Razalli, M. R., & Abdul-Talib, A. N. (2014). The Influence of Environmental Dynamism on Strategic Outsourcing Success: A Partial Least Squares Structural Equation Modelling Approach. *International Journal of Modelling in Operations Management, 4*(3/4), 229-247. doi:10.1504/IJMOM.2014.067382

Hassim, A. A., Asmat-Nizam, A.-T., & Addul Rahim, A. B. (2011). The effects of entrepreneurial orientation on firm organisational innovation and market orientation toward firm business performance. *International on Sociality and Economics Development, 10*, 280–284.

Ho, K. L. P., Nguyen, C. N., Adhikari, R., Miles, M. P., & Bonney, L. (2017). Exploring market orientation, innovation, and financial performance in agricultural value chains in emerging economies. *Journal of Innovation & Knowledge*, 1–12. doi:10.1016/j.jik.2017.03.008

Jiang, X., Liu, H., Fey, C., & Jiang, F. (2018). Entrepreneurial orientation, network resource acquisition, and firm performance: A network approach. *Journal of Business Research, 87*, 46–57. doi:10.1016/j.jbusres.2018.02.021

Kajalo, S., & Lindblom, A. (2015). Market orientation, entrepreneurial orientation and business performance among small retailers. *International Journal of Retail & Distribution Management, 43*(7), 580–596. doi:10.1108/IJRDM-04-2014-0044

Kanibir, H., Saydan, R., & Nart, S. (2014). Determining the antecedents of marketing competencies of SMEs for international market performance. *Procedia - Social and Behavioral Sciences*, (1), 12–23. doi:10.1016/j.sbspro.2014.09.003

Karami, M., & Tang, J. (2019). Entrepreneurial orientation and SME international performance: The mediating role of networking capability and experiential learning. *International Small Business Journal, 37*(2), 105–124. doi:10.1177/0266242618807275

Keskin, H. (2006). Market orientation, learning orientation, and innovation capabilities in SMEs: An extended model. *European Journal of Innovation Management, 9*(4), 396–417. doi:10.1108/14601060610707849

Kohli, A. K., & Jaworski, B. J. (1990). Market orientation: The construct, research propositions and managerial implications. *Journal of Marketing, 54*(2), 1–18. doi:10.1177/002224299005400201

Lee, Y. K., Kim, S. H., Seo, M. K., & Hight, S. K. (2015). Market orientation and business performance: Evidence from franchising industry. *International Journal of Hospitality Management, 44*, 28–37. doi:10.1016/j.ijhm.2014.09.008

Lonial, S. C., & Carter, R. E. (2015). The impact of organizational orientations on medium and small firm performance: A resource-based perspective. *Journal of Small Business Management, 53*(1), 94–113. doi:10.1111/jsbm.12054

Lorenzoni, G., & Lipparini, A. (1999). The leveraging of interfirm relationships as a distinctive organizational capability: A longitudinal study. *Strategic Management Journal*, *20*(4), 317–338. doi:10.1002/(SICI)1097-0266(199904)20:4<317::AID-SMJ28>3.0.CO;2-3

Mambula, C. J. (2002). Perceptions of SMEs growth constraints in Nigeria. *Journal of Small Business Management*, *40*(1), 58–65. doi:10.1111/1540-627X.00039

Mohamed, M.A., & Abdul-Talib, A.N. (2020). Non-pecuniary Factors Influencing Diaspora Homeland Investment. *Transcending Cultural Frontiers*, 125–139. doi:10.1007/978-981-15-4454-5_8

Muddaha, G., Kheng, Y. K., & Sulaiman, Y. (2018). Impact of management capabilities and environmental dynamism on Nigerian SMEs marketing innovation performance. *International Journal of Management Research & Review*, *8*(1), 20–35.

Nakos, G., Dimitratos, P., & Elbanna, S. (2019). The mediating role of alliances in the international market orientation-performance relationship of SMEs. *International Business Review*, *28*(3), 603–612. doi:10.1016/j.ibusrev.2018.12.005

Narver, J., & Slater, S. (1990). The effect of a market orientation on business profitability. *Journal of Marketing*, *54*(4), 20–35. doi:10.1177/002224299005400403

Nasir, W. M. N., Al Mamun, A., & Breen, J. (2017). Strategic orientation and performance of SMEs in Malaysia. *SAGE Open*, *7*(2). Advance online publication. doi:10.1177/2158244017712768

Palmer, C., Niemand, T., Stöckmann, C., Kraus, S., & Kailer, N. (2017). The interplay of entrepreneurial orientation and psychological traits in explaining firm performance. *Journal of Business Research*. Advance online publication. doi:10.1016/j.jbusres.2017.10.005

Panayides, P. M. (2007). The impact of organizational learning on relationship orientation, logistics service effectiveness and performance. *Industrial Marketing Management*, *36*(1), 68–80. doi:10.1016/j.indmarman.2005.07.001

Papastamatelou, J., Busch, R., Begun, O., Okan, E. Y., & Gassemi, K. (2016). Effects of network capabilities on firm performance across cultures. *International Journal of Management and Economics*, *49*(1), 79–105. doi:10.1515/ijme-2016-0005

Parida, V., Pesämaa, O., Wincent, J., & Westerberg, M. (2017). Network capability, innovativeness, and performance: A multidimensional extension for entrepreneurship. *Entrepreneurship and Regional Development*, *29*(1–2), 94–115. doi:10.1080/08985626.2016.1255434

Peltier, J. W., & Naidu, G. M. (2012). Social networks across the SMEs organisational lifecycle. *Journal of Small Business and Enterprise Development*, *19*(1), 56–73. doi:10.1108/14626001211196406

Pinho, J. C. (2008). TQM and performance in small medium entreprises: The mediating effect of customer orientation and innovation. *International Journal of Quality & Reliability Management*, *25*(3), 256–275. doi:10.1108/02656710810854278

Polat, I., & Mutlu, H. M. (2012). The impacts of market orientation, entrepreneurial orientation, environmental uncertainty and internationalization speed on firm performance. *European Researcher*, *27*(8), 1248–1254.

Ra'ed, M., Al-Henzab, J., Tarhini, A., & Obeidat, B. Y. (2018). The associations among market orientation, technology orientation, entrepreneurial orientation and organizational performance. *Benchmarking*, *25*(8), 3117–3142. doi:10.1108/BIJ-02-2017-0024

Sa'id, K. S., Talib, A. B. A., & Hassan, R. (2019a). The role of access to capital and the component of strategic orientations on smes performance: A conceptual framework. *International Journal of Business. Economics and Law*, *19*(5), 311–321.

Sa'id, K. S., Talib, A. B. A., & Hassan, R. (2019b). The role of access to finance, relational capabilities and the omponent of strategic on SMEs performance in Nigeria: A pilot study. *Asian Journal of Multidisciplinary Studies*, *7*(12), 8–19.

Sarstedt, M., Ringle, C. M., Smith, D., Reams, R., & Hair, J. F. Jr. (2014). Partial least squares structural equation modeling (PLS-SEM): A useful tool for family business researchers. *Journal of Family Business Strategy*, *5*(1), 105–115. doi:10.1016/j.jfbs.2014.01.002

Sekeran, U., & Bougie, R. (2010). *Research methods for business: A skill building approach* (5th ed.). John Wiley and Sons.

Sekeran, U., & Bougie, R. (2013). *Researh methods for business: a skill building approach* (6th ed.). John Wiley & Sons Ltd.

Shehu, A. M., & Mahmood, R. (2014). The relationship between market orientation and business performance of Nigerian SMEs: The role of organizational culture. *International Journal of Business and Social Science*, *5*(9), 159–168.

Slater, S., & Narver, J. C. (1994). Market orientation, customer value and superior performance. *Business Horizons*, 22–28.

Slater, S. F., & Narver, J. C. (1995). Market orientation and the learning organization. *Journal of Marketing*, *59*(3), 63–74. doi:10.1177/002224299505900306

SMEDAN. (2012). Survey on Micro, Small and Medium enterprises (MSMEs) in Nigeria. SMEDAN.

SMEDAN. (2013). Smedan and National Bereau of Statistics Collaborative Survey: Selected Findings. SMEDAN.

Smirnova, M., Naudé, P., Henneberg, S. C., Mouzas, S., & Kouchtch, S. P. (2011). The impact of market orientation on the development of relational capabilities and performance outcomes: The case of Russian industrial firms. *Industrial Marketing Management*, *40*(1), 44–53. doi:10.1016/j.indmarman.2010.09.009

Smirnova, M. M., & Kushch, S. P. (2006). Understanding the role of relational capabilities in buyer-seller relationships. *22nd IMP Conference*, 7–9.

Solano Acosta, A., Herrero Crespo, Á., & Collado Agudo, J. (2018). Effect of market orientation, network capability and entrepreneurial orientation on international performance of small and medium enterprises (SMEs). *International Business Review*, *27*(6), 1128–1140. doi:10.1016/j.ibusrev.2018.04.004

Spillan, J., & Parnell, J. (2006). Marketing resources and firm performance among SMEs. *European Management Journal*, *24*(2–3), 236–245. doi:10.1016/j.emj.2006.03.013

Srivastava, R. K., Shervani, T. A., & Fahey, L. (1998). Market-based assets and shareholder value: A framework for analysis. *Journal of Marketing*, *62*(1), 2–18. doi:10.1177/002224299806200102

Tehseen, S., Ahmed, F. U., Qureshi, Z. H., Uddin, M. J., & Ramayah, T. (2019). Entrepreneurial competencies and SMEs' growth: The mediating role of network competence. *Asia-Pacific Journal of Business Administration*, *11*(1), 2–29. doi:10.1108/APJBA-05-2018-0084

Tsougkou, E., Cadogan, J. W., Hodgkinson, I. R., Oliveira, J. S., Abdul-Talib, A. N., Story, V. M., & Lioliou, E. (2019). *Achieving export competitive advantage: can global orientation and export product adaptation be reconciled.* In *2019 AMA Global Marketing SIG Conference*, Buenos Aires, Argentina.

Wang, Y. (2016). What are the biggest obstacles to growth of SMEs in developing countries? An empirical evidence from an enterprise survey. *Borsa Istanbul Review*, *16*(3), 167–176. doi:10.1016/j.bir.2016.06.001

Weerawardena, J., & O'Cass, A. (2004). Exploring the characteristics of the market-driven firms and antecedents to sustained competitive advantage. *Industrial Marketing Management*, *33*(5), 419–428. doi:10.1016/j.indmarman.2003.07.002

Zahra, S. A., & Garvis, D. (2000). International corporate entrepreneurship and company performance: The moderating effect of international environmental hostility. *Journal of Business Venturing*, *10*, 43–58. doi:10.1016/0883-9026(94)00004-E

Zakaria, N., & Abdul-Talib, A. N. (2010). Applying Islamic market-oriented cultural model to sensitize strategies towards global customers, competitors, and environment. *Journal of Islamic Marketing*, *1*(1), 51–62. doi:10.1108/17590831011026222

Zakaria, N., Abdul-Talib, A. N., & Amelinckx, A. (Eds.). (2020). *Transcending Cultural Frontiers: Practices, Challenges, and Strategy for International Business*. Springer. doi:10.1007/978-981-15-4454-5

Zakaria, N., Abdul-Talib, A.N., & Amelinckx, A. (2020). Advancing Cultural Frontiers to Champion Global Business in Emerging Markets. *Transcending Cultural Frontiers*, 1–10. doi:10.1007/978-981-15-4454-5_1

Zakaria, N., Abdul-Talib, A. N., & Othman, N. (Eds.). (2016). *Handbook of research on impacts of international business and political affairs on the global economy*. IGI Global. doi:10.4018/978-1-4666-9806-2

Zamani, M. N. S., Ashari, H., & Abdul-Talib, A. N. (2017). The strategic fit of multiple strategic orientations and new product development performance in Malaysian manufacturing firms. *Journal for Studies in Management and Planning*, *3*(1), 87–101.

Zamani, S. N. M., & Abdul-Talib, A. N. (2016). Strategic orientations and new product success: The mediating impact of innovation speed. International Information Institute (Tokyo), 19(7B), 2785–2790.

Chapter 14
Iron Silk Road Trans-Caspian East-West-Middle Corridor Initiative and Baku-Tbilisi-Kars Railway Line: Impact on International Trade

Özlem Karadağ Albayrak
https://orcid.org/0000-0003-0832-0490
Kafkas University, Turkey

Başak Çelik
https://orcid.org/0000-0002-5753-5458
Kafkas University, Turkey

ABSTRACT

The East-West Middle Corridor (Middle Corridor) with the Caspian Transit, which starts from Turkey with the Baku Tbilisi Kars Railway line, reaches the Caucasus region. From here it travels over the Caspian Sea through Turkmenistan and Kazakhstan to Central Asia and China and is one of the most important components of historical silk road resuscitation project. With this study, the contribution of Baku Tbilisi Kars railway line and Kars Logistics Center, which is the European and Turkish gateway of the middle corridor, to the silk railway in terms of international leasing is explored.

INTRODUCTION

Located in both Asia and Europe, Turkey has an important advantage in terms of logistics activities provided by two-way material flow from Asia to Europe. The road and belt project, introduced by China in 2013, has supported Turkey in using this advantage. Based on this opportunity, Baku Tbilisi Kars Railway line and Kars Logistics Center initiatives, which provide the connection of the middle belt of

DOI: 10.4018/978-1-7998-9071-3.ch014

this initiative, have been completed. Turkey will become one of the most significant actors of world trade by such investments. In addition to the economic contributions to economic growth and regional development, these projects will also develop the rail silk route in Turkey and cultural communication with Turkish States.

The aim of this study is to investigate passenger and freight transport activities in the context of railway in Turkey, which is located at one of the two ends of the iron silk road within the scope of the belt road project. In the Belt Road project, it is expected that the expectations of globalization, infrastructure development activities, trade development and economic gains will be met mutually for all member countries. For this, the applications of the railway silk road, Baku Tbilisi Kars Railway Line and Kars Logistics Center for Turkey were examined in relation to the belt road project.

BACKGROUND

Railroads are an important issue in economic, social and political organizations in modern societies. For developed industries, general capabilities such as specialized industry, mass production, membership in world markets and logistics activities carried out with efficient means of transportation throughout the supply chain are of importance. Cultural transcendence, which has developed thanks to globalization, enables the international trade of international businesses to increase more and more (Zakaria et al, 2021). In this sense, the BRI project has turned into a truly global system covering many regions, countries and cities with the aim of establishing connections between different regions (Grydehøj et al, 2020). Within the scope of this project, it is planned to carry out a significant number of railway projects, since railways are the most efficient means of transportation (. Turkey is in an important position especially as it will be one of the European gateways of this network.

In logistics sector, different types of transportation, namely modes, are generally used in freight and passenger transportation. These modes have specific advantages and disadvantages. For example, while road transport is considered the most flexible mode, railway has the lowest transportation cost and is a suitable mode for the transportation of bulky goods despite high investment cost.

Development in foreign trade activities directly affects countries' growth. Increase in mass production by advancing technology necessitates bulk shipments. In this regard, railroad transportation is the most important alternative to sea transportation regarding mass transportation.

There is evidence that the use and quality of infrastructure to be provided in different projects positively affects trade flows and volume (Ramasamy and Yeung, 2019). Belt and Road project is mainly based on traditional and underdeveloped logistics trade routes covering both the terrestrial and oceanic Silk Road (An et al., 2018). The re-activation of the economic belt of the Great Silk Road within the globalization steps with the Belt Road project provides new and important opportunities for the economies of the countries on this road (Raimbekov et al, 2021). Today, the main factors of the integration of these countries are logistics, international trade and tourism Raimbekov et al., 2018. (.Using the Silk Road, Asian and European explorers have traded many products and shared cultural elements for nearly 1000 years. This cooperation and openness and as a route of mutual benefit in international trade are thought to contribute to the welfare of the countries through which it passes (Wang et al, 2019). The ring road project will increase the flow and volume of trade. Because the venture project includes infrastructure development, human knowledge and international relations to improve business relations (Kong et al.,

2020). In addition, the demand in information and coordinated logistics services due to the Belt and Road Initiative project shows an increasing interest in frequent international trade transactions (Li et al., 2020).

Turkey is a country located in both Asia and Europe. It is also located in an alternative transit zone that can be used for passenger and freight transportation between China and Europe. Researchers interest in creating a lower cost transportation network by utilizing this location of Turkey. For this reason, the Baku Tbilisi Kars (BTK) railway line, which is the stop of the Iron Silk Road and aims both freight and passenger transportation with the railway network on the China-London line from Asia to Europe, was established. This railroad is entirely 838.6 km, of which 503 km passes through Azerbaijan, 259 km through Georgia and 76 km through Turkey.

MAIN FOCUS OF THE CHAPTER

The Belt and Road project includes social-economic and political cooperation between the participating countries. Although this project is generally described as a center for infrastructure development, it is a comprehensive initiative that also includes policy dialogue, barrier-free trade, financial support and people-to-people exchange (Huang, 2016). With this project, Turkey aims to contribute to the development of basic structural elements such as transportation corridors, logistics centers, infrastructure and field development, especially in the field of trade and investment, which are built for integration. While Turkey is exporting raw materials and semi-finished products to China, it is purchasing technology and capital-intensive products from China. This results in Turkey's low export income but high export expenditure. This result shows that the trade between Turkey and China is asymmetrical. Turkey runs one third of its total current account deficit against China. With this project, cooperation to be made in the fields of renewable energy (especially solar energy), information technologies, robotics and 5G, where China is quite good with a win-win principle, may be beneficial for Turkey (Nuroğlu, 2019). In this study, an analysis will be conducted on Turkey's connections with other existing railway corridors in China. The middle corridor, to which the Baku Tbilisi Kars railway line will be connected to, will be discussed in terms of the chains established and being established from China to Europe.

ISSUES, CONTROVERSIES, PROBLEMS

Production moves from Asia to Europe in the world. While approximately 18% of total import was made in (United States of America: 14%) American continent and approximately 23% in Europe (Germany: 7%), the remaining major part was made in Asian (China and Taiwan: 14%) countries. In addition, whereas approximately 15% of total export was made in (United States of America: 8%) American continent and approximately 30% in Europe (Germany: 8%), the remaining major part was made in Asian (China and Taiwan: 17%) countries (Republic of Turkey Ministry of Trade, 2020). This shows that the material movement takes place in two-way from Asia to Europe. In this regard, all roads (railway, seaway, highway…) on this movement route and the countries where these roads are located are of paramount importance. With a high strategical importance, Turkey is a country serving as a bridge between Asia and Europe. For this reason, any logistics research that will affect international trade activities regarding Turkey draws attention.

International Trade activities have important effects on the economic growth of countries. One of the expectations regarding Belt and Road Initiative (BRI) project introduced by China in 2013 is its contribution to international trade and economic growth. In the literature, the studies on green logistics have been focused on recently, and different approaches, investigating the effect of foreign trade for the countries within the BRI project, have been discussed. Khan et al (2021) has concluded that this initiative would have a positive effect on renewable energy in 69 countries that participated in BRI initiative. An et al (2021) have argued that better quality of transportation infrastructure, efficiency of customs clearance and adequacy of logistics services in China have reduced carbon emission level significantly due to energy saving in the supply chain process.

Wu et al (2021) has investigated the effect of foreign trade activities in China on the emission in BRI countries. It has been concluded that while import intensity from China reduced emission, export intensity increased emission. According to the research carried out by Majeed et al (2021) in 102 BRI countries, trade gap has increased financial development in Asia, Europe and Latin America but decreased in Africa. According to Belt and Road industrial robot trade relationship, several countries such as China, Turkey and India are in the central position (Li et al, 2021). A study (Feng et al, 2020) comparing competitive advantages of countries with regard to trade has argued that Turkey and Russia are the countries with the largest competitive trade advantages, while China has the strongest mediation capacity with BRI countries.

As an element of the BRI project, BTK Railway Line is one of the actors of international trade, and the trade volume on this line will increase rapidly in the following years. In order to use this potential properly and to make future plans, investigations and applications should be conducted and submitted to policymakers.

BELT AND ROAD INITIATIVE (BRI)

Technological developments and globalization have made cooperation between countries obligatory. Regarding this cooperation, the "Belt and Road Initiative" (BRI) was launched by the Chinese government in 2013. In his state visits to Kazakhstan and Indonesia in 2013, President Xi Jinping stated that the BRI was developed to promote infrastructure and trade across land and sea-based routes, which would accelerate the economy under growing feelings of globalization and protectionism (Buckley, 2020: 311; Du ve Zhang, 2018; Li et al, 2019). This initiative covers 72 countries with 65% of the whole world population (OECD, 2018). BRI initiative is of importance as it connects different regions in the world (Hussain et al., 2020:2). This initiative, by which technology, infrastructure, resource mobilization and labor mobility will be shared, will support countries in terms of industrial growth and economic progress (Rauf et al, 2018: 2). Financial investment flows of this investment change between USD 4 to 8 trillion, and more share has been assigned to the developing countries from this fund in order to develop their economies. Within the scope of BRI plans, 7000 projects will be completed by focusing on energy projects, infrastructure development, export and trade, market integration and skills diversification (Khan et al, 2021:480). For this reason, two significant financial funds have been established to finance the Belt and Road project. These are as follows: Silk Road Fund (2014) and Asian Infrastructure Investment Bank (AIIB (2015) (Zhang et al, 2018:136).

Despite these advantages, it is discussed that this initiative, funded by China and of which infrastructure projects have been established, is focused on China while the roles of other project countries have not been considered (Calabrese and Cao, 2021). It is claimed that the goals of BRI are in accordance with the development aims of possible host countries, however, some infrastructure projects implemented have shown that little importance has been attached on long-term needs of the host countries. Even before the COVID-19 pandemic, these issues caused tensions and fractures between China and several host countries regarding the design, development and execution of SME infrastructure projects mostly due to burden of debt and related 'asset acquisitions' (Buckley, 2020: 311).

Turkey has a significant role in the Belt and Road project due to its geopolitical position, stability and NATO membership. Turkey may act as a gate for China to Balkans and Europe as well as a key ally in the Middle East. Furthermore, as Turkey controls many strategic transitions, it is considered an integral country of the Belt and Road project (Akçay and Qingye, 2020: 2). Turkey is located in China's economic corridor of China-Central West Asia with Kazakhstan, Kyrgyzstan, Tajikistan, Uzbekistan, Turkmenistan and Iran, six belts that are rich in terms of energy and resources in the world.

SILK ROAD ECONOMIC BELT (SREB)

The Republic of Turkey provides favorable business opportunities for Foreign Direct Investment (FDI) and domestic businesses (Christansen et al, 2016).With the BRI project, seaway, railway and road transportation systems of countries will be developed and extended. This initiative has two components called Silk Road Economic Belt (SREB) and 21st Century Maritime Silk Road (MSR). Of these, Silk Road Economic Belt focuses on gathering China, Central Asia, Russia and Europe (Baltic) and connecting China to the Persian Gulf and the Mediterranean via Central Asia and the Indian Ocean. On the other hand, 21st Century Maritime Silk Road has been designed to arrive in Europe from the coast of China via the South China Sea and the Indian Ocean on the one hand and to go to South Pacific from the coast of China via the South China Sea on the other hand (Xinhua, 2016).

In the 21st century, China and Turkey are two countries located at two edges of the old silk road, which is closely related to "One Belt, One Road", a Chinese initiative (Jinghon and Kuzmin, 2021). When this initiative is considered in terms of railway networks, it is argued in terms of geography that Poland is the most proper center to connect railways from post-Soviet countries of Silk Road Economic Belt (SREB) to railways planned from the Balkans and the Greek port of Piraeus. In addition, it is urged that the projection of Germany as a center in this respect is wrong as the Budapest-Belgrade railway goes further north. In addition, the Czech Republic is considered an alternative rail center, if not as much as Poland (Górski, 2018: 115).

Trans-Caspian East-West-Middle Corridor (Middle Corridor), which starts from Turkey and reaches the Caucasus region, and then Central Asia and the People's Republic of China (PRC) by crossing the Caspian Sea after Turkmenistan and Kazakhstan, is one of the most important components of the project of reviving the historical Silk Road. The Middle Corridor starts in our country and then reaches Georgia, Azerbaijan and the Caspian Sea, respectively with railway and highway connections, which then extends to PRC by following the route of Turkmenistan- Uzbekistan-Kyrgyzstan or Kazakhstan (via Caspian Pass). To this end, Baku/Alat (Azerbaijan), Aktau/Kuryk (Kazakhstan) and Turkmenbashi (Turkmenistan) ports are used for combined transport in the Caspian Pass (mfa.gov.tr, 2021).

Turkey has joined Trans-Caspian East-West-Middle Corridor initiative, starting in China and then crossing Central Asia (Kazakhstan or Kyrgyzstan, Uzbekistan, Turkmenistan) and then the Caspian Sea, Azerbaijan and Georgia and which is known to be Middle Corridor, in order to adapt to these developments. This initiative mainly focuses on a network of road and railway transport modes with transitions in the Caspian Sea. If this corridor is used effectively, it is expected to help Turkey and Central Asian countries benefit from China-Europe trade and infrastructure investments (TEPAV, 2019).

There are many bilateral and multilateral cooperation initiatives among Azerbaijan, Georgia, Kazakhstan, Kyrgyzstan, Turkmenistan, Turkey, Uzbekistan, Afghanistan and China. Some of these are as follows: Turkey signed "Memorandum of Understanding Between The Government of The Republic of Turkey and The Government of The People's Republic Of China On Cooperation Within The Framework Of The Silk Road Economic Belt and The 21st Century Maritime Silk Road Initiative" on 14 November 2015 at the G20 Leaders' Summit held in Antalya (TBMM, 2015). In addition, Turkey signed Joint Cooperation Protocol with Azerbaijan and Central Asian Republics, and established a Coordinatination Council. The Lapis Lazuli-Transportation Corridor Agreement was signed to provide a regional cooperation among Turkey, Georgia, Azerbaijan, Turkmenistan and Afghanistan to serve the belt road initiative (portseurope.com, 2021).

Although it is not within the scope of BRI, Trans Anatolian Natural Gas Pipeline Project (TANAP) is important for Turkey as it will transport natural gas from the Caspian Sea to Europe via Turkey, as a part of the European Union's Southern Gas Corridor. This line, in 1850 km length, will pass through 20 provinces of Ardahan, Kars, Erzurum, Erzincan, Bayburt, Gümüşhane, Giresun, Sivas, Yozgat, Kırşehir, Kırıkkale, Ankara, Eskişehir, Bilecik, Kütahya, Bursa, Balıkesir, Çanakkale, Tekirdağ and Edirne, and will end in the İpsala district of Edirne on the Greek border (TANAP, 2021).

In addition to its economic contribution, the iron silk road, to which the BTK line is connected, will also contribute to the unity and integrity of the Turkish World (Özpay, 2018). This historical railway line has important effects on the Turkish World in terms of economy, strategy and management, and the importance of the "logistics" sector is better understood in the globalizing world trade, where competition is getting live day each passing day by using the latest technologies (Bucsky and Kenderdine, 2020).

Figure 1. Trans-Caspian East-West Middle Corridor (Bulut, 2018).

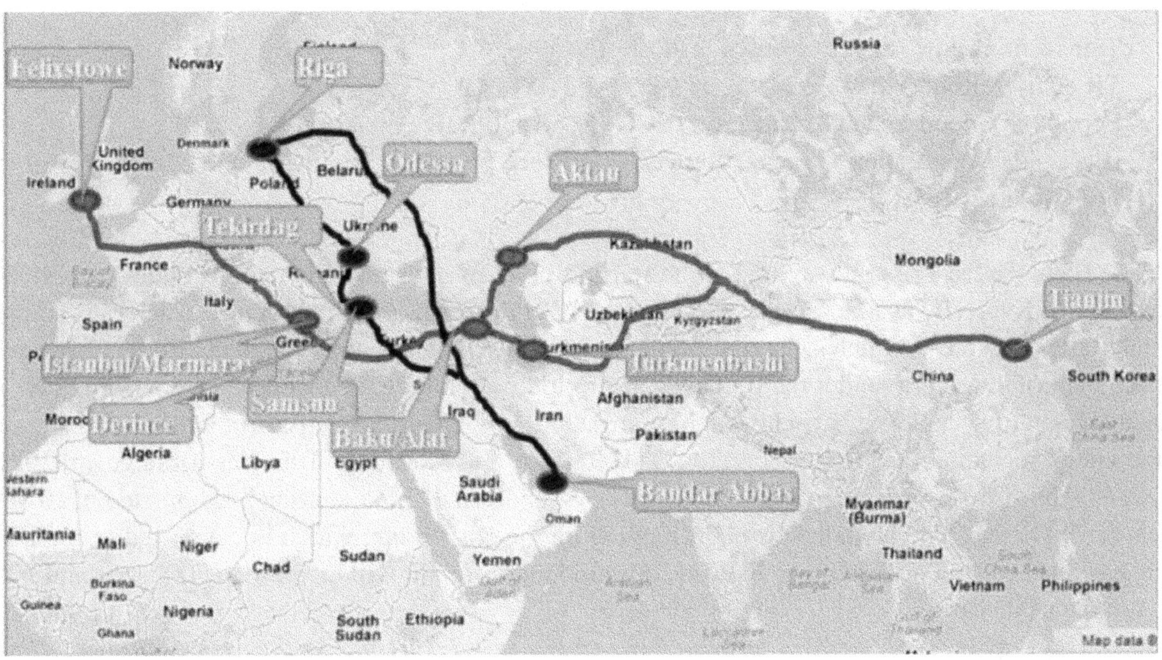

Figure 2. Alternative Routes from China to Europe (bakuresearchinstitute.org, 2021).

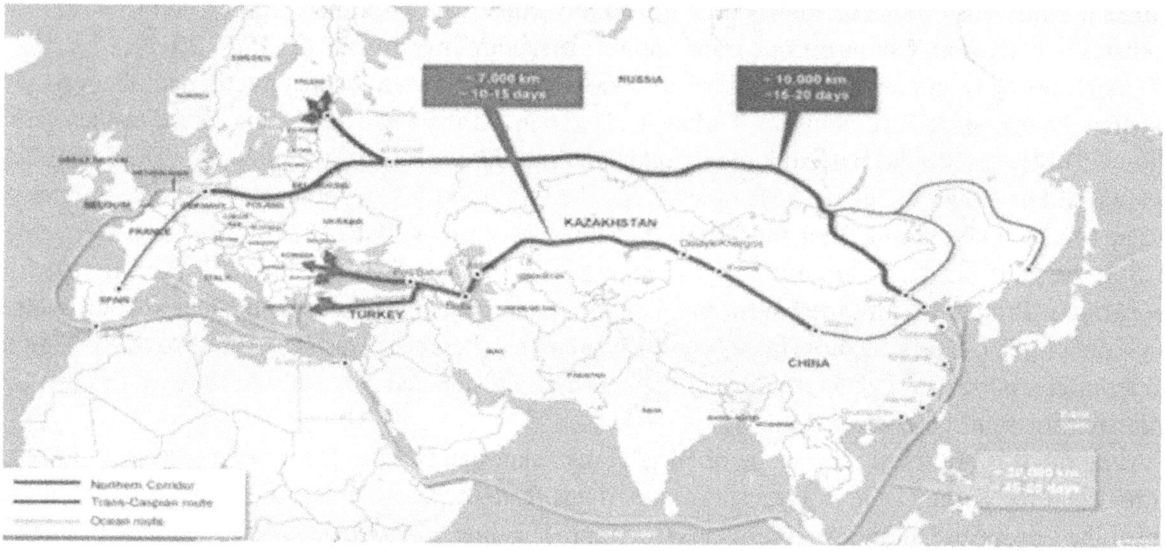

BAKU TBILISI KARS RAILWAY LINE (BTK)

Turkey is a part of international transportation routes due to its advantage caused by its location. Some of these roads are as follows:

- United Nations Economic and Social Commission for Europe (UNECE) E-roads,

Trans-European North-South Motorway (TEM), Trans-European Railway (TER) Projects and Euro-Asian Transport Links (EATL)

- Trans-European Transport Networks (TEN-T)
- TRACECA Routes
- Economic Cooperation Organization (ECO) Road and Rail Corridors
- Black Sea Cooperation Organization (BSEC) Black Sea Ring Highways and Motorways of the Sea (Bulut, 2018)

The Baku Tbilisi Kars railway line is the starting point of the middle corridor in our country. The Baku Tbilisi Kars railway line was put into service in 2017 in terms of infrastructure. Chang'an Train of China Railway Express, which is the first freight train arrived in our country over the Middle Corridor (6 November 2019, Ankara) under the Belt and Road Initiative, completed its journey from China's Xi'an city to Prague, the capital of Czech Republic, in 18 days by using the transportation infrastructure of our country, including the Middle Corridor, BTK Railway and Marmaray Tube Pass (mfa.gov.tr, 2021). Now, Istanbul-China journey is completed in 12 days, and Kars-China journey is completed in 10 days with the BTK line. The amount of freight moving on the Kars route, which is connected to the BTK line, has reached 4000 tons per day. In 2021, this amount of freight will increase to 7000 tons and 9000 tons in the next year.

The BTK route, which is a Middle Corridor initiative, represents a Turkish policy aiming to establish an efficient transport connection with China. With this network, the Turkish railway network has established a railway connection to Kazakhstan and then to Central Asia and China via the Caspian roll-on/roll-off (RORO) connection through the Transcaucasian countries (Georgia and Azerbaijan) (Prokic and Stanimirović, 2019).

In the BTK line, 1160 containers of import and 8239 containers of export were carried out until now. All these activities were made to the Turkic Republics and China in the middle belt. In the BTK line, while Citrus, Marble, Soybean Meal, Miscellaneous Food, Iron Ore, Construction Material, White Goods, Pipe, Borax, Manganese Ore are exported, Lentil, Wheat, Feed, Adipic Acid, Copper Cathode, Paper, Walnut, Silicone, Coil and Billet Sheet, Sunflower, Steel Construction are imported (Muharrem Toraman, face to face interview, June 2021).

Figure 3. Baku Tbilisi Kars Railway (mfa.gov.tr, 2021).

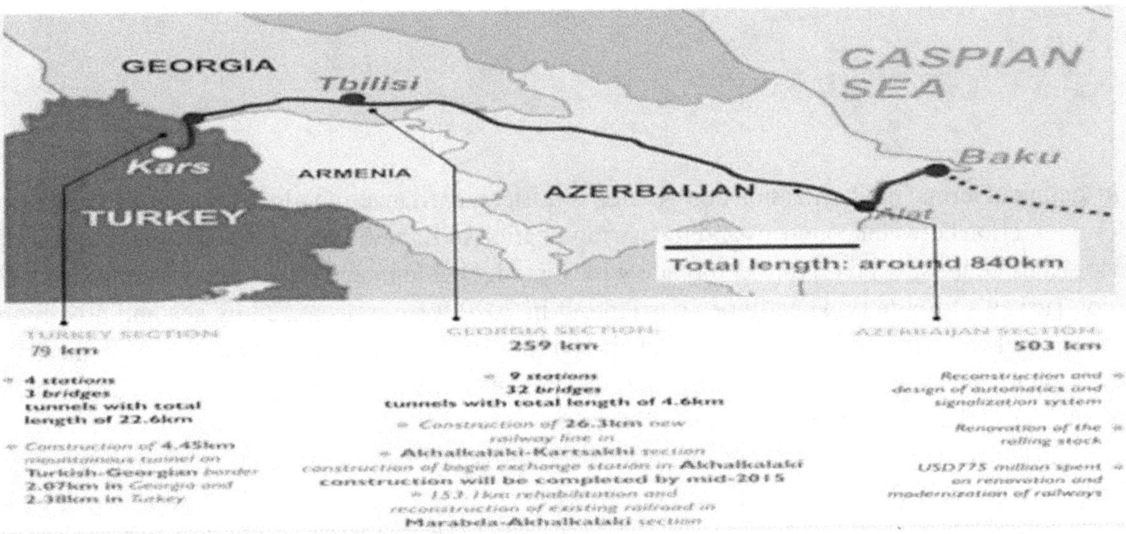

KARS LOGISTICS CENTER (KLC)

The necessity and importance of integrated and value-added logistics activities are increasing each passing day to meet customer expectations. Logistics villages, in which such activities can be fulfilled by a holistic approach, have begun to become widespread so that logistics activities can be met (Bay and Erol, 2016: 124). These places are stated as *Logistics Centres, Logistic Bases or Logistic Villages* in the literature. Logistics Centres are the places, where all national and international logistics and transportation operations are managed and various business operations are directed (Yazdani et al, 2020).

Figure 4. Logistics Centers in Turkey (TCDD[2021)

In technical terms, modernization contributes significantly to meeting global freight demand through better interaction between countries and the harmonization of related operations (Bersenev et al., 2020). The logistics centres, which have been made widespread, enable intermodal transport activities. While 60% of Turkey's foreign trade activities carried out in 2020 were transported by sea and 30% by road, the rate of railway remained at 0.5%. This rate is too low for railway transport mode, which has the biggest advantage in terms of cost after maritime transport mode. It is also very low for Turkey, which has a railway network from one end to other (1280 km).

Kars Logistics Center (KLC) will increase this rate by means of the Asian trade that will be connected with the BTK Railway line. Kars Logistics Center is established on a 400000 m^2 area, which is very close to the city center and organized industrial zone. This center has a highway connection, and its distance to airport is 12 km and the nearest port is 277 km. While the theoretical capacity of KLC was approximately 1700 tons per day, its actual capacity was approximately 1190 tons until the opening date of 21/05/2021. Following its opening, theoretical capacity will be achieved rapidly.

SOLUTIONS AND RECOMMENDATIONS

The followings are suggested so that Turkey provides advantage regarding competition in the markets of other countries and becomes an effective actor in the BRI initiative: first of all, in order to show that the idea of reviving the Great Silk Road between China and Turkey is not a dream and to draw the interests of investors in this regard, it will be beneficial to increase mutual cooperation between China and Turkey. Secondly, the developments in the BTK line should be monitored well and the extent of its potential should be determined. This may provide Turkey with a leader role among BRI countries. Thirdly, Turkey and Russia have been determined as the countries with the most competitive advantage in international trade among the BRI countries. This advantage should be evaluated by a professional network system.

Fourthly, the movements on the middle belt line should be made more effective by determining the regional cooperation of the countries on the middle belt line, their areas of expertise in production and the advantages specific to these countries. Lastly, it should be ensured to remove the factors to decrease speed such as communication, information sharing, lack of experience, hardware deficiencies that may cause a slowdown in international trade activities on this network. One of the activities to be performed in this respect has been fulfilled in the Turkish side of BTK. The first dual gauge rail was established in Turkey in order to prevent any problem that may be caused due to the difference of the rail line with a width of 1520 millimetres used in countries such as Russia, Azerbaijan, Georgia, Kazakhstan and the rails of 1435 millimetre standards used in Turkey and Europe.

FUTURE RESEARCH DIRECTIONS

The most significant contribution of this study is to discuss the BTK line as a gate of the BRI project, located on the iron silk road and introduced by the Chinese government in 2013, in the middle belt. In this study, a general perspective has been provided, and BTK specific evaluations have been made. In further studies, models, which will reveal the effects of this line on macro variables by various econometric models, may be established. Such models will be useful for policy-makers in future planning. In addition, its benefits to regional development can also be analyzed.

In addition to these, the rates of using railway instead of maritime transport can be estimated for Turkey by using different estimation methods. This is important for the preparation of a future projection.

CONCLUSION

Turkey is one of the most important countries of the road silk road that will be revived by the BRI. It is one of the rare countries, which is a bridge between Asia and Europe, in which all modes of transport such as martime, railway, road, airway, pipeline, inland waterway are made. This provides Turkey with a great advantage in terms of intermodal transportation. BTK railway line and KLC, which have been established for this purpose, will provide many advantages to Turkey in terms of using these advantages. Turkey opens the Europen gate of the material flow that will start from China, Asia to Europe. Public institutions, private establishment, universities and non-governmental organizations, which will contribute in this regard, should work together and share their knowledge and skills.

This research received no specific grant from any funding agency in the public, commercial, or not-for-profit sectors.

REFERENCES

Abdul-Talib, A. N., & Keung, C. W. (2021). Impact of organisational capabilities on R&D project innovation performance of E&E manufacturing firms in malaysia. *International Journal of Business Innovation and Research*, *1*(1), 10042101. doi:10.1504/IJBIR.2021.10042101

Akçay, N., & Qingye, T. (2020). Turkey's perceptions of China's Belt and Road initiative (2013–2017): Media and think-tanks discourse analysis. *Bölgesel Araştırmalar Dergisi, 56*(December), 73–96. doi:10.1177/0009445520916877

Akman, M.S., & Tepav. (2019). *Turkey's Middle Corridor and Belt and Road Initiative: Coherent or Conflicting?* Retrieved May 01, 2021, from https://think-asia.org/handle/11540/11336

An, H., Razzaq, A., Nawaz, A., Noman, S. M., & Khan, S. A. R. (2021). Nexus between green logistic operations and triple bottom line: Evidence from infrastructure-led Chinese outward foreign direct investment in Belt and Road host countries. *Environmental Science and Pollution Research International, 28*(37), 51022–51045. Advance online publication. doi:10.100711356-021-12470-3 PMID:33977429

Andri'c, J. M., Wang, J., & Zhong, R. (2019). Identifying the critical risks in railway projects based on fuzzy and sensitivity analysis: A case study of Belt and Road projects. *Sustainability, 11*(5), 1302. doi:10.3390u11051302

bakuresearchinstitute.org. (2020). *The Trans-Caspian Corridor: the shortest path or a difficult bridge between East and West?* Retrieved May 01, 2021, from https://bakuresearchinstitute.org/en/the-trans-caspian-corridor-the-shortest-path-or-a-difficult-bridge-between-east-and-west/

Bay, M., & Erol, F. (2016). Lojistik Köylerin Önemi ve İntermodal Taşımacılık Faaliyetleriyle Desteklenmesi: Karaman İlinde Bir Uygulama. *KMÜ Sosyal ve Ekonomik Araştırmalar Dergisi, 18*(30), 124–134.

Bersenev, A., Chikilevskaya, M., & Rusinov, I. (2020). Silk road rail corridors outlook and future perspectives of development. *Procedia Computer Science, 167*, 1080–1087.

Buckley, P. J. (2020). China's Belt and Road initiative and the Covid-19 crisis. *Journal of International Business Policy, 3*(3), 311–314.

Bucsky, P., & Kenderdine, T. (2020). Is the iron silk road really so important? Rail freight use on China's "Silk road economic belt. *Вестник МГИМО-Университета, 13*(5), 168–193. doi:10.24833/2071-8160-2020-5-74-168-193

Bulut, E. B. (2018). Governance of transport corridors' perspective of Turkey. *11th meeting of comcec transport and communications working group on governance of transport corridors in the OIC member states: Challenges, cases and policy lessons.* (Report)

Calabrese, L., & Cao, Y. (2021). Managing the Belt and Road: Agency and development in cambodia and myanmar. *World Development, 141*, 105297.

Christansen B., Dirikan,T., Dirikan, C., Kasarcı, F. (2016). *Turkey's Economic Sustainability in Global Hypercompetition.* Academic Press.

Feng, L. Y., Xu, H. L., Wu, G., Zhao, Y., & Xu, J. L. (2020). Exploring the structure and influence factors of trade competitive advantage network along the Belt and Road. *Physica A, 559*, 125057.

Górski, J. (2018). China's Strategy Toward Central and Eastern Europe Within the Framework of 16 + 1 Group: The Case of Poland. In China's Belt and Road Initiative in Changing the Rules of Globalization (pp. 115-134). Palgrave MacMillan.

Grydehøj, A., Davis, S., Guo, R., & Zhang, H. (2020). Silk road archipelagos: Islands in the Belt and Road Initiative. *Island Studies Journal, 15*(2), 3–12.

Hassan, M. G., Razalli, M. R., & Abdul-Talib, A. N. (2014). The influence of environmental dynamism on strategic outsourcing success: A partial least squares Structural Equation Modelling approach. *International Journal of Modelling in Operations Management, 4*(3/4), 229–247.

Hassan, M. G., Razali, M. R., & Abdul-Talib, A. N. (2015). The impact of industrial supplier-manufacturer relationship on strategic outsourcing success. *Jurnal Teknologi, 74*(1), 83–90.

Huang, Y. (2016). Understanding China's Belt & Road initiative: Motivation, framework and assessment. *China Economic Review, 40*, 314–321.

Hussein, J., Khan, A., & Zhou, K. (2020). The impact of natural resource depletion on energy use and CO2emission in Belt&Road initiative countries: A cross-country analysis. *Energy, 199*, 1174092.

Jinghon, T., & Kuzmin, V. A. (2021). Development of Chinese -Turkish relations under "One Belt, One Road" initiative. *Nauchnyi Dialog, 3*, 438-451. DOI: doi:10.24224/2227-1295-2021-3-438-451

Khan, A., Chenggang, Y., Hussain, J., & Kui, Z. (2021). Impact of technological innovation, financial development and foreigndirect investment on renewable energy, non-renewable energy andthe environment in Belt and Road Initiative countries. *Renewable Energy, 171*, 479–491.

Kong, E., Wei, W. X., Swallow, P., & Thomson, S. B. (2020). Belt-and-Road Initiative: Driving the need to understand intellectual capital in Chinese multinational enterprises. *Thunderbird International Business Review, 62*(3), 279–290. doi:10.1002/tie.22088

Li, G., Zhang, Q., Bai, Z., & Sabeeh, P. (2020). Research on logistics service supply chain information sharing mechanism in the belt and road initiative. *IEEE Access: Practical Innovations, Open Solutions, 8*, 189684–189701.

Li, Y. Y., Li, Y. L., Pan, A., Pan, X., & Veglianti, E. (2021). The network structure characteristics and determinants of the Belt and Road industrial robot trade. *Emerging Markets Finance & Trade*, 1–11. doi:10.1080/1540496X.2021.1897315

Majeed, A., Jiang, P., Ahmad, M., Khan, M. A., & Olah, J. (2021). The impact of foreign direct investment on financial development: New evidence from panel cointegration and causality analysis. *Journal of Competitiveness, 13*(1), 95–112. https://doi.org/10.7441/joc.2021.01.06

Nuroğlu, E. (2019). *Turkey-China relations within the framework of the Belt-Road Project*. Retrieved September 2, 2012 from https://www.aa.com.tr/tr/analiz/kusak-yol-projesi-cercevesinde-turkiye-cin-iliskileri/1538112

OECD. (2018). *China's Belt and Road Initiative in the Global Trade, Investment and Finance, Landscape*. Retrieved April 13, 2021, from https://www.oecd.org/general/searchresults/?q=china%20belt%20and&cx=012432601748511391518:xzeadub0b0a&cof=FORID:11&ie=UTF-8

Özpay, G. A. (2018). The Baku-Tbilisi-Kars railway and its geopolitical importance in terms of Turkey. *Marmara Geographical Review, 37*, 103–111.

portseurope.com. (2021). *Turkey ratifies Lapis Lazuli transport corridor route,* Retrieved May 05, 2021, from https://www.portseurope.com/turkey-ratifies-lapis-lazuli-transport-corridor-route/

Prokic, M., & Stanimirović, U. (2019). *Eu-China Rail Economic Corridors and Their Role In Trade In Goods.* Retrieved May 29, 2001, from https://www.researchgate.net/publication/339103201_EU-CHINA_RAIL_ECONOMIC_CORRIDORS_AND_THEIR_ROLE_IN_TRADE_IN_GOODS

Raimbekov, Z., Syzdykbayeva, B., Rakhmetulina, Z., & Zhenskhan, D. (2018). The effectiveness of logistics development and its impact on the economies of the countries along the silk road passing through kazakhstan. *Transport Problems*, *13*(4), 127–14.

Ramasamy, B., & Yeun, M. C. H. (2019). China's One Belt One Road initiative: The impact of trade facilitation versus physical infrastructure on exports. *World Economy*, *42*, 1673–1694.

Rauf, A., Liu, X., Amin, W., Ozturk, I., Rehman, O. U., & Sarwar, S. (2018). Energy and ecological sustainability: Challenges and panoramas in Belt and Road initiative countries. *Sustainability*, *10*(8), 1–21. https://doi.org/10.3390/su10082743

Repuclic of Turkey Ministry of Foreing Affairs. (2021). *Türkiye'nin Çok taraflu Ulaştırma Politikası*, Retrieved May 01, 2021, from https://www.mfa.gov.tr/turkiye_nin-cok-tarafli-ulastirma-politikasi.tr.mfa

Repuplic of Turkey Ministry of Trade. (2020). *World Trade by Countries (2005-2020).* Retrieved May 28, 2021, from https://ticaret.gov.tr/istatistikler/dis-ticaret-istatistikleri/ulkelere-gore-dunya-ticareti-2005-2020

TANAP. (2021). *Tanap Nedir?* Retrieved May 20, 2021, from https://www.tanap.com/tanap-projesi/tanap-nedir/

TCDD. (2021). *Lojistik Merkezler*. Retrieved May 28, 2021, from https://www.tcdd.gov.tr/harita/lojistik-merkezleri

The Grand National Assembly of Turkey (TBMM). (2015, November). The Draft Law (1/673) and the Foreign Affairs Commission Report on the Approval of the Memorandum of Understanding between the Government of the Republic of Turkey and the Government of the People's Republic of China on the Harmonization of the Silk Road Economic Belt, the 21st Century Silk Road at Sea and the Middle Corridor Initiative.

Wang, M. L., Qiub, Q., & Choic, C. H. (2019). How will the Belt and Road initiative advance China's exports? *Asia Pacific Business Review*, *25*(1), 81–89. https://doi.org/10.1080/13602381.2018.1525855

Wu, Y., Chen, C., & Hu, C. (2021). The impacts of trade intensity with China on carbon emissions in belt and road countries. *Journal of the Asia Pacific Economy*, 1–20. doi:10.1080/13547860.2021.1924601

Xinhua. (2016). *Chronology of China's Belt and Road Initiative, last modified 24 June.* Retrieved April 21, 2021, from http://news.xinhuanet.com/english/2016-06/24/c_135464233.htm

Yazdani, M., Chatterjee, P., Pamucar, D., & Chakraborty, S. (2020). Development of an integrated decision making model for location selection of logistics centers in the Spanish autonomous communities. *Expert Systems with Applications*, *148*(113208), 1–21.

Zakaria, N., Abdul-Talib, A. N., & Amelinckx, A. (Eds.). (2020). *Transcending Cultural Frontiers: Practices, Challenges, and Strategy for International Business*. Springer.

Zakaria, N., Abdul-Talib, A. N., & Amelinckx, A. (2020). Advancing cultural frontiers to champion global business in emerging markets. In *Transcending Cultural Frontiers* (pp. 1–10). Springer.

Zakaria, N., Abdul-Talib, A. N., & Othman, N. (Eds.). (2016). *Handbook of research on impacts of international business and political affairs on the global economy*. IGI Global.

Zhang, W., Alon, I., & Lattemann, C. (2018). *China's Belt and Road Initiative: Changing the Rules of Globalization*. Palgrave.

ADDITIONAL READING

Anderson, P. (2020). Not a Silk Road: Trading networks between China and the Middle East as a dynamic interaction of competing Eurasian geographies. *Global Networks-A Journal Of Transnational Affairs*, *20*(4), 708–724. doi:10.1111/glob.12271

Ehteshami, A., & Horesh, N. (Eds.). (2018). *China's Presence in the Middle East: The Implications of the One Belt, One Road Initiative*. Routledge.

Gui, Q., Liu, C., & DeBin, D. (2019). The structure and dynamic of scientific collaboration network among countries along the Belt and Road. *Sustainability*, *11*(19), 5187, 1-17.

Hashim, F., Bakar, A. R. A., & Abdul-Talib, A. N. (2010). *International Business* (2nd ed.). Oxford Fajar Press.

Zakaria, N., Abdul-Talib, A. N., & Amelinckx, A. (Eds.). (2020). *Transcending Cultural Frontiers: Practices, Challenges, and Strategy for International Business*. Springer. doi:10.1007/978-981-15-4454-5

Zakaria, N., Abdul-Talib, A. N., & Othman, N. (Eds.). (2016). *Handbook of research on impacts of international business and political affairs on the global economy*. IGI Global. doi:10.4018/978-1-4666-9806-2

Zamani, M. N. S., Ashari, H., & Abdul-Talib, A. N. (2017). The strategic fit of multiple strategic orientations and new product development performance in Malaysian manufacturing firms. *Journal for Studies in Management and Planning*, *3*(1), 87–101.

Zamani, S. N. M., & Abdul-Talib, A. N. (2016). Strategic orientations and new product success: The mediating impact of innovation speed. International Information Institute (Tokyo), 19(7B), 2785–2790.

KEY TERMS AND DEFINITIONS

Baku Tbilisi Kars Railway Line (BTK): It is a regional railway line that directly connects Azerbaijan, Georgia and Turkey.

Belt and Road Initiative (BRI): The initiative announced by Chinese President Xi Jinping during a series of visits to Central Asian and South Asian countries at the end of 2013.

Middle Corridor: The Trans-Caspian East-West-Middle Corridor Initiative.

Modes: Expresses the direction used in transportation. Seaway, railway, highway, airway, etc.

Silk Road Economic Belt (SREB): It is a world-famous trade route starting from China and extending to Europe through Anatolia and the Mediterranean.

Chapter 15
Exploring Cultural Factors Impacting Female Digital Entrepreneurs in Underdeveloped Countries:
A Comparative Analysis

Areeba Waseem Shaikh
University of Wollongong in Dubai, UAE

Norhayati Zakaria
https://orcid.org/0000-0002-3970-1694
University of Wollongong in Dubai, UAE

ABSTRACT

This chapter aims at understanding the cultural influence on female digital entrepreneurs in underdeveloped countries and the possible effects of cyberostracism by integrating the significance of culture and its influence on females providing a holistic view of how women with entrepreneurial desires experience challenges due to the identified existing gaps in underdeveloped countries. Besides sociocultural dynamics, education is a factor observed to be extremely impactful. Basic and digital literacy are considered essential to progress in conducting businesses across borders. From a digital perspective, "cyberostracism" is identified as a potential issue women could encounter due to lack of education. In this study, a comparative analysis on female digital entrepreneurs of the Asian and European region is conducted based on the view of a collectivistic and individualistic society concluded by providing a framework to minimize gaps and establish an environment for women to pursue digital entrepreneurship in their societies, mitigating the possible effects of cyberostracism.

DOI: 10.4018/978-1-7998-9071-3.ch015

INTRODUCTION

The field of entrepreneurship has been a popular topic in modern literature. The advantage of doing what interests you and establishing a business by putting your skills and capabilities to the best of its use has attracted many to pursue entrepreneurship as a career. In conjunction with entrepreneurship, adopting and implementing global strategies is a key factor in conducting cross border trade and businesses. The convenience that information age provides, has created a new economy and therefore given rise to "digital entrepreneurship" amongst all genders. This concept further explains the growth of an economy in relation to modern business processes and digitalization.

An entrepreneur is a person who has the willingness and capacity of developing, organizing, and managing a business. Entrepreneurship, specifically that incorporates innovation, is a vital component in fostering the growth of an economy (Fang and Collier, 2016). However, based on the following factors: political, technological, human resources and natural resources, it has been recognized that entrepreneurial activities differ in different economies.

The European and Asian regions are two such economies that have been identified, that differ from each other based on these factors. While it is noted that these factors may cause interruption with entrepreneurial activities, they will further result in obstruction of operating businesses across borders. A comparative study of these economies provides us with a comprehensive understanding of the impact on their respective economies and ultimately its results on conducting cross border trade and businesses. Research shows that the effect of the economies' socio-cultural dynamics and governmental support has had a great impact on the activities for conducting businesses within and outside, for its population. The difference in operations with regards to their human resources in the case of entrepreneurship has been observed closely in both the European and Asian economies (Kamberidou, 2020).

This chapter explains the socio-cultural aspect that has led to comparison of the entrepreneurial intention and activity in a digital environment, particularly with regards to women of the Asian region i.e., the underdeveloped region, with that of the European region i.e., the developed region. Majority of the females in underdeveloped countries undergo cultural and societal pressures along with the unsupportive economic environment, limiting them from progressing in conducting businesses.

Though the digital age has come about opening doors to many opportunities, the required infrastructure has not been adopted or established by many of the Asian countries, as opposed to European countries. Hence, digital activities have been severely constrained (Nambisan, 2017). This chapter explores the cultural factor from a view of the famous Dutch psychologist Greet Hofstede's cultural dimension. In particular, *individualism* and *collectivism*, with briefly incorporating the element of gender disparity to support the concept of having a wider perspective in conducting businesses globally.

Further to that the difference in literacy rates amongst women in the two societies, proves that education contributes greatly towards success of women being able to progress in different fields in developed countries as opposed to underdeveloped countries (Islami, 2019). Therefore, another challenge in conduction of cross border trade is little or no implementation of global strategies and policies in conducting business, the lack of technological know-how and ignorance of the issues the lack of knowledge can bring about. Though the digital age has come across many negative psychological and behavioural outcomes. The feeling of exclusion on digital platforms, a phenomenon known as cyberostracism, has shown a drastic decline in the well-being of people who are unable to handle this issue (Schneider et al., 2017). Therefore, our research question is: How do cultural factors impact female digital entrepreneurs in underdeveloped countries and the possible effects of cyberostracism on them?

It is firstly imperative to identify the existing gap between desired activities of female digital entrepreneurs and the socio-economic condition. Secondly, the possibilities of these females facing cyberostracism, a potential issue due to lack of ICT and STEM education and finally the impact on the country's economy to thrive and sustainably perform.

Past patterns of women entrepreneurial initiatives and leadership styles have not seen much of a change. The two regions, Asia and Europe have been taken into account for the purpose of conducting a comparative analysis from the view of a collectivistic and an individualistic society respectively, one of Hofstede's popular cultural dimensions (Kamberidou, 2020). As the terms suggest, in a collectivistic society decisions and judgements are group based, while an individualistic society is much liberal and allows for individuals to foster independently. Research articles and current statistics provide sufficient evidence in this context, addressing the identified issue.

Additionally, cyberostracism has been studied and analyzed from the perspective of digital entrepreneurs and how the appropriate education attained can influence the cognitive dimension of an individual and aid in overcoming the effects of this phenomenon (Schneider et al., 2017). Higher education permits for digital literacy i.e., the basic skills set needed to pursue digital activities. It acts as an enabler to overcome the digital skills gap. To carry forward and execute with these knowledge and expertise, support is extremely crucial, whether from home, society, or the government. In the European region it has been on the rise, while in the case of underdeveloped countries what adds on is gender disparity with regards to entrepreneurship. The structure of the chapter is followed by highlighting and discussing key findings on cultural factors influencing female digital entrepreneurs in underdeveloped countries as opposed to developed countries in the light of education and effect of cyberostracism. In accordance with that a proposed framework based on Hofstede's cultural dimension has been presented. Further a correlation analysis has been performed to support our research question, that provides a holistic view of the economic freedom on literacy outcome of females with finally discussing the challenges faced by stakeholders in operating businesses across the globe.

LITERATURE REVIEW

Individualism vs Collectivism

Geert Hofstede (1984) defines culture as "the collective programming of the mind that distinguishes the members of one group or category of people from others." While there are five of Hofstede's cultural dimensions; power distance, individualism vs collectivism, masculinity vs femininity, uncertainty avoidance and long-term orientation, this chapter focuses on individualistic vs collectivistic societies with consideration to masculinity vs femininity. This particular dimension has been taken into consideration as it relates closely with female digital entrepreneurs in underdeveloped countries and helps define the gaps and issues (Kamberidou, 2020).

From an entrepreneurial perspective, key points presented in research in relation to the success of an economy from the cultural dimension, (Gorodnichenko and Roland, 2017) in their research argue that individualistic cultures encourage more innovation as opposed to collectivistic culture. The European region is an example that has embedded an individualistic culture where they provide high social status for people that have made valuable inventions. The emphasis is on personal freedom and accomplishments, hence important innovations are awarded. These innovations are stimulated by governmental support such as monetary rewards and robust encouragement to innovate. The stimulation of radical innovations adds further towards operating and managing businesses in other countries. In comparison, the Asian cultural values are aligned with collectivism, where actions are taken collectively, and people are discouraged to make decisions based on their personal thoughts and ideas. In terms of operating and managing businesses across borders, "individualism has a dynamic effect whereas collectivism has a static effect."

Brush et al. (2018) in their research emphasize on the effect of gender in an entrepreneurial environment, proposing that women are at a disadvantage on different levels of the entrepreneurial ecosystem, organizational level, institutional level and individual level. Asian collectivists countries may consider gender roles to be social norms or standards that determine responsibilities as well as opportunities. Characteristics of entrepreneurs such as ambition, risk-takers and bold have been coupled to masculine behaviourism. To support their study, they have presented data from the World Economic Forum that identifies seven components out of which, culture, education and finance are most relevant. Considering that the regulatory institution is designed by the government, it is likely that there is a hidden angle towards gender, decreasing the probability and interest of women entrepreneurs. (Brush et al., 2018) from their analysis of 28 countries prove that countries with normative institutional support such as childcare, gender equality, tax regulations property ownership and so on, are more likely to aid women in maintaining a work-life balance, overcoming the gender role conflict, similar to what (Gorodnichenko and Roland, 2017) have mentioned in their research.

WOMEN ENTREPRENEURS/DIGITAL ENTREPRENEURS

This chapter explains that women entrepreneurs are continuously facing the multitasking behaviors which could be described as juggling through personal, professional and social obligations along with trying to pursue their goals, eventually experiencing a role conflict. The multitasking whirlpool is mainly the result of gender role expectations. Evidence of some Asian countries like Pakistan, India, Jordan and Egypt shows that dual role is a great obstacle which prevails in career imbalance with support of the same claim from western culture. Kamberidou (2020) further identifies the need of implementation of policies in support of women that enable them to pursue careers as digital entrepreneurs, as well as accommodating women in ICT and STEM education to attract more females in the tech field. In comparison with the western society, women in developing countries face many more challenges due to sociocultural barriers. Such challenges are often unidentified or not taken into consideration and therefore makes it difficult for women to manage businesses inside or outside of their economies. These challenges include, gender inequality, lack of education, lack of opportunities, financial resources and digital exclusion.Whilst, Nsengimana et al. (2018) in her research claims that culture strengthens gender gaps. She further provides data on the level of education for women; while 61% received primary education, 26.3% received high school education and only 11.7% achieved tertiary education. While social media provides new opportunities, lack of education or of basic digital skills set becomes an obstacle to identify or make use of these opportunities.

Besides, Kamberidou (2020) illustrates that entrepreneurship is most often linked to innovation which allows sustenance of economic viability by applying technology. Their contribution is responsible for increase in income per capita and likewise solves unemployment issues. In her research she further implies that the European region has been involved in discussions for implementing policies and procedures towards initiatives to increase the number of women working in cybercommunity.

In line with the above, McAdam, Crowley and Harrison (2019) take three pillars of entrepreneurial system; policy, infrastructure and culture, similar to the research of Brush et al., (2018) which provide evidence that an underdeveloped institutional framework and unsupportive culture is a major limitation towards female entrepreneurship. It further takes into consideration the concept of gender disparity, creating an unsupportive environment for females to grow as entrepreneurs in Saudi Arabia. The economy of Saudi Arabia is wealthy, but male dominated. There may be ample entrepreneurial resources as well as financial resources, but entrepreneurial support also requires strong social and cultural structures with quality education and well-established infrastructures. Two of the four key social and cultural voids identified in this paper, relevant to our research issues are gender segregation and expectations of the society from women. Additionally, their research agrees with the importance of implementing policies towards development of an entrepreneurial environment.

Moving forward, Nambisan (2017) in his research emphasizes greatly on digital platforms and digital infrastructure with relevant implications of digital entrepreneurship to innovators and entrepreneurship. He demonstrates that digital platforms are a big contribution to opportunities for entrepreneurs. For example, at the time of the global pandemic due to COVID-19, regulatory authorities compelled companies to have their employees work from home, a drastic shift took place towards digitizing studies, work and other businesses related activities. The digital infrastructure that comprises technology, tools and systems provide a favorable environment to innovation and individual entrepreneurs as well as companies for communication and collaboration across borders which is identified to be extremely necessary if the world is in a crisis like a global pandemic. With the illustration of Davidson's entrepreneurial opportunity framework proves that digital infrastructure works as an external support mechanism in the process of the outcome. Further to that while digital platforms allow for value creation, digital platforms allow groups to engage in their entrepreneurial initiatives. Additionally, he highlights that the individuals in these groups are dynamic and take initiatives centered around their goals and capabilities. In terms of governance, individuals can easily bring into action their skills and capabilities in open structures as opposed to closed structures. It is also been highlighted that the implication on entrepreneurial cognition stating that entrepreneurs draw on their memory and prior experiences to compare and analyze the superficial features of a new stimulus in deciphering a new opportunity (Nambisan 2017). New digital infrastructures together with the associated social, cognitive, and institutional elements may shape the entrepreneurial processes and outcomes, making them less predictable.

Similarly, Ryan, Allen, Gray, and Mclnerny (2017) have examined digital literacy, (computer and internet) correlating with digital intent. They claim that the intention towards entrepreneurship is connected to entrepreneurial behavior through digital literacy. Their method provides results of 30% theoretical knowledge while 70% practical knowledge with emphasis being on digital entrepreneurship, their research suggests that more focus on practical learning with digital platforms and e-commerce has a meaningful effect alongside necessary theoretical knowledge of marketing strategies on social media and other online platforms.

CYBEROSTRACISM AND ITS POSSIBLE EFFECTS ON WOMEN ENTREPRENEURS

Adding to Ryan, Allen, Gray, and Mclnerny's research we look at the issue of cyberostracism. Conducting businesses across borders through the digital platform requires an individual to handle two types of cultures, real and virtual, simultaneously. While the real culture comes from the society a person is living in, the virtual culture comes from the cybersociety a person is operating their business in. Societal culture is inevitably embedded in individuals from childhood, it is not something to be learnt but rather a set of values and beliefs that shape your thoughts and leads to a similar behavior to that of the people in the society (Gorodnichenko and Roland, 2017). On the other hand, virtual culture is a universe of its own, especially if one would want to conduct businesses related operations through digitalization. Cyberostracism is well described in the research of Ryan, Allen, Gray, and Mclnerny (2017) as a phenomenon that occurs when internet users feel excluded or perceive lack of feedback from online community members. The sense of belonging to a community can be psychologically satisfying primarily for contentment with life and increased welfare. The same has been agreed by Kamberidou in her findings, entrepreneurial initiatives taken by women are mostly for personal fulfilment and not just profit. In addition, her findings prove a strong correlation between female entrepreneurship and digital media (Kamberidou, 2020). Similarly, Nambisan in his research mentions the cognitive effect on entrepreneurs from engaging in social media and how high constraints lead to negative outcomes. According to Ryan, Allen, Gray, and Mclnerny (2017) females may lack sense of usability of the online platform and tools as well as not realize the time that should be devoted to these activities. Thus, their time for offline interactions may be taken up resulting in harmful psychological effects. The sense of usability can come from practical education of digital tools. Hence, understanding the virtual culture and its effects on a person's psychology and behavior, requires quality education in the digital context.

In these fast-paced times an individual's mind towards the virtual culture has been programmed in such a manner that they may expect to receive instant responses, attain a loyal following on social media platforms and get offended by negative feedback (Schneider et al., 2017). Psychologically, women may experience feelings of exclusion from the cybercommunity leading to frustration and further impacting their behavior negatively. Thus, impacting their entrepreneurial performance resulting in either completely abandoning the idea of pursuing digital entrepreneurship or reduced positive outcome of their business. Therefore, in accordance with the research of (Kamberidou, 2020) women should be provided with ICT and STEM education to encourage their perusal.

RESEARCH METHODOLOGY

This research is based on secondary data presented in journal articles in the past five years by different scholars and researchers which we developed a comparative analysis. The articles selected are from the area of management, psychology, behavior, culture, economics and information technology. These research areas and articles have been chosen with relevance to key themes of this research paper: Culture, Cross border trade, Female Digital Entrepreneurs and Cyberostracism. Cultural study is an area that is still applied in various research that connect human psychology and behaviorism. In academic resources, culture in its simplest form is defined as the shared set of values, beliefs and behavioral patterns common in groups of people (Gorodnichenko and Roland, 2017). Culture has been observed to differ in different regions, countries, and societies and therefore to answer our research question we firstly explore the cultural dimension in our chosen regions, Asia and Europe. In accordance with our chosen regions, we examine Greet Hofstede's study on culture, particularly studying individualism and collectivism in depth. The cultural theme has been further investigated in relation to females. Given the cultural difference we identify the factors within the cultural context that contribute towards successful female digital entrepreneurs in these regions allowing for a better scope to digitally conduct businesses and trade across borders. To prove the contribution of the cultural framework towards economic well-being, of individualistic and collectivistic societies, we create a linkage of the cultural pattern followed in these regions to their economic standing.

Secondly, we explore the studies focusing particularly on female digital entrepreneurs with relevance to culture, providing an insight to gender roles, societal pressures, governmental support and education in the developed and underdeveloped regions. The study further leads to recognizing the impact of these factors on entrepreneurial opportunities for females, their intent to pursue digital entrepreneurship and the outcome of entrepreneurial performance, a major point of study of this research. Moving forward, analyzing the impact of education further leads to an interesting phenomenon, known as cyberostracism, important to acknowledge in the case of digital entrepreneurship. Therefore, existing literature on virtual culture versus the real culture in the context of cyberostracism has been explored. The study of cyberostracism aided in comprehension of the possible negative effects it could have on females in underdeveloped countries due lack of digital literacy (Bandera and Passerini, 2018).

We further examine how these effects could cause harm to an economy as whole, and not just individuals, in the development of conducting businesses globally, and were able to conclude that females with inadequate basic or digital literacy could likely experience psychological insecurity leading to adverse behaviorism. In our research we highlight cyberostracism as a possible issue that could cause deterioration in the intention, desires and performance of female digital entrepreneurs leading to economies deteriorating. On that account we contribute our gathered data and literature to define a framework based on Hofstede's cultural dimension explaining how effects of cyberostracism can be minimized through a systematic structure and further increase not only the economic wellbeing of underdeveloped countries but also aid in conducting businesses outside their country with efficient use of technology. Lastly, a correlation analysis has been performed by collecting data of the economic freedom score and women literacy rates to prove the significance of high standard economic environment towards individuals.

DATA ANALYSIS

Below tables present a comparative analysis of the countries in the European region and the Asian region with the highest and lowest 10 countries' ranking by tech, data and business skills.

Figure 1. Asian Countries ranking by tech, data and business skills
Source: Harvard Business Review, 2020

Lowest	Business skill	Tech skill	Data skill
No. 51	Ecuador	South Korea	India
No. 52	U.A.E	Vietnam	Indonesia
No. 53	Nigeria	Turkey	Kenya
No. 54	Indonesia	Indonesia	Vietnam
No. 55	South Korea	Philippines	Egypt
No. 56	Turkey	Bangladesh	Turkey
No. 57	Pakistan	Egypt	Bangladesh
No. 58	Saudi Arabia	Kenya	Saudi Arabia
No. 59	Bangladesh	Pakistan	Pakistan
No. 60	Egypt	Nigeria	Nigeria

Figure 2. European Countries ranking by tech, data and business skills
Source: Harvard Business Review, 2020

Highest	Business skill	Tech skill	Data skill
No. 1	Finland	Argentina	Israel
No. 2	Switzerland	Czech Republic	Switzerland
No. 3	Austria	Austria	Belgium
No. 4	Netherlands	Spain	Austria
No. 5	Belgium	Poland	Sweden
No. 6	New Zealand	Belarus	Czech Republic
No. 7	Germany	Germany	Germany
No. 8	Sweden	Sweden	France
No. 9	Australia	Belgium	United Kingdom
No. 10	Canada	Finland	Poland

Figure 1 consists of countries mostly from the Asian region and Figure 2 consists of countries from the European region. This is in agreement with Gorodnichenko and Roland (2017) research that "people from an individualistic culture should be working in research-oriented occupations as independent thinking will result in better idea generation". In addition to the above, the charts below illustrate countries from the European and Asian region from the context of individualism and collectivism.

Figure 3. Country Comparison; European countries
Source: Greet Hofstede, 2020

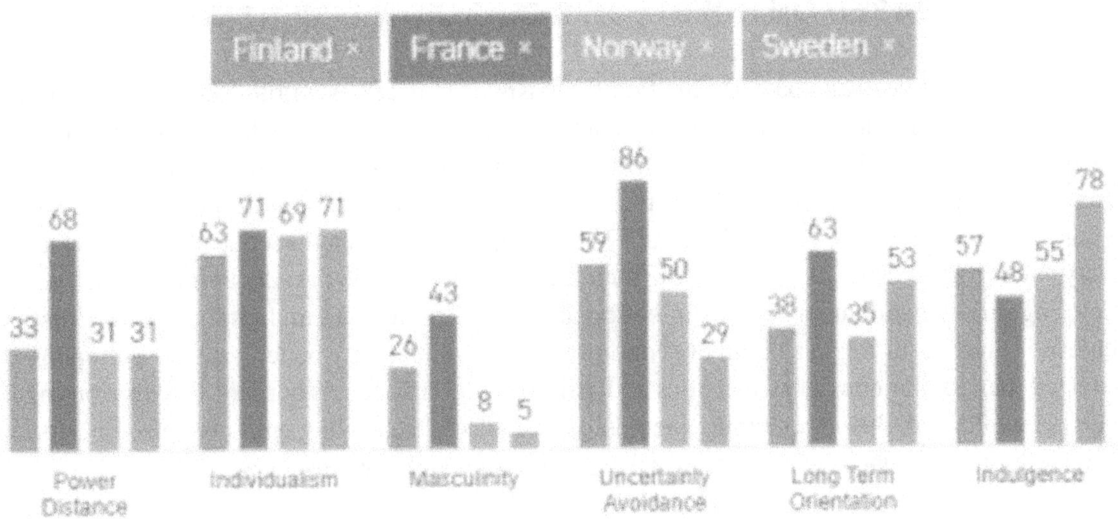

Figure 4. Country Comparison; Asian Countries
Source: Greet Hofstede, 2020

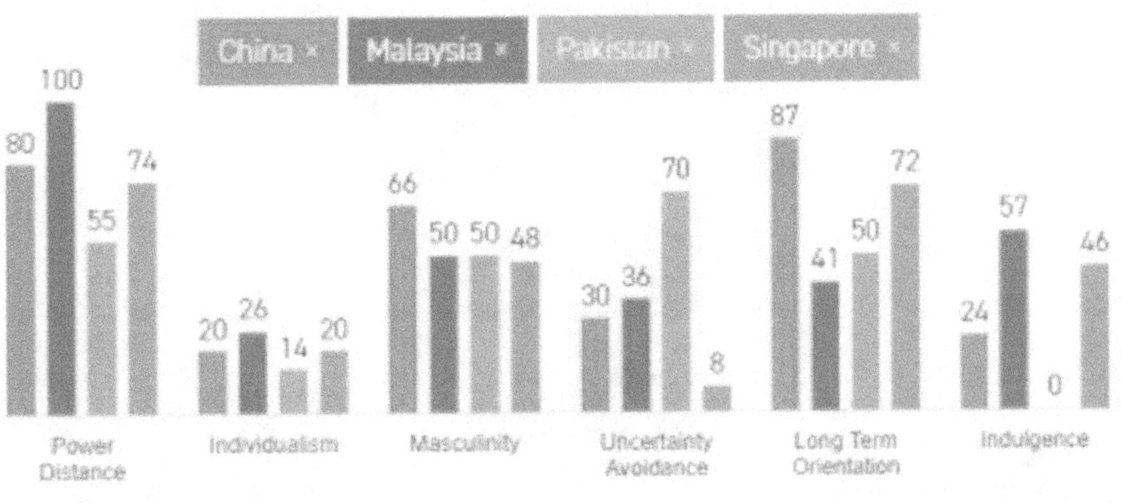

The data supports our findings from the literature review that the European region being an individualistic society has better economic stability as opposed to the Asian region being a collectivistic society and hence better scope to survive a global crisis, such as a pandemic that disrupts the business activities of the world, as it has a well-established infrastructure in place.

FRAMEWORK BASED ON HOFSTEDE'S CULTURAL DIMENSION

The following framework has been defined on the basis of Hofstede's cultural dimension. Firstly, the focus on individualism and collectivism allows us to identify key factors such as socio-cultural, socio-economic, governmental laws, digital infrastructure and financial support that have a remarkable influence on female digital entrepreneurs. While these factors allow to build opportunities, it can also bring in challenges of overcoming the digital skills gap. Therefore, it is important that education is provided, after a society or economy invests in strengthening their foundation. Through the education of basic and digital literacy, cognitive development towards intention and desire to innovate in digital entrepreneurship can be achieved. Thus, resulting in a boom of economic welfare by enabling better ways for entrepreneurs to operate and manage their business decisions and activities digitally across borders, by contributing to the income per capita and closing unemployment gaps. And lastly improving entrepreneurial performance by understanding the challenges cyberostracism can cause and mitigating its effects.

Figure 5. Framework based on cultural dimension

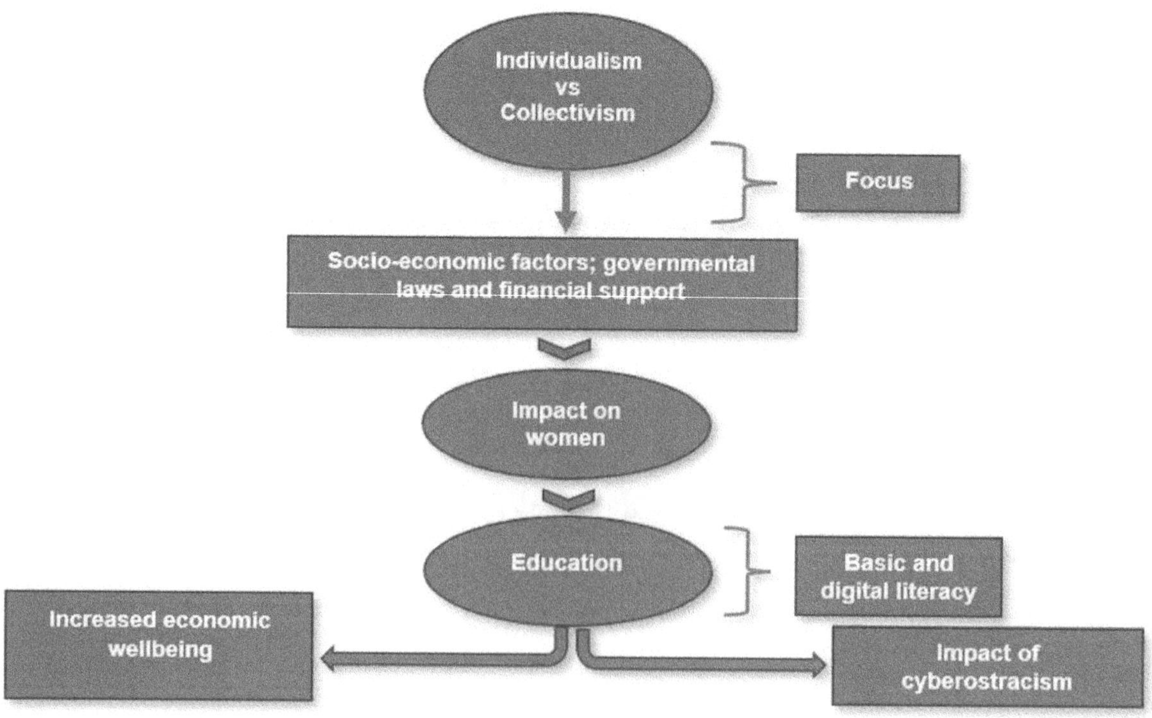

CORRELATION ANALYSIS

To further support our argument about the impact of economic support for women contributing greatly towards higher female literacy rates, to aid with conducting businesses outside of their countries, we conducted a correlation analysis. The two variables are the female literacy rates and economic freedom score. The term "economic freedom" is defined as the ability of people from a society to take economic actions. The table below includes female literacy rates of countries from both regions studied in this research as well as the economic freedom score of each country.

Table 1. Country Rankings: World & Global Economy Rankings on Economic Freedom

Countries	Female Literacy Rate %	Economic Freedom Score
Pakistan	**42.73**	**54.8**
India	**62.98**	**56.5**
Bangladesh	**58.31**	**56.4**
Egypt	**68.06**	**54.0**
U.A.E	**95.10**	**76.2**
Saudi Arabia	**91.84**	**62.4**
Spain	**99.60**	**66.9**
Poland	**99.80**	**69.1**
Austria	**99.00**	**73.3**
Germany	**99.00**	**73.5**
Sweden	**99.00**	**74.9**
Finland	**99.00**	**75.7**
	Correlation coefficient 'r'	**0.87469**

(Index of Economic Freedom, 2020)

From the analysis above, the correlation coefficient value 'r' 0.87469 indicates a positive correlation between the two variables proving that greater economic freedom correlates with higher literacy rates. In accordance with our research, a higher literacy rate aids in better entrepreneurial performance leading to better conduction of cross border trade and businesses which would ultimately lead improved economic standing.

Figure 6. Correlation Graphical Analysis

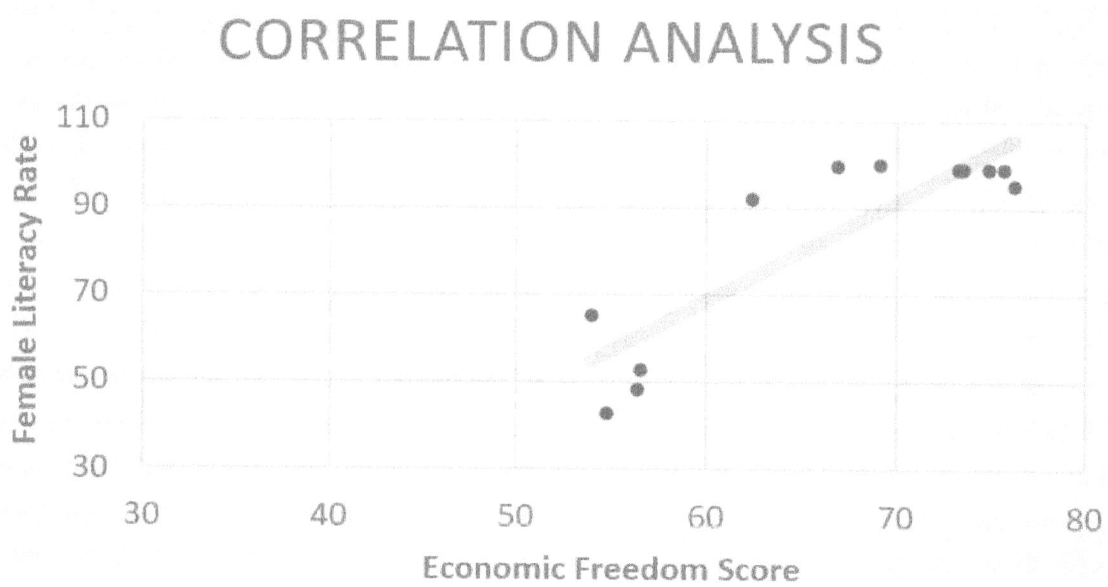

LIMITATIONS

Though there is sufficient research study on the topic of cyberostracism in the context of virtual culture, a lack of previous research study is noticed especially in the context of real culture, gender and age. Moreover, it is primarily available from the perspective of youngsters, students, customers and daily users of social media, without any direct effects on adults or digital entrepreneurs. Additionally, to a great extent, research papers included data from either a collectivistic dimension or an individualistic dimension, in the context of culture, a cross-culture viewpoint was not given due consideration as that could have probably provided us with an understanding of how a balanced society operates. Although there is evidence of collectivistic societies acknowledging to propel towards the balanced approach. The cultural dimension was implied for women residing in particular regions and did not take into account the impact on psychology or behavior of women who may have migrated to an individualistic society from a collectivistic one. Furthermore, researching the gender aspect could provide more insight in terms of comparing the contribution each gender brings to the economic welfare of a country by carrying out business activities within their economy or outside of it.

CONCLUSION

Culture is observed to be a significant factor of economic development in terms of innovation, growth and conducting businesses across borders. In our discussion we highlight that while sociocultural factors have a great impact on individuals, they also impact economic well-being of a country. Thus, establishment of a digital infrastructure as well as implementation of legislation and policies with regards to e-business is necessary, to allow for opportunities for women to innovate, increase their parameters of conducting businesses and provide them with financial support. Since there is demand in countries like Pakistan for women run business (Kamberidou, 2020) providing the right infrastructure and educating women would encourage development of female digital entrepreneurs in underdeveloped countries. Further to that females in underdeveloped countries are more vulnerable to impacts of cyberostracism and therefore with education, psychological impact of cyberostracism can be minimized, hence improving entrepreneurial activity and performance. From the proposed framework we recognize that embedding standards and procedures in citizens requires an optimum education system, from an early on stage. It is empirical that education builds a foundation of psychological, behavioral and political aspects as citizens with higher education have a better understanding of their emotional thoughts and feelings and therefore better self-control. It further moulds their minds towards identifying meaningful opportunities in the smallest of problems.

REFERENCES

Ahmed, Z., Su, L., Rafique, K., Khan, S., & Jamil, S. (2017). A study on the factors affecting consumer buying behavior towards online shopping in Pakistan. *Journal of Asian Business Strategy*, *7*(2), 44–56.

Al Majali, S. (2020). The digital world for children and its relationship with personality disorders: Exploring emerging technologies. *International Journal of Emerging Technologies in Learning*, *15*(01), 213. doi:10.3991/ijet.v15i01.11412

Ashraf, A., Razzaque, M., & Thongpapanl, N. (2016). The role of customer regulatory orientation and fit in online shopping across cultural contexts. *Journal of Business Research*, *69*(12), 6040–6047. doi:10.1016/j.jbusres.2016.05.019

Bandera, C., & Passerini, K. (2018). Personality traits and the digital entrepreneur: A new breed or same actor? *Twenty-fourth Americas Conference on Information Systems*, 1-10.

Baruh, L., & Cemalcılar, Z. (2018). When more is more? The impact of breadth and depth of information disclosure on attributional confidence about and interpersonal attraction to a social network site profile owner. *Cyberpsychology (Brno)*, *12*(1), 1. doi:10.5817/CP2018-1-1

Brush, C., Edelman, L., Harrison, R., Hechavarria, D., Justo, R., & McAdam, M. (2018). A gendered look at entrepreneurship ecosystems. *Academy of Management Proceedings*, *2018*(1), 16912. doi:10.5465/AMBPP.2018.16912symposium

Choi, H. (2015). The young generation and their social media. *Sociétés*, *129*(3), 105. doi:10.3917oc.129.0105

Dy, A., Marlow, S., & Martin, L. (2016). A Web of opportunity or the same old story? Women digital entrepreneurs and intersectionality theory. *Human Relations*, *70*(3), 286–311. doi:10.1177/0018726716650730

Gorodnichenko, Y., & Roland, G. (2017). Culture, Institutions, and the Wealth of Nations. *The Review of Economics and Statistics*, *99*(3), 402–416. doi:10.1162/REST_a_00599

Gudmanian, A., Drotianko, L., Sydorenko, S., Zhuravliova, O. & Yahodzinskyi, S. (2019). Social transformations of speech culture in information age. *E3S Web of Conferences*, *135*.

Harvard Business Review. (2020). *Ranking Countries And Industries By Tech, Data, And Business Skills*. Available at: https://hbr.org/2019/05/ranking-countries-and industries-by-tech-data-and-business-skills

Hashim, F., Bakar, A. R. A., & Talib, A. N. (2010). *International Business* (2nd ed.). Oxford Fajar Press.

Heritage.org. (2020). *Country Rankings: World & Global Economy Rankings On Economic Freedom*. Available at: https://www.heritage.org/index/ranking

Hofstede Insights. (2020). *Country Comparison - Hofstede Insights*. Available at: https://www.hofstede-insights.com/country-comparison/

Islami, N. (2019). The effect of digital literacy toward enterpreneur behaviors through students' intention enterpreneurship on Economics Education Study Program at Jember. *IOP Conference Series. Earth and Environmental Science*, *243*, 1–9. doi:10.1088/1755-1315/243/1/012084

Kamberidou, I. (2020). "Distinguished" women entrepreneurs in the digital economy and the multitasking whirlpool. *Journal of Innovation and Entrepreneurship*, *9*(1), 3. doi:10.118613731-020-0114-y

Kothgassner, O., Griesinger, M., Kettner, K., Wayan, K., Völkl-Kernstock, S., Hlavacs, H., Beutl, L., & Felnhofer, A. (2017). Real-life prosocial behavior decreases after being socially excluded by avatars, not agents. *Computers in Human Behavior*, *70*, 261–269. doi:10.1016/j.chb.2016.12.059

McAdam, M., Crowley, C., & Harrison, R. (2019). "To boldly go where no [man] has gone before" - Institutional voids and the development of women's digital entrepreneurship. *Technological Forecasting and Social Change*, *146*, 912–922. doi:10.1016/j.techfore.2018.07.051

Nambisan, S. (2017). Digital entrepreneurship: Toward a digital technology perspective of entrepreneurship. *Entrepreneurship Theory and Practice*, *41*(6), 1029–1055. doi:10.1111/etap.12254

Nonnenmacher, V., Oliveira, L., Villamil, M., & Bodmann, B. (2014). Modeling and visualization individual and collective opinions towards extremism in a society. *Procedia Computer Science*, *29*, 2412–2421. doi:10.1016/j.procs.2014.05.225

Robinson, L., Cotten, S., Ono, H., Quan-Haase, A., Mesch, G., Chen, W., Schulz, J., Hale, T., & Stern, M. (2015). Digital inequalities and why they matter. *Information Communication and Society*, *18*(5), 569–582. doi:10.1080/1369118X.2015.1012532

Roser, M., & Ortiz-Ospina, E. (2020). *Literacy*. Our World in Data. Available at: https://ourworldindata.org/literacy

Ryan, T., Allen, K., Gray, D., & McInerney, D. (2017). How Social Are Social Media? A Review of Online Social Behaviour and Connectedness. *Journal of Relationships Research*, *8*, 8. doi:10.1017/jrr.2017.13

Schneider, F., Zwillich, B., Bindl, M., Hopp, F., Reich, S., & Vorderer, P. (2017). Social media ostracism: The effects of being excluded online. *Computers in Human Behavior*, *73*, 385–393. doi:10.1016/j.chb.2017.03.052

Tandon, U., Kiran, R., & Sah, A. (2017). Analyzing customer satisfaction: Users perspective towards online shopping. *Nankai Business Review International*, *8*(3), 266–288. doi:10.1108/NBRI-04-2016-0012

Zakaria, N., Abdul-Talib, A. N., & Amelinckx, A. (Eds.). (2020). *Transcending Cultural Frontiers: Practices, Challenges, and Strategy for International Business*. Springer. doi:10.1007/978-981-15-4454-5

Zakaria, N., Abdul-Talib, A. N., & Amelinckx, A. (2020). Advancing cultural frontiers to champion global business in emerging markets. In *Transcending Cultural Frontiers* (pp. 1–10). Springer. doi:10.1007/978-981-15-4454-5_1

Zakaria, N., Abdul-Talib, A. N., & Othman, N. (Eds.). (2016). *Handbook of research on impacts of international business and political affairs on the global economy*. IGI Global. doi:10.4018/978-1-4666-9806-2

Chapter 16
COVID-19's Impact on Tertiary Institutions in Nigeria and Its Effects on the Economy

Temitope Teniola Onileowo
https://orcid.org/0000-0001-7136-6403
Universiti Teknologi Malaysia, Malaysia & Ekiti State University, Nigeria

Farrah Merlinda Muharam
https://orcid.org/0000-0002-6429-2044
Universiti Teknologi Malaysia, Malaysia

Mohd Khairuddin Ramliy
https://orcid.org/0000-0002-2114-5896
Universiti Teknologi Malaysia, Malaysia

ABSTRACT

This chapter addressed Coronavirus disease 2019 (COVID-19) impact on tertiary institutions in Nigeria, its effect on the economy, and possible coping strategies in a time of global pandemic and national disaster. COVID-19 was reported as a pandemic by the World Health Organization (WHO) on March 11, 2020, discovered in Wuhan, China, in December 2019, spread to several nations, forcing the closure of tertiary institutions all over the world. The effect has also disrupted the school academic calendar at tertiary institutions, decreased international education, Suspension of local and international conferences, etc. And the economy, leading to job losses, revenue loss in the informal sector, business closure, agricultural production and food insecurity, a sharp drop in oil revenues, and economic uncertainties. Which, thus, harms the economy. This chapter makes recommendations to assist Nigeria's government and the educational institutions in coping with the effect of the outbreak and similar pandemics soon.

DOI: 10.4018/978-1-7998-9071-3.ch016

INTRODUCTION

In history, humankind has experienced various pandemics where some of which were disastrous than others. The 1918 pandemic, popularly referred to as the Spanish Flu, killed more than 50 million people worldwide, where more than 14 million people died in India and Britain alone. The impact of the pandemic had grown broader and more global. It had a significant effect on World War I. Imperial borders and large-scale deprivation are exacerbated by unemployment and inflation through a range of countries. The pandemic increased the movements of liberation in former colonies and pushed nations to implement universal healthcare policies. It has also led to advances in epidemiology, virology, and vaccine production.

Fast forward a century, the Covid-19 pandemic went on its disastrous course at various timelines in different parts of the world. The pandemic has wreaked havoc on economies around the globe. Experts anticipate that the outbreak will cause the country to enter a worldwide financial crisis (Ozili, 2020). This virus has claimed many lives all around the world. Table 1 summarises the number of reported cases and deaths worldwide since the start of the Covid-19 pandemic. There were 5,203,796 cases and 336,559 deaths worldwide as of the 24th of May 2020, as shown in the table below.

Table 1. Global Covid-19 statistics as of 24th May 2020.

Region	Total confirmed cases	Total deaths
Africa	77,295	2,073
Americas	2,338,124	138,116
Eastern Mediterranean	415,806	10,988
Europe	2,006,984	173,886
South-East Asia	191,966	5,748
Western Pacific	173,621	5,748
Total	**5,203,796**	**336,559**

Source: WHO

In December 2019, a novel coronavirus outbreak was first reported in Wuhan, Province of Hubei, China. Nigeria recorded its first case on the 27th of February 2020 (Ohia, Bakarey, & Ahmad, 2020). According to the Nigeria Centre for Disease Control (NCDC), the virus has spread to over 30 states. The number of reported cases and deaths is rising daily (Nigeria Centre for Disease Control, 2020). Table 2 shows the number of reported cases and deaths recorded by the NCDC from 17th to 23rd May 2020.

Table 2 shows that the pandemic has caused Nigerians immense hardships. Many individuals have lost their lives, jobs, and their businesses as a result of the disaster. The economy of Nigeria has also suffered significant damage. The outbreak has harmed several economic sectors, including Education, manufacturing, banking, agriculture, sports, hospitality, aviation, and transportation, to name a few. For example, the pandemic has resulted in enormous flight cancellations in the airline industry. People have been unable to travel overseas for further studies, business, or personal reasons as a result of the worldwide travel prohibition. The hospitality business has also been hit hard by the pandemic. Several guesthouses have closed due to the lockdown rule, and their operations, revenues, and sales have all suffered. Including several hotel bookings were cancelled, as expected. Based on this specific pandemic, the national authority enforced a higher degree of restrictions on individuals and businesses alike. The nation's customers are required to participate in social distance activities. This virus has triggered so many calamities in the education sector and the world economy.

Table 2. Nigeria's Covid-19 statistics from 17th to 23rd May 2020.

Date	Total confirmed cases	Total deaths
17/05/20	5,621	176
18/05/20	5,959	182
19/05/20	6,175	191
20/05/20	6,401	192
21/05/20	6,677	200
22/05/20	7,016	211
23/05/20	7,261	221

Source: WHO

In many respects, the post-coronavirus world would be different-economically, socially, and health-wise (Donthu & Gustafsson, 2020). Nobody is going to get out of this crisis without losing something. Ironically, this pandemic has targeted one of the essential things in modern society: human freedom, as this has a direct and severe effect on every sector, most especially on education and the economy worldwide, particularly those requiring physical contact. While everyone anticipated a turnaround in the economy, the Corona Pandemic has tossed almost a knocking punch affecting the global education sector, economic activity and adding a supply shock to the economy. Many of the nation's commercial outlets were forced to remain closed. Educational institutions' operations across the globe have been disrupted, resulting in total shutdowns of all tertiary institutions. Many were losing their jobs, connections, loss of income and revenues, increased government expenditure, accumulated debts, and a drop in government allocation to the education sector, among others, due to the Covid-19 (He & Harris, 2020).

Moreover, adequate financial support plays a significant role in maintaining and improving the quality of Education and effectively transforming the institution's landscape. Hence, the importance of appropriate financial support in any institution's organisational growth and development, be it social, economic, business, political, educational, among others, cannot be overemphasised. It should be noted that a properly funded institution provides a template for quality education through guaranteed academic pursuit where an expected high-level workforce is generated. Apart from human capital, adequate funding has been described as probably the most critical factor in sustaining and enhancing the quality of Education, particularly for effective and continued operations of educational institutions in this COVID-19 era (Idialu & Idialu, 2012; Onileowo T. T., 2021).

Meanwhile, there are also evaluations of what kind of world we will inherit in the next decade, following the 2020 cataclysmic transition. Based on evolution hypotheses that countries are already involved in a pandemic firefight. Nonetheless, there is plenty of material to sift through and create a model of what the future will look like for Education and trade in the months and years to come when life comes back to a new one. It becomes urgent for Nigeria's Government to evaluate the current situation, plan future challenges, and develop coping strategies to minimise the effect of the pandemic on the education sector and the country's economic crisis.

Indeed, the first beneficiaries of this chapter will undoubtedly be Nigerians and the Nigerian Government. This chapter will also be beneficial to citizens and governments from other countries. And can also be a source of information for future studies. The aim is to discuss the impact of Covid-19 on tertiary institutions and the effect on the Economy and give recommendations accordingly. The following is a breakdown of how this chapter is structured. The next section will examine the Covid-19 pandemic, followed by the title on Covid-19's impact on Tertiary institutions. Next is the effects of Covid-19 on the economy. And lastly, the chapter will explore recommendations for assisting Nigeria's Government and tertiary institutions in coping with the severe impact of Covid-19 and then conclude.

CONCEPT OF COVID-19 PANDEMIC

The novel Coronavirus disease 2019 (COVID-19) was discovered in Wuhan, China, in December 2019 and has spread to nearly every country on the planet. Severe Acute Respiratory Syndrome Coronavirus 2 is the virus that causes the disease, which is a rare but dangerous form of Coronavirus (SARS- COV-2). According to the World Health Organization, the virus has become a global pandemic with fatal consequences (WHO, 2020). As of April 9, 2020, 1,603,428 cases were reported, with 356,440 recoveries and 95,714 deaths (Jacob, Abigeal, & Lydia, 2020). On February 27, 2020, an Italian citizen became the COVID-19 index case in Nigeria. There were 288 hospital-reported cases of COVID-19 in Nigeria as of April 9, 2020, including 51 discharges and seven fatalities (Nigeria Centre for Diseases Control, 2020). To stop the virus from spreading further, civil society groups and government agencies initiated public awareness campaigns about the importance of good hygiene and social distance. At airports, travellers were subjected to temperature screenings, and those returning from countries where COVID-19 had been reported were advised to isolate themselves.

COVID-19, a member of the Coronavirus family, also includes SARS, Hemagglutinin Type 5 and Neuraminidase Type 1 (H5N1), Hemagglutinin Type 1 and Neuraminidase Type 1 (H1N1), and Middle East Respiratory Syndrome (MERS), is a viral infection through the eyes, nose, and mouth droplets transmitted via sneezing, coughing as well as immediate contact with an infected person. It takes one to fourteen days for it to grow. Fever, cough, and dizziness are symptoms, and it's detected through a lab experiment. The virus can cause severe breathing difficulties and even death, notably among the elderly or those with chronic illnesses. On the other hand, infected individuals are asymptomatic carriers of the virus, while others can only have a mild infection but recover quickly (Obododike & Cokekeokosisi, 2020). COVID-19 has no cure, though the vaccines have been discovered in some advanced countries, and vaccination has begun in most countries globally; this is to ensure citizens' safety. As of 18 February 2021, at least seven different vaccines across three platforms have been rolled out in countries. Vulnerable populations in all countries are the highest priority for vaccination. Vaccines are a critical new tool in the battle against COVID-19, and it is hugely encouraging to see so many vaccines proving successful and going into development.

Scientists worldwide are collaborating and innovating to bring us tests, treatments, and vaccines to collectively save lives and end this pandemic (WHO, COVID-19 Vaccines, 2021). However, safe and effective vaccines will be a game-changer for the foreseeable future. Individuals must continue wearing masks, daily hand washing, sanitisers, social distancing, avoiding crowds, clinical etiquette, and self-isolation while sick are all valuable knowledge to reduce widespread infection. Being vaccinated does not mean that individuals should throw caution to the wind and put themselves and others at risk, mainly because it is still unclear how the vaccines can protect against disease, infection, and transmission (Leppin & Aro, 2009). As a result, people can be educated about infection risks to take the appropriate precautions. Preventive measures are needed in the early stages of a pandemic to protect against possible threats and slow the spread of the disease. In compliance with this, the Nigerian Government (along with other governments worldwide) implemented various containment policies that have caused significant social and economic instability. It disrupted people's daily lives, except for healthcare professionals and critical commercial operations. Also, the pandemic has forced citizens to stay at home, including industries and institutions. The lockdown has put the livelihoods of Nigerians who make a living in the informal sector in jeopardy since most of their operations require face-to-face interaction. In Nigeria, there is also a lack of social security system, zero provision for humanitarian assistance, and most people struggle each day to earn a living. Thus, this chapter highlights the impact of Covid-19 on tertiary institutions in Nigeria.

COVID-19 IMPACT ON NIGERIA'S TERTIARY INSTITUTIONS

The Covid-19 outbreak, coupled with the lockdown of schools at various levels of education in Nigeria, has served as a test for the education technology interventions for teaching-learning activities. Unfortunately, the Nigerian education system arrived at this point not fully prepared. Also, with the move to reopen schools for the learners in terminal classes, there will be adequate time to prepare them for their respective terminal examinations. But this can only be possible if the Government and the schools' authorities make available preventive measures and facilities to prevent the spread of coronavirus in various schools. The good question here is will this move be effective now that the Government and the nation at large are experiencing economic meltdown? Nobody knows the answer to this until the activity has been re-evaluated after a period of operation in that trend.

ACADEMIC CALENDAR INTERRUPTIONS AT TERTIARY INSTITUTIONS

All Nigerian tertiary institutions have been ordered to close and students to return home by the Federal Ministry of Education. On March 19, Sonny Echono, a Permanent Secretary in the Ministry of Education, informed journalists that the decision formed one of the country's ultimate decisions in controlling the virus from spreading. Nigeria is now on the rising list of African nations that have shut down educational institutions. Before the announcement by the permanent secretary, several universities had already sent their students' home. COVID-19 has interrupted Nigeria's academic calendar since several tertiary institutions have begun their first semester exams. According to Jacob et al. (2020), the closing across all academic institutions, from elementary schools to educational institutions, will affect students' degree programs, including projects. Nations throughout other South and Southeast Asia had also ordered the closing of their colleges and universities with at least two weeks to curb the problem of the COVID-19 virus, which the World Health Organization has proclaimed a global pandemic (Alwis, Saif, & Niazi, 2020). However, authorities in many countries agree that the closures may last much longer than expected. The closings came strong and forcefully the week, several weeks after the number of deaths increased and several weeks after universities across North-East Asia, including Japan, South Korea, Singapore, and China – where the virus first emerged – shutdown during February and March. The city's universities, including those in Hong Kong and Taiwan, have yet to start classes. According to Simon & Hans (2020) a global shutdown of educational institutions would result in significant (or undoubtedly unfair) disruptions of students' Education, interruptions of internal evaluations, or the absence of substitution of national qualification examinations inferior option.

DECREASED INTERNATIONAL EDUCATION

The COVID-19 has caused most international students studying in Nigeria to return to their respective homes. The Nigerian Government declared that educational institutions be closed to prevent the further spread of the virus. The deadly COVID-19 epidemic has had a detrimental impact on international Education. Most Nigerian international students have returned home. Those intending to travel for studies abroad will be unable to do so due to the global closure of educational institutions and a travel restriction imposed by various countries.

In contrast, Zakaria et al. (2005) stated that China's grand plan to be the world's largest importer of international students is in jeopardy. Future exchange programmes on Chinese campuses would be difficult to recommend without reservation to university deans and recruiters. Nearly three out of ten students in a QS poll of over 2,000 students from Africa, Asia, and Australia, mentioned the virus had forced them to change their plans. Thus, challenging to say how many students who took part in the study attended school in China.

SUSPENSION OF LOCAL AND INTERNATIONAL CONFERENCES

The COVID-19 pandemic has forced the suspension of several conferences on different programmes scheduled for the first and second quarters of 2020. For the time being, discoveries and findings in the educational sectors have been restricted because many tertiary institutions in Nigeria have not fully integrated Information communication technology (ICT) into their students' educational activities. Most academic programs, including science, will be cancelled, except for international students and those having medical or other emergencies, which may be permitted to stay in their hall of residence with specific approval from the director with restricted messing (catering) services. In an official statement by Subhasis Chaudhuri, director of IIT Bombay in Maharashtra, the Indian state is most affected by the virus, with hundreds of reported deaths. The 2019–20 coronavirus pandemic affected educational institutions, resulting in widespread school and university closures (Onyema, et al., 2020). More than 421 million students were out of school on 3 April 2020 related to school closing in response to COVID-19. According to UNESCO statistics, about 200 countries have introduced national restrictions, affecting nearly 98 percent of the global education system. Cambridge International Examinations (CIE) issued a press release on March 23, 2020, declaring a suspension of the Cambridge IGCSE, Cambridge O Level, Cambridge International AS & A Level, Cambridge AICE Diploma, and Cambridge Pre-U exams for all countries in the May/June 2020 set. Exams for the International Baccalaureate have since been postponed.

BUDGET CUTS IN EDUCATIONAL INSTITUTIONS

Health crises and the economic downturn have wreaked havoc on the higher education sector, with universities, students, and most households losing significant income. During the fall semester, the sudden shift from face-to-face to online learning resulted in unexpected expenses. In order to plan for the fall semester, more money was spent on health prevention initiatives. Many students with inadequate financial resources may drop out of college or move to less expensive public institutions, resulting in a revenue loss, especially for institutions that rely solely on tuition fees. It's reasonable to anticipate a flood of mergers in the public and private sectors, with many private institutions closing their doors permanently. The results in many developing economies, where public support for higher learning has been inadequate, typically less than 0.5 per cent of GDP—could be disastrous. Decreased government budgets, coupled with a lower probability of increased private funding, could cause many students to drop out of college, risking institutions' capacity to maintain high standards of teaching and study.

According to Akanni & Gabriel (2020), the Nigerian federal budget for the financial year 2020 was planned with significant profit estimates, though with controversial discoveries (2020). In the authorised budget, revenue collections were projected to be N 8.24 trillion, up around 20% in 2019. With a price of oil index at $57 per barrel and an oil supply of approximately 2.18 million barrels a day, the revenue projections were based upon overall international oil production and a competitive economy. The advent of COVID-19 and the increasing prevalence across Nigeria also necessitated a thorough analysis and revision of previous revenue estimates and fiscal forecasts. In contrast to the problems that caused the global economy to hit a downturn in 2016. The present growth of the world economy faces more significant challenges today, since the price of oil is now around US$30, amid predictions it will continue to fall due to a trade war among major industry players. Sadly, the country has failed miserably to set aside adequate reserves for rainy days like those ahead. The latest considerations to adjust the budget downward are unavoidable in light of these overwhelming economic challenges.

The Academic Staff Union of Universities (ASUU) also criticised the Federal Government's plan to slash the Universal Basic Education Commission's budget from 111.78 billion to 50.76 billion dollars. According to the academic union, the same proposal for healthcare will be a damaging wind that would further damage the sector. He claims that a realistic and proactive government will not use resources on public building renovations or bus purchases to the detriment of crucial industries like Education and healthcare. As a result, the academic staff union of Universities (ASUU) has cautioned President Muhammadu Buhari from cutting health and education budgets in the proposed revenue account for 2020. The budget cuts will directly affect the country's school budget, which experts have characterised as insufficient. Several infrastructure projects and school development plans scheduled for this year will be scrapped due to budget cuts (Ajayi, 2020). Africa's growth rate, which was 3.4 percent in 2019, will increase to 3.9 percent in 2020, according to (Damtew Teferra, 2020).

Unfortunately, this is now likely to remain a pipe dream, as the country's economy and educational institutions are likely to be severely impacted. The effect on educational institutions will most probably be noticed on two fronts: first, is a sharp drop in public funding to educational institutions as a result of low productivity and growth; and second, a related reduction in development partner contributions, primarily to research, with which African Education has become overly reliant. Education can once again be dismissed as a luxury that West African countries cannot afford. It is crucial to overcoming obstacles such as COVID-19 – and a slew of various human-made and environmental hazards. Table 3 shows the budget allocation to Education in Nigeria from 2010 to 2019.

Table 3. Nigeria Budgetary allocation to Education (2010 - 2019)

Year	Budget (₦Trillion)	Educational Allocation (₦ Billion)	Percentage of Budget (%)
2010	5.160	249.09	4.83
2011	4.972	306.30	6.16
2012	4.877	400.15	8.20
2013	4.987	426.53	8.55
2014	4.962	493.00	9.94
2015	5.068	392.20	7.74
2016	6.061	369.60	6.10
2017	7.444	550.00	7.38
2018	8.612	605.80	7.03
2019	8.830	620.50	7.03
Total	**60.973**	**4413.17**	**7.24**

Source: (Ndujihe, 2019)- Vanguard Newspaper; (Ameh & Aluko, 2019) –Punch Newspaper

The table above shows that the education sector received an average of 7.24 percent over ten years, opposed to UNESCO's recommendation of 15-20 percent. Infrastructures like power supply, digital platforms, training programmes, and others required for student learning to expand in Nigeria would not be available as a result. It means that using e-learning for instructional delivery in Nigeria is plagued with challenges.

STUDENT SAFETY

Colleges in low- and middle-income countries are concerned about the safety of their students throughout school closings, even though their capacity to communicate with them and offer support has been restricted. According to a study, COVID-19 affected 62 per-cent of members of the Global Schools Forum's willingness to adopt child safety rules. Administrators, including the teachers and social workers, have lost touch with students, making it challenging to detect bullying or offer face-to-face assistance and therapy (GSF, 2020). Prolonged school closings could put any out-of-school children in danger at home, given the increased violence against children during lockdowns (Edwards, 2020). Furthermore, shareholders indicated that school administration is worried over the safety and health of students when schools reopen, as so many would not have the financial resources to comply with government-mandated Standard Operating Procedures. Most school administrators anticipate that additional room for social distancing will be required, but that fee revenue will not be sufficient to cover the expense.

EDUCATION-LEARNING GAPS

In all Nigerian educational institutions, the COVID-19 virus has disrupted student learning. As a result, learning activities have been suspended in all universities, polytechnics, and colleges of Education across the world. In addition, many Nigerian students were absent from school for a month or longer, meaning that they were inactive. Likewise, a study conducted in May by the Nigerian non-profit SEED revealed that only 25 out of 100 parents had smartphones, and only two had sufficient data coverage to remain online (SEED, 2020). As a result, privately-owned schools in low- and middle-income countries have tried other delivery methods (Text messaging, media, printed version materials). And study results show that significant numbers of students had no interaction with their institutions throughout the period (GSL, 2020; Young Lives, 2020a).

Consequently, these privately owned schools from low-income and middle-income countries expect their students to experience significant learning loss whenever they resume. They lack adequate resources to include the tailored approaches needed to address this, given the other constraints they face. As a result, the findings indicate that the sector will immediately require adequate assistance to protect the Education of students, especially those who are already experiencing numerous levels of vulnerability and are at risk of learning losses.

EXAMINATION DEFERMENT

Before the advent of the COVID-19, which forced the closure of all Nigerian educational institutions, several higher education institutions in Nigeria had started their first semester exams. According to Simon & Hans (2020), school, college, and university closures disrupt students worldwide and coincide with a crucial assessment period, causing several exams to be deferred or cancelled. Internal evaluations are perhaps viewed as less significant, and many have been cancelled. However, they aim to provide information about a child's development to parents and teachers. Because of the lack of this knowledge takes longer to recognise all high-potential learning disabilities, which can negatively affect children. Simon & Hans (2020) investigated the impact of a major IT failure in Denmark's testing program. As a result, several students were unable to finish the examination. The authors discovered that taking an examination improved a two-year entrance exam by 9% of a confidence interval, with comparable results in mathematics. Children from low-income families are most affected. Notably, the institutional lockdown affects more than just internal evaluations. For instance, in the UK, both examinations for primary national qualifications such as GCSEs and A levels were cancelled for the whole batch.

Moreover, If Nigeria's digital technology had been robust and highly developed, it would have played a vital role in accelerating recovery from the severe shock of the COVID-19 pandemic disaster. For example, Nigerian schools, universities, and educators can post schoolwork online so that students quarantined at home do not miss substantial portions of their Education when school is closed or unable to attend. On the other hand, E-learning is a platform that can enable continuous teaching and learning without the learners leaving their homes.

THE EFFECTS OF COVID-19 ON THE ECONOMY

The Covid-19 pandemic has a wide range of social, political, cultural, and economic consequences. Some may claim that it is too soon to discuss the pandemic's impact. But, more importantly, when will the pandemic most likely end? Experts believe that the Covid-19 pandemic will not be eradicated soon (Croda, et al., 2020). The United Nations Educational, Scientific, and Cultural Organization stated that the COVID-19 outbreak had unprecedented effects on global well-being, economy, businesses, and education systems, with 1.6 billion students impacted by school closings (UIS, 2020). Therefore, it's critical to discuss the consequences early so that the appropriate quarters can take steps to mitigate the pandemic's effects. With that in mind, the following are the effects of Covid-19 on the economy.

JOB LOSSES

Several individuals have lost their employment position due to the Covid-19 pandemic, and more are in danger of losing their jobs in the near term. Nigeria's unemployment rate has risen as a result of the pandemic. Before the outbreak, Nigeria's unemployment rate was 23.1 percent (National Bureau of Statisticsa, 2019). However, the unemployment rate increases to almost 33 percent by the end of 2020 due to the pandemic (Innocent Otache, 2020). The economy suffers as unemployment rises. When unemployment peaks, criminal behaviours, and social vices are more likely to rise, putting the country in great danger. Moreover, a rise in unemployment may result in increased starvation and poverty in the country.

REVENUE LOSS IN THE INFORMAL SECTOR

Workers in the informal sector and the under-priviledged are the most affected by the outbreak since they rely on the day-to-day proceeds made from their businesses. This group of people comprises Street sellers or hawkers, taxi drivers, petty traders, craftsmen, motorbike (or "Okada") riders, waste collectors, and hairdressers are among those who fall into this group. They undertake various business activities for their sustenance. Sadly, the lockdown and movement control policies made their businesses forced closed, causing them to suffer from starvation and poverty. It is worth noting that the informal sector accounts for 60 percent of the worldwide workforce and survives on less than $2 per day (International Labour Orgnization, 2020).

BUSINESS CLOSURE

The Covid-19 pandemic has resulted in the closure of several businesses, most specifically small and medium enterprises (SMEs). It is related to their limited resources and vulnerability. Various measures adopted to control the spread of the virus, such as social distancing, self-isolation or quarantine, a restriction on public gatherings, and market closures, have affected their activities, revenues, and incomes. Also, many small business enterprises have encountered demand and supply chain disruptions, including a sharp drop in demand for commodities and services due to the lockdown and transportation restriction. In addition, supply channels have suffered significant damage. Nigerian business enterprises, for example, import Chinese goods (Ozili, 2020). Now that there is a restriction on overseas travels, commodities from such countries would be interrupted. Border restrictions, of course, harm foreign trade.

AGRICULTURAL PRODUCTION AND FOOD INSECURITY

The Covid-19 epidemic has impacted agriculture output and trade. It has undoubtedly compounded the country's food insecurity problem. The various movement restrictions to curtail the virus spread have affected agricultural products' demand and supply channels and commodities both inside and abroad. Seedlings, insecticides, fertilisers, and farm equipment are hard to come by for farmers. In addition, due to the absence of labour and logistical problems, industrial processes have been disrupted. The emergence of the pandemic in Nigeria occurred at an unexpected time, causing widespread disruption.

Moreover, the advent of the pandemic in Nigeria disrupts agricultural projects. For some agriculturists, the pandemic strikes during plantation, while for others, it strikes during the harvesting period. Without a doubt, these interruptions harm agricultural production and commercialization.

A SHARP DROP IN OIL REVENUES

Nigeria's economy is based solely on a single product (National Bureau of Statisticsa, 2019). And it is primarily reliant on petroleum exports for its development and economic prosperity. The advent of the Covid-19 pandemic has significantly impacted the global price of petroleum. For instance, the cost of crude oil has decreased from around $60 per barrel to less than $30 per barrel, significantly impacting Nigeria's crude oil sales revenues (Ozili, 2020). The pandemic has severely affected the market for Nigerian crude oil. Also, the drop in crude oil prices has affected Nigeria's economy in significant ways. It has a direct impact on Nigeria's budget for the year 2020. Due to a sharp fall in oil income, the budget was reviewed. Initially, the budget was set at N10.594 trillion but has now decreased to N10.276 trillion.

ECONOMIC UNCERTAINTY

The economic situation of Nigeria is weak on the verge of entering a recession as a result of the Covid-19 outbreak. There are a plethora of indicators pointing to a downturn in the economy. During this pandemic, the cost of products and services has soared, the unemployment rate has risen, currency value has become more erratic, and business operations have been severely interrupted due to the outbreak. The economy is becoming more volatile due to this circumstance—likewise, strain by the loss of revenue and employment and a swing in purchasing habits. Consequently, Nigeria's foreign reserves anticipated drained due to the significant loss of revenues caused by the sharp drop in oil prices, leaving its economy uncertain.

RECOMMENDATIONS

Based on the preceding discussions, this chapter presents the following recommendations to assist Nigeria's government and educational institutions in coping with the impact of the Covid-19 and similar pandemics soon.

Adoption Of E-Learning

Online education or virtual classrooms or systems (i.e., e-learning) has become essential due to the Covid-19 pandemic. Students can learn from home with the help of an online education system. Also, due to the shutdown and movement control policies implemented during the pandemic, several institutions have established a virtual teaching system to ensure that student learning programmes are not interrupted. Surprisingly, many institutions, notably in affluent nations, had already implemented the digital student learning system prior to the Covid-19 outbreak. Along with the conventional classroom method, Nigeria must adopt online learning. The Nigerian Government must provide online education facilities and equipment to accomplish this. The Government should subsidise laptops for students and instructors in this regard. Also, to encourage online student learning, institutions should provide accessible internet service. Electricity should also be available at all times. More importantly, educator training courses should be designed to learn digital or e-learning skills that will allow them to teach effectively online. Similarly, to boost productivity, students should also learn basic ICT abilities for productive virtual education.

Acquisition of Relevant Ict Skills

Due to the closure of businesses, workplaces, and several institutions, ICT skills have become essential because of the pandemic. During the pandemic, many people work from home (teleworking), many governments and corporate gatherings are conducted digitally using teleconferencing technologies like Skype, Zoom, and WhatsApp video. And for employees to preserve their jobs, employees must learn necessary ICT skills. Teleworking or telecommuting (also known as working-from-home [WFH]) could become the new norm. Additionally, job applicants must learn essential ICT, media, and e-business skills to improve their chances. For job seekers, having ICT skills is an advantage. Understanding the basic operations of ICT hardware is very important in today's world. This hardware comprises scanners, printers, projectors, laptops, smartphones, photocopiers, and tablets. Also, use of the internet, such as searching for information using search engines. Typing, which is the capacity to utilise word processing software to generate letters or agendas. E-mails and their handling, and the use of media platforms (LinkedIn, Instagram, Twitter, and Facebook). Including communication and networking platforms such as Zoom, Slack, G-suite, Office 365, WebEx, and Skype, among others.

Adoption of the E-Business Model

Businesses must accept e-business as a legitimate business strategy. Using the lessons learned from the Covid-19 pandemic. If a firm intends to stay in business and compete, it needs to go online (Onileowo, Muharam, Ramily, & Saleh, 2021). Due to the pandemic's lockdown and movement regulations, many buyers have turned to internet shopping. Surprisingly, online buying allows the buyer to have their purchases delivered to them in the convenience of their own home. Nevertheless, we live in a technologically advanced environment. As a result, business processes must become more digital. They must incorporate new automation technology into their operations, such as robotics and artificial intelligence. Also, organisations must ensure that their staff has the necessary ICT or technology literacy to adapt to the new business environment.

Monetary Policy Measures

The Nigerian Government, through the Central Bank of Nigeria (CBN), has declared several monetary policy measures aimed at minimising the impact of the Covid-19 pandemic on the country's economy. The Central Bank of Nigeria, for example, has launched an N3.5 trillion economic stimulus programme (PKF, 2020). The CBN has also granted a loan facility of N50 billion ($138.89 million) for individuals and Enterprises that the outbreak has severely impacted. Likewise, the health sector has been allocated another N100 billion ($277.78 million), and a loan facility of N1 trillion ($2.78 billion) has also been authorised to the manufacturing sector. In addition, all CBN initiatives have had their interest rates slashed from 9 to 5 percent with a one-year freeze imposed on all CBN investments. While the monetary policy actions listed above have already been implemented, there's more work to be done. Commercial banks' lending rate to small businesses, for example, is too high and should be lowered. The official rate of interest is currently 13.5 percent (United Capital, 2020). This proposal is critical because small business owners are not eligible for the CBN's SMEs loan facility. In addition, Government should strengthen foreign exchange flow through the CBN to facilitate international trade as all of these initiatives would enhance the economy by stimulating economic growth in the country.

Fiscal Policy Measures

The Nigerian Government needs to take specific monetary policy initiatives to minimise the economic impacts of the pandemic. Doing this might, for example, lower the current tax rate or provide tax benefits to selected SMEs. Thus, it would increase support for the business performance. Besides this, Government should enhance investment in essential infrastructure. The Government, for instance, should invest in power. The cost of conducting business in Nigeria has risen due to many SMEs producing their electricity. Without a doubt, a steady supply of energy will lower the cost of goods and services in Nigeria tremendously. The Nigerian Government needs to make significant investments in the healthcare industry. The Covid-19 outbreak has revealed the country's weak healthcare infrastructure. Investment in the healthcare industry would prepare the country to deal with future pandemics, as Covid-19 may not be the last. The Government should explore providing direct financial support for those that have lost their jobs as a welfare state scheme.

Economic Diversification Through Agriculture

Nigeria must diversify its economy in light of the sharp drop in oil income caused by the Covid-19 epidemic. In truth, diversification of the national economy has been long overdue. Nigeria should explore other avenues for supporting its economy other than the oil sector in light of the unexpected and sharp drop in oil prices. Prioritising agriculture is the available option to Nigeria in its diversification efforts. Nigeria must concentrate on agriculture and invest heavily in the area to realise the full benefits. Agriculture can contribute to the country's economic development (Innocent Otache, 2020; Praburaj, Design, & Nadu, 2018). Agriculture gives jobs, revenue, and food, according to the literature (Otache, 2017). It primarily feeds farmers and guarantees that the country's food supply is secure. Agricultural output is a source of revenue for the Government and a means of income for farmers. Agriculture also employs the growing youth population. To fully realise the agricultural sector's potential, the Government must establish agricultural practices that favour individuals to pursue careers in farming and agriculture vocations. The Government, for example, might provide current and prospective farmers with financial assistance in low-interest soft loans.

Similarly, the Government may purchase fertilisers, seedlings, herbicides, and agriculture equipment and discount their sale or donate them to farmers for free, including Mechanised and irrigated farming technologies to encourage them. Nigerian youth, remarkably fresh graduates, could pursue farming and agriculture. Nigerian youngsters should exploit the abundant farmland and agribusiness prospects available in the country (Otache, 2017). They may choose to farm maize and millet, fish, and poultry.

Redesigning of The Manufacturing Industry

The manufacturing industry is the economy's nerve centre (Uma, et al., 2019). The Nigerian Government, on the other hand, has long denied manufacturing its legitimate position in the country's development and sustainability. It is due to the 1970s oil boom. Nigeria has thus evolved into a consumer country. Its economy is significantly reliant on imports (Innocent Otache, 2020; Uma, et al., 2019). Nigeria's excessive reliance on imported commodities reveals why the country's economy is often hit hard in global crises. The Covid-19 pandemic has undoubtedly harmed Nigeria's budget. Nigeria, for example, buys mainly from China, but now with the pandemic's quarantine and restriction on international travel, purchase commodities from China has become impossible (Ozili, 2020).

Further, the drop in oil income during the outbreak has demonstrated that depending solely on the petroleum industry as the base can be hazardous. As a result, the economy needs to be diversified. In addition to agriculture, Nigeria's policy should concentrate on the manufacturing industry in its economic diversification drive (EDD). The manufacturing industry's contribution to Gross Domestic Product (GDP) has dropped significantly in recent years. According to published data, the sector contributed only 9.20 percent of GDP in 2018 (National Bureau of Statisticsa, 2019). This figure indicates there is still much to improve the sector's performance. The Government should make significant investments in the industry in this regard. Besides providing financial assistance to enterprises, the Government must invest in energy and road construction infrastructure. In Nigeria, addressing the difficulties of energy and roads would enhance the sector's performance considerably. Also, manufacturers could be given tax breaks by the Government. It would both excite them and motivate more people to pursue careers in the manufacturing industry. When the sector is revitalised, it will contribute to its economic sustainability and provide employment possibilities. In the end, it will aid Nigeria's unemployment crisis to be significantly alleviated.

The Need for Several Income Streams

The emergence of this outbreak also highlighted the importance of having several income streams. Many people have lost their jobs to the attack. Those who rely on a single enterprise for a living have seen it fail. One of the lessons learned from the pandemic is depending on a single income source is equivalent to placing all the eggs in a basket, which may be devastating if that revenue source is gone. Having several revenue streams is beneficial since it ensures that you will have other options if one source of income is blocked. Salaried workers should develop additional sources of income coupled with their primary jobs. For example, engage in enterprises such as rentals, blogging, online advertisement or marketing, virtual assistant, publishing e-books, high-yield stock investment, website or application design, real estate investment, fish farming, small-scale livestock, etc.

CONCLUSION

The outbreak of Covid-19 has shaken the educational sector and the world economy off its strength. Nigeria's Economy was inclusive. This chapter examines the impact of the Covid-19 pandemic on Nigeria's tertiary institutions and its effect on the Economy and suggests viable survival solutions. The outbreak in Nigeria has had religious, social, political, and economic consequences. In fact, looking at the pandemic trend, it could be something we will live with for a long time. There is no doubt that there will be a severe setback in Nigeria's education system and the Economy if the Government and concerned personnel do not adequately manage the pandemic lockdown. Schools' calendars have been disrupted; the oil sector, which serves as a significant source of revenue to Nigeria, has been hit hard. There is a reduction in the country's economic development, which has affected education finance as well. Since the family income depends on the economic growth of any country, most of the families in Nigeria are experiencing economic hardship. As a result of the pandemic lockdown, some vulnerable families having their children under the federal government free feeding scheme face the challenge of searching for food for their children while with them at home. Unfortunately, the illiteracy level of some parents in Nigeria is not helping the matter because not every parent or guidance could handle the black and white teaching of their children. Thus, it will cause children in these categories to experience a significant setback in their academic endeavours in the long run. Many of them may drop out of school and become unruly and thus, might increase the level of social vices, which can be detrimental to society. Generally, the Covid -19 outbreak in Nigeria has had social, religious, political, and economic repercussions. Precisely, the Covid-19 impact on Nigeria's Education includes Academic calendar interruptions at tertiary institutions, Decreased international education, Suspension of local and international conferences, Education-learning gaps, Budget cuts in educational institutions, Student safety, and Examination deferment. And its effects on the Economy include Job losses, Revenue loss in the informal sector, Business closure, Agricultural production and food insecurity, A sharp drop in oil revenues, and Economic uncertainty.

ACKNOWLEDGMENT

This research received no particular grant, either from a government, private, or non-profit funding organisation.

REFERENCES

Ajayi, O. (2020). *ASUU faults FG's proposed slash of education, health budget.* Ibadan: Vanguard Nigeria News. Retrieved 25 April, 2021, from https://www.vanguardngr.com/2020/04/asuu-faults-fgs-proposed-slash-of-education-health-budget/

Akanni, L. O., & Gabriel, S. C. (2020). *The implication of Covid-19 pandemic on the Nigerian Economy.* Retrieved 5 August, 2021, from cseaafrica. org/the-implication-ofcovid19-on-the-nigerian-economy

Alwis, D. D., Saif, S. K., & Niazi, S. (2020). *Universities shut down across South and Southeast Asia. University World News.* University World News. Retrieved 26 April, 2021, from https://www. universityworldnews. com/post. php

Ameh, J., & Aluko, O. (2019). *2019 budget: Education gets 620.5bn, against UNESCO "s advice.* Retrieved 2 August, 2021, from https://punchng.com/2019-budget-education-gets-n620-5bnagainst-unesco-advice/

Croda, J., Oliveira, W. D., Frutuoso, R. L., Mandetta, L. H., Baia-da-Silva, D. C., Brito-Sousa, J. D., & Lacerda, M. G. (2020). *COVID-19 in Brazil: Advantages of a socialized unified health system and preparation to contain cases.* Retrieved 5 August, 2021, from https://www.scielo.br/j/rsbmt/a/bwLKCs6ZfGhyFn3mp4RDhdQ/?format=html&lang=en

Damtew, T. (2020). *COVID-19- A Vindictive messenger for multilateralism.* School of Education, University of KwaZulu-Natal. Retrieved 25 April, 2021, from https://soe.ukzn.ac.za/news/2020/05/covid-19-a-vindictive-messenger-for-multilateralism/

Donthu, N., & Gustafsson, A. (2020). Effects of COVID-19 on business and research. *Journal of Business Research, 117*, 284–289. doi:10.1016/j.jbusres.2020.06.008 PMID:32536736

Edwards, J. (2020). *Protect a Generation: The impact of COVID-19 on children's lives.* Save the Children International. Retrieved 6 May, 2021, from https://www.savethechildren.org/content/dam/usa/reports/emergency-response/protect-a-generation-report.pdf

GSF. (2020). *GSF Member COVID-19 Survey. All children should have access to quality education.* Global Schools Forum. Retrieved 6 May, 2021, from https://www.globalschoolsforum.org/

GSL. (2020). *School Leaders' Response to COVID-19.* Retrieved 2020 May, 2020, from https://internationalednews.com/2020/04/08/global-school-leaders-respond-to-covid-19/

Hashim, F., Bakar, A. R. A., & Abdul-Talib, A. N. (2010). *International Business* (2nd ed.). Oxford Fajar Press.

He, H., & Harris, L. (2020). The impact of Covid-19 pandemic on corporate social responsibility and marketing philosophy. *Journal of Business Research, 116*(8), 176–182. doi:10.1016/j.jbusres.2020.05.030 PMID:32457556

Idialu, J. O., & Idialu, E. E. (2012). Entity, ownership, educational subsidies and funding of Nigerian tertiary institutions: Current research. *Journal of Social Sciences, 4*(1), 56–61.

Innocent, O. (2020). The Effects of the Covid-19 Pandemic on the Nigeria's Economy and Possible Coping Strategies. *Asian Journal of Social Sciences and Management Studies, 7*(3), 173–179.

International Labour Orgnization. (2020). *COVID-19 crisis and the informal economy Immediate responses and policy challenges.* Retrieved 3 August, 2021, from https://www.ilo.org/global/topics/employment-promotion/informal-economy/publications/WCMS_743623/lang--en/index.htm.1-8

Jacob, O. N., Abigeal, I., & Lydia, A. E. (2020). Impact of COVID-19 on the higher institutions development in Nigeria. *Electronic Research Journal of Social Sciences and Humanities, 2*(2), 126–135.

Leppin, A., & Aro, A. R. (2009). Risk perception related to SARS and avian influenza: Theoretical foundations of current behavioral research. *International Journal of Behavioral Medicine, 16*(1), 7–29. doi:10.100712529-008-9002-8 PMID:19214752

National Bureau of Statisticsa. (2019). *Nigerian gross domestic product Report.* Retrieved 3 August, 2021, from https://www.nigerianstat.gov.ng/pdfuploads/GDP_Report_Q3_2019.pdf

Ndujihe, C. (2019). *Education sector gets paltry N3.9 trillion out of N55.19 trillion in 10 years.* Retrieved 2 August, 2021, from https://www.vanguardngr.com/2018/04/educationfree-fall/

Nigeria Centre for Disease Control. (2020). *Covid-19 situation Report: Situation Report 85, saturday, 23rd may, 2020.* Retrieved 3 August, 2021, from https://reliefweb.int/report/world/coronavirus-disease-2019-covid-19-situation-report-85-14-april-2020

Obododike, M. P., & Cokekeokosisi, J. O. (2020). Challenges Of Implementing E-Learning In Nigeria Educational System In The Covid-19 Pandemic Era. *Social Sciences and Education Research Review, 7*(2), 152–171.

Ohia, C., Bakarey, A. S., & Ahmad, T. (2020). COVID-19 and Nigeria: Putting the realities in context. *International Journal of Infectious Diseases, 95*, 279–281. doi:10.1016/j.ijid.2020.04.062 PMID:32353547

Onileowo, T. T. (2021). Women Entrepreneurship Challenges in Ekiti State Southwest Nigeria: Way Forward. *Albukhary Social business Journal, 2*(1), 1-9.

Onileowo, T. T., Muharam, F. M., Ramily, M. K., & Saleh, F. K. (2021). The Nexus between Innovation and Business Competitive Advantage: A Conceptual Study. *Universal Journal of Accounting and Finance, 9*(3), 352–361. doi:10.13189/ujaf.2021.090309

Onyema, E. M., Eucheria, N. C., Obafemi, F. A., Sen, S., Atonye, F. G., Sharma, A., & Alsayed, A. O. (2020). Impact of Coronavirus pandemic on education. *Journal of Education and Practice, 11*(13), 108–121.

Otache, I. (2017). Agripreneurship development: A strategy for revamping Nigeria's economy from recession. *African Journal of Economic and Management Studies, 8*(4), 474–483. doi:10.1108/AJEMS-05-2017-0091

Ozili, P. K. (2020). *Covid-19 pandemic and economic crisis: The Nigerian experience and structural causes.* Retrieved from https://pkf-ng.com/media/10046217/pkf-nigeria-covid-19-bulletin-final-ed.pdf

PKF. (2020). *Covid-19 PKF Nigeria update.* Retrieved 3 August 2021, from https://pkf-ng.com/media/10046217/pkf-nigeria-covid-19-bulletin-final-ed.pdf. 1-5

Praburaj, L., Design, F., & Nadu, T. (2018). Role of agriculture in the economic development of a country. *International Journal of Commerce, 6*(3), 1–5.

SEED. (2020). *Impact of COVID-19 on Education for Vulnerable Children.* Sustainable Education and Enterprise Development. Retrieved 6 May, 2021, from https://www.seed.com.ng/impact-of-covid-19-on-education-for-vulnerable-children/

Simon, B., & Hans, H. S. (2020). *Schools, skills, and learning: The impact of COVID-19 on education.* Retrieved 5 August 2021, from https://voxeu.org/article/impact-covid-19-education. https://www.universityworldnews.com/post.php?story=20200324065639773

Terwase, I. T., Abdul-Talib, A. N., & Zengeni, K. T. (2014). Nigeria, Africa's largest economy: International business perspective. *International Journal of Management Sciences, 3*(7), 534–543.

UIS. (2020). *Recalculating Proficiency in Schools: COVID-19 Related Learning Losses and Dropping Out.* Sustainable Development Goals. Retrieved 6 May, 2021, from https://sdg.uis.unesco.org/author/uisblog/

Uma, K. E., Obidike, P. C., Chukwu, C. O., Kanu, C., Ogbuagu, R. A., Osunkwo, F. O., & Ndubuisi, P. (2019). Revamping the Nigerian manufacturing sub-sector as a panacea for economic progress: Lessons from South Korea. *Mediterranean Journal of Social Sciences, 10*(4), 111–123. doi:10.2478/mjss-2019-0057

United Capital. (2020). *Nigeria outlook 2020: A different playing field.* Retrieved 3 August, 2021, from https://www.unitedcapitalplcgroup.com/wpcontent/uploads/2020/01/Nigeria-Outlook-2020_A-different-playing-field-3.pdf

WHO. (2020). *WHO Director-General's opening remarks at the media briefing on COVID-19-11 March 2020.* Retrieved 26 April, 2021, from https://www.who.int/director-general/speeches/detail/who-director-general-s-opening-remarks-at-the-media-briefing-on-covid-19---11-march-2020

WHO. (2021). *COVID-19 Vaccines.* Retrieved 26 April, 2021, from https://www.who.int/emergencies/diseases/novel-coronavirus-2019/covid-19-vaccines

Young Lives. (2020a). *Interrupted Education in Ethiopia: Support for Students During COVID-19 School Closures.* Young Lives. Retrieved 6 May, 2021, from https://www.younglives.org.uk/content/interrupted-education-ethiopia-support-students-during-covid-19-school-closures

Zakaria, F., Liu, M., Caryl, C., Miller, K. L., Punoose, R., & Barry, J. (2005). Does the future belong to China. *Newsweek.*

Zakaria, N., Abdul-Talib, A. N., & Amelinckx, A. (Eds.). (2020). *Transcending Cultural Frontiers: Practices, Challenges, and Strategy for International Business.* Springer. doi:10.1007/978-981-15-4454-5

Zakaria, N., Abdul-Talib, A. N., & Amelinckx, A. (2020). Advancing cultural frontiers to champion global business in emerging markets. In *Transcending Cultural Frontiers* (pp. 1–10). Springer. doi:10.1007/978-981-15-4454-5_1

Zakaria, N., Abdul-Talib, A. N., & Othman, N. (Eds.). (2016). *Handbook of research on impacts of international business and political affairs on the global economy. IGI Global.*

KEY TERMS AND DEFINITIONS

COVID-19: It's an illness caused by a novel coronavirus now called severe acute respiratory syndrome coronavirus 2 (SARS-CoV-2; formerly called 2019-nCoV), which was first identified amid an outbreak of respiratory illness cases in Wuhan City, Hubei Province.

Economy: Refers to the state of a country or region in terms of the production and consumption of goods and services and the supply of money.

Tertiary: Refers to higher Education, or post- secondary Education received at (Government or privately funded), monotechnics, polytechnics and colleges of Education.

WHO: The World Health Organization (WHO) is a United Nations specialised organisation in charge of global public health.

Chapter 17
Reflections and Future Directions for the Green Maritime Supply Chain in Malaysia

Muhamad Fairuz Ahmad Jasmi
https://orcid.org/0000-0003-0171-2125
Universiti Utara Malaysia, Malaysia

Yudi Fernando
Universiti Malaysia Pahang, Malaysia

Rusdi Omar
Universiti Utara Malaysia, Malaysia

Muhammad Shabir Shaharudin
https://orcid.org/0000-0002-3453-7813
Universiti Sains Malaysia

ABSTRACT

The maritime sector and shipping industry have been argued to be effective drivers of international trade. Internationalization has become a strategic business plan by entrepreneurs and industry players to expand the business, especially when their business was already established in the domestic market. However, current international laws began to be tightened by requiring each exporting and shipping firms to implement green sea transport practices and documentations. A limited number of empirical-based evidence has forced the maritime practitioners to conduct business without clear green concepts knowledge and availability of best business practices to be benchmarked. With this in mind, the aim of this chapter is to examine current issues, differences, and dilemmas confronting practitioners, governments, stakeholders, and scholars. This chapter has developed a green maritime supply chain concept based on practitioners' reflections and provides future direction to scholars interested in studying green logistics and supplying chain management in the maritime sector.

DOI: 10.4018/978-1-7998-9071-3.ch017

INTRODUCTION

As a global trade facilitator, the maritime supply chain plays a central role in providing a relatively low-cost and efficient mode of transportation compared to the value of the goods being shipped worldwide. Maritime supply chain contributed to about 90% of entire world trade volumes through commodities movement by seaway (Lister, Poulsen, & Ponte, 2015). Currently, the function of seaborne trade has been an important backbone to Malaysia's economic growth and development (Jeevan, Ghaderi, Bandara, Saharuddin, & Othman, 2015). The effectiveness and proficient management of materials, products, and information systems depended on maritime ports and shipping as the key components of Malaysian maritime supply chain activities. In addition to this, a myriad of Malaysian industries ranging from foods, industrial merchandise, and energy resources are much dependent on a relatively secure handling logistic and safe delivery process of the global shipping industry. As part of life-line trade for many global companies, the maritime sector is essential to maintain economic development and prosperity distribution throughout the nation, thus satisfying a critical societal role as part of Malaysia's imperative economic function.

Conversely, in the decade after the onset of climate change and global warming concerns, a greater focus has been put on the maritime sector's sustainability (Jasmi, Fernando, & Ismail, 2020). Although sea transportation has comparatively the 'greener image' because of its less emitting CO^2 per ton-mile than other transportation, given its scale and rapid development, it could be a major contributor towards climate change globally (Lister et al., 2015). The rising public interest and consciousness regarding environmental issues caused by maritime operations are a major challenge within the maritime circle (Jasmi & Fernando, 2021). Moreover, the current inclination towards climate change, conservation, and environmental sustainability has been extensively discussed by industry players, stakeholders, and worldwide political leaders (Jasmi & Fernando, 2018; Revkin, 2009; Rosenthal, 2009). The significant connotation of this mounting issue could be reflected through the course of research devoted to addressing climate change issues within the business environment. Facilitating the role of the intermediary global supply chain, maritime industries globally have begun to act in response to environmental concerns by embracing sustainable practices in their operations (Jasmi & Fernando, 2018; Sarkis, Zhu, & Lai, 2011). From an environmental perspective, the rising pressure as depicted by worldwide concerns on environmental problems also affects Malaysian maritime sectors. The Malaysian maritime sector that occupies diverse activities that utilise hydrocarbon resources also discharge hazardous emissions that may contribute to the climatic problem. In this sense, there is mounting pressure on Malaysia's maritime industry to side with sustainable operation following the international trend in sustainability.

Additionally, the International Maritime Organization (IMO) regulatory amendments related to emissions, ballast water discharge, and ship design will put additional strain on the maritime sectors to increase their sustainability agenda (Makkonen & Inkinen, 2021). Moreover, international regulations based upon green practices and documents began to be tightened up by requiring each shipping country to implement sustainable practices in its operation. However, international regulations set up by the International Maritime Organization (IMO) are insufficient to mitigate the marine pollution and environmental damage resulting from the increasing population of shipping traffic each year (Sardain, Sardain, & Leung, 2019). According to a survey by Asian Port Association (2004), the overlapping problems with this implementation of regulations and guidelines regarding shipping efficiency and optimum utilisation of resources are usually dampened by the stakeholders' attitudes. In these remarks, the awareness level within the stakeholder's community is still in its infancy state (Fernando, Jasmi, & Shaharudin, 2019).

The resulting predicament of this situation may be seen through a lack of incentive and concrete effort regarding proper action or mitigation plan on environmental issues surrounding the maritime industry. Qi, Zou, & Xie (2020) have also indicated in their study that even though various policies developed, the government and corporate sector have not paid much attention to monitoring environmental issues.

Furthermore, Fernando et al. (2019) deposited that amongst the problems maritime sectors face comprises the expenditure and cost of conforming to green regulations, deficiency of green technology to be adopted, and appeasing opposite interests and priorities in their daily business, the industry as well as society. For that reason, it is critical for stakeholders in the industry to "fine-tune" the actions and efforts to ensure an impending sustainable future and to measure existing industrial practices in this sector to curb carbon production from their routine activities and, along the way, contribute in addressing bigger issues of climate change.

In retrospect, many efforts and studies on sustainability have been conducted in many other sectors. However, studies on sustainability within the maritime domain are still limited. It is primarily so with regards to the maritime sector in Malaysia. Since the research on sustainability in Malaysia's maritime sector is inadequate, further research and observation should be conceded in this exacting area. In addressing these gaps, the purpose of this paper thus is fourfold:

1. To elevate the importance of maritime supply chain (discussing in overview chapter as well as the component of maritime supply chain chapter) and highlight why maritime supply chain is a primary component in achieving environmental sustainability within Malaysian maritime industry;
2. To discuss the concept of sustainability in the maritime supply chain
3. To examine the present state of the environmental laws and policy in Malaysia as well as its potentialities, challenges, and constraints
4. To classify the diverse 'imperative' or goals that must be met to implement sustainability and the action needed to achieve them – probability of acquiring appropriate actions by the relevant regulatory bodies and the many maritime stakeholders. Inevitably the goals here are not to be conceived as a measurement of empirical results but rather an expression of the intention of a desirable future state that industry players can achieve.

BACKGROUND OF MARITIME SECTOR IN MALAYSIA

Overview of Malaysian Maritime Sector

The maritime industry in Asia, one of the world's most promising economic regions, has developed into an extensive expansion course in modern times. Maritime industries in this region have seen an augmented growth in their throughput resulting from their competitiveness and capability to cater to regional trade and economic growth in their respective countries. In Malaysia, maritime sectors' progression evolved through a diverse growth phase in reaction to various policy initiatives, guidelines, regulations, and other factors in the maritime supply chain system. Historically, the maritime industry development in Malaysia started in the 15th century where Malacca became the most important maritime port for domestic and international trade. This period's significance in maritime trade was reflected through Malaysia's strategic location for trading in the heart of seaborne traffic from the Indian Ocean to East Malaysia (Drabble, 2004). Later, the Melaka Kingdom's fall in the year 1511, due to Portuguese intrusion, has made the Malacca seaport lose its dominant status as the leading trading port in the region. These current circumstances present a handful of challenges to Malaysia, as an aspiring maritime nation, to traverse the competition posed by maritime sectors in this Asia Pacific region.

Currently, being a homeland surrounded by the ocean, Malaysia's reliance on the sea is ubiquitous. This dependence broadens into an extensive scope of key areas such as trading businesses, energy resources, transportation, employment, commodities movement, tourism, and military defences. Following the regional Exclusive Economic Zone authority, Malaysia has a relatively outsized sea area than its modest landmass (Thirugnana et al., 2021). Malaysia's maritime attribute is highlighted by the very fact that it is a land fragmented by the prevailing ocean, with the South China Sea untying Peninsular Malaysia from Sabah and Sarawak. In recent years, Malaysia's maritime sector has gone through various transformations in the 1980s and 1990s due to its rapid economic growth. This is due to rapid industrialisation resulting from the various ventures of Foreign Direct Investment (FDI) in the state (Jasmi, 2019). This economic development's notable outcome has made Malaysia's maritime supply chain activities imperative to extensive import-export operations. Malaysia's maritime industries have developed extensively in the preceding decade, with Port Klang being the world's 12th largest container handling port and Port of Tanjung Pelepas being the fastest-growing transhipment port in the world.

Moreover, marine natural resources also add to Malaysia's economic prosperity, with hydrocarbon fuel such as petroleum and gas representing Malaysia's peculiarity as the largest single export commodity. In addition to this, the maritime field has become more and more imperative in economic and security conditions. All of these developments emphasise the significance of the maritime sector to the nation's socio-economic and well-being. As Malaysia desires to become a developed industrial nation, the maritime division's involvement in the direction of the Malaysian economy's expansion and dynamism will become ever more important. Therefore, the fundamental concept of stewardship of these sectors must be commenced in a sustainable approach to ensure efficient use of its assets and resources for many generations to come (Jasmi & Fernando, 2021).

THE COMPONENTS OF THE MALAYSIAN MARITIME SUPPLY CHAIN SYSTEM

The maritime supply chain's complex and globalise nature is well established by various governmental regulations and policy-making processes related to global shipping industries. In general, within these complex supply chain systems, shipping companies, port authorities, trading companies, and stevedores typically collaborate and cooperate with each other in the immense management of maritime logistics (Cheng, Farahani, Lai, & Sarkis, 2015). In this regard, various stakeholders of diverse nationalities are players in the daily business and trade of shipping operations. These players are concerned in the design, production, ownership, construction, procedure, administration, crewing of maritime trader vessels and training, classification, investment, finance, liability, and insurance aspects of shipping operations. The remaining major stakeholders could be categorised as freight owners and definitive customers and ancillary services such as stevedore, pilotage, equipment maintenance service, vessel traffic services, towage, and consolidator (Lam, 2011).

In Malaysia, the maritime supply chain exists under many shore infrastructures such as port and warehousing facilities as well as workforce for cargo handling and support services to ensure efficient and reliable shipping operations. The Malaysian maritime supply chain acts as an imperative linkage between the international logistics supply chain and the Malaysian domestic supply chain by moving cargo worldwide to cater to global trade and economic development. Hence, each and everyone in the chains are mutually crucial to work cohesively to function efficiently. For better understanding, Figure 1 shows the structure of maritime supply chain members in Malaysia in general categorised by:

1. Carriers, including operators and shipping linear (international and domestically operation), road haulier (conventional trucking, container truck transportation, and bonded truck), railway and airlines carrier;
2. The terminal operator that includes maritime port, inland port system, freight terminal, and inland container depot;
3. Carrier intermediaries, including shipping agent, air cargo agent, off dock depot operator, non-vessel operating common carrier, shipbroker, and i-port;
4. Cargo intermediaries, including freight forwarders, customs agents, multimodal transport operator, warehouse operator (bonded and non-bonded), private warehouse (bonded and non-bonded), International Procurement Centers and regional distribution Centers;
5. Inland water transport, including barges, tugs, and riverine vessels;
6. Ancillary services providers including cargo handler or stevedoring companies, packaging service providers, cargo consolidators, and equipment maintenance and material handling suppliers;
7. Integrated Logistic Service Providers including third-party logistics providers (3PLs) and lead logistic providers (LLPs), often called fourth party logistic providers (4PLs)

Figure 1. Structure of Freight Logistics
Source: Roadmap on the Freight Transport in Malaysia (2012)

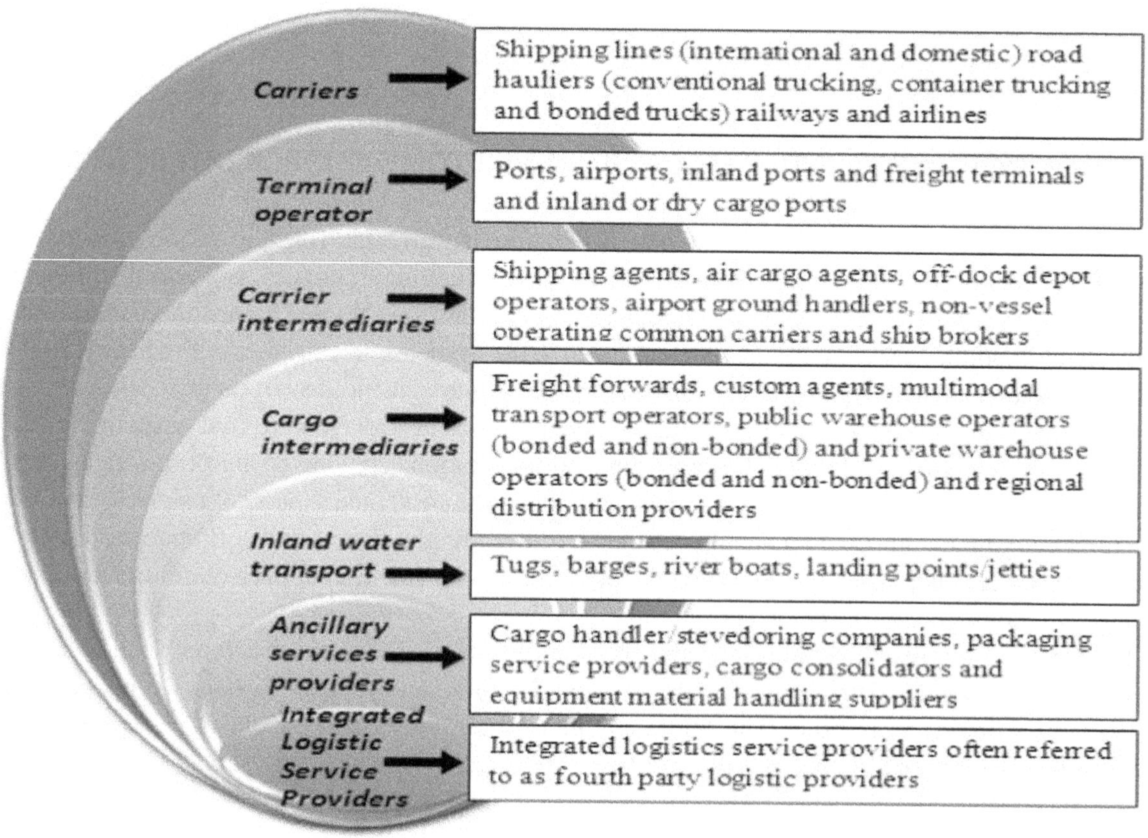

The maritime supply chain has several multitudes of industrial players, making it the most complicated industry in the world. Given these significant roles to each player in the maritime supply chain, many issues were raised regarding integration and coordination function between the players (Fernando et al., 2019). The maritime supply chain flow of operation proved to be challenging to operate efficiently from an operational context. The problem lies in competitiveness amongst industry players, compliance with international and local regulations, health and safety issues, and environmental problems. This complex structure of the maritime sector, in general, provides the fundamental idea to this paper to determine the nature of its operation and identify sustainability dimension that can be included in the line of its supply chain operation and its distinctive challenge. Thus, in the subsequent chapter, the sustainability in the maritime supply chain, regulations, and challenges are briefly explained based on this supply chain structure.

SUSTAINABILITY IN MARITIME SUPPLY CHAIN

The Notion of Sustainable Maritime Supply Chain

The conceptual notion of "sustainable development" has been an important area of apprehension to current society and industry in general. In this context, sustainable development can be described as "one that meets the present generation's needs and desires without jeopardising future generations' ability to satisfy their own" (Avesani, 2020). According to Meadows and Meadows (1972), sustainable development from the perspective of limits to global growth has been an issue for decades. In recent years, the conception of sustainability is diverted from that anticipated early concept in the seventies. The 'Limits to Growth' concept is no longer be acknowledged by societies and industries in recent years. Nowadays, the real challenge to industries towards sustainability is to make certain that the particular industries could potentially sustain economic growth while at the same time ensuring environmental protection (Rao & Yan, 2020). The climate change crisis can also be perceived as one portion of the sustainability dilemma that posed the greatest challenge facing civilisation today.

The notion of sustainability, in general, has been applied to various sectors, communities, and economies, often leading to a range of definitions and understanding of the expression. It was a thought that gained considerable discussion with the Brundtland Report published in 1987 and was further ingrained into public awareness and discussion at the Rio Earth Summit in 1992. To further strengthen this respective agenda, the World Summit for Sustainable Development held in January 2002 called for the world's attention to the various challenges of sustainability issues. As previously stated, sustainability itself can be defined as an advancement that assembles the requisite needs of the present without compromising prospects' capacity to meet their own potential needs. Thus, sustainability in this exacting context is about constructing a society that shapes an appropriate balance between economic, social, and environmental aims (Destek, 2020). For organisations in general, this involves satisfying economic development, investor value, industrial reputation, consumer relations, and the value of products and services. From a broader perspective, sustainability also means adopting and pursuing ethical and moral-driven business practices, creating sustainable jobs, building value for all the company's stakeholders, and attending to the underserved's needs (Kolk, 2016). Additionally, balancing economic and environmental performance has become increasingly imperative for organisations to face competition, regulation, and social pressures (Escobar & Vredenburg, 2011).

Various literature emphasised sustainability within logistic and shipping line operations in the perspective of sustainability in the maritime supply chain. As such, Fernando et al. (2019) define sustainability in the maritime supply chain as a conceptual term as maritime green supply chain management (MGSCM) that emphasise five dimensions of sustainable conduct, which include green financial flow, integration of green information, and green practices, green value-added services and green shipping design to enhance efficiency and environmental performance. The term green maritime logistics used by Psaraftis (2016) emphasises sustainability as a persistent attempt to accomplish acceptable environmental and economic performance. In comparison, Cheng, Farahani, Lai and Sarkis (2015a) defined a sustainable maritime supply chain as integrating maritime managerial and organisational units, materials flow, information, communication, and monetary flows to meet customer needs and improve competitiveness to achieve social performance by reducing environmental impact impacts. While Jasmi & Fernando (2018) sustainability in the maritime supply chain can be defined as integrating maritime organisational units (ports, shipping companies, etc.) along a supply chain and coordinating material (container, bulk, and general cargoes), knowledge, and financial flows in order to meet consumer demands and increase the supply chain's competitiveness in order to benefit; subject to compliance with regulations governing social and environmental impacts.

The theoretical term "green shipping practice" (GSP) by Lun, Lai, Wong, and Cheng (2014) and "green management practice" (GMP) by Lun (2011) in defining maritime sustainability has also become prominently used in the literature. GSP and GMP capability focuses principally on enhancing profitable operation and efficiency in operational conditions as well as reducing the harmful impact of maritime supply chain actions on the environment. In contrast, others defined sustainability in the maritime supply chain as a decision approach and actions that meet the maritime sector's current and potential needs for future industry and its stakeholders while sufficiently sustaining environmental resources (American Association of Port Authorities, 2007). It is beyond this modest scope of the paper to elaborate much literature on the sustainable concept. Still, it has appeared that incorporating sustainability into maritime management approaches has become progressively significant to attain a significant competitive advantage and lessen the environmental impact. However, many maritime organisations generally are still hesitant to take a more aggressive approach to implement these sustainability practices due to a perceived lack of evidence that the benefits exceed the costs of pursuing these initiatives (Li, Ye, Dai, Zhao, & Sheu, 2019), the complexity of the maritime supply chain nature as well as regulatory and governance problems.

ENVIRONMENTAL REGULATION IN MARITIME SUPPLY CHAIN

To recapitulate, operation in the maritime supply chain is a firmly regulated activity because of its global nature and the various parties involved along its chain. These sectors' complex nature can only be efficiently managed with a set of well-documented and stringently enforced laws, conventions, protocols, policies, regulations, and standards (Ashari, Yusof, Mohd Zamani, & Abdul Talib, 2018). This is well established that as merchant ships navigate around the globe and load and unload all kinds of cargoes at the diverse port system, the transhipment of goods can only be managed with a set of protocols, agreement, and policies restricted to its operation that cross beyond the boundaries. In this regard, the earliest global bodies concerning the need for standardisation and association of transportation means came into being in the nineteenth century (Zacher & Sutton, 1996). Urgent needs and awareness eventually sparked a need to institute a global body dealing with the comprehensive safety of maritime shipping operations. The central agreement of policies and protocols amongst countries is currently regulated through United Nation's International Maritime Organization (IMO). IMO is the major source of about 60 legal mechanisms that funnel its member states' laws and regulatory development to develop comprehensive safety and security dimension at sea, facilitate trade among maritime states, and keep the marine environment protected. The International Convention for the Safety of Life at Sea (SOLAS) and the International Convention on Oil Pollution Preparedness, Response, and Cooperation (OPRC) are the two most relevant regulations. Others include the International Oil Pollution Compensation Funds. It also functions as a depository of yet to be ratified treaties, such as the International Convention on Liability and Compensation for Damage in Connection with the Carriage of Hazardous and Noxious Substances by Sea, 1996 (HNS Convention) and 2007, Nairobi International Convention of Removal of Wrecks (Hao,2008).

The International Maritime Organization often endorses maritime regulations that are broadly implemented by international and national maritime authorities in member countries, such as the International Regulations for the Prevention of Collisions at Sea (COLREG). In promoting environmentally friendly maritime industries, the International Maritime Organization (IMO) has been required by the United Nations Framework Convention on Climate Change (UNFCCC) to spearhead green shipping efforts. According to Khalid et al. (2010), the IMO has initiated several instruments and programmes aimed at reducing toxic emissions from maritime supply chain operations. These include the following:

1. Encouraging industry players by adopting guidelines and procedures for environmentally-friendly ship recycling, ballast water management, curbing GHG emissions.
2. Allocating susceptible environmental, maritime areas as Particularly Sensitive Sea Areas (PSSA) and Special Areas.
3. Instil the awareness on the need to protect the environment to industry players and the public stakeholders

The list of key IMO conventions to prevent and control ships' pollution and moderating the effects of any harm arising from maritime operations and accidents are listed in Table 1.

Accentuating its importance in highlighting the marine environment protection while facilitating shipping activities, Malaysia has adopted a few of its conventions as its maritime policies. Of the conventions established, there is none significant other than the International Convention for the Prevention of Pollution from Ships, or better known as MARPOL 73/78, as the central international convention covering the hindrance of pollution by ships from its operational or unintended accident causes. It was created to eradicate the undesirable impact of shipping operations of every type of vessel on the environment by regulating pollutants' discharge.

MARPOL 73/78 enclosed six annexes that institute the release standards for six key groups of pollutants, as summarised in Table 2:

Table 1. Key IMO conventions on pollution and environmental protection

Convention/code/ law	Remarks
Pollution prevention	
International Convention for the Prevention of Pollution from Ships (MARPOL 73/78)	It concerns accidental oil pollution in operation and pollution by chemicals, consignment in packaged form, sewage, rubbish, and air pollution.
International Convention on Prevention of Marine Pollution by Dumping of Waste and Other Matters 1972	The International Convention on Liability and Compensation for Damage in Connection with the Carriage of Hazardous and Noxious Substances by Sea was restructured in 1996.
Oil pollution	
International Convention on Oil Pollution Preparedness, Response, and Cooperation (OPRC)	It is a comprehensive international framework for structural cooperation in dealing with huge incidents of maritime pollution
International Convention on Civil Liability for Oil Pollution Damage (CLC) 1969	A law is adopted to guarantee that sufficient payment is available to persons who undergo oil pollution harm resulting from naval casualties involving oil-carrying transportations. It puts a considerable liability for such harm on the vessel's possessor from which the pollution of oil originates
Safety and security of merchant ships	
International Convention for the Safety of Life at Sea (SOLAS) 1974	The major convention includes all worldwide treaties concerning the global safety and security of trader's vessels.
International Convention for Standards, Training, Certification, and Watchkeeping for Seafarers (STCW) 1978	It deposits the global standards of competence that are accepted by the international regulatory body for seafarers globally.
Convention on the International Regulations for the Prevention of Collisions at Sea (COLREG) 1972	It provides ample guidance and guidelines concerning safe sailing speed, collision risk, and the conduct of vessels operation in or close to traffic separation schemes.
Protection of the marine environment	
International Convention on the Control of Harmful Anti-Fouling Systems on Ship (AFS) 2001	It prohibits the utilisation of hazardous organotin in anti-fouling paints used on vessels and ships. It establishes an instrument of actions needed to prevent the possible upcoming usage of other hazardous substances in anti-fouling systems.
International Convention for the Control and Management of Ships" Ballast Water and Sediments (BWM) 2004	It is divided into Articles, and an Annex consists of practical standards and requirements in the Regulations and Laws for controlling and administering ships' ballast water and sediments.

Source: International Maritime Organisation (2015)

Table 2. MARPOL 73/78 Annexes

Annex	Remarks
Annex I	Regulations for the prevention of pollution by oil
Annex II	Regulations for the control of pollution by the noxious liquid substance in bulk
Annex III	Regulations for the prevention of pollution by harmful substances carried by sea in packaged forms, or freight containers, portable tanks, or road and rail wagons
Annex IV	Regulations for the prevention of pollution by sewage
Annex V	Regulations for the prevention of pollution by garbage from ships
Annex VI	Regulations for the prevention of air pollution from ships

Source: International Maritime Organization (2015)

Both Annexes I and II are collectively obligatory, while Annexes II, IV, V, and VI are voluntary. Malaysia has agreed to MARPOL 73/78 on January 31, 1997, which entered into force in Malaysia on May 1, 1997 (Khalid et al., 2010). As Annexes I, II, and V were endorsed, Malaysia is also lawfully bounced to act under these annexes' provisions. The introduction of these conventions highlights the significance of IMO, its Member Governments, the shipping industry players, and stakeholders to participate and play their part to lessen the maritime supply chain's environmental impact. In addition to these conventions, Malaysia's Maritime Department (MARDEP) has taken a tentative step toward developing a clean, stable, and comprehensive sea communication system by adopting the 1974 International Convention for the Safety of Life at Sea (SOLAS) to ensure marine conservation and the quality development of the country's maritime policy. Adoption of this convention entails the following:

1. International Convention for the Prevention of Pollution from Ships (MARPOL) 73/78, Annexes I, II, and V
2. International Convention on Tonnage Measurement of Ships, 1969
3. International Regulations for Preventing Collision at Sea (COLREGS), 1972
4. International Convention on Load Lines, 1966 or as amended
5. International Convention on Civil Liability for Oil Pollution Damage (CLC) 1969, Protocol of 1992
6. International Convention on Civil Liability for Oil Pollution Damage (CLC) 1969, Protocol of 1992
7. International Convention on Load Lines, 1966 or as amended
8. International Convention on Civil Liability for Oil Pollution Damage (CLC) 1969, Protocol of 1992
9. International Convention on Civil Liability for Oil Pollution Damage (CLC) 1969, Protocol of 1992
10. International Regulations for Preventing Collision at Sea (COLREGS), 1972
11. International Convention on Load Lines, 1966 or as amended
12. International Convention on Civil Liability for Oil Pollution Damage (CLC) 1969, Protocol of 1992
13. International Convention on Civil Liability for Oil Pollution Damage (CLC) 1969, Protocol of 1992
14. International Convention on Load Lines, 1966 or as amended
15. International Convention on Civil Liability for Oil Pollution Damage (CLC) 1969, Protocol of 1992

MARDEP, as one of the regulatory bodies of the Malaysian maritime sector (Osnin & Rahman, 2018), has embraced these international policies to ensure safe navigation of international merchant vessels, providing services to merchant vessels such as ship inspection, certification, registration, and licensing, providing unparallel services to ships navigating in Malaysian waters and ports as well as supervising examinations of seafarers to help smoothen the flow of maritime supply chain operation. Highlighting the importance of maritime sectors to the country, these conventions and policies are needed to ensure environmentally sound and efficient maritime supply chain systems. The broad scope of its mandate means that IMO is well placed to support the maritime supply chain system's cohesion and good functioning and contribute to its sustainable development worldwide. The organisation's potential to make a real difference lies in capacity-building measures to develop and strengthen maritime transport sectors in developing countries.

Finally, it is important to remember that, while the IMO's mandate is primarily focused on vessels engaging in international trade (Molenaar, 2014), there are genuine opportunities for the organisation to play a direct and significant role in promoting policy cooperation at the national and regional levels as well. This is because of its standing in the world as the most respected competent body in all technical matters pertaining to shipping. Thus, it can assist with the coordination of the different players in the maritime supply chain system. It can also provide valuable feedback on the effects of measures implemented throughout the supply chain system.

MALAYSIA AND ENVIRONMENTAL STEWARDSHIP: THE CURRENT AGENDA

As a developing country, Malaysia has emphasised socio-economic development as the fundamental element to achieving prosperity. With its vast ocean area and its plentiful resources, Malaysian maritime industries bear enormous management and administration responsibilities, especially regarding environmental stewardship and sustainable development of its marine resources (Othman, Bruce, & Hamid, 2011). Affirmation with these obligations, Malaysia is dedicated to numerous worldwide maritime policy conventions, which it has ratified accordingly, such as IMO policies and regulations. The commitments to protect its environment are shown with the well-established adoption of several internal policies. The National Policy on the Environment (NPE) has been drafted in the Seventh Malaysian Plan, which stresses a wide-ranging strategy to protect the environment and its natural resources and accomplish the sustainable goal of green consumption and production. As articulated in the NPE, Malaysia has acquired a positive and active approach to regional and worldwide ecological and green issues by cooperating with neighbouring countries and relevant organisations on transboundary maritime issues and environmental concerns. The sustainable actions taken by Malaysia are reflected through several meaningful precaution steps that accentuate its seriousness to embrace sustainability principles that include several national environmental policies and regulations in Malaysia which apply to the maritime sector, as listed b Table 3.

Table 3. Key policies and governances on pollution and environmental protection

Act/Law/Policy/Governance	Remark
i) Merchant Shipping Ordinance 1952	Merchant Shipping Ordinance 1952 (MSO 1952) is the Act that administrates international merchant shipping in Malaysia. Ever since its establishment, it is in the course of numerous amendments. This is due to the governments' imitative to replace the new Merchant Shipping Act with MSO 1952. However, this new Act will integrate quite a few amendments to agree with the international conventions to which Malaysia is a member. Besides, being a member of the United Nations Convention on the Law of the Seas (UNCLOS) 1982, Malaysia has to alter several maritime environmental norms as noted in the convention to be integrated into Malaysian domestic law.
ii) Environmental Quality Act 1974	The Environmental Quality Act 1974 (EQA 1974) is Malaysia's most important legislation system to oversee environmental security. However, the Act is only pertinent within the territorial waters of Malaysia's ocean boundary, which may widen up to 12 nautical miles from the baselines, respectively. Consequently, the Act is not relevant to the Exclusive Economic Zone (which may broaden up to 200 nautical miles from the baselines) and Malaysia's Continental Shelf. Moreover, the EQA 1974 has only two provisions openly related to marine pollution.
iii) Merchant Shipping (Oil Pollution) Act (amended in 2005)	The Act was revised in 2005 to fulfil the 1992 Civil Liability Convention and 1992 Fund Convention for oil pollution. The noteworthy enhancement of the Act is the extension of its territorial appliance to incorporate the Exclusive Economic Zone regarding marine pollution. This, in return, had successfully filled the loopholes of the Environmental Quality Act 1974 and the Merchant Shipping Ordinance 1952.
iv) Exclusive Economic Zone Act 1984	The EEZ Act establishment has included several aspects of UNCLOS 1982 while providing authorised rights to Malaysia, extending to 200 nautical miles from the baselines and control maritime operations to Malaysia's continental ridge. In this sense, the Act deals with protecting and conserving ecological marine life and the environment. Moreover, the Act assured Malaysia's independent rights to exploit its natural resources in the EEZ area.
v) Malaysian Maritime Enforcement Agency Act 2004	The Malaysian Maritime Enforcement Agency (MMEA) is a primary organisation that upholds law, policies, regulations, and peace, safety, and security in the maritime zone. In this sense, Malaysia has also established the National Policy on Climate Change (NPCC), which provides a structure and regulatory framework to assemble and guide numerous governmental agencies, industry players, communities, and other stakeholders in addressing the dispute of climate change. The NPCC, administered by the Ministry of Natural Resources and Environment, offers directional guidelines in the shape of premeditated thrusts and solutions for the country to take significant conduct and recognise the opportunities towards sustainable development within the industries.

Source: Mustafa & Ariffin (2011)

Despite these endless efforts, the Malaysian maritime supply chain still confronts threats and challenges. While Malaysia's government has made many attempts to address the sustainability issue, there is a serious necessity to obtain a stock of sustainable approaches in which they have been undertaken. This is because the active policies and existing maritime sustainability regulations were designed a relatively long ago when environmental resources were far better and healthier. New challenges and constraints have arisen nowadays (Zakaria, Abdul-Talib, & Osman, 2016), requiring more practical, definite, and sensitive actions and policies to convey sustainability in its maritime activities. The required judgments of course actions must be prepared based on a significant understanding of these activities' possible contribution and effect to the environment and its economic structure according to the existing improvement of maritime and environmental issues. Underlying these serious issues, the subsequent chapter would briefly explain the challenge faced by the Malaysian maritime industry.

THE CHALLENGE OF MALAYSIAN MARITIME SUPPLY CHAIN

Historically, the maritime supply chain's challenge lies in the regulatory authorities concerning the development of environmental regulations. Since the 1950s, there has been an increasing number of environmental rules and regulations in position at diverse government levels to manage environmental effects by maritime supply chain operations. In this regard, the most prominent rule-making authority is the International Maritime Organisation (IMO), which administers more than 20 global conventions concerning environmental issues related to maritime operations. The green initiatives regimes established by the IMO are nevertheless defective in quite a few respects. Even though the implementation and updating of IMO conventions have accelerated in recent years, the procedure and process of bilateral resolution-making are very time-consuming. Many years may go by between agenda-setting up, approval, implementation, and entry-into-force of a particular convention (Wuisan, van Leeuwen, (Kris) van Koppen, Leeuwen, & Koppen, 2012). Besides, incentives and encouragement for maritime organisations to act according to the conventions are lacking, and efficient enforcement of instruments to deal with non-compliance parties is limited and inadequate (Tan, 2005). For that reason, it is extremely uncertain whether the IMO can make certain instantaneous and effective actions in avoiding further ecological degradation from maritime supply chain operation.

Furthermore, the Malaysian maritime supply chain, as part of a cross-border distribution system of cargoes from a solitary place to another, frequently over vast distances, is subjected to a complex issue of policies, laws, and regulations. In this sense, before the cargoes being transhipped to Malaysian soil, they will first be subjected to the regulations and policies of naval infrastructure (port system), economic, societal, and environmental setting of their respective country of origin. The goods then travel across a port system into the international carriage, where various rules apply. This is where important international policies are imposed on the respective system. The policies and regulations are based on globally accepted commercial regulations as well as international standards, rules, and regulations developed by IMO (Joung, Kang, Lee, & Ahn, 2020). Once the goods finally reach their intended destination, they are yet to land at ports that have their own set of domestic infrastructure, regulations, and policies in a different country. Commencing from here then, they may be further distributed to multiple destinations, where, in turn, another state of affairs, law and policies may affect. This complex nature of multiple successive phases of the distribution chain adding up to individual whole and interconnected operation where the reality of this chain goes beyond diverse interests and priorities of involving players in each phase of the maritime supply chain. On the other hand, this complicated system of this maritime supply chain as a whole is required for the wide-ranging global transhipment to function. Unnecessary competition could disturb this global cohesion, which adversely impacts the efficiency of moving freight worldwide.

Maritime supply chain system must remain a big business endeavour and venture, which carry an essential public service to the globe at a rather low cost while functioning under many changing sets of laws and regulations in diverse jurisdictions (Voyer et al., 2018). The underlying problem is not always about the regulations but the implementation of those laws and policies. Besides, this set of laws is not inert and depends on its jurisdiction area's regulatory body. For example, international freight transporter may be subjected to an IMO set of regulations. Still, the domestic partner of its operation is not subjected to IMO's regulation standard but rather depends on domestic regulations on the country's jurisdiction. Since Malaysia only implements several IMO regulations and its own set of laws, the problem lies with Malaysia's weaker or non-comprehensive environmental laws. This posed a problem for the sustainability agenda, as domestic actors are not bound by stringent international environmental protection standards. However, the changes are always introduced to hold new challenges and adversities in the industries, such as technological and industrial advances in the maritime industry as well as augmented public expectations for collectively improved safety, protection, and environmental performance, but the time needed to respond to this change is slow in the Malaysian context. For that reason, the shipping industry in Malaysia must continuously strive to enhance its measures and be equipped to adjust to varying regulatory and compliance requirements with extra supervision and intervention from governmental bodies. Nevertheless, if regulations grow too demanding and the increasing cost of shipments, the operational dimension of the catering movement of huge volumes of basic materials and cargo at comparatively low cost could be threatened. This would not be in the general public and country's interest and would negatively impact society's development and prosperity.

Besides these contemplations concerning the equilibrium between expenditure (cost) and benefit, it is imperative to bear in mind that value creation and the flow of value in Malaysia's maritime supply chain system, which contains a chain of industry players, all of whom must allocate and distribute values, should be protected. In this sense, if each player in the Malaysian maritime sector fulfils their diverse functions and works collectively in mutual support of this value chain, the maritime supply chain will operate efficiently for the entire stakeholders concerned and society and society whole. To summarise, cargoes' movement by the maritime supply chain is subjected to economic goals, social well-being, environmental responsibilities, and mutual requirements on many different levels. The challenge here lies in how the maritime supply chain complex system can be translated into justifiably, equitably, and comparatively fair across the chain of players to put together the whole supply chain system in sustainable order. This is predominantly a difficult task in the Malaysian context since coordination and integration involving shore-side maritime players, and the international shipping sector is not well-established as far as policies are concerned. This problem is due to the fact of a general inclination towards profit orientation by every player in the industries, who may be successful in shunting costs to other players, and this may in turn influence the sustainability of those other players' operations, and in the end, have an effect on the maritime supply chain as a whole. This could be translated into a loss of flexibility and sustainability in one linkage in the chain that could risk degrading the whole supply chain over a period of time.

Besides, all players in the maritime supply chain system are subjected to peripheral and external costs. Nevertheless, several of these costs will eventually involve all players (Abdul-Talib & Teong, 2019). In this sense, if the costs affect specific parts within the maritime supply chain system, it will inevitably affect the whole maritime supply chain system or just a link in the respective supply chain system. A coherent approach is needed to overcome this problem through comprehensive regulation and policies and educate the players by overseeing governmental bodies regarding this issue. Thus, a noteworthy mention should be made of the maritime supply chain role in Malaysia, where an efficient and coherent system is a precondition for facilitating import-export growth and development in this industry. The further progress of maritime industries in Malaysia is a necessity that must be met to enhance its efficiency. Therefore, Malaysia must participate and embrace new trading patterns around the world. Sustainability agendas and more comprehensive policies and regulations should be adopted concurrently to align domestic maritime industries with global needs and requirements for gaining a competitive advantage. For Malaysia, incredible opportunities arise from a more comprehensive engagement with the shipping sector, and Malaysia should play its role as a part of the global chain.

TOWARDS SUSTAINABLE DEVELOPMENT FOR MALAYSIAN MARITIME SUPPLY CHAIN

Although the law-making, policy, and regulatory frameworks for certain environmental elements such as forestry and land use are well recognised, similar and parallel requirements and provisions for maritime environmental protection are not all-inclusive and are spread over different sets of laws and agencies. In this regard, it is disputable that the lack of a complete and comprehensive maritime policy has turned into an obstruction to the expansion of coordinated development of maritime economic operations in addressing environmental issues and resources. This adversity is highlighted by the exclusion of maritime management as the most important part of the functions of central or federal agencies associated with maritime dealings, such as the National Maritime Council and Cabinet Committee on Maritime Affairs. The schemes undertaken by such associations are prepared in an uncoordinated approach, missing in a distinctive approach and plan to expand and systematically administer the Malaysian maritime operations. This state of affairs has resulted in multiple problems in the Malaysian maritime sector, which comprises deficient policy remedies, inter-organisational conflicts within the maritime sector occurring from inconsistency in development patterns, and insufficient authority maritime sectors to commence assigned tasks clash of jurisdictions between federal and state.

Consecutively, to mitigate this problem and to endow with reliable provisions and services most proficiently, the Malaysian maritime supply chain system must convey a safe, secure, and consistent efficiency of transportation of goods transversely around the globe while still putting an effort in decreasing harmful pollution, increasing energy efficiency as well as resource preservation. To achieve this sustainable agenda, the complicated inter-relationship among players in the Malaysian maritime supply chain system should be first acknowledged and considered when tackling specific sustainable actions. To put into perspective, sustainability in the maritime supply chain requires well-ordered, integrated, and efficient administration that collaborates closely with global and domestic partners and encourages compliance with international standards, supported by relevant institutions with technical know-how and expertise. In this sense, sustainability in the maritime supply chain must involve synchronised and coordinated support from the shore-side entity essential to shipping, such as port facilities, cargo-handling infrastructure, and land logistics systems to ensure a transparent and holistic approach to sustainability in its operation. This collaboration of shore-side players from both industry and governmental bodies could provide sustainable provision and care for maritime operations and environmental protection to ensure that the supply chain integrity and sustainability concept does not become eroded in the long run.

The qualified, skilled, and competent workforce (Zakaria, Abdul-Talib, & Amelinckx, 2020b) is also important for a sustainable maritime supply chain. In the Malaysian maritime context, the most challenging issue facing the shipping industry today is how to draw and maintain adequate people of the sufficiently trained and qualified workforce and industry professionals with the right understanding of the "green" concept, motivation, information, and skills for sustainable application of developing green technologies and measures. The challenges will increase significantly as global trade continues (Zakaria, Abdul-Talib, & Amelinckx, 2020a) to develop and shipping activities increase accordingly. With this kind of backdrop, an all-inclusive approach and strategy for advancing maritime supply chain operation are indispensable for the sustainable utilisation of the marine environment and its resources. Maritime supply chain operations must be cautiously planned and well-managed in an organised, systematic and integrated approach to reduce the loss of biodiversity and pollution and ensure maritime resources are preserved at points that can sustainably hold present and future generations. In this sense, a coherent plan should include the subsequent approaches:

1. Applicable policies, regulations, conventions, set of laws, and plans must be comprehensively set up and researched accordingly (Hashim, Bakar, & Talib, 2010). It supports maritime supply chain operation in a comportment that could be enhanced, particularly in a distinctive development in specific sectors that require sustainability attention.
2. Assisting diverse governmental bodies, departments, organisations, and institutions engaged in maritime supply chain activities in concentrating their attention, intelligence, and effort, and sharing their established expertise among themselves and with other related sectors of the maritime supply chain.
3. Developing reliable, transparent, and accurate measurement methods (Abdul Talib & Keung, 2022) for assessing the maritime supply chain's sustainable development.
4. Increasing collaboration and cooperation among stakeholders in the maritime supply chain, including individuals, private companies, non-governmental organisations (NGOs), communities, and governmental bodies involved in maritime sectors. Additionally, these organisations need to strengthen their relationships with international maritime agencies to ensure that their operations adhere to global standards and requirements.
5. Financial support from financial sectors or government bodies should be carefully considered to support the changing existence of the maritime supply chain and to ensure long-term resource allocation efficiency to advance the three pillars of sustainable growth.
6. Collaborating closely with academic institutions and other research and development organisations to match current understanding with emerging green technologies and organisational practices will allow maritime businesses to advance toward this sustainability agenda continuously.

To reiterate, the most critical aspect of a sustainable maritime supply chain's efficiency is the application of comprehensive and global principles that ensure global "level playing fields" by adhering to international safety and environmental regulations, focusing on technical and operational aspects of shipping vessels, as well as adequate education and training of crews and experts. In this context, a sustainable maritime supply chain should prioritise pollution management, environmental biodiversity conservation, and maritime governance values, all of which should be perpetually expressed in IMO conventions to ensure the long-term incorporation of sustainability into the supply chain.

In summary, given the critical role of the maritime supply chain as a major contributor to the Malaysian economy, it is also critical that all stakeholders in the maritime supply chain collaborate to address the sustainability challenges demanded and capitalise on the existing opportunities provided by this concept of sustainable growth. Due to the critical nature of maritime supply chain growth, Malaysia should adopt a more holistic, sustainable approach to planning its maritime supply chain following the principles espoused by sustainable development values. Such attitudes and outlooks on sustainability will lay the groundwork for a variety of appropriate environmental policies regulating maritime supply chain operations that are aligned with the sector's sustainability objectives of economic growth, social development, and environmental protection.

CONCLUSION

Given the significance of the maritime supply chain to the Malaysian economy, Malaysia needs to maintain and improve its efforts and actions towards balancing this sector's growth with environmentally sustainable development of its operations and marine resources. In this regard, the environmental thought of sustainability should be given greater importance in the planning, coordination, management, execution, and monitoring of maritime supply chain operations in this sector. Thorough and responsive planning in this operational management sector, reducing pollution and ecosystem protection is critical to protecting Malaysia's maritime wealth and preserving its natural maritime environment. Additionally, the ocean's vast nature requires the unparallel commitment and involvement of all stakeholders concerned with maritime supply chain operations to ensure long-term sustainability in their development. Thus, the imperative action by adopting an incorporated approach towards maritime management via the recruitment of all stakeholders – governmental bodies, private enterprises, NGOs, academicians, and societies – in satisfying their societal responsibilities could help contribute to the planning and development of sustainable maritime supply chain operation. Activities in areas such as environmental, maritime protection policies and strategies, maritime cooperation initiatives, and maritime economics that will encourage sustainability and protection of resources and excellent maritime management should be planned deliberately well to guarantee their effectiveness. The required coordination of plausible strategies across the multi-layers of maritime supply chain operation based on sustainability values and their execution by the stakeholder's commitment will certify the strengthening efforts to protect the environment optimally. Countless other elements beyond this intended paper must be developed to construct an environment favourable to achieve this gracious and significant goal. A dynamic integration between maritime supply chain players and a conducive environment for efficient decision-making and intensive collaboration among agencies and nations would be required and coordinated accordingly to provide a sustainable platform for maritime supply chain operations to function effectively. Therefore, an innovative approach of sustainable maritime supply chain development policy based on the above priorities should be synchronised and coordinated by capable leadership and supported by a well-organised support system – e.g., governmental bodies, NGOs, IMO, and academic institutions- could turn the Malaysian progress towards the ideals of sustainability and twirl the country into a flourishing and successful maritime nation in the future.

REFERENCES

Abdul Talib, A. N., & Keung, C. W. (2021). Impact of organisational capabilities on R&D project innovation performance of E&E manufacturing firms in Malaysia. *International Journal of Business Innovation and Research, 1*(1), 10042101. doi:10.1504/IJBIR.2021.10042101

Abdul-Talib, A.-N., & Teong, N. H. (2019). Internet sales channel and manufacturers' brand: A transaction cost analysis. *International Journal of Supply Chain Management, 8*(6), 957–966.

American Association of Port Authorities. (2007). *Embracing the concept of sustainability as a standard practice for ports and the association*. Author.

Ashari, H., Yusof, Y., Mohd Zamani, S. N., & Abdul Talib, A. N. (2018). A study of the effect of market orientation on Malaysian automotive industry supply chain performance. *International Journal of Technology, 9*(8), 1651–1657. doi:10.14716/ijtech.v9i8.2749

Asian Port Association. (2004). *Best Practices Manual on Port Safety, Health, Environment and Security.* Retrieved April 26, 2021, from https://www.scribd.com/document/41805028/1-TEXT-Best-Practices-Manual-Safety-Security-Health-Environment-Rcaversion

Avesani, M. (2020). Sustainability, sustainable development, and business sustainability. In *Life Cycle Sustainability Assessment for Decision-Making* (pp. 21–38). Elsevier. doi:10.1016/B978-0-12-818355-7.00002-6

Cheng, T. C. E., Farahani, R. Z., Lai, K. H., & Sarkis, J. (2015). Sustainability in maritime supply chains: Challenges and opportunities for theory and practice. *Transportation Research Part E, Logistics and Transportation Review, 78*, 1–2. doi:10.1016/j.tre.2015.03.007

Destek, M. A. (2020). Investigation on the role of economic, social, and political globalization on environment: Evidence from CEECs. *Environmental Science and Pollution Research International, 27*(27), 33601–33614. doi:10.100711356-019-04698-x PMID:30864029

Escobar, L. F., & Vredenburg, H. (2011). Multinational oil companies and the adoption of sustainable development: A resource-based and institutional theory interpretation of adoption heterogeneity. *Journal of Business Ethics, 98*(1), 39–65. doi:10.100710551-010-0534-x

Fernando, Y., Jasmi, M. F. A. M. F. A., & Shaharudin, M. S. M. S. (2019). Maritime green supply chain management: Its light and shadow on the bottom line dimensions of sustainable business performance. *International Journal of Shipping and Transport Logistics, 11*(1), 60. doi:10.1504/IJSTL.2019.096872

Hashim, F., Bakar, A. R. A., & Talib, A. N. A. (2010). *International Business*. Oxford University Press.

International Maritime Organization. (2015). *List of IMO Conventions*. Retrieved from https://www.imo.org/en/About/Conventions/ListOfConventions/Pages/Default.aspx

Jasmi, F., & Fernando, Y. (2018). Notions of Maritime Green Supply Chain Management. In *Encyclopedia of Information Science and Technology* (4th ed., pp. 5465–5475). IGI Global.

Jasmi, M. F. A. (2019). *Maritime Green Supply Chain Management (MGSCM) and Financial Performance: A Mediating Effect of Energy Efficiency and Low Carbon Performance*. Universiti Malaysia Pahang.

Jasmi, M. F. A., & Fernando, Y. (2021). A Review of Future Energy Efficiency Measures and CO2 Emission Reduction in Maritime Supply Chain. Encyclopedia of Organizational Knowledge, Administration, and Technology, 2431–2442.

Jasmi, M. F. A., Fernando, Y., & Ismail, I. (2020). Adoption level of maritime green supply chain management: Preliminary findings from a pilot study. *International Journal of Logistics Systems and Management, 37*(4), 556–575. doi:10.1504/IJLSM.2020.111826

Jeevan, J., Ghaderi, H., Bandara, Y. M. M., Saharuddin, A. H. H., & Othman, M. R. R. (2015). The implications of the growth of port throughput on the port capacity: The case of Malaysian major container seaports. *International Journal of E-Navigation and Maritime Economy, 3*, 84–98. doi:10.1016/j.enavi.2015.12.008

Joung, T.-H., Kang, S.-G., Lee, J.-K., & Ahn, J. (2020). The IMO initial strategy for reducing Greenhouse Gas (GHG) emissions, and its follow-up actions towards 2050. *Journal of International Maritime Safety, Environmental Affairs, and Shipping, 4*(1), 1–7. doi:10.1080/25725084.2019.1707938

Kolk, A. (2016). The social responsibility of international business: From ethics and the environment to CSR and sustainable development. *Journal of World Business, 51*(1), 23–34. doi:10.1016/j.jwb.2015.08.010

Lam, J. J. S. L. (2011). Patterns of maritime supply chains: Slot capacity analysis. *Journal of Transport Geography, 19*(2), 366–374. doi:10.1016/j.jtrangeo.2010.03.016

Li, Y., Ye, F., Dai, J., Zhao, X., & Sheu, C. (2019). The adoption of green practices by Chinese firms. *International Journal of Operations & Production Management, 39*(4), 550–572. doi:10.1108/IJOPM-12-2017-0753

Lister, J., Poulsen, R. T., & Ponte, S. (2015). Orchestrating transnational environmental governance in maritime shipping. *Global Environmental Change, 34*, 185–195. doi:10.1016/j.gloenvcha.2015.06.011

Lun, Y. (2011). Green management practices and firm performance: A case of container terminal operations. *Resources, Conservation and Recycling, 55*(6), 559–566. doi:10.1016/j.resconrec.2010.12.001

Lun, Y. H. V., Lai, K., Wong, C. W. Y., & Cheng, T. C. E. (2014). Green shipping practices and firm performance. *Maritime Policy & Management, 41*(2), 134–148. doi:10.1080/03088839.2013.819133

Makkonen, T., & Inkinen, T. (2021). Systems of environmental innovation: Sectoral and technological perspectives on ballast water treatment systems. *WMU Journal of Maritime Affairs, 20*(1), 81–98. doi:10.100713437-021-00226-2

Meadows, D., & Meadows, D. (1972). The limits to growth. Academic Press.

Molenaar, E. J. (2014). Options for regional regulation of merchant shipping outside imo, with particular reference to the arctic region. *Ocean Development and International Law, 45*(3), 272–298. doi:10.1080/00908320.2014.929474

Mustafa, M., & Ariffin, M. (2011). Protection of marine biodiversity from pollution : Legal strategies in malaysia. *International Journal of Bioscience, Biochemistry, Bioinformatics, 1*, 276–281. doi:10.7763/IJBBB.2011.V1.52

Osnin, N. A., & Rahman, N. S. F. A. (2018). Assessment and ranking of inland navigation practices in Malaysia: The case of Kenyir lake. *The Asian Journal of Shipping and Logistics, 34*(4), 289–296. doi:10.1016/j.ajsl.2018.12.002

Othman, M. R., Bruce, G. J., & Hamid, S. A. (2011). The strength of Malaysian maritime cluster: The development of maritime policy. *Ocean and Coastal Management, 54*(8), 557–568. doi:10.1016/j.ocecoaman.2011.02.004

Psaraftis, H. N. (2016). Green maritime logistics: The quest for win-win solutions. *Transportation Research Procedia, 14*, 133–142. doi:10.1016/j.trpro.2016.05.049

Qi, G., Zou, H., & Xie, X. (2020). Governmental inspection and green innovation: Examining the role of environmental capability and institutional development. *Corporate Social Responsibility and Environmental Management, 27*(4), 1774–1785. doi:10.1002/csr.1924

Rao, C., & Yan, B. (2020). Study on the interactive influence between economic growth and environmental pollution. *Environmental Science and Pollution Research International, 27*(31), 39442–39465. doi:10.100711356-020-10017-6 PMID:32651783

Revkin, A. (2009). *Disaster Hot Spots on a Crowding Planet*. Academic Press.

Rosenthal, E. (2009). Biggest obstacle to global climate deal may be how to pay for it. *Herald Tribune*.

Sardain, A., Sardain, E., & Leung, B. (2019). Global forecasts of shipping traffic and biological invasions to 2050. *Nature Sustainability, 2*(4), 274–282. doi:10.103841893-019-0245-y

Sarkis, J., Zhu, Q. H., & Lai, K. H. (2011). An organizational theoretic review of green supply chain management literature. *International Journal of Production Economics, 130*(1), 1–15. doi:10.1016/j.ijpe.2010.11.010

Tan, A. K.-J. (2005). *Vessel-source marine pollution: The law and politics of international regulation* (Vol. 45). Cambridge University Press. doi:10.1017/CBO9780511494628

Thirugnana, S., Jaafar, A. B., Yasunaga, T., Nakaoka, T., Ikegami, Y., & Su, S. (2021). Estimation of ocean thermal energy conversion resources in the east of Malaysia. *Journal of Marine Science and Engineering, 9*, 22. doi:10.3390/jmse9010022

Voyer, M., Schofield, C., Azmi, K., Warner, R., McIlgorm, A., & Quirk, G. (2018). Maritime security and the blue economy: Intersections and interdependencies in the Indian Ocean. *Journal of the Indian Ocean Region, 14*(1), 28–48. doi:10.1080/19480881.2018.1418155

Wuisan, L., & van Leeuwen, J., van Koppen, C. S. A., Leeuwen, J. van, & Koppen, C. van. (2012). Greening international shipping through private governance: A case study of the Clean Shipping Project. *Marine Policy, 36*, 165–173. doi:10.1016/j.marpol.2011.04.009

Zacher, M. W., & Sutton, B. A. (1996). *Governing global networks: International regimes for transportation and communications*. Cambridge University Press.

Zakaria, N., Abdul-Talib, A.-N., & Amelinckx, A. (2020a). Advancing cultural frontiers to champion global business in emerging markets. In *Transcending Cultural Frontiers* (pp. 1–10). Springer. doi:10.1007/978-981-15-4454-5_1

Zakaria, N., Abdul-Talib, A.-N., & Amelinckx, A. (2020b). *Transcending Cultural Frontiers*. Springer. doi:10.1007/978-981-15-4454-5

Zakaria, N., Abdul-Talib, A.-N., & Osman, N. (2016). *Handbook of research on impacts of international business and political affairs on the global economy*. IGI Global. doi:10.4018/978-1-4666-9806-2

Chapter 18
Travel Motivations and Travel Careers of Malaysian Backpackers

Samshul Amry Abdul Latif
https://orcid.org/0000-0002-0791-8514
International Islamic University Malaysia, Malaysia

Mazni Saad
International Islamic University Malaysia, Malaysia

Nuraini Ismail
International Islamic University Malaysia, Malaysia

Murodjon Matniyozov
Urgench State University, Uzbekistan

Mona Fairuz Ramli
Kolej Universiti Islam Perlis, Malaysia

ABSTRACT

The study's two primary goals are to determine the main travel motives of Malaysian backpackers and to examine the variations in travel motivations across three categories of backpackers: first-time, repeat, and serial. The results were collected using a self-administered online survey adopting a convenience sample technique. The non-normally distributed data were examined using exploratory factor analysis, median score assessment, and Kruskal-Wallis H tests on a sample of 249. Stimulation is the most crucial factor motivating backpackers, while recognition is the least important. The study also found that backpackers' motivation varied with travel experience. Due to limited research on Asian motivational travel determinants, notably among Malaysian backpackers, this study's motivational features are drawn from other countries. Future research should focus on non-Western motivators impacting backpackers. There is a need for more research on Asian tourism, notably Malaysian backpackers at various stages of their travel careers.

DOI: 10.4018/978-1-7998-9071-3.ch018

INTRODUCTION

Over the last two decades, with mass tourism at its core, backpacking has been an uncommon aspect of travel, significantly distinct from the conventional modes of leisure travel (Ee and Kahl, 2016). Previous studies have suggested that backpacking tourism is a phenomenon that contributes significantly to the economies of developed as well as developing countries (Scheyvens, 2002, 2006; Richards and Wilson, 2003). This is because backpackers typically spend a substantial sums of money at their destinations. These expenditures may translate to economic benefits to the host population. Among others, this may be due to backpackers' longer or extended duration of stay (Alves *et al.*, 2016).

Backpackers are categorically distinct from mass tourism. Since backpackers are passionate about finding new tourism vistas, they are frequently seen as pioneers of new locations and travel trailblazers, rendering them as an extremely interesting category of tourists. They are frequently self-organized and travel in a flexible manner to a variety of areas (Jensen and Hjalager, 2018). The majority of experts defined backpackers as those who value low-cost lodging, extended vacations, itinerary simplicity, meeting other travellers, and partaking in a variety of activities (Chen, Bao, & Huang, 2014; Loker-Murphy & Pearce, 1995; Pearce & Foster, 2007).

Previous research on backpacking tourism mostly adopted Euro-centric perspectives (Cohen & Cohen, 2015) for travelers from developed countries (Allon & Anderson, 2010; Brenner & Fricke, 2007; Chitty, Ward, & Chua, 2007; Huxley, 2004; Nash, Thyne, & Davies, 2006; Pearce & Foster, 2007). Several earlier studies, however, have emphasised the significance of intensifying and broadening the scope of the research to include demographics such as Asian backpackers (Cai, Cohen, & Tribe, 2019; Cohen, 2006; Teo & Leong, 2006; Winter, Teo, & Chang, 2009). Recent efforts examined backpackers from Asia (Bui, Wilkins and Lee, 2014; Cai, Cohen and Tribe, 2019; Yang, Yang and Khoo-Lattimore, 2019; Wantono and McKercher, 2020), which may contribute to a deeper understanding of Asian independent youth travelers or tourists' culture, norms, and behaviors.

Interestingly, the definition of a backpacker is not in consensus due to conflicting views of "scholars who contest the conflicting claims to its origin, the entrepreneurs who seek to extend it as a label, to the backpackers who wish to distance themselves from it" (O' Regan, 2018, p. 193). In this study, a backpacker is viewed as an independent traveler who prefers budget accommodation, longer holidays, itinerary flexibility, predominantly under 40 years of age, likes meeting other travelers, and involve themselves with social and participatory holiday activities (Pearce, 1990; Loker-Murphy and Pearce, 1995; Pearce, Murphy and Brymer, 2009).

Since its inception, the backpacking phenomenon has evolved continuously in response to changes in the social-historical context, affecting physical institutional arrangements and travel habits, such as destinations visited and attractions, as well as who to travel with (Uriely, Yonay and Simchai, 2002; Miao and Bao, 2007). Moreover, it involves intangible psychological characteristics, including the motives of travelers, their attachments to home cultures, and the significance they give to their journeys (Filep, 2014; Pearce & Foster, 2007).

Backpackers are not merely a sociological category; they are a term indicating their social identity. Previous research on backpacker identity issues has largely been based on Western conceptions, with an emphasis on Western backpackers and their interactions with Asian hosts (Winter, Teo and Chang, 2009). Although research on Asian backpackers emerged from the early 2000s (Muzaini, 2006; Teo & Leong, 2006, among others), the numbers are still quite limited. With an increase in Asians travelling to their homelands or engaging in domestic tourism (Mohamed, Omar and Lau, 2010), in their backyard or regional tourism (Paris, Musa and Thirumoorthi, 2015) and further afield internationally (Cai, Cohen and Tribe, 2019) for leisure, business, and other purposes, this leads to non-Western tourism and academic research advances (Chang, 2015). As a result, it is equally important to examine their usefulness for Malaysian backpackers. The main objectives of this study are to identify the push and pull factors that motivate Malaysian backpackers to go on a backpacker trip and to investigate how the importance of those motivational factors differs according to the travel careers; first-time, repeat, and serial backpackers. This research attempts to examine these issues.

LITERATURE REVIEW

Backpacking is a concept used to explain how individuals vary in several ways from other tourists or passengers (Cohen, 2011; Pearce, 1990). There are some questions, however, as to where the mark for backpackers started. Pearce (1990) noted that the rise of backpackers in the 1960s and 1970s was due in part to the "marginal" behavior of the hippie or drifter sort (O' Regan, 2018). Certain labels applied including solo travelers (Hyde and Lawson, 2003), drifters (Cohen, 2010) and volunteer travelers (Kohler, Stribl and Stieger, 2016), to name a few (see review by O' Regan (2018).

BACKPACKERS' TRAVEL MOTIVATIONS

Dann (1977, 1981) established the push and pull paradigm that divided the incentive of visitors to travel into two types: internal socio-psychological forces and external forces. Internal socio-psychological forces are the driving forces encouraging visitors to travel, including flight, popularity, self-actualization, or adventure. In contrast, external forces are known to attract tourists to a specific destination, such as natural landscapes, sunlight or historic sites. In brief, push factors triggered visitors to travel, while pull factors decide where they are heading (Jensen and Hjalager, 2018).

These motivational factors were viewed to function and take effect in two different approaches; either as temporal sequencing or naturally taking effect simultaneously (Crompton, 1979; Uysal and Jurowski, 1994). Crompton (1979) divided motivational factors into two classes and classified seven push factors (prestige, relaxation, regression, escape from a routine environment, relationships enhancement, exploration and evaluation of self, and social interaction facilitation) and two pull factors (education and novelty).

Over the decades, the push and pull factors were examined by many studies with different settings on different types of travellers (Fodness, 1994; Kozak, 2002; Caber and Albayrak, 2016; Jensen and Hjalager, 2018). It was found that the motivations to travel to the same destination may differ according to the tourists' country (Kozak, 2002). This leads to the notion that tourists' motivations are not to be generalized to everyone, and may vary between destinations and travel type, including backpackers.

Equally the anthropological and survey-based research on backpacking have much focused on the motivations. The anthropological approach examined various parts of backpackers including social, spatial, organizational matters of backpacker activity, motivations, among others, towards a comprehensive understanding of backpackers (Maoz, 2007; Jensen and Hjalager, 2018). On the other hand, the survey and other recent approaches (Pearce and Foster, 2007; Paris and Teye, 2010; Chen, Bao and Huang, 2014; Chen and Huang, 2017) focused on distinct motivational factors primarily based on the push and pull theory.

Among the motivational differences between the conventional tourists and backpackers revealed from previous studies were a break from routine job, a drive for independence, personal development, meeting new people, a sense of exploration, and exposure to new cultures and settings (Maoz, 2007; Alves *et al.*, 2016; Jensen and Hjalager, 2018). Often, traveling as a backpacker is seen as a form of personal self-development (Pearce, Murphy and Brymer, 2009; Chen, Bao and Huang, 2014).

One of the most commonly cited motivations in backpackers literature are the desire for independence and the pursuit of adventure (Alves *et al.*, 2016), which is crucial in building a backpacker's self-identity and personal development (Chen, Huang and Hu, 2019). Previous studies also suggested that backpackers were driven by three push factors (Adventure Tourism, Heritage and Escapism) and three pull factors (Historical/Cultural Attractions, Ecological and Service Delivery) and observed that the motivation of backpackers varied by background, namely Age, Gender, and Nationality (Dayour, 2013).

Several studies have suggested that individuals may have different travel motives to de-stress and fulfill their inner needs (Chen et al., 2014). Based on the backpacking motives identified, backpackers are classed into four categories; escapers/relaxers, social/excitement seekers, self-developers, and achievers (Loker-Murphy, 1997). It is crucial to understand that backpackers are not an absolute homogenous group (Pearce and Foster, 2007; Oliveira-Brochado and Gameiro, 2013; Chen, Bao and Huang, 2014). There are many motivational similarities between the conventional tourists and backpackers, with differences lies in need of luxury and relaxation, among others (Oliveira-Brochado and Gameiro, 2013; Brochado, Rita and Gameiro, 2015).

The idea of heterogeneity in backpackers' motivational was long suggested by Cohen (1972), which distinctively differentiate between drifters and explorers. While certain backpackers seek pleasure or adventure in their travels, others may seek experiences to improve oneself, self-development or empowerment (Riley, 1988; Osman, Brown and Phung, 2019). Further classification into sub-categories revealed more homogenous groups based on the backpackers' type-related attributes such as "the tendency to hold anti-establishment or ambivalent views toward their own culture, a quest for adventure, authenticity, profound experiences; and a self-perception as travelers rather than tourists" (Uriely, 2009, p. 308). The country-related differences between backpackers' motivations were also examined (Mohsin and Ryan, 2003; Oliveira-Brochado and Gameiro, 2013).

BACKPACKERS' TRAVEL CAREER

Following the idea of travel career by Pearce (1993), several studies proposed that backpackers' motives are quite complex. These motives are likely to evolve from the first to the future succeeding journeys (Uriely, Yonay and Simchai, 2002; Paris and Teye, 2010). Observations have already been made, but little is grasped about the inspiration that drives ongoing backpacker trips to reshape and restore (Jensen and Hjalager, 2018). Personal or social growth (Paris and Teye, 2010), intra-group status (Srensen, 2003), and perceived risk (Adam, 2015) are less important to experienced backpackers. This is illustrated by Kelman's social theory (1958), a well-established model for explaining how people behave.

Kelman (1958) identified three types of behavioural and emotional adaption mechanisms; compliance, recognition, and internalization. Compliance applies to the acknowledgement to gain or avoid social chastisement from other relevant parties. Here, the personality is mainly motivated by external forces, such as a willingness to please certain people or prepare for future careers. Compliance seems important to first-time backpackers, who often undertake their backpacking trip between college and their first work in a transition span (Snee, 2014). Whereas, in the recognition phase, the person is no longer motivated by external forces, but rather by an inner need to be accepted within the group. For example, they are feeling attached to a backpacker community and belonging to it. This phase was intended for return backpackers, where trips are inspired by the need to preserve, improve or establish a backpacker social identity. For instance, re-experience the backpacker's lifestyle, and ultimately reunite with past hiking trip pals. Then, the latter phase, internationalisation, is the triggered conduct that reflects the ideals of the entity and becomes part of their desires and norms. Backpacking trips, for example, become an integral part of an individual's lifestyle.

The research on differences in travel encouragement between the first-time, repeat, and serial backpackers is limited. Most studies accepted that motives for travel are fundamentally subjective and, thus, evolve over time. As an example, a traveler's experience through a destination or method of travel could, or may not, influence the reasons for future travel decisions, being the same travel style or location.

RESEARCH METHODS

Measurement Instruments

This study used self-administered online questionnaire approach so that the researchers were able "to reach a large sample of backpackers with varying degrees of experience as backpackers" (Jensen & Hjalager, 2018, p. 3). Using Google Form, the questionnaire was divided into sections, namely, the travel motivation, backpackers' experience and socio-demographic variables such as gender, age, and education. There were two screening questions to exclude non-Malaysian and non-backpackers at the beginning of the questionnaire. The respondents were requested to attempt the questionnaire based on their most recent backpacking trip.

The 36 motivational items in the questionnaire were obtained from the motivation of backpacking literature. Guided by Jensen & Hjalager (2018), these previous studies included Chen et al., (2014); Chen, Zhao, and Huang (2019); Chen and Huang (2017); Hsu, Wang, and Huang, (2014); Larsen, Øgaard, and Brun, (2011); and Paris and Teye (2010).

The Sun and Beach factor from Jensen and Hjalager (2018) was not included and replaced with Destination Attributes from Kim (2014). This was because the items were less suitable to the general Malaysian respondents such as "visiting countries where the sun shines every day, Traveling in sunny countries, and Getting a lot of sun" as Malaysia is a sunny tropical country. The motivation items were measured using the 5-point Likert Scale ranging from 1 = strongly disagree, 2 = disagree, 3 = neutral, 4 = agree and 5 = strongly agree.

The respondents were asked on the frequency of backpacking trips they made as a backpacker, the destination they have visited which were categorized as Asian, European, African, Middle Eastern, American countries or domestic destinations. The respondents can make multiple selections for this question. Then the respondents were asked about the duration of their last backpacking trip as well who their traveling partner(s) were if any.

SAMPLING PROCEDURE

The study used a non-random convenience sampling approach by disseminating the link to the online questionnaire to potential respondents through several electronic channels such as WhatsApp and Facebook groups. Through Whatsapp, potential respondents were personally approached and requested for participation if they have been on a backpacking trip. Once completed, the researchers requested that the link be snowballed and passed on to their backpacking friends. The link was also shared in several private Whatsapp groups. Similarly, on Facebook, the request for participation and the questionnaire link on several Facebook pages on backpacking such as Backpackers Buddies Malaysia and Malaysia Backpackers were posted. The request and link were also posted in the researchers' personal Facebook page.

SAMPLE PROFILE

A total of 364 respondents responded to our request. However, 108 respondents were removed as they have yet to travel as a backpacker. Additionally, another seven respondents were also excluded as they were non-Malaysians, leaving 249 respondents available for analysis. Based on the formula N>50+8m (where m = number of independent variables) provided by Tabachnick and Fidell (2007, p. 123), the sample size is acceptable. Table 1 below displays the sample profile.

The majority of the respondents were females (76.7%), and 74.4% were categorized as under the 30-year-old group. The respondents were reported to have bachelor's degree (72.3%), followed by master's degree (12.9%) and certificate/diploma (12.0%).

Based on their previous backpacking trips, the respondents were categorized into three different levels of travel experience (first-time, repeat, and serial). The respondents who have travelled only once were grouped into the first-time backpackers category (n=33). The respondents who have travelled twice or three times as backpackers were grouped into the repeat backpackers category (n=79), while those who had travelled four times or more were categorized as serial backpackers (n= 137). It was reported that 13.3% of the respondents had travelled once as a backpacker, 31.7% travelled twice or three times and 55.0% travelled four times or more.

While 42% of the respondents were categorized as students, 51% were employed. The largest employment category (30%) indicated that the respondents were employed in the private sector. Of the total respondents, 6% of the respondents were classified as unemployed, and 30% had no source of income. The income of the employed respondents were primarily (23%) less than MYR 1,500 per month. The second-largest group by income (20%) earned a monthly income of between MYR 1501 to MYR 3,000. This is followed by the next group (17%) of which the respondents earned more than MYR 7,001 per month.

A total of 36 items were subjected to principal components analysis (PCA) using SPSS version 24. Prior to PCA, the data suitability for factor analysis was assessed. The result of the correlation matrix revealed the presence of many coefficients of .3 and above. The Kaiser- Meyer-Olkin value was .922, exceeding the recommended value of .6 (Kaiser, 1970, 1974) and Bartlett's Test of Sphericity (Bartlett, 1954) reached statistical significance, supporting the factorability of the correlation matrix.

Table 1. Profile of survey respondents

	Total sample. *n= 249*	**First-time backpackers,** *n= 33*	**Repeat backpackers,** *n= 79*	**Serial backpackers,** *n= 137*
Gender	%	%	%	%
Male	23.3	27.3	24.1	21.9
Female	76.7	72.7	75.9	78.1
Age				
< 20	4.1	15.2	5.1	0.7
21-25	55.4	72.7	74.7	40.1
26-30	14.9	0.0	12.7	19.7
31-35	12.4	9.1	1.3	19.7
36-40	6.0	3.0	1.3	9.5
41-45	2.8	0.0	1.3	4.4
46-50	1.6	0.0	0.0	2.9
51+	2.8	0.0	3.8	2.9
Education				
Primary School	0.4	3.0	0.0	0.0
Secondary School	1.2	0.0	0.0	2.2
Certificate/Diploma	12.0	12.1	8.9	13.9
Bachelor's Degree	72.3	84.8	86.1	61.3
Master's Degree	12.9	0.0	3.8	21.2
Ph. D	0.8	0.0	0.0	1.5
No formal education	0.4	0.0	1.3	0.0
Occupation				
Public Sector	12.4	3.0	5.1	19.0
Private Sector	30.5	27.3	15.2	40.1
Student	42.6	54.5	60.8	29.2
Freelance	8.4	9.1	10.1	7.3
Unemployed	6.1	6.1	8.9	4.4
Income (MYR)				
<1500	23.3	30.3	29.1	18.2
1501-3000	20.5	18.2	16.5	23.4
3001-4500	0.3	0.0	5.1	14.6
4501-6000	7.2	0.0	1.3	12.4
6001-7000	0.8	0.0	0.0	1.5
>7001	17.4	9.1	1.3	11.7
No Income	30.5	42.4	46.8	18.2
Destination*				
Domestic		57.6	68.4	65.0
Asia		36.4	50.6	75.9
Europe		6.1	10.1	27.7
Africa		0.0	2.5	1.5
America		0.0	0.0	3.6
No of days based on the last trip				
<3 days		42.4	43.0	16.8
4-6 days		48.5	43.0	45.3
7-10 days		6.1	8.9	20.4
>11 days		3.0	5.1	17.5

* Sum of percentage exceeds 100% as respondents could mark more than one destination.

With one item removed (FS3), principal components analysis revealed the presence of twelve (12) components with eigenvalues exceeding 1, as depicted in Table 2 of the variance, respectively. The scree plot was inspected, and twelve (12) breaks were revealed. The twelve (12) component solution explained a total of 85.95% of the variance and converged in seven (7) iterations. Varimax rotation was performed to aid in the interpretation, and the presence of a simple structure was revealed (Thurstone, 1947), with strong loadings accordingly to the factors. All of the correlations were found to be weak (ranging from -0.04 to 0.356) except for one component (r = 0.62) suggesting the scales are separated (Watson, Clark and Tellegen, 1988). The structure was found to be almost similar to Jensen & Hjalager (2018).

RESULTS

Assessment of the Motivational Factors' Importance

Table 2. Factor analysis with Varimax rotation for travel motivations of Malaysian backpackers

Motivational factors and items	Loadings	EV	% of variance	Reliability	Median
Factor 1: Host-site Involvement (HSI) - Push HI2 Learn about other cultures HI1 Explore other cultures HI3 Interact with the local people HI4 Get authentic and genuine experiences	.783 .759 .635 .577	2.378	6.795	.888	4.25
Factor 2: Self-actualization (SA) - Push SA2 Understand more about myself SA3 Gain a new perspective of my own life SA1 Challenge myself mentally	.825 .814 .685	1.275	3.643	.889	4.000
Factor 3: Gastronomic Experiences (GEX) - Pull GE2 Experience different food cultures GE3 Taste food prepared in other cultures GE1 Get gastronomic experiences	.855 .848 .791	1.735	4.958	.896	4.000
Factor 4: Nature (NAT) – Pull N1 Have nature experiences N2 Be closed to nature N3 View beautiful nature sceneries	.819 .785 .659	1.203	3.437	.895	4.667
Factor 5: Low-budget travel (LBT) – Pull LB3 Travel far away without paying a fortune LB2 Use cheap way to travel LB1 Get many travel experiences for a modest budget	.837 .829 .734	1.404	4.012	.928	4.333
Factor 6: Escape (ESC) – Push E2 Get away from everyday duties E1 Get away from daily routine E3 Temporarily not worrying about future	.870 .846 .833	16.368	46.765	.904	4.667
Factor 7: Recognition (RECOG) – Push R2 To be recognized for having traveled as a backpacker R1 Visit sites that will impress my friends and family R3 To get experiences that are worth telling others about	.874 .853 .582	.940	2.686	.845	3.333
Factor 8: Volunteering / Creating Friendship (VOL) - Push VF2 To create joy and value for the local people VF1 To have the opportunity to perform charity work VF3 To create new friendships	.851 .846 .763	1.855	5.3	.913	4.000
Factor 9: Stimulation (STI) – Push S2 To have once in a lifetime experiences S3 To explore the unknown S1 To have fun	.602 .559 .540	.530	1.514	.976	5.000
Factor 10: Autonomy (AUT) – Push A1 To plan my trip A2 To do what I want A3 To be independent	.793 .728 .624	1.022	2.921	.927	4.667
Factor 11: Famous Sites and Attractions (FS) - Pull FA1 To visit famous sites and attractions FA2 To visit cultural and historical sites	.757 .719	.723	2.067	.961	4.500
Factor 12: Destination Attributes (DA) - Pull DA2 To experience well-preserved area DA1 To visit different "ecology zone" (climate, land-forms, and land-covers) DA3 To experience awe-inspiring landscape	.758 .756 .754	.649	1.855	.966	4.500

As recommended by Pallant (2010), the data underwent preliminary analyses. The data were found to be non-normally distributed. It is a better alternative to use median to measure the central tendency of non-normally distributed data as it reflects the distribution's centre more accurately.

Table 2 presents the findings showing that Stimulation has the highest median value (5.0) and followed by Nature, Autonomy, and Escape (4.67), with identical median value. Both Destination Attributes, and Famous Sites and Attractions have identical median value (4.5). It is then followed by in descending order of importance, Low-budget travel (4.33), Host site involvement (4.25), Volunteering / Creating Friendship (4.0), Gastronomic Experiences (4.0), Self-actualization (4.0), and lastly Recognition (3.33).

The results show that the top three highest-ranked motivational factors are push motivations. This suggests that the backpackers' travel motivations are internally motivated. From the total of twelve motivations, only one factor (Recognition) was below the midpoint scale of 3.0.

COMPARISON OF THE MOTIVATIONAL FACTORS AMONG FIRST-TIME, REPEAT, AND SERIAL BACKPACKERS

Kruskal-Wallis H test was used to examine the non-normally distributed data. The analysis examined the differences in motivation score among the three different groups; first-time, repeat, and serial backpackers. The Kruskal-Wallis H test (also known as the "one-way ANOVA on ranks") is a rank-based nonparametric test to determine statistically significant differences between two or more groups of an independent variable on a continuous or ordinal dependent variable (Laerd-Statistics, 2015).

The Kruskal-Wallis H test makes four assumptions: 1) that there is one continuous or ordinal dependent variable, 2) that there is one independent variable composed of two or more categorical independent groups, 3) that observations are independent, and 4) that the score distributions across each independent variable group have a similar shape (Laerd-Statistics, 2015).

Each of the twelve (12) motivational factors was subjected to an individual Kruskal-Wallis H test to evaluate if there were any differences in score between the three groups of backpackers. As determined by visual inspection of the boxplots for each motivating factor, the distributions of all factor scores were similar across groups. Prior to the examination, any outliers for each factor were identified and removed.

Posthoc analyses were then performed on the medians of motivational scores that were shown to be statistically and substantially different between the groups. These pairwise comparisons were carried out using a process that included a Bonferroni correction for multiple comparisons (Dunn, 1964). The posthoc analyses were conducted largely to ascertain the existence of differences.

According to Table 3, there are four (4) motivational factors that vary by group. The first motivational factor is Host Site Involvement (HSI), which demonstrates a significant difference in motivation between repeat backpackers and serial backpackers ($p = .020$). Low Budget Travel (LBT) is the second motivational factor, with a significant difference between repeat backpackers and serial backpackers ($p = .018$). Stimulation (STI) is the third motivational factor, with a significant difference between repeat and serial backpackers ($p = .018$). Finally, the fourth and final motivational factor is Autonomy (AUT), which indicates that there are substantial differences between repeat backpackers and serial backpackers ($p = .003$), as well as between first-time backpackers and serial backpackers ($p = .049$).

Table 3. Sample size by group, Chi Square values and difference results

HSI	"First-time" (n = 30) "Repeat" (n = 75) "Serial" (n = 137)	$\chi 2(2) = 7.425$, $p = .024$	Significant difference between repeat backpacker (4.00) and serial backpacker (4.50) (p = .020)
SA	"First-time" (n = 33) "Repeat" (n = 79) "Serial" (n = 137)	$\chi 2(2) = 2.087$, $p = .352$	No significant difference between the groups
GEX	"First-time" (n = 32) "Repeat" (n = 78) "Serial" (n = 137)	$\chi 2(2) = .786$, $p = .675$	No significant difference between the groups
NAT	"First-time" (n = 33) "Repeat" (n = 77) "Serial" (n = 134)	$\chi 2(2) = 1.446$, $p = .485$	No significant difference between the groups
LBT	"First-time" (n = 33) "Repeat" (n = 77) "Serial" (n = 129)	$\chi 2(2) = 7.529$, $p = .023$	Significant difference between repeat backpacker (4.00) and serial backpacker (4.33) (p = .018)
ESC	"First-time" (n = 33) "Repeat" (n = 79) "Serial" (n = 137)	$\chi 2(2) = 3.094$, $p = .213$	No significant difference between the groups
RECOG	"First-time" (n = 32) "Repeat" (n = 77) "Serial" (n = 137)	$\chi 2(2) = 5.821$, $p = .540$	No significant difference between the groups
VOL	"First-time" (n = 33) "Repeat" (n = 78) "Serial" (n = 137)	$\chi 2(2) = .799$, $p = .671$	No significant difference between the groups
STI	"First-time" (n = 32) "Repeat" (n = 77) "Serial" (n = 116)	$\chi 2(2) = 7.852$, p zzx= .023	Significant difference between repeat backpacker (5.00) and serial backpacker (5.00) (p = .018)
AUT	"First-time" (n = 33) "Repeat" (n = 77) "Serial" (n = 133)	$\chi 2(2) = 13.361$, $p = .001$	Significant difference between repeat backpacker (4.33) and serial backpacker (5.00) (p = .003) Significant difference between first -time backpacker (4.00) and serial backpacker (5.00) (p = .049)
FS	"First-time" (n = 31) "Repeat" (n = 78) "Serial" (n = 135)	$\chi 2(2) = 2.472$, $p = .291$	No significant difference between the groups
DA	"First-time" (n = 31) "Repeat" (n = 79) "Serial" (n = 136)	$\chi 2(2) = 3.275$, $p = .194$	No significant difference between the groups

According to the findings, the most important motivational factor for Malaysian backpackers is Stimulation. This result is consistent with Jensen & Hjalager's earlier work (2018). Nature is the second most popular pull factor among Malaysian backpackers, indicating that they are interested in nature-related experiences. When both push and pull motivations are considered, both are equally represented in the top 50% of factors. Unlike prior research (Hecht and Martin, 2006; Jensen and Hjalager, 2018), our conclusion indicates that, on a more or less equal footing, both push and pull factors are critical for Malaysian backpackers. Interestingly, Gastronomic experience ranks with Self-Actualization and Volunteering as the least important factor (median score of 4). As with earlier findings, Recognition is the least important motivational factor for backpackers (median score of 3.33).

DISCUSSION

This study examined travel motivations among first-time, repeat and serial backpackers. The current findings indicate that the pattern of backpacking was influenced by previous travel experiences and demographic factors like gender and age. Additionally, twelve motivation factors were verified, including three that significantly differed between backpackers with first-time, repeat, and serial travel experience, and those with low-budget travel, stimulation, and autonomy. Contradicting to Hsu, Wang and Huang (2014) and Jensen and Hjalager (2018), which acknowledged the findings for general travel motivation, priorities for backpacker travel motivation could be suggested by two significant differences in relation to previous travel experience, namely, *self-actualization* and *recognition*. The four motivation factors at the core of backpacker travel motivation in this recent study were stimulation, nature, escape, and autonomy. Hecht and Martin (2006) noted that the stimulation factor was the most crucial including three motivation items: having a once-in-a-lifetime experience, exploring the unknown, and having fun, which are closely identical to the most important motivational items in this study.

Studies have shown that backpacking travelers are the trendsetters in leisure tourism. Their tendency of spending more money due to a longer duration stays, create an advantage for the destination hosts (Alves et al., 2016; Chen et al., 2014; Ee & Kahl, 2016; Scheyvens, 2006). In this study, Malaysian backpackers were found to have adopted the preference for an independent traveling style for a longer duration of outbound tourism. This finding is similar to the previous findings on Western travelers (Allon & Anderson, 2010; Jensen & Hjalager, 2018; Pear & Foster, 2007) and Asian backpackers preferences (Cai et al., 2019; Teo & Leong, 2006; Wantono & McKercher, 2020; Yang et al., 2019). This result serves to add to the present findings on Asian backpackers (Chang, 2015; Mohamed et al., 2010; Paris et al., 2015) by specifying the Malaysian backpackers' identity based on their tourism practices and preference for outbound tourism, and their motivational factors at different experience levels.

Recent advancements in gender equality have resulted in significant increases in women's work opportunities in both developed and developing countries (Yang, Khoo-Lattimore and Arcodia, 2018). In recent years, women have had more opportunities and choices including tourism and traveling, thanks to their increased economic independence (Su, Johnson and O'Mahony, 2020). As a result, there has been a considerable increase in the number of women who are using their independence to travel on their own in search of freedom, independence, and empowerment. Although the bulk of the respondents were young females (aged 21 to 25) with limited income, the paper suggests that they are nevertheless willing to organise their trips and go backpacking.

Though most of the backpackers who participated in this study have low income, they are young (aged 21 to 25 years old) and educated (with a higher level of education). Perhaps similar to other low budget travelers, this type of backpackers tend to travel in groups to save costs, and their preferred destinations are towards Asian countries as well as domestic. The choice of destinations for first-time backpackers tend to be domestic destinations may be due to lack of backpacking experience. However, with enough experience, they would progress further and begin to explore international destinations. The results also suggest that experienced backpackers prefer Asian countries (75.9%) as their international destinations. These destinations were chosen perhaps due to proximity or even favorable currency exchange leading to lower costs (Park *et al.*, 2019; Verma, 2020; Xie and Tveterås, 2020).

The findings also suggest that serial backpackers may expand their travels abroad to Asian countries as they earn better (employed) compared to repeat backpackers (mainly students). Serial backpackers are the dominant travelers in this study, and this group is distinctively different compared to repeat backpackers.

Reflecting by the demographic, young backpackers with low budgets prefer to be independent when it comes to the trip arrangement and have the desire to be away from routines. This group of backpackers are also attracted to experience nature, be close and to appreciate the beautiful natural sceneries. This is then followed by in descending order of importance, Low-budget travel, Host Site involvement, Volunteering / Creating Friendship, Gastronomic Experiences, Self-actualization, and lastly Recognition. Similar to Jensen and Hjalager (2018) and Sorensen (2003), Malaysian backpackers are not motivated to impress others and thus, the Recognition is ranked lowest as backpackers are particularly reluctant to admit prestige and recognition as an underlying motive for their travel choices (Crompton, 1979).

In terms of the distinct motivational factors, the finding showed that Malaysian backpackers are similar with recent approaches (Chen et al., 2014; Chen & Huang, 2017; Paris & Teye, 2010). The results, however, demonstrated that 36 motivational items produced four (4) factors underlying the Malaysian backpackers' motivation. When carefully examined, the push and pull motivations factors are equally represented as the top 50% motivational factors. The push factors are Host Site Involvement, and Stimulations while the pull factors are Low Budget and Nature. This finding suggests that both push and pull factors are more or less equally crucial to Malaysian backpackers. This result, however, contradicts the findings by Hecht and Martin (2006) and Jensen and Hjalager (2018).

The results suggest that Malaysia backpackers are mostly motivated to travel due to the Stimulation push factor that drives the backpackers to have a once-in-a-lifetime experience, explore the unknown and have fun. Stimulated backpackers, according to Fridgin (1991), is best for a person who seeks out activities through travel as an individual. In comparing push travel motivation between repeated and serial backpackers, the study verified the results of several studies on backpackers (Hecht and Martin, 2006; Park *et al.*, 2019). In line with this, the present research finds that the attributes are equally shared with Autonomy (push), Escape (push) and Nature (pull) where the results are very much similar to Jensen and Hjalager (2018).

The results also suggest that there are differences in motivational factors at a different stage of backpackers' travel careers. The results indicate that the repeat and serial backpackers have different levels of motivations for HSI, LBT, STI, and AUT. These findings can perhaps be justified as first-time backpackers gained more experiences after a few backpacking trips. As a result, they become more confident to explore and experience new cultures, interact with the local people and thus obtain a genuine travelling experience (HSI). Through their initial backpacking experience, they may discover the cheapest way to travel with a modest budget (LBT). This may include seeking budget transport, accommodation and meals. After being more experienced backpackers, they are stimulated to explore the unknown parts of the world, have more fun while backpacking, and search for once-in-a-lifetime experiences (STI). With enough backpacking experiences, they tend to be more knowledgeable in planning their subsequent trips, resulting in a more independent traveling movement and itineraries (AUT). This results may suggest the characteristics, identity and behavior of Malaysian backpackers as they progress through their travel career.

Based on the results, only a small percentage (3%) of the first-time backpackers stayed beyond eleven (11) days. A large percentage of first-time (48%) and repeating backpackers (43%) spend less than seven (7) days on their last backpacking trip. This indicates that as backpackers gained enough experience, they tend to extend their stay longer. This trend may be useful to the destination or tourism-related service marketers to strategize capturing these segments. Further, the income of these backpackers seems to determine the choice of destination and the average length of stay. Future studies can examine whether such analogy affects the backpackers' behavior.

CONCLUSION

This study provides essential information for researchers and experts alike. Firstly, the information on Malaysian backpackers has created the possibility of distinguishing backpackers' motivating factors and behaviors around Asian countries. This research provides a better foundation for a thorough understanding of the current pattern among Malaysian backpackers by identifying their highest push and pull travel motivation factors. While previous studies (Uriely, Yonay and Simchai, 2002; Paris and Teye, 2010; Hsu, Wang and Huang, 2014; Jensen and Hjalager, 2018) have identified variations in the travel motivation of backpackers according to their the travel career (from the first and to the sequential backpacker trips), this research has shown otherwise. The findings suggest that Malaysian backpackers have the same travel motivation trend across three separate experiential categories. Lastly, this research makes a significant difference between frequent backpackers with the first time and repeat backpackers in terms of the destination reached during a backpacking trip. In this sense, it illustrates the need for a more comprehensive grouping of backpackers to define their desires and priorities.

Travel inspiration has for decades, become a staple of tourism studies. It is seen as one of the critical elements of recognizing the patterns of visitors' decision making. Comprehensive knowledge of travel motivation plays a crucial role in anticipating potential travel trends. By examining the characteristics of backpackers and understanding their travel motivations, service providers can strategize to seize any business opportunity by satisfying the demands of these individuals.

LIMITATION AND FUTURE DIRECTION

Several limitations need to be considered in the current study. First, there are a limited number of previous studies available to investigate motivational travel variables, particularly on Malaysian backpackers. The motivational elements used in this research, therefore, were based on previous studies from other countries. Future studies should investigate other emerging or potential non-Western (Cai, Cohen and Tribe, 2019) motivational factors on backpackers. Accordingly, as suggested by Chen et al. (2014), future studies could use qualitative methods to generate more detailed Asian-based variables. This enables a more in-depth understanding of the travel motivation of Malaysian backpackers. Second, this study is heavily skewed towards females. The outcome would, therefore, be one-sided since gender may impact choices. Future studies can attempt to balance the number of males and females in the samples. Third, motivational elements should include several religious or spiritual qualities, such as attending places of worship, knowing certain religious rituals, enhancing religious knowledge, and recognizing the beauty of holy or sacred architecture. The holy or sacred architecture may include mosque, synagogue, church, temples, among others (Raj, 2012; Fattah and Eddy-U, 2016). The findings may provide the foundation for business operators relevant to tourism in expanding and targeting their market. Finally, the fourth, this study did not evaluate the respondents' responses based on their recent specific backpacking trip. Perhaps, future studies could evaluate based on specific backpackers' domestic, regional or international trips.

REFERENCES

Allon, F., & Anderson, K. (2010). Intimate encounters: The embodied transnationalism of backpackers and independent travellers. *Population Space and Place*, *16*(1), 11–22. doi:10.1002/psp.574

Alves, S., Abrantes, J. L., Antunes, M. J., Seabra, C., & Herstein, R. (2016). WOM antecedents in backpacker travelers. *Journal of Business Research*, *69*(5), 1851–1856. doi:10.1016/j.jbusres.2015.10.068

Bartlett, M. S. (1954). A note on the multiplying factors for various χ 2 approximations. *Journal of the Royal Statistical Society. Series B. Methodological*, *16*(2), 296–298. doi:10.1111/j.2517-6161.1954.tb00174.x

Brenner, L., & Fricke, J. (2007). The evolution of backpacker destinations: The case of Zipolite, Mexico. *International Journal of Tourism Research*, *9*(3), 217–230. doi:10.1002/jtr.604

Brochado, A., Rita, P., & Gameiro, C. (2015). Exploring backpackers' perceptions of the hostel service quality. *International Journal of Contemporary Hospitality Management*, *27*(8), 1839–1855. doi:10.1108/IJCHM-03-2014-0145

Bui, H. T., Wilkins, H., & Lee, Y.-S. (2014). Liminal experience of East Asian backpackers. *Tourist Studies*, *14*(2), 126–143. doi:10.1177/1468797614532179

Caber, M., & Albayrak, T. (2016). 'Push or pull? Identifying rock climbing tourists' motivations. *Tourism Management*, *55*, 74–84. doi:10.1016/j.tourman.2016.02.003

Cai, W., Cohen, S. A., & Tribe, J. (2019). Harmony rules in Chinese backpacker groups. *Annals of Tourism Research*, *75*, 120–130. doi:10.1016/j.annals.2018.12.010

Chang, T. C. (2015). The asian wave and critical tourism scholarship. *International Journal of Asia-Pacific Studies*, *11*(1), 83–101.

Chen, G., Bao, J., & Huang, S. (2014). Segmenting chinese backpackers by travel motivations. *International Journal of Tourism Research*, *16*(1), 355–367. doi:10.1002/jtr.1928

Chen, G., Huang, S., & Hu, X. (2019). Backpacker personal development, generalized self-efficacy, and self-esteem: Testing a structural model. *Journal of Travel Research*, *58*(4), 680–694. doi:10.1177/0047287518768457

Chen, G., & Huang, S. S. (2017). Toward a theory of backpacker personal development : Cross-cultural validation of the BPD scale. *Tourism Management*, *59*, 630–639. doi:10.1016/j.tourman.2016.09.017

Chen, G., Zhao, L., & Huang, S. (2019). Backpacker identity: Scale development and validation. *Journal of Travel Research*, *59*(2), 1–14. doi:10.1177/0047287519829255

Chitty, B., Ward, S., & Chua, C. (2007). An application of the ECSI model as a predictor of satisfaction and loyalty for backpacker hostels. *Marketing Intelligence amd. Planning (Chicago, Ill.)*, *25*, 563–580.

Cohen, E. (2006). Pai—A backpacker enclave in transition. *Tourism Recreation Research*, *31*(3), 11–27. doi:10.1080/02508281.2006.11081502

Cohen, E., & Cohen, S. A. (2015). Beyond Eurocentrism in tourism: A paradigm shift to mobilities. *Tourism Recreation Research, 40*(2), 157–168. doi:10.1080/02508281.2015.1039331

Cohen, S. A. (2010). *Re-conceptualising lifestyle travellers: Contemporary'drifters*. Channel View Publications.

Cohen, S. A. (2011). Lifestyle travellers. Backpacking as a way of life. *Annals of Tourism Research, 38*(4), 1535–1555. doi:10.1016/j.annals.2011.02.002

Dann, G. M. S. (1977). Anomie, ego-enhancement and tourism. *Annals of Tourism Research, 4*(4), 184–194. doi:10.1016/0160-7383(77)90037-8

Dann, G. M. S. (1981). Tourist motivation an appraisal. *Annals of Tourism Research, 8*(2), 187–219. doi:10.1016/0160-7383(81)90082-7

Ee, T., & Kahl, C. (2016). Self discovery and backpackers: A conceptual paper about liminal experience. *International Journal of Religious Tourism and Pilgrimage, 4*(1), 49–58.

Fattah, A. A., & Eddy-U, M. E. (2016). Mosque-visiting: Motivations and experiences of non-Muslim visitors at the Al-Azhar mosque in Egypt. *Turizam, 20*(3), 105–127. doi:10.5937/Turizam1603105F

Filep, S. (2014). Moving beyond subjective well-being: A tourism critique. *Journal of Hospitality & Tourism Research (Washington, D.C.), 38*(2), 266–274. doi:10.1177/1096348012436609

Fodness, D. (1994). Measuring tourist motivation. *Annals of Tourism Research, 21*(3), 555–581. doi:10.1016/0160-7383(94)90120-1

Fridgin, J. D. (1991). *Dimensions of Tourism*. Educational Institute of the American Hotel and Motel Association.

Hashim, F., Bakar, A. R. A., & Abdul-Talib, A. N. (2010). *International Business* (2nd ed.). Oxford Fajar Press.

Hsu, J. L., Wang, T. C. T., & Huang, P. Y. H. (2014). Motivations for first-time and repeat backpackers in Shanghai. *Tourism Management Perspectives, 12*, 57–61. doi:10.1016/j.tmp.2014.08.001

Huxley, L. (2004). Western backpackers and the global experience: An exploration of young people's interaction with local cultures. *Tourism, Culture & Communication, 5*(1), 37–44. doi:10.3727/1098304042781472

Hyde, K. F., & Lawson, R. (2003). The nature of independent travel. *Journal of Travel Research, 42*(1), 13–23. doi:10.1177/0047287503253944

Jensen, J. M., & Hjalager, A. M. (2018). Travel motivations of first-time, repeat, and serial backpackers. *Tourism and Hospitality Research, 19*(4), 465–477. doi:10.1177/1467358418781440

Kaiser, H. F. (1970). *A second generation little jiffy*. Springer. doi:10.1007/BF02291817

Kaiser, H. F. (1974). An index of factorial simplicity. *Psychometrika, 39*(1), 31–36. doi:10.1007/BF02291575

Kim, J.-H. (2014). The antecedents of memorable tourism experiences: The development of a scale to measure the destination attributes associated with memorable experiences. *Tourism Management, 44*, 34–45. doi:10.1016/j.tourman.2014.02.007

Kohler, T., Stribl, A., & Stieger, D. (2016). Innovation for Volunteer Travel: Using Crowdsourcing to Create Change. In Open Tourism: Open Innovation, Crowdsourcing and Co-Creation Challenging the Tourism Industry. Springer. doi:10.1007/978-3-642-54089-9

Kozak, M. (2002). Comparative analysis of tourist motivations by nationality and destinations. *Tourism Management, 23*(3), 221–232. doi:10.1016/S0261-5177(01)00090-5

Laerd-Statistics. (2015). *Kruskal-Wallis H test using SPSS Statistics. Statistical tutorials and software guides.* Available at: https://statistics.laerd.com/

Larsen, S., Øgaard, T., & Brun, W. (2011). Backpackers and mainstreamers: Realities and Myths. *Annals of Tourism Research, 38*(2), 690–707. doi:10.1016/j.annals.2011.01.003

Loker-Murphy, L. (1997). Backpackers in Australia : A Motivation-Based Segmentation Study. *Journal of Travel & Tourism Marketing, 5*(4), 23–45. doi:10.1300/J073v05n04_02

Loker-Murphy, L., & Pearce, P. L. (1995). Young budget travelers: Backpackers in Australia. *Annals of Tourism Research, 22*(4), 819–843. doi:10.1016/0160-7383(95)00026-0

Maoz, D. (2007). Backpackers' motivations the role of culture and nationality. *Annals of Tourism Research, 34*(1), 122–140. doi:10.1016/j.annals.2006.07.008

Miao, X., & Bao, J. (2007). Grounded theory of non-standardized groups travel. *Luyou Xuekan, 22*(8), 48–54.

Mohamed, B., Omar, S. I., & Lau, P. M. (2010). Malaysian youth tourism market: A lucrative but overlooked tourist segment. *Malaysian Journal of Youth Market, 3*(August), 1–21.

Mohsin, A., & Ryan, C. (2003). Backpackers in the Northern Territory of Australia?motives, behaviours and satisfactions. *International Journal of Tourism Research, 5*(2), 113–131. doi:10.1002/jtr.421

Muzaini, H. (2006). Backpacking Southeast Asia: Strategies of "looking local"'. *Annals of Tourism Research, 33*(1), 144–161. doi:10.1016/j.annals.2005.07.004

Nash, R., Thyne, M., & Davies, S. (2006). An investigation into customer satisfaction levels in the budget accommodation sector in Scotland: A case study of backpacker tourists and the Scottish Youth Hostels Association. *Tourism Management, 27*(3), 525–532. doi:10.1016/j.tourman.2005.01.001

O'Regan, M. (2018). Backpacking's future and its drifter past. *Journal of Tourism Futures, 4*(3), 193–204. doi:10.1108/JTF-04-2018-0019

Oliveira-Brochado, A., & Gameiro, C. (2013). Toward a better understanding of backpackers' motivations. *Tékhne. Instituto Politécnico do Cávado e do Ave, 11*(2), 92–99. doi:10.1016/j.tekhne.2013.11.001

Osman, H., Brown, L., & Phung, T. M. T. (2019). The travel motivations and experiences of female Vietnamese solo travellers. *Tourist Studies, 63*, 12–22. doi:10.1177/1468797619878307

Paris, C. M., Musa, G., & Thirumoorthi, T. (2015). A comparison between Asian and Australasia backpackers using cultural consensus analysis. *Current Issues in Tourism, 18*(2), 175–195. doi:10.1080/13683500.2014.920771

Paris, C. M., & Teye, V. (2010). Backpacker Motivations : A Travel Career Approach. *Journal of Hospitality Marketing & Management, 19*(3), 244–259. doi:10.1080/19368621003591350

Park, J. (2019). Travel motivation among cross border tourists : Case study of Langkawi. *Tourism Management Perspectives, 31*, 63–71. doi:10.1016/j.tmp.2019.03.004

Pearce, P. L. (1990). *The backpacker phenomenon: Preliminary answers to basic questions*. Department of Tourism, James Cook University of North Queensland.

Pearce, P. L. (1993). Fundamentals of tourist motivation. In *Tourism research: Critiques and challenges*. Routledge.

Pearce, P. L., & Foster, F. (2007). A "university of travel": Backpacker learning. *Tourism Management, 28*(5), 1285–1298.

Pearce, P. L., Murphy, L. & Brymer, E. (2009). *Evolution of the Backpacker Market and the Potential for Australian Tourism, Sustainable Tourism Cooperative Research Centre's (STCRC's)*. Academic Press.

Raj, R. (2012). Religious tourist's motivation for visiting religious sites. *International Journal of Tourism Policy, 4*(2), 95–105.

Richards, G., & Wilson, J. (2003). *New horizons in independent youth and student travel. A report to the international student travel confederation (ISTC) and the association of tourism and leisure education (ATLAS)*. International Student Travel Confederation.

Riley, P. J. (1988). Road culture of international long-term budget travelers. *Annals of Tourism Research, 15*(3), 313–328. doi:10.1016/0160-7383(88)90025-4

Scheyvens, R. (2002). Backpacker tourism and third world development article. *Annals of Tourism Research, 29*(1), 144–164. doi:10.1016/S0160-7383(01)00030-5

Scheyvens, R. (2006). Sun, sand, and beach fale: Benefiting from backpackers—the samoan way. *Tourism Recreation Research, 31*(3), 75–86. doi:10.1080/02508281.2006.11081507

Snee, H. (2014). *A cosmopolitan journey? Difference, distinction and identity work in gap year travel*. Ashgate Publishing, Ltd.

Su, D. N., Johnson, L. W., & O'Mahony, B. (2020). Analysis of push and pull factors in food travel motivation. *Current Issues in Tourism, 23*(5), 572–586.

Tabachnick, B. G., & Fidell, L. S. (2007). Using Multivariate Statistics. In PsycCRITIQUES (5th ed.). Boston, MA: Pearson Education Inc. doi:10.1037/022267

Teo, P., & Leong, S. (2006). A postcolonial analysis of backpacking. *Annals of Tourism Research, 33*(1), 109–131.

Thurstone, L. L. (1947). *Multiple-factor analysis: A development and expansion of The Vectors of Mind.* University of Chicago Press.

Uriely, N. (2009). Deconstructing tourist typologies: The case of backpacking. *International Journal of Culture, Tourism and Hospitality Research, 3*(4), 306–312. doi:10.1108/17506180910994523

Uriely, N., Yonay, Y., & Simchai, D. (2002). Backpacking experiences: A type and form analysis. *Annals of Tourism Research, 29*(2), 520–538.

Verma, S. (2020). A study on the impact of fluctuation in exchange rate (inr to usd) and mean monthly temperature on foreign tourist arrivals in india. *Studies in Indian Place Names*, (50), 4605–4612.

Wantono, A., & McKercher, B. (2020). Backpacking and risk perception: The case of solo Asian women. *Tourism Recreation Research, 45*(1), 19–29. doi:10.1080/02508281.2019.1636180

Watson, D., Clark, L. A., & Tellegen, A. (1988). Development and validation of brief measures of positive and negative affect: The PANAS scales. *Journal of Personality and Social Psychology, 54*(6), 1063.

Winter, T., Teo, P., & Chang, T. C. (2009). Asian tourism and the retreat of anglo-western centrism in tourism theory. *Current Issues in Tourism, 12*(1), 21–31.

Xie, J., & Tveterås, S. (2020). Economic decline and the birth of a tourist nation. *Scandinavian Journal of Hospitality and Tourism, 20*(2), 1–19. doi:10.1080/15022250.2020.1719882

Yang, E. C. L., Khoo-Lattimore, C., & Arcodia, C. (2018). Power and empowerment: How Asian solo female travellers perceive and negotiate risks. *Tourism Management, 68*, 32–45.

Yang, E. C. L., Yang, M. J. H., & Khoo-Lattimore, C. (2019). The meanings of solo travel for Asian women. *Tourism Review, 74*(5), 1047–1057. doi:10.1108/TR-10-2018-0150

Zakaria, N., Abdul-Talib, A. N., & Amelinckx, A. (Eds.). (2020). *Transcending Cultural Frontiers: Practices, Challenges, and Strategy for International Business*. Springer.

Zakaria, N., Abdul-Talib, A. N., & Amelinckx, A. (2020). Advancing cultural frontiers to champion global business in emerging markets. In *Transcending Cultural Frontiers* (pp. 1–10). Springer.

Zakaria, N., Abdul-Talib, A. N., & Othman, N. (Eds.). (2016). *Handbook of research on impacts of international business and political affairs on the global economy.* IGI Global.

Compilation of References

Abaex, B. (1992). *Brazilian Footwear*. Brazilian Association of Export Agents.

Abd-Razak, I. S., & Abdul-Talib, A. N. (2009). Explorative study of proactive and responsive export market orientation: an in-depth interview. In *Australian and New Zealand Marketing Academy (ANZMAC) Conference*. Retrieved from www. duplication. net. au/ANZMAC09/papers/ANZMAC2009-288. pdf

Abdul Majid, N., Ramli, Z., Md Sum, S., & Awang, A. H. (2021). Sustainable palm oil certification scheme frameworks and impacts: A systematic literature review. *Sustainability*, *13*(6), 3263. doi:10.3390u13063263

Abdul Talib, A. N. (2005). *Differences in market-oriented behaviour levels accross firms' domestic and export marketing operation: A study of antecedents and consequences*. Aston University.

Abdul Talib, A., & Teong, N. (2019). Internet Sales Channel and Manufacturers' Brand: A Transaction Cost Analysis. *International Journal of Supply Chain Management*, *8*(5), 1130–1340.

Abdul-Latif, S.-A., & Abdul-Talib, A. N. (2017). Consumer Racism: A Scale Modification. *Asia Pacific Journal of Marketing and Logistics*, *29*(3), 616–633. doi:10.1108/APJML-02-2016-0026

Abdul-Talib, A. N., & Abd-Razak, I.-S. (2020). Proactive and responsive export market orientation behaviours, antecedents, and firm performance. *Leveraging Consumer Behavior and Psychology in the Digital Economy*, 191–204.

Abdul-Talib, A. N., & Arshad, S. (2021). Searching the effects of viral marketing via customer-based brand equity on purchase intentions. Handbook of Research on Technology Applications for Effective Customer Engagement, 66–75. doi:10.4018/978-1-7998-4772-4.ch005

Abdul-Talib, A. N., & Japeri, N. (2020). Brand consciousness and brand loyalty. *Economic, Educational, and Touristic Development in Asia*, 106–126. doi:10.4018/978-1-7998-2239-4.ch006

Abdul-Talib, A. N., & Yusof, M. (2020). Antecedents of global brands preference among generation y in malaysia. *Leveraging Consumer Behavior and Psychology in the Digital Economy*, 153–171. doi:10.4018/978-1-7998-3042-9.ch009

Abdul-Talib, A. N., & Abd-Razak, I. S. (2012). Export market oriented behaviours within the medical tourism industry: A case study. *International Journal of Tourism Policy*, *4*(4), 289–301. doi:10.1504/IJTP.2012.052546

Abdul-Talib, A. N., & Abd-Razak, I. S. (2012). Export market oriented behaviours within the medical tourism industry: A case study. *International Journal of Tourism*, *4*(4), 289–301.

Abdul-Talib, A. N., & Adnan, M. M. (2017). Determinants of consumer's willingness to boycott surrogate products. *Journal of Islamic Marketing*, *8*(3), 345–360. doi:10.1108/JIMA-08-2015-0065

Abdul-Talib, A. N., & Keung, C. W. (2021). Impact of Organisational Capabilities on R&D Project Innovation Performance of E&E Manufacturing Firms in Malaysia. *International Journal of Business Innovation and Research.*, *1*(1), 10042101. doi:10.1504/IJBIR.2021.10042101

Abdul-Talib, A. N., Salleh, M. F. M., Shamsuddin, F. M., & Ashari, H. (2011). The effects of firm size and international business experience on export attitudes. *Journal of Competitiveness Studies*, *19*(1&2), 4–14.

Abdul-Talib, A. N., & Teong, N. (2019). Internet sales channel and manufacturers' brand: A transaction cost analysis. *International Journal of Supply Chain Management*, *8*(5), 1130–1340.

Abor, J., & Quartey, P. (2010). Issues in SME development in Ghana and South Africa. *International Research Journal of Finance and Economics*, *39*(6), 215–228.

Acquaah, M., & Agyapong, A. (2015). The relationship between competitive strategy and firm performance in micro and small businesses in Ghana: The moderating role of managerial and marketing capabilities. *Africa Journal of Management*, *1*(2), 172–193. doi:10.1080/23322373.2015.1025684

Ado, A., Su, Z., & Wanjiru, R. (2017). Learning and knowledge transfer in Africa-China JVs: Interplay between informalities, culture, and social capital. *Journal of International Management*, *23*(2), 166–179. doi:10.1016/j.intman.2016.11.003

Agbiboa, D. E. (2013). No retreat, no surrender: Understanding the religious terrorism of Boko Haram in Nigeria. *African Study Monographs*, *34*(2), 65–84.

Agbiboa, D. E. (2013). Why Boko Haram exists: The relative deprivation perspective. *African Conflict and Peacebuilding Review*, *3*(1), 144–157. doi:10.2979/africonfpeacrevi.3.1.144

Agbiboa, D. E., & Maiangwa, B. (2013). Boko Haram, religious violence, and the crisis of national identity in Nigeria: Towards a non-killing approach. *Journal of Developing Societies*, *29*(4), 379–403. doi:10.1177/0169796X13503198

Aghedo, I. (2012). Winning the war, losing the peace: Amnesty and the challenges of post- conflict peace-building in the Niger delta, Nigeria. *Journal of Asian and African Studies*, *48*(3), 267–280. doi:10.1177/0021909612453987

Agreement on Subsidies and Countervailing Measures, Apr. 15, 1994, Marrakesh Agreement Establishing the World Trade Organization, Annex 1A, 1869 U.N.T.S. 14.

Ahmed, Z., Su, L., Rafique, K., Khan, S., & Jamil, S. (2017). A study on the factors affecting consumer buying behavior towards online shopping in Pakistan. *Journal of Asian Business Strategy*, *7*(2), 44–56.

Ajayi, O. (2020). *ASUU faults FG's proposed slash of education, health budget.* Ibadan: Vanguard Nigeria News. Retrieved 25 April, 2021, from https://www.vanguardngr.com/2020/04/asuu-faults-fgs-proposed-slash-of-education-health-budget/

Akanni, L. O., & Gabriel, S. C. (2020). *The implication of Covid-19 pandemic on the Nigerian Economy.* Retrieved 5 August, 2021, from cseaafrica. org/the-implication-ofcovid19-on-the-nigerian-economy

Akçay, N., & Qingye, T. (2020). Turkey's perceptions of China's Belt and Road initiative (2013–2017): Media and think-tanks discourse analysis. *Bölgesel Araştırmalar Dergisi*, *56*(December), 73–96. doi:10.1177/0009445520916877

Akman, M.S., & Tepav. (2019). *Turkey's Middle Corridor and Belt and Road Initiative: Coherent or Conflicting?* Retrieved May 01, 2021, from https://think-asia.org/handle/11540/11336

Al Ariss, A., & Özbilgin, M. (2010). Understanding self- initiated expatriates: Career experiences of Lebanese self-initiated expatriates in France. *Thunderbird International Business Review*, *52*(4), 275–285. doi:10.1002/tie.20355

Al Majali, S. (2020). The digital world for children and its relationship with personality disorders: Exploring emerging technologies. *International Journal of Emerging Technologies in Learning*, *15*(01), 213. doi:10.3991/ijet.v15i01.11412

Albaity, M., & Rahman, M. (2012). Behavioral finance and Malaysian culture. *International Business Research*, *5*(11), 65–76. doi:10.5539/ibr.v5n11p65

Ali, A., & Badhani, K. N. (2020). Beta-anomaly: Evidence from the Indian equity market. *Asia-Pacific Financial Markets*, *8*, 1–24.

Alkholifey, A. (2000). *The Saudi Arabian Stock Market: Efficient Market Hypothesis and Investors Behavior* [PhD Thesis]. Colorado State University.

Allon, F., & Anderson, K. (2010). Intimate encounters: The embodied transnationalism of backpackers and independent travellers. *Population Space and Place*, *16*(1), 11–22. doi:10.1002/psp.574

Aloulou, W. J. (2019). Impacts of strategic orientations on new product development and firm performances: Insights from Saudi industrial firms. *European Journal of Innovation*, *22*(2), 257–280. doi:10.1108/EJIM-05-2018-0092

Al-Razeen, A. M. (1997). *The Weak-Form Efficiency of the Saudi Stock Market* [Ph.D. Thesis]. University of Leicester.

Al-Sa'di, A. F., Abdallah, A. B., & Dahiyat, S. E. (2017). The mediating role of product and process innovations on the relationship between knowledge management and operational performance in manufacturing companies in Jordan. *Business Process Management Journal*, *23*(2), 349–376. doi:10.1108/BPMJ-03-2016-0047

Altman, Y., & Shortland, S. (2008). Women and international assignments: Taking stock—A 25-year review. *Human Resource Management*, *47*(2), 199–216. doi:10.1002/hrm.20208

Altuntaş, G., Semerciöz, F., & Eregez, H. (2013). Linking strategic and market orientations to organizational performance: The role of innovation in private healthcare organizations. *Procedia: Social and Behavioral Sciences*, *99*, 413–419. doi:10.1016/j.sbspro.2013.10.509

Al-Twaijry, A. A. (2007). Saudi stock market historical view and crisis effect: Graphical and statistical analysis. *Journal of Human Sciences*, *34*(1), 80–95.

Álvarez Espinoza, R., & González Tissinetti, A. (2020). *Competition, selection, and productivity growth in the Chilean manufacturing industry*. Universidad de Chile.

Alves, S., Abrantes, J. L., Antunes, M. J., Seabra, C., & Herstein, R. (2016). WOM antecedents in backpacker travelers. *Journal of Business Research*, *69*(5), 1851–1856. doi:10.1016/j.jbusres.2015.10.068

Alwis, D. D., Saif, S. K., & Niazi, S. (2020). *Universities shut down across South and Southeast Asia. University World News*. University World News. Retrieved 26 April, 2021, from https://www. universityworldnews. com/post. php

Amador, J., & Cabral, S. (2016). Global value chains: A survey of drivers and measures. *Journal of Economic Surveys*, *30*(2), 278–301. doi:10.1111/joes.12097

Ameh, J., & Aluko, O. (2019). *2019 budget: Education gets 620.5bn, against UNESCO"s advice*. Retrieved 2 August, 2021, from https://punchng.com/2019-budget-education-gets-n620-5bnagainst-unesco-advice/

American Association of Port Authorities. (2007). *Embracing the concept of sustainability as a standard practice for ports and the association*. Author.

Anair, D., & Mahmassani, A. (2013). Cattle, Cleared Forests, and Climate Change. Academic Press.

Analysis of the impact of the epidemic on China's metal mineral imports. (2020, March 28). My steel.com.

Anand, V. K. (1999). Informal sector and its role in employment creation in developing countries. *Journal of the Indian Institute of Economics*, *41*(3), 542–556.

Ananthalakshmi, A., Sipalan, J., & Brock, J. (2019)., *Exclusive: EU risks 'trade war' with Malaysia over palm oil – Mahathir*. Reuters. Retrieved September 23, 2021, from Reuters at https://www.reuters.com/article/us-malaysia-politics-mahathir-exclusive-idUSKCN1R917W

Anderson, J. (1979). A theoretical foundation for the gravity equation. *The American Economic Review*, *69*(1), 106–116.

Anderson, J., & Wincoop, E. (2003). Gravity with gravitas: A solution to the border puzzle. *The American Economic Review*, *93*(1), 170–192. doi:10.1257/000282803321455214

Andresen, M., & Bergdolt, F. (2017). A systematic literature review on the definitions of global mindset and cultural intelligence – Merging two different research streams. *International Journal of Human Resource Management*, *28*(1), 170–195. doi:10.1080/09585192.2016.1243568

Andresen, M., Biemann, T., & Pattie, M. W. (2015). What makes them move abroad? Reviewing and exploring differences between self-initiated and assigned expatriation. *International Journal of Human Resource Management*, *26*(7), 932–947. doi:10.1080/09585192.2012.669780

Andri'c, J. M., Wang, J., & Zhong, R. (2019). Identifying the critical risks in railway projects based on fuzzy and sensitivity analysis: A case study of Belt and Road projects. *Sustainability*, *11*(5), 1302. doi:10.3390u11051302

Anh, D. T. (2016). *The causes and effects of Korean pop culture on Vietnamese consumer behavior the causes and effects of Korean pop* (Unpublished Master's thesis). College of Interdisciplinary Studies Thammasat University.

An, H., Razzaq, A., Nawaz, A., Noman, S. M., & Khan, S. A. R. (2021). Nexus between green logistic operations and triple bottom line: Evidence from infrastructure-led Chinese outward foreign direct investment in Belt and Road host countries. *Environmental Science and Pollution Research International*, *28*(37), 51022–51045. Advance online publication. doi:10.100711356-021-12470-3 PMID:33977429

Anh, C. P. T. T., & Baughn, C. (2013). Antecedents and consequence of International Joint Venture Learning: The case of Vietnam. *Journal of Economic Development*, *13*(3), 58–71.

Anh, P. T. T., Baughn, C. C., Hang, N. T. M., & Neupert, K. E. (2006). Knowledge acquisition from foreign parents in international joint ventures: An empirical study in Vietnam. *International Business Review*, *15*(5), 463–487. doi:10.1016/j.ibusrev.2006.05.004

Annuar, M. N., Ariff, M., & Shamsher, M. (1992). A test of semi-strong efficiency of the KLSE. *Malaysian Journal of Economic Studies*, *22*(2), 1–18.

Annuar, M., Shamsher, M., & Ali, M. (1988). Stock Returns and the Weekend Effect: The Malaysian Experience. *Pertanika*, *11*(1), 107–114.

Annuar, M., Shamsher, M., & Zainal, M. (1987). An empirical study of the treasury bill in malaysia: Part 1 – using treasury bills as predictor of inflation. *Pertanika*, *10*(3), 349–355.

Anyadike, N. O. (2013). Boko Haram and national security challenges in Nigeria: Causes and solutions. *Journal of Economics and Sustainable Development*, *4*(5).

Arango, T. (2009, June 23). Cable TV's big worry: Taming the web. *The New York Times*. Retrieved from https://www.nytimes.com/2009/06/24/business/media/24pay.html?_r=1

Araújo, I. F., Perobelli, F. S., & Faria, W. R. (2021). Regional and global patterns of participation in value chains: Evidence from Brazil. *Inter Economics*, *I*(165), 154–171. doi:10.1016/j.inteco.2020.12.009

Arief, R. A., Cangara, A. R., Badu, M. N., Baharuddin, A., & Apriliani, A. (2020, October). The impact of the European Union (EU) renewable energy directive policy on the management of Indonesian palm oil industry. *IOP Conference Series. Earth and Environmental Science*, *575*(1), 012230. doi:10.1088/1755-1315/575/1/012230

Arnold, G. C. (2008). *Corporate Financial Management* (4th ed.). Pearson Education Limited.

Arora, N., & Lohani, P. (2017). Does foreign direct investment spillover total factor productivity growth? A study of Indian drugs and pharmaceutical industry. *Benchmarking*, *24*(7), 1937–1955. doi:10.1108/BIJ-09-2016-0148

Arshad, S., Shahid, M., Laeeq, M., & Ashfaq, M. Which school of thought better measure the concept of market orientation. *International Journal of Research, 2*(12), 1178-1180.

Ashari, H., Yusof, Y., Zamani, M., Norhashmaedayu, S., Talib, A., & Nizam, A. (2018). A study of effect of market orientation on Malaysian automotive industry supply chain performance. *International Journal of Technology*, *9*(8), 1651–1657. doi:10.14716/ijtech.v9i8.2749

Ashraf, A., Razzaque, M., & Thongpapanl, N. (2016). The role of customer regulatory orientation and fit in online shopping across cultural contexts. *Journal of Business Research*, *69*(12), 6040–6047. doi:10.1016/j.jbusres.2016.05.019

Asian Port Association. (2004). *Best Practices Manual on Port Safety, Health, Environment and Security.* Retrieved April 26, 2021, from https://www.scribd.com/document/41805028/1-TEXT-Best-Practices-Manual-Safety-Security-Health-Environment-Rcaversion

Asness, C. S., Frazzini, A., & Pedersen, L. H. (2013). *Quality Minus Junk. Working Paper.* AQR Capital Management and New York University.

Asness. (2011). Momentum in Japan. The exception that proves the rule. *The Journal of Portfolio Management. Summer*, *37*(4), 67-75.

Athanassakos, G. (2009). Value versus growth stock returns and the value premium: The Canadian experience 1985-2005. *Canadian Journal of Administrative Sciences / Revue Canadienne des Sciences de Administration*, *26*(2), 109 - 121.

Athukorala, P. C., & Yamashita, N. (2006). Production fragmentation and trade integration: East Asia in a global context. *The North American Journal of Economics and Finance*, *17*(3), 233–256. doi:10.1016/j.najef.2006.07.002

Autio, E. (2005). Creative tension: The significance of Ben Oviatt's and Patricia McDougall's article 'toward a theory of international new ventures'. *Journal of International Business Studies*, *36*(1), 9–19. doi:10.1057/palgrave.jibs.8400117

Autio, E., George, G., & Alexy, O. (2011). International entrepreneurship and capability development: Qualitative evidence and future research directions. *Entrepreneurship Theory and Practice*, *3*(1), 11–37. doi:10.1111/j.1540-6520.2010.00421.x

Autio, E., Sapienza, H. J., & Almeida, J. G. (2000). Effects of age at entry, knowledge intensity, and imitability on international growth. *Academy of Management Journal*, *43*(5), 909–924.

Autio, E., Sapienza, H. J., & Arenius, P. (2005). International social capital, technology sharing, and foreign market learning in internationalizing entrepreneurial firms. *Advances in Entrepreneurship, Firm, Emergence, and Growth*, *8*, 9–42. doi:10.1016/S1074-7540(05)08002-5

Avesani, M. (2020). Sustainability, sustainable development, and business sustainability. In *Life Cycle Sustainability Assessment for Decision-Making* (pp. 21–38). Elsevier. doi:10.1016/B978-0-12-818355-7.00002-6

Baard, P. P., Deci, E. L., & Ryan, R. M. (2004). A motivational basis of performance and weil-being in two work settings. *Journal of Applied Social Psychology*, *34*(10), 2045–2068. doi:10.1111/j.1559-1816.2004.tb02690.x

Bader Abdulaziz Alkhaldi, J. D. (2015). The Saudi capital market: The crash of 2006 and lessons to be learned. *International Journal of Business, Economics and Law*, *8*(4), 235–250.

Bae, E., Chang, M., Park, E., & Kim, D. (2017). The effect of Hallyu on tourism in Korea. *Journal of Open Innovation*, *3*(22), 2–12. doi:10.118640852-017-0075-y

Bai, S. (2019). Study on the impact of international public health emergency response measures on international trade and countermeasures. *Port Health Control*, (4), 1–3.

Bai, W., Holmström-Lind, C., & Johanson, M. (2018). Leveraging networks, capabilities and opportunities for international success: A study on returnee entrepreneurial ventures. *Scandinavian Journal of Management*, *34*(1), 51–62. doi:10.1016/j.scaman.2017.12.001

Bajgar, M., Berlingieri, G., Calligaris, S., Criscuolo, C., & Timmis, J. (2019). *Industry concentration in Europe and North America.* London School of Economics and Political Science.

Bakker, A. B., & Demerouti, E. (2007). The job demands-resources model: State of the art. *Journal of Managerial Psychology*, *22*(3), 309–328. doi:10.1108/02683940710733115

bakuresearchinstitute.org. (2020). *The Trans-Caspian Corridor: the shortest path or a difficult bridge between East and West?* Retrieved May 01, 2021, from https://bakuresearchinstitute.org/en/the-trans-caspian-corridor-the-shortest-path-or-a-difficult-bridge-between-east-and-west/

Balik, R., & Mehran, J. (2008). *Benjamin Graham revisited.* Available from: http://www. academy financial. org/09Conference/09Proceedings/(5D)% 0Balik,% 0Mehran.pdf

Balkiz, O. (2003). Testing informational market efficiency on Kuala Lumpur stock exchange. *Jurnal Ekonomi Malaysia*, *37*(3), 3–20.

Baltagi, B. H. (2021). *Econometric analysis of panel data.* Springer Nature. doi:10.1007/978-3-030-53953-5

Bandera, C., & Passerini, K. (2018). Personality traits and the digital entrepreneur: A new breed or same actor? *Twenty-fourth Americas Conference on Information Systems*, 1-10.

Baranowska-Prokop, E., & Sikora, T. (2017). Competitiveness of polish international new ventures from managerial perspective. In A. Vlachvei (Ed.), *ABSCA) book series. Factors affecting firm competitiveness and performance in the modern business world, Business Science Reference* (pp. 83–107). doi:10.4018/978-1-5225-0843-4.ch003

Barberis, N., & Shleifer, A. (2003). Style investing. *Journal of Financial Economics*, *68*(2), 161–199. doi:10.1016/S0304-405X(03)00064-3

Barclay, D., Higgins, C., & Thompson, R. (1995). *The Partial Least Squares (PLS) approach to casual modeling: personal computer adoption ans use as an illustration.* Academic Press.

Barney, J. B. (1991). Firm resources and sustained competitive advantage. *Journal of Management*, *17*(1), 99–120. doi:10.1177/014920639101700108

Barreda, A. A., Bilgihan, A., Nusair, K., & Okumus, F. (2015). Generating brand awareness in online social networks. *Computers in Human Behavior*, *50*, 600–609. doi:10.1016/j.chb.2015.03.023

Bartlett, M. S. (1954). A note on the multiplying factors for various χ 2 approximations. *Journal of the Royal Statistical Society. Series B. Methodological*, *16*(2), 296–298. doi:10.1111/j.2517-6161.1954.tb00174.x

Bartusevicius, H. (2013). The inequality-conflict nexus re-examined: Income, education and popular rebellions. *Journal of Peace Research*, *51*(1), 35–50. doi:10.1177/0022343313503179

Baruh, L., & Cemalcılar, Z. (2018). When more is more? The impact of breadth and depth of information disclosure on attributional confidence about and interpersonal attraction to a social network site profile owner. *Cyberpsychology (Brno), 12*(1), 1. doi:10.5817/CP2018-1-1

Basu, S. (1977). Investment performance of common stocks in relation to their price-earnings ratios: A test of the efficient market hypothesis. *The Journal of Finance, 32*(3), 663–682. doi:10.1111/j.1540-6261.1977.tb01979.x

Battistella, C., De Toni, A. F., & Pillon, R. (2016). Inter-organisational technology/knowledge transfer: A framework from critical literature review. *The Journal of Technology Transfer, 41*(5), 1195–1234. doi:10.100710961-015-9418-7

Bay, M., & Erol, F. (2016). Lojistik Köylerin Önemi ve İntermodal Taşımacılık Faaliyetleriyle Desteklenmesi: Karaman İlinde Bir Uygulama. *KMÜ Sosyal ve Ekonomik Araştırmalar Dergisi, 18*(30), 124–134.

Bekaert, G., & Hodrick, R. (2017). *International Financial Management.* Cambridge University Press. doi:10.1017/9781316282274

Bembom, M., & Schwens, C. (2018). The role of networks in early internationalizing firms: A systematic review and future research agenda. *European Management Journal, 36*(6), 679–694. doi:10.1016/j.emj.2018.03.003

Bengtsson, L. (2004). Explaining born globals: An organisational learning perspective on the internationalisation process. *International Journal of Globalisation and Small Business, 1*(1), 28–41. doi:10.1504/IJGSB.2004.005616

Bernama. (2019). M'sia to switch to Chinese fighter jets if palm oil ban continues: Mahathir. *The Sun Daily.* Retrieved September 25, 2021, from https://www.thesundaily.my/local/m-sia-to-switch-to-chinese-fighter-jets-if-palm-oil-ban-continues-mahathir-DM718306

Bernard, V., Thomas, J., & Wahlen, J. (1997). Accounting-based stock price anomalies: Separating market inefficiencies from risk. *Contemporary Accounting Research, 14*(2), 89–136. doi:10.1111/j.1911-3846.1997.tb00529.x

Bernstein, M. S., Bakshy, E., Burke, M., & Karrer, B. (2013, April). Quantifying the invisible audience in social networks. In *Proceedings of the SIGCHI conference on human factors in computing systems* (pp. 21–30). ACM 10.1145/2470654.2470658

Bersenev, A., Chikilevskaya, M., & Rusinov, I. (2020). Silk road rail corridors outlook and future perspectives of development. *Procedia Computer Science, 167*, 1080–1087.

Biemann, T., & Andresen, M. (2010). Self-initiated foreign expatriates versus assigned expatriates: Two distinct types of international careers? *Journal of Managerial Psychology, 25*(4), 430–448. doi:10.1108/02683941011035313

Bildersee, J. S., Cheh, J. J., & Zutshi, A. (1993). The performance of Japanese common stocks in relation to their net current asset values. *Japan and the World Economy, 5*(3), 197–215. doi:10.1016/0922-1425(93)90011-R

Bilgen, İ. (2019). Fuarcılıkta Bugünün Geleneği: Sanal Fuarlar. In Pazarlama Düşüncesiyle Sürdürüleblir Fuarcılık ve istihdam (pp. 227-238). Sokak Yayın Grubu.

Bingham, C. B., & Davis, J. P. (2012). Learning sequences: Their existence, effect, and evolution. *Academy of Management Journal, 55*(3), 611–641. doi:10.5465/amj.2009.0331

BirdR. G.GerlachR. H. (2013). *The Good and the Bad of Value Investing: Applying a Bayesian Approach to Develop Enhancement Models.* https://ssrn.com/abstract=391686 doi:10.2139/ssrn.391686

Bloodgood, J. M., Sapienza, H. J., & Almeida, J. G. (1996). The internationalization of new high potential U.S. ventures: Antecedents and outcomes. *Entrepreneurship Theory and Practice, 20*(4), 61–76. doi:10.1177/104225879602000405

Bloomberg, L.P. (2015). *Net current asset value and market value.* Author.

Bodie, Z., Kane, A., & Marcus, A. (2007). *Essentials of investments* (6th ed.). McGraw-Hill/Irwin.

Bolt-Lee, C., & Foster, S. (2003). The core competency framework: A new element in continuing call for accounting education change in the United States. *Accounting Education, 12*(1), 33–47. doi:10.1080/0963928031000074486

Bondarouk, E., & Ruël, H. (2012). Lobbying of commercial diplomats: institutional setting as a determining factor. In H. Ruël (Ed.), *Commercial diplomacy and international business: A conceptual and empirical exploration, Advanced Series in Management* (Vol. 9, pp. 251–291). Emerald Group Publishing Limited. doi:10.1108/S1877-6361(2012)0000009013

Boso, N., Story, V., & Cadogan, J. (2013). Entrepreneurial orientation, market orientation, networks ties and performance: Study of entrepreneurial firms in a developing economy. *Journal of Business Venturing, 28*(6), 708–727. doi:10.1016/j.jbusvent.2013.04.001

Bournakis, I. (2021). Spillovers and productivity: Revisiting the puzzle with EU firm level data. *Economics Letters, 201*, 109804. doi:10.1016/j.econlet.2021.109804

BPS (Badan Pusat Statistik). (2015). *Annual Manufactuirng Survey.* Badan Pusat Statistik Republik Indonesia.

Brazil exported 33.68m tonnes of iron ore in June, the highest level in nearly nine months. (2021). *Economic and trade information.* https://www.tjgportnet.com/m/news-33899.aspx

Brenner, L., & Fricke, J. (2007). The evolution of backpacker destinations: The case of Zipolite, Mexico. *International Journal of Tourism Research, 9*(3), 217–230. doi:10.1002/jtr.604

Brochado, A., Rita, P., & Gameiro, C. (2015). Exploring backpackers' perceptions of the hostel service quality. *International Journal of Contemporary Hospitality Management, 27*(8), 1839–1855. doi:10.1108/IJCHM-03-2014-0145

Brouthers, K. D., Nakos, G., & Dimitratos, P. (2015). SME entrepreneurial orientation, international performance, and the moderating role of strategic alliances. *Entrepreneurship Theory and Practice, 39*(5), 1161–1187. doi:10.1111/etap.12101

Brush, C., Edelman, L., Harrison, R., Hechavarria, D., Justo, R., & McAdam, M. (2018). A gendered look at entrepreneurship ecosystems. *Academy of Management Proceedings, 2018*(1), 16912. doi:10.5465/AMBPP.2018.16912symposium

Buckley, P. J. (2020). China's Belt and Road initiative and the Covid-19 crisis. *Journal of International Business Policy, 3*(3), 311–314.

Buckley, P. J., & Casson, M. (2021). Thirty years of International Business Review and international business research. *International Business Review, 30*(2), 101795. doi:10.1016/j.ibusrev.2021.101795

Bucsky, P., & Kenderdine, T. (2020). Is the iron silk road really so important? Rail freight use on China's "Silk road economic belt. *Вестник МГИМО-Университета, 13*(5), 168–193. doi:10.24833/2071-8160-2020-5-74-168-193

Bui, H. T., Wilkins, H., & Lee, Y.-S. (2014). Liminal experience of East Asian backpackers. *Tourist Studies, 14*(2), 126–143. doi:10.1177/1468797614532179

Buli, B. M. (2017). Entrepreneurial orientation, market orientation and performance of SMEs in the manufactiuring industry: Evidence from Ethiopian entreprises. *Management Research Review, 40*(3), 292–309. doi:10.1108/MRR-07-2016-0173

Bulut, E. B. (2018). Governance of transport corridors' perspective of Turkey. *11th meeting of comcec transport and communications working group on governance of transport corridors in the OIC member states: Challenges, cases and policy lessons.* (Report)

Bustamante, J. C. (2019). Intellectual property rights as branding services for exports value-adding: An analysis of Chile-s-Sello de Origen-programme. *International Journal of Intellectual Property Management, 9*(3-4), 315–341. doi:10.1504/IJIPM.2019.103044

Butler, K., & Malaikah, S. J. (1992). Efficiency and inefficiency in thinly traded stock markets: Kuwait and Saudi Arabia. *Journal of Banking & Finance, 16*(197), 108–209. doi:10.1016/0378-4266(92)90085-E

Caber, M., & Albayrak, T. (2016). 'Push or pull? Identifying rock climbing tourists' motivations. *Tourism Management, 55*, 74–84. doi:10.1016/j.tourman.2016.02.003

Cai, W., Cohen, S. A., & Tribe, J. (2019). Harmony rules in Chinese backpacker groups. *Annals of Tourism Research, 75*, 120–130. doi:10.1016/j.annals.2018.12.010

Calabrese, L., & Cao, Y. (2021). Managing the Belt and Road: Agency and development in cambodia and myanmar. *World Development, 141*, 105297.

Calvet, A. L. (1983). A synthesis of foreign directinvestment theories and theories of the multinational firm. *International Accounting and Transnational Decisions,* 315-334.

Carl-LeVan, A. (2013). Sectarian rebellions in post-transition Nigeria compared. *Journal of Intervention and Statebuilding, 7*(3), 335–352. doi:10.1080/17502977.2013.783999

Carr, J. E. (2005). Multiple-Baseline Designs Across Participants. *Behavioral Interventions, 20*(3), 219–224. doi:10.1002/bin.191

Cassiman, B., & Veugelers, R. (2006). In search of complementarity in innovation strategy: Internal R&D and external knowledge acquisition. *Management Science, 52*(1), 68–82. doi:10.1287/mnsc.1050.0470

Cavusgil, S. T., & Knight, G. (2015). The born global firm: An entrepreneurial and capabilities perspective on early and rapid internationalization. *Journal of International Business Studies, 46*(1), 3–16. doi:10.1057/jibs.2014.62

Cazura, A. C., Mary, M. M., & Manrakhan, S. (2007). Causes of the difficulties in internationalization. *Journal of International Business Studies, 38*(5), 709–725. doi:10.1057/palgrave.jibs.8400295

Cerdin, J. L., & Selmer, J. (2014). Who is a self-initiated expatriate? Towards conceptual clarity of a common notion. *International Journal of Human Resource Management, 25*(9), 1281–1301. doi:10.1080/09585192.2013.863793

Cesar, A. S. S. J. (in press). Brazil and the COVID-19 pandemic. *Kidney International Reports.*

Chambers, D. B. (2013). *There* was a country: Achebe's final work. *Journal of Asian and African Studies, 48*(6), 752–759. doi:10.1177/0021909613506454

Chang, D. (2012). Testing some of Benjamin Graham's stock selection criteria: A case of the FTSE Bursa Malaysia Emas Index from year 2000 to 2009. *Jurnal Manajemen Dan Kewirausahaan/Journal of Management and Entrepreneurship, 13*(2), 99-106.

Chang, F. K. (2021). *Palm oil: Malaysian economic interests and foreign relations.* Foreign Policy Research Institute. https://www.fpri.org/article/2021/04/palm-oil-malaysian-economic-interests-and-foreign-relations/

Chang, T. C. (2015). The asian wave and critical tourism scholarship. *International Journal of Asia-Pacific Studies, 11*(1), 83–101.

Chang, Y., & Peng, M. W. (2012). Expatriate knowledge transfer, subsidiary absorptive capacity, and subsidiary performance. National Taiwan University of Science and Technology Hong Kong University of Science and Technology. *Academy of Management Journal, 55*(4), 927–948. doi:10.5465/amj.2010.0985

Chan, L. K., Hamao, Y., & Lakonishok, J. (1991). Fundamentals and stock returns in Japan. *The Journal of Finance, 46*(5), 1739–1764. doi:10.1111/j.1540-6261.1991.tb04642.x

Chan, L. K., & Lakonishok, J. (2004). Value and growth investing: Review and update. *Financial Analysts Journal, 3*(2), 71–86. doi:10.2469/faj.v60.n1.2593

Chao, M. C., & Spillan, J. E. (2010). The journey from market orientation to firm performance: A comparative study of US and Taiwanese SMEs. *Management Research Review, 33*(5), 472–483. doi:10.1108/01409171011041901

Chapman, S., Buttler, A., Francez, A. J., Laggoun-Défarge, F., Vasander, H., Schloter, M., Combe, J., Grosvernier, P., Harms, H., Epron, D., Mitchell, E., & Gilbert, D. (2003). Exploitation of northern peatlands and biodiversity maintenance: A conflict between economy and ecology. *Frontiers in Ecology and the Environment, 1*(10), 525–532. doi:10.1890/1540-9295(2003)001[0525:EONPAB]2.0.CO;2

Che Rose, R., Sri Ramalu, S., Uli, J., & Kumar, N. (2010). Expatriate Performance in International Assignments: The Role of Cultural Intelligence as Dynamic Intercultural Competency. *International Journal of Business and Management, 5*(8), 76–85. doi:10.5539/ijbm.v5n8p76

Chee, S., Sloan, R., & Uysal, A. (2013). A framework for value investing. *Australian Journal of Management, 38*(3), 599–633. doi:10.1177/0312896213510715

Chen, N. (2017). China's economic and trade development under the international economic and trade situation. University of International Business and Economics, (4).

Chen, W. H. (2020). *Bilateral trade between China and Brazil has bucked the trend.* Gwangmyong Net. https://www.sohu.com/a/433634676_162758

Chen, C.-J., Hsiao, Y.-C., & Chu, M.-A. (2014). Transfer mechanisms and knowledge transfer: The cooperative competency perspective. *Journal of Business Research, 67*(12), 2531–2541. doi:10.1016/j.jbusres.2014.03.011

Chen, G., Bao, J., & Huang, S. (2014). Segmenting chinese backpackers by travel motivations. *International Journal of Tourism Research, 16*(1), 355–367. doi:10.1002/jtr.1928

Chen, G., & Huang, S. S. (2017). Toward a theory of backpacker personal development : Cross-cultural validation of the BPD scale. *Tourism Management, 59*, 630–639. doi:10.1016/j.tourman.2016.09.017

Chen, G., Huang, S., & Hu, X. (2019). Backpacker personal development, generalized self-efficacy, and self-esteem: Testing a structural model. *Journal of Travel Research, 58*(4), 680–694. doi:10.1177/0047287518768457

Chen, G., Zhao, L., & Huang, S. (2019). Backpacker identity: Scale development and validation. *Journal of Travel Research, 59*(2), 1–14. doi:10.1177/0047287519829255

Cheng, T. C. E., Farahani, R. Z., Lai, K. H., & Sarkis, J. (2015). Sustainability in maritime supply chains: Challenges and opportunities for theory and practice. *Transportation Research Part E, Logistics and Transportation Review, 78*, 1–2. doi:10.1016/j.tre.2015.03.007

Chen, L., Xie, X. Z., & Liu, L. (2018). China's export trade efficiency and trade potential: 1980~2015. *International Economic and Trade Exploration, 34*(1), 33–50.

Chen, S. (2016). Cultural technology: A framework for marketing cultural exports – analysis of Hallyu (the Korean wave). *International Marketing Review, 33*(1), 25–50. doi:10.1108/IMR-07-2014-0219

Chen, T. J., & Tang, D. P. (1987). Comparing technical efficiency between import-substitution-oriented and export-oriented foreign firms in a developing economy. *Journal of Development Economics, 26*(2), 277–289. doi:10.1016/0304-3878(87)90030-7

Chetty, S., & Campbell-Hunt, C. (2004). A strategic approach to internationalization: A traditional versus a "born-global" approach. *Journal of International Marketing, 12*(1), 57–81. doi:10.1509/jimk.12.1.57.25651

Chi-Koffi, L. C. Y., & Wang, W. D. (2021). Effects of Covid-19 Pandemic on International Financial Management. *International Journal of Trend in Scientific Research and Development, 5*(3), 321–323.

Chiluwa, I. (2012). Social media networks and the discourse of resistance: A sociolinguistic CDA of Biafra Online discourses. *Discourse & Society, 23*(3), 217–244. doi:10.1177/0957926511433478

Chima, O. (2017, September 27). New Vista for MSMEs. *Thisday*. Retrieved from https://www.pressreader.com/nigeria/thisday/20170927/281724089743223

Chin, W. W., Marcolin, B. L., & Newsted, P. R. (2003). A partial least squares latent variable modeling approach for measuring interaction effects: Results from a monte carlo simulation study and an electronic-mail emotion/ adoption study. *Information Systems Research, 14*(2), 1–18. Retrieved from file:///F:/Mendeley/2003/Material/Material - 2003 - Moderators 82-95.pdf

China imports iron ore and soybeans from Brazil, while Brazil imports mechanical, electrical and chemical products from China. (2018). https://www.sohu.com/a/256885828_100110525

China Money Network. (2020, April 15). *Forecast of large market trend of various varieties.* Qishun Investment.

China Social Science Network. (2020). *The price of iron ore in Brazil has risen after the closure of a mine because of the outbreak.* http://ex.cssn.cn/hqxx/ywhg/202006/t20200625_5147651.shtml?ivk_sa=1023197a

China Trade News Net. (2020). http://www.guangrunwuliu.com/xwzx/xydt/102375.shtml; https://baijiahao. baidu. com/s?id=1669830382126371019&wfr=spider&for=pc

Chinedu, E. A., Titus, O. C., & Thaddeus, E. O. (2010). Achieving vision 2020 in Nigeria: A review of the economic and market-oriented business reforms. *Journal of Sustainable Development in Africa, 12*(4), 58–71.

Ching, L. (2000, Winter). Globalising the Regional, Regionalising the Global: Mass Culture and Asianism in the Age of Late Capital. *Public Culture, 12*(1), 233–257. doi:10.1215/08992363-12-1-233

Chinta, R., Cheung, M.-S., & Capar, N. (2015). Double whammy or double advantage: "Foreignness" and "newness" as determinants of success in international business. *Journal of Management and Strategy, 6*(1), 76–87. doi:10.5430/jms.v6n1p76

Chin, W. W. (2010). *How to write up and report PLS analyses. In Handbook of partial least squares.* Springer.

Chitty, B., Ward, S., & Chua, C. (2007). An application of the ECSI model as a predictor of satisfaction and loyalty for backpacker hostels. *Marketing Intelligence amd. Planning (Chicago, Ill.), 25*, 563–580.

Choi, H. (2015). The young generation and their social media. *Sociétés, 129*(3), 105. doi:10.3917oc.129.0105

Choi, J., & Jeon, H. H. (2020). Are all Asian tourists the same? Chinese versus Japanese dining satisfaction. *British Food Journal, 122*(11), 3529–3545. doi:10.1108/BFJ-06-2019-0454

Christansen B., Dirikan,T., Dirikan, C., Kasarcı, F. (2016). *Turkey's Economic Sustainability in Global Hypercompetition.* Academic Press.

Chui, A., Wei, J., & Titman, S. (2010). Individualism and momentum around the world. *The Journal of Finance, 65*(1), 361–392. doi:10.1111/j.1540-6261.2009.01532.x

Cohen, E. (2006). Pai—A backpacker enclave in transition. *Tourism Recreation Research, 31*(3), 11–27. doi:10.1080/02508281.2006.11081502

Cohen, E., & Cohen, S. A. (2015). Beyond Eurocentrism in tourism: A paradigm shift to mobilities. *Tourism Recreation Research, 40*(2), 157–168. doi:10.1080/02508281.2015.1039331

Cohen, M. J. (2020). Does the COVID-19 outbreak mark the onset of a sustainable consumption transition? *Sustainability: Science, Practice, and Policy, 16*(1), 1–3. doi:10.1080/15487733.2020.1740472

Cohen, S. A. (2010). *Re-conceptualising lifestyle travellers: Contemporary'drifters.* Channel View Publications.

Cohen, S. A. (2011). Lifestyle travellers. Backpacking as a way of life. *Annals of Tourism Research, 38*(4), 1535–1555. doi:10.1016/j.annals.2011.02.002

Colchester, M., Chao, S., Dan, V. T., & Villanueva, J. (2011). Oil palm expansion in south East Asia. *Bogor, Moreton-in-Marsh: Forest People Programme and Perkumpulan Sawit Watch.*

Committee on the Environment, Public Health and Food Safety. (2017). *On Palm Oil and Deforestation of Rainforest* (2016/2222(INI)). European Parliament. https://www.europarl.europa.eu/doceo/document/A-8-2017-0066_EN.html

Companhia Vale do Rio Doce. (n.d.). In *Baidupedia.* https://baike.baidu.com/item/%E5%B7%B4%E8%A5%BF%E6%B7%A1%E6%B0%B4%E6%B2%B3%E8%B0%B7%E5%85%AC%E5%8F%B8/3372019?fr=aladdin

Constantinescu, C., Mattoo, A., & Ruta, M. (2019). Does vertical specialisation increase productivity? *World Economy, 42*(8), 2385–2402. doi:10.1111/twec.12801

Costinot, A., & Rodriguez-Clare, A. (2013). Trade Theory with Numbers: Quantifying the Consequences of Globalization. Handbook of International Economics, 4.

Coviello, N., & Yli-Renko, H. (2016). *Handbook of measures for international entrepreneurship research: multi-item scales crossing disciplines and contexts.* Edward Elgar Publishing. doi:10.4337/9781784711405

Croda, J., Oliveira, W. D., Frutuoso, R. L., Mandetta, L. H., Baia-da-Silva, D. C., Brito-Sousa, J. D., & Lacerda, M. G. (2020). *COVID-19 in Brazil: Advantages of a socialized unified health system and preparation to contain cases.* Retrieved 5 August, 2021, from https://www.scielo.br/j/rsbmt/a/bwLKCs6ZfGhyFn3mp4RDhdQ/?format=html&lang=en

Ćuzović, S., Sokolov Mladenović, S., & Ćuzović, Đ. (2019). The impact of social and cultural factors on success of trade internationalization. *Poslovna Izvrsnost, 13*(1), 57–76. doi:10.22598/pi-be/2019.13.1.57

da Silva, P. A., & da Rocha, A. (2001). Perception of export barriers to Mercosur by Brazilian firms. *International Marketing Review, 18*(6), 589–610. doi:10.1108/EUM0000000006296

Damodoran. (2012). *Investment valuation: Tools and technique for determining the value of any asset.* Wiley Finance.

Damtew, T. (2020). *COVID-19- A Vindictive messenger for multilateralism.* School of Education, University of Kwa-Zulu-Natal. Retrieved 25 April, 2021, from https://soe.ukzn.ac.za/news/2020/05/covid-19-a-vindictive-messenger-for-multilateralism/

Daniel, E. (2016). The usefulness of qualitative and quantitative approaches and methods in researching problem-solving ability in science education curriculum. *Journal of Education and Practice, 7*(15), 91–100.

Dann, G. M. S. (1977). Anomie, ego-enhancement and tourism. *Annals of Tourism Research, 4*(4), 184–194. doi:10.1016/0160-7383(77)90037-8

Dann, G. M. S. (1981). Tourist motivation an appraisal. *Annals of Tourism Research, 8*(2), 187–219. doi:10.1016/0160-7383(81)90082-7

Dauvergne, P. (2018). The global politics of the business of "sustainable" palm oil. *Global Environmental Politics, 18*(2), 34–52. doi:10.1162/glep_a_00455

David, N. (1995). Analyst forecasting errors and their implications for security analysis. *Financial Analysts Journal, 51*(3), 30–41. doi:10.2469/faj.v51.n3.1903

Dawu, S. (2021). *Export participation and productivity: Evidence from the Ghana manufacturing industry* [Master Theses]. UMEA University.

Dayang Norwana, A. A. B., Kanjappan, R., Chin, M., Schoneveld, G. C., Potter, L., & Andriani, R. (2011). The local impacts of oil palm expansion in malaysia; an assessment based on a case study in Sabah state. *Center for International Forestry Research (CIFOR) Working Paper, 78*, 1-17.

Day, G. S. (1994). The capabilities of market-driven organisation. *Journal of Marketing, 58*(4), 37–52. doi:10.1177/002224299405800404

De Chernatony, L., & Dall'Olmo Riley, F. (1998). Defining a" brand": Beyond the literature with experts' interpretations. *Journal of Marketing Management, 14*(5), 417–443. doi:10.1362/026725798784867798

De Loecker, J. (2007). Do exports generate higher productivity? Evidence from Slovenia. *Journal of International Economics, 73*(1), 69-98. doi: .2007.03.003 doi:10.1016/j.jinteco

Deci, E. L., & Ryan, R. M. (2000). The "what" and "why" of goal pursuits: Human needs and the self-determination of behavior. *Psychological Inquiry, 11*(4), 227–268. doi:10.1207/S15327965PLI1104_01

DeSarbo, W. S., Anthony Di Benedetto, C., & Sinha, I. (2005). Revisiting the Miles and Snow strategic framework: Uncovering interrelationships between strategic types, capabilities, environmental uncertainty, and firm performance. *Strategic Management Journal, 26*(1), 47–74. doi:10.1002mj.431

Destek, M. A. (2020). Investigation on the role of economic, social, and political globalization on environment: Evidence from CEECs. *Environmental Science and Pollution Research International, 27*(27), 33601–33614. doi:10.100711356-019-04698-x PMID:30864029

Devinney, T. M., Markman, G., Pedersen, T., & Tihanyi, L. (2016). *Global Entrepreneurship: Past, Present & Future.* Emerald Group Publishing. doi:10.1108/S1571-5027201629

Dhanaraj, C., Lyles, M. A., Steensma, H. K., & Tihanyi, L. (2004). Managing tacit and explicit knowledge transfer in IJVs: The role of relational embeddedness and the impact on performance. *Journal of International Business Studies, 35*(5), 428–442. doi:10.1057/palgrave.jibs.8400098

Dibb, S., Simkin, L., Pride, W. M., & Ferrell, O. C. (1994). *Marketing: Concepts and strategies* (2nd ed.). Houghton Mifflin.

Ding, J. (2020). Three essential problems of the spread of COVID-19 and the acceleration of globalization. *Xinhua Finance.* http://news.xinhua08.com/a/20200623/1943879.shtml

Djankov, S., & Hoekman, B. (2000). Foreign investment and productivity growth in Czech enterprises. *The World Bank Economic Review, 14*(1), 49–64. doi:10.1093/wber/14.1.49

Doherty, N. T. (2013). Understanding the self-initiated expatriate. A review and directions for future research. *International Journal of Management Reviews, 15*, 447–469. doi:10.1111/ijmr.12005

Doherty, N. T., & Dickmann, M. (2012). Measuring the return on investment in international assignments: An action research approach. *International Journal of Human Resource Management*, *23*(16), 3434–3454. doi:10.1080/09585192.2011.637062

Donthu, N., & Gustafsson, A. (2020). Effects of COVID-19 on business and research. *Journal of Business Research*, *117*, 284–289. doi:10.1016/j.jbusres.2020.06.008 PMID:32536736

Dornbusch, R., Fischer, S., & Startz, R. (2011). *Macroeconomics* (11th ed.). The McGraw-Hill Companies.

DoukasJ. A.BalaA.CogginT. D. (1998). Multifactor Asset Pricing Analysis of International Value Investment Strategies. https://ssrn.com/abstract=54002 doi:10.2139/ssrn.54002

Drew, M. E., & Veeraraghanan, M. (2002). A closer look at the size and value premium in emerging markets: Evidence from the Kuala Lumpur Stock Exchange. *Asian Economic Journal*, *16*(4), 337–351. doi:10.1111/1467-8381.00156

Duan, B. L. (2011). *Research on Iron Ore Trade and Investment between China and Brazil* [Unpublished master dissertation]. University of International Business and Economics, Chaoyang District, Beijing, China.

Dubai Statistics Center. (n.d.). *Dubai Socioeconomic Statistics*. Retrieved from https://www.dsc.gov.ae/en-us/Themes/Pages/National-Accounts.aspx?Theme=24

Dy, A., Marlow, S., & Martin, L. (2016). A Web of opportunity or the same old story? Women digital entrepreneurs and intersectionality theory. *Human Relations*, *70*(3), 286–311. doi:10.1177/0018726716650730

Easterby-Smith, M., Lyles, M. A., & Tsang, E. W. (2008). Inter-organizational knowledge transfer: Current themes and future prospects. *Journal of Management Studies*, *45*(4), 677–690. doi:10.1111/j.1467-6486.2008.00773.x

Ebrahim, S., Hudson, R., Iqbal, A., & Shah, E. (2016). Dispelling the myth of value premium: Contrary evidence of Malaysian crony capitalism. *International Journal of Banking, Accounting and Finance*, *7*(1), 1–33.

Economic development in Brazil. (2015). https://wenku.baidu.com/view/695b0014680203d8cf2f245c.html

Edstrom, A., & Galbraith, J. R. (1977). Transfer of Managers as a Coordination and Control Strategy in Multinational Organizations. *Cornell Univers.*, *22*(2), 248–263.

Edwards, J. (2020). *Protect a Generation: The impact of COVID-19 on children's lives.* Save the Children International. Retrieved 6 May, 2021, from https://www.savethechildren.org/content/dam/usa/reports/emergency-response/protect-a-generation-report.pdf

Ee, T., & Kahl, C. (2016). Self discovery and backpackers: A conceptual paper about liminal experience. *International Journal of Religious Tourism and Pilgrimage*, *4*(1), 49–58.

Ekwe-Ekwe, H. (2013). The Achebean restoration. *Journal of Asian and African Studies*, *48*(6), 698–709. doi:10.1177/0021909613506485

Elliot, B., Docherty, P., Easton, S., & Lee, D. (2018). Profitability and investment-based factor pricing models. *Accounting and Finance*, *58*(2), 397–421. doi:10.1111/acfi.12217

Embas, D. U. (2012). Statement by The Honourable Dato' Sri Douglas Unggah Embas, Minister of Natural Resources and Environment, *Malaysia. The United Nations Conference on Sustainable Development*, Rio De Janeiro.

Engelen, A., Gupta, V., Strenger, L., & Brettel, M. (2015). Entrepreneurial orientation, firm performance, and the moderating role of transformational leadership behaviors. *Journal of Management*, *41*(4), 1069–1097. doi:10.1177/0149206312455244

Esch, F.-R., Moll, T., Schmitt, B., Elger, C. E., Neuhaus, C., & Weber, B. (2012). Brands on the brain: Do consumers use declarative information or experienced emotions to evaluate brands. *Journal of Consumer Psychology*, *22*(1), 75–85. doi:10.1016/j.jcps.2010.08.004

Escobar, L. F., & Vredenburg, H. (2011). Multinational oil companies and the adoption of sustainable development: A resource-based and institutional theory interpretation of adoption heterogeneity. *Journal of Business Ethics*, *98*(1), 39–65. doi:10.100710551-010-0534-x

Espino-Rdriguez, T. F., & Rodriguez-Diaz, M. (2008). Effect of internal and relational capabilities on outsourcing: An intergrated model. *Industrial Management & Data Systems*, *108*(3), 328–345. doi:10.1108/02635570810858750

Esquivias, M. A., & Harianto, S. K. (2020). Does competition and foreign investment spur industrial efficiency?: Firm-level evidence from Indonesia. *Heliyon*, *6*(8), 1–10. doi:10.1016/j.heliyon.2020.e04494 PMID:32904310

Eun, C. S., & Resnick, B. G. (2010). *International Financial Mgmt* (4th ed.). Tata McGraw-Hill Education.

Evangelista, F., & Hau, L. N. (2009). Organizational context and knowledge acquisition in IJVs: An empirical study. *Journal of World Business*, *44*(1), 63–73. doi:10.1016/j.jwb.2008.03.016

Evers, N., Gliga, G., & Rialp-Criado, A. (2019). Strategic orientation pathways in international new ventures and born global firms—Towards a research agenda. *Journal of International Entrepreneurship*, *17*(3), 287–304. doi:10.100710843-019-00259-y

Eyland, G. (2020). *A Brief History of Value Investing. Fundamental Finance Playbook.* Available: https://fundamentalfinanceplaybook.com/histories/what-is-value-investing/

Ezeani, N. S. (2012). The teacher and skills acquisition at business education: From the perspective of accounting skills. *Arabian Journal of Business and Management Review*, *2*(4), 25–36.

Fafunwa, A. B. (2002). *History of Education in Nigeria.* NPS Educational Publishers Ltd.

Falko, F., Presseau, S. J., & Vera, A. S. (2014). Time to retire the theory of planned behavior. *Health Psychology Review*, *8*(1), 1–7. doi:10.1080/17437199.2013.869710 PMID:25053004

Falk, R. F., & Miller, N. B. (1992). *A primer for soft modeling.* University of Akron Press.

Fama, E.F., & French, K.R. (2012). *Size, value and momentum in international stock returns.* Academic Press.

Fama, E. (1970). Efficient capital markets: A review of theory and empirical work. *The Journal of Finance*, *25*(2), 383–417. doi:10.2307/2325486

Fama, E. F. (1998). Market efficiency, long-term returns, and behavioral finance. *Journal of Financial Economics*, *49*(3), 283–306. doi:10.1016/S0304-405X(98)00026-9

Fama, E. F., & French, K. R. (1992). The cross-section of expected stock returns. *The Journal of Finance*, *47*(2), 427–465. doi:10.1111/j.1540-6261.1992.tb04398.x

Fama, E. F., & French, K. R. (1993). Common risk factors in the returns on stocks and bonds. *Journal of Financial Economics*, *33*(1), 3–56. doi:10.1016/0304-405X(93)90023-5

Fama, E. F., & French, K. R. (1995). Size and Book-to-Market Factors in Earnings and Returns. *The Journal of Finance*, *50*(1), 131–155. doi:10.1111/j.1540-6261.1995.tb05169.x

Fama, E. F., & French, K. R. (1998). Value versus growth: The international evidence. *The Journal of Finance*, *53*(6), 1975–1999. doi:10.1111/0022-1082.00080

Fama, E. F., & French, K. R. (2015). A five-factor asset pricing model. *Journal of Financial Economics, 105*(3), 457–472. doi:10.1016/j.jfineco.2012.05.011

Fama, E. F., & French, K. R. (2017). International tests of a five-factor asset pricing model. *Journal of Financial Economics, 123*(3), 441–463. doi:10.1016/j.jfineco.2016.11.004

Fan Fah, C., Shamsher, M., & Annuar, M. N. (2008). Earning announcements: The impact of firm size on share prices. *Journal of Money. Investment and Banking, 3*(3), 36–46.

Fan, T., & Phan, P. (2018). International new ventures: revisiting the influences behind the 'bornGlobal' firm. *International Entrepreneurship: The Pursuit of Opportunities across National Borders*, 131–172.

Fang, J., Collins, A., & Yao, S. (2021). On the global COVID-19 pandemic and China's FDI. *Journal of Asian Economics, 1*(74), 101300. doi:10.1016/j.asieco.2021.101300

Fattah, A. A., & Eddy-U, M. E. (2016). Mosque-visiting: Motivations and experiences of non-Muslim visitors at the Al-Azhar mosque in Egypt. *Turizam, 20*(3), 105–127. doi:10.5937/Turizam1603105F

Federal Republic of Nigeria. (2013). *National Policy on Education.* NERDC Press.

Feng, L. Y., Xu, H. L., Wu, G., Zhao, Y., & Xu, J. L. (2020). Exploring the structure and influence factors of trade competitive advantage network along the Belt and Road. *Physica A, 559*, 125057.

Ferencikova, S., & Ferencikova, S. (2016). The International New Ventures: Applicability of the Theory on the Slovak Innovative Start-Ups. In *Internet of Things. IoT Infrastructures. IoT360.* Springer. doi:10.1007/978-3-319-47075-7_16

Fernando, Y., Jasmi, M. F. A. M. F. A., & Shaharudin, M. S. M. S. (2019). Maritime green supply chain management: Its light and shadow on the bottom line dimensions of sustainable business performance. *International Journal of Shipping and Transport Logistics, 11*(1), 60. doi:10.1504/IJSTL.2019.096872

Ferraro, R., Bettman, J. R., & Chartrand, T. L. (2009). The power of strangers: The effect of incidental consumer brand encounters on brand choice. *The Journal of Consumer Research, 35*(5), 729–741. doi:10.1086/592944

Ferson, W. E., & Harvey, C. R. (1994). Sources of risk and expected returns in global equity markets. *Journal of Banking & Finance, 18*(4), 775–803. doi:10.1016/0378-4266(93)00020-P

Filep, S. (2014). Moving beyond subjective well-being: A tourism critique. *Journal of Hospitality & Tourism Research (Washington, D.C.), 38*(2), 266–274. doi:10.1177/1096348012436609

Fillis, I. (2001). Small firm internationalization: An investigate survey and future research direction. *Management Decision, 39*(9), 767–783. doi:10.1108/00251740110408683

Fodness, D. (1994). Measuring tourist motivation. *Annals of Tourism Research, 21*(3), 555–581. doi:10.1016/0160-7383(94)90120-1

Foresight Industrial Research Institute. (2019). *Report on in-depth interpretation of bilateral trade between China and major countries in the Americas in 2019.* Author.

Fornell, C., & Larcker, D. F. (1981). *Structural equation models with unobservable variables and measurement error: Algebra and statistics.* Academic Press.

Fornell, C., & Larcker, D. J. (1994). Partial Least Squares. Cambridge, MA: Blackwell Publishers.

Fornell, C., & Larcker, D. F. (1981). Evaluating structural equation models with unobservable variables and measurement error. *JMR, Journal of Marketing Research, 18*(1), 39–50. doi:10.1177/002224378101800104

Foye, J. (2018). A comprehensive test of the Fama-French five-factor model in emerging markets. *Emerging Markets Review*, *37*(1), 199–222. doi:10.1016/j.ememar.2018.09.002

Freeman, J., Carroll, G. R., & Hannan, M. T. (1983). The liability of newness: Age dependence in organizational death rates. *American Sociological Review*, *48*(5), 692–710. doi:10.2307/2094928

Fridgin, J. D. (1991). *Dimensions of Tourism*. Educational Institute of the American Hotel and Motel Association.

FRN. (2004). *National Policy on Education Lagos*. NERDC Press.

Froese, F. J. (2012). Motivation and adjustment of self-initiated expatriates: The case of expatriate academics in South Korea. *International Journal of Human Resource Management*, *23*(6), 1095–1112. doi:10.1080/09585192.2011.561220

GATS. General Agreement on Trade in Services, Apr. 15, 1994, Marrakesh Agreement Establishing the World Trade Organization, Annex 1B, 1869 U.N.T.S. 183, 33 I.L.M. 1167 (1994)

GATT 1994:General Agreement on Tariffs and Trade 1994, Apr. 15, 1994, Marrakesh Agreement Establishing the World Trade Organization, Annex 1A, 1867 U.N.T.S. 187, 33 I.L.M. 1153 (1994)

GębarowskiM.WiażewiczJ. (2014). Trade shows as a place of knowledge sharing about tourism Products. In *Human Capital without Borders: Knowledge and Learning for Quality of Life, Proceedings of the Management, Knowledge and Learning International Conference 2014, 25-27 June 2014, Portorož*. https://ssrn.com/abstract=2706205

Geisser, S. (1974). A predictive approach to the random effect model. *Biometrika*, *61*(1), 101–107. doi:10.1093/biomet/61.1.101

Gharghori, P., Sebastian, S., & Madhu, V. (2012). Value versus growth: Australian evidence. *Accounting and Finance*, *53*(1), 393–417.

Gil, R. B., Andres, E. F., & Salinas, E. M. (2007). Family as a source of consumer-based brand equity. *Journal of Product and Brand Management*, *16*(3), 188–199. doi:10.1108/10610420710751564

Global Exhibition Barometer, U. F. I. (2021). *Report based on the results of a survey concluded in January 2021* (26th ed.). The Global Association of the Exhibition Industry.

Global Recovery Insights, U. F. I. (2020). *Part 2: The future of digital and hybrid events*. The Global Association of the Exhibition Industry.

Gnizy, I., Cadogan, J. W., Oliveira, J. S., Abdul-Talib, A. N., & Nizam, A. (2017). National Regional Diversification Strategy and Export Performance: An Extended Abstract. *2016 Academy of Marketing Science (AMS) World Marketing Congress*, 29–33. 10.1007/978-3-319-47331-4_5

Golfetto, F., & Rinallo, D. (2014). Trade show events, from live to digital: towards the development of new competencies. *Spatial Aspects Concerning Economic Structure, 12*(3), 1-24.

Gorodnichenko, Y., & Roland, G. (2017). Culture, Institutions, and the Wealth of Nations. *The Review of Economics and Statistics*, *99*(3), 402–416. doi:10.1162/REST_a_00599

Górski, J. (2018). China's Strategy Toward Central and Eastern Europe Within the Framework of 16 + 1 Group: The Case of Poland. In China's Belt and Road Initiative in Changing the Rules of Globalization (pp. 115-134). Palgrave MacMillan.

Götz, O., Liehr-Gobbers, K., & Krafft, M. (2010). *Evaluation of structural equation models using the partial least squares (PLS) approach. In Handbook of partial least squares*. Springer.

Graham, B. (1949). The Intelligent Investor. Harper & Brothers.

Graham, B. (1976). A conversation with Benjamin Graham. *Financial Analysts Journal, 2*(1), 20–23. doi:10.2469/faj.v32.n5.20

Graham, B. (2003). *The intelligent investor* (Revised ed.). Harper Collins.

Graham, B., & Dodd, D. L. (1934). *Security analysis: principles and technique*. McGraw-Hill.

Grant, R. M. (1996). Toward a knowledge-based theory of the firm. *Strategic Management Journal, 17*(S2), 109–122. doi:10.1002mj.4250171110

Gregersen, H. B., & Black, J. S. (1990). A multifaceted approach to expatriate retention in international assignments. *Group & Organization Management, 15*(4), 461–485. doi:10.1177/105960119001500409

Gruber-Muecke, T., & Hofer, K. M. (2015). Market orientation, entrepreneurial orientation and performance in emerging markets. *International Journal of Emerging Market, 10*(3), 560–571. doi:10.1108/IJoEM-05-2013-0076

Grydehøj, A., Davis, S., Guo, R., & Zhang, H. (2020). Silk road archipelagos: Islands in the Belt and Road Initiative. *Island Studies Journal, 15*(2), 3–12.

GSF. (2020). *GSF Member COVID-19 Survey. All children should have access to quality education.* Global Schools Forum. Retrieved 6 May, 2021, from https://www.globalschoolsforum.org/

GSL. (2020). *School Leaders' Response to COVID-19.* Retrieved 2020 May, 2020, from https://internationalednews.com/2020/04/08/global-school-leaders-respond-to-covid-19/

Guadalupe, M., Kuzmina, O., & Thomas, C. (2012). Innovation and Foreign Ownership. *The American Economic Review, 102*(7), 3594–3627. doi:10.1257/aer.102.7.3594

Gudmanian, A., Drotianko, L., Sydorenko, S., Zhuravliova, O. & Yahodzinskyi, S. (2019). Social transformations of speech culture in information age. *E3S Web of Conferences, 135.*

Gujarati, D. N., & Porter, D. C. (2009). *Basic econometrics (international edition)*. McGraw-Hills Inc.

Gunday, G., Ulusoy, G., Kilic, K., & Alpkan, L. (2011). Effects of innovation types on firm performance. *International Journal of Production Economics, 133*(2), 662–676. doi:10.1016/j.ijpe.2011.05.014

Guo, H. (2020, June 12). *The COVID-19 epidemic will not affect the broad prospects of Sino-Brazilian economic and trade cooperation, said Brazilian Ambassador to China.* China Radio International Online. http://www.cri.cn/

Guo, B., Zhang, W., Zhang, Y., & Zhang, H. (2017). The five-factor asset pricing model tests for the Chinese stock market. *Pacific-Basin Finance Journal, 43*(2), 84–106. doi:10.1016/j.pacfin.2017.02.001

Haddad, M., & Harrison, A. (1993). Are there positive spillovers from direct foreign investment?: Evidence from panel data for Morocco. *Journal of Development Economics, 42*(1), 51–74. doi:10.1016/0304-3878(93)90072-U

Hair, J. F., Black, W. C., Babin, B. J., Anderson, R. E., & Tatham, R. L. (2010). *Multivariate data analysis: A global perspective.*

Hair, J. F., Black, W. C., Babin, B. J., Anderson, R. E., & Tatham, R. L. (2006). *Multivariate data analysis* (Vol. 6). Pearson Prentice Hall.

Hair, J. F., Hult, G. T. M., Ringle, C. M., & Sarsteddt, M. (2017). *A primer on partial least square structural equation modeling (PLS-SEM)* (2nd ed.). Sage.

Hair, J. F. Jr, Hult, G. T. M., Ringle, C., & Sarstedt, M. (2016). *A primer on partial least squares structural equation modeling (PLS-SEM).* Sage Publications.

Hair, J. F. Jr, Sarstedt, M., Hopkins, L., & Kuppelwieser, V. (2014). Partial least squares structural equation modeling (PLS-SEM). *European Business Review*, *26*(2), 106–121. doi:10.1108/EBR-10-2013-0128

Hair, J. F., Ringle, C. M., & Sarstedt, M. (2011). PLS-SEM: Indeed a silver bullet. *Journal of Marketing Theory and Practice*, *19*(2), 139–152. doi:10.2753/MTP1069-6679190202

Hakala, H., & Kohtamäki, M. (2011). Configurations of entrepreneurial- customer- and technology orientation: Differences in learning and performance of software companies. *International Journal of Entrepreneurial Behaviour & Research*, *17*(1), 64–81. doi:10.1108/13552551111107516

Halbesleben, J. R. B., & Wheeler, A. R. (2008). The relative roles of engagement and embeddedness in predicting job performance and intention to leave. *Work and Stress*, *22*(3), 242–256. doi:10.1080/02678370802383962

Han, P. M. (2016). *Influences of Korean Wave on the Intention of Visiting Korea in Generation Y Malaysia*. http://eprints.intimal.edu.my/id/eprint/914

Hanauer, M. X., & Lauterbach, J. G. (2019). The cross-section of emerging market stock returns. *Emerging Markets Review*, *38*(1), 265–286. doi:10.1016/j.ememar.2018.11.009

Hansen, W. W., & Musa, U. A. (2013). Fanon, the wretched and Boko Haram. *Journal of Asian and African Studies*, *48*(3), 281–296. doi:10.1177/0021909612467277

Hanson, D., & Fraser, J. (2013). ESG Investing in Graham & Doddsville. *Journal of Applied Corporate Finance, 25*(3), 20–31. Available: https://us.jflglobal.com/media/uploads/news/2015-09/Hanson-2013

Harvard Business Review. (2020). *Ranking Countries And Industries By Tech, Data, And Business Skills*. Available at: https://hbr.org/2019/05/ranking-countries-and industries-by-tech-data-and-business-skills

Harzing, A. (2001). Spiders : The Role of Expatriates in Controlling Foreign. *Journal of World Business*, *36*(4), 366–379. doi:10.1016/S1090-9516(01)00061-X

Ha, S., Chan, G., & Lee, A. (2018). A Phenomenological study on the effects of Korean TV dramas on Chinese. *Journal of Tourism & Hospitality (Los Angeles, Calif.)*, *2018*(02), 1–7. doi:10.29011/THOA

Hasan, A., & Ramzan, M. (2018). Exploring effect of challenge on employee engagement. *Merit Research Journal of Education and Review*, *6*(6), 92–100.

Hashim, F., Bakar, A. R. A., & Abdul-Talib, A. N. (2010). *International Business* (2nd ed.). Oxford Fajar Press.

Hassan, M. G., Razalli, M. R., & Abdul-Talib, A. N. (2014). The Influence of Environmental Dynamism on Strategic Outsourcing Success: A Partial Least Squares Structural Equation Modelling Approach. *International Journal of Modelling in Operations Management, 4*(3/4), 229-247. doi:10.1504/IJMOM.2014.067382

Hassan, M. G., Razalli, M. R., & Abdul-Talib, A. N. (2014). The influence of environmental dynamism on strategic outsourcing success: A partial least squares Structural Equation Modelling approach. *International Journal of Modelling in Operations Management*, *4*(3/4), 229–247.

Hassan, M. G., Razali, M. R., & Abdul-Talib, A. N. (2015). The impact of industrial supplier-manufacturer relationship on strategic outsourcing success. *Jurnal Teknologi*, *74*(1), 83–90.

Hassan, S. S., & Craft, S. (2012). Examining world market segmentation and brand positioning strategies. *Journal of Consumer Marketing*, *29*(5), 344–356. doi:10.1108/07363761211247460

Hassim, A. A., Asmat-Nizam, A.-T., & Addul Rahim, A. B. (2011). The effects of entrepreneurial orientation on firm organisational innovation and market orientation toward firm business performance. *International on Sociality and Economics Development, 10*, 280–284.

He, H., & Harris, L. (2020). The impact of Covid-19 pandemic on corporate social responsibility and marketing philosophy. *Journal of Business Research, 116*(8), 176–182. doi:10.1016/j.jbusres.2020.05.030 PMID:32457556

Henderson, A. D. (1999). Firm strategy and age dependence: A contingent view of the liabilities of newness, adolescence, and obsolescence. *Administrative Science Quarterly, 44*(2), 281–314. doi:10.2307/2666997

Hengeveld, J. (2021). *Using CSR within emerging markets to gain legitimacy* [Master dissertation]. University of Southampton.

Henseler, J., Ringle, C. M., & Sinkovics, R. R. (2009). *The use of partial least squares path modeling in international marketing. In New challenges to international marketing.* Emerald Group Publishing Limited.

Heritage.org. (2020). *Country Rankings: World & Global Economy Rankings On Economic Freedom.* Available at: https://www.heritage.org/index/ranking

He, S., & Guo, K. (2021). What factors contribute to the mutual dependence degree of China in its crude oil trading relationship with oil-exporting countries? *Energy, 228*, 120–547. doi:10.1016/j.energy.2021.120547

Hill, J. N. C. (2013). Religious extremism in northern Nigeria past and present: Parallels between the Pseudo-Tijanis and Boko Haram. *The Round Table: The Commonwealth Journal of International Affairs, 102*(3), 235–244. doi:10.1080/00358533.2013.796146

Hill, R. C., Griffiths, W. E., & Lim, G. C. (2018). *Principles of econometrics.* John Wiley & Sons.

Hinkes, C. (2019). Adding (bio) fuel to the fire: Discourses on palm oil sustainability in the context of European policy development. *Environment, Development and Sustainability, 22*(8), 7661–7682. doi:10.100710668-019-00541-y

Hippler, T. (2009). Why do they go? Empirical evidence of employees' motives for seeking or accepting relocation. *International Journal of Human Resource Management, 20*(6), 1381–1401. doi:10.1080/09585190902909889

Hirschmann, R. (2021). *Export volume of palm oil from Malaysia to the EU 2011-2020.* Statista. Retrieved September 23, 2021, from https://www.statista.com/statistics/1091983/export-volume-palm-oil-malaysia-eu/#:~:text=In%20 2020%2C%20Malaysia%20exported%20around,oil%2C%20after%20India%20and%20China

Ho, K. L. P., Nguyen, C. N., Adhikari, R., Miles, M. P., & Bonney, L. (2017). Exploring market orientation, innovation, and financial performance in agricultural value chains in emerging economies. *Journal of Innovation & Knowledge*, 1–12. doi:10.1016/j.jik.2017.03.008

Hoechle, D. (2007). Robust standard errors for panel regressions with cross-sectional dependence. *The Stata Journal, 7*(3), 281–312. doi:10.1177/1536867X0700700301

Hofstede Insights. (2020). *Country Comparison - Hofstede Insights.* Available at: https://www.hofstede-insights.com/country-comparison/

Holmes, O'Connor, R. C., Perry, V. H., Tracey, I., Wessely, S., Arseneault, L., Ballard, C., Christensen, H., Cohen Silver, R., Everall, I., Ford, T., John, A., Kabir, T., King, K., Madan, I., Michie, S., Przybylski, A. K., Shafran, R., Sweeney, A., ... Bullmore, E. (2020). Multidisciplinary research priorities for the COVID-19 pandemic: A call for action for mental health science. *The Lancet. Psychiatry, 7*(6), 547–560. doi:10.1016/S2215-0366(20)30168-1 PMID:32304649

Holopainen, J., & Björkman, I. (2005). The personal characteristics of the successful expatriate: A critical review of the literature and an empirical investigation. *Personnel Review*, *34*(1), 37–50. doi:10.1108/00483480510578476

Ho, M. H.-W., & Wang, F. (2015). Unpacking knowledge transfer and learning paradoxes in international strategic alliances: Contextual differences matter. *International Business Review*, *24*(2), 287–297. doi:10.1016/j.ibusrev.2014.08.002

Homburg, C., Klarmann, M., & Schmitt, J. (2010). Brand awareness in business markets: When is it related to firm performance? *International Journal of Research in Marketing*, *27*(3), 201–212. doi:10.1016/j.ijresmar.2010.03.004

Hong, X. T. (2021). Latest official data from Brazil: Iron ore exports reached 33.68 million tons in June, the highest level in nearly 9 months. *Sina Finance*. https://baijiahao.baidu.com/s?id=1682950467157288988&wfr=spider&for=pc

Horner, S., & Swarbrooke, J. (2012). *Leisure marketing*. Routledge. doi:10.4324/9780080478937

Howe-Walsh, L., & Schyns, B. (2010). Self-initiated expatriation: Implications for hrm. *International Journal of Human Resource Management*, *21*(2), 260–273. doi:10.1080/09585190903509571

Hsiao, C. (2014). *Analysis of panel data*. Cambridge university press. doi:10.1017/CBO9781139839327

Hsu, J. L., Wang, T. C. T., & Huang, P. Y. H. (2014). Motivations for first-time and repeat backpackers in Shanghai. *Tourism Management Perspectives*, *12*, 57–61. doi:10.1016/j.tmp.2014.08.001

Huang, R., & Sarigollu, E. (2014). How brand awareness relates to market outcome, brand equity, and the marketing mix. In *Fashion branding and consumer behaviors* (pp. 113–132). Springer. doi:10.1007/978-1-4939-0277-4_8

Huang, Y. (2016). Understanding China's Belt & Road initiative: Motivation, framework and assessment. *China Economic Review*, *40*, 314–321.

Hult, G. T. M., Hurley, R. F., & Knight, G. A. (2004). Innovativeness: Its antecedents and impact on business performance. *Industrial Marketing Management*, *33*(5), 429–438. doi:10.1016/j.indmarman.2003.08.015

Hung, J.-L., & Yang, D. (2017). The validation of an instrument for evaluating the effectiveness of professional development program on teaching online. *Journal of Educational Technology Development and Exchange*, *8*(1). Advance online publication. doi:10.18785/jetde.0801.02

Hung, R. Y. Y., Lien, B. Y.-H., Yang, B., Wu, C.-M., & Kuo, Y.-M. (2011). Impact of TQM and organizational learning on innovation performance in the high-tech industry. *International Business Review*, *20*(2), 213–225. doi:10.1016/j.ibusrev.2010.07.001

Hussein, J., Khan, A., & Zhou, K. (2020). The impact of natural resource depletion on energy use and CO2emission in Belt&Road initiative countries: A cross-country analysis. *Energy*, *199*, 1174092.

Huxley, L. (2004). Western backpackers and the global experience: An exploration of young people's interaction with local cultures. *Tourism, Culture & Communication*, *5*(1), 37–44. doi:10.3727/1098304042781472

Huynh, T. D. (2018). Explaining anomalies in Australia with a five-factor asset pricing model. *International Review of Finance*, *18*(1), 123–135. doi:10.1111/irfi.12125

Hwang, J., Kim, S. S., Choe, J. Y. J., & Chung, C. H. (2018). Exploration of the successful glocalisation of ethnic food: A case of Korean food. *International Journal of Contemporary Hospitality Management*, *30*(12), 3656–3676. doi:10.1108/IJCHM-07-2017-0452

HWU. (2015). Cultural guide to Malaysia. *HWU Malaysia Cultural Awareness*, (March), 1–9. Retrieved from https://www.hw.ac.uk/documents/HWU_Malaysia_Cultural_awareness_document_190315(1).pdf

Hyde, K. F., & Lawson, R. (2003). The nature of independent travel. *Journal of Travel Research*, *42*(1), 13–23. doi:10.1177/0047287503253944

Hymer, S. H. (1976). *The international operations of national firms: A study in direct foreign investment*. MIT Press.

Ibrahim, I., & Yong, O. (1994). *The Behavior of Far Eastern Stocks*. Leeds Publication.

Ibrahim, M. B., Abdul-Talib, A. N., & Jedin, M. H. (2018). Determinants of knowledge sharing among banks employees and its effect on service innovation: A conceptual framework. *Journal of Business and Management*, *20*(5), 39–45.

Idialu, J. O., & Idialu, E. E. (2012). Entity, ownership, educational subsidies and funding of Nigerian tertiary institutions: Current research. *Journal of Social Sciences*, *4*(1), 56–61.

Ilardi, B. C., Leone, D., Kasser, T., & Ryan, R. M. (1993). Richard m. ryan. *Journal of Applied Social Psychology*, *23*(21), 1789–1805. doi:10.1111/j.1559-1816.1993.tb01066.x

ILO. (2000). *InFocus Programme on Skills, Knowledge and Employability*. Series on the Informal Economy.

IMF. (2004) Definition of foreign direct investment (FDI) terms, IMF committee on balance of payments statistics and OECD. In *Workshop on International Investment Statistics, Direct Investment Technical Expert Group (DITEG)*. Issues Paper (DITEG) #20, Statistics Canada.

Inkinen, H., & Inkinen, H. (2016). Review of empirical research on knowledge management practices and firm performance. *Journal of Knowledge Management*, *20*(2), 230–257. doi:10.1108/JKM-09-2015-0336

Inkpen, A. (1998). Learning, knowledge acquisition, and strategic alliances. *European Management Journal*, *16*(2), 223–229. doi:10.1016/S0263-2373(97)00090-X

Inkson, K., Arthur, M. B., Pringle, J., & Barry, S. (1997). Expatriate assignment versus overseas experience: Contrasting models of international human resource development. *Journal of World Business*, *32*(4), 351–368. doi:10.1016/S1090-9516(97)90017-1

Innocent, O. (2020). The Effects of the Covid-19 Pandemic on the Nigeria's Economy and Possible Coping Strategies. *Asian Journal of Social Sciences and Management Studies*, *7*(3), 173–179.

International Labour Orgnization. (2020). *COVID-19 crisis and the informal economy Immediate responses and policy challenges*. Retrieved 3 August, 2021, from https://www.ilo.org/global/topics/employment-promotion/informal-economy/publications/WCMS_743623/lang--en/index.htm.1-8

International Maritime Organization. (2015). *List of IMO Conventions*. Retrieved from https://www.imo.org/en/About/Conventions/ListOfConventions/Pages/Default.aspx

InvestorP. (2020). *Home*. Available: http://pragmaticinvestor.com/

Islami, N. (2019). The effect of digital literacy toward enterpreneur behaviors through students' intention enterpreneurship on Economics Education Study Program at Jember. *IOP Conference Series. Earth and Environmental Science*, *243*, 1–9. doi:10.1088/1755-1315/243/1/012084

Ismail, N. A., & Kuivalainen, O. (2015). The effect of internal capabilities and external environment on small-and medium-sized enterprises' international performance and the role of the foreign market scope: The case of the Malaysian halal food industry. *Journal of International Entrepreneurship*, *13*(4), 418–451. doi:10.100710843-015-0160-x

Isumonah, V. A. (2012). Armed society in the Niger Delta. *Armed Forces and Society*, *39*(2), 331–358. doi:10.1177/0095327X12446925

ITC. (1987). *Commercial representation: Handbook for official trade representatives.* International Trade Center UNCTAD/GATT.

Ivancic, H., & Koh, L. P. (2016). Evolution of sustainable palm oil policy in Southeast Asia. *Cogent Environmental Science, 2*(1), 1195032. doi:10.1080/23311843.2016.1195032

Jackson, M. O. (2005). The economics of social networks, based on a lecture. *Proceedings of the 9th World Congress of the Econometric Society,* 1–86. http://scholar.google.com/scholar?q=related:fmyMXEu64lQJ:scholar.google.com/&hl=en&num=30&as_sdt=0,5%5Cnpapers2://publication/uuid/C2505DB7-3CD1-410F-BF91-B71C3B22812E

Jackson, A. (2007). Nigeria: A security overview. *The Round Table: The Commonwealth Journal of International Affairs, 96*(392), 587–603. doi:10.1080/00358530701626040

Jacob, O. N., Abigeal, I., & Lydia, A. E. (2020). Impact of COVID-19 on the higher institutions development in Nigeria. *Electronic Research Journal of Social Sciences and Humanities, 2*(2), 126–135.

Jacobs, H. (2016). Market maturity and mispricing. *Journal of Financial Economics, 122*(2), 270–287. doi:10.1016/j.jfineco.2016.01.030

Jafari-Sadeghi, V., Nkongolo-Bakenda, J. M., Dana, L. P., Anderson, R. B., & Biancone, P. P. (2020). Home country institutional context and entrepreneurial internationalization: The significance of human capital attributes. *Journal of International Entrepreneurship, 18*(2), 165–195. doi:10.100710843-019-00264-1

Jaguli, A. R., Malek, M. M., & Palil, M. R. (2014). Do MNCS'high quality and standard requirements matter? A channel for vertical spillovers. *International Journal of Business and Society, 15*(1), 127.

Jang, H., & Park, M. (2020). Social media, media and urban transformation in the context of overtourism. *International Journal of Tourism Cities, 6*(1), 233–260. doi:10.1108/IJTC-08-2019-0145

Jasmi, M. F. A. (2019). *Maritime Green Supply Chain Management (MGSCM) and Financial Performance: A Mediating Effect of Energy Efficiency and Low Carbon Performance.* Universiti Malaysia Pahang.

Jasmi, M. F. A., & Fernando, Y. (2021). A Review of Future Energy Efficiency Measures and CO2 Emission Reduction in Maritime Supply Chain. Encyclopedia of Organizational Knowledge, Administration, and Technology, 2431–2442.

Jasmi, F., & Fernando, Y. (2018). Notions of Maritime Green Supply Chain Management. In *Encyclopedia of Information Science and Technology* (4th ed., pp. 5465–5475). IGI Global.

Jasmi, M. F. A., Fernando, Y., & Ismail, I. (2020). Adoption level of maritime green supply chain management: Preliminary findings from a pilot study. *International Journal of Logistics Systems and Management, 37*(4), 556–575. doi:10.1504/IJLSM.2020.111826

Jaworski, B. J., & Kohli, A. K. (1993). Market orientation: Antecedents and consequences. *Journal of Marketing, 57*(3), 53–70. doi:10.1177/002224299305700304

Jeevan, J., Ghaderi, H., Bandara, Y. M. M., Saharuddin, A. H. H., & Othman, M. R. R. (2015). The implications of the growth of port throughput on the port capacity: The case of Malaysian major container seaports. *International Journal of E-Navigation and Maritime Economy, 3,* 84–98. doi:10.1016/j.enavi.2015.12.008

Jensen, J. M., & Hjalager, A. M. (2018). Travel motivations of first-time, repeat, and serial backpackers. *Tourism and Hospitality Research, 19*(4), 465–477. doi:10.1177/1467358418781440

Jiang, X., Liu, H., Fey, C., & Jiang, F. (2018). Entrepreneurial orientation, network resource acquisition, and firm performance: A network approach. *Journal of Business Research, 87,* 46–57. doi:10.1016/j.jbusres.2018.02.021

Jinghon, T., & Kuzmin, V. A. (2021). Development of Chinese -Turkish relations under "One Belt, One Road" initiative. *Nauchnyi Dialog, 3*, 438-451. Doi:10.24224/2227-1295-2021-3-438-451

Johanson, J., & Vahlne, J. E. (2009). The Uppsala internationalization process model revisited: From liability of foreignness to liability of outsidership. *Journal of International Business Studies, 40*(9), 1411–1431. doi:10.1057/jibs.2009.24

Johanson, J., & Vahlne, J.-E. (1977). The internationalization process of the firm. *Journal of International Business Studies, 8*(1), 23–32. doi:10.1057/palgrave.jibs.8490676

Johanson, J., & Vahlne, J.-E. (1990). The mechanism of internationalization. *International Marketing Review, 7*(4), 11–24. doi:10.1108/02651339010137414

Johanson, J., & Wiedersheim-Paul, F. (1975). The internationalization of the firm—Four Swedish cases. *Journal of Management Studies, 12*(3), 305–322. doi:10.1111/j.1467-6486.1975.tb00514.x

Jokinen, T., Brewster, C., & Suutari, V. (2008). Career capital during international work experiences: Contrasting self-initiated expatriate experiences and assigned expatriation. *International Journal of Human Resource Management, 19*(6), 979–998. doi:10.1080/09585190802051279

Jolly, V. K., Alahuhta, M., & Jeannet, J. P. (1992). Challenging the incumbents: How high technology start-ups compete globally. *Strategic Change, 1*(2), 71–82. doi:10.1002/jsc.4240010203

Jones, M. V., Coviello, N. E., & Tang, Y. K. (2011). International entrepreneurship research (1989–2009): A domain ontology and thematic analysis. *Journal of Business Venturing, 26*(6), 632–659. doi:10.1016/j.jbusvent.2011.04.001

Jones, R., Kierzkowski, H., & Lurong, C. (2005). What does evidence tell us about fragmentation and outsourcing? *International Review of Economics & Finance, 14*(3), 305–316. doi:10.1016/j.iref.2004.12.010

Jong, H. N. (2019). *Malaysia calls on Southeast Asia to back palm oil against EU's 'unfair' claims*. Eco-Business. Retrieved September 23, 2021, from https://www.eco-business.com/news/malaysia-calls-on-southeast-asia-to-back-palm-oil-against-eus-unfair-claims/

Joshi, R., & Garg, P. (2021). Role of brand experience in shaping brand love. *International Journal of Consumer Studies, 45*(2), 259–272. doi:10.1111/ijcs.12618

Joung, T.-H., Kang, S.-G., Lee, J.-K., & Ahn, J. (2020). The IMO initial strategy for reducing Greenhouse Gas (GHG) emissions, and its follow-up actions towards 2050. *Journal of International Maritime Safety, Environmental Affairs, and Shipping, 4*(1), 1–7. doi:10.1080/25725084.2019.1707938

Ju, H. (2010). *Glocalization of the Korean popular culture in East Asia: Theorising the Korean wave*. The University of Oklahoma.

Kaboudarahangi, M., Tahir, O. M., & Kamal, M. (2013). Malaysia's three major ethnic group preferences in creating a malaysian garden identity. *The Australian Geographer, 44*(2), 197–213. doi:10.1080/00049182.2013.789588

Kaiser, H. F. (1970). *A second generation little jiffy*. Springer. doi:10.1007/BF02291817

Kaiser, H. F. (1974). An index of factorial simplicity. *Psychometrika, 39*(1), 31–36. doi:10.1007/BF02291575

Kajalo, S., & Lindblom, A. (2015). Market orientation, entrepreneurial orientation and business performance among small retailers. *International Journal of Retail & Distribution Management, 43*(7), 580–596. doi:10.1108/IJRDM-04-2014-0044

Kamberidou, I. (2020). "Distinguished" women entrepreneurs in the digital economy and the multitasking whirlpool. *Journal of Innovation and Entrepreneurship, 9*(1), 3. doi:10.118613731-020-0114-y

Kang, S., Kumar, S. S., & Ku, B. (2021). The liability of foreignness in early-stage corporate venture capital investment. *Humanities and Social Sciences Letters*, *9*(1), 72–85. doi:10.18488/journal.73.2021.91.72.85

Kanibir, H., Saydan, R., & Nart, S. (2014). Determining the antecedents of marketing competencies of SMEs for international market performance. *Procedia - Social and Behavioral Sciences*, (1), 12–23. doi:10.1016/j.sbspro.2014.09.003

Karami, M., & Tang, J. (2019). Entrepreneurial orientation and SME international performance: The mediating role of networking capability and experiential learning. *International Small Business Journal*, *37*(2), 105–124. doi:10.1177/0266242618807275

Karolyi. (2016). Home bias, an academic puzzle. *Review of Finance*, *20*(6), 2049-2078.

Kartika, I. T., Cangara, A. R., Nasrun, M., & Marifat, I. D. N. (2020, October). Interaction between the European Union's renewable energy directives and Indonesia's sustainable palm oil policy. *IOP Conference Series. Earth and Environmental Science*, *575*(1), 012228. doi:10.1088/1755-1315/575/1/012228

Keller, W. (2010). International trade, foreign direct investment, and technology spillovers. In *Handbook of the Economics of Innovation* (Vol. 2, pp. 793–829). North-Holland. doi:10.1016/S0169-7218(10)02003-4

Keskin, H. (2006). Market orientation, learning orientation, and innovation capabilities in SMEs: An extended model. *European Journal of Innovation Management*, *9*(4), 396–417. doi:10.1108/14601060610707849

Khalifah, N. A., & Jafaar, Z. (2017). Technical efficiency of establishments in Malaysia's electrical electronics industries: Exporting or vertical trade? *Jurnal Ekonomi Malaysia*, *51*(1), 15–30.

Khamis, R., Anasweh, M., & Hamdan, A. (2018). Oil prices and stock market returns in oil-exporting countries: Evidence from Saudi Arabia. *International Journal of Energy Economics and Policy*, *8*(3), 301–306.

Khan, A., Chenggang, Y., Hussain, J., & Kui, Z. (2021). Impact of technological innovation, financial development and foreigndirect investment on renewable energy, non-renewable energy andthe environment in Belt and Road Initiative countries. *Renewable Energy*, *171*, 479–491.

Kianto, A., Ritala, P., Spender, J.-C., & Vanhala, M. (2014). The interaction of intellectual capital assets and knowledge management practices in organizational value creation. *Journal of Intellectual Capital*, *15*(3), 362–375. doi:10.1108/JIC-05-2014-0059

Kiendrebeogo, Y. (2020). Learning by exporting or self-selection into exporting? *Middle East Development Journal*, *12*(2), 304–325. doi:10.1080/17938120.2020.1756105

Kikechi, W., Owano, A., Ayodo, T. M. O., & Ejakait, E. (2013). Do entrepreneurial skills acquired from technical subjects help secondary school graduates in self employment in kenya. *International Journal of Education and Research*, *1*(8), 1–12.

Kim, D., Cho, S.-D., & Jung, G. O. (2016). Wave of home culture and MNC performance: The Korean Wave (Hallyu). *International Marketing in Rapidly Changing Environments*, *24*, 193–216. doi:10.1108/S1474-7979(2013)0000024012

Kim, J.-H. (2014). The antecedents of memorable tourism experiences: The development of a scale to measure the destination attributes associated with memorable experiences. *Tourism Management*, *44*, 34–45. doi:10.1016/j.tourman.2014.02.007

Kim, K. H., Kim, K. S., Kim, D. Y., Kim, J. H., & Kang, S. H. (2008). Brand equity in hospital marketing. *Journal of Business Research*, *1*(61), 75–82. doi:10.1016/j.jbusres.2006.05.010

Kim, M. S., & Stepchenkova, S. (2019). Altruistic values and environmental knowledge as triggers of pro-environmental behavior among tourists. *Current Issues in Tourism*, *23*(13), 1575–1580. doi:10.1080/13683500.2019.1628188

Kim, S. (2010). Extraordinary experience: Re-enacting and photographing at screen tourism locations. *Tourism and Hospitality Planning & Development*, *7*(1), 59–75. doi:10.1080/14790530903522630

Kim, S., & O'Connor, N. (2011). A cross-cultural study of screen-tourists' profiles. *Worldwide Hospitality and Tourism Themes*, *3*(2), 141–158. doi:10.1108/17554211111123005

Kimura, F., Takahashi, Y., & Hayakawa, K. (2007). Fragmentation and parts and components trade: Comparison between East Asia and Europe. *The North American Journal of Economics and Finance*, *18*(1), 23–40. doi:10.1016/j.najef.2006.12.002

Kindleberger, C. P. (1969). *American business abroad: Six lectures on direct investment*. Yale University Press.

Klepper, G. (2018)., *Winners and losers from the proposed ban on palm oil*. EcoBusiness. Retrieved September 23, 2021, from https://www.iscc-system.org/eco-business-winners-and-losers-from-the-proposed-ban-on-palm-oil/

Klerck, W. G., & Maritz, A. C. (1997). A test of Graham's stock selection criteria on industrial shares traded on the JSE. *The Investment Analysts Journal*, *26*(45), 25–33. doi:10.1080/10293523.1997.11082374

Knight, G. A., & Cavusgil, S. T. (1996). The born global firm: A challenge to traditional internationalization theory. *Advances in Intemational Marketing*, *8*, 11–26.

Knight, G. A., & Cavusgil, S. T. (2004). Innovation, organizational capabilities, and the born global firm. *Journal of International Business Studies*, *35*(2), 124–141. doi:10.1057/palgrave.jibs.8400071

Knight, G. A., & Liesch, P. W. (2016). Internationalization: From incremental to born global. *Journal of World Business*, *51*(1), 93–102. doi:10.1016/j.jwb.2015.08.011

Knight, J. (1997). A shared vision? Stakeholders' perspectives on the internationalization of higher education in Canada. *Journal of Studies in International Education*, *1*(1), 27–44. doi:10.1177/102831539700100105

Knudsen, M. P., & Servais, P. (2007). Analyzing internationalization configurations of SME's: The purchaser's perspective. *Journal of Purchasing and Supply Management*, *13*(2), 137–151. doi:10.1016/j.pursup.2007.06.002

Ko, E., & Lee, S. (2011). Cultural heritage fashion branding in Asia. *Tourism Sensemaking: Strategies to Give Meaning to Experience*, 89–109. doi:10.1108/S1871-3173(2011)0000005008

Kocak, A., & Abimbola, T. (2009). The effects of entrepreneurial marketing on born global performance. *Journal of International Marketing Review*, *26*(4/5), 439–452. doi:10.1108/02651330910971977

Koctecky, M., & Naray, O. (2007). Commercial Diplomacy and International Business, Clingendael Discussion Papers in Diplomacy. *Clingendael Institute, 107*.

Kogut, B. (2002). International management and strategy. Handbook of strategy management, 261-278.

Kohler, T., Stribl, A., & Stieger, D. (2016). Innovation for Volunteer Travel: Using Crowdsourcing to Create Change. In Open Tourism: Open Innovation, Crowdsourcing and Co-Creation Challenging the Tourism Industry. Springer. doi:10.1007/978-3-642-54089-9

Kohli, A. K., & Jaworski, B. J. (1990). Market orientation: The construct, research propositions and managerial implications. *Journal of Marketing*, *54*(2), 1–18. doi:10.1177/002224299005400201

Kohpaiboon, A. (2009). Vertical and horizontal FDI technology spillovers: evidence from Thai manufacturing. *ERIA Discussion Paper, 8*.

Kolk, A. (2016). The social responsibility of international business: From ethics and the environment to CSR and sustainable development. *Journal of World Business*, *51*(1), 23–34. doi:10.1016/j.jwb.2015.08.010

Kondak, N. E. (1997). The efficient market hypothesis revisited: Some evidence from the Istanbul Stock Exchange. *Capital Board of Turkey*, *83*(1), 23–35.

Kong, E., Wei, W. X., Swallow, P., & Thomson, S. B. (2020). Belt-and-Road Initiative: Driving the need to understand intellectual capital in Chinese multinational enterprises. *Thunderbird International Business Review*, *62*(3), 279–290. doi:10.1002/tie.22088

Koo, C., Chung, N., Kim, D. J., & Hlee, S. (2016). The impact of destination websites and cultural exposure: A comparison study of experienced and inexperienced travelers. *International Journal of Tourism Cities*, *2*(1), 1–16. doi:10.1108/IJTC-04-2015-0009

Kothgassner, O., Griesinger, M., Kettner, K., Wayan, K., Völkl-Kernstock, S., Hlavacs, H., Beutl, L., & Felnhofer, A. (2017). Real-life prosocial behavior decreases after being socially excluded by avatars, not agents. *Computers in Human Behavior*, *70*, 261–269. doi:10.1016/j.chb.2016.12.059

Kovjanic, S., Schuh, S. C., & Jonas, K. (2013). Transformational leadership and performance: An experimental investigation of the mediating effects of basic needs satisfaction and work engagement. *Journal of Occupational and Organizational Psychology*, *86*(4), 543–555. doi:10.1111/joop.12022

Kozak, M. (2002). Comparative analysis of tourist motivations by nationality and destinations. *Tourism Management*, *23*(3), 221–232. doi:10.1016/S0261-5177(01)00090-5

Krejcie, R. V., & Morgan, D. W. (1970). Determining sample size for research activities. *Educational and Psychological Measurement*, *30*(3), 607–610. doi:10.1177/001316447003000308

Kubota, K., & Takehara, H. (2017). Does the Fama and French Five-Factor Model Work Well in Japan? *International Review of Finance*, *18*(1), 137–146. doi:10.1111/irfi.12126

Kuivalainen, O., Saarenketo, S., & Puumalainen, K. (2012). Start-up patterns of internationalization: A framework and its application in the context of knowledge intensive SMEs. *European Management Journal*, *30*(4), 372–385. doi:10.1016/j.emj.2012.01.001

Kunene, N., & Chung, Y. C. (2020). Sustainable production policy impact on palm oil firms' performance: Empirical analysis from Indonesia. *Sustainability*, *12*(20), 8750. doi:10.3390u12208750

Laerd-Statistics. (2015). *Kruskal-Wallis H test using SPSS Statistics. Statistical tutorials and software guides.* Available at: https://statistics.laerd.com/

Lafaurie, J. (2018). Deux monnaiesmérovingiennestrouvées à Reculver (Kent). *Bulletin de la Société Nationale des Antiquaires de France*, *1971*(1), 209–219. doi:10.3406/bsnaf.1973.8048

Lakonishok, J., Shleifer, A., & Vishny, R. W. (1994). Contrarian investment, extrapolation, and risk. *The Journal of Finance*, *49*(5), 1541–1578. doi:10.1111/j.1540-6261.1994.tb04772.x

Lam, J. J. S. L. (2011). Patterns of maritime supply chains: Slot capacity analysis. *Journal of Transport Geography*, *19*(2), 366–374. doi:10.1016/j.jtrangeo.2010.03.016

Lamouchi, R. A. (2020). Long Memory and Stock Market Efficiency: Case of Saudi Arabia. *International Journal of Economics and Financial Issues*, *10*(3), 29–34. doi:10.32479/ijefi.9568

Lamouchi, R. A., & Alawi, S. M. (2020). Dynamic linkages between the oil spot, oil futures, and stock markets: Evidence from Dubai. *International Journal of Energy Economics and Policy, 10*(1), 377–383. doi:10.32479/ijeep.8705

Lane, P. J., Salk, J. E., & Lyles, M. A. (2001). Absorptive capacity, learning, and performance in international joint ventures. *Strategic Management Journal, 22*(12), 1139–1161. doi:10.1002mj.206

Lanjong, M. N. (1983). *A study of market efficiency and risk return relationship in the Malaysian stock market* [Unpublished Ph.D Thesis]. Katholieke Universitiet Te Leuven, Belgium.

Larsen, S., Øgaard, T., & Brun, W. (2011). Backpackers and mainstreamers: Realities and Myths. *Annals of Tourism Research, 38*(2), 690–707. doi:10.1016/j.annals.2011.01.003

Laura, P. S., Raúl, V. F., & Giampietro, M. (2021). The international division of labor and embodied working time in trade for the US, the EU and China. *Ecological Economics*, (180), 106909.

Lauterbach, B., & Vu, J. D. (1993). Ben Graham's net current asset value rule revisited: The size-adjusted returns. *Quarterly Journal of Business and Economics, 3*(2), 82–108.

Le Mens, G., Hannan, M. T., & Pólos, L. (2014). Organizational obsolescence, drifting tastes, and age dependence in organizational life chances. *Organization Science, 26*(2), 550–570. doi:10.1287/orsc.2014.0910

Lee, C. M. C. (2014). Value Investing: Bridging Theory and Practice. *China Accounting and Finance Review, 16*(2), 10–38. doi:10.760340570-014-0005-3

Lee, C.-K., Reisinger, Y., Ahmad, M. S., Park, Y.-N., & Kang, C.-W. (2021). The influence of Hanok experience on tourists' attitude and behavioral intention: An interplay between experiences and a Value-Attitude-Behavior model. *Journal of Vacation Marketing, 27*(4), 449–465. doi:10.1177/13567667211011761

Lee, C., Park, C.-S., & Vertinsky, I. (2012). *Relational Capital, Knowledge Transfer and Performance in International Joint Ventures (IJVs) in Korea. In Korean Science and Technology in an International Perspective.* Springer.

Lee, D. (2004). The growing influence of business in UK diplomacy. *International Studies Perspectives, 5*(1), 50–54. doi:10.1111/j.1528-3577.2004.00154.x

Lee, J. M., Paik, Y., Horak, S., & Yang, I. (2021). Turning a liability into an asset of foreignness: Managing informal networks in Korea. *Business Horizons.* Advance online publication. doi:10.1016/j.bushor.2021.04.002

Lee, M. J. (2020). Touring the land of romance: Transnational Korean television drama consumption from online desires to offline intimacy. *Journal of Tourism and Cultural Change, 18*(1), 67–80. doi:10.1080/14766825.2020.1707467

Lee, S., Lee, K., Kwak, G., & Kim, H. (2017). The effect of the Korean wave on Malaysian university students' perception. *Culinary Science & Hospitality Research, 23*(1), 79–83. doi:10.20878/cshr.2017.23.1.009009009

Lee, Y. K., Kim, S. H., Seo, M. K., & Hight, S. K. (2015). Market orientation and business performance: Evidence from franchising industry. *International Journal of Hospitality Management, 44*, 28–37. doi:10.1016/j.ijhm.2014.09.008

Lenaerts, K., & Merlevede, B. (2018). Indirect productivity effects from foreign direct investment and multinational firm heterogeneity. *Review of World Economics, 154*(2), 377–400. doi:10.100710290-017-0298-9

Leppin, A., & Aro, A. R. (2009). Risk perception related to SARS and avian influenza: Theoretical foundations of current behavioral research. *International Journal of Behavioral Medicine, 16*(1), 7–29. doi:10.100712529-008-9002-8 PMID:19214752

Lerner, J. O. S., Leamon, A., & Dew, S. T. E. (2017). *The CMA and the Saudi Stock Market Crash of 2006.* BELLA Research Group, Saudi Capital Market Authority.

Levine, S. S., & Prietula, M. J. (2012). How knowledge transfer impacts performance: A multilevel model of benefits and liabilities. *Organization Science, 23*(6), 1748–1766. doi:10.1287/orsc.1110.0697

Li, C., & Luo, Y. (2019). Spillover effects of foreign direct investment: Evidence from the west midlands of England. *Economic Issues, 24*(Part 1).

Li, H. (2010). Sustainable Development of International Trade. *Modern Economy*, (3).

Li, X. (2021, April). FDI and International Trade: A Review. In *2021 6th International Conference on Social Sciences and Economic Development (ICSSED 2021)* (pp. 904-909). Atlantis Press. 10.2991/assehr.k.210407.171

Lian, K. K., & Leng, K. G. (1994). Weak Form Efficiency in the KLSE: New Evidence. *Capital Market Review*, *2*(1), 45–58.

Lian, Z. (2020). *China Baowu and Brazil's Vale realize RMB cross-border settlement.* Observer Network.

Li, B. D. (2020). *The Epidemic and the Changing World.* Boao Forum for Asia.

Lichtenthaler, U. (2009). Absorptive capacity, environmental turbulence, and the complementarity of organizational learning processes. *Academy of Management Journal*, *52*(4), 822–846. doi:10.5465/amj.2009.43670902

Li, E. P. H., Min, H. J., & Lee, S. (2020). Soft power and nation rebranding. *International Marketing Review*, *38*(1), 141–162. doi:10.1108/IMR-01-2019-0053

Li, G., Zhang, Q., Bai, Z., & Sabeeh, P. (2020). Research on logistics service supply chain information sharing mechanism in the belt and road initiative. *IEEE Access: Practical Innovations, Open Solutions*, *8*, 189684–189701.

Li, H. B., & Zou, J. Y. (2019). Research on the Potential and Efficiency of Trade between China and Brazil-Based on the Analysis of Stochastic Frontier Gravity Model. *Economic Research Guide*, (10), 184–189.

Li, H., & Atuahene-Gima, K. (2001). Product innovation strategy and the performance of new technology ventures in China. *Academy of Management Journal*, *44*(6), 1123–1134.

Lim, T. L. (1980). *The Efficient Market Hypothesis and Weak Form Test on the KLSE* [Unpublished dissertation (MBA)]. University of Sheffield.

Limenta, M. (2020). Palm oil for fuels: WTO rules and environmental protection. *Global Trade and Customs Journal, 15*(7).

LimK. P.BrooksR. D. (2006). The evolving and relative efficiencies of stock markets: empirical evidence from rolling bi-correlation test statistics. *Social Science Research Network.* Available from: http://ssrn.com/abstract=931071

Lin, Q. (2017). Noisy prices and the Fama–French five-factor asset pricing model in China. *Emerging Markets Review*, *31*, 141–163. doi:10.1016/j.ememar.2017.04.002

Lin, W. B. (2007). Factors affecting the correlation between interactive mechanism of strategic alliance and technological knowledge transfer performance. *The Journal of High Technology Management Research*, *17*(2), 139–155. doi:10.1016/j.hitech.2006.11.003

Lister, J., Poulsen, R. T., & Ponte, S. (2015). Orchestrating transnational environmental governance in maritime shipping. *Global Environmental Change*, *34*, 185–195. doi:10.1016/j.gloenvcha.2015.06.011

Liu, C. H., Chang, A. Y. P., & Fang, Y. P. (2020). Network activities as critical sources of creating capability and competitive advantage. *Management Decision*, *58*(3), 544–568. doi:10.1108/MD-08-2017-0733

Li, Y. Y., Li, Y. L., Pan, A., Pan, X., & Veglianti, E. (2021). The network structure characteristics and determinants of the Belt and Road industrial robot trade. *Emerging Markets Finance & Trade*, 1–11. doi:10.1080/1540496X.2021.1897315

Li, Y., Ye, F., Dai, J., Zhao, X., & Sheu, C. (2019). The adoption of green practices by Chinese firms. *International Journal of Operations & Production Management*, *39*(4), 550–572. doi:10.1108/IJOPM-12-2017-0753

Loker-Murphy, L. (1997). Backpackers in Australia : A Motivation-Based Segmentation Study. *Journal of Travel & Tourism Marketing*, *5*(4), 23–45. doi:10.1300/J073v05n04_02

Loker-Murphy, L., & Pearce, P. L. (1995). Young budget travelers: Backpackers in Australia. *Annals of Tourism Research*, *22*(4), 819–843. doi:10.1016/0160-7383(95)00026-0

Long, Y., Li, P., & You, B. (2014). Knowledge transfer, governance mechanisms in alliance and environmental uncertainty: An empirical study. *Chinese Management Studies*, *8*(3), 438–472. doi:10.1108/CMS-07-2013-0129

Lonial, S. C., & Carter, R. E. (2015). The impact of organizational orientations on medium and small firm performance: A resource-based perspective. *Journal of Small Business Management*, *53*(1), 94–113. doi:10.1111/jsbm.12054

Lopes, S. de F., Ramos, M. B., & de Almeida, G. R. (2017). The role of mountains as refugia for biodiversity in Brazilian Caatinga: Conservationist implications. *Tropical Conservation Science*, *10*. Advance online publication. doi:10.1177/1940082917702651

Lopez, C., & Fan, Y. (2009). Internationalisation of the Spanish fashion brand Zara. *Journal of Fashion Marketing and Management*, *13*(2), 279–296. doi:10.1108/13612020910957770

Lorenzoni, G., & Lipparini, A. (1999). The leveraging of interfirm relationships as a distinctive organizational capability: A longitudinal study. *Strategic Management Journal*, *20*(4), 317–338. doi:10.1002/(SICI)1097-0266(199904)20:4<317::AID-SMJ28>3.0.CO;2-3

Lounsbury, M., & Glynn, M. A. (2001). Cultural entrepreneurship: Stories, legitimacy, and the acquisition of resources. *Strategic Management Journal*, *22*(6/7), 545–564. doi:10.1002mj.188

Love, J. H., Roper, S., & Zhou, Y. (2016). Experience, age and exporting performance in UK SMEs. *International Business Review*, *25*(4), 806–819. doi:10.1016/j.ibusrev.2015.10.001

Lun, Y. (2011). Green management practices and firm performance: A case of container terminal operations. *Resources, Conservation and Recycling*, *55*(6), 559–566. doi:10.1016/j.resconrec.2010.12.001

Lun, Y. H. V., Lai, K., Wong, C. W. Y., & Cheng, T. C. E. (2014). Green shipping practices and firm performance. *Maritime Policy & Management*, *41*(2), 134–148. doi:10.1080/03088839.2013.819133

Luostarinen, R., & Gabrielsson, M. (2006). Globalization and marketing strategies of born globals in SMOPECs. *Thunderbird International Business Review*, *48*(6), 773–801. doi:10.1002/tie.20122

Lyles, M. A., & Salk, J. E. (1996). Knowledge acquisition from foreign parents in international joint ventures: An empirical examination in the Hungarian context. *Journal of International Business Studies*, *27*(5), 877–903. doi:10.1057/palgrave.jibs.8490155

Madsen, T. K., & Servais, P. (1997). The internationalization of born globals: An evolutionary process? *International Business Review*, *6*(6), 561–583. doi:10.1016/S0969-5931(97)00032-2

Mafabi, S., Munene, J., & Ntayi, J. (2012). Knowledge management and organisational resilience: Organisational innovation as a mediator in Uganda. *Parastatals. J. Strateg. Manag*, *5*(1), 57–80. doi:10.1108/17554251211200455

Magbadelo, J. O. (2012). Defence transformation in Nigeria: A critical issue for national security concerns. *India Quarterly. Journal of International Affairs*, *68*(3), 251–266. doi:10.1177/0974928412454603

Maier-Knapp, N. (2020). *The European Commission's palm oil conundrum*. East Asia Forum. Australia at https://www.eastasiaforum.org/2020/02/28/the-european-commissions-palm-oil-conundrum/?utm_source=rss&utm_medium=rss&utm_campaign=the-european-commissions-palm-oil-conundrum

Majeed, A., Jiang, P., Ahmad, M., Khan, M. A., & Olah, J. (2021). The impact of foreign direct investment on financial development: New evidence from panel cointegration and causality analysis. *Journal of Competitiveness*, *13*(1), 95–112. https://doi.org/10.7441/joc.2021.01.06

Makkonen, T., & Inkinen, T. (2021). Systems of environmental innovation: Sectoral and technological perspectives on ballast water treatment systems. *WMU Journal of Maritime Affairs*, *20*(1), 81–98. doi:10.100713437-021-00226-2

Malaysia, B. (2013). Bursa Malaysia Annual Report 2012. Kuala Lumpur, Malaysia: Bursa Malaysia

Malaysian Palm Oil Council. (2021a). *The implications of EU resolution to the Malaysian palm oil industry*. http://mpoc.org.my/the-implications-of-eu-resolution-to-the-malaysian-palm-oil-industry/

Malaysian Palm Oil Council. (2021b)., *96.04% of Oil Palm Estates have achieved MSPO Certification* – MPOB. http://mpoc.org.my/96-04-of-oil-palm-estates-have-achieved-mspo-certification-mpob/

Malkiel, B. G. (1973). *A random walk down Wall Street*. W.W. Norton and Co.

Malkiel, B. G. (2003). The efficient market hypothesis and its critic. *The Journal of Economic Perspectives*, *17*(3), 59–82. doi:10.1257/089533003321164958

Mambula, C. J. (2002). Perceptions of SMEs growth constraints in Nigeria. *Journal of Small Business Management*, *40*(1), 58–65. doi:10.1111/1540-627X.00039

Maoz, D. (2007). Backpackers' motivations the role of culture and nationality. *Annals of Tourism Research*, *34*(1), 122–140. doi:10.1016/j.annals.2006.07.008

Marylene, G., & Edward, D. (2005). Self-determination theory and work motivation. *Journal of Organizational Behavior*, *26*(4).

Masaaki, O. (2018). Another "oil war": the birth and development of unhealthy palm oil and its counter discourse; 岡本正明. (2018). もう一つの油戦争—不健康なパーム油という言説, その対抗言説の誕生と発展—. 東南アジア研究, *55*(2), 217-239.

Mason, K. J., & Leek, S. (2008). Learning to build a supply network: An exploration of dynamic business models. *Journal of Management Studies*, *45*(4), 774–799. doi:10.1111/j.1467-6486.2008.00769.x

Maurya, U. K., & Mishra, P. (2012). What is a brand? A Perspective on Brand Meaning. *European Journal of Business and Management*, *4*(3), 122–133.

May, I. A., Arogundadade, B.B., & Ekundayo, H.T. (2007). Assessing realities and challenges of technical education in imo state secondary school education system. *Nigeria Journal of Educational Administration and Planning, 7.*

Mayaki, I. A. (2010). *South-South mutual learning: A priority for national capacity development in Africa.* Retrieved from /WBI/Resources/213798-1286217829056/mayaki.pdf

Mayr, S., Hollaus, B., & Madner, V. (2021). Palm oil, the RED II and WTO law: EU sustainable biofuel policy tangled up in green? *Review of European, Comparative & International Environmental Law*, *30*(2), 233–248. doi:10.1111/reel.12386

Mbionwu, U. (2008). *School Administration in a Dwindling Economy: Nigeria Case*. Awka: Erudite Printers.

McAdam, M., Crowley, C., & Harrison, R. (2019). "To boldly go where no [man] has gone before" - Institutional voids and the development of women's digital entrepreneurship. *Technological Forecasting and Social Change*, *146*, 912–922. doi:10.1016/j.techfore.2018.07.051

McDougal, P. P., & Oviatt, B. M. (2000). International entrepreneurship: The intersection of two research paths. *Academy of Management Journal*, *43*, 902–908.

McDougal, P. P., Shane, S., & Oviatt, B. M. (1994). Explaining the Formation of International New Ventures: The limits of theories from international business research. *Journal of Business Venturing*, *9*(6), 469–487. doi:10.1016/0883-9026(94)90017-5

Mckenna, S., & Richardson, J. (2007). The increasing complexity of the internationally mobile professional: Issues for research and practice. *Cross Cultural Management*, *14*(4), 307–320. doi:10.1108/13527600710830331

McKinsey & Co. (1993). *Emerging Exporters*. Australian Manufacturing Council.

McMahon, D. (2021). As Australia loses its trump card, China and Brazil strike a trade deal. *Global Times*. https://new.qq.com/rain/a/20210707A070PD00

Meadows, D., & Meadows, D. (1972). The limits to growth. Academic Press.

Mehar, M. R., Naeem, M., Nazeer, M., & Arshad, S. (2018). Relationship of Economic and Financial variables with behavior of Stock Prices: A case of Pakistan Stock Exchange. *Merit Research Journal of Education and Review*, *6*(6), 92-100.

Meijaard, E., Brooks, T. M., Carlson, K. M., Slade, E. M., Garcia-Ulloa, J., Gaveau, D., Lee, J. S. H., Santika, T., Juffe-Bignoli, D., Struebig, M. J., Wich, S. A., Ancrenaz, M., Koh, L. P., Zamira, N., Abrams, J. F., Prins, H. H. T., Sendashonga, C. N., Murdiyarso, D., Furumo, P. R., ... Sheil, D. (2020). The environmental impacts of palm oil in context. *Nature Plants*, *6*(12), 1418–1426. doi:10.103841477-020-00813-w PMID:33299148

Miao, X., & Bao, J. (2007). Grounded theory of non-standardized groups travel. *Luyou Xuekan*, *22*(8), 48–54.

Michailof, S. (2013). Africa 2050: Jobs and prosperity in a multipolar global economy moving out of fragility and conflict. *Global Journal of Emerging Market Economies*, *5*(2), 117–149. doi:10.1177/0974910113494537

Milanzi, M. A. (2012). Export barrier perceptions in Tanzania: The influence of social networks. *Journal of African Business*, *13*(1), 29–39. doi:10.1080/15228916.2012.657941

Minbaeva, D., Park, C., Vertinsky, I., & Cho, Y. S. (2018). Disseminative capacity and knowledge acquisition from foreign partners in international joint ventures. *Journal of World Business*, *53*(5), 712–724. doi:10.1016/j.jwb.2018.03.011

Min, H. J. (2013). New women and modern girls: Consuming foreign goods in colonial Seoul. *Journal of Historical Research in Marketing*, *5*(4), 494–520. doi:10.1108/JHRM-01-2013-0004

Ministry of Trade, Republic of Turkey. (n.d.). https://ticaret.gov.tr/ihracat/fuarlar

Mladenović, S. S., Mladenović, I., & Ranđelović, M. P. (2020). Emerging Markets And Internationalization Of Retail: The Case Of Bric Countries. *Economic Themes*, *58*(4), 479–500. doi:10.2478/ethemes-2020-0027

Mohamad, M. (2019). Dr. Mahathir: Britain should break with Europe on palm oil. *New Straits Times*. Retrieved September 23, 2021, from, August 19, https://www.nst.com.my/news/nation/2019/08/514041/dr-mahathir-britain-should-break-europe-palm-oil

Mohamad, M. (2019, September 27). *Statement by the General Debate of the 74th session of the United Nation General Assembly, New York*. https://www.nst.com.my/news/nation/2019/09/525269/dr-ms-full-speech-text-74th-unga

Mohamed, M. A., Abdul-Talib, A. N., & Ramlee, A. (2022). Determinants of the firm performance of returnee entrepreneurs in Somalia: the effects of external environmental conditions. *Journal of Enterprising Communities: People and Places in the Global Economy*.

Mohamed, M.A., & Abdul-Talib, A.N. (2020). Non-pecuniary Factors Influencing Diaspora Homeland Investment. *Transcending Cultural Frontiers*, 125–139. doi:10.1007/978-981-15-4454-5_8

Mohamed, B., Omar, S. I., & Lau, P. M. (2010). Malaysian youth tourism market: A lucrative but overlooked tourist segment. *Malaysian Journal of Youth Market*, *3*(August), 1–21.

Mohammed, K. (2021). The state and the fight against Boko Haram insurgency in Nigeria. In *The Routledge Handbook of Counterterrorism and Counterinsurgency in Africa* (pp. 395–407). Routledge. doi:10.4324/9781351271929-26

Mohanram, P. (2005). Separating winners from losers among low book-to-market stocks using financial statement analysis. *Review of Accounting Studies*, *10*(2), 133–170. doi:10.100711142-005-1526-4

Mohsin, A., & Ryan, C. (2003). Backpackers in the Northern Territory of Australia?motives, behaviours and satisfactions. *International Journal of Tourism Research*, *5*(2), 113–131. doi:10.1002/jtr.421

Molenaar, E. J. (2014). Options for regional regulation of merchant shipping outside imo, with particular reference to the arctic region. *Ocean Development and International Law*, *45*(3), 272–298. doi:10.1080/00908320.2014.929474

Momoh, O. A. (2012). Revitalization of technical education in Nigeria as a vehicle for transformation. *Proceedings of COREN 21st Engineering Assembly*, 53 – 81.

Montoya, M. A., Allegretti, G., Sleimann Bertussi, L. A., & Talamini, E. (2021). Renewable and Non-renewable in the energy-emissions-climate nexus: Brazilian contributions to climate change via international trade. *Journal of Cleaner Production*, *312*, 127700. doi:10.1016/j.jclepro.2021.127700

Moore, K., & Reid, S. (2008). The Birth of Brand: 4000 Years of Branding History. *Business History*, *50*(4), 419–432. doi:10.1080/00076790802106299

Morais, F., & Ferreira, J. J. (2020). SME internationalisation process: Key issues and contributions, existing gaps and the future research agenda. *European Management Journal*, *38*(1), 62–77. doi:10.1016/j.emj.2019.08.001

Moralles, H. F., & Moreno, R. (2020). FDI productivity spillovers and absorptive capacity in Brazilian firms: A threshold regression analysis. *International Review of Economics & Finance*, *70*, 257–272. doi:10.1016/j.iref.2020.07.005

Muddaha, G., Kheng, Y. K., & Sulaiman, Y. (2018). Impact of management capabilities and environmental dynamism on Nigerian SMEs marketing innovation performance. *International Journal of Management Research & Review*, *8*(1), 20–35.

Muhammad, H., Pasha, M. F., & Ghani, I. (2020). Combined measures to control the COVID-19 pandemic in Wuhan, Hubei, China: A narrative review. *Journal of Biosafety and Biosecurity*, *2*(2), 51–57. doi:10.1016/j.jobb.2020.10.001 PMID:33521592

Murugiah, S. (2014). KLCI Week Ahead – KLCI to trend higher, support seen at 1,870. *The Edge Malaysia*. Available at: http://www.theedgemalaysia.com/business news/289984-klci-week-ahead-klci-to-trend-higher-support-seen-at-1870.html

Mustafa, M., & Ariffin, M. (2011). Protection of marine biodiversity from pollution : Legal strategies in malaysia. *International Journal of Bioscience, Biochemistry, Bioinformatics*, *1*, 276–281. doi:10.7763/IJBBB.2011.V1.52

Muzaini, H. (2006). Backpacking Southeast Asia: Strategies of "looking local"'. *Annals of Tourism Research*, *33*(1), 144–161. doi:10.1016/j.annals.2005.07.004

Myers, B., & Pringle, J. K. (2005). Self-initiated foreign experience as accelerated development: Influences of gender. *Journal of World Business*, *40*(4), 421–431. doi:10.1016/j.jwb.2005.08.009

Najafi-Tavani, S., Najafi-Tavani, Z., Naudé, P., Oghazi, P., & Zeynaloo, E. (2018). How collaborative innovation networks affect new product performance: Product innovation capability, process innovation capability, and absorptive capacity. *Industrial Marketing Management*, *73*, 193–205. doi:10.1016/j.indmarman.2018.02.009

Nakos, G., Dimitratos, P., & Elbanna, S. (2019). The mediating role of alliances in the international market orientation-performance relationship of SMEs. *International Business Review*, *28*(3), 603–612. doi:10.1016/j.ibusrev.2018.12.005

Nambisan, S. (2017). Digital entrepreneurship: Toward a digital technology perspective of entrepreneurship. *Entrepreneurship Theory and Practice*, *41*(6), 1029–1055. doi:10.1111/etap.12254

Narver, J., & Slater, S. (1990). The effect of a market orientation on business profitability. *Journal of Marketing*, *54*(4), 20–35. doi:10.1177/002224299005400403

Nash, R., Thyne, M., & Davies, S. (2006). An investigation into customer satisfaction levels in the budget accommodation sector in Scotland: A case study of backpacker tourists and the Scottish Youth Hostels Association. *Tourism Management*, *27*(3), 525–532. doi:10.1016/j.tourman.2005.01.001

Nasir, W. M. N., Al Mamun, A., & Breen, J. (2017). Strategic orientation and performance of SMEs in Malaysia. *SAGE Open*, *7*(2). Advance online publication. doi:10.1177/2158244017712768

Nathrah, Y. (2006). *The evidence of size effect during bull and bear markets* [Unpublished MSc thesis]. Universiti Putra Malaysia.

National Bureau of Statisticsa. (2019). *Nigerian gross domestic product Report.* Retrieved 3 August, 2021, from https://www.nigerianstat.gov.ng/pdfuploads/GDP_Report_Q3_2019.pdf

Natsuda, K., & Thoburn, J. (2020). *Automotive Industrialisation: Industrial Policy and Development in Southeast Asia*. Routledge. doi:10.4324/9780429445354

Ndlovu-Gatsheni, S. J. (2012). Beyond the equator there are no sins: Coloniality and violence in Africa. *Journal of Developing Societies*, *28*(419), 419–440. Advance online publication. doi:10.1177/0169796X12463143

Ndujihe, C. (2019). *Education sector gets paltry N3.9 trillion out of N55.19 trillion in 10 years.* Retrieved 2 August, 2021, from https://www.vanguardngr.com/2018/04/educationfree-fall/

Negash, E. S., Zhu, W., Lu, Y., & Wang, Z. (2020). Does chinese inward foreign direct investment improve the productivity of domestic firms? Horizontal linkages and absorptive capacities: Firm-level evidence from Ethiopia. *Sustainability*, *12*(7), 3000–3023. doi:10.3390u12073023

Neoh, H. K. (1986). *An Examination of the Efficiency of the Malaysian Stock Market* [PhD Dissertation]. University of Edinburg.

Ng, K. Y., Van Dyne, L., & Ang, S. (2009). From experience to experiential learning: Cultural intelligence as a learning capability for global leader development. *Academy of Management Learning & Education*, *8*(4), 511–526. doi:10.5465/amle.8.4.zqr511

Ngoni, C. S., Felicity, N. N., & Precious, M. (2021). Exhibitors' preference at trade fairs: The case of Zimbabwe International Trade Fair (ZITF). *Journal of Convention & Event Tourism*, 1–21. Advance online publication. doi:10.1080/15470148.2021.1893241

Nguyen, N. T. D., & Aoyama, A. (2014). Achieving efficient technology transfer through a specific corporate culture facilitated by management practices. *The Journal of High Technology Management Research, 25*(2), 108–122. doi:10.1016/j.hitech.2014.07.001

Nguyen, N. T. D., & Aoyama, A. (2015). The impact of cultural differences on technology transfer: Management practice moderation. *Journal of Manufacturing Technology Management, 26*(7), 926–954. doi:10.1108/JMTM-09-2013-0130

Nguyen, T. X. H., Pham, T. H., Dao, T. N., Nguyen, T. N., & Tran, T. K. N. (2020). the impact of foreign ownership and management on firm performance in Vietnam. *The Journal of Asian Finance, Economics, and Business, 7*(9), 409–418. doi:10.13106/jafeb.2020.vol7.no9.409

Nicholson, W., & Snyder, C. M. (2012). *Microeconomic theory: Basic principles and extensions* (11th ed.). Nelson Education.

Nigeria Centre for Disease Control. (2020). *Covid-19 situation Report: Situation Report 85, saturday, 23rd may, 2020.* Retrieved 3 August, 2021, from https://reliefweb.int/report/world/coronavirus-disease-2019-covid-19-situation-report-85-14-april-2020

Nonaka, I., & Takeuchi, H. (1995). *The knowledge-creating company: How Japanese companies create the dynamics of innovation.* Oxford University Press.

Nonnenmacher, V., Oliveira, L., Villamil, M., & Bodmann, B. (2014). Modeling and visualization individual and collective opinions towards extremism in a society. *Procedia Computer Science, 29*, 2412–2421. doi:10.1016/j.procs.2014.05.225

Noor, F. M. M., Gassner, A., Terheggen, A., & Dobie, P. (2017). Beyond sustainability criteria and principles in palm oil production: Addressing consumer concerns through in setting. *Ecology and Society, 22*(2), 1–5. PMID:29780429

Norli, A., Annuar, M. N., Taufik, H., & Sazali, Z. A. (2010). Short-run stock overreaction: Evidence from Bursa Malaysia. *International Journal of Economics and Management, 4*(2), 319–333.

Nossal, K. R., & Stubbs, R. (1997). Mahathir's Malaysia: an emerging middle power? In Niche diplomacy (pp. 147-163). Palgrave Macmillan. doi:10.1007/978-1-349-25902-1_8

Nowiński, W., & Rialp, A. (2013). Drivers and strategies of international new ventures from a Central European transition economy. *Journal for East European Management Studies, 18*(2), 191–231. doi:10.5771/0949-6181-2013-2-191

Nuroğlu, E. (2019). *Turkey-China relations within the framework of the Belt-Road Project.* Retrieved September 2, 2012 from https://www.aa.com.tr/tr/analiz/kusak-yol-projesi-cercevesinde-turkiye-cin-iliskileri/1538112

Nuru, A. (2007). *The Relevance of National Vocational Education Qualification (NVQS) in TVE in Nigeria.* Unpublished Conference Paper.

O'Regan, M. (2018). Backpacking's future and its drifter past. *Journal of Tourism Futures, 4*(3), 193–204. doi:10.1108/JTF-04-2018-0019

Obododike, M. P., & Cokekeokosisi, J. O. (2020). Challenges Of Implementing E-Learning In Nigeria Educational System In The Covid-19 Pandemic Era. *Social Sciences and Education Research Review, 7*(2), 152–171.

OECD. (2009). *OECD benchmark definition of foreign direct investment 2008.* Organisation for Economic Co-operation and Development Publishing.

OECD. (2009). *Top Barriers and Drivers to SME Internationalisation. Report by the OECD Working Party on SMEs and Entrepreneurship.* OECD.

OECD. (2018). *China's Belt and Road Initiative in the Global Trade, Investment and Finance, Landscape*. Retrieved April 13, 2021, from https://www.oecd.org/general/searchresults/?q=china%20belt%20and&cx=012432601748511391518:xzeadub0b0a&cof=FORID:11&ie=UTF-8

Ogundele, M.O., Oluwolara, F.K., & Adegbemi, F.O. (2011). *Fundamentals of Organizational Behaviors*. Ilorin: Ramfik Concepts.

Oh, Y. (2020). *From concrete walls to digital walls: Transmedia construction of place myth in Ihwa Mural Village, South Korea*. doi:10.1177/0163443720916410

Ohia, C., Bakarey, A. S., & Ahmad, T. (2020). COVID-19 and Nigeria: Putting the realities in context. *International Journal of Infectious Diseases*, *95*, 279–281. doi:10.1016/j.ijid.2020.04.062 PMID:32353547

Okafor, L. E. (2021). Export market destinations, imported intermediates, and productivity: Firm-level evidence from Ghana. *The International Trade Journal*, *35*(4), 383–410. doi:10.1080/08853908.2020.1718567

Okeke, S. O. C., Egbuonu, R. N., & Ugbaja, J. N. (2009). Entrepreneurship skills acquisition of biology education students through design project. *50th STAN Annual Conference Proceedings*, 106 – 108.

Okeke, B. C. (2007). Vocational and technical education: Meeting goals, objectives and visions of national economic empowerment development strategies (NEEDS) and MDGS. *Journal of Science Education*, *9*(1), 11–20.

Okunade, S. K., Faluyi, O. T., & Matambo, E. (2021). Evolving patterns of insurgency in Southern and West Africa: Refocusing the Boko Haram lens on Mozambique. *African Security Review*, •••, 1–17. doi:10.1080/10246029.2021.1959360

Oladeji, O. F. (2019). The skills acquisition programme and youth empowerment in ondo state of Nigeria. *Global Journal of Human Social Science: A Arts and Humanity Psychology*, *19*(6).

Oliveira-Brochado, A., & Gameiro, C. (2013). Toward a better understanding of backpackers' motivations. *Tékhne. Instituto Politécnico do Cávado e do Ave*, *11*(2), 92–99. doi:10.1016/j.tekhne.2013.11.001

Olmo, J. C., Hassoun, S. S., & Fernández, P. M. (2020). Spatial relationship between economic growth and renewable energy consumption in 26 European countries. *Energy Econ*, *92*, 104962. doi:10.1016/j.eneco.2020.104962

Olufadewa, I. J., Adesina, M. A., Ekpo, M. D., Akinloye, S. J., Iyanda, T. O., Nwachukwu, P., & Kodzo, L. D. (2020). Lessons from the coronavirus disease 2019 (COVID-19) pandemic response in China, Italy, and the U.S.: A guide for Africa and low- and middle-income countries. *Global Health Journal*, *5*(1), 56–61. doi:10.1016/j.glohj.2021.02.003 PMID:33585052

Olutoyin, D. S. (2009). Developing entrepreneurial skills through chemistry education. *50th STAN Annual Conference Proceedings*, 190 – 194.

Onah, N., & Okwuosa, L. (2016). Youth employment and peace in Nigerian society. *Mediterranean Journal of Social Sciences*, *7*(1), 52–58.

Onapajo, H., Uzodike, U. O., & Whetho, A. (2012). Boko Haram terrorism in Nigeria: The international dimension. *South African Journal of International Affairs*, *19*(3), 337–357. doi:10.1080/10220461.2012.740319

Onileowo, T. T. (2021). Women Entrepreneurship Challenges in Ekiti State Southwest Nigeria: Way Forward. *Albukhary Social business Journal*, *2*(1), 1-9.

Onileowo, T. T., Muharam, F. M., Ramily, M. K., & Saleh, F. K. (2021). The Nexus between Innovation and Business Competitive Advantage: A Conceptual Study. *Universal Journal of Accounting and Finance*, *9*(3), 352–361. doi:10.13189/ujaf.2021.090309

Onuche, U., & Ogbe, F. G. (2021). Comparative analysis of Nigeria's aquaculture and capture fisheries development across different policy regimes from 1960 to 2016: A case for an inclusive and sustainable fisheries development. *University-Led Knowledge and Innovation for Sustainable Development*, 143.

Onyema, E. M., Eucheria, N. C., Obafemi, F. A., Sen, S., Atonye, F. G., Sharma, A., & Alsayed, A. O. (2020). Impact of Coronavirus pandemic on education. *Journal of Education and Practice*, *11*(13), 108–121.

Oosterveer, P. (2020). Sustainability of palm oil and its acceptance in the EU. *Journal of Oil Palm Research*, *32*(3), 365–376.

Oppenheimer, H. R. (1984). A test of Benjamin Graham's stock selection criteria. *Financial Analysts Journal*, *40*(5), 68–74. doi:10.2469/faj.v40.n5.68

Oppenheimer, H. R. (1986). Ben Graham's net current asset values: A performance update. *Financial Analysts Journal*, *8*(1), 40–47. doi:10.2469/faj.v42.n6.40

Oppenheimer, H. R., & Schlarbaum, G. G. (1981). Investing with Benjamin Graham: An ex ante test of the efficient markets hypothesis. *Journal of Financial and Quantitative Analysis*, *16*(3), 341–360. doi:10.2307/2330242

Oranu, R. N. (2004*). Vocational and technical education in Nigeria*. Academic Press.

Ordoyo, A. F. P., Menor, J. C., & Felecia, M. L. D. (2021). A case study on the effect of K-Drama in choosing South Korea as a Travel Destination. *International Journal of Sciences, Basic and Applied Research*, *58*(2).

Orlic, E., Hashi, I., & Hisarciklilar, M. (2018). Cross sectoral FDI spillovers and their impact on manufacturing productivity. *International Business Review*, *27*(4), 777–796. doi:10.1016/j.ibusrev.2018.01.002

Osman, H., Brown, L., & Phung, T. M. T. (2019). The travel motivations and experiences of female Vietnamese solo travellers. *Tourist Studies*, *63*, 12–22. doi:10.1177/1468797619878307

Osnin, N. A., & Rahman, N. S. F. A. (2018). Assessment and ranking of inland navigation practices in Malaysia: The case of Kenyir lake. *The Asian Journal of Shipping and Logistics*, *34*(4), 289–296. doi:10.1016/j.ajsl.2018.12.002

Otache, I. (2017). Agripreneurship development: A strategy for revamping Nigeria's economy from recession. *African Journal of Economic and Management Studies*, *8*(4), 474–483. doi:10.1108/AJEMS-05-2017-0091

Othman, M. R., Bruce, G. J., & Hamid, S. A. (2011). The strength of Malaysian maritime cluster: The development of maritime policy. *Ocean and Coastal Management*, *54*(8), 557–568. doi:10.1016/j.ocecoaman.2011.02.004

Oviatt, B. M., & McDougall, P. P. (2005). The internationalization of entrepreneurship. *Journal of International Business Studies*, *36*(1), 2–8. doi:10.1057/palgrave.jibs.8400119

Oviatt, B. M., & McDougal, P. (1994). Toward a theory of international new ventures. *Journal of International Business Studies*, *25*(1), 45–64. doi:10.1057/palgrave.jibs.8490193

Oviatt, B. M., & McDougal, P. (1997). Challenges for Internationalization Process Theory: The Case of International New Ventures. *Management International Review*, *37*(2), 85–99.

Ozili, P. K. (2020). *Covid-19 pandemic and economic crisis: The Nigerian experience and structural causes.* Retrieved from https://pkf-ng.com/media/10046217/pkf-nigeria-covid-19-bulletin-final-ed.pdf

Özpay, G. A. (2018). The Baku-Tbilisi-Kars railway and its geopolitical importance in terms of Turkey. *Marmara Geographical Review*, *37*, 103–111.

Özsoy, S., Ergüzel, O. Ş., Ersoy, A. Y., & Saygılı, M. (2021). The impact of digitalization on export of high technology products: A panel data approach. *The Journal of International Trade & Economic Development*, 1–22. doi:10.1080/09638199.2021.1965645

Paik, Y., & Sohn, J. D. (2004). Expatriate managers and MNC's ability to control international subsidiaries: The case of Japanese MNCs. *Journal of World Business*, *39*(1), 61–71. doi:10.1016/j.jwb.2003.08.003

Pak, Y. S., Ra, W., & Lee, J. M. (2015). An integrated multi-stage model of knowledge management in international joint ventures: Identifying a trigger for knowledge exploration and knowledge harvest. *Journal of World Business*, *50*(1), 180–191. doi:10.1016/j.jwb.2014.02.006

Palazzo, V., Savoia, J. R., Securato, J. R., & Bergmann, D. R. (2018). Análise de carteiras de valor no mercado brasileiro. *Revista Contabilidade & Finanças*, *29*(78), 452–468. doi:10.1590/1808-057x201804810

Palmer, C., Niemand, T., Stöckmann, C., Kraus, S., & Kailer, N. (2017). The interplay of entrepreneurial orientation and psychological traits in explaining firm performance. *Journal of Business Research*. Advance online publication. doi:10.1016/j.jbusres.2017.10.005

Panayides, P. M. (2007). The impact of organizational learning on relationship orientation, logistics service effectiveness and performance. *Industrial Marketing Management*, *36*(1), 68–80. doi:10.1016/j.indmarman.2005.07.001

Papastamatelou, J., Busch, R., Begun, O., Okan, E. Y., & Gassemi, K. (2016). Effects of network capabilities on firm performance across cultures. *International Journal of Management and Economics*, *49*(1), 79–105. doi:10.1515/ijme-2016-0005

Parc, J., & Moon, H. (2013). *Korean dramas and films: Key factors for their international competitiveness*. doi:10.1163/15685314-12341295

Parida, V., Pesämaa, O., Wincent, J., & Westerberg, M. (2017). Network capability, innovativeness, and performance: A multidimensional extension for entrepreneurship. *Entrepreneurship and Regional Development*, *29*(1–2), 94–115. doi:10.1080/08985626.2016.1255434

Paris, C. M., Musa, G., & Thirumoorthi, T. (2015). A comparison between Asian and Australasia backpackers using cultural consensus analysis. *Current Issues in Tourism*, *18*(2), 175–195. doi:10.1080/13683500.2014.920771

Paris, C. M., & Teye, V. (2010). Backpacker Motivations : A Travel Career Approach. *Journal of Hospitality Marketing & Management*, *19*(3), 244–259. doi:10.1080/19368621003591350

Park, C., Vertinsky, I., & Minbaeva, D. (2013). *The influence of foreign partners' disseminative capacities on knowledge transfers to international joint ventures*. Academic Press.

Park, B. I. (2011). Knowledge transfer capacity of multinational enterprises and technology acquisition in international joint ventures. *International Business Review*, *20*(1), 75–87. doi:10.1016/j.ibusrev.2010.06.002

Park, J. (2019). Travel motivation among cross border tourists : Case study of Langkawi. *Tourism Management Perspectives*, *31*, 63–71. doi:10.1016/j.tmp.2019.03.004

Park, J. M., Lee, J. E., & Jeong, Y. H. (2018). The effect of strategic orientation on the speed of internationalization in small and medium-sized enterprises in South Korea. *Muyeog Yeon'gu*, *14*(5), 21–42.

Paul, J., & Rosado-Serrano, A. (2019). Gradual internationalization vs born-global. International new venture models. *International Marketing Review*, *36*(6), 830–858. doi:10.1108/IMR-10-2018-0280

Pavlou, P. A., & El Sawy, O. A. (2006). From IT leveraging competence to competitive advantage in turbulent environments: The case of new product development. *Information Systems Research, 17*(3), 198–227. doi:10.1287/isre.1060.0094

Pearce, P. L. (1993). Fundamentals of tourist motivation. In *Tourism research: Critiques and challenges*. Routledge.

Pearce, P. L., Murphy, L. & Brymer, E. (2009). *Evolution of the Backpacker Market and the Potential for Australian Tourism, Sustainable Tourism Cooperative Research Centre's (STCRC's)*. Academic Press.

Pearce, P. L. (1990). *The backpacker phenomenon: Preliminary answers to basic questions*. Department of Tourism, James Cook University of North Queensland.

Pearce, P. L., & Foster, F. (2007). A "university of travel": Backpacker learning. *Tourism Management, 28*(5), 1285–1298.

Peltier, J. W., & Naidu, G. M. (2012). Social networks across the SMEs organisational lifecycle. *Journal of Small Business and Enterprise Development, 19*(1), 56–73. doi:10.1108/14626001211196406

Peltokorpi, V., & Froese, F. J. (2009). Organizational expatriates and self-initiated expatriates: Who adjusts better to work and life in Japan? *International Journal of Human Resource Management, 20*(5), 1096–1112. doi:10.1080/09585190902850299

Penrose, E. T. (2009). *The Theory of the Growth of the Firm*. Oxford University Press.

Petroman, I., Petroman, C., Marin, D., Ciolac, R., Vaduva, L., & Pandur, I. (2013). Types of cultural tourism. *Lucrari Stiintifice. Zootehnie si Biotehnologii, 46*(1), 385–388.http://search.ebscohost.com/login.aspx?direct=true&db=a9h&AN=90641216&site=ehost

Pham, J. P. (2012, April). *Boko Haram's evolving threat, African security briefs*. Retrieved https://www.questia.com/read/1P3-2711932791/boko-haram-s-evolving-threat

Pham, T. T. T., Hoang, T. A. N., Pham, H. H., & Ngo, M. T. (2014). *Does exporting spur firm productivity and promote inclusive growth? Evidence from Vietnam.* https://idl-bnc-idrc.dspacedirect.org/bitstream/handle/10625/54699/IDL-54699.pdf?sequence=1&isAllowed=y

Pinchera, V., & Rinallo, D. (2017). The emergence of Italy as a fashion country: Nation branding and collective meaning creation at Florence's fashion shows (1951–1965). *Business History*, 1–29.

Pinho, J. C. (2008). TQM and performance in small medium entreprises: The mediating effect of customer orientation and innovation. *International Journal of Quality & Reliability Management, 25*(3), 256–275. doi:10.1108/02656710810854278

Piotroski, J. (2000). Value investing: The use of historical financial statement information to separate winners from losers. *Journal of Accounting Research, 38*, 1–41. doi:10.2307/2672906

Pirouz, B., Shaffiee Haghshenas, S., Pirouz, B., Shaffiee Haghshenas, S., & Piro, P. (2020). Development of an assessment method for investigating the impact of climate and urban parameters in confirmed cases of Covid-19: A new challenge in sustainable development. *International Journal of Environmental Research and Public Health, 17*(8), 2801. doi:10.3390/ijerph17082801 PMID:32325763

PKF. (2020). *Covid-19 PKF Nigeria update.* Retrieved 3 August 2021, from https://pkf-ng.com/media/10046217/pkf-nigeria-covid-19-bulletin-final-ed.pdf. 1-5

Polat, I., & Mutlu, H. M. (2012). The impacts of market orientation, entrepreneurial orientation, environmental uncertainty and internationalization speed on firm performance. *European Researcher, 27*(8), 1248–1254.

Ponomarov, S. Y., & Holcomb, M. C. (2009). Understanding the concept of supply chain resilience. *International Journal of Logistics Management, 20*(1), 124–143. doi:10.1108/09574090910954873 portseurope.com. (2021). *Turkey ratifies Lapis Lazuli transport corridor route,* Retrieved May 05, 2021, from https://www.portseurope.com/turkey-ratifies-lapis-lazuli-transport-corridor-route/

Praburaj, L., Design, F., & Nadu, T. (2018). Role of agriculture in the economic development of a country. *International Journal of Commerce, 6*(3), 1–5.

Prasad, B., & Junni, P. (2017). Understanding top management team conflict, environmental uncertainty and firm innovativeness: Empirical evidence from India. *International Journal of Conflict Management, 28*(1), 122–143. doi:10.1108/IJCMA-02-2016-0006

Preece, S. B., Miles, G., & Baetz, M. C. (1999). Explaining the international intensity and global diversity of early-stage technology-based firms. *Journal of Business Venturing, 14*(3), 259–281. doi:10.1016/S0883-9026(97)00105-5

Prokic, M., & Stanimirović, U. (2019). *Eu-China Rail Economic Corridors and Their Role In Trade In Goods.* Retrieved May 29, 2001, from https://www.researchgate.net/publication/339103201_EUCHINA_RAIL_ECONOMIC_CORRIDORS_AND_THEIR_ROLE_IN_TRADE_IN_GOODS

Psaraftis, H. N. (2016). Green maritime logistics: The quest for win-win solutions. *Transportation Research Procedia, 14*, 133–142. doi:10.1016/j.trpro.2016.05.049

Pukall, T. J., & Calabro, A. (2014). The internationalization of family firms: A critical review and integrative model. *Family Business Review, 27*(2), 103–125. doi:10.1177/0894486513491423

Pye, O., & Bhattacharya, J. (Eds.). (2013). *The palm oil controversy in Southeast Asia: A transnational perspective.* Institute of Southeast Asian Studies.

Pyper, K. L., Gounaris, S., & Doherty, A. M. (2015). *Export to expand: A conceptual examination of branding as a deterministic parameter in export performance.* Academic Press.

Pyper, K., Doherty, A. M., Gounaris, S., & Wilson, A. (2019). Investigating international strategic brand management and export performance outcomes in the B2B context. *International Marketing Review, 37*(1), 98–129. doi:10.1108/IMR-02-2019-0087

Qi, G., Zou, H., & Xie, X. (2020). Governmental inspection and green innovation: Examining the role of environmental capability and institutional development. *Corporate Social Responsibility and Environmental Management, 27*(4), 1774–1785. doi:10.1002/csr.1924

Ra'ed, M., Al-Henzab, J., Tarhini, A., & Obeidat, B. Y. (2018). The associations among market orientation, technology orientation, entrepreneurial orientation and organizational performance. *Benchmarking, 25*(8), 3117–3142. doi:10.1108/BIJ-02-2017-0024

Radzuan, M. I. S., Inho, S., & Ahmad, Y. (2015). A rethink of the incentives programme in the conservation of South Korea's historic villages. *Journal of Cultural Heritage Management and Sustainable Development, 5*(2), 176–201. doi:10.1108/JCHMSD-02-2014-0006

Raei, M. F., Ignatenko, A., & Mircheva, M. (2019). *Global Value Chains: What are the Benefits and Why Do Countries Participate?* International Monetary Fund.

Raimbekov, Z., Syzdykbayeva, B., Rakhmetulina, Z., & Zhenskhan, D. (2018). The effectiveness of logistics development and its impact on the economies of the countries along the silk road passing through kazakhstan. *Transport Problems, 13*(4), 127–14.

Raj, M. P. M. (2018). Film induced tourism Model-A qualitative research study. *Asian Journal of Research in Marketing, 7*(2), 28. doi:10.5958/2277-6621.2018.00005.1

Raj, R. (2012). Religious tourist's motivation for visiting religious sites. *International Journal of Tourism Policy*, *4*(2), 95–105.

Rakodi, C. (2012). Inter-religious violence and its aftermath: Insights from Indian and Nigerian cities. *Journal of Asian and African Studies*, *48*(5), 557-576. DOI: 10.1177/0021909612464339

Ramasamy, B., & Yeun, M. C. H. (2019). China's One Belt One Road initiative: The impact of trade facilitation versus physical infrastructure on exports. *World Economy*, *42*, 1673–1694.

Ramli, B. N. (2016, October 10). *Big Bang entertains over 10,000 fans in KL with music, fun, and games*. Retrieved from New Straits Times: Retrieved from https://www.nst.com.my/news/2016/10/179225/bigbang-entertains-over-10000-fans-kl-musicfun-and-games

Rana, K. S. (2016). *Bilateral Diplomacy*. Manas Publication.

Rao, M. (2017, May 1). *Dimsum brings more Korean drama content to Malaysia*. Retrieved May 7, 2017, from Marketing Interactive: https://www.marketing-interactive.com/dimsum-bringsmore-korean-dramas-to-malaysia/

Rao, C., & Yan, B. (2020). Study on the interactive influence between economic growth and environmental pollution. *Environmental Science and Pollution Research International*, *27*(31), 39442–39465. doi:10.100711356-020 10017-6 PMID:32651783

Rasmussen, E. S., & Madsen, T. K. (2002). The born global concept. *Proceedings of the 28th EIBA 2002 Conference*, 1-26.

Rauch, J. E. (2001). Business and social networks in international trade. *Journal of Economic Literature*, *39*(4), 1177–1203. doi:10.1257/jel.39.4.1177

Rauf, A., Liu, X., Amin, W., Ozturk, I., Rehman, O. U., & Sarwar, S. (2018). Energy and ecological sustainability: Challenges and panoramas in Belt and Road initiative countries. *Sustainability*, *10*(8), 1–21. https://doi.org/10.3390/su10082743

Rennie, M. W. (1993). Global competitiveness: Born global. *The McKinsey Quarterly*, *4*, 45–52.

Repuclic of Turkey Ministry of Foreing Affairs. (2021). *Türkiye'nin Çok taraflu Ulaştırma Politikası*, Retrieved May 01, 2021, from https://www.mfa.gov.tr/turkiye_nin-cok-tarafli-ulastirma-politikasi.tr.mfa

Repuplic of Turkey Ministry of Trade. (2020). *World Trade by Countries (2005-2020)*. Retrieved May 28, 2021, from https://ticaret.gov.tr/istatistikler/dis-ticaret-istatistikleri/ulkelere-gore-dunya-ticareti-2005-2020

Research on the situation, strategy and policy of mineral resources in China. (2020). In *Baidu Encyclopaedia online*. https://baike.baidu.com/item/Researchonthesituation,strategyandpolicyofmineralresourcesinChina/56513210?fr=aladdin

Reuber, A. R., Knight, G. A., Liesch, P. W., & Zhou, L. (2018). International entrepreneurship: The pursuit of entrepreneurial opportunities across national borders. *Journal of International Business Studies*, *49*(4), 395–406. doi:10.105741267-018-0149-5

Reuters. (2018a). *European move to ban palm oil from biofuels is 'crop apartheid'—Malaysia*. Retrieved September 23, 2021, from https://www.reuters.com/article/malaysia-palmoil-eu-idUSL3N1PD1NJ

Reuters. (2019). *Malaysia, Indonesia send protest letter to EU on palm o il curbs.*, Malaysiakini. Retrieved September 23, 2021, from https://www.malaysiakini.com/news/471322

Reuters. (2021). *Malaysia takes WTO legal action against EU over palm biofuel curbs*. Retrieved January 23, 2021 from https://www.reuters.com/article/us-malaysia-palmoil-eu-idUSKBN29L054

Revkin, A. (2009). *Disaster Hot Spots on a Crowding Planet*. Academic Press.

Rialp, A., Rialp, J., & Knight, G. A. (2005). The phenomenon of early internationalizing firms: What do we know after a decade (1993-2003) of scientific inquiry? *International Business Review*, *14*(2), 147–166. doi:10.1016/j.ibusrev.2004.04.006

Rialp, A., Rialp, J., Urbano, D., & Vaillant, Y. (2005). The born-global phenomenon: A comparative case study research. *Journal of International Entrepreneurship*, *3*(2), 133–171. doi:10.100710843-005-4202-7

Richards, G., & Wilson, J. (2003). *New horizons in independent youth and student travel. A report to the international student travel confederation (ISTC) and the association of tourism and leisure education (ATLAS)*. International Student Travel Confederation.

Richardson, J., & McKenna, S. (2003). International experience and academic careers: What do academics have to say? *Personnel Review, 32*(6), 774-795+802. doi:10.1108/00483480310498710

Richardson, J., & Mallon, M. (2005). Career interrupted? The case of the self-directed expatriate. *Journal of World Business*, *40*(4), 409–420. doi:10.1016/j.jwb.2005.08.008

Richardson, J., & Mckenna, S. (2002). Leaving and experiencing: Why academics expatriate and how they experience expatriation. *Career Development International*, *7*(2), 67–78. doi:10.1108/13620430210421614

Richardson, J., & McKenna, S. (2006). Exploring relationships with home and host countries: A study of self-directed expatriates. *Cross Cultural Management*, *13*(1), 6–22. doi:10.1108/13527600610643448

Riley, P. J. (1988). Road culture of international long-term budget travelers. *Annals of Tourism Research*, *15*(3), 313–328. doi:10.1016/0160-7383(88)90025-4

Rinallo, D., Bathelt, H., & Golfetto, F. (2017). Economic geography and industrial marketing views on trade shows: Collective marketing and knowledge circulation. *Industrial Marketing Management*, *61*, 93–103. doi:10.1016/j.indmarman.2016.06.012

Rinallo, D., Borghini, S., & Golfetto, F. (2010). Exploring visitor experiences at trade shows. *Journal of Business and Industrial Marketing*, *25*(4), 249–258. doi:10.1108/08858621011038207

Ritter, J. R. (1991). The long-run performance of initial public offerings. *The Journal of Finance*, *46*(1), 3–27. doi:10.1111/j.1540-6261.1991.tb03743.x

Roberts, N. (2015). Absorptive capacity, organizational antecedents, and environmental dynamism. *Journal of Business Research*, *68*(11), 2426–2433. doi:10.1016/j.jbusres.2015.02.019

Robinson, L., Cotten, S., Ono, H., Quan-Haase, A., Mesch, G., Chen, W., Schulz, J., Hale, T., & Stern, M. (2015). Digital inequalities and why they matter. *Information Communication and Society*, *18*(5), 569–582. doi:10.1080/1369118X.2015.1012532

Rojec, M., & Knell, M. (2018). Why is there a lack of evidence on knowledge spillovers from foreign direct investment? *Journal of Economic Surveys*, *32*(3), 579–612. doi:10.1111/joes.12207

Romanowski, M. H., & Nasser, R. (2015). Identity issues: Expatriate professors teaching and researching in Qatar. *Higher Education*, *69*(4), 653–671. doi:10.100710734-014-9795-0

Rosenberg, B., Reid, K., & Lanstein, R. (1984). Persuasive evidence of market inefficiency. *Journal of Portfolio Management*, *11*(2), 9–17.

Rosenthal, E. (2009). Biggest obstacle to global climate deal may be how to pay for it. *Herald Tribune*.

Roser, M., & Ortiz-Ospina, E. (2020). *Literacy*. Our World in Data. Available at: https://ourworldindata.org/literacy

Rotsios, K., Sklavounos, N., & Hajidimitriou, Y. (2018). *Knowledge Transfer and Trust Among Partners: The Case of Greek IJVs. In Economy, Finance and Business in Southeastern and Central Europe.* Springer.

Ruël, H. J. M., & Zuidema, L. (2012). *The effectiveness of commercial diplomacy; a survey among Dutch embassies and consulates.* Discussion Papers in Diplomacy, Clingendael Institute, March 2012(123), 1-54. http://www.clingendael.nl/cdsp/publications/discussion-papers/archive.html

Rugman, A., & Brain, C. (2003). Multinational enterprises are regional, not global. *Multinational Business Review, 11*(1), 3–12. doi:10.1108/1525383X200300001

Ryan, R. M., & Deci, E. L. (2000). Intrinsic and extrinsic motivations: Classic definitions and new directions. *Contemporary Educational Psychology, 25*(1), 54–67. doi:10.1006/ceps.1999.1020 PMID:10620381

Ryan, T., Allen, K., Gray, D., & McInerney, D. (2017). How Social Are Social Media? A Review of Online Social Behaviour and Connectedness. *Journal of Relationships Research, 8*, 8. doi:10.1017/jrr.2017.13

S. Korea seeks Malaysia's expertise for its Muslim-Friendly Hospitality. (2019, May 22). *Malay mail.* Retrieved from https://www.malaymail.com/news/malaysia/2019/05/22/s.-korea-seeksmalaysias-expertise-for-its-muslim-friendly-hospitality/1755357

Sa'id, K. S., Talib, A. B. A., & Hassan, R. (2019a). The role of access to capital and the component of strategic orientations on smes performance: A conceptual framework. *International Journal of Business. Economics and Law, 19*(5), 311–321.

Sa'id, K. S., Talib, A. B. A., & Hassan, R. (2019b). The role of access to finance, relational capabilities and the omponent of strategic on SMEs performance in Nigeria: A pilot study. *Asian Journal of Multidisciplinary Studies, 7*(12), 8–19.

Saad, M., Kamarizzaman, N. A., Ishak, N., & Pratt, T. J. (2021). The influence of Pahang heritage food on behavioral intentions among Malaysian domestic tourists. *Environment-Behaviour Proceedings Journal, 6*(16), 163–169. doi:10.21834/ebpj.v6i16.2680

Salaam, A. O. (2012). Boko Haram: Beyond religious fanaticism. *Journal of Policing, Intelligence and Counter Terrorism, 7*(2), 147-162. DOI: .2012.719096 doi:10.1080/18335330

SAMA. (n.d.). *Annual Report 1997-2013.* SAMA Press.

Samuelson, P. A., & Nordhaus, W. D. (2019) Economics (19th ed.). New York: McGraw-Hill Education.

Santos, I. M. (2020). The effect of exports on a wealth of a country: A comment on the role of natural capital in the Amazon basin. *PRACS: Revista Eletrônica de Humanidades do Curso de Ciências Sociais da UNIFAP, 13*(2), 17–30. doi:10.18468/pracs.2020v13n2.p17-30

Sapienza, H. J., Autio, E., George, G., & Zahra, S. A. (2006). A capabilities perspective on the effects of early internationalization on firm survival and growth. *Academy of Management Review, 31*(4), 917–933. doi:10.5465/amr.2006.22527465

Sardain, A., Sardain, E., & Leung, B. (2019). Global forecasts of shipping traffic and biological invasions to 2050. *Nature Sustainability, 2*(4), 274–282. doi:10.103841893-019-0245-y

Sareewiwatthana, P., & Janin, P. (2017). Test of Quantitative Investing Strategies of Famous Investors: Case of Thailand. *Journal of Investment Management & Financial Innovation, 12*(2), 13–25. doi:10.21511/imfi.14(3-1).2017.06

Sari, D. W. (2019). The potential horizontal and vertical spillovers from foreign direct investment on Indonesian manufacturing industries. *Economic Papers: A Journal of Applied Economics and Policy, 38*(4), 299-310.

Sari, D. W., & Restikasari, W. (2021). Global Trade Pattern on High-Tech Firms. *Jurnal Ekonomi dan Pembangunan Indonesia, 21*(1), 77-94. doi:10.21002/jepi.v21i1.1342

Sari, D. W., Khalifah, N. A., & Suyanto, S. (2016). The spillover effects of foreign direct investment on the firms' productivity performances. *Journal of Productivity Analysis, 46*(2), 199–233. doi:10.100711123-016-0484-0

Sari, D. W., Restikasari, W., & Haryanto, T. (2020). Global Trading of Electronic Component in Indonesia Manufacturing Industry. *Elementary Education Online, 19*(4), 639–646. doi:10.17051/ilkonline.2020.04.167

Sarkis, J., Zhu, Q. H., & Lai, K. H. (2011). An organizational theoretic review of green supply chain management literature. *International Journal of Production Economics, 130*(1), 1–15. doi:10.1016/j.ijpe.2010.11.010

Sarstedt, M., Ringle, C. M., Smith, D., Reams, R., & Hair, J. F. Jr. (2014). Partial least squares structural equation modeling (PLS-SEM): A useful tool for family business researchers. *Journal of Family Business Strategy, 5*(1), 105–115. doi:10.1016/j.jfbs.2014.01.002

Saudi Arabian Monetary Agency. (2004). 40th Annual Report. Author.

Saudi Arabian Monetary Agency. (2006). 42nd Annual Report. Author.

Saudi Arabian Monetary Agency. (2020). 56th Annual Report. Author.

Saudi Chamber of Commerce in Riyadh. (2005). *Explore to What Extend the Efficiency of the Local Stock Market and its Role in Supporting the National Economy.* In the 15th Annual Meeting of Saudi Economic Association, Riyadh, Saudi Arabia.

Scheyvens, R. (2002). Backpacker tourism and third world development article. *Annals of Tourism Research, 29*(1), 144–164. doi:10.1016/S0160-7383(01)00030-5

Scheyvens, R. (2006). Sun, sand, and beach fale: Benefiting from backpackers—the samoan way. *Tourism Recreation Research, 31*(3), 75–86. doi:10.1080/02508281.2006.11081507

Schiuma, G., Andreeva, T., & Kianto, A. (2012). Does knowledge management really matter? Linking knowledge management practices, competitiveness and economic performance. *Journal of Knowledge Management, 16*(4), 617–636. doi:10.1108/13673271211246185

Schmidheiny, S., & Zorraquin, F. J. (1998). *Financing change: the financial community, eco-efficiency, and sustainable development*. MIT Press.

Schmitz, H. (1999). *Global Competition and Local Cooperation: Success and Failure in the Sinos Valley, Brazil* [Unpublished doctoral dissertation]. University of Sussex, Brighton, UK.

Schneider, F., Zwillich, B., Bindl, M., Hopp, F., Reich, S., & Vorderer, P. (2017). Social media ostracism: The effects of being excluded online. *Computers in Human Behavior, 73*, 385–393. doi:10.1016/j.chb.2017.03.052

SEED. (2020). *Impact of COVID-19 on Education for Vulnerable Children.* Sustainable Education and Enterprise Development. Retrieved 6 May, 2021, from https://www.seed.com.ng/impact-of-covid-19-on-education-for-vulnerable-children/

Sekeran, U., & Bougie, R. (2010). *Research methods for business: A skill building approach* (5th ed.). John Wiley and Sons.

Sekeran, U., & Bougie, R. (2013). *Researh methods for business: a skill building approach* (6th ed.). John Wiley & Sons Ltd.

Selmer, J., Lauring, J., Eleanor, L., & Charlotte, Z. (2016). *Global Talent Management and Staffing in MNEs*. doi:10.1108/S1876-066X20160000032018

Selmer, J., & Lauring, J. (2010). Self-initiated academic expatriates: Inherent demographics and reasons to expatriate. *European Management Review, 7*(3), 169–179. doi:10.1057/emr.2010.15

Selmer, J., & Lauring, J. (2013). Cognitive and affective reasons to expatriate and work adjustment of expatriate academics. *International Journal of Cross Cultural Management*, *13*(2), 175–191. doi:10.1177/1470595813485382

Selmer, J., & Lauring, J. (2015). Host country language ability and expatriate adjustment: The moderating effect of language difficulty. *International Journal of Human Resource Management*, *26*(3), 401–420. doi:10.1080/09585192.2011.561238

Seng, T. L., & Taha, A. Z. (2017). Interpartner relation fit, knowledge transfer, and IJVs innovativeness: The Malaysian context. *International Journal of Advanced and Applied Sciences*, *4*(1), 47–54. doi:10.21833/ijaas.2017.01.007

Seringhaus, F. H. R., & Rosson, P. J. (1994). International trade fairs and foreign market involvement: Review and research directions. *International Business Review*, *3*(3), 311–329. doi:10.1016/0969-5931(94)90008-6

Seringhaus, F. H. R., & Rosson, P. J. (1995). Visitor and exhibitor industrial trade fairs interaction. *Journal of Business Research*, *32*, 81–90. doi:10.1016/0148-2963(94)00012-4

Severo, E. A., Guimaraes, J. C. F. D., & Dellarmelin, M. L. (2021). Impact of the COVID-19 pandemic on environmental awareness, sustainable consumption and social responsibility: Evidence from generations in Brazil and Portugal. *Journal of Cleaner Production*, *286*, 124947. doi:10.1016/j.jclepro.2020.124947 PMID:33173257

Seyedghorban, Z., Matanda, M. J., & LaPlaca, P. (2016). Advancing theory and knowledge in the business-to-business branding literature. *Journal of Business Research*, *69*(8), 2664–2677. doi:10.1016/j.jbusres.2015.11.002

Shaffer, M. A., Harrison, D. A., & Matthew Gilley, K. (1999). Dimensions, determinants, and differences in the expatriate adjustment process sixteen to forty percent of assignments. *Journal of International Business Studies*, *30*(3), 557–581. doi:10.1057/palgrave.jibs.8490083

Shahbaz, M., Nasreen, S., Ahmed, K., & Hammoudeh, S. (2017). Trade openness-carbon emissions nexus: The importance of turning points of trade openness for country panels. *Energy Econ*, *61*, 221–232. doi:10.1016/j.eneco.2016.11.008

Shanghai Municipal Commission of Commerce. (2020). *What is the impact of the epidemic on China's overseas mining investment, out of service port.* Author.

Shehu, A. M., & Mahmood, R. (2014). The relationship between market orientation and business performance of Nigerian SMEs: The role of organizational culture. *International Journal of Business and Social Science*, *5*(9), 159–168.

Sheil, D., Casson, A., Meijaard, E., Van Noordwijk, M., Gaskell, J., Sunderland-Groves, J., Wertz, K., & Kanninen, M. (2009). *The impacts and opportunities of oil palm in Southeast Asia: What do we know and what do we need to know?* (Vol. 51). Center for International Forestry Research.

Sheng, Y., Wu, Y., Shi, X., & Zhang, D. (2014). Market Integration and Energy Trade Efficiency: An Application of Malmqvist Index to Analyse Multi-Product Trade. Energy Market Integration in East Asia: Energy Trade, Cross Border Electricity, and Price Mechanism, 29, 135-161.

Shen, G. (2020). Impact of the global spread of COVID-19 on international trade and mitigation measures. *People's Forum Academic Frontiers*, *2*, 2–7.

Shimbov, B., Alguacil, M., & Suárez, C. (2013). Fragmentation and parts and components trade in the Western Balkan countries. *Post-Communist Economies*, *25*(3), 371–391. doi:10.1080/14631377.2013.813142

Shuai, J., Chen, J. H., Leng, Z. H., Wang, Z. H., & Shi, Z. Y. (2018). Research on the International Competitiveness of Chinese Renewable Energy Products under the Background of "One Belt And One Road". *China Soft Science*, 7.

Shuai, J., Leng, Z., Cheng, J., & Shi, Z. (2020). China's renewable energy trade potential in the "Belt-and-Road" countries: A gravity model analysis. *Renewable Energy*, *161*, 1025–1035. doi:10.1016/j.renene.2020.06.134

Simon, B., & Hans, H. S. (2020). *Schools, skills, and learning: The impact of COVID-19 on education.* Retrieved 5 August 2021, from https://voxeu.org/article/impact-covid-19-education. https://www.universityworldnews.com/post.php?story=20200324065639773

Simonin, B. L. (2004). An empirical investigation of the process of knowledge transfer in international strategic alliances. *Journal of International Business Studies, 35*(5), 407–427. doi:10.1057/palgrave.jibs.8400091

Singh, D. A. (2009). Export performance of emerging market firms. *International Business Review, 18*(4), 321–330. doi:10.1016/j.ibusrev.2009.03.002

Singh, J., & Kaur, K. (2014). Testing Benjamin Graham's stock selection criteria in Indian stock market. *Management and Labor Studies, 39*(1), 43–62. doi:10.1177/0258042X14535156

Sinkula, J. M., Baker, W. E., & Noordewier, T. (1997). A framework for market-based organizational learning: Linking values, knowledge, and behavior. *Journal of the Academy of Marketing Science, 25*(4), 305–318. doi:10.1177/0092070397254003

Sino-Brazilian economic and trade cooperation in 2020. (2020). *Information on CPEC.* Author.

Sipilä, K. (2021). *Finnish SMEs' manifestation of agility in the uncertain US business environment* [Master Dissertation]. University of Vaasa.

Slater, S., & Narver, J. C. (1994). Market orientation, customer value and superior performance. *Business Horizons*, 22–28.

Slater, S. F., & Narver, J. C. (1995). Market orientation and the learning organization. *Journal of Marketing, 59*(3), 63–74. doi:10.1177/002224299505900306

SMEDAN. (2012). Survey on Micro, Small and Medium enterprises (MSMEs) in Nigeria. SMEDAN.

SMEDAN. (2013). Smedan and National Bereau of Statistics Collaborative Survey: Selected Findings. SMEDAN.

Smirnova, M. M., & Kushch, S. P. (2006). Understanding the role of relational capabilities in buyer-seller relationships. *22nd IMP Conference*, 7–9.

Smirnova, M., Naudé, P., Henneberg, S. C., Mouzas, S., & Kouchtch, S. P. (2011). The impact of market orientation on the development of relational capabilities and performance outcomes: The case of Russian industrial firms. *Industrial Marketing Management, 40*(1), 44–53. doi:10.1016/j.indmarman.2010.09.009

Snee, H. (2014). *A cosmopolitan journey? Difference, distinction and identity work in gap year travel.* Ashgate Publishing, Ltd.

Söderbom, M., & Teal, F. (2001). *Are African manufacturing firms really inefficient?: Evidence from firm-level panel data.* UNIDO.

Solaja, O. M., & Adenuga, O. A. (2016). Investigating the impact of skill acquisition programmes on graduates unemployment dilemma in Lagos state, Nigeria. St. Theresa. *Journal of the Humanities and Social Sciences, 2*(2), 16–39.

Solano Acosta, A., Herrero Crespo, Á., & Collado Agudo, J. (2018). Effect of market orientation, network capability and entrepreneurial orientation on international performance of small and medium enterprises (SMEs). *International Business Review, 27*(6), 1128–1140. doi:10.1016/j.ibusrev.2018.04.004

Solomon, H. (2012). Counter-terrorism in Nigeria. *RUSI Journal, 157*(4), 6–11. doi:10.1080/03071847.2012.714183

Som, A. P. M., Marzuki, A., & Yousefi, M. (2012). Factors influencing visitors' revisit behavioral intentions: A case study of Sabah, Malaysia. *International Journal of Marketing Studies, 4*(4), 39–50.

Song, H., & Kim, H. (2019). *Value-Based Profiles of Visitors to a World Heritage Site: The Case of Suwon Hwaseong Fortress (in South Korea).* doi:10.3390/su11010132

Song, M., & Montoya-Weiss, M. M. (2001). The effect of perceived technological uncertainty on Japanese new product development. *Academy of Management Journal, 44*(1), 61–80.

Spencer-Oatey, H. (2015). *What is Culture? A Compilation of Quotations.* Retrieved from http://www.warwick.ac.uk/globalpadintercultural

Spender, J.-C. (1996). Organizational knowledge, learning and memory: Three concepts in search of a theory. *Journal of Organizational Change Management, 9*(1), 63–78. doi:10.1108/09534819610156813

Spillan, J., & Parnell, J. (2006). Marketing resources and firm performance among SMEs. *European Management Journal, 24*(2–3), 236–245. doi:10.1016/j.emj.2006.03.013

Spross, H. (2018). *Does EU biofuel deal compromise the environment for trade with Southeast Asia?* Deutsche Welle. Retrieved September 23, 2021, from, https://p.dw.com/p/305XJ

Spyropoulou, S., Skarmeas, D., & Katsikeas, C. S. (2011). An examination of branding advantage in export ventures. *European Journal of Marketing, 45*(6), 910–935. doi:10.1108/03090561111119967

Srholec, M. (2007). High-tech exports from developing countries: A symptom of technology spurts or statistical illusion? *Review of World Economics, 143*(2), 227–255. doi:10.100710290-007-0106-z

Srivastava, R. K., Shervani, T. A., & Fahey, L. (1998). Market-based assets and shareholder value: A framework for analysis. *Journal of Marketing, 62*(1), 2–18. doi:10.1177/002224299806200102

Srivastava, V., & Pandey, P. M. (2012). Effect of process parameters on the performance of EDM process with ultrasonic assisted cryogenically cooled electrode. *Journal of Manufacturing Processes, 14*(3), 393–402. doi:10.1016/j.jmapro.2012.05.001

Statista. (2016). Retrieved August 30, 2021, from https://www.statista.com/statistics/898274/south-korea-inbound-tourists-from-malaysia/

Statista. (2019). Retrieved August 30, 2021, from https://www.statista.com/statistics/1017835/south-korea-korean-drama-popularity-malaysia/

Sterner, T. (1990). Ownership, technology, and efficiency: An empirical study of cooperatives, multinationals, and domestic enterprises in the Mexican cement industry. *Journal of Comparative Economics, 14*(2), 286–300. doi:10.1016/0147-5967(90)90073-I

Stiglitz, J. E. (2021). The proper role of government in the market economy: The case of the post-COVID recovery. *Journal of Government and Economics, 1*, 100004. doi:10.1016/j.jge.2021.100004

Stinchcombe, A. L. (1965). Social structure and organizations. In J. G. March (Ed.), *Handbook of organizations.* Rand McNally.

Stocker, F., Abib, G., Jhunior, R. D. O. S., & Irigaray, H. A. R. (2021). Brazilian craft breweries and internationalization in the born global perspective. *Revista de Gestão, 28*(2), 163–178. doi:10.1108/REGE-01-2021-0014

Stone, M. (1974). Cross-validatory choice and assessment of statistical predictions. *Journal of the Royal Statistical Society. Series B. Methodological, 36*(2), 111–147. doi:10.1111/j.2517-6161.1974.tb00994.x

Straub, D., Boudreau, M.-C., & Gefen, D. (2004). Validation guidelines for IS positivist research. *Communications of the Association for Information Systems, 13*(1), 1–63.

Stray, S., Bridgewater, S., & Murray, G. (2001). The internationalisation process of small, technology-based firms: Market selection, mode choice and degree of internationalisation. *Journal of Global Marketing*, *15*(1), 7–29. doi:10.1300/J042v15n01_02

Stylidis, K., Hoffenson, S., Rossi, M., Wickman, C., Soderman, M., & Soderberg, R. (2020). Transforming brand core values into perceived quality: A Volvo case study. *International Journal of Product Development*, *24*(1), 43–67. doi:10.1504/IJPD.2020.106448

Su, D. N., Johnson, L. W., & O'Mahony, B. (2020). Analysis of push and pull factors in food travel motivation. *Current Issues in Tourism*, *23*(5), 572–586.

Suleiman, M. N., & Karim, M. A. (2015). Cycle of bad governance and corruption: The rise of Boko Haram in Nigeria. *SAGE Open*, *5*(1), 1–11. doi:10.1177/2158244015576053

Sullivan, D. (1994). Measuring the degree of internationalization of a firm. *Journal of International Business Studies*, *25*(2), 325–342. doi:10.1057/palgrave.jibs.8490203

Sustainable Development. (n.d.). In *Baidu Encyclopaedia online*. https://baike.baidu.com/item/sustainabledevelopment/360491?fr=aladdin

Suutari, V., & Brewster, C. (2000). Making their own way: International experience through self-initiated foreign assignments. *Journal of World Business*, *35*(4), 417–436. doi:10.1016/S1090-9516(00)00046-8

Suutari, V., Brewster, C., Mäkelä, L., Dickmann, M., & Tornikoski, C. (2018). The effect of international work experience on the career success of expatriates: A comparison of assigned and self-initiated expatriates. *Human Resource Management*, *57*(1), 37–54. doi:10.1002/hrm.21827

Swim, J. K., Stern, P. C., Doherty, T. J., Clayton, S., Reser, J. P., Weber, E. U., Gifford, R., & Howard, G. S. (2011). Psychology's contributions to understanding and addressing global climate change. *The American Psychologist*, *66*(4), 241–250. doi:10.1037/a0023220 PMID:21553950

Szulanski, G., Ringov, D., & Jensen, R. J. (2016). Overcoming stickiness: How the timing of knowledge transfer methods affects transfer difficulty. *Organization Science*, *27*(2), 304–322. doi:10.1287/orsc.2016.1049

Tabachnick, B. G., & Fidell, L. S. (2007). Using Multivariate Statistics. In PsycCRITIQUES (5th ed.). Boston, MA: Pearson Education Inc. doi:10.1037/022267

Tadawul, A. S. R. (2020). Annual Report. Academic Press.

Tala, A., Ahmad, A., & Amjad, A. (2016). Do behavioral finance factors influence stock investment decisions of individual investors? Evidence from Saudi stock market. *American International Journal of Contemporary Research*, *6*(3), 234–250.

Tan, T. (2019). Stop palm oil discrimination. *The Star*. Retrieved September 25, 2021, from https://www.thest ar.com.my/news/nation/2019/03/21/stop-palm-oil-discrimination/

Tan, A. K.-J. (2005). *Vessel-source marine pollution: The law and politics of international regulation* (Vol. 45). Cambridge University Press. doi:10.1017/CBO9780511494628

TANAP. (2021). *Tanap Nedir?* Retrieved May 20, 2021, from https://www.tanap.com/tanap-projesi/tanap-nedir/

Tandon, U., Kiran, R., & Sah, A. (2017). Analyzing customer satisfaction: Users perspective towards online shopping. *Nankai Business Review International*, *8*(3), 266–288. doi:10.1108/NBRI-04-2016-0012

Tang, F. Y. (2018). *Countries along the "One Belt And One Road" should increase the use of renewable energy*. China Economic Times.

Tan, W.-K. (2017). Repeat visitation: A study from the perspective of leisure constraint, tourist experience, destination images, and experiential familiarity. *Journal of Destination Marketing & Management*, *6*(3), 233–242. doi:10.1016/j.jdmm.2016.04.003

TCDD. (2021). *Lojistik Merkezler*. Retrieved May 28, 2021, from https://www.tcdd.gov.tr/harita/lojistik-merkezleri

Teh, P. Y. (2016). *The role of Korean drama promoting tourism among Malaysians* (PhD thesis). University of Malaya.

Teh, P. Y., & Goh, H. C. (2018). Does Korean drama have a real influence? An analysis of Malaysia outbound tourists to South Korea. *Tourism, Culture & Communication*, *16*, 147–160.

Tehseen, S., Ahmed, F. U., Qureshi, Z. H., Uddin, M. J., & Ramayah, T. (2019). Entrepreneurial competencies and SMEs' growth: The mediating role of network competence. *Asia-Pacific Journal of Business Administration*, *11*(1), 2–29. doi:10.1108/APJBA-05-2018-0084

Tenenhaus, M., Vinzi, V. E., Chatelin, Y.-M., & Lauro, C. (2005). PLS path modeling. *Computational Statistics & Data Analysis*, *48*(1), 159–205. doi:10.1016/j.csda.2004.03.005

Teo, P., & Leong, S. (2006). A postcolonial analysis of backpacking. *Annals of Tourism Research*, *33*(1), 109–131.

Terwase, I. T., Abdul-Talib, A. N., Zengeni, K. T., & Terwase, J. M. (2015). The psychological trauma on Boko Haram victims in Nigeria: Conflict resolution perspective. *Mediterranean Journal of Social Sciences*, *6*(S4), 519-519.

Terwase, I. T., Abdul-Talib, A. N., Siben, N. E., Puldu, G. S., & Adesina, O. S. (2017). The AU/Nepad peace and security governance in Africa. *Otoritas: Jurnal Ilmu Pemerintahan*, *7*(2), 93–99. doi:10.26618/ojip.v7i2.825

Terwase, I. T., Abdul-Talib, A. N., & Zengeni, K. T. (2014). Nigeria, Africa's largest economy: International business perspective. *International Journal of Management Sciences*, *3*(7), 534–543.

Terwase, I. T., Abdul-Talib, A. N., & Zengeni, K. T. (2015). The role of ECOWAS on economic governance, peace and security perspectives in West Africa. *Mediterranean Journal of Social Sciences*, *6*(3), 257. doi:10.5901/mjss.2015.v6n3p257

Terwase, I. T., Adesina, O. S., Puldu, G. S., & Abdul-Talib, A. N. (2018). The role of ecowas on peace and conflict resolution in Nigeria and Gambia. *IRA-. International Journal of Management and Social Sciences*, *12*(3), 55–61.

Terwase, J. M., Terwase, I. T., Puldu, G. S., & Abdul Talib, A. N. (2018). Unemployment, psychological trauma, militancy and Boko Haram conflict in Nigeria. IRA. *International Journal of Education and Multidisciplinary Studies*, *13*(3), 27–40. doi:10.21013/jems.v13.n3.p1

Tharenou, P. (2003). The initial development of receptivity to working abroad: Self-initiated international work opportunities in young graduate employees. *Journal of Occupational and Organizational Psychology*, *76*(4), 489–515. doi:10.1348/096317903322591604

Tharenou, P., & Caulfield, N. (2010). Will i stay or will i go? Explaining repatriation by self-initiated expatriates. *Academy of Management Journal*, *53*(5), 1009–1028. doi:10.5465/amj.2010.54533183

The Grand National Assembly of Turkey (TBMM). (2015, November). The Draft Law (1/673) and the Foreign Affairs Commission Report on the Approval of the Memorandum of Understanding between the Government of the Republic of Turkey and the Government of the People's Republic of China on the Harmonization of the Silk Road Economic Belt, the 21st Century Silk Road at Sea and the Middle Corridor Initiative.

The OECD predicts the global economic losses caused by the new crown epidemic by the end of 2021 . (2020, September 17). Kommersant.

Thi Thuc Anh, P. (2017). Toward A Comprehensive Model of International Joint Venture Learning. *Journal of Economic Development, 19*(1), 51.

Thirugnana, S., Jaafar, A. B., Yasunaga, T., Nakaoka, T., Ikegami, Y., & Su, S. (2021). Estimation of ocean thermal energy conversion resources in the east of Malaysia. *Journal of Marine Science and Engineering, 9*, 22. doi:10.3390/jmse9010022

Thornhill, S., & Amit, R. (2003). Learning about failure: Bankruptcy, firm age, and the resource based view. *Organization Science, 14*(5), 497–509. doi:10.1287/orsc.14.5.497.16761

Thorn, K. (2009). The relative importance of motives for international self-initiated mobility. *Career Development International, 14*(5), 441–464. doi:10.1108/13620430910989843

Thurstone, L. L. (1947). *Multiple-factor analysis: A development and expansion of The Vectors of Mind.* University of Chicago Press.

Thuy Pham, N., & Swierczek, F. W. (2006). Facilitators of organizational learning in design. *The Learning Organization, 13*(2), 186–201. doi:10.1108/09696470610645502

Toma, P. (2020). Size and productivity: A conditional approach for Italian pharmaceutical sector. *Journal of Productivity Analysis, 54*(1), 1–12. doi:10.100711123-020-00580-y

Torbiörn, I. (1994). Operative and strategic use of expatriates in new organizations and market structures. *International Studies of Management & Organization, 24*(3), 5–17. doi:10.1080/00208825.1994.11656634

Torsekar, M. P., & VerWey, J. (2019). East Asia-Pacific's participation in the global value chain for electronic products. *Journal of International Commerce Economics, 1*, 1–21.

Tourists flock to Korean drama 'Goblin" filming sites. (2017, January 12). Retrieved from The Jakarta Post: https://www.thejakartapost.com/travel/2017/01/12/tourists-flock-to-korean-drama-goblin-filming-sites

Trembath, J. L. (2016). The professional lives of expatriate academics: Construct clarity and implications for expatriate management in higher education. *Journal of Global Mobility, 4*(2), 112–130. doi:10.1108/JGM-04-2015-0012

TRIPS. Agreement on Trade-Related Aspects of Intellectual Property Rights, Apr. 15, 1994, Marrakesh Agreement Establishing the World Trade Organization, Annex 1C, 1869 U.N.T.S. 299, 33 I.L.M. 1197 (1994)

Trolan, J. (2017). A look into Korean popular culture and its tourism benefits. *International Journal of Educational Policy Research and Review, 4*(9), 203–209. doi:10.15739/ijeprr.17.022

Truong, C. (2009). Value investing using price earnings ratio in New Zealand. *University of Auckland Business Review, 12*(1), 1–7.

Tsang, E. W., Nguyen, D. T., & Erramilli, M. K. (2004). Knowledge acquisition and performance of international joint ventures in the transition economy of Vietnam. *Journal of International Marketing, 12*(2), 82–103. doi:10.1509/jimk.12.2.82.32901

Tsougkou, E., Cadogan, J. W., Hodgkinson, I. R., Oliveira, J. S., Abdul-Talib, A. N., Story, V. M., & Lioliou, E. (2019). *Achieving export competitive advantage: can global orientation and export product adaptation be reconciled.* In *2019 AMA Global Marketing SIG Conference*, Buenos Aires, Argentina.

Tybout, A. M., & Sternthal, B. (2012). Developing a compelling brand positioning. *Kellogg on Marketing*, 73-91.

UIS. (2020). *Recalculating Proficiency in Schools: COVID-19 Related Learning Losses and Dropping Out.* Sustainable Development Goals. Retrieved 6 May, 2021, from https://sdg.uis.unesco.org/author/uisblog/

Ukhuegbe, S., & Fenemigho, A. I. (2021). Determining the termination of a non-international armed conflict: an analysis of the Boko Haram insurgency in northern Nigeria. In *Nigerian Yearbook of International Law 2018/2019* (pp. 299–327). Springer. doi:10.1007/978-3-030-69594-1_14

Uma, K. E., Obidike, P. C., Chukwu, C. O., Kanu, C., Ogbuagu, R. A., Osunkwo, F. O., & Ndubuisi, P. (2019). Revamping the Nigerian manufacturing sub-sector as a panacea for economic progress: Lessons from South Korea. *Mediterranean Journal of Social Sciences, 10*(4), 111–123. doi:10.2478/mjss-2019-0057

UNHCR. (2021). *Nigeria Emergency.* Retrieved from https://www.unhcr.org/afr/nigeria-emergency.html

United Capital. (2020). *Nigeria outlook 2020: A different playing field.* Retrieved 3 August, 2021, from https://www.unitedcapitalplcgroup.com/wpcontent/uploads/2020/01/Nigeria-Outlook-2020_A-different-playing-field-3.pdf

Urbany, J. E., Dickson, P. R., & Wilkie, W. L. (1989). Buyer uncertainty and information search. *The Journal of Consumer Research, 16*(2), 208–215. doi:10.1086/209209

Urgal, B., Quintás, M. A., & Arévalo-Tomé, R. (2013). Knowledge resources and innovation performance: The mediation of innovation capability moderated by management commitment. *Technology Analysis and Strategic Management, 25*(5), 543–565. doi:10.1080/09537325.2013.785514

Uriely, N. (2009). Deconstructing tourist typologies: The case of backpacking. *International Journal of Culture, Tourism and Hospitality Research, 3*(4), 306–312. doi:10.1108/17506180910994523

Uriely, N., Yonay, Y., & Simchai, D. (2002). Backpacking experiences: A type and form analysis. *Annals of Tourism Research, 29*(2), 520–538.

Ursachi, G., Horodnic, I. A., & Zait, A. (2015). How reliable are measurement scales? External factors with indirect influence on reliability estimators. *Procedia Economics and Finance, 20*, 679–686. doi:10.1016/S2212-5671(15)00123-9

Uwaifo, V. O. (2009). Technical Education and its Challenges in Nigeria in the 21st Century. *International NGO Journal, 5*(2), 40–44.

Uzodike, U. O., & Maiangwa, B. (2012). Boko Haram terrorism in Nigeria: Causal factors and central problematic. *African Renaissance, 9*(1), 91–118.

Vale looks forward to meeting you at the 4th CIIE. (2021, October 11). *Vale.*

Vale. (2020, February 11). In the fourth quarter, iron ore production fell 22.4% year-on-year, and sales fell 3.2% year-on-year. *U.S. Stock News.*

Vallerand, R. J. (2000). Deci and Ryan's self-determination theory: A view from the hierarchical model of intrinsic and extrinsic motivation. *Psychological Inquiry, 11*(4), 312–318.

Van Den Broeck, A., Vansteenkiste, M., De Witte, H., & Lens, W. (2008). Explaining the relationships between job characteristics, burnout, and engagement: The role of basic psychological need satisfaction. *Work and Stress, 22*(3), 277–294. doi:10.1080/02678370802393672

Van Ha, Holmes, & Hassan. (2019). Does foreign investment benefit the exporting activities of Vietnamese firms? *The World Economy.* doi:10.1111/twec.12912

Vansteenkiste, M., Neyrinck, B., Niemiec, C. P., Soenens, B., De Witte, H., & Van Den Broeck, A. (2007). On the relations among work value orientations, psychological need satisfaction and job outcomes: A self-determination theory approach. *Journal of Occupational and Organizational Psychology, 80*(2), 251–277. doi:10.1348/096317906X111024

Varkkey, H. (2013). Patronage politics, plantation fires and transboundary haze. *Environmental Hazards, 12*(3-4), 200–217. doi:10.1080/17477891.2012.759524

Varkkey, H., Tyson, A., & Choiruzzad, S. A. B. (2018). Palm oil intensification and expansion in Indonesia and Malaysia: Environmental and socio-political factors influencing policy. *Forest Policy and Economics, 92*, 148–159. doi:10.1016/j.forpol.2018.05.002

Verma, S. (2020). A study on the impact of fluctuation in exchange rate (inr to usd) and mean monthly temperature on foreign tourist arrivals in india. *Studies in Indian Place Names*, (50), 4605–4612.

Vernon, R. (1966). International investment and international trade in the product cycle. *The Quarterly Journal of Economics, 80*(2), 190–207. doi:10.2307/1880689

Vinh, V. X. (2019). Foreign Ownership and Firm Performance-Evidence in Vietnam. *Journal of Economic Development*, 85–104.

Viotti, P. R., & Kauppi, M. V. (2014). *Uluslararası ilişkiler ve dünya siyaseti* [International relations and world politics]. Nobel.

Voyer, M., Schofield, C., Azmi, K., Warner, R., McIlgorm, A., & Quirk, G. (2018). Maritime security and the blue economy: Intersections and interdependencies in the Indian Ocean. *Journal of the Indian Ocean Region, 14*(1), 28–48. doi:10.1080/19480881.2018.1418155

Vu, H. T., & Lee, T.-T. (2013). Soap operas as a matchmaker: A cultivation analysis of the effects of South Korean TV dramas on Vietnamese women's marital intentions. *Journalism & Mass Communication Quarterly, 90*(2), 308–330. doi:10.1177/1077699013482912

Vu, J. D. (1988). An empirical analysis of Benjamin Graham's net current asset value. *Financial Review, 23*(2), 215–225. doi:10.1111/j.1540-6288.1988.tb00787.x

Wagner, J. (2007). Exports and productivity: A survey of the evidence from firm-level data. *The World Economy, 30*(1), 60-82. DOI: .00872.x doi:10.1111/j.1467-9701.2007

Waheed, A., Khan, S. Z., Arshad, S., Rafique, K., & Laeeq, M. (2018). How Market Orientation Helps to Gain Competitive Advantages in New Product Offering. *IJAMEE, 3*(3), 1-7.

Waldek, L., & Jayasekara, S. (2011). Boko Haram: The evolution of Islamist extremism in Nigeria. *Journal of Policing. Intelligence and Counter Terrorism, 6*(2), 168–178. doi:10.1080/18335330.2011.605217

Wang, H. L. (2019). Analysis on the relationship between international trade and the ecological environment under the background of sustainable development. *Science Technology and Industry, 8*.

Wang, J. (2011). Vale accounts for 80% of Brazil's $20 billion worth of iron ore exports. *China Finance and Economics.* http://news.xinhua08.com/

Wang, C. L., & Ahmed, P. K. (2004). The development and validation of the organisational innovativeness construct using confirmatory factor analysis. *European Journal of Innovation Management, 7*(4), 303–313. doi:10.1108/14601060410565056

Wang, C. L., Sarkar, A., & Sarkar, J. G. (2018). Building the holy brand: Towards a theoretical model of brand religiosity. *International Journal of Consumer Studies, 42*(6), 736–743. doi:10.1111/ijcs.12430

Wang, M. L., Qiub, Q., & Choic, C. H. (2019). How will the Belt and Road initiative advance China's exports? *Asia Pacific Business Review, 25*(1), 81–89. https://doi.org/10.1080/13602381.2018.1525855

Wang, X. (2013). Forming mechanisms and structures of a knowledge transfer network: Theoretical and simulation research. *Journal of Knowledge Management, 17*(2), 278–289. doi:10.1108/13673271311315213

Wang, Y. (2016). What are the biggest obstacles to growth of SMEs in developing countries? An empirical evidence from an enterprise survey. *Borsa Istanbul Review, 16*(3), 167–176. doi:10.1016/j.bir.2016.06.001

Wantono, A., & McKercher, B. (2020). Backpacking and risk perception: The case of solo Asian women. *Tourism Recreation Research, 45*(1), 19–29. doi:10.1080/02508281.2019.1636180

Watson, D., Clark, L. A., & Tellegen, A. (1988). Development and validation of brief measures of positive and negative affect: The PANAS scales. *Journal of Personality and Social Psychology, 54*(6), 1063.

Weerawardena, J., & O'Cass, A. (2004). Exploring the characteristics of the market-driven firms and antecedents to sustained competitive advantage. *Industrial Marketing Management, 33*(5), 419–428. doi:10.1016/j.indmarman.2003.07.002

Wei, Y., Liu, H., & Park, K.-S. (2021). Examining the structural relationships among heritage proximity, perceived impacts, attitude and residents' support in intangible cultural heritage tourism. *Sustainability, 13*(15), 8358. doi:10.3390u13158358

What's On. (2021, May 30). *Dubai World Trade Center.* https://www.dwtc.com/en/events

White, B., Borras, S. M. Jr, Hall, R., Scoones, I., & Wolford, W. (2012). The new enclosures: Critical perspectives on corporate land deals. *The Journal of Peasant Studies, 39*(3-4), 619–647. doi:10.1080/03066150.2012.691879

WHO. (2020). *WHO Director-General's opening remarks at the media briefing on COVID-19-11 March 2020.* Retrieved 26 April, 2021, from https://www.who.int/director-general/speeches/detail/who-director-general-s-opening-remarks-at-the-media-briefing-on-covid-19---11-march-2020

WHO. (2021). *COVID-19 Vaccines.* Retrieved 26 April, 2021, from https://www.who.int/emergencies/diseases/novel-coronavirus-2019/covid-19-vaccines

Wiklund, J. (1999). The sustainability of the entrepreneurial orientation–performance relationship. *Entrepreneurship Theory and Practice, 24*(1), 37–48. doi:10.1177/104225879902400103

Wiklund, J., Baker, T., & Shepherd, D. A. (2010). The age-effect of financial indicators as buffers against the liability of newness. *Journal of Business Venturing, 25*(4), 423–437. doi:10.1016/j.jbusvent.2008.10.011

Williams, C. (2007). Transfer in context: Replication and adaptation in knowledge transfer relationships. *Strategic Management Journal, 28*(9), 867–889. doi:10.1002mj.614

Winter, T., Teo, P., & Chang, T. C. (2009). Asian tourism and the retreat of anglo-western centrism in tourism theory. *Current Issues in Tourism, 12*(1), 21–31.

Wong, R., & Nanoo, A. (2020). Palm Oil: A Case for Conciliation over Confrontation. *Asia Global Online Journal.* https://www.asiaglobalonline.hku.hk/palm-oil-case-conciliation-over-confrontation

Wooldridge, J. M. (2015). *Introductory econometrics: A modern approach.* Cengage Learning.

World Bank. (2019). *Belt & Road Economics: Opportunities and Risks of Transport Corridors.* World Bank.

World Benchmarking Alliance. (2020). *The impact of multinationals in developing countries: A framework of Benchmarking.* worldbenchmarkingalliance.org

World Federation Exchanges. (2014). *Monthly Report February 2014.* https://www.world-exchanges.org/statistics/monthly-reports

World Trade Organization. (2021a). *European Union and certain Member states – certain measures concerning palm oil and oil palm crop-based biofuels – Request for consultations by Malaysia* (G/L/1384; G/SCM/D131/1; G/TBT/D/54; WT/DS600/1). https://docs.wto.org/dol2fe/Pages/FE_Search/FE_S_S006.aspx?Query=(%20@Symbol=%20(wt/ds600/1%20))&Language=ENGLISH&Context=FomerScriptedSearch&languageUIChanged=true#

World Trade Organization. (2021b). *Understanding the WTO Basics, Principles of the trading system.* https://www.wto.org/english/thewto_e/whatis_e/tif_e/fact2_e.htm

World Wildlife Fund. (n.d.). *8 things to know about palm oil.* Retrieved September 23, 2021, from https://www.wwf.org.uk/updates/8-things-know-about-palm-oil

Worthington, A., & Higgs, H. (2005). *Weak-form Market Efficiency in Asian Emerging and Developed Equity Markets: Comparative Tests of Random Walk Behavior.* University of Wollongong, School of Accounting and Finance Working Paper Series, No. 05/03.

Wuisan, L., & van Leeuwen, J., van Koppen, C. S. A., Leeuwen, J. van, & Koppen, C. van. (2012). Greening international shipping through private governance: A case study of the Clean Shipping Project. *Marine Policy*, *36*, 165–173. doi:10.1016/j.marpol.2011.04.009

Wu, Y., Chen, C., & Hu, C. (2021). The impacts of trade intensity with China on carbon emissions in belt and road countries. *Journal of the Asia Pacific Economy*, 1–20. doi:10.1080/13547860.2021.1924601

Xiao, Y., & Arnold, G. C. (2008). Testing Benjamin Graham's net current asset value strategy in London. *Journal of Investing*, *17*(4), 11–19. doi:10.3905/JOI.2008.17.4.011

Xie, F., & Zhang, G. (2020). Brazil's countermeasures and enlightenment to deal with the impact of the epidemic and stabilize the economic and financial system. *Contemporary Financial Research, 4*, 54-61.

Xie, J., & Tveterås, S. (2020). Economic decline and the birth of a tourist nation. *Scandinavian Journal of Hospitality and Tourism*, *20*(2), 1–19. doi:10.1080/15022250.2020.1719882

Xing, Y. (2014). China's high-tech exports: The myth and reality. *Asian Economic Papers*, *13*(1), 109–123. doi:10.1162/ASEP_a_00256

Xinhua. (2016). *Chronology of China's Belt and Road Initiative, last modified 24 June.* Retrieved April 21, 2021, from http://news.xinhuanet.com/english/2016-06/24/c_135464233.htm

Xu, F. B. (2020, April 28). Expert: How does the world epidemic affect China's economy. *China International Import Expo.*

Yakob, N. (2001). *Monetary Uncertainty and Stock Prices: The Case of Malaysia. Department of Finance*. Universiti Kebangsaan Malaysia.

Yakubu, M. J., & Falode, A. J. (2021). Analyzing Nigerian army-Boko Haram's conflict through the prisms of Marx's theory of economic determinism. *Društvene i humanističke studije*, *6*(3), 299-320.

Yalϭin, K. C. (2010). Market rationality: Efficient market hypothesis versus market anomalies. *European Journal of Economic and Political Studies*, *2*(1), 23–38.

Yang, E. C. L., Khoo-Lattimore, C., & Arcodia, C. (2018). Power and empowerment: How Asian solo female travellers perceive and negotiate risks. *Tourism Management*, *68*, 32–45.

Yang, E. C. L., Yang, M. J. H., & Khoo-Lattimore, C. (2019). The meanings of solo travel for Asian women. *Tourism Review*, *74*(5), 1047–1057. doi:10.1108/TR-10-2018-0150

Yang, J. (2008). General or vocational? The tough choice in the Chinese education policy. *International Journal of Educational Development, 18*(4), 289–304. doi:10.1016/S0738-0593(98)00026-1

Yasar, M., & Paul, C. J. M. (2007). International linkages and productivity at the plant level: Foreign direct investment, exports, imports and licensing. *Journal of International Economics, 71*(1), 373–388. doi:10.1016/j.jinteco.2006.03.004

Yatim, P. (2017). CSR in a controversial industry: The case of Malaysian oil palm companies. *International Journal of Sustainable Society, 9*(4), 327–345. doi:10.1504/IJSSOC.2017.090521

Yazdani, M., Chatterjee, P., Pamucar, D., & Chakraborty, S. (2020). Development of an integrated decision making model for location selection of logistics centers in the Spanish autonomous communities. *Expert Systems with Applications, 148*(113208), 1–21.

Yoo, B., Donthu, N., & Lee, S. (2000). An examination of selected marketing mix elements and brand equity. *Journal of the Academy of Marketing Science, 28*(2), 195–211. doi:10.1177/0092070300282002

Young Lives. (2020a). *Interrupted Education in Ethiopia: Support for Students During COVID-19 School Closures.* Young Lives. Retrieved 6 May, 2021, from https://www.younglives.org.uk/content/interrupted-education-ethiopia-support-students-during-covid-19-school-closures

Yuan, Y. (2020, June 5). *The epidemic has profoundly affected the prospects of global economic development.* China Economic Net.

Yusuf, B. N. M., Zakaria, N., & Abdul-Talib, A. N. (2021). Using social network tools to facilitate cultural adjustment of self-initiated Malaysian female expatriate nurses in Saudi Arabia. *Journal of Infection and Public Health, 14*(3), 380–384. doi:10.1016/j.jiph.2020.11.008 PMID:33621801

Yusuf, H. O. (2013). Harvest of violence: The neglect of basic rights and the Boko Haram insurgency in Nigeria. *Critical Studies on Terrorism, 6*(3), 371–391. doi:10.1080/17539153.2013.835528

Zacher, M. W., & Sutton, B. A. (1996). *Governing global networks: International regimes for transportation and communications.* Cambridge University Press.

Zaheer, S. (1995). Overcoming the liability of foreignness. *Academy of Management Journal, 38*, 341–363.

Zaheer, S., & Mosakowski, E. (1997). The dynamics of the liability of foreignness: A global study of survival in financial services. *Strategic Management Journal, 18*(6), 439–446. doi:10.1002/(SICI)1097-0266(199706)18:6<439::AID-SMJ884>3.0.CO;2-Y

Zahra, A. S., Sapienza, H. J., & Davidsson, P. (2006). Entreprenuership and Dynamic Capabilities: A review model and research agenda. *Journal of Management Studies, 43*(4), 917–955. doi:10.1111/j.1467-6486.2006.00616.x

Zahra, S. A. (2005). A theory of international new ventures: A decade of research. *Journal of International Business Studies, 36*(1), 20–28. doi:10.1057/palgrave.jibs.8400118

Zahra, S. A., & Garvis, D. (2000). International corporate entrepreneurship and company performance: The moderating effect of international environmental hostility. *Journal of Business Venturing, 10*, 43–58. doi:10.1016/0883-9026(94)00004-E

Zahra, S. A., & Hayton, J. C. (2008). The effect of international venturing on firm performance: The moderating influence of absorptive capacity. *Journal of Business Venturing, 23*(2), 195–220. doi:10.1016/j.jbusvent.2007.01.001

Zahra, S. A., Ireland, R. D., & Hitt, M. A. (2000). International expansion by new venture firms: International diversity, mode of market entry, technological learning and performance. *Academy of Management Journal, 43*(5), 925–950.

Zakaria, F., Liu, M., Caryl, C., Miller, K. L., Punoose, R., & Barry, J. (2005). Does the future belong to China. *Newsweek.*

Zakaria, N., Abdul-Talib, A. N., & Amelinckx, A. (2020). Advancing Cultural Frontiers to Champion Global Business in Emerging Markets. *Transcending Cultural Frontiers*, 1–10.

Zakaria, N., & Abdul-Talib, A. N. (2010). Applying Islamic market-oriented cultural model to sensitize strategies towards global customers, competitors, and environment. *Journal of Islamic Marketing*, *1*(1), 51–62. doi:10.1108/17590831011026222

Zakaria, N., Abdul-Talib, A. N., & Amelinckx, A. (2020). Advancing cultural frontiers to champion global business in emerging markets. In *Transcending Cultural Frontiers* (pp. 1–10). Springer. doi:10.1007/978-981-15-4454-5_1

Zakaria, N., Abdul-Talib, A. N., & Amelinckx, A. (Eds.). (2020). *Transcending Cultural Frontiers: Practices, Challenges, and Strategy for International Business*. Springer. doi:10.1007/978-981-15-4454-5

Zakaria, N., Abdul-Talib, A. N., & Othman, N. (Eds.). (2016). *Handbook of research on impacts of international business and political affairs on the global economy. IGI Global.*

Zakaria, N., Abdul-Talib, A. N., & Othman, N. (Eds.). (2016). *Handbook of research on impacts of international business and political affairs on the global economy*. IGI Global. doi:10.4018/978-1-4666-9806-2

Zakaria, N., Wan-Ismail, W.-N. A., & Abdul-Talib, A. N. (2021). Seriously, Conspicuous Consumption? The Impact of Culture, Materialism and Religiosity on Malaysian Generation Y Consumers' Purchasing of Foreign Brands. *Asia Pacific Journal of Marketing and Logistics*, *33*(2), 526–560. doi:10.1108/APJML-07-2018-0283

Zamani, S. N. M., & Abdul-Talib, A. N. (2016). Strategic orientations and new product success: The mediating impact of innovation speed. International Information Institute (Tokyo), 19(7B), 2785–2790.

Zamani, M. N. S., Ashari, H., & Abdul-Talib, A. N. (2017). The strategic fit of multiple strategic orientations and new product development performance in Malaysian manufacturing firms. *Journal for Studies in Management and Planning*, *3*(1), 87–101.

Zaremba, A., & Czapkiewicz, A. (2017). Digesting anomalies in emerging European markets: A comparison of factor pricing models. *Emerging Markets Review*, *31*(3), 1–15. doi:10.1016/j.ememar.2016.12.002

Zaremba, A., Maydybura, A., Czapkiewicz, A., & Arnaut, M. (2019). Explaining equity anomalies in frontier markets: A horserace of factor pricing models. *Emerging Markets Review*, *35*(3), 211–230.

Zhang, Z., Zhao, J., & Liu, L. (2018). Analysis of iron ore trade between China and Brazil, China Economic and Trade Guide I. *Foreign Investment Economic and Trade*, 26.

Zhang, W., Alon, I., & Lattemann, C. (2018). *China's Belt and Road Initiative: Changing the Rules of Globalization*. Palgrave.

Zhao, Y. (2020, December 8). *Brazilian Expert: Adhering to the people-centered approach is the key to China's success in fighting the epidemic.* International Online Report.

Zheng, S. Y. (2019). *Research on Innovative Human Resource Management Model—Taking Brazilian companies as an example*. Academic Press.

Zhonghong National Research Institute. (2020, May 8). *Affected by the epidemic How are the preparations for the 3rd China International Import Expo*. Zhonghong State Research Institute of Information Technology. http://www.china-cer.com.cn/guwen/202005185134.html

Zhou, Z. (2020). Prospects of Sino-Brazilian economic and trade cooperation in post-epidemic era. *Maritime China, 1*(9).

Zhou, N., & Guillén, M. F. (2015). From home country to home base: A dynamic approach to the liability of foreignness. *Strategic Management Journal*, *36*(6), 907–917. doi:10.1002mj.2242

Zhu, D. J. (2020). Many Latin American countries are actively promoting economic recovery. *City Financial Newspaper.* https://baijiahao.baidu.com/s?id=1677520127105244128&wfr=spider&for=pc

Zizek, S. (2020). *PANDEMIC!: Covid-19 Shakes the World.* John Wiley & Sons. doi:10.2307/j.ctv16t6n4q

About the Contributors

Asmat-Nizam Abdul-Talib teaches international business and marketing at the Universiti Utara Malaysia. He received his PhD in International Marketing from Aston Business School, Aston University, UK, his MBA in International Business from Cardiff University, UK, and a Bachelors Degree in Economics from Concordia University, Canada. At current, his academic research has received financial support or support in kind from various institutions. His research interests lie primarily in international marketing and strategic marketing, especially in export market intelligence, and the use of export market intelligence in the firm's export decision process.

Norhayati Zakaria has a Ph.D. in Information Science and Technology and MPhil. of Information Transfer, both at Syracuse University and MSc. Management at Rensselaer Polytechnic Institute, Troy, NY. As an Associate Professor, she is currently attached at Faculty of Business and Management at University of Wollongong in Dubai, United Arab of Emirates. Her educational training bridges interdisciplinary fields of cross-cultural management, international human resource management, and information science. With her educational training abroad and experiences as an expatriate, she is culturally competent to the myriad culturally-attuned behaviors of global workforces. With her research program looking at an innovative work structure called global virtual teams and a new form of expatriates such as self-initiated expatriates, she explores key questions of 'how do we manage the impact of culture on global talents face-to-face and virtually and how do we inculcate cultural intelligence among them?' by using qualitative research methods. She is also engaged in research to explore a new way business is conducted via the digital platform and how such business model shapes the culture of the consumerism and entice them to buy goods and services in different forms for different reasons.

Samshul-Amry Abdul-Latif is currently attached with the Department of Tourism, Kulliyyah of Languages and Management, International Islamic University Malaysia (IIUM) in Pagoh campus. He graduated from the University of Otago, New Zealand in 1999 and started his career by joining a private limited company in Kuala Lumpur right after graduation, involving sales and marketing of consumer goods. He moved on to another private company with similar portfolio but was later absorbed into agriculture and palm oil plantation consultation department. He was then promoted to managerial level after three years. After that, he served in a Government-Linked Agency, Perbadanan Nasional Berhad (PERNAS) under the Special Programmes Department which he handled the operations of Women and Graduates Development Franchise Programme. After two years, he was appointed as a vice president of a private limited company handling investments of oil and gas facility (Labuan), silica (Yemen) and coal (Mozambique). After a short stint, he moved on join a family-owned agriculture project in Kedah involving cash crops and fruits. While working, he pursued his Master's degree and graduated in 2012. He pursued his doctorate in 2012 and was appointed as a research assistant to his Ph.D Supervisor. Prior to his graduation in 2016, his articles were accepted in several international conferences including Malaysian Social Science Association Conference and Australia New Zealand International Business Association Conference held in Melbourne, Australia, among others. His research articles were published in several renowned Scopus-indexed international journals including Journal of Islamic Marketing and Asia Pacific Journal of Marketing and Logistics, and others since 2016. He actively reviews journal articles from Journal of Islamic Marketing, Emerald Emerging Case Studies, The CASE Journal among many others. His areas of interests include destination marketing, tourists' behavior, tourism marketing, consumer boycott, consumer racism, consumer ethnocentrism, and consumer animosity. He won the '2017 Highly Commended Article' award from Journal of Islamic Marketing and won 4th place in Emerald-UUM Case Writing Competition in 2015. Among the research grants he secured was Jamalullail Research Grant Scheme in 2021 and Research Initiative Grant Scheme in 2017. He actively participates as a team member for several research grants and sponsored research at national level. Currently, he heads the Malay Food Heritage Branding flagship project under IIUM and recently appointed as the Deputy Dean of Postgraduate and Responsible Research in his faculty.

* * *

Abdul Rahim Abu Bakar received his PhD from Aston Business School, Aston University U.K. in 2004. He has taught in numerous institutions in the U.K., Malaysia and currently in Saudi Arabia. His main research interest is in adoption and diffusion of technology, digital marketing, strategic management/marketing, service marketing and entrepreneurship. He has served as an editorial board in numerous journals as well as guest editors. His recent venture in entrepreneurship research looks at crowdfunding as an alternative source of funding.

Muhamad Fairuz Ahmad Jasmi received his PhD in Industrial Management from Universiti Malaysia Pahang (UMP). Born and raised in Penang, Malaysia, he has developed a passion for interdisciplinary approaches to solving the sustainability challenge in business and maritime supply chain environments. Prior to enrolling at UMP, he received his Master in Business Administration (MBA) in Sustainable Development from the Universiti Sains Malaysia (USM). Realizing his passion for teaching and knowledge, he pursues his vision in higher learning to become an academician and respected scholar in the future. His current research interest is focusing on green supply chain management, sustainable development, value chain cluster as well as maritime logistics and supply chain.

Sana Arshad is a faculty member in Marketing and Management in the Department of Management Sciences at Curtin University. She is currently undertaking her Ph.D. in Marketing at the Universiti Utara Malaysia, Malaysia.

Muharrem Can has been working at Turkish Ministry of Trade since1995. He worked as Commercial Counsellor ın Albania between 2011-2015. He has B.A degree in Istanbul University, master degree in Marmara University and PhD dagree in economics from Necmettin Erbakan University. He study in international relations and International policy economy. He mainly study at diplomacy, commercial diplomacy, international economic relations, international investment and export. He is fluent in English and intermediate in French, Arabic and Albanian. He is married with three children.

Ahmet Canli has been working as Commercial Attaché at the Consulate General of Turkey in Dubai since 2018, and in New York between 2009 and 2013. Previously, he worked at the Turkish Ministry of Trade, in different positions, such as Head of Department, Head of Section, and Foreign Trade Expert for more than 25 years. He earned his Ph.D. degree in history from Gazi University, M.S. degree in international affairs from Florida State University, and B.A. degree in international affairs from Ankara University. He is native in Turkish, fluent in English, and intermediate in Arabic. His academic focus is on economic history, international affairs, and economic development. He is married with two children.

Yudi Fernando, Ph.D., is an Editor in Chief of International Journal of Industrial Management and Managing Editor of Journal Governance and Integrity at Faculty of Industrial Management Universiti Malaysia Pahang. He is an honorary lecturer at Binus Online Learning. He has been working in the electronics industry for several years. His current research interests are green operations management, service management, logistics, and sustainable issues in supply chain management. He is a Research Committee Chair and founding member of Academy of Business and Management (ABM). Dr. Yudi is also a member of the Society of Logisticians, Malaysia/Pertubuhan Pakar Logistik Malaysia (LogM). Dr. Yudi serves as a technical committee in international conferences and invited speaker in various universities. He enjoys his daily work as an operation management scholar while actively teaching and having research papers published in the related field.

Fariza Hashim is an Associate Professor at University Kuala Lumpur, Malaysia She graduated from Aston University, in the UK for Ph.D.; Cardiff University for the Master, and Oklahoma State University for her bachelor's degree. Fariza has taught in several universities in Malaysia and Saudi Arabia. She specializes in International Business Strategy and Entrepreneurship and has been teaching at both undergraduate and postgraduate levels. She has published numerous articles in international and Scopus indexed journals and written several books in international business. Her research interest includes Internationalization, Entrepreneurship, FDI and Organizational Behavior.

Jiayi He is an independent researcher. Her research interests include international trade and Chinese business.

Nor Azilah Husin, PhD, is an Associate Professor and the Deputy Dean in the Faculty of Business and Accountancy, Universiti Selangor. She is the recipient of the Malaysian BRIGHT student Scholarship at the University of Wisconsin, USA. She is also a recipient of a Postgraduate Study Scholarship. In her illustrious 32 years in academia, she received the Excellent Service award three times and was nominated as The Best Paper presenter in several conferences. She has been the Principal Researcher for several grants. Her passionate research interests are Business Management, Educational Management, Human Resource Management, Quality of Life, Well-being, Work-life Balance, and Retrenchment. She has written a couple of books, published, and reviewed various journals.

Norafidah Ismail is a Senior Lecturer at Universiti Utara Malaysia, Kedah. Her area of specialization is the International Relations of the Middle East, Foreign Policy Analysis and International Political

Economy. Dr. Ismail earned a B.A. from International Islamic University, Malaysia, an M.A. in International Political Economy from the University of Leeds, and a Ph.D. in Arab and Islamic Studies from University of Exeter, United Kingdom.

Nuraini Ismail is a graduate with a Bachelor's Degree in Tourism Planning and Hospitality Management from International Islamic University Malaysia (IIUM) in Pagoh campus. She interned at IMG Travel and Tours in 2018 and Korea Tourism Organization (KTO) in 2019. Currently, she works as Business Relationship Executive at SimplifiJohan Sdn. Bhd. for almost one year and a half.

Kamilah Kamaludin is an Assistant Professor in the Accounting Department at Prince Sultan University. She received her PhD in Accounting and Finance from University of Manchester, United Kingdom. Her research interests and publications are in the areas of organisational performance, corporate governance, organisational change, and management performance.

Özlem Karadağ Albayrak was born in Turkey in 1977. She is married and has a son. She completed his primary, secondary and high school education in Istanbul. She then moved to Sakarya for university education. She graduated from Sakarya University, Department of Industrial Engineering in 1999. She worked in various companies in Istanbul for 12 years in quality, production planning and production responsibility positions. She has been working as a faculty member at Kafkas University since 2013. In 2019, she received my PhD from Atatürk University, Department of Econometrics. She makes use of my experience in the private sector in the lectures he teaches at the university. Later, with his academic career, he turned to new research areas. These areas are renewable energy, logistics and econometrics.

Nida Malik is a research scholar at Universiti Utara Malaysia. Nida Malik worked for a several companies in a managerial capacity at Pakistan and currently serving at Symtera Analytics, LLC as HR Manager. Her research interest includes performance management, talent acquisition and strategic HR policies and implementation.

Fahad Manzoor is associated with ENBD and facilitates the people in marketing and sales division as brand service ambassador.

Murodjon Matniyozov is currently attached with the Department of Tourism and Hospitality Management, Urgench State University (UrSU) in Urgench City. He graduated from the Urgench State University, Uzbekistan in 2017 and started his career in the Department of Finance and Planning of Urgench State University as an economist. He started his professional teaching activity in 2019 after graduating with a master's degree in the department of Tourism and Hospitality management at Tourism and Economics faculty. After that, while he was working as an assistant teacher he won a grant from the United Nations World Tourism Organization (UNWTO) and funded by European Bank for Reconstruction and Development (EBRD). He was involved in the cooperation agreement between the World Tourism Organization and Urgench State University for the project "Understanding the international and domestic tourists in Khorezm and the attitudes of Ichan kala residents", which he was appointed as the coordinator of the project from October, 2019 to March, 2020. His areas of interests include planning, destination marketing, business etiquette,hotel branding, tourism marketing, restaurant business, touring, hospitality management and ecotourism. He participated in several other projects, and recently won a 6-month internship in Italy on Erasmus+ mobility.

Farrah Merlinda Muharam holds a Ph.D in Financial Economics, Master of Research and Advance Diploma in Entrepreneurship and Management from Universitat Autonoma de Barcelona, Spain on top of her MBA (Universiti Utara Malaysia) and B. Accounting with honours (UNITEN). Currently, she is a Senior Lecturer in Universiti Teknologi Malaysia. She has an interest in real options and investment analysis, entrepreneurship including social entrepreneurship, technology audit and strategic management. At the moment, she involves in technology evaluation team with government agency, has built entrepreneurship modules for higher education institution (a research in knowledge transfer program in higher education institution), a team member in 2 community transformation through social entrepreneurship projects and conducting research in technology audit towards better firms' performance. She is also passionate in organizing charity events for the purpose of fundraising.

Rusdi Omar is the Assistant Vice-Chancellor of UUM COLGIS and the Dean of Ghazali Shafie School of Government, College of Government, Law and International Studies, Universiti Utara Malaysia, Kedah, Malaysia. He received his PhD in Politics and International Relations from Adelaide University, Australia. Dr. Rusdi Omar's research interests include Southeast Asian politics, political leadership, foreign policy analysis, and ASEAN politics.

Temitope Teniola Onileowo is a Lecturer II at the Department of Entrepreneurship, Faculty of Management Sciences, Ekiti State University, Ado-Ekiti, Nigeria. She received her B.Sc. in Banking &Finance from Ekiti State University, Ado – Ekiti, Nigeria, and M.Sc. degree in Business Administration from National Open University of Nigeria. She is a Senior Member of Institute of Classic Entrepreneurs of Nigeria (ICENT). She is currently a doctoral student in Azman Hashim International Business School, Faculty of Management Sciences Universiti Teknologi Malaysia. Her research interests are in Financing, Entrepreneurship and SMEs Development.

Nur Zafirah Ramlee has just graduated with her first degree in Tourism Planning and Hospitality Management in Kulliyyah of Languages and Management, International Islamic University Malaysia.

Mona Fairuz Ramli is currently a senior lecturer at Department of Marketing, Faculty of Business and Sciences Management, College University Islam Perlis Malaysia. She received her MBA from University Utara Malaysia in October 2011 and Bachelor in Marketing from University Technology MARA, Malaysia. She obtained his Ph.D. in Marketing, in 2016 at University of Utara Malaysia. Her areas of Interests include consumer behavior, digital marketing, environmental sustainable and tourist behaviour. Her current research in nature-based tourism, tourism sustainability, mobile app in heritage art and culture, and online learning. She has been involved in many collaborative research projects marketing especially consumer behavior by various instances including the Jamalullail Research Grant Scheme (JRGS)-UIAM, Universitas Islam Riau (Matching Grant) and 1+3 UUM Research Grant. She currently serves as the advisor of the KUIPs Marketing Division. She started her journey as an educator teaching her university's marketing and integrated marketing communication courses. Now, she teaches both at the undergraduate and graduate level for Business Administration programs. Dr Mona is committed to the following three principles. These principles are also at the heart of her research because of their importance to her personal teaching philosophy. It is an iterative cycle in which her teaching philosophy guides her research and in turn, her research findings enhance her teaching practice. Through her experiences as a student, teaching assistant, and financial executive in the disciplines of Marketing, marketing management studies, retailing and banking industry, she have had the opportunity to reflect on her approaches to teaching and learning. Here, she shares what she believe to be the underlying theoretical and philosophic approaches she brings to and apply in the classroom as part of a teaching team. Dr Mona believes that there are multiple ways to learn as she place this philosophy into practise by centering her classes on Kolb's experiential learning cycle and paying attention to students' various learning styles. The courses she teaches are designed to provide students with real-world experiences. When she looks at experiential learning from a course-wide perspective, she see assignments as developing skills that are then reinforced by the following activity.

Mohd Khairuddin Ramliy is currently Senior Lecturer in the Business Administration Department of Azman Hashim International Business School (AHIBS). He has M.Sc. in IT Entrepreneurship & PhD of Management (Innovation) from UTM Skudai in 2009-2017. He formerly held several positions in non-academic and academic in the private organisation, business consultant, and an entrepreneur since 2007. He is very passionate about Innovation, Entrepreneurship, Technology Commercialisation, and SMEs Development.

Mazni Saad is an Assistant Professor and Head of Tourism at the International Islamic University Malaysia. She previously worked in the Universiti Selangor and at Management, Science University, Universiti Kuala Lumpur, and Universiti Teknologi MARA. While working in the electronic company, Dr Mazni has held managerial positions in various departments for eleven years. She holds a PhD in Hotel and Tourism Management (Universiti Teknologi MARA), a Master's degree in Technology Management with a focus on Occupational Safety and Health (Universiti Sains Malaysia) and an undergraduate degree was in Tourism and Travel (Western Michigan University). She writes journal articles and books, attends conferences, and trains the public. At international conferences, she has won gold, silver, and best paper awards.

Mohammed Sambo is a Lecturer in the Department of Political Science, Federal University of Kashere. Dr. Abubakar Sambo holds PhD from the Universiti Utara Malaysia.

Michael Sampat is an independent researcher working in a number of different disciplines including Sociology, Political Science, Ethics, and Biblical Studies.

Safwan Sani is a Lecturer in the Department of Political Science, Federal University of Kashere, Nigeria.

Muhammad Shabir Shaharudin received his MBA in International Business from Universiti Sains Malaysia and bachelor's degree in international business from Limkokwing University, Malaysia. He is currently pursuing PhD at Faculty of Industrial Management, Universiti Malaysia Pahang. He has two years working experience in two SMEs in transport & logistics and retail & distribution industries. His current research is in Carbon Footprint of supply chain and his area of interest includes sustainable development and supply chain & operations. He is part of the editorial board member and was promoted to Associate Editor for International Journal of Productivity Management and Assessment Technologies (IJPMAT), USA. He is also a reviewer for Sustainable Energy Technologies and Assessments Journal and a reviewer for IGI Global. Currently, he is the Journal Manager for Journal of Governance & Integrity (JGI), Malaysia. He has several journal publications including in Journal of Cleaner Production, International Journal of Shipping and Transport Logistics, Journal of Manufacturing Technology Management and International Journal of Services and Operations Management.

Subramaniam Sri Ramalu is an Associate Professor of Organizational Behavior and Leadership. His current position is Director of Postgraduate Studies Unit, College of Business, UUM. Dr. Subramaniam's research interest includes leadership, organizational behaviour and human resource management. He has successfully supervised many doctoral and Master students. To date, he has completed 16 research projects and published more than 60 articles in both local and international journals.

Isaac Terwase is a Lecturer in the Department of Political Science, Federal University of Kashere, Nigeria. He holds a PhD in Political Science from the Universiti Utara Malaysia.

Ratnaria Wahid, Bachelor of Laws (LLB) (Hons), International Islamic University Malaysia (IIUM; Masters of Law (LLM) Australian National University, Canberra, Australia (ANU); PhD University of East Anglia, Norwich, United Kingdom(UEA); Advocate and Solicitor (Malaya) (Non-Practising), was a postdoctoral fellow in the University of Ottawa, Canada is currently an Associate Professor at the School of International Studies, College of Law, Government and International Studies, Universiti Utara Malaysia. She teaches public international law, politics in international law, international environmental law and organizational leadership at both Undergraduate and Postgraduate programs. Her doctorate is on the Flexibilities within the International Copyright System for teaching, research and study, particularly in the Higher Educational Institutions. Her research interests lie in the field of copyright law, human rights and education, public international law as well as leadership. She is also currently a Fellow in the Institute of Excellence for Islamicjerusalem Studies and the Chief Editor of the Journal of International Studies.

Poshan (Sam) Yu is a Lecturer in Accounting and Finance in the International Cooperative Education Program of Soochow University (China). He is also an External Professor of FinTech and Finance at SKEMA Business School (China), a Visiting Professor at Krirk University (Thailand) and a Visiting Researcher at the Australian Studies Centre of Shanghai University (China). Sam leads FasterCapital (Dubai, UAE) as a Regional Partner (China) and serves as a Startup Mentor for AIC RAISE (Coimbatore, India). His research interests include financial technology, regulatory technology, public-private partnerships, mergers and acquisitions, private equity, venture capital, start-ups, intellectual property, art finance, and China's "One Belt One Road" policy.

Muhammad Yusuf is a Lecturer in the Department of Political Science, Federal University of Kashere, Nigeria.

Nadisah Zakaria has 17 years of experience in academia. Her main research interest is in the pricing and mispricing of the stock market quoted shares, corporate restructuring, and investment. Nadisah has published her works in several journal publications and conference articles on the aforementioned topics and has received research grants locally and internationally. Her current research project focuses on the performance of crowdfunding in property and real estate and the impact of covid-19 in share performance.

Index

A

absorptive capacity 63, 72, 92-93, 95, 99, 103-106, 108-110, 128-129
accommodation 291, 301, 305
Algeria 92, 95, 98, 105-106

B

backpackers 290-295, 297-306
Baku Tbilisi Kars Railway Line (BTK) 228, 235
Belt and Road Initiative (BRI) 225, 235
Belt and Road project 222-226
Boko Haram 76-91
born global 46-49, 51-52, 56, 58, 60, 62
brand awareness 15-19, 21-24, 26, 54
Brand Loyalty 15, 21, 23, 26
Brand Satisfaction 21, 26
branding 15-26, 34-35, 43, 189
Brazil 132-141, 143-153, 267
business 1-2, 4, 10-12, 14, 16-17, 22-26, 29, 41-42, 45-47, 49-50, 52-55, 57-63, 68, 70-75, 77, 82, 84-87, 89, 91-92, 95, 99-100, 106-111, 116-117, 126, 128-129, 131-132, 134-135, 142-143, 145, 147, 149-150, 153, 169-170, 172-173, 175, 178, 180-182, 184, 186, 189-190, 194, 200-203, 207, 209-210, 213-214, 216-221, 223, 226, 229, 231-235, 238, 242-244, 246, 248-254, 261-264, 266-273, 275, 282, 286-287, 289, 292, 302-304, 307
buy-and-hold abnormal return 155, 166-167

C

Chad 76-78, 80, 83-88
China 2, 7-8, 10, 12, 34-35, 69, 96, 98, 106, 108, 130, 132-154, 159, 173, 222, 224-236, 252-253, 255, 257, 265, 269, 273
climate change 2-3, 7, 10-11, 75, 136, 151, 271-272, 275, 277
collectivism 238-240, 243, 245-246
commercial diplomacy 176, 183-184, 189-190
communication 16-18, 21-22, 44-45, 97, 113, 146, 177-178, 181, 184-185, 200, 223, 231, 241, 250, 257, 263, 276, 279, 304
competitive advantage 19, 26, 47, 57, 60, 65, 68, 109, 130, 205, 215-216, 221, 230, 232, 268, 276, 283
COVID-19 30, 132-134, 140, 142, 145, 147-152, 154, 176-177, 185, 188, 226, 232, 241, 252-269
cross-border international trade 112, 115, 118, 125
Cultural Intelligence 57, 64, 68, 72, 74
culture 26-35, 39-42, 44, 50, 65-70, 82, 96, 106, 109, 146, 169, 204, 206, 210, 220, 237, 239-244, 248-249, 291, 293, 304-307
Customer Equity 26
cyberostracism 237-239, 242-243, 246, 248-249

D

development 1-6, 8, 10, 12-13, 16, 18-19, 22-23, 25, 27, 29, 41-42, 44, 47, 52, 57, 60, 66-69, 71, 73-75, 77-82, 89-90, 95, 105-106, 109-111, 113, 116, 118, 127-130, 132-139, 141, 144, 146-153, 156, 161, 163, 177-178, 180, 188-189, 191-195, 197, 199-205, 209, 214, 216-221, 223-226, 231-235, 241, 243, 246, 248-250, 254-255, 258, 260, 262, 264-269, 271-275, 277, 279-288, 293, 303, 305-307
digital 16, 21, 23, 28, 31, 43, 147, 177, 184-185, 189, 216, 237-243, 246, 248-250, 259-260, 263
digital entrepreneurship 237-238, 241-243, 246, 250
digital literacy 237, 239, 241, 243, 246, 250
digital skills 237, 239-240, 246
Digitalization of the Fairs 176
discussions 20, 22, 46-47, 241, 262
dissemination of information 105
diversity 49, 55, 61, 63, 68, 79, 179
Dubai 173, 176-177, 185-190, 237

E

economic freedom 239, 243, 247, 250
economy 4, 7, 9, 11, 14, 21, 23, 26, 29, 45, 54, 61, 63, 68, 75-77, 80, 90-91, 95, 98, 110-111, 127, 130-133, 136-137, 142, 144-147, 151-153, 170, 174-175, 186, 190-192, 194, 201-202, 205, 216, 221, 225, 227, 234-235, 238-239, 241, 243, 246-248, 250-255, 258, 260-262, 264-269, 273, 285, 287-289, 307
Education 24-25, 35, 42, 50, 55, 60, 64, 67-68, 74-75, 79, 82, 89, 91, 129-130, 150, 169, 191-194, 200-202, 237-243, 246, 249-250, 252-261, 263, 266-269, 284, 292, 294, 300, 306
elementary 130, 256
emerging countries 155, 158, 204-207
entrepreneurship 46, 57-62, 105, 170, 191, 197, 201, 205, 214-216, 219, 221, 237-243, 246, 249-250, 268
environmental uncertainty 92-93, 97-99, 103, 105-107, 109-111, 219
epidemic 132-133, 135, 139-140, 143-154, 168, 188, 257, 262, 264
European Union 1-4, 10-12, 14, 146, 227
export 2, 4, 10, 12, 15, 17-26, 41, 49, 88, 98, 110, 112-116, 119, 123-127, 129-130, 135-137, 139-142, 144, 146, 149, 176, 178-179, 183, 192, 194, 200, 203-205, 210, 215-216, 221, 224-225, 229, 273
export intensity 49, 112-113, 115-116, 119, 123-124, 126, 225
Export Performance 15, 25-26, 110, 127

F

FDI 60, 113, 128-129, 142, 150, 226, 273
females 36, 237-243, 249, 295, 300, 302
film-induced 27-28
firm 20, 23-24, 47, 49, 51-54, 56-63, 94-96, 99, 105, 107-110, 112, 115-119, 124-130, 145, 149, 157, 163, 168, 172, 181, 203, 205-210, 214, 216-220, 263, 287
first-time 32, 290, 292-295, 298, 300-301, 304
foreign 1-2, 11, 15-17, 19, 21, 26, 28, 34, 43, 47, 49-57, 59, 64-66, 69, 71-73, 75, 87-88, 92-95, 98-99, 105-106, 109, 113-119, 124-131, 133, 135-136, 138, 140-146, 149, 153, 159, 178-179, 183-184, 186, 190, 203-205, 208-209, 214, 223, 225-226, 230, 232-234, 261-262, 264, 273, 307
foreign policy 1-2, 11, 209, 214
foreignness 53-55, 57-60, 63

G

globalization 15, 17, 19, 26, 46-47, 54-55, 60, 64, 67-68, 132-133, 148, 150, 223, 225, 232, 235, 286
governance 1-2, 78, 80-81, 90-91, 109, 111, 148-149, 232, 241, 276, 284, 287-288
green supply chain 270, 276, 286-288

H

high-tech manufacturing industry 112, 114-115, 122, 124-126

I

importation 191, 205
individualism 170, 238-240, 243, 245-246
innovativeness 92-95, 99, 103-105, 108, 110-111, 208, 219
Internally Displaced Persons and Refugees 76
International and Performance 203
international community 1, 76, 86
International Joint Venture 92, 106, 110
International Marketing 15, 20, 24-26, 42-43, 50-51, 58-61, 108, 111
international new ventures 46-48, 51, 56-58, 61, 63
international trade 8, 16, 25, 55, 60, 62, 77-78, 84, 112-113, 115, 118, 125, 128-129, 132-137, 145-146, 148-149, 151-153, 176-178, 180, 182-183, 186, 189-190, 205, 222-225, 230-231, 264, 270, 272, 279
iron silk road 222-224, 227, 231-232

K

Kars Logistics Center 222-223, 229-230
K-drama 27-31, 33, 38, 40, 43
knowledge acquisition 92-98, 103-109, 111, 179
knowledge management practices 92-93, 96-97, 99, 103-106, 108, 110

L

Learning Advantage of Newness 46, 52
liabilities of newness 46, 53, 59
local consumption 191-193, 198-200
logistics 23, 26, 145, 152, 219, 222-225, 227, 229-230, 233-234, 270, 273-274, 276, 283, 286-288

M

Mahathir 1, 4, 6-8, 11, 13
Malaysia 1-15, 23, 27-32, 41-42, 44, 46, 64, 68-69, 73, 128, 155, 158, 160-162, 164-170, 173-175, 216, 219, 231, 252, 270-274, 277, 279-283, 285-288, 290, 294-295, 301
Malaysian 2-11, 13-14, 26-31, 35-36, 39-41, 43-44, 59, 68, 73, 75, 110, 155, 161-165, 167-169, 171, 173-174, 216, 221, 235, 271-273, 279-288, 290, 292, 294, 297, 299-302, 305
Maritime Law 270
maritime supply chain 270-277, 279-285, 287
market 2, 7, 10, 15-16, 18, 20-25, 41, 46-47, 49-50, 52-57, 59, 62-64, 68, 75-76, 84, 90, 96-97, 99, 108, 110, 115-117, 119, 124-126, 129, 133-135, 137-141, 144, 146-150, 152, 155-181, 183-184, 190, 194, 203-210, 212-220, 225, 261-262, 270, 286, 302, 305-306
market efficiency 155, 158, 162, 168, 170-171, 173, 175
mathematics 260
mental health 151
Middle Corridor 222, 224, 226-229, 232, 234, 236
modes 8, 34, 49, 223, 227, 231, 236, 291
Modification 23
motivation 27, 29, 47, 64-67, 69-70, 72-73, 75, 98, 194, 233, 284, 290, 293-294, 298, 300-302, 304, 306

N

Nigeria 4, 76-91, 191-205, 207-209, 214-215, 217, 219-220, 252-269
Nigeria's economy 80, 252, 262, 266-268

O

online education 263
online platform 242

P

palm oil 1-14
Perceived Quality 25-26
psychological needs satisfaction 64, 68
Purchase Intentions 23, 26

R

repeat 26-27, 34, 41, 44, 290, 292, 294-295, 298, 300-302, 304
revisit intention 27, 30, 34-36, 38-40

S

Saudi Arabia 75, 155, 158, 162-163, 166-168, 170, 172-174, 241
school 23, 81, 85, 127, 175, 177, 201, 240, 252, 257-261, 266-267, 269
school education 201, 240
Science 9, 11-12, 26, 42-43, 57, 59-60, 62, 72-73, 107-108, 110, 127, 137, 141, 150-153, 173, 191, 201, 220, 232, 250, 257, 286, 288
self-reliance 191, 193-194
serial backpackers 290, 292, 294-295, 298, 300-301, 304
shipping 10, 141-142, 270-271, 273-274, 276-277, 279, 282-284, 286-288
Silk Road Economic Belt (SREB) 226, 236
Skill 68, 191-200, 202, 205-206, 209, 220
Small and Medium Enterprise 203, 212
strategic 7, 25, 47, 53-54, 58-61, 63, 65, 75, 80, 83, 93, 97, 107-111, 134, 136-137, 180, 203-206, 208, 213-216, 218-221, 226, 233, 235, 270, 272
supervision 97, 282
Supply Chain Management 23, 188, 276, 286-288
sustainability 1-3, 5-7, 9-13, 19, 45, 56, 62, 129, 132-133, 146, 148, 150, 193, 232, 234-235, 265, 270-272, 275-276, 280-286, 288
sustainable development 3, 5-6, 10, 12, 44, 89-90, 132-134, 136, 146, 148-149, 151-153, 217, 269, 275, 279-280, 283-287

T

teachers 259-260
technical education 191, 193-194, 200-202
technology 10, 23, 31, 40, 42, 57, 59, 64, 72, 92, 94-95, 97, 99-100, 107-109, 111, 115-118, 125, 128-130, 133-134, 137, 144, 153-154, 161-162, 168, 177, 181, 184-186, 191-192, 194, 216-217, 220, 223-225, 240-243, 250, 256-257, 260, 263, 272, 286-287
terrorism 76-79, 83-84, 87-91
tertiary 137, 191, 200, 240, 252, 254-257, 266-267, 269
tertiary institutions 191, 200, 252, 254-257, 266-267
Tourism 16, 27-29, 32, 34-35, 39, 41-45, 183, 189, 216, 223, 273, 290-293, 300, 302-307
trade 1, 3-4, 6-12, 14, 16-17, 19, 25, 54-55, 58, 60, 62, 76-78, 83-85, 87-88, 98, 112-113, 115-116, 118-119, 121-130, 132-154, 176-190, 194, 204-206, 222-225, 227, 230-234, 236, 238, 242-243, 247, 254, 258, 261-262, 264, 270-274, 277, 279, 284
trade fairs 176-180, 182-186, 188-190

transfer mechanisms 92-93, 95-96, 99, 103-107
travel career 290, 293, 301-302, 306
travel motivation 290, 294, 300-302, 306

U

unemployment 79, 81-82, 91, 141, 191-192, 200, 202, 240, 246, 253, 261-262, 265
University 5, 27, 41-44, 59, 62, 64, 68-69, 71-72, 76, 81-82, 92, 109, 112, 127-128, 132, 149-150, 152, 155, 169, 173-175, 191-192, 203, 215, 217, 222, 237, 252, 257, 260, 266-267, 286, 288, 290, 306-307

V

value investing 155-158, 160, 164, 166, 168-171, 173-175
vertical trade integration 112-113, 115-116, 119, 123-124
videos 29, 87
Virtual fairs 176, 185, 188
vocational education 192-194, 200-201

W

WOM 22, 26, 303
work engagement 64, 68-69, 73
World Health Organization 252, 255-256, 269
WTO 1-2, 6, 8-9, 11-14, 17, 137

www.ingramcontent.com/pod-product-compliance
Lightning Source LLC
LaVergne TN
LVHW062119300926
849161LV00010B/2495